REPAIRS AND OVERHAUL

Engine and Associated Systems

Transmission

Brakes and suspension

Body equipment

Wiring diagrams

WITHDRAWN FROM STOCK

REFERENCE

Index

0•4 Introduction

The Ford Transit covered by this manual was introduced in the UK in October 2000 and continued in production until 2006 when it was replaced by an entirely new version. Seemingly innumerable variations of body types and styles are available, mounted on a long, medium or short wheelbase chassis.

The Transit is available with 2.0 and 2.4 litre turbocharged diesel engines and a 2.3 litre petrol engine (not covered by this manual). The diesel engines are DOHC 16-valve units with direct diesel injection or common rail diesel injection. As a departure from previous Transit vehicles, the models covered in this manual are available in either front wheel drive or rear wheel drive configuration. 2.0 litre models are all front wheel drive with the engine and transmission mounted transversely at the front. Rear wheel drive models utilise the 2.4 litre engine, mounted in-line with the transmission.

2.0 litre models are equipped with a 5-speed all synchromesh manual transmission, whereas the transmission on 2.4 litre models is either a 5- or 6- speed unit, according to engine power output.

Front suspension is fully independent on all models, with a beam axle or live axle, supported on semi-eliptic leaf springs employed at the rear.

All models are fitted with dual-circuit servo-assisted brakes, with discs at the front and self-adjusting drum brakes at the rear.

A wide range of standard and optional equipment is available within the Transit range, including power steering, air conditioning, remote central locking, electric windows, anti-lock braking system, electronic engine immobiliser and supplemental restraint systems.

For the home mechanic, the Transit is a relatively straightforward vehicle to maintain, and most of the items requiring frequent attention are easily accessible.

Your Ford Transit manual

The aim of this manual is to help you get the best value from your vehicle. It can do so in several ways. It can help you decide what work must be done (even should you choose to get it done by a garage), provide information on routine maintenance and servicing, and give a logical course of action and diagnosis when random faults occur. However, it is hoped that you will use the manual by tackling the work yourself. On simpler jobs, it may even be quicker than booking the vehicle into a garage and going there twice, to leave and collect it. Perhaps most important, a lot of money can be saved by avoiding the costs a garage must charge to cover its labour and overheads.

The manual has drawings and descriptions to show the function of the various components, so that their layout can be understood. Then the tasks are described and photographed in a clear step-by-step sequence.

References to the 'left' or 'right' are in the sense of a person in the driver's seat, facing forward.

Project vehicles

The main vehicle used in the preparation of this manual, and which appears in many of the photographic sequences, was a Ford Transit rear wheel drive van with a 2.4 litre engine. Additional work was carried out on a Transit front wheel drive van with a 2.0 litre engine.

Acknowledgements

Certain illustrations are the copyright of Ford Motor Company Limited, and are used with their permission. Thanks are due to Draper Tools Limited, who provided some of the workshop tools, to Eurocams Limited who provided engine components and technical assistance, and to all those people at Sparkford who helped in the production of this manual.

We take great pride in the accuracy of information given in this manual, but vehicle manufacturers make alterations and design changes during the production run of a particular vehicle of which they do not inform us. No liability can be accepted by the authors or publishers for loss, damage or injury caused by any errors in, or omissions from, the information given.

Working on your car can be dangerous. This page shows just some of the potential risks and hazards, with the aim of creating a safety-conscious attitude.

General hazards

Scalding

• Don't remove the radiator or expansion tank cap while the engine is hot.
• Engine oil, automatic transmission fluid or power steering fluid may also be dangerously hot if the engine has recently been running.

Burning

• Beware of burns from the exhaust system and from any part of the engine. Brake discs and drums can also be extremely hot immediately after use.

Crushing

• When working under or near a raised vehicle, always supplement the jack with axle stands, or use drive-on ramps. *Never venture under a car which is only supported by a jack.*

• Take care if loosening or tightening high-torque nuts when the vehicle is on stands. Initial loosening and final tightening should be done with the wheels on the ground.

Fire

• Fuel is highly flammable; fuel vapour is explosive.
• Don't let fuel spill onto a hot engine.
• Do not smoke or allow naked lights (including pilot lights) anywhere near a vehicle being worked on. Also beware of creating sparks (electrically or by use of tools).
• Fuel vapour is heavier than air, so don't work on the fuel system with the vehicle over an inspection pit.
• Another cause of fire is an electrical overload or short-circuit. Take care when repairing or modifying the vehicle wiring.
• Keep a fire extinguisher handy, of a type suitable for use on fuel and electrical fires.

Electric shock

• Ignition HT voltage can be dangerous, especially to people with heart problems or a pacemaker. Don't work on or near the ignition system with the engine running or the ignition switched on.

• Mains voltage is also dangerous. Make sure that any mains-operated equipment is correctly earthed. Mains power points should be protected by a residual current device (RCD) circuit breaker.

Fume or gas intoxication

• Exhaust fumes are poisonous; they often contain carbon monoxide, which is rapidly fatal if inhaled. Never run the engine in a confined space such as a garage with the doors shut.
• Fuel vapour is also poisonous, as are the vapours from some cleaning solvents and paint thinners.

Poisonous or irritant substances

• Avoid skin contact with battery acid and with any fuel, fluid or lubricant, especially antifreeze, brake hydraulic fluid and Diesel fuel. Don't syphon them by mouth. If such a substance is swallowed or gets into the eyes, seek medical advice.
• Prolonged contact with used engine oil can cause skin cancer. Wear gloves or use a barrier cream if necessary. Change out of oil-soaked clothes and do not keep oily rags in your pocket.
• Air conditioning refrigerant forms a poisonous gas if exposed to a naked flame (including a cigarette). It can also cause skin burns on contact.

Asbestos

• Asbestos dust can cause cancer if inhaled or swallowed. Asbestos may be found in gaskets and in brake and clutch linings. When dealing with such components it is safest to assume that they contain asbestos.

Special hazards

Hydrofluoric acid

• This extremely corrosive acid is formed when certain types of synthetic rubber, found in some O-rings, oil seals, fuel hoses etc, are exposed to temperatures above 400ºC. The rubber changes into a charred or sticky substance containing the acid. *Once formed, the acid remains dangerous for years. If it gets onto the skin, it may be necessary to amputate the limb concerned.*
• When dealing with a vehicle which has suffered a fire, or with components salvaged from such a vehicle, wear protective gloves and discard them after use.

The battery

• Batteries contain sulphuric acid, which attacks clothing, eyes and skin. Take care when topping-up or carrying the battery.
• The hydrogen gas given off by the battery is highly explosive. Never cause a spark or allow a naked light nearby. Be careful when connecting and disconnecting battery chargers or jump leads.

Air bags

• Air bags can cause injury if they go off accidentally. Take care when removing the steering wheel and/or facia. Special storage instructions may apply.

Diesel injection equipment

• Diesel injection pumps supply fuel at very high pressure. Take care when working on the fuel injectors and fuel pipes.

⚠️ *Warning: Never expose the hands, face or any other part of the body to injector spray; the fuel can penetrate the skin with potentially fatal results.*

Remember...

DO

• Do use eye protection when using power tools, and when working under the vehicle.

• Do wear gloves or use barrier cream to protect your hands when necessary.

• Do get someone to check periodically that all is well when working alone on the vehicle.

• Do keep loose clothing and long hair well out of the way of moving mechanical parts.

• Do remove rings, wristwatch etc, before working on the vehicle – especially the electrical system.

• Do ensure that any lifting or jacking equipment has a safe working load rating adequate for the job.

DON'T

• Don't attempt to lift a heavy component which may be beyond your capability – get assistance.

• Don't rush to finish a job, or take unverified short cuts.

• Don't use ill-fitting tools which may slip and cause injury.

• Don't leave tools or parts lying around where someone can trip over them. Mop up oil and fuel spills at once.

• Don't allow children or pets to play in or near a vehicle being worked on.

The following pages are intended to help in dealing with common roadside emergencies and breakdowns. You will find more detailed fault finding information at the back of the manual, and repair information in the main chapters.

If your vehicle won't start and the starter motor doesn't turn

☐ Move the driver's seat fully forward, open the battery box cover and make sure that the battery terminals are clean and tight.

☐ Switch on the headlights and try to start the engine. If the headlights go very dim when you're trying to start, the battery is probably flat. Get out of trouble by jump starting (see next page) using a friend's car.

If your vehicle won't start even though the starter motor turns as normal

☐ Is there fuel in the tank?

☐ Is there moisture on electrical components under the bonnet? Switch off the ignition, then wipe off any obvious dampness with a dry cloth. Spray a water-repellent aerosol product (WD-40 or equivalent) on engine and fuel system electrical connectors like those shown in the photos. (Note that diesel engines don't usually suffer from damp).

1 Check that the airflow meter wiring is connected securely.

2 Check the security and condition of the battery connections.

3 Check all multi-plugs and wiring connectors for security.

4 Check that all fuses are still in good condition and none have blown.

Check that electrical connections are secure (with the ignition switched off) and spray them with a water-dispersant spray like WD-40 if you suspect a problem due to damp

Jump starting

When jump-starting a vehicle using a booster battery, observe the following precautions:

✔ Before connecting the booster battery, make sure that the ignition is switched off.

✔ Ensure that all electrical equipment (lights, heater, wipers, etc) is switched off.

✔ Take note of any special precautions printed on the battery case.

✔ Make sure that the booster battery is the same voltage as the discharged one in the vehicle.

✔ If the battery is being jump-started from the battery in another vehicle, the two vehicles MUST NOT TOUCH each other.

✔ Make sure that the transmission is in neutral (or PARK, in the case of automatic transmission).

 Jump starting will get you out of trouble, but you must correct whatever made the battery go flat in the first place. There are three possibilities:

1 The battery has been drained by repeated attempts to start, or by leaving the lights on.

2 The charging system is not working properly (alternator drivebelt slack or broken, alternator wiring fault or alternator itself faulty).

3 The battery itself is at fault (electrolyte low, or battery worn out).

1 Lift up the cover over the flat battery's positive (+) cable terminal box in the engine compartment and connect one end of the red jump lead to the terminal.

2 Connect the other end of the red lead to the positive (+) terminal of the booster battery.

3 Connect one end of the black jump lead to the negative (-) terminal of the booster battery

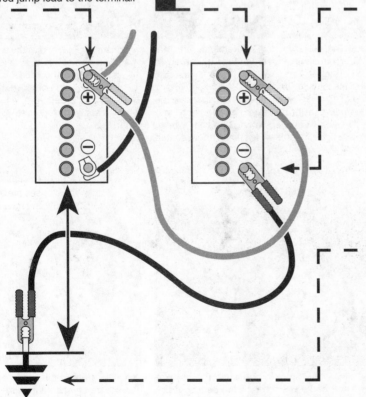

4 Connect the other end of the black jump lead to a bolt or bracket on the engine block, well away from the battery, on the vehicle to be started.

5 Make sure that the jump leads will not come into contact with the fan, drive-belts or other moving parts of the engine.

6 Start the engine using the booster battery and run it at idle speed. Switch on the lights, rear window demister and heater blower motor, then disconnect the jump leads in the reverse order of connection. Turn off the lights etc.

Wheel changing

 Warning: Do not change a wheel in a situation where you risk being hit by other traffic. On busy roads, try to stop in a lay-by or a gateway. Be wary of passing traffic while changing the wheel – it is easy to become distracted by the job in hand.

Preparation

☐ When a puncture occurs, stop as soon as it is safe to do so.

☐ Park on firm level ground, if possible, and well out of the way of other traffic.

☐ Use hazard warning lights if necessary.

☐ If you have one, use a warning triangle to alert other drivers of your presence.

☐ Apply the handbrake and engage first or reverse gear.

☐ Chock the wheel diagonally opposite the one being removed – a couple of large stones will do for this.

☐ If the ground is soft, use a flat piece of wood to spread the load under the jack.

Changing the wheel

1 The jack, jack handle and wheelbrace are located in a stowage compartment in the front right-hand stepwell. Release the catches and remove the stowage compartment cover, then unclip the retaining straps and remove the jack, handle and wheelbrace.

2 The spare wheel is located under the rear of the vehicle, held in place by a bracket attached to a steel cable. To access the mechanism that lowers the wheel, locate the guide hole which will be either above the bumper, right of centre, or on the right-hand side of the vehicle, behind the rear wheel. Where fitted, unscrew the security bolt located above the guide hole.

3 Insert the flat end of the wheelbrace or the short arm of the jack handle (according to model) into the guide hole and engage the mechanism. Turn the wheelbrace or jack handle anticlockwise until the spare wheel rests on the ground and there is slack in the cable.

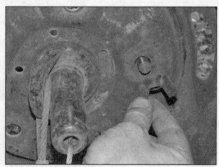

4 Slide the spare wheel out from under the vehicle and disengage the cable bracket by unscrewing the wing nut.

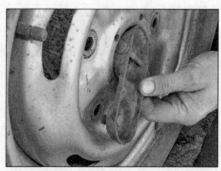

5 Twist the bracket and push the bracket and cable out through the centre of the wheel.

6 Where applicable, prise off the wheel nut covers or wheel trim, using the flat end of the wheelbrace, for access to the wheel nuts. Slacken each wheel nut by half a turn.

7 Position the jack under the jacking point nearest the punctured wheel. The front jacking points are the rear bolts for the front subframe which engage with recesses in the flap on top of the jack. Turn the jack handle clockwise until the wheel is raised clear of the ground.

8 The rear jacking points for front wheel drive vehicles are under the rear eyes of the leaf spring, or under the axle as near to the wheel as possible. The rear jacking points for rear wheel drive vehicles are under the axle as near to the wheel as possible. The flap on top of the jack should be flipped to the open position for positive engagement. Turn the jack handle clockwise until the wheel is raised clear of the ground.

9 Unscrew the wheel nuts, noting which way round they fit, and remove the wheel. Fit the spare wheel and screw on the nuts. Lightly tighten the nuts with the wheelbrace.

10 Lower the vehicle to the ground and fully tighten the wheel nuts. On vehicles with 5-stud wheels, tighten the nuts in the sequence shown. On vehicles with 6-stud wheels, tighten the nuts in a diagonal sequence. Refit the wheel nut covers or wheel trim, as applicable.

Finally . . .

- [ ] Remove the wheel chocks.
- [ ] Secure the punctured wheel back under the vehicle using the cable and bracket, then stow the jack and tools in the stowage compartment.
- [ ] Check the tyre pressure on the wheel just fitted. If it is low, or if you don't have a pressure gauge with you, drive slowly to the nearest garage and inflate the tyre to the correct pressure.
- [ ] Have the damaged tyre or wheel repaired, or renew it, as soon as possible.
- [ ] Don't leave the spare wheel cradle empty and unsecured – it could drop onto the ground while the vehicle is moving.
- [ ] Have the wheel bolts tightened to the correct torque (see Chapter 10) at the earliest opportunity.

Towing

When all else fails, you may find yourself having to get a tow home – or of course you may be helping somebody else. Long-distance recovery should only be done by a garage or breakdown service. For shorter distances, DIY towing using another vehicle is easy enough, but observe the following points:
- [ ] Use a proper tow-rope – they are not expensive. The vehicle being towed must display an ON TOW sign in its rear window.
- [ ] Always turn the ignition key to the 'On' position when the vehicle is being towed, so that the steering lock is released, and the direction indicator and brake lights work.
- [ ] Only attach the tow-rope to the towing eyes located in the front bumper and below the rear bumper.
- [ ] Before being towed, release the handbrake and select neutral on the transmission.
- [ ] Note that greater-than-usual pedal pressure will be required to operate the brakes, since the vacuum servo unit is only operational with the engine running.
- [ ] Greater-than-usual steering effort will also be required.
- [ ] The driver of the vehicle being towed must keep the tow-rope taut at all times to avoid snatching.
- [ ] Make sure that both drivers know the route before setting off.
- [ ] Only drive at moderate speeds and keep the distance towed to a minimum. Drive smoothly and allow plenty of time for slowing down at junctions.

Identifying leaks

Puddles on the garage floor or drive, or obvious wetness under the bonnet or underneath the car, suggest a leak that needs investigating. It can sometimes be difficult to decide where the leak is coming from, especially if the engine bay is very dirty already. Leaking oil or fluid can also be blown rearwards by the passage of air under the car, giving a false impression of where the problem lies.

Warning: Most automotive oils and fluids are poisonous. Wash them off skin, and change out of contaminated clothing, without delay.

 The smell of a fluid leaking from the car may provide a clue to what's leaking. Some fluids are distinctively coloured. It may help to clean the car carefully and to park it over some clean paper overnight as an aid to locating the source of the leak. Remember that some leaks may only occur while the engine is running.

Sump oil

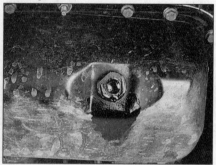

Engine oil may leak from the drain plug...

Oil from filter

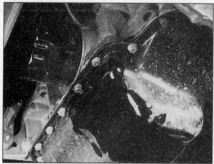

...or from the base of the oil filter.

Gearbox oil

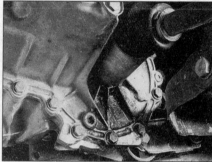

Gearbox oil can leak from the seals at the inboard ends of the driveshafts.

Antifreeze

Leaking antifreeze often leaves a crystalline deposit like this.

Brake fluid

A leak occurring at a wheel is almost certainly brake fluid.

Power steering fluid

Power steering fluid may leak from the pipe connectors on the steering rack.

Introduction

There are some very simple checks which need only take a few minutes to carry out, but which could save you a lot of inconvenience and expense.

These *Weekly checks* require no great skill or special tools, and the small amount of time they take to perform could prove to be very well spent, for example:

☐ Keeping an eye on tyre condition and pressures, will not only help to stop them wearing out prematurely, but could also save your life.

☐ Many breakdowns are caused by electrical problems. Battery-related faults are particularly common, and a quick check on a regular basis will often prevent the majority of these.

☐ If your vehicle develops a brake fluid leak, the first time you might know about it is when your brakes don't work properly. Checking the level regularly will give advance warning of this kind of problem.

☐ If the oil or coolant levels run low, the cost of repairing any engine damage will be far greater than fixing the leak, for example.

Underbonnet check points

◀ **2.0 litre engines**

1 *Engine oil level dipstick*

2 *Engine oil filler cap*

3 *Coolant reservoir (expansion tank)*

4 *Washer fluid reservoir*

5 *Fuse/relay box*

6 *Power steering fluid reservoir*

7 *Brake and clutch fluid reservoir*

◀ **2.4 litre engines**

1 *Engine oil level dipstick*

2 *Engine oil filler cap*

3 *Coolant reservoir (expansion tank)*

4 *Washer fluid reservoir*

5 *Fuse/relay box*

6 *Power steering fluid reservoir*

7 *Brake and clutch fluid reservoir*

Engine oil level

Before you start
✔ Make sure that the vehicle is on level ground.
✔ The oil level must be checked with the engine at normal operating temperature, however, wait at least 5 minutes after the engine has been switched off.

HAYNES HiNT *If the oil is checked immediately after driving the vehicle, some of the oil will remain in the upper engine components, resulting in an inaccurate reading on the dipstick.*

The correct oil
Modern engines place great demands on their oil. It is very important that the correct oil for your vehicle is used (see *Lubricants and fluids*).

Vehicle care
● If you have to add oil frequently, you should check whether you have any oil leaks. Place some clean paper under the vehicle overnight, and check for stains in the morning. If there are no leaks, then the engine may be burning oil.
● Always maintain the level between the upper and lower dipstick marks (see photo 3). If the level is too low, severe engine damage may occur. Oil seal failure may result if the engine is overfilled by adding too much oil.

1 The dipstick is brightly coloured for easy identification (see *Underbonnet check points* on page 0•11 for exact location). Withdraw the dipstick.

2 Using a clean rag or paper towel remove all oil from the dipstick. Insert the clean dipstick into the tube as far as it will go, then withdraw it again.

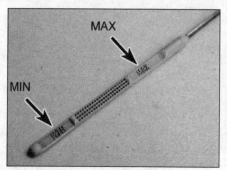
3 Note the level on the end of the dipstick, which should be between the upper (MAX) mark and lower (MIN) mark. Approximately 2.0 litres of oil will raise the level from the lower mark to the upper mark.

4 Oil is added through the filler cap. Unscrew the cap and top-up the level. A funnel may help to reduce spillage. Add the oil slowly, checking the level on the dipstick frequently. Avoid overfilling (see *Vehicle care*).

Coolant level

 Warning: Do not attempt to remove the expansion tank pressure cap when the engine is hot, as there is a very great risk of scalding. Do not leave open containers of coolant about, as it is poisonous.

Vehicle care
● Adding coolant should not be necessary on a regular basis. If frequent topping-up is required, it is likely there is a leak. Check the radiator, all hoses and joint faces for signs of staining or wetness, and rectify as necessary.

● It is important that antifreeze is used in the cooling system all year round, not just during the winter months. Don't top up with water alone, as the antifreeze will become diluted.

1 The coolant level varies with the temperature of the engine and is visible through the expansion tank. When the engine is cold, the coolant level should be between the MAX and MIN marks on the side of the tank. When the engine is hot, the level will rise slightly.

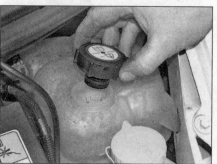
2 If topping-up is necessary, **wait until the engine is cold**. Slowly unscrew the expansion tank cap, to release any pressure present in the cooling system, and remove it.

3 Add a mixture of water and antifreeze to the expansion tank until the coolant is up to the MAX level mark. Refit the cap and tighten it securely.

Brake (and clutch) fluid level

Warning:
- *Brake fluid can harm your eyes and damage painted surfaces, so use extreme caution when handling and pouring it.*

- *Do not use fluid that has been standing open for some time, as it absorbs moisture from the air, which can cause a dangerous loss of braking effectiveness.*

 The fluid level in the reservoir will drop slightly as the brake pads wear down, but the fluid level must never be allowed to drop below the MIN mark.

Before you start
✔ Make sure that your vehicle is on level ground.
✔ Cleanliness is of great importance when dealing with the braking system, so take care to clean around the reservoir cap before topping up. Use only clean brake fluid.

Safety first!
● If the reservoir requires repeated topping-up this is an indication of a fluid leak somewhere in the system, which should be investigated immediately.
● If a leak is suspected, the vehicle should not be driven until the braking system has been checked. Never take any risks where brakes are concerned

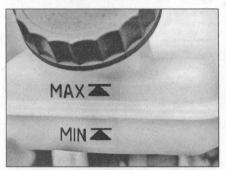

1 The MAX and MIN marks are indicated on the front of the reservoir. The fluid level must be kept between the marks at all times.

2 If topping-up is necessary, first wipe clean the area around the filler cap to prevent dirt entering the hydraulic system. Unscrew the reservoir cap.

3 Carefully add fluid, taking care not to spill it onto the surrounding components. Use only the specified fluid as mixing different types can cause damage to the system. After topping-up to the correct level, securely refit the cap and wipe off any spilt fluid.

Power steering fluid level

✔ Park the vehicle on level ground.
✔ Set the steering wheel straight-ahead.
✔ The engine should be turned off.

 For the check to be accurate, the steering must not be turned once the engine has been stopped.

Safety first!
● The need for frequent topping-up indicates a leak, which should be investigated immediately.

1 The fluid level is visible through the reservoir body. When the engine is cold, the level should be up to the MAX mark on the side of the reservoir.

2 If topping-up is required, wipe clean the area around the reservoir filler neck and unscrew the filler cap from the reservoir.

3 When topping-up, use the specified type of fluid and do not overfill the reservoir. When the level is correct, securely refit the cap.

Tyre condition and pressure

It is very important that tyres are in good condition, and at the correct pressure - having a tyre failure at any speed is highly dangerous. Tyre wear is influenced by driving style - harsh braking and acceleration, or fast cornering, will all produce more rapid tyre wear. As a general rule, the front tyres wear out faster than the rears. Interchanging the tyres from front to rear ("rotating" the tyres) may result in more even wear. However, if this is completely effective, you may have the expense of replacing all four tyres at once! Remove any nails or stones embedded in the tread before they penetrate the tyre to cause deflation. If removal of a nail does reveal that

the tyre has been punctured, refit the nail so that its point of penetration is marked. Then immediately change the wheel, and have the tyre repaired by a tyre dealer.

Regularly check the tyres for damage in the form of cuts or bulges, especially in the sidewalls. Periodically remove the wheels, and clean any dirt or mud from the inside and outside surfaces. Examine the wheel rims for signs of rusting, corrosion or other damage. Light alloy wheels are easily damaged by "kerbing" whilst parking; steel wheels may also become dented or buckled. A new wheel is very often the only way to overcome severe damage.

New tyres should be balanced when they are fitted, but it may become necessary to re-balance them as they wear, or if the balance weights fitted to the wheel rim should fall off. Unbalanced tyres will wear more quickly, as will the steering and suspension components. Wheel imbalance is normally signified by vibration, particularly at a certain speed (typically around 50 mph). If this vibration is felt only through the steering, then it is likely that just the front wheels need balancing. If, however, the vibration is felt through the whole car, the rear wheels could be out of balance. Wheel balancing should be carried out by a tyre dealer or garage.

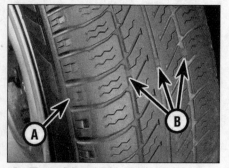

1 Tread Depth - visual check
The original tyres have tread wear safety bands (B), which will appear when the tread depth reaches approximately 1.6 mm. The band positions are indicated by a triangular mark on the tyre sidewall (A).

2 Tread Depth - manual check
Alternatively, tread wear can be monitored with a simple, inexpensive device known as a tread depth indicator gauge.

3 Tyre Pressure Check
Check the tyre pressures regularly with the tyres cold. Do not adjust the tyre pressures immediately after the vehicle has been used, or an inaccurate setting will result.

Tyre tread wear patterns

Shoulder Wear

Underinflation (wear on both sides)
Under-inflation will cause overheating of the tyre, because the tyre will flex too much, and the tread will not sit correctly on the road surface. This will cause a loss of grip and excessive wear, not to mention the danger of sudden tyre failure due to heat build-up.
Check and adjust pressures
Incorrect wheel camber (wear on one side)
Repair or renew suspension parts
Hard cornering
Reduce speed!

Centre Wear

Overinflation
Over-inflation will cause rapid wear of the centre part of the tyre tread, coupled with reduced grip, harsher ride, and the danger of shock damage occurring in the tyre casing.
Check and adjust pressures

If you sometimes have to inflate your car's tyres to the higher pressures specified for maximum load or sustained high speed, don't forget to reduce the pressures to normal afterwards.

Uneven Wear

Front tyres may wear unevenly as a result of wheel misalignment. Most tyre dealers and garages can check and adjust the wheel alignment (or "tracking") for a modest charge.
Incorrect camber or castor
Repair or renew suspension parts
Malfunctioning suspension
Repair or renew suspension parts
Unbalanced wheel
Balance tyres
Incorrect toe setting
Adjust front wheel alignment
Note: *The feathered edge of the tread which typifies toe wear is best checked by feel.*

Screen washer fluid level

● Screenwash additives not only keep the windscreen clean during bad weather, they also prevent the washer system freezing in cold weather – which is when you are likely to need it most. Don't top-up using plain water, as the screenwash will become diluted, and will freeze in cold weather.

⚠ **Warning: On no account use engine coolant antifreeze in the screen washer system – this may damage the paintwork.**

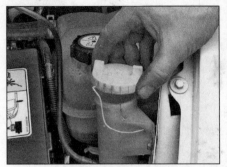

1 The reservoir for the windscreen and rear window (where applicable) washer systems is located on the front left-hand side of the engine compartment. If topping-up is necessary, remove the filler cap.

2 When topping-up the reservoir a screenwash additive should be added in the quantities recommended on the bottle.

Wiper blades

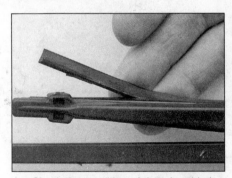

1 Check the condition of the wiper blades. If they are cracked or show any signs of deterioration, or if the glass swept area is smeared, renew them. Wiper blades should be renewed annually.

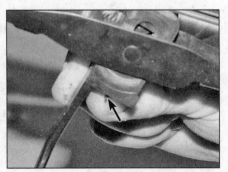

2 To remove a windscreen wiper blade, pull the arm fully away from the screen until it locks. Swivel the blade through 90°, then squeeze the locking clip, and detach the blade from the arm. When fitting the new blade, make sure that the blade locks securely into the arm, and that the blade is orientated correctly.

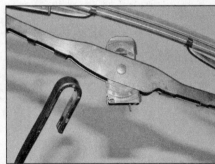

3 Don't forget to check the tailgate wiper blade as well (where applicable) which is removed in the same way.

Battery

Caution: Before carrying out any work on the vehicle battery, read the precautions given in 'Safety first!' at the start of this manual.

✔ Make sure that the battery tray is in good condition, and that the clamp is tight. Corrosion on the tray, retaining clamp and the battery itself can be removed with a solution of water and baking soda. Thoroughly rinse all cleaned areas with water. Any metal parts damaged by corrosion should be covered with a zinc-based primer, then painted.

✔ Periodically (approximately every three months), check the charge condition of the battery as described in Chapter 5.

✔ If the battery is flat, and you need to jump start your vehicle, see *Roadside Repairs*.

1 The battery is located in a compartment beneath the driver's seat. Move the driver's seat fully forward, and open the battery box cover. The exterior of the battery should be inspected periodically for damage such as a cracked case or cover.

2 Check the tightness of battery clamps to ensure good electrical connections. You should not be able to move them. Also check each cable for cracks and frayed conductors.

HAYNES HiNT

Battery corrosion can be kept to a minimum by applying a layer of petroleum jelly to the clamps and terminals after they are reconnected.

3 If corrosion (white, fluffy deposits) is evident, remove the cables from the battery terminals, clean them with a small wire brush, then refit them. Automotive stores sell a tool for cleaning the battery post . . .

4 . . . as well as the battery cable clamps

Electrical systems

✔ Check all external lights and the horn. Refer to the appropriate Sections of Chapter 12 for details if any of the circuits are found to be inoperative.

✔ Visually check all accessible wiring connectors, harnesses and retaining clips for security, and for signs of chafing or damage.

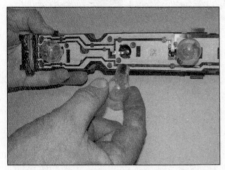

1 If a single indicator light, stop-light or headlight has failed, it is likely that a bulb has blown and will need to be replaced. Refer to Chapter 12 for details. If both stop-lights have failed, it is possible that the switch has failed (see Chapter 9).

2 If more than one indicator light or headlight has failed, it is likely either that a fuse has blown or that there is a fault in the circuit (see Chapter 12). To gain access to the fuses in the engine compartment fuse/relay box, release the catches at the front and lift up the lid.

3 Additional fuses are located in the passenger compartment fuse/relay box on the passenger's side of the facia. To gain access, lift out the storage compartment using the grab handle . . .

4 . . . then release the clips and lift off the fuse/relay box cover.

5 To replace a blown fuse, remove it, where applicable, using the plastic tool provided. Fit a new fuse of the same rating, available from car accessory shops. It is important that you find the reason that the fuse blew (see *Electrical fault finding* in Chapter 12).

Lubricants and fluids

Engine:

Preferred specification . . . . Multigrade engine oil, viscosity SAE 5W/30 to
Ford specification WSS-M2C913-B

Alternative specification*. . . . . Multigrade engine oil, viscosity SAE 5W/30, 5W/40 or 10W/40
to specification ACEA A1/B1 or ACEA A3/B3 or higher

Manual transmission . . . . Transmission oil to Ford specification WSD-M2C200-C

Power steering reservoir . . . . Automatic transmission fluid to Ford specification
WSA-M2C195-A

Cooling system . . . . Motorcraft Super Plus 2000 antifreeze to Ford specification
WSS-M97B44-D

Brake/clutch fluid reservoir . . . . Super DOT 4 brake fluid to Ford specification ESD-M6C57-A

Rear axle . . . . SAE 90W/140 gear oil to Ford specification WSL-M2C192-A

**Wheel hub bearings, propeller shaft universal joints and
general greasing** . . . . Grease to Ford specification SAM-1C-9111-A

** Use of the alternative specification engine oils may result in longer cold start cranking time, reduced engine performance,
reduced fuel economy and increased emission levels.*

Tyre pressures

Vehicle specific information on tyre pressures and wheel and tyre data is contained on a label attached to the driver's door pillar. Additional information is also contained in the driver's handbook supplied with the vehicle.

Chapter 1
Routine maintenance and servicing

Contents

Degrees of difficulty

Easy, suitable for novice with little experience 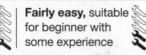	**Fairly easy,** suitable for beginner with some experience 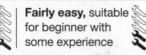	**Fairly difficult,** suitable for competent DIY mechanic 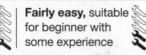	**Difficult,** suitable for experienced DIY mechanic 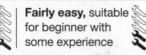	**Very difficult,** suitable for expert DIY or professional 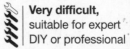

Lubricants and fluids. . . . .   Refer to the end of *Weekly checks* on page 0•18

Capacities

Engine oil:
  2.0 litre engines:
    With filter. . . . .   6.5 litres
    Without filter . . . .   6.0 litres
  2.4 litre engines:
    With filter. . . . .   7.0 litres
    Without filter . . . .   6.5 litres
  Difference between dipstick minimum and maximum marks. . . . . . .   2.0 litres
Cooling system. . . . .   10.0 litres
Fuel tank. . . . .   80.0 litres
Rear axle . . . .   2.6 litres
Transmission:
  2.0 litre engines . . . .   2.25 litres
  2.4 litre engines with 5-speed transmissions. . . . .   1.3 litres
  2.4 litre engines with 6-speed transmissions. . . . .   2.2 litres

Cooling system

Coolant protection at 40% antifreeze/water mixture ratio:
  Slush point . . . .   -25°C (-13°F)
  Solidifying point . . . .   -30°C (-22°F)

Braking system

Minimum front brake pad lining thickness. . . . .   1.5 mm
Minimum rear brake shoe lining thickness.   1.0 mm

Torque wrench settings

	Nm	lbf ft
Alternator mounting bracket (2.0 litre engines)	47	35
Engine oil drain plug.	23	17
Rear axle filler/level plug:		
Filler/level plug located on the differential housing cover	34	25
Filler level plug located on the drive pinion housing	30	22
Roadwheel nuts	200	148
Transmission filler/level plug.	35	26

The maintenance intervals in this manual are provided with the assumption that you, not the dealer, will be carrying out the work. These are the minimum maintenance intervals recommended by us for vehicles driven daily. If you wish to keep your vehicle in peak condition at all times, you may wish to perform some of these procedures more often. We encourage frequent maintenance, because it enhances the efficiency, performance and resale value of your vehicle.

If the vehicle is driven in dusty areas, used to tow a trailer, or driven frequently at slow speeds (idling in traffic) or on short journeys, more frequent maintenance intervals are recommended.

When the vehicle is new, it should be serviced by a dealer service department (or other workshop recognised by the vehicle manufacturer as providing the same standard of service) in order to preserve the warranty. The vehicle manufacturer may reject warranty claims if you are unable to prove that servicing has been carried out as and when specified, using only original equipment parts or parts certified to be of equivalent quality.

Every 250 miles (400 km) or weekly

☐ Refer to *Weekly checks*

Every 7500 miles or 6 months, whichever occurs first

☐ Renew the engine oil and filter (Section 3)*

*Note: *The manufacturers recommend that the engine oil and filter are changed every 15 000 miles or 12 months if the vehicle is being operated under normal conditions. However, oil and filter changes are good for the engine and we recommend that the oil and filter are renewed more frequently, especially if the vehicle is driven in dusty areas, used to tow a trailer, or driven frequently at slow speeds (idling in traffic) or on short journeys.*

Every 15 000 miles or 12 months, whichever occurs first

In addition to the item listed in the previous service, carry out the following:

☐ Check the battery and clean the terminals (Section 4)
☐ Check the auxiliary drivebelt (Section 5)
☐ Check the electrical system (Section 6)
☐ Check under the bonnet for fluid leaks and hose condition (Section 7)
☐ Check the condition of the fuel filter and drain the water (Section 8)
☐ Renew the fuel filter according to condition (Section 9)
☐ Check the condition of all engine compartment wiring (Section 10)
☐ Check the condition of all air conditioning system components (Section 11)
☐ Check the seat belts (Section 12)
☐ Check the antifreeze concentration (Section 13)
☐ Check the steering, suspension and roadwheels (Section 14)
☐ Check the driveshaft rubber gaiters and CV joints – front wheel drive models (Section 15)

Every 15 000 miles or 12 months, whichever occurs first (continued)

☐ Check the propeller shaft and centre bearing for wear – rear wheel drive models (Section 16)
☐ Lubricate the propeller shaft universal joints – rear wheel drive models (Section 17)
☐ Check the exhaust system (Section 18)
☐ Check the underbody, and all fuel/brake lines (Section 19)
☐ Check the brake pad and brake shoe lining thickness (Section 20)
☐ Check the operation and adjustment of the handbrake (Section 21)
☐ Check the doors and bonnet, and lubricate their hinges and locks (Section 22)
☐ Check the security of all roadwheel nuts (Section 23)
☐ Road test (Section 24)
☐ Reset the service interval indicator (Section 25)

Every 30 000 miles or 2 years, whichever occurs first

In addition to the relevant items listed in the previous services, carry out the following:

☐ Renew the air filter element (Section 26)
☐ Check the transmission oil level (Section 27)
☐ Check the rear axle oil level – rear wheel drive models (Section 28)
☐ Renew the brake fluid (Section 29)
☐ Renew the coolant (Section 30)*

*Note: *Vehicles using Ford purple Super Plus coolant do not need the coolant renewed on a regular basis.*

Every 100 000 miles or 10 years, whichever occurs first

In addition to the relevant items listed in the previous services, carry out the following:

☐ Renew the auxiliary drivebelts (Section 31)

Underbonnet view of a 2.0 litre engine model

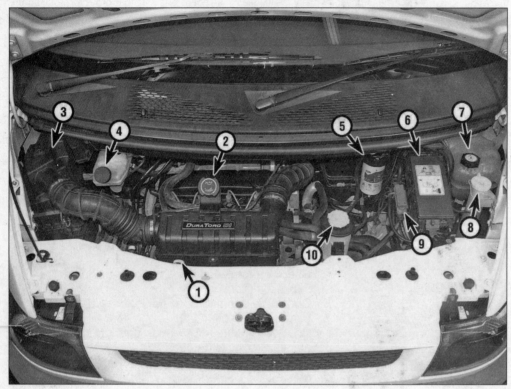

1   Engine oil level dipstick
2   Engine oil filler cap
3   Air cleaner assembly
4   Brake (and clutch) fluid
    reservoir
5   Fuel filter
6   Fuse/relay box
7   Coolant expansion tank
8   Screen washer fluid
    reservoir
9   Positive (+) cable terminal
    box
10 Power steering fluid
    reservoir

Underbonnet view of a 2.4 litre engine model

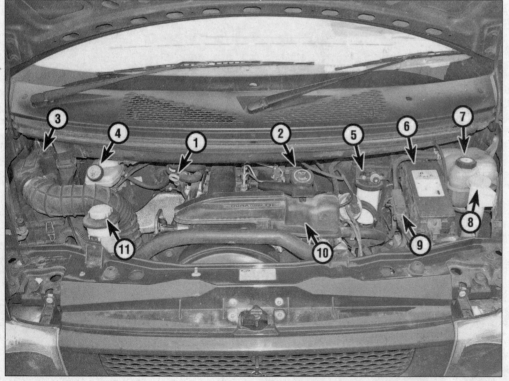

1   Engine oil level dipstick
2   Engine oil filler cap
3   Air cleaner assembly
4   Brake (and clutch) fluid
    reservoir
5   Fuel filter
6   Fuse/relay box
7   Coolant expansion tank
8   Screen washer fluid
    reservoir
9   Positive (+) cable terminal
    box
10 Auxiliary drivebelt cover
11 Power steering fluid
    reservoir

Front underbody view of a front wheel drive model

1 Engine oil drain plug
2 Oil filter
3 Front brake calipers
4 Intercooler
5 Screen washer fluid
   reservoir
6 Transmission
7 Steering track rods
8 Front suspension lower
   arms
9 Front subframe
10 Engine/transmission rear
   mounting
11 Exhaust front pipe
12 Driveshaft intermediate
   shaft

Front underbody view of a rear wheel drive model

1 Engine oil drain plug
2 Oil filter
3 Exhaust front pipe
4 Transmission
5 Front subframe
6 Front suspension lower
   arms
7 Engine crossmember
8 Alternator
9 Intercooler
10 Radiator cooling fan
11 Horn
12 Fuel filter

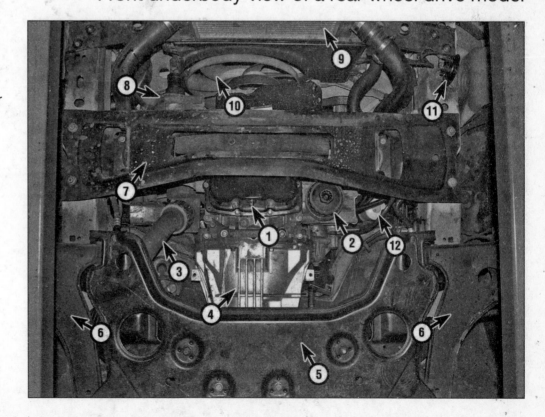

Rear underbody view of a front wheel drive model

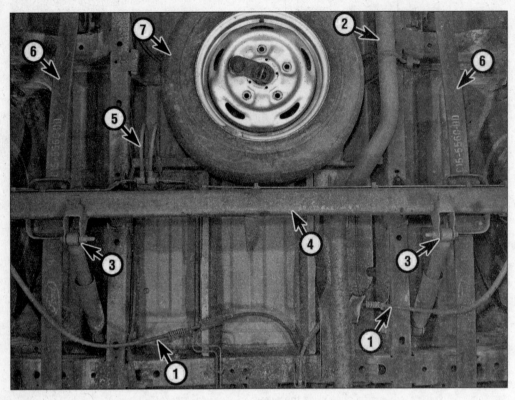

1 Handbrake cables
2 Exhaust tailpipe
3 Shock absorber lower mountings
4 Beam axle
5 Brake hydraulic hoses
6 Leaf springs
7 Spare wheel

Rear underbody view of a rear wheel drive model

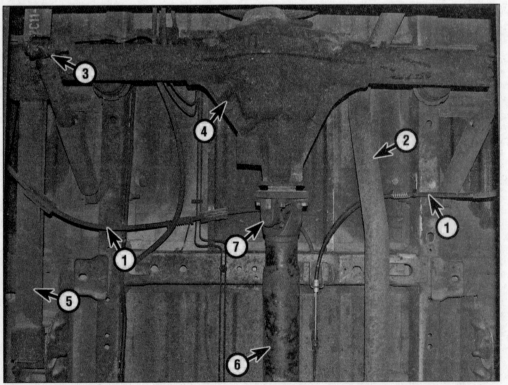

1 Handbrake cables
2 Exhaust tailpipe
3 Shock absorber lower mounting
4 Rear axle
5 Leaf spring
6 Propeller shaft
7 Universal joint

1 General information

1 This Chapter is designed to help the home mechanic maintain his/her vehicle for safety, economy, long life and peak performance.
2 The Chapter contains a master maintenance schedule, followed by Sections dealing specifically with each task in the schedule. Visual checks, adjustments, component renewal and other helpful items are included. Refer to the accompanying illustrations of the engine compartment and the underside of the vehicle for the locations of the various components.
3 Servicing your vehicle in accordance with the mileage/time maintenance schedule and the following Sections will provide a planned maintenance programme, which should result in a long and reliable service life. This is a comprehensive plan, so maintaining some items but not others at the specified service intervals, will not produce the same results.
4 As you service your vehicle, you will discover that many of the procedures can – and should – be grouped together, because of the particular procedure being performed, or because of the proximity of two otherwise unrelated components to one another. For example, if the vehicle is raised for any reason, the exhaust can be inspected at the same time as the suspension and steering components.
5 The first step in this maintenance pro-gramme is to prepare yourself before the actual work begins. Read through all the Sections relevant to the work to be carried out, then make a list and gather all the parts and tools required. If a problem is encountered, seek advice from a parts specialist, or a dealer service department.

2 Regular maintenance

1 If, from the time the vehicle is new, the routine maintenance schedule is followed closely, and frequent checks are made of fluid levels and high-wear items, as suggested throughout this manual, the engine will be kept in relatively good running condition, and the need for additional work will be minimised.
2 It is possible that there will be times when the engine is running poorly due to the lack of regular maintenance. This is even more likely if a used vehicle, which has not received regular and frequent maintenance checks, is purchased. In such cases, additional work may need to be carried out, outside of the regular maintenance intervals.
3 If engine wear is suspected, a compression test or leak-down test (refer to Chapter 2A or 2B) will provide valuable information regarding the overall performance of the main internal components. Such a test can be used as a basis to decide on the extent of the work to be carried out. If, for example, a compression or leak-down test indicates serious internal engine wear, conventional maintenance as described in this Chapter will not greatly improve the performance of the engine, and may prove a waste of time and money, unless extensive overhaul work is carried out first.
4 The following series of operations are those most often required to improve the performance of a generally poor running engine:

Primary operations

a) Clean, inspect and test the battery (see 'Weekly checks' and Section 4).
b) Check all the engine related fluids (refer to 'Weekly checks').
c) Check the condition and tension of the auxiliary drivebelt (Section 5).
d) Check the condition of all hoses, and check for fluid leaks (Sections 7 and 19).
e) Renew the fuel filter (Section 9).
f) Check the condition of the air filter, and renew if necessary (Section 26).

5 If the above operations do not prove fully effective, carry out the following secondary operations:

Secondary operations

All items listed under *Primary operations*, plus the following:

a) Check the charging system (refer to Chapter 5).
b) Check the pre/post-heating system (refer to Chapter 5).
c) Check the fuel system and emissions control systems (refer to Chapter 4A and 4B).

Every 7500 miles or 6 months

3 Engine oil and filter renewal

> **HAYNES HiNT**
> *Frequent oil and filter changes are the most important preventative maintenance procedures which can be undertaken by the DIY owner. As engine oil ages, it becomes diluted and contaminated, which leads to premature engine wear.*

1 Before starting this procedure, gather together all the necessary tools and materials. Also, make sure that you have plenty of clean rags and newspapers handy, to mop up any spills. Ideally, the engine oil should be warm, as it will drain more easily and more built-up sludge will be removed with it. Take care not to touch the exhaust or any other hot parts of the engine when working under the vehicle. To avoid any possibility of scalding and to protect yourself from possible skin irritants and other harmful contaminants in used engine oils, it is advisable to wear gloves when carrying out this work.

2 Access to the underside of the vehicle will be greatly improved if it can be raised on a lift, driven onto ramps, or jacked up and supported on axle stands (see *Jacking and vehicle support*). Whichever method is chosen, make sure that the vehicle remains level, or if it is at an angle, that the drain plug is at the lowest point.
3 Remove the oil filler cap, then unscrew the engine oil drain plug (located at the lowest point of the sump) about half a turn. Position the draining container under the drain plug, then remove the plug completely – recover the sealing washer **(see illustration and Haynes Hint).**
4 Allow some time for the oil to drain, noting that it may be necessary to reposition the container as the oil flow slows to a trickle.
5 After all the oil has drained, wipe off the

3.3 Engine oil drain plug location (arrowed)

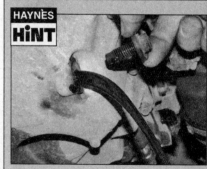

> **HAYNES HiNT**
> *Keep the plug pressed into the sump while unscrewing it by hand the last couple of turns. As the plug releases from the threads, move it away sharply, so the stream of oil issuing from the sump runs into the pan, not up your sleeve.*

3.7a Unscrew the oil filter housing cover . . .

3.7b . . . and discard the paper element

3.8 Removing the O-ring seal

drain plug with a clean rag, and fit a new sealing washer. Clean the area around the drain plug opening, and refit the plug. Tighten the plug to the specified torque.

6 Move the container into position under the oil filter, which is located on the front of the cylinder block (front wheel drive models), or the left-hand side of the cylinder block (rear wheel drive models).

7 Unscrew the oil filter plastic cover from the bottom of the oil filter housing, then remove and discard the paper element **(see illustrations)**.

8 Remove the O-ring seal and obtain a new one **(see illustration)**. Clean the filter housing and cover.

9 Fit the new O-ring seal onto the cover and lubricate it with a little engine oil.

10 Locate the new paper element on the cover, then screw the assembly into the filter housing and tighten securely by hand.

11 Remove the old oil and all tools from under the vehicle, then lower the vehicle to the ground.

12 Remove the dipstick, then unscrew the oil filler cap from the camshaft cover. Fill the engine, using the correct grade and type of oil (see *Weekly checks*). An oil can spout or funnel may help to reduce spillage. Pour in half the specified quantity of oil first, then wait a few minutes for the oil to fall to the sump. Continue adding oil, a small quantity at a time, until the level is up to the lower mark on the dipstick. Refit the filler cap.

13 Start the engine and run it for a few minutes, then check for leaks. Note that there

may be a delay of a few seconds before the oil pressure warning light goes out when the engine is first started, as the oil circulates through the engine oil galleries and the new oil filter before the pressure builds up.

14 Switch off the engine, and wait a few minutes for the oil to settle in the sump once more. With the new oil circulated and the filter completely full, recheck the level on the dipstick, and add more oil as necessary.

15 Dispose of the used engine oil and filter safely, with reference to *General repair procedures* in the Reference Chapter of this manual. Do not discard the old filter with domestic household waste. The facility for waste oil disposal provided by many local council refuse tips and/or recycling centres generally has a filter receptacle alongside.

Every 15 000 miles or 12 months

4 Battery maintenance and charging

⚠️ *Warning: Certain precautions must be followed when checking and servicing the battery. Hydrogen gas, which is highly flammable, is always present in the battery cells, so keep lighted tobacco and all other open flames and sparks away from the battery. The electrolyte inside the battery is actually dilute sulphuric acid, which will cause injury if splashed on your skin or in your eyes. It will also ruin clothes and painted surfaces.*

General

1 A routine preventive maintenance programme for the battery in your vehicle is the only way to ensure quick and reliable starts. For general maintenance, refer to *Weekly checks* at the start of this manual. Also, at the front of the manual, is information on jump starting. For details of removing and installing the battery, refer to Chapter 5.

Battery electrolyte level

2 On models not equipped with a sealed or 'maintenance-free' battery, check the electrolyte level of all six battery cells.

3 The level must be approximately 10 mm above the plates; this may be shown by maximum and minimum level lines marked on the battery's casing.

4 If the level is low, use a coin or screwdriver to release the filler/vent cap, and add distilled water. To improve access to the centre caps, it may be helpful to remove the battery hold-down clamp.

5 Install and securely retighten the cap, then wipe up any spillage.

Caution: Overfilling the cells may cause electrolyte to spill over during periods of heavy charging, causing corrosion or damage.

Charging

⚠️ *Warning: When batteries are being charged, hydrogen gas, which is very explosive and flammable, is produced. Do not smoke, or allow open flames, near a charging or a recently charged battery. Wear eye protection when near the battery during charging. Also, make sure the charger is unplugged before connecting or disconnecting the battery from the charger.*

6 Slow-rate charging is the best way to restore a battery that's discharged to the point where it will not start the engine. It's also a good way to maintain the battery charge in a vehicle

that's only driven a few miles between starts. Maintaining the battery charge is particularly important in winter, when the battery must work harder to start the engine, and electrical accessories that drain the battery are in greater use.

7 Check the battery case for any instructions regarding charging the battery. Some maintenance-free batteries may require a particularly low charge rate or other special conditions, if they are not to be damaged.

8 It's best to use a one- or two-amp battery charger (sometimes called a 'trickle' charger). They are the safest, and put the least strain on the battery. They are also the least expensive. For a faster charge, you can use a higher amperage charger, but don't use one rated more than 1/10th the amp/hour rating of the battery (ie, no more than 5 amps, typically). Rapid boost charges that claim to restore the power of the battery in one to two hours are hardest on the battery, and can damage batteries not in good condition. This type of charging should only be used in emergency situations.

9 The average time necessary to charge a battery should be listed in the instructions that come with the charger. As a general rule, a trickle charger will charge a battery in 12 to 16 hours.

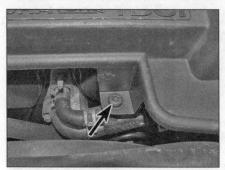

5.6a Undo the auxiliary drivebelt cover right-hand retaining bolt (arrowed) . . .

5.6b . . . and centre retaining bolt (arrowed) . . .

5.6c . . . then release the wiring harness and/or hoses and lift the cover off the engine

5 Auxiliary drivebelt check

General

1 On 2.0 litre engines, two auxiliary drivebelts are fitted. The main auxiliary drivebelt is of flat, multi-ribbed type, and is located on the right-hand end of the engine. It drives the alternator and, where fitted, the air conditioning compressor from the engine's crankshaft pulley. A separate multi-ribbed drivebelt drives the power steering pump and coolant pump from the left-hand end of the inlet camshaft.

2 On 2.4 litre engines, a single, flat, multi-ribbed drivebelt is used and is located on the front of the engine. The belt drives the alternator, power steering pump, coolant pump, radiator cooling fan, brake servo vacuum pump and, where fitted, the air conditioning compressor, from the engine's crankshaft pulley.

3 The good condition and proper tension of the auxiliary drivebelts are critical to the operation of the engine. They must, therefore, be regularly inspected.

Check

4 With the engine switched off, open and support the bonnet.

5 On 2.0 litre engines, firmly apply the handbrake, then jack up the front of the vehicle and support it securely on axle stands (see *Jacking and vehicle support*). Remove the right-hand roadwheel, then remove the auxiliary drivebelt cover (two fasteners) from under the wheel arch.

6 On 2.4 litre engines, undo the two bolts securing the auxiliary drivebelt cover to the top of the engine. The centre bolt may be located under a plastic cover on certain models. There may also be an additional bolt at the left-hand side of the cover; if so, undo this bolt also. Release the wiring harness and/or hoses at the rear of the cover and lift the cover off the engine **(see illustrations)**.

7 Using an inspection light or a small electric torch, and rotating the engine with a spanner applied to the crankshaft pulley bolt, check the whole length of the drivebelt for cracks, separation of the rubber, and torn or worn ribs. Also, check for fraying and glazing, which gives the drivebelt a shiny appearance.

8 Both sides of the drivebelt should be inspected, which means you will have to twist the drivebelt to check the underside. Use your fingers to feel the drivebelt where you can't see it. If you are in any doubt as to the condition of the drivebelt, renew it as described below.

9 In addition, on 2.0 litre engines, remove the power steering pump drivebelt cover from the top of the engine. Inspect the drivebelt as described in paragraphs 7 and 8.

Drivebelt tension

10 On all except 2.0 litre engines without air conditioning, the auxiliary drivebelts are tensioned by an automatic tensioner; regular checks are not required, and manual 'adjustment' is not possible. On 2.0 litre engines without air conditioning, the main auxiliary drivebelt is of the 'stretchy' type and a tensioner is not used.

11 If you suspect that a drivebelt is slipping and/or running slack, or that the tensioner is otherwise faulty, it must be renewed.

Drivebelt renewal

12 Refer to Section 31.

6 Electrical system check

1 Check the operation of all external lights and indicators (front and rear).

2 Check for satisfactory operation of the instrument panel, its illumination and warning lights, the switches and their function lights.

3 Check the horn(s) for satisfactory operation.

4 Check all other electrical equipment for satisfactory operation.

7 Underbonnet check for fluid leaks and hose condition

1 Visually inspect the engine joint faces, gaskets and seals for any signs of water or oil leaks. Pay particular attention to the areas around the camshaft cover, cylinder head, oil filter and sump joint faces. Bear in mind that, over a period of time, some very slight seepage from these areas is to be expected – what you are really looking for is any indication of a serious leak. Should a leak be found, renew the offending gasket or oil seal by referring to the appropriate Chapters in this manual.

2 Also check the security and condition of all the engine related pipes and hoses, and all braking system pipes and hoses and fuel lines. Ensure that all cable ties or securing clips are in place, and in good condition. Clips which are broken or missing can lead to chafing of the hoses, pipes or wiring, which could cause more serious problems in the future.

3 Carefully check the radiator hoses and heater hoses along their entire length. Renew any hose which is cracked, swollen or deteriorated. Cracks will show up better if the hose is squeezed. Pay close attention to the hose clips that secure the hoses to the cooling system components. Hose clips can pinch and puncture hoses, resulting in cooling system leaks. If the crimped type hose clips are used, it may be a good idea to replace them with standard worm-drive clips.

4 Inspect all the cooling system components (hoses, joint faces, etc) for leaks **(see Haynes Hint)**.

5 Where any problems are found on system components, renew the component or gasket with reference to Chapter 3.

HAYNES HINT

A leak in the cooling system will usually show up as white- or rust-coloured deposits on the area adjoining the leak.

8.1a The fuel filter service indicator (arrowed) is either screwed into the filter housing . . .

8.1b . . . or incorporated in the fuel supply pipe adjacent to the filter housing (arrowed)

8 Fuel filter condition check and water draining

Fuel filter condition check

1 The fuel filter is located at the rear of the engine compartment, on the left-hand side of the bulkhead. The filter assembly incorporates a service indicator either screwed into the filter housing, or incorporated in the fuel supply pipe adjacent to the filter housing (see illustrations). The service indicator is a clear plastic capsule containing an internal spring and movable sector, and marked externally with green, clear and red areas which indicate the condition of the filter. When the service indicator is being used, the movable sector will align with one of the three coloured areas giving an indication of filter condition. To operate the service indicator, proceed as follows.

2 On vehicles with 2.4 litre 120 PS and 125 PS engines, start the engine and allow it to idle. On all other engines leave the ignition switched off.

3 Press the yellow button on the top of the service indicator and keep it depressed for three seconds to reset the unit (see illustration).

4 Start the engine (if it is not already running).

5 Run the engine at 4000 RPM for 5 seconds, then return it to idle. On models without a tachometer, fully depress the accelerator for 3 seconds, then release it.

6 Check the condition of the service indicator. If the movable sector is in the green area, this indicates that the filter is in good condition and no action is necessary. If it is in the clear area, this indicates that the filter condition is marginal and the filter should be renewed at the next service interval. If it is in the red area, this indicates that the filter is in poor condition and should be renewed immediately (see Section 9).

7 On completion of the check, switch off the engine.

Fuel filter water draining

Caution: Before starting any work on the fuel filter, wipe clean the filter assembly and the surrounding area as it is essential that no dirt or other foreign matter is allowed into the system. Obtain a suitable container into which the filter can be drained and place rags or similar material under the filter assembly to catch any spillages. Do not allow diesel fuel to contaminate components such as the alternator and starter motor, the coolant hoses and engine mountings, and any wiring.

8 If the fuel filter service indicator indicates that the fuel filter should be renewed immediately, proceed as described in Section 9. If the filter is still in a serviceable condition, drain the water from the filter as follows.

9 In addition to taking the precautions noted above to catch any fuel spillages, connect a tube to the drain screw on the base of the fuel filter (see illustration). Place the other end of the tube in a clean jar or can.

10 Loosen the drain screw approximately one complete turn and allow the filter to drain until clean fuel, free of dirt or water, emerges from the tube (approximately 100 cc is usually sufficient).

11 Tighten the drain screw securely and remove the drain tube.

12 On completion, dispose of the drained fuel safely.

9 Fuel filter renewal

Caution: Before starting any work on the fuel filter, wipe clean the filter assembly and the surrounding area as it is essential that no dirt or other foreign matter is allowed into the system. Place rags or similar material under the filter assembly to catch any spillages. Do not allow diesel fuel to contaminate components such as the alternator and starter motor, the coolant hoses and engine mountings, and any wiring.

Note 1: *The fuel filter assembly incorporates a service indicator which can be used to check the filter condition (see Section 8). If the service indicator is in the green or clear areas, it is not strictly necessary to renew the filter at this service interval, however the filter condition should continue to be checked periodically, using the service indicator.*

Note 2: *Before carrying out the following procedure, read carefully the precautions given in the appropriate Sections of Chapter 4A.*

8.3 Press the yellow button on the service indicator for three seconds to reset the unit

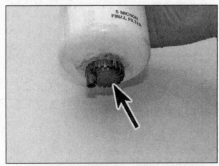

8.9 Fuel filter drain screw (arrowed)

1 The fuel filter is located at the rear of the engine compartment, on the left-hand side of the bulkhead.

2 Where fitted, disconnect the wiring connector from the water-in-fuel sensor at the base of the filter.

Vehicles manufactured up to November 2004

3 Rotate the fuel filter locking collar clockwise (as viewed from above), to release the filter from the housing, then remove the filter and locking collar from the engine compartment (see illustrations).

4 Where fitted, remove the water-in-fuel sensor from the old filter and transfer it to the new filter.

5 Position the new filter together with the locking collar on the filter housing. Engage the locking collar with the housing and rotate the collar anticlockwise to lock it in position. An audible click will be heard when the locking collar is correctly secured. Where fitted, reconnect the wiring connector to the water-in-fuel sensor at the base of the filter.

6 Wipe away any spilled fuel, then prime and bleed the fuel system as described in Chapter 4A.

7 On completion, dispose of the old filter safely.

Vehicles manufactured from November 2004 onward

8 Rotate the fuel filter body clockwise (as viewed from above), to release the filter from the housing, then remove the filter from the engine compartment.

9 Where fitted, remove the water-in-fuel sensor from the old filter and transfer it to the new filter.

10 Align the mark on the filter body with the first mark on the housing and engage the filter with the housing. Turn the filter body anticlockwise until the mark on the filter body aligns with the second mark on the filter housing. Where fitted, reconnect the wiring connector to the water-in-fuel sensor at the base of the filter.

11 Wipe away any spilled fuel, then prime and bleed the fuel system as described in Chapter 4A.

12 On completion, dispose of the old filter safely.

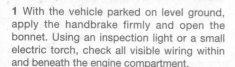

10 Engine compartment wiring check

1 With the vehicle parked on level ground, apply the handbrake firmly and open the bonnet. Using an inspection light or a small electric torch, check all visible wiring within and beneath the engine compartment.

2 What you are looking for is wiring that is obviously damaged by chafing against sharp edges, or against moving suspension/transmission components and/or the auxiliary

9.3a On pre-November 2004 vehicles, rotate the fuel filter locking collar clockwise . . .

drivebelt, by being trapped or crushed between carelessly refitted components, or melted by being forced into contact with the hot engine castings, coolant pipes, etc. In almost all cases, damage of this sort is caused in the first instance by incorrect routing on reassembly after previous work has been carried out.

3 Depending on the extent of the problem, damaged wiring may be repaired by rejoining the break or splicing-in a new length of wire, using solder to ensure a good connection, and remaking the insulation with adhesive insulating tape or heat-shrink tubing, as appropriate. If the damage is extensive, given the implications for the vehicle's future reliability, the best long-term answer may well be to renew that entire section of the loom, however expensive this may appear.

4 When the actual damage has been repaired, ensure that the wiring loom is re-routed correctly, so that it is clear of other components, and not stretched or kinked, and is secured out of harm's way using the plastic clips, guides and ties provided.

5 Check all electrical connectors, ensuring that they are clean, securely fastened, and that each is locked by its plastic tabs or wire clip, as appropriate. If any connector shows external signs of corrosion (accumulations of white or green deposits, or streaks of 'rust'), or if any is thought to be dirty, it must be unplugged and cleaned using electrical contact cleaner. If the connector pins are severely corroded, the connector must be renewed; note that this may mean the renewal of that entire section of the loom – see your local Ford dealer for details.

6 If the cleaner completely removes the corrosion to leave the connector in a satisfactory condition, it would be wise to pack the connector with a suitable material which will exclude dirt and moisture, preventing the corrosion from occurring again. A Ford dealer may be able to recommend a suitable product.

7 Use the same techniques to ensure that all earth points in the engine compartment provide good electrical contact through clean, metal-to-metal joints, and that all are securely fastened.

9.3b . . . then remove the filter and locking collar from the engine compartment

11 Air conditioning system check

1 The following maintenance checks will ensure that the air conditioner operates at peak efficiency:
   a) Check the auxiliary drivebelt (see Section 5).
   b) Check the system hoses for damage or leaks.
   c) Inspect the condenser fins for leaves, insects and other debris. Use a clean paint brush to clean the condenser.
   d) Check that the drain tube from the front of the evaporator is clear – note that it is normal to have clear fluid (water) dripping from this while the system is in operation, to the extent that quite a large puddle can be left under the vehicle when it is parked.

2 It's a good idea to operate the system for about 30 minutes at least once a month, particularly during the winter. Long term non-use can cause hardening of the seals, and subsequent failure.

3 Because of the complexity of the air conditioning system and the special equipment necessary to service it, in-depth fault diagnosis and repairs are not included in this manual.

4 The most common cause of poor cooling is simply a low system refrigerant charge. If a noticeable drop in cool air output occurs, the following quick check will help you determine if the refrigerant level is low.

5 Warm the engine up to normal operating temperature.

6 Place the air conditioning temperature selector at the coldest setting, and put the blower at the highest setting. Open the doors – to make sure the air conditioning system doesn't cycle off as soon as it cools the passenger compartment.

7 With the compressor engaged – the clutch will make an audible click, and the centre of the clutch will rotate – feel the inlet and outlet pipes at the compressor. One side should be cold, and one hot. If there's no perceptible difference between the two pipes, there's something wrong with the compressor or the system. It might be a low charge – it might be

14.4 Checking for wear in the front suspension and hub bearings

something else. Take the vehicle to a dealer service department or an automotive air conditioning specialist.

12 Seat belt check

1 Check the seat belts for satisfactory operation and condition. Inspect the webbing for fraying and cuts. Check that they retract smoothly and without binding into their reels.
2 Check that the seat belt mounting bolts are tight, and if necessary tighten them to the specified torque wrench setting (Chapter 11).

13 Antifreeze concentration check

1 The cooling system should be filled with the recommended antifreeze and corrosion protection fluid. Over a period of time, the concentration of fluid may be reduced due to topping-up (this can be avoided by topping-up with the correct antifreeze mixture) or fluid loss. If loss of coolant has been evident, it is important to make the necessary repair before adding fresh fluid. The exact mixture of antifreeze-to-water which you should use depends on the relative weather conditions. The mixture should contain at least 40% antifreeze, but not more than 70%. Consult the mixture ratio chart on the antifreeze container before adding coolant. Use antifreeze

14.9 Rear spring U-bolt nuts (two of four arrowed)

which meets the vehicle manufacturer's specifications.
2 With the engine cold, carefully remove the cap from the expansion tank. If the engine is not completely cold, place a cloth rag over the cap before removing it, and remove it slowly to allow any pressure to escape.
3 Antifreeze checkers are available from car accessory shops. Draw some coolant from the expansion tank and observe how many plastic balls are floating in the checker. Usually, 2 or 3 balls must be floating for the correct concentration of antifreeze, but follow the manufacturer's instructions.
4 If the concentration is incorrect, it will be necessary to either withdraw some coolant and add antifreeze, or alternatively drain the old coolant and add fresh coolant of the correct concentration.

14 Steering, suspension and roadwheel check

Front suspension and steering

1 Firmly apply the handbrake, then jack up the front of the vehicle and support it securely on axle stands (see *Jacking and vehicle support*).
2 Visually inspect the balljoint dust covers and the steering rack-and-pinion gaiters for splits, chafing or deterioration. Any wear of these components will cause loss of lubricant, together with dirt and water entry, resulting in rapid deterioration of the balljoints or steering gear.
3 Check the power steering fluid hoses for chafing or deterioration, and the pipe and hose unions for fluid leaks. Also, check for signs of fluid leakage under pressure from the steering gear rubber gaiters, which would indicate failed fluid seals within the steering gear.
4 Grasp the roadwheel at the 12 o'clock and 6 o'clock positions, and try to rock it **(see illustration)**. Very slight free play may be felt, but if the movement is appreciable, further investigation is necessary to determine the source. Continue rocking the wheel while an assistant depresses the footbrake. If the movement is now eliminated or significantly reduced, it is likely that the hub bearings are at fault. If the free play is still evident with the footbrake depressed, then there is wear in the suspension joints or mountings.
5 Now grasp the wheel at the 9 o'clock and 3 o'clock positions, and try to rock it as before. Any movement felt now may again be caused by wear in the hub bearings or the steering track rod balljoints. If the outer track rod balljoint is worn, the visual movement will be obvious. If the inner joint is suspect, it can be felt by placing a hand over the rack-and-pinion rubber gaiter and gripping the track rod. If the wheel is now rocked, movement will be felt at the inner joint if wear has taken place.

6 Using a large screwdriver or flat bar, check for wear in the suspension mounting bushes by levering between the relevant suspension component and its attachment point. Some movement is to be expected, as the mountings are made of rubber, but excessive wear should be obvious. Also check the condition of any visible rubber bushes, looking for splits, cracks or contamination of the rubber.
7 With the car standing on its wheels, have an assistant turn the steering wheel back-and-forth, about an eighth of a turn each way. There should be very little, if any, lost movement between the steering wheel and roadwheels. If this is not the case, closely observe the joints and mountings previously described. In addition, check the steering column universal joints for wear, and also check the rack-and-pinion steering gear itself.

Rear suspension

8 Chock the front wheels, then jack up the rear of the vehicle and support securely on axle stands (see *Jacking and vehicle support*).
9 Working as described previously for the front suspension, check the rear hub bearings, the leaf spring mounting bushes and the shock absorber mountings for wear. Also check that the rear spring U-bolt nuts are tightened to the specified torque as given in Chapter 10 **(see illustration)**.

Shock absorbers

10 Check for any signs of fluid leakage around the shock absorber body, or from the rubber gaiter around the piston rod. Should any fluid be noticed, the shock absorber is defective internally, and should be renewed.
Note: *Shock absorbers should always be renewed in pairs on the same axle.*
11 The efficiency of the shock absorber may be checked by bouncing the vehicle at each corner. Generally speaking, the body will return to its normal position and stop after being depressed. If it rises and returns on a rebound, the shock absorber is probably suspect. Also examine the shock absorber upper and lower mountings for any signs of wear.

Roadwheels

12 Periodically remove the roadwheels, and clean any dirt or mud from the inside and outside surfaces. Examine the wheel rims for signs of rusting, corrosion or other damage. Light alloy wheels are easily damaged by 'kerbing' whilst parking, and similarly, steel wheels may become dented or buckled. Renewal of the wheel is very often the only course of remedial action possible.
13 The balance of each wheel and tyre assembly should be maintained, not only to avoid excessive tyre wear, but also to avoid wear in the steering and suspension components. Wheel imbalance is normally signified by vibration through the vehicle's bodyshell, although in many cases it is particularly noticeable through the steering

wheel. Conversely, it should be noted that wear or damage in suspension or steering components may cause excessive tyre wear. Out-of-round or out-of-true tyres, damaged wheels and wheel bearing wear/maladjustment also fall into this category. Balancing will not usually cure vibration caused by such wear.

15 Driveshaft rubber gaiter and CV joint check

1 The driveshaft rubber gaiters on front wheel drive vehicles are very important, because they prevent dirt, water and foreign material from entering and damaging the constant velocity (CV) joints. External contamination can cause the gaiter material to deteriorate prematurely, so it's a good idea to wash the gaiters with soap and water occasionally.

2 With the vehicle raised and securely supported on axle stands (see *Jacking and vehicle support*), turn the steering onto full-lock, then slowly rotate each front wheel in turn. Inspect the condition of the outer constant velocity (CV) joint rubber gaiters, squeezing the gaiters to open out the folds **(see illustration)**. Check for signs of cracking, splits, or deterioration of the rubber, which may allow the escape of grease, and lead to the ingress of water and grit into the joint. Also check the security and condition of the retaining clips. Repeat these checks on the inner CV joints. If any damage or deterioration is found, the gaiters should be renewed as described in Chapter 8.

3 At the same time, check the general condition of the outer CV joints themselves, by first holding the driveshaft and attempting to rotate the wheels. Repeat this check on the inner joints, by holding the inner joint yoke and attempting to rotate the driveshaft.

4 Any appreciable movement in the CV joint indicates wear in the joint, wear in the driveshaft splines, or a loose driveshaft retaining nut.

16 Propeller shaft universal joint and centre bearing check

1 Ideally, the vehicle should be raised at the front and rear and securely supported on axle stands (see *Jacking and vehicle support*) with the rear wheels free to rotate.

2 Check around the rubber portion of the centre bearings for any signs of cracks, oil contamination or deformation of the rubber **(see illustration)**. If any of these conditions are apparent, the centre bearing(s) should be renewed as described in Chapter 8.

3 At the same time, check the condition of the universal joints by holding the propeller shaft in one hand and the transmission or rear axle flange in the other **(see illustration)**. Try to twist the two components in opposite

15.2 Check the driveshaft gaiters by hand for cracks and/or leaking grease

directions and look for any movement in the universal joint spiders. Repeat this check at the centre bearing(s), and in all other areas where the individual parts of the propeller shaft or universal joints connect. If any wear is evident, refer to Chapter 8 for repair procedures. If grating or squeaking noises have been heard from below the vehicle, or if there is any sign of rust-coloured deposits around the universal joint spiders, this indicates an advanced state of wear, and should be seen to immediately.

17 Propeller shaft universal joint lubrication

1 Chock the front wheels then jack up the rear of the vehicle and securely support it on axle stands (see *Jacking and vehicle support*).

2 Wipe clean the area around the grease nipples on the propeller shaft universal joints **(see illustration)**.

3 Using a grease gun filled with the specified grease (see *Lubricants and fluids*) and applied firmly to the nipple, give the gun a few strokes to lubricate the universal joint spiders and needle roller bearings.

4 Lower the vehicle to the ground on completion.

18 Exhaust system check

1 With the engine cold, check the complete

16.3 Check the condition of the propeller shaft universal joints

16.2 Check the rubber portion of the propeller shaft centre bearings for signs of cracks, oil contamination or deformation

exhaust system, from its starting point at the engine to the end of the tailpipe. If necessary, raise the front and rear of the vehicle and support it on axle stands (see *Jacking and vehicle support*).

2 Check the exhaust pipes and connections for evidence of leaks, severe corrosion, and damage. Make sure that all brackets and mountings are in good condition and that all relevant nuts and bolts are tight. Leakage at any of the joints or in other parts of the system will usually show up as a black sooty stain in the vicinity of the leak.

3 Rattles and other noises can often be traced to the exhaust system, especially the brackets and rubber mountings. Try to move the pipes and silencers. If the components are able to come into contact with the body or suspension parts, secure the system with new mountings. Otherwise separate the joints (if possible) and twist the pipes as necessary to provide additional clearance.

19 Underbody and fuel/brake line check

1 With the vehicle raised and supported on axle stands (see *Jacking and vehicle support*), thoroughly inspect the underbody and wheel arches for signs of damage and corrosion. In particular, examine the bottom of the side sills, and any concealed areas where mud can collect.

2 Where corrosion and rust is evident, press

17.2 Propeller shaft universal joint grease nipple (arrowed)

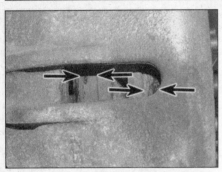

20.2 Check the thickness of the pad friction material through the caliper inspection window

and tap firmly on the panel with a screwdriver, and check for any serious corrosion which would necessitate repairs.

3 If the panel is not seriously corroded, clean away the rust, and apply a new coating of underseal. Refer to Chapter 11 for more details of body repairs.

4 Inspect the fuel tank and filler neck for punctures, cracks and other damage. The connection between the filler neck and tank is especially critical. Sometimes a rubber filler neck or connecting hose will leak due to loose retaining clamps or deteriorated rubber.

5 Carefully check all rubber hoses and metal fuel lines leading away from the fuel tank. Check for loose connections, deteriorated hoses, crimped lines, and other damage. Pay particular attention to the vent pipes and hoses, which often loop up around the filler neck and can become blocked or crimped. Follow the lines to the front of the vehicle, carefully inspecting them all the way. Renew damaged sections as necessary. Similarly, whilst the vehicle is raised, take the opportunity to inspect all underbody brake fluid pipes and hoses.

6 From within the engine compartment, check the security of all fuel, vacuum, power steering and brake hose attachments and pipe unions, and inspect all hoses for kinks, chafing and deterioration.

20 Brake pad and brake shoe wear check

Front disc brakes

1 Apply the handbrake, then jack up the front of the vehicle and support it on axle stands (see *Jacking and vehicle support*). For better access to the brake calipers, remove the roadwheels.

2 Look through the inspection window in the caliper, and check that the thickness of the friction lining material on each of the pads is not less than the recommended minimum thickness given in the Specifications **(see illustration)**.

3 If it is difficult to determine the exact thickness of the pad linings, or if you are at

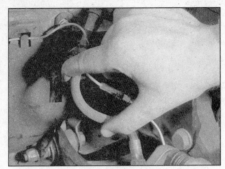

20.7 Checking the condition of a flexible brake hose

all concerned about the condition of the pads, then remove them from the calipers for further inspection (refer to Chapter 9).

4 Check the caliper on the other side in the same way.

5 If any one of the brake pads has worn down to, or below, the specified limit, *all four* pads must be renewed as a set.

6 Check both front brake discs with reference to Chapter 9.

7 Before refitting the wheels, check all brake lines and flexible hoses with reference to Chapter 9. In particular, check the flexible hoses in the vicinity of the calipers, where they are subjected to most movement. Bend them between the fingers and check that this does not reveal previously hidden cracks, cuts or splits **(see illustration)**.

8 On completion, refit the roadwheels and lower the vehicle to the ground. Tighten the wheel nuts to the specified torque.

Rear drum brakes

9 Chock the front wheels, then jack up the rear of the vehicle, and support it securely on axle stands (see *Jacking and vehicle support*).

10 For a quick check, the thickness of friction material remaining on one of the brake shoes can be observed through the hole in the brake backplate which is exposed by prising out the sealing grommet. If a rod of the same diameter as the specified minimum friction material thickness is placed against the shoe friction material, the amount of wear can be assessed. An electric torch or inspection light will probably be required. If the friction

21.5 Handbrake cable adjuster nut (arrowed)

material on any shoe is worn down to the specified minimum thickness or less, all four shoes must be renewed as a set.

11 For a comprehensive check, the brake drum should be removed and cleaned. This will allow the wheel cylinders to be checked, and the condition of the brake drum itself to be fully examined (see Chapter 9).

21 Handbrake operation and adjustment check

1 With the vehicle on a slight slope, apply the handbrake lever, and check that it holds the vehicle stationary, then release the lever and check that there is no resistance to movement of the vehicle.

2 If necessary, adjust the handbrake as follows. First, position the vehicle on level ground.

3 Chock the front wheels then jack up the rear of the vehicle and securely support it on axle stands (see *Jacking and vehicle support*).

4 Firmly apply the handbrake lever, then release it three or four times.

5 From under the vehicle, locate the handbrake cable adjuster nut at the cable compensator plate **(see illustration)**.

6 With the handbrake lever released, tighten the cable adjuster nut until the brake shoes just start to drag on the brake drums and slight resistance is felt when the roadwheel is rotated.

7 Slacken the handbrake cable adjuster nut three full turns and check that the rear wheels are free to rotate without binding.

8 On completion, lower the vehicle to the ground.

22 Door and bonnet check and lubrication

1 Check that the doors, bonnet and, where applicable, the tailgate close securely. Check that the bonnet safety catch operates correctly. Check the operation of the door check straps.

2 Lubricate the hinges, door check straps, the striker plates and the bonnet catch sparingly with a little oil or grease.

23 Roadwheel nut tightness check

1 Apply the handbrake, chock the wheels, and engage 1st gear.

2 Remove the wheel nut covers (or wheel centre cover), using the flat end of the wheel brace supplied in the tool kit.

3 Check the tightness of all wheel nuts using a torque wrench (refer to the Specifications).

24 Road test

Instruments and electrical equipment

1 Check the operation of all instruments and electrical equipment.
2 Make sure that all instruments read correctly, and switch on all electrical equipment in turn, to check that it functions properly.

Steering and suspension

3 Check for any abnormalities in the steering, suspension, handling or road 'feel'.
4 Drive the vehicle, and check that there are no unusual vibrations or noises.
5 Check that the steering feels positive, with no excessive 'sloppiness', or roughness, and check for any suspension noises when cornering and driving over bumps.

Drivetrain

6 Check the performance of the engine, clutch, transmission and driveshafts/propeller shaft.
7 Listen for any unusual noises from the engine, clutch and transmission.

8 Make sure that the engine runs smoothly when idling, and that there is no hesitation when accelerating.
9 Check that the clutch action is smooth and progressive, that the drive is taken up smoothly, and that the pedal travel is not excessive. Also listen for any noises when the clutch pedal is depressed.
10 Check that all gears can be engaged smoothly without noise, and that the gear lever action is smooth and not abnormally vague or 'notchy'.
11 On front wheel drive models, listen for a metallic clicking sound from the front of the vehicle, as the vehicle is driven slowly in a circle with the steering on full-lock. Carry out this check in both directions. If a clicking noise is heard, this indicates wear in a driveshaft joint (see Chapter 8).

Braking system

12 Make sure that the vehicle does not pull to one side when braking, and that the wheels do not lock when braking hard (models with ABS).
13 Check that there is no vibration through the steering when braking.
14 Check that the handbrake operates correctly, without excessive movement of the lever, and that it holds the vehicle stationary on a slope.
15 Test the operation of the brake servo unit as follows. Depress the footbrake four or five times to exhaust the vacuum, then start the engine. As the engine starts, there should be a noticeable 'give' in the brake pedal as vacuum builds up. Allow the engine to run for at least two minutes, and then switch it off. If the brake pedal is now depressed again, it should be possible to detect a hiss from the servo as the pedal is depressed. After about four or five applications, no further hissing should be heard, and the pedal should feel considerably harder.

25 Service interval indicator reset

1 Switch the ignition on (position II) without starting the engine.
2 Simultaneously depress the brake pedal and accelerator pedal fully for at least 15 seconds until the service interval indicator light flashes. With the light flashing, turn the ignition off.

Every 30 000 miles or 2 years

26 Air filter element renewal

1 The air filter element is located in the air cleaner assembly on the right-hand side of the engine compartment.
2 Release the clip and detach the air outlet duct from the air cleaner cover (see illustration).
3 Disconnect the wiring connector from the mass air flow sensor on the air cleaner cover (see illustration).
4 Disconnect the vacuum hose from the air cleaner cover (see illustration).
5 Pull the water drain pipe down to release it from the water drain channel (see illustration).

6 Release the two clips securing the air cleaner cover to the air cleaner housing. Move the water drain pipe to one side, then lift the

air cleaner cover up at the front, disengage it at the rear and manipulate it out from the engine compartment (see illustration).

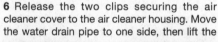

26.2 Release the clip and detach the air outlet duct from the air cleaner cover

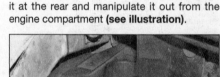

26.3 Disconnect the wiring connector from the mass air flow sensor

26.4 Disconnect the vacuum hose from the air cleaner cover

26.5 Pull the water drain pipe down to release it from the water drain channel

26.6 Move the water drain pipe to one side, then lift the air cleaner cover up and off the air cleaner housing

26.7 Lift out the filter element and wipe out the housing

7 Lift out the element, noting its direction of fitting, and wipe out the housing **(see illustration)**.
8 If carrying out a routine service, the element must be renewed regardless of its apparent condition.
9 If you are checking the element for any other reason, inspect its lower surface; if it is oily or very dirty, renew the element. If it is only moderately dusty, it can be re-used by blowing it clean with compressed air.
10 Fit the new element using a reversal of the removal procedure.

27 Transmission oil level check

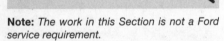

Note: *The work in this Section is not a Ford service requirement.*
1 To check the oil level, raise the vehicle and support it securely on axle stands (see *Jacking and vehicle support*), making sure that the vehicle is level.
2 The filler/level plug is situated in the following location, according to model:
Front wheel drive models – *on the lower front side of the transmission housing.*
Rear wheel drive models with 5-speed transmissions – *on the left-hand side of the transmission housing.*
Rear wheel drive models with 6-speed transmissions – *on the right-hand side of the transmission housing.*
3 Using a suitable Allen key or socket, unscrew and remove the filler/level plug – take care, as it will probably be very tight.
4 If the lubricant level is correct, the oil should be up to, or just below, the lower edge of the filler/level plug hole.
5 If the transmission needs topping-up, use a syringe or a plastic bottle and tube, to add more lubricant of the specified type (refer to *Lubricants and fluids*) **(see illustration)**.
6 Stop filling the transmission when the lubricant begins to run out of the hole, then wait until the flow of oil ceases.
7 Refit the filler/level plug, and tighten it to the specified torque setting. Drive the vehicle a short distance, then check for leaks.
8 A need for regular topping-up can only be

27.5 Topping-up the transmission oil

due to a leak, which should be found and rectified without delay.

28 Rear axle oil level check

Note: *The work in this Section is not a Ford service requirement.*
1 To check the oil level, raise the vehicle and support it securely on axle stands (see *Jacking and vehicle support*), making sure that the vehicle is level.
2 Depending on axle type, the filler/level plug will be located either on the differential housing cover, or on the left-hand side of the drive pinion housing.
3 Using a suitable Allen key or socket, unscrew and remove the filler/level plug – take care, as it will probably be very tight.
4 On axles with the filler/level plug located on the differential housing cover, the oil level should be between 6 and 14 mm below the lower edge of the filler/level plug hole. On axles with the filler level plug located on the drive pinion housing, the oil level should be up to the lower edge of the filler/level plug hole.
5 The best way to check the level is to use a 'dipstick' made up from a bent piece of wire. Put the wire in the hole (but don't drop it in) and check the level **(see illustration)**.
6 If the axle needs topping-up, use a syringe, or a plastic bottle and tube, to add more lubricant of the specified type (refer to *Lubricants and fluids*). Stop filling the transmission when the lubricant either begins

28.5 Using a home-made dipstick to check the rear axle oil level

to run out of the hole, or is at the correct level on the 'dipstick'.
7 Refit the filler/level plug, and tighten it to the specified torque.
8 A need for regular topping-up can only be due to a leak, which should be found and rectified without delay.

29 Brake fluid renewal

The procedure is similar to that for the bleeding of the hydraulic system as described in Chapter 9, except that the brake fluid reservoir should be emptied by syphoning, and allowance should be made for the old fluid to be removed from the circuit when bleeding a section of the circuit.

30 Coolant renewal

Note: *If the antifreeze used is Ford's purple Super Plus, or of similar quality, Ford state that coolant renewal is only necessary every ten years. If the vehicle's history is unknown, if the antifreeze is of lesser quality, or if you prefer to follow conventional servicing intervals, the coolant should be changed as follows.*

⚠ **Warning: Refer to Chapter 3 and observe the warnings given. In particular, never remove the expansion tank filler cap when the engine is running, or has just been switched off, as the cooling system will be hot, and the consequent escaping steam and scalding coolant could cause serious injury. If the engine is hot, the electric cooling fan may start rotating even if the engine is not running, so be careful to keep hands, hair and loose clothing well clear when working in the engine compartment.**

Cooling system draining

⚠ **Warning: Wait until the engine is cold before starting this procedure.**

1 To drain the system, first remove the expansion tank filler cap. Place a thick cloth over the expansion tank cap, then turn the cap anticlockwise as far as the first stop and wait for any pressure to be released, then depress it and turn it further anticlockwise to remove it.
2 If additional working clearance is required, apply the handbrake, then jack up the front of the vehicle and support it on axle stands (see *Jacking and vehicle support*).
3 Place a large drain tray underneath the radiator, and unscrew the radiator drain plug **(see illustration)**. Allow the coolant to drain into the tray.
4 The cylinder block may also be drained

by removing the drain plug located on the exhaust manifold side of the engine at the flywheel end **(see illustration)**.

5 On completion, retighten the drain plugs securely. Where necessary, lower the vehicle to the ground.

Cooling system flushing

6 If coolant renewal has been neglected, or if the antifreeze mixture has become diluted, then in time, the cooling system may gradually lose efficiency, as the coolant passages become restricted due to rust, scale deposits, and other sediment. The cooling system efficiency can be restored by flushing the system clean.

7 The radiator should be flushed independently of the engine, to avoid unnecessary contamination.

Radiator flushing

8 Disconnect the top and bottom hoses and any other relevant hoses from the radiator, with reference to Chapter 3.

9 Insert a garden hose into the radiator top inlet. Direct a flow of clean water through the radiator, and continue flushing until clean water emerges from the radiator bottom outlet.

10 If after a reasonable period, the water still does not run clear, the radiator can be flushed with a good proprietary cleaning agent. It is important that the manufacturer's instructions are followed carefully. If the contamination is particularly bad, remove the radiator, insert the hose in the radiator bottom outlet, and reverse-flush the radiator.

Engine flushing

11 Remove the thermostat as described in Chapter 3 then, if the radiator top hose has been disconnected from the engine, temporarily refit the thermostat housing cover and reconnect the hose.

12 With the top and bottom hoses disconnected from the radiator, insert a garden hose into the radiator top hose. Direct a clean flow of water through the engine, and continue flushing until clean water emerges from the radiator bottom hose.

13 On completion of flushing, refit the thermostat and reconnect the hoses with reference to Chapter 3.

Cooling system filling

14 Before attempting to fill the cooling

30.3 Radiator drain plug (shown with radiator removed)

system, make sure that all hoses and clips are in good condition, and that the clips are tight. Note that an antifreeze mixture must be used all year round, to prevent corrosion of the engine components.

15 Fill the system via the expansion tank, with the correct antifreeze mixture, until the coolant level reaches the MAX mark on the side of the expansion tank. Refit the expansion tank filler cap.

16 Start the engine and allow it to idle until it reaches normal operating temperature, then allow it to idle for a further 5 minutes.

17 Switch off the engine and allow it to cool for at least 30 minutes.

18 Remove the filler cap and top-up the coolant level to the MAX mark on the expansion tank. Refit and tighten the cap.

Antifreeze mixture

19 Ford state that, if the only antifreeze used is Ford's own purple Super Plus, it will last for ten years. This is subject to it being used in the recommended concentration, unmixed with any other type of antifreeze or additive, and topped-up when necessary using only that antifreeze type, mixed with clean water. If any other type of antifreeze is (or has been) added, the ten year life period no longer applies; in this case, the system must be drained and thoroughly flushed before fresh coolant mixture is poured in.

20 If any antifreeze other than Ford's is to be used, the coolant must be renewed at regular intervals to provide an equivalent degree of protection. The conventional recommendation is to renew the coolant every two years.

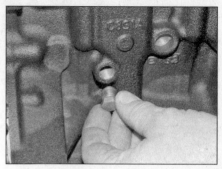

30.4 Cylinder block drain plug

21 If the antifreeze used is to Ford's specification, the levels of protection it affords are indicated in the Specifications Section of this Chapter. To give the recommended *standard* mixture ratio for this antifreeze, 40% (by volume) of antifreeze must be mixed with 60% of clean, soft water. If you are using any other type of antifreeze, follow its manufacturer's instructions to achieve the correct ratio.

22 It is best to make up slightly more than the system's specified capacity, so that a supply is available for subsequent topping-up. However, note that you are unlikely to fully drain the system at any one time (unless the engine is being completely stripped), and the capacities quoted are therefore slightly academic for routine coolant renewal.

23 Before adding antifreeze, the cooling system should be completely drained, preferably flushed, and all hoses checked for condition and security. Fresh antifreeze will rapidly find any weaknesses in the system.

24 After filling with antifreeze, a label should be attached to the expansion tank, stating the type and concentration of antifreeze used, and the date installed. Any subsequent topping-up should be made with the same type and concentration of antifreeze. If topping-up using antifreeze to Ford's specification, note that a 50/50 mixture is permissible, purely for convenience.

25 Do not use engine antifreeze in the windscreen/tailgate washer system, as it will damage the vehicle's paintwork. A screen wash additive should be added to the washer system in its maker's recommended quantities.

Every 100 000 miles or 10 years

31 Auxiliary drivebelt renewal

2.0 litre engines

Main drivebelt – models without air conditioning

Note: *The drivebelt is of the 'stretchy' type and a tensioner is not used. The belt is designed to*

be used once only and after removal, a new belt must always be fitted.

1 Move the driver's seat fully forward, open the battery box cover and disconnect the battery negative terminal (refer to *Disconnecting the battery* in the Reference Chapter).

2 Firmly apply the handbrake, then jack up the front of the vehicle and support it securely on axle stands (see *Jacking and vehicle support*). Remove the right-hand front roadwheel.

3 Undo the two fasteners and remove the splash shield around the crankshaft pulley.

4 Remove the auxiliary drivebelt by cutting through it with a sharp knife.

5 Check the two pulleys, ensuring that their grooves are clean, and removing all traces of oil and grease.

6 The new drivebelt will be supplied with a fitting tool which should be positioned over the crankshaft pulley grooves at the 3 o'clock position. Use the holes in the pulley to locate the tool in position.

7 Locate the new drivebelt in the grooves of the alternator pulley so that it is centred in the

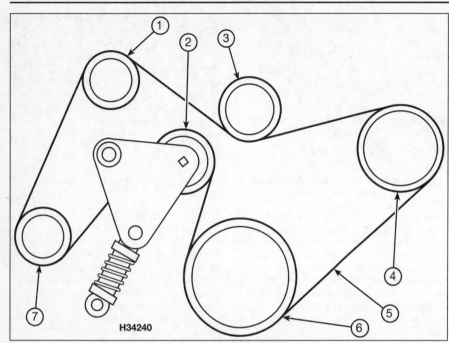

**31.24 Main auxiliary drivebelt routing –
2.0 litre engines with air conditioning**

1 Idler pulley	4 Air conditioning	5 Auxiliary drivebelt
2 Tensioner pulley	compressor	6 Crankshaft pulley
3 Idler pulley	pulley	7 Alternator pulley

grooves, and not overlapping the raised sides. Position the belt over the top of the crankshaft pulley and over the fitting tool.

8 Rotate the crankshaft clockwise, by means of the crankshaft pulley, until the fitting tool is at the 9'oclock position and the belt is seated in the grooves of the pulley. Remove the fitting tool.

9 Rotate the crankshaft clockwise, through at least two full turns to settle the drivebelt on the pulleys, then check that the drivebelt is properly installed.

10 Refit the splash shield around the crankshaft pulley, then refit the roadwheel and tighten the wheel nuts to the specified torque.

11 Lower the vehicle to the ground and reconnect the battery.

Main drivebelt – models with air conditioning

12 Move the driver's seat fully forward, open the battery box cover and disconnect the battery negative terminal (refer to *Disconnecting the battery* in the Reference Chapter).

13 Firmly apply the handbrake, then jack up the front of the vehicle and support it securely on axle stands (see *Jacking and vehicle support*). Remove the right-hand front roadwheel.

14 Undo the two fasteners and remove the splash shield around the crankshaft pulley.

15 If the existing drivebelt is to be refitted, mark it, or note the maker's markings on its flat surface, so that it can be installed the same way round.

16 Rotate the tensioner pulley clockwise to release its pressure on the drivebelt. Depending on model and equipment, the tensioner will either have a hex fitting for a spanner or socket, or a square hole into which a ratchet handle from a socket set can be fitted.

17 Slip the drivebelt off the drive pulley, and release the tensioner again. Working from the wheel arch or engine compartment as necessary, slip the drivebelt off the remaining pulleys.

18 Remove the alternator as described in Chapter 5.

19 Undo the three bolts securing the alternator mounting bracket to the cylinder block. Move the alternator mounting bracket and drivebelt tensioner assembly to one side and remove the auxiliary drivebelt.

20 Check all the pulleys, ensuring that their grooves are clean, and removing all traces of oil and grease. Check that the tensioner works properly, with strong spring pressure being felt when its pulley is rotated clockwise, and a smooth return to the limit of its travel when released.

21 If the original drivebelt is being refitted, use the marks or notes made on removal, to ensure that it is installed to run in the same direction as it was previously.

22 Locate the drivebelt behind the alternator mounting bracket and drivebelt tensioner assembly, then place the mounting bracket in position on the cylinder block. Refit the three retaining bolts and tighten them to the specified torque.

23 Refit the alternator as described in Chapter 5.

24 To fit the drivebelt, arrange it on the grooved pulleys so that it is centred in their grooves, and not overlapping their raised sides (note that the flat surface of the drivebelt is engaged on one or more pulleys) and routed correctly **(see illustration)**. Start at the top, and work down to finish at the bottom pulley. Rotate the tensioner pulley clockwise, slip the drivebelt onto the bottom pulley, then release the tensioner again.

25 Rotate the crankshaft clockwise, by means of the crankshaft pulley, through at least two full turns to settle the drivebelt on the pulleys, then check that the drivebelt is properly installed.

26 Refit the splash shield around the crankshaft pulley, then refit the roadwheel and tighten the wheel nuts to the specified torque.

27 Lower the vehicle to the ground and reconnect the battery.

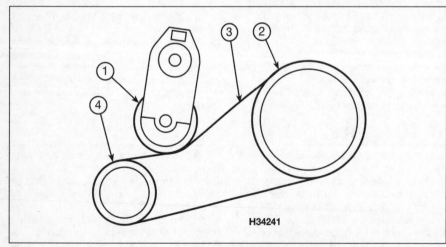

**31.34 Power steering pump drivebelt routing –
2.0 litre engines**

1 Tensioner pulley	3 Auxiliary drivebelt
2 Camshaft pulley	4 Power steering pump pulley

Power steering pump drivebelt

28 Move the driver's seat fully forward, open the battery box cover and disconnect the battery negative terminal (refer to *Disconnecting the battery* in the Reference Chapter).

29 Remove the intake air resonator and air ducts as described in Chapter 4A.

30 Release the retaining clips and remove the EGR valve air duct.

31 Remove the power steering pump drivebelt cover from the top of the engine.

32 Undo the two bolts and move the EGR valve tube to one side.

33 If the existing drivebelt is to be refitted, mark it, or note the maker's markings on its flat surface, so that it can be installed the same way round.

34 Rotate the tensioner pulley clockwise to release its pressure on the drivebelt **(see illustration)**. The tensioner pulley bracket has a square hole into which a ratchet handle from a socket set can be fitted.

35 Slip the drivebelt off the two pulleys, and release the tensioner again.

36 Check the pulleys, ensuring that their grooves are clean, and removing all traces of oil and grease. Check that the tensioner works properly, with strong spring pressure being felt when its pulley is rotated clockwise, and a smooth return to the limit of its travel when released.

37 If the original drivebelt is being refitted, use the marks or notes made on removal, to ensure that it is installed to run in the same direction as it was previously.

38 To fit the drivebelt, arrange it on the lower pulley so that it is centred in their grooves, and not overlapping their raised sides. Rotate the tensioner pulley clockwise, slip the drivebelt onto the upper pulley, then release the tensioner again.

39 Refit the components removed for access, then reconnect the battery negative terminal.

2.4 litre engines

40 Move the driver's seat fully forward, open the battery box cover and disconnect the battery negative terminal (refer to *Disconnecting the battery* in the Reference Chapter).

41 Undo the two bolts securing the auxiliary drivebelt cover to the top of the engine. The centre bolt may be located under a plastic cover on certain models. There may also be an additional bolt at the left-hand side of the cover; if so, undo this bolt also. Release the wiring harness at the rear of the cover and lift the cover off the engine **(see illustrations 5.6a to 5.6c)**.

42 If the existing drivebelt is to be refitted, mark it, or note the maker's markings on its flat surface, so that it can be installed the same way round.

43 Rotate the tensioner pulley anticlockwise to release its pressure on the drivebelt. The tensioner pulley bracket has a square hole into which a ratchet handle from a socket set can be fitted.

44 Slip the drivebelt off the drive pulley, release the tensioner again, and slip the drivebelt off the remaining pulleys. Manipulate the belt around the fan and remove it from the engine.

45 Check all the pulleys, ensuring that their grooves are clean, and removing all traces of oil and grease. Check that the tensioner works properly, with strong spring pressure being felt when its pulley is rotated clockwise, and a smooth return to the limit of its travel when released.

46 If the original drivebelt is being refitted, use the marks or notes made on removal, to ensure that it is installed to run in the same direction as it was previously.

47 To fit the drivebelt, arrange it on the grooved pulleys so that it is centred in their grooves, and not overlapping their raised sides (note that the flat surface of the drivebelt is engaged on one or more pulleys) and routed correctly **(see illustrations overleaf)**. Start at the bottom, and work up to finish at the idler pulley. Rotate the tensioner pulley anticlockwise, slip the drivebelt onto the idler pulley, then release the tensioner again.

48 Rotate the crankshaft clockwise, by means of the crankshaft pulley, through at least two full turns to settle the drivebelt on the pulleys, then check that the drivebelt is properly installed.

49 Refit the drivebelt cover, then reconnect the battery.

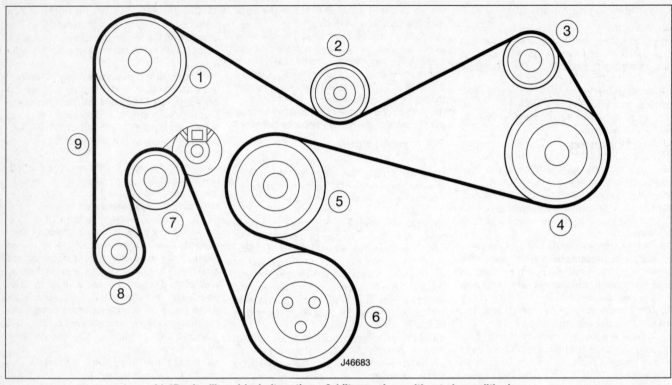

31.47a Auxiliary drivebelt routing – 2.4 litre engines without air conditioning

1 Power steering pump pulley	2 Idler pulley	4 Coolant pump pulley	6 Crankshaft pulley	8 Alternator pulley
	3 Vacuum pump pulley	5 Cooling fan pulley	7 Tensioner pulley	9 Auxiliary drivebelt

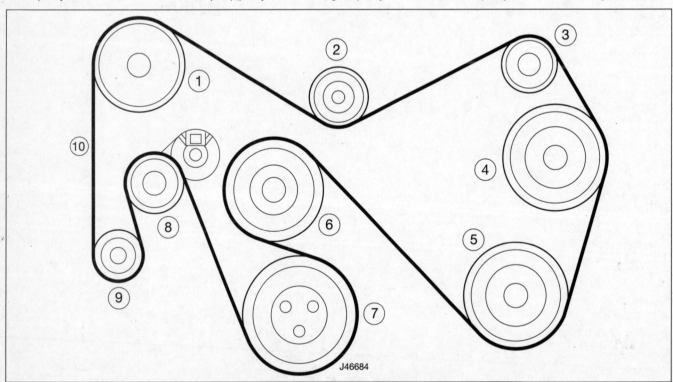

31.47b Auxiliary drivebelt routing – 2.4 litre engines with air conditioning

1 Power steering pump pulley	4 Coolant pump pulley	6 Cooling fan pulley	9 Alternator pulley
2 Idler pulley	5 Air conditioning compressor pulley	7 Crankshaft pulley	10 Auxiliary drivebelt
3 Vacuum pump pulley		8 Tensioner pulley	

Chapter 2 Part A:
2.0 litre engine in-vehicle repair procedures

Contents

Degrees of difficulty

Easy, suitable for novice with little experience	**Fairly easy,** suitable for beginner with some experience	**Fairly difficult,** suitable for competent DIY mechanic	**Difficult,** suitable for experienced DIY mechanic	**Very difficult,** suitable for expert DIY or professional

Specifications

General

Engine type.	Four-cylinder, in-line, double overhead camshaft
Designation	DuraTorq-Di and TDCi
Engine codes:	
DuraTorq-Di (75 PS – direct injection)	D3FA
DuraTorq-Di (85 PS – direct injection)	F3FA
DuraTorq-Di (100 PS – direct injection)	ABFA
DuraTorq-TDCi (125 PS – common rail injection).	FIFA
Capacity.	1998 cc
Bore	86.0 mm
Stroke.	86.0 mm
Compression ratio	19 : 1
Power output:	
D3FA.	55 kW (75 PS) at 3300 rpm
F3FA	63 kW (85 PS) at 3800 rpm
ABFA.	74 kW (100 PS) at 4000 rpm
FIFA.	92 kW (125 PS) at 3800 rpm
Firing order	1-3-4-2 (No 1 cylinder at timing chain end)
Direction of crankshaft rotation	Clockwise (seen from right-hand side of vehicle)

Cylinder head

Piston protrusion:	
Engine codes D3FA, F3FA and ABFA:	**Thickness of cylinder head gasket**
0.300 to 0.400 mm	1.10 mm (1 hole/tooth)
0.401 to 0.450 mm	1.15 mm (2 holes/teeth)
0.451 to 0.500 mm	1.20 mm (3 holes/teeth)
Engine code FIFA:	
0.430 to 0.520 mm	1.10 mm (1 hole/tooth)
0.521 to 0.570 mm	1.15 mm (2 holes/teeth)
0.571 to 0.620 mm	1.20 mm (3 holes/teeth)
Maximum permissible gasket surface distortion	0.10 mm

Lubrication

Engine oil capacity	See Chapter 1
Oil pressure – maximum (engine at operating temperature):	
At idle	1.25 bars
At 2000 rpm	2.00 bars

Torque wrench settings

	Nm	lbf ft
Alternator mounting bracket bolts	47	35
Auxiliary drivebelt idler pulley bolt	53	39
Big-end bearing cap bolts:*		
Stage 1	25	19
Stage 2	37	27
Stage 3	Angle-tighten a further 90°	
Camshaft carrier bolts		
Stage 1 – bolts 1 to 22	23	17
Stage 2 – bolts 23 to 25	10	7
Camshaft cover	10	7
Camshaft position sensor	10	7
Camshaft sprocket bolts	33	24
Catalytic converter support bracket bolts	25	19
Coolant pump bolts	23	17
Crankshaft oil seal carrier bolts*	10	7
Crankshaft position sensor	7	5
Crankshaft pulley bolts:*		
Stage 1	30	22
Stage 2	Angle-tighten a further 95°	
Cylinder head bolts:		
Stage 1 – bolts 1 to 10	10	7
Stage 2 – bolts 11 to 18	10	7
Stage 3 – bolts 1 to 10	20	15
Stage 4 – bolts 11 to 18	20	15
Stage 5 – bolts 1 to 10	35	26
Stage 6 – bolts 11 to 18	26	19
Stage 7 – bolts 1 to 10	45	33
Stage 8 – bolts 1 to 10	Angle-tighten a further 90°	
Stage 9 – bolts 11 to 18	Angle-tighten a further 90°	
Stage 10 – bolts 1 to 10	Angle-tighten a further 90°	
Stage 11 – bolts 11 to 18	Angle-tighten a further 90°	
Engine/transmission mountings:		
Vehicles manufactured up to July 2003:		
Left-hand mounting:		
To inner wing panel	70	52
To transmission	150	111
Right-hand mounting:		
To engine bracket – bolts*	103	76
To engine bracket – nut*	150	111
To inner wing panel	70	52
Rear mounting:		
Rear mounting-to-subframe	23	17
Rear mounting through-bolt*	103	76
Vehicles manufactured from July 2003 onward:		
Left-hand mounting:		
To inner wing panel*	70	52
To transmission – bolts	115	85
To transmission – nut	133	98
Right-hand mounting:		
To engine bracket – bolts	115	85
To engine bracket – nut.	133	98
To inner wing panel.	70	52
Rear mounting:		
Mounting-to-subframe	23	17
Mounting through-bolt*	103	76
Exhaust manifold and turbocharger nuts and bolts	40	30
Exhaust manifold heat shield	8	6
Exhaust manifold to catalytic converter	40	30

Torque wrench settings (continued)

	Nm	lbf ft
Flywheel bolts:		
Stage 1	15	11
Stage 2	30	22
Stage 3	75	55
Stage 4	Angle-tighten a further 45°	
Fuel injection pump sprocket	32	24
Fuel injectors:		
D3FA, F3FA and ABFA engines	52	38
FIFA engines	47	35
Fuel pressure pipe union nuts	40	30
Fuel return line unions	8	6
Glow plugs	12	9
Inlet manifold bolts	16	12
Lower crankcase/ladder to cylinder block	23	17
Main bearing cap bolts:*		
Stage 1	15	11
Stage 2	20	15
Stage 3	35	26
Stage 4	80	59
Stage 5	Angle-tighten a further 90°	
Oil cooler bolts	23	17
Oil pump bolts	10	7
Oil pump chain tensioner	16	12
Oil pump pick-up pipe	10	7
Power steering pump	22	16
Power steering pump drivebelt pulley	64	47
Roadwheel nuts	200	148
Rocker shaft bolts:		
Stage 1	13	10
Stage 2	Angle-tighten a further 45°	
Starter motor	25	19
Sump bolts:		
Stage 1	7	5
Stage 2	14	10
Sump oil drain plug	23	17
Thermostat housing-to-cylinder head	23	17
Timing chain cover:		
Nuts	10	7
Bolts	14	10
Timing chain guide retaining bolts	15	11
Timing chain tensioner	15	11
Transmission-to-engine bolts	40	30
Turbocharger oil feed pipe union	14	10
Turbocharger oil return pipe bolts	10	7

* Use new nuts/bolts

1 General information

How to use this Chapter

This Part of Chapter 2 is devoted to repair procedures possible while the engine is still installed in the vehicle. Since these procedures are based on the assumption that the engine is installed in the vehicle, if the engine has been removed and mounted on a stand, some of the preliminary dismantling steps outlined will not apply.

Information concerning engine/transmission removal and refitting and engine overhaul can be found in Part C of this Chapter.

Engine description

The 2.0 litre diesel engines covered in this Part of Chapter 2 are all in-line four-cylinder, turbocharged units, with 16-valve, double overhead camshaft (DOHC) arrangement. The DI engines are of the direct fuel injection type, with the TDCI engine being a common rail design. The engine is mounted transversely at the front of the vehicle, with the transmission on its left-hand end.

The engine cylinder block casting is of cast-iron and has a lower aluminium crankcase which is bolted to the underside of the cylinder block, with a pressed steel sump bolted under that.

The crankshaft runs in five main bearings, the centre main bearing's upper half incorporating thrust washers to control crankshaft endfloat. The connecting rods rotate on horizontally-split bearing shells at their big-ends. The pistons are attached to the connecting rods by gudgeon pins which are a floating fit in the connecting rod small-end eyes, secured by circlips. The aluminium alloy pistons are fitted with three piston rings – two compression rings and an oil control ring.

The inlet and exhaust valves are each closed by coil springs, and they operate in guides which are a shrink-fit in the cylinder head, as also are the valve seat inserts.

The double overhead camshaft sprockets and the fuel injection pump are driven by a chain from a sprocket on the crankshaft. The camshafts operate the sixteen valves via rockers which are mounted on rocker shafts that run parallel with the camshafts. Each camshaft rotates in five bearings that are machined directly in the cylinder head and the (bolted on) bearing caps. This means that the bearing caps are not available separately from the cylinder head, and must not be interchanged with caps from another engine.

The vacuum pump (used for the brake

servo and other vacuum actuators) is located on the transmission end of the cylinder head, driven by a slot in the end of the exhaust camshaft.

Lubrication is by means of a chain driven oil pump driven from a sprocket on the crankshaft. The oil pump is mounted below the lower crankcase, and draws oil through a strainer located in the sump. The pump forces oil through an externally-mounted full-flow cartridge-type filter. From the filter, the oil is pumped into a main gallery in the cylinder block/crankcase, from where it is distributed to the crankshaft (main bearings) and cylinder head. On some models, an oil cooler is fitted next to the oil filter, at the rear of the block. The cooler is supplied with coolant from the engine cooling system.

While the crankshaft and camshaft bearings receive a pressurised supply, the camshaft lobes and valves are lubricated by splash, as are all other engine components. The undersides of the pistons are cooled by oil, sprayed from nozzles fitted above the upper main bearing shells. The turbocharger receives its own pressurised oil supply.

Repairs with the engine in the vehicle

The following major repair operations can be accomplished without removing the engine from the vehicle. However, owners should note that any operation involving the removal of the timing chain, camshafts or cylinder head requires careful forethought, depending on the level of skill and the tools and facilities available. Refer to the relevant text for details.

a) Compression pressure – testing.
b) Camshaft cover – removal and refitting.
c) Timing chain cover – removal and refitting.
d) Timing chain – renewal.
e) Timing chain tensioner and sprockets – removal and refitting.
f) Camshaft oil seal – renewal.
g) Camshafts and hydraulic rockers – removal and refitting.
h) Cylinder head – removal, overhaul and refitting.
i) Crankshaft pulley – removal and refitting.
j) Sump – removal and refitting.
k) Pistons, connecting rods and big-end bearings – removal and refitting*.
l) Crankshaft oil seals – renewal.
m) Oil pump – removal and refitting.
n) Flywheel – removal and refitting.
o) Engine/transmission mountings – removal and refitting.
p) Inlet manifold – removal and refitting.
q) Exhaust manifold – removal and refitting.

*Although the operation marked with an asterisk can be carried out with the engine in the vehicle (after removal of the sump), it is preferable for the engine to be removed, in the interests of cleanliness and improved access. For this reason, the procedure is described in Chapter 2C.

2 Compression and leakdown tests – description and interpretation

Compression test

Note 1: *A compression tester suitable for use with diesel engines will be required for this test.*

Note 2: *The following procedure is likely to log a fault code in the powertrain control module memory. If the engine management warning light is illuminated after the test, it will be necessary to have the fault code cleared by a Ford dealer or suitably equipped garage using specialist diagnostic equipment.*

1 When engine performance is down, or if misfiring occurs which cannot be attributed to the fuel or emissions systems, a compression test can provide diagnostic clues as to the engine's condition. If the test is performed regularly, it can give warning of trouble before any other symptoms become apparent.

2 The engine must be fully warmed-up to normal operating temperature and the battery must be fully charged. The aid of an assistant will also be required.

3 Remove the glow plugs as described in Chapter 5.

4 Open the engine compartment fuse/relay box and remove the glow plug relay (R2). The relay is located at the rear of the fuse/relay box on the right-hand side (engine side).

5 On direct injection engines, disconnect the wiring connector at the rear of the fuel injection pump. On engines with common rail injection, disconnect the wiring connectors from the fuel injectors.

6 Fit a compression tester to the No 1 cylinder glow plug hole. The type of tester which screws into the plug thread is preferred.

7 Crank the engine for several seconds on the starter motor. After one or two revolutions, the compression pressure should build up to a maximum figure and then stabilise. Record the highest reading obtained.

8 Repeat the test on the remaining cylinders, recording the pressure in each.

9 The cause of poor compression is less easy to establish on a diesel engine than on a petrol engine. The effect of introducing oil into the cylinders (wet testing) is not conclusive, because there is a risk that the oil will sit in the recess on the piston crown, instead of passing to the rings. However, the following can be used as a rough guide to diagnosis.

10 An actual compression pressure value is not stated by Ford, however all cylinders should produce very similar pressures. Any significant difference indicates the existence of a fault. Note that the compression should build-up quickly in a healthy engine. Low compression on the first stroke, followed by gradually increasing pressure on successive strokes, indicates worn piston rings. A low compression reading on the first stroke, which

does not build-up during successive strokes, indicates leaking valves or a blown head gasket (a cracked head could also be the cause).

11 A low reading from two adjacent cylinders is almost certainly due to the head gasket having blown between them and the presence of coolant in the engine oil will confirm this.

12 On completion, remove the compression tester, and refit the glow plugs as described in Chapter 5.

13 On direct injection engines, reconnect the wiring connector to the fuel injection pump. On engines with common rail injection, reconnect the wiring connectors to the fuel injectors.

14 Refit the glow plug relay to the fuse/relay box.

Leakdown test

15 A leakdown test measures the rate at which compressed air fed into the cylinder is lost. It is an alternative to a compression test, and in many ways it is better, since the escaping air provides easy identification of where pressure loss is occurring (piston rings, valves or head gasket).

16 The equipment required for leakdown testing is unlikely to be available to the home mechanic. If poor compression is suspected, have the test performed by a suitably equipped garage.

3 Engine timing – setting

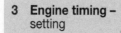

Note: *Only turn the engine in the normal direction of rotation – clockwise viewed from the right-hand side of the vehicle.*

General information

1 Top Dead Centre (TDC) is the highest point in the cylinder that each piston reaches as it travels up and down when the crankshaft turns. Each piston reaches TDC at the end of the compression stroke and again at the end of the exhaust stroke, but TDC generally refers to piston position on the compression stroke. No 1 piston is at the timing chain end of the engine.

2 Setting No 1 piston at 50° before top dead centre (BTDC) is an essential part of many procedures, such as timing chain removal, cylinder head removal and camshaft removal.

3 The design of the engines covered in this Chapter is such that piston-to-valve contact may occur if the camshaft or crankshaft is turned with the timing chain removed. For this reason, it is important to ensure that the camshaft and crankshaft do not move in relation to each other once the timing chain has been removed from the engine.

Setting

Note 1: *Ford service tool 303-675 (for engines with direct injection) or 303-698 (for engines*

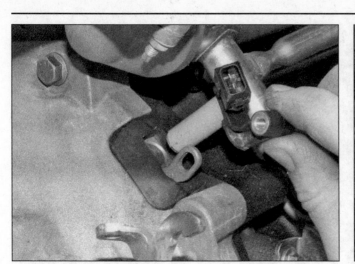

3.9 Undo the retaining bolt and withdraw the crankshaft position sensor

3.10 Ford timing tool inserted into the crankshaft sensor bracket (transmission removed for clarity)

with common rail injection) – obtainable from Ford dealers or a tool supplier will be required to set the timing at 50° BTDC.

Note 2: A new crankshaft position sensor will be required for refitting.

4 Move the driver's seat fully forward, open the battery box cover and disconnect the battery negative terminal (refer to Disconnecting the battery in the Reference Chapter).

5 Firmly apply the handbrake, then jack up the front of the vehicle and support it securely on axle stands (see Jacking and vehicle support). Remove the right-hand roadwheel, then remove the auxiliary drivebelt cover (two fasteners) from under the wheel arch.

6 The engine can now be rotated using the crankshaft pulley.

7 A timing hole is provided on the top of the transmission, to permit the crankshaft position sensor to be located.

8 Refer to Chapter 4A and remove the intake air resonator and air ducts.

9 Disconnect the wiring connector from the crankshaft position sensor, undo the retaining bolt and withdraw the sensor from the bellhousing **(see illustration)**. Note that a new sensor will be required for refitting.

10 The special tool can now be inserted into the sensor hole to set the timing at 50° BTDC **(see illustration)**.

11 Turn the crankshaft in the direction of engine rotation, until the end of the tool drops into a recess in the outer toothed part of the flywheel, this will be in the 50° BTDC position.

12 If the engine is being set to 50° BTDC as part of the timing chain removal/renewal procedure, further confirmation of the position can be gained once the timing chain outer cover has been removed. At 50° BTDC, 6 mm timing pins are inserted into the camshaft and fuel pump sprockets, see Section 7.

13 If the holes in the camshaft sprockets do not align, remove the timing pin from the crankshaft and rotate the engine one full turn, then re-install the timing pin.

14 Before rotating the crankshaft again, make sure that the timing pin (and where fitted the camshaft sprocket timing pins) are removed. When operations are complete, fit the new crankshaft position sensor as described in Chapter 4A. Refit all other components removed for access. **Do not** use the crankshaft timing setting tool to prevent the crankshaft from rotating.

4 Camshaft cover – removal and refitting

Caution: Do not carry out any work on the fuel system with the engine running. Wait for at least 2 minutes after the engine has been stopped before any work is carried out on the fuel system, to make sure the fuel pressure and temperature has dropped sufficiently. Make sure that all the fuel lines are kept clean. Fit blanking plugs to the end of the fuel lines when they are disconnected, to prevent foreign matter entering the components.

Removal

D3FA, F3FA and ABFA engines

1 Remove the inlet manifold as described in Section 19.

2 Using a spanner to hold the injectors in position, slacken the fuel supply pipe unions. Note the position of the fuel supply pipes before removal.

3 Slacken the fuel supply pipe unions at the fuel injection pump, then disconnect the fuel supply pipes and discard them. New supply pipes will be required on refitting. Fit blanking caps to the injectors and fuel pump unions, to prevent dirt ingress.

4 Disconnect the fuel injector return pipe from the fuel injection pump.

5 Release the retaining clips and disconnect the fuel return pipe from the injectors. Discard

the return pipe and sealing washers as new ones will be required on refitting.

6 Disconnect the crankcase ventilation hose from the rear of the camshaft cover.

7 Unscrew the retaining bolts and lift the camshaft cover off the cylinder head. Recover the gasket and discard it – a new gasket and seals will be required on refitting.

FIFA engine

8 Move the driver's seat fully forward, open the battery box cover and disconnect the battery negative terminal (refer to Disconnecting the battery in the Reference Chapter).

9 Refer to Chapter 4A and remove the intake air resonator and air ducts, then remove the engine upper cover.

10 Before proceeding further, use a brush and suitable solvent to clean the area around the injector high-pressure fuel pipe unions. It is essential that no dirt enters the system. Allow time for any solvent used to dry.

11 Disconnect the electrical connectors from the fuel injectors **(see illustration)**, make sure the wiring connectors are kept clean.

12 Release the retaining clips and withdraw the fuel return lines at the injectors **(see illustrations)**. Discard the O-ring seals as new ones will be required on refitting.

13 Using a spanner to hold the injectors in

4.11 Disconnecting the electrical connectors from the fuel injectors

4.12a Release the retaining clips and pull the fuel return lines from the injectors

4.12b On later models, release the collar around the injector . . .

4.12c . . . and withdraw the return pipe

4.13 Using a spanner to hold the injectors in position, slacken the fuel supply pipe unions

4.14 Slacken the fuel supply pipes at the fuel rail

4.17 Where applicable, withdraw the fuel return pipe collars

position, slacken the fuel supply pipe unions **(see illustration)**. Note the position of the fuel supply pipes before removal.

14 Slacken the fuel supply pipe unions at the fuel rail **(see illustration)**.

15 Once the unions are loose, wrap clean absorbent tissue or rag around them briefly, to soak away any dirt which may otherwise enter. If available, Ford recommend using a vacuum line to suck any dirt away from the opening union – do not use an airline, as this may blast dirt inwards, rather than cleaning it away.

16 Disconnect the fuel supply pipes and discard them. New supply pipes will be required for refitting. Fit blanking caps to the injectors and fuel rail unions, to prevent dirt ingress.

17 Temporarily remove the blanking caps from the injectors and withdraw the fuel return pipe collars (where fitted) from the injectors **(see illustration)**. Refit the blanking plugs.

18 Carefully prise out the four fuel injector seals from the camshaft cover **(see illustration)**. Discard the seals as new ones will be required for refitting.

19 Disconnect the crankcase ventilation hose from the rear of the camshaft cover **(see illustration)**.

20 Unscrew the retaining bolts and remove the two fuel rail securing brackets from the camshaft cover **(see illustration)**.

21 Unscrew the retaining bolts and lift the camshaft cover off the cylinder head **(see illustration)**. Recover the gasket and discard it – a new gasket and seals will be required for refitting.

4.18 Prise out the four camshaft cover fuel injector seals

4.19 Disconnect the crankcase ventilation hose from the camshaft cover

Refitting

22 Clean the sealing surfaces of the cover and the head, and check the condition of the rubber seals fitted to the cover bolts.

23 Refitting is a reversal of removal, noting the following points:

a) *Renew all seals, gaskets and supply pipes as noted on removal.*

b) *Ensure the gasket is correctly seated on the cylinder head, and take care to avoid displacing it as the camshaft cover is lowered into position.*

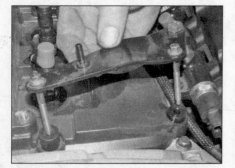

4.20 Remove the securing brackets from the camshaft cover

4.21 Remove the camshaft cover

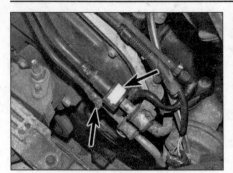

5.8a Disconnect the fuel lines (arrowed) . . .

5.8b . . . then undo the retaining nut and bolt, and detach the fuel line bracket from the cylinder head

5.10 Undo the retaining bolts/nuts and remove the engine mounting (arrowed)

c) *Ensure that the new fuel supply pipes are routed as noted on removal.*

d) *Screw on all the fuel supply pipe unions finger tight initially to ensure that they are not cross-threaded, then tighten the unions to the specified torque. Ensure that the injectors are held with a spanner to prevent them turning as the pipe unions are tightened.*

e) *Check the ventilation hose is securely reconnected.*

f) *Tighten the camshaft cover retaining bolts to the specified torque.*

g) *On completion, prime and bleed the fuel system as described in Chapter 4A.*

24 When the engine has been run for some time, check for signs of oil leakage from the gasket joint.

---

5 Timing chain cover –
removal and refitting

Note 1: *To carry out this task with the engine/transmission installed in the vehicle will require the equipment necessary to raise and support the front of the vehicle. Ford technicians use an engine support bar, which locates in the channels at the top of each inner wing, and a further beam attached to this, which rests on the front crossmember. If such an arrangement is not available, use an engine crane; either way, use a suitable length of chain and hooks to attach the lifting gear to the engine lifting eye. If the engine must be supported from*

below, use a large piece of wood on a trolley jack to spread the load and reduce the chance of damage to the sump. Precise details of the procedure will depend on the equipment available and the following description is typical.

Note 2: *Ford technicians use special tools for removing the oil seal and aligning the timing chain cover – see text. A new timing chain cover will be required for refitting, as the cover will be irreparably distorted during removal.*

Removal

1 Move the driver's seat fully forward, open the battery box cover and disconnect the battery negative terminal (refer to *Disconnecting the battery* in the Reference Chapter).

2 Firmly apply the handbrake, then jack up the front of the vehicle and support it securely on axle stands (see *Jacking and vehicle support*). Remove the right-hand roadwheel.

3 Remove the auxiliary drivebelt as described in Chapter 1.

4 If not already done as part of the auxiliary drivebelt removal procedure, remove the alternator as described in Chapter 5. Undo the three bolts securing the alternator mounting bracket to the cylinder block and remove the alternator mounting bracket and drivebelt tensioner assembly.

5 Remove the crankshaft pulley as described in Section 6.

6 Remove the crankshaft timing chain end oil seal as described in Section 16.

7 Remove the retaining bolts and nuts from the lower part of the timing chain cover.

8 Disconnect the fuel lines at the quick-release connectors, then undo the retaining nut and bolt and detach the fuel line bracket from the cylinder head **(see illustrations)**.

9 Depending on the equipment available, support the engine either from the top using a support bar or from underneath the sump using a suitable jack.

10 Undo the retaining bolts and nuts, then remove the engine mounting from the right-hand inner front wing panel **(see illustration)**.

11 Undo the retaining nut and slide the idler pulley (where fitted) from the mounting bracket **(see illustration)**. **Note:** *This will not come all the way off the stud at this point.*

12 Undo the retaining bolts, and remove the mounting bracket, complete with idler pulley from the timing chain cover **(see illustrations)**.

13 Remove the retaining bolts/nuts from the upper part of the timing chain cover.

14 Using a couple of scrapers or similar, carefully work your way around the timing chain cover and prise it away from the engine. The cover will become distorted on removal, discard it, as a new cover must be used on refitting.

15 Measure the length of the timing chain cover retaining bolts. On early engines M6 x 14 mm bolts were used, whereas M6 x 16 mm bolts were fitted to later engines. If M6 x 14 mm bolts are currently fitted, these must be discarded and a new set of the longer bolts must be obtained.

Refitting

16 Make sure that the mating surfaces of the cover and the engine casing are clean.

5.11 Undo the retaining nut (arrowed) and slide the idler pulley away from the engine

5.12a Undo the retaining bolts, including the one (arrowed) behind the idler pulley . . .

5.12b . . . and remove the mounting bracket, complete with idler pulley

Apply a 3 mm bead of sealant (Loctite 510, or equivalent) around the mating surface of the timing chain cover, ensuring that the sealant bead passes around the inside of the retaining bolt holes.

Caution: Install the timing chain cover within 5 minutes of applying the sealer to the engine casing. Make sure the cover does not come into contact with the engine casing, until the correct position for fitting is obtained.

17 Fit the new timing chain cover and install the retaining nuts and bolts hand-tight.

18 Using a cover aligning tool (Ford special tool 303-682), insert the tool over the end of the crankshaft to align the cover **(see illustration)**, then tighten all the timing chain cover retaining nuts and bolts to the specified torque. Remove the tool once the cover is in position.

19 Further refitting is a reversal of removal. Noting the following points:

a) *Fit a new crankshaft oil seal as described in Section 16.*

b) *Refit the crankshaft pulley as described in Section 6.*

c) *Where removed, refit the alternator as described in Chapter 5.*

d) *Refit the auxiliary drivebelt as described in Chapter 1.*

6 Crankshaft pulley – removal and refitting

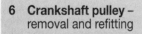

Removal

Note: *New crankshaft pulley retaining bolts will be required for refitting.*

1 Move the driver's seat fully forward, open the battery box cover and disconnect the battery negative terminal (refer to *Disconnecting the battery* in the Reference Chapter).

2 Firmly apply the handbrake, then jack up the front of the vehicle and support it securely on axle stands (see *Jacking and vehicle support*). Remove the right-hand roadwheel.

3 Remove the auxiliary drivebelt, as described in Chapter 1.

4 The three bolts which secure the crankshaft pulley must now be slackened. Ensure that

5.18 Insert the tool over the end of the crankshaft to align the cover, before tightening the retaining bolts

the vehicle is adequately supported, as considerable effort may be needed to slacken the bolts.

5 Ford technicians use a special holding tool (205-072) which locates in the outer holes of the pulley and prevents it from turning. If this is not available, select a gear, and have an assistant firmly apply the hand- brake and footbrake as the bolts are loosened. If this method is unsuccessful, remove the starter motor as described in Chapter 5, and jam the flywheel ring gear, using a suitable tool, to prevent the crank- shaft from rotating.

6 Unscrew the bolts securing the pulley to the crankshaft, and remove the pulley **(see illustration)**. Discard the bolts and obtain new bolts for refitting.

7 With the pulley removed, it is advisable to check the crankshaft oil seal for signs of oil leakage **(see illustration)**. If necessary, fit a new seal as described in Section 16.

Refitting

8 Refit the pulley to the end of the crankshaft, then fit the new pulley securing bolts and tighten them as far as possible before the crankshaft starts to rotate.

9 Holding the pulley against rotation as for removal, first tighten the bolts to the specified Stage 1 torque.

10 Stage 2 involves tightening the bolts though an angle, rather than to a torque. The bolts must be rotated through the specified angle – special angle gauges are available from tool outlets. As a guide, a 90° angle is equivalent to a quarter-turn, and this is easily judged by

assessing the start and end positions of the socket handle or torque wrench.

11 Refit and tension the auxiliary drivebelt as described in Chapter 1.

12 Refit the roadwheel, lower the vehicle to the ground, and reconnect the battery negative lead. Tighten the wheel nuts to the specified torque.

7 Timing chain – removal, inspection and refitting

Note: *Only turn the engine in the normal direction of rotation – clockwise from the right-hand side of the vehicle.*

Removal

1 Remove the timing chain cover, as described in Section 5.

2 Referring to the information in Section 3, set the engine to 50° BTDC on No 1 cylinder. In this position, insert a 6 mm timing pin (6 mm drill bit) in each camshaft sprocket and one in the fuel pump sprocket **(see illustration)**. Note that on the FIFA engine (common rail injection), there may be a timing hole in the sprocket, but no corresponding hole in the pump for the pin to engage. As the injection pump on engines with common rail injection does not need to be timed, the use of a timing pin is not strictly necessary.

3 If the timing chain is not being fitted straight away (or if the chain is being removed as part of another procedure, such as cylinder head removal), temporarily refit the engine right-hand mounting and tighten the bolts securely.

4 Slacken the timing chain tensioner by inserting a small screwdriver into the access hole in the tensioner and releasing the pawl mechanism. Press against the timing chain guide to depress the piston into the tensioner housing, when fully depressed, insert a locking pin (approximately 1.5 mm) to lock the piston in its compressed position **(see illustration)**.

5 To remove the tensioner, undo the two retaining bolts and remove the timing chain tensioner from the cylinder block, taking care not to remove the locking pin **(see illustration)**.

6 Undo the retaining bolts and remove the tensioner timing chain guide and the fixed

6.6 Unscrew the bolts and remove the crankshaft pulley

6.7 Check the crankshaft oil seal for signs of oil leakage

7.2 Insert 6 mm timing pins (6 mm drill bits), to align the camshaft sprockets

7.4 Insert a pin (arrowed) to lock the piston in its compressed position

7.5 Remove the timing chain tensioner from the cylinder block, taking care not to remove the locking pin

7.6a Undo the retaining bolts and remove the tensioner timing chain guide . . .

7.6b . . . the upper fixed chain guide bolts (arrowed) . . .

7.6c . . . the middle fixed chain guide . . .

timing chain guides from the cylinder block (see illustrations).

7 Holding the fuel injection pump sprocket in position, slacken the retaining bolts and remove the sprocket (see illustration). **Note:** *Do not rely on the timing pin (6 mm drill bit) to hold the sprocket in position.*

8 With the camshafts held in position, undo the camshaft sprocket retaining bolts and remove the camshaft sprockets and timing chain. Do not rotate the crankshaft until the timing chain is refitted. **Note:** *Do not rely on the timing pins (6 mm drill bit) to hold the sprockets in position.*

9 Check the condition of the timing chain, tensioner and guides before refitting them. When fitting a new timing chain, a new tensioner should be fitted as a matter of course, especially if the engine has completed a large mileage.

10 To remove the timing chain sprocket from the crankshaft, the oil pump drive chain will need to be removed first. Hold the tensioner in and insert a locking pin (approximately 1.5 mm) to lock the piston in its compressed position (see illustration). Undo the two retaining bolts and remove the oil pump drive chain tensioner from the engine. The chain can now be removed from the sprocket. Undo the retaining bolt and withdraw the sprocket from the crankshaft (see illustration).

7.6d . . . and the lower fixed timing chain guide

7.7 Remove the fuel pump sprocket

7.10a Insert a locking pin (drill bit) to lock the piston in its compressed position

7.10b Undo the retaining bolt and withdraw the sprocket from the crankshaft

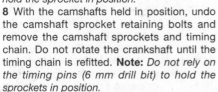
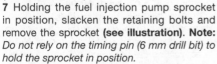

7.19 Refit the timing chain and sprockets

7.20a With the timing pins/6 mm drill bits (arrowed) inserted into the sprockets . . .

Inspection

Note: *Keep all components identified for position to ensure correct refitting.*

11 Clean all components thoroughly and wipe dry.

12 Examine the chain tensioner and tensioner guide for excessive wear or other damage. Check the guides for deep grooves made by the timing chain.

13 Examine the timing chain for excessive wear. Hold it horizontally and check how much movement exists in the chain links. If there is any doubt, compare it to a new chain. Renew as necessary.

14 Examine the teeth of the camshaft and crankshaft sprockets for excessive wear and damage.

15 Before refitting the timing chain tensioner, the piston must be compressed and locked until refitted (if not already done on removal). To do this, insert a small screwdriver into the access hole in the tensioner and release the pawl mechanism. Now lightly clamp the tensioner in a soft-jawed vice and slowly compress the piston. Do not apply excessive force, and make sure that the piston remains aligned with its cylinder. When completely compressed, insert a locking pin/1.5 mm

diameter wire rod into the special hole to lock the piston in its compressed position.

Refitting

16 Ensure that the crankshaft and camshaft are still set to 50° BTDC on No 1 cylinder, as described in Section 3.

17 If not already fitted, refit the crankshaft drive sprocket onto the crankshaft and securely tighten the retaining bolt. Refit the oil pump drive chain and tensioner, then hold pressure against the tensioner guide and withdraw the tensioner locking pin. (see Section 13, for further information on refitting the oil pump).

18 Refit the fuel pump sprocket and the exhaust camshaft sprocket, DO NOT tighten the retaining bolts at this stage.

19 With the timing chain around the inlet camshaft sprocket, and with the copper link on the chain aligned with the timing mark on the sprocket, refit the timing chain and sprocket. Feed the timing chain around the crankshaft drive sprocket, fuel pump sprocket and exhaust camshaft sprocket **(see illustration)**.

20 With the timing pins (6 mm drill bits) inserted into the sprockets to re-align them, the copper links on the timing chain must line

up with the timing marks on the sprockets **(see illustrations)**.

21 Refit the tensioner to the cylinder block and tighten the retaining bolts to the specified torque. Take care not to remove the locking pin.

22 Refit the timing chain tensioner guide on the upper pivot pin and tighten the retaining bolt to the specified torque setting. Hold pressure against the bottom of the tensioner guide and withdraw the tensioner locking pin. This will then tension the timing chain **(see illustration)**.

23 Refit the three fixed timing chain guides and tighten the retaining bolts to the specified torque setting.

24 Tighten the camshaft sprocket retaining bolts and the fuel injection pump sprocket retaining bolts, to the specified torque setting shown at the beginning of this Chapter. **Note:** *Do not rely on the timing pins (6 mm drill bits) to hold the sprockets in position.*

25 Check that the engine is still set to 50° BTDC (as described in Section 3), and remove the timing pins (6 mm drill bits) from the sprockets and the timing peg from the crankshaft sensor hole.

26 Turn the engine (in the direction of engine

7.20b . . . realign the copper links on the timing chain with the timing mark (arrowed) on the camshaft sprockets . . .

7.20c . . . and the timing mark (arrowed) on the fuel pump sprocket

7.22 Hold pressure against the tensioner guide (arrowed) and withdraw the locking pin

rotation) two full turns. Refit the timing pins and crankshaft timing peg to make sure the engine timing is still set at 50° BTDC (see Section 3 for further information).

27 Check the tension of the chain then remove the timing pins (6 mm drill bits) from the sprockets and the timing peg from the crankshaft sensor hole. Refit the crankshaft sensor.

28 Refit the timing chain cover as described in Section 5.

---

8 Timing chain tensioner and sprockets – removal, inspection and refitting

Timing chain tensioner

1 The timing chain tensioner is removed as part of the timing chain renewal procedure, in Section 7.

Camshaft sprockets

2 The camshaft sprockets are removed as part of the timing chain renewal procedure, in Section 7.

Crankshaft sprocket

3 The crankshaft sprocket is removed as part of the timing chain renewal procedure, in Section 7.

Fuel injection pump sprocket

4 Removal of the injection pump sprocket is described as part of the timing chain renewal procedure, in Section 7

---

9 Camshafts and hydraulic rockers – removal and refitting

Note 1: *A new camshaft oil seal and suitable sealant will be required for refitting. New rocker shaft retaining bolts will also be required.*

Note 2: *Only turn the engine in the normal direction of rotation – clockwise from the right-hand side of the vehicle.*

Removal

1 Remove the timing chain cover, as described in Section 5.

9.6 The rocker shafts are marked at the timing chain end of each shaft: IN for inlet shaft

2 Referring to the information in Section 3, set the engine to 50° BTDC on No 1 cylinder. In this position, insert a 6 mm timing pin (6 mm drill bit) in each camshaft sprocket and one in the fuel injection pump sprocket (see Section 7).

3 Remove the camshaft cover, as described in Section 4.

4 Remove the power steering pump drivebelt as described in Chapter 1. Undo the retaining bolt and remove the power steering pump pulley from the end of the camshaft. Prevent the pulley from rotating as the retaining bolt is slackened using a suitable forked tool engaged with the slots in the pulley.

5 Undo the retaining bolts and remove the brake vacuum pump from the transmission end of the exhaust camshaft, as described in Chapter 9.

6 Slacken and remove the rocker shaft retaining bolts, and discard them as new ones will be required on refitting. Lift out the rocker shafts, complete with rocker arms and store them in a clean and safe area. **Note:** *They are marked at the timing chain end of the shaft, IN for inlet shaft and EX for exhaust shaft (see illustration).*

7 Slacken the timing chain tensioner and remove the tensioner timing chain guide, the upper timing chain guide and the camshaft sprockets **(see illustration)** as described in Section 7.

8 Slacken the camshaft carrier retaining bolts in the **reverse** of the sequence shown **(see illustration 9.14)**, then lift the camshaft carrier from the cylinder head.

9.7 Removing the upper timing chain guide

9 Carefully lift out the camshafts, and place them somewhere clean and safe – the lobes must not be scratched. Remove the camshaft oil seals from the transmission end of the camshafts and discard them, new ones will be required for refitting.

10 Before removing the hydraulic rocker arms from the rocker shaft, first mark the rockers so that they are fitted in the same position on re-assembly. The rocker arms can then be withdrawn from the rocker shaft along with the springs.

Refitting

11 Make sure that the top surfaces of the cylinder head, and in particular the camshaft bearing surfaces and the mating surfaces for the camshaft carrier, are completely clean.

12 Lubricate the camshafts and cylinder head bearing journals with clean engine oil, then carefully lower the camshafts into position in the cylinder head **(see illustrations)**.

13 Apply a 2.5 mm bead of sealant (Loctite 510, or equivalent) around the outer mating surface of the camshaft carrier **(see illustration)**. **Note:** *Install the timing camshaft carrier within 5 minutes of applying the sealer to the mating surface. Make sure the carrier does not come into contact with the cylinder head, until the correct position for fitting is obtained.*

14 Install the camshaft carrier retaining bolts and tighten them to the specified torque in the sequence shown **(see illustration)**.

15 Refit the timing chain, sprockets, guides and tensioner as described in Section 7.

9.12a Lubricate the cylinder head bearing journals with clean engine oil . . .

9.12b . . . then carefully lower the camshafts into position

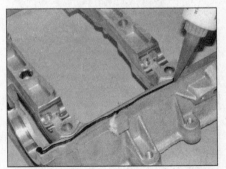

9.13 Apply a 2.5 mm bead of sealant around the outer mating surface of the camshaft carrier

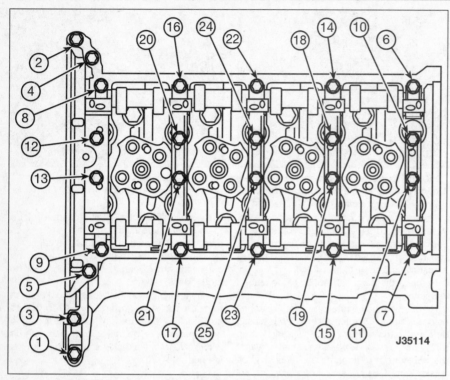

9.14 Tightening sequence for the camshaft carrier retaining bolts

16 Install the rocker shafts using new retaining bolts, making sure the oil bores point downwards and that they are fitted in the correct position as noted on removal (see paragraph 6). Tighten the retaining bolts to the specified torque.

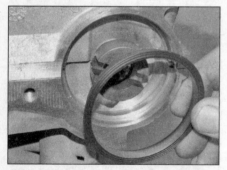

9.17 Fit a new oil seal before refitting the brake vacuum pump

10.2 Undo the retaining bolt and remove the power steering pump pulley

17 Fit a new oil seal **(see illustration)**, then refit the brake vacuum pump to the transmission end of the exhaust camshaft, as described in Chapter 9.
18 Fit a new camshaft oil seal and refit the power steering pump pulley to the end of the camshaft as described in Section 10.
19 Refit the camshaft cover, as described in Section 4.
20 Refit the timing chain cover, as described in Section 5.

10 Camshaft oil seal – renewal

1 Remove the power steering pump drivebelt as described in Chapter 1.
2 Undo the retaining bolt and remove the power steering pump pulley from the end of the camshaft **(see illustration)**. Prevent

10.5 Fitting the oil seal over the end of the camshaft, using the sleeve supplied with the new oil seal

the pulley from rotating as the retaining bolt is slackened using a suitable forked tool engaged with the slots in the pulley.
3 Remove the camshaft oil seal. Ford technicians have a special seal extractor for this (tool No 303-293). In the absence of this tool, do not use any removal method which might damage the sealing surfaces, or a leak will result when the new seal is fitted **(see Haynes Hint)**.

> **HAYNES HINT** *One of the best ways to remove an oil seal is to carefully drill or punch two holes through the seal, opposite each other (taking care not to damage the surface behind the seal as this is done). Two self-tapping screws are then screwed into the holes. By pulling on the screw heads alternately with a pair of pliers, the seal can be extracted.*

4 Clean out the seal housing and the sealing surface of the camshaft by wiping it with a lint-free cloth. Remove any swarf or burrs that may cause the seal to leak.
5 Apply a little oil to the new camshaft oil seal, and fit it over the end of the camshaft, using the sleeve supplied with the new oil seal **(see illustration)**. If a sleeve is not supplied, to avoid damaging the seal lips, wrap a little tape over the end of the camshaft.
6 Ford technicians have a special tool for pressing the seal into the cylinder head (tool No 303-683), but if this is not available, a deep socket of suitable size can be used. **Note:** *Select a socket that bears only on the hard outer surface of the seal, not the inner lip which can easily be damaged. It is important that the seal is fitted square to the shaft, and is fully seated.*
7 The remaining procedure is a reversal of removal.

11 Cylinder head – removal, inspection and refitting

Removal

1 Move the driver's seat fully forward, open the battery box cover and disconnect the battery negative terminal (refer to *Disconnecting the battery* in the Reference Chapter).
2 Drain the cooling system as described in Chapter 1.
3 Remove the camshafts and hydraulic rockers as described in Section 9.
4 Remove the exhaust manifold as described in Section 20.
5 Undo the retaining nut and disconnect the bracket for the cylinder head temperature sensor wiring block connector. Unclip the wiring from the end of the cylinder head **(see illustration)**.

11.5 Undo the retaining nut (arrowed) and remove the bracket for the wiring block connector

11.11a Disconnect the wiring connector (common rail injection engines) from the end of the fuel rail

11.11b Disconnect the wiring connector from the camshaft position sensor

6 Release the retaining clip and disconnect the expansion tank hose from the thermostat housing.

7 Disconnect the electrical connector and vacuum hose at the EGR valve.

8 Undo the retaining nuts and bolts and remove the EGR valve mounting bracket, valve and metal connecting pipe.

9 Release the clip and detach the EGR cooler pipe from the EGR cooler.

10 Disconnect the remaining connectors (as applicable), then undo the retaining bolts and remove the inlet manifold.

11 On the FIFA engine (common rail injection), disconnect the wiring connector from the end of the fuel rail and the camshaft position sensor (see illustrations).

12 Undo the retaining nut and disconnect the glow plug wiring connector (see illustration).

13 On the FIFA engine (common rail injection), remove the fuel supply pipe clamp and slacken the supply line at the fuel pump (see illustrations). Slacken the fuel supply pipe at the fuel rail then remove and discard (see illustration), as a new pipe will be required on refitting. Install blanking plugs to the open ports on the fuel pump and supply rail to prevent dirt ingress. Release the retaining clip and disconnect the return pipe from the fuel injection pump. Discard the return pipe as a new one will be required on refitting.

14 On all other engines, undo the retaining bolts and remove the fuel supply and return pipes from the fuel pump (see illustration).

15 Slacken the fuel injector locking sleeves and remove the fuel injectors (for further information see Chapter 4A).

16 Check around the head and the engine bay that there is nothing still attached to the cylinder head, nor anything which would prevent it from being lifted away.

17 Working in the reverse order of the tightening sequence (see illustration 11.41), loosen the cylinder head bolts by half a turn at a time, until they are all loose. Remove the head bolts, and discard them – Ford state that they must not be re-used, even if they appear to be serviceable.

18 Lift the cylinder head away, and use assistance if possible, as it is a heavy assembly. Do not, under any circumstances, lever the head between the mating surfaces, as this will certainly damage the sealing surfaces for the gasket, leading to leaks.

19 Once the head has been removed, recover the gasket from the two dowels and discard the gasket, as a new one will be required on refitting, see paragraph 21.

Inspection

20 If required, dismantling and inspection of the cylinder head is covered in Part C of this Chapter.

Cylinder head gasket selection

21 Examine the old cylinder head gasket for manufacturer's identification markings. These will be in the form of teeth (one, two or three) on the front edge of the gasket and/or holes in the gasket, which indicate the gasket's thickness (see illustration).

22 Unless new components have been fitted, or the cylinder head has been machined (skimmed), the new cylinder head gasket must

11.12 Undo the retaining nut (arrowed) and disconnect the glow plug wiring connector

11.13a On common rail injection engines, remove the clamp bolt (arrowed) and slacken the fuel supply pipe union . . .

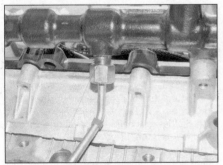

11.13b . . . then slacken the fuel supply pipe at the fuel rail

11.13c Release the retaining clip (arrowed) and disconnect the return pipe from the fuel injection pump

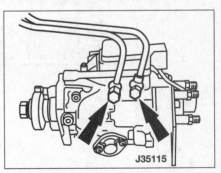

11.14 Remove the fuel supply and return pipes (arrowed) from the fuel pump

11.21 Teeth and holes in the gasket (arrowed), which indicate the gasket's thickness

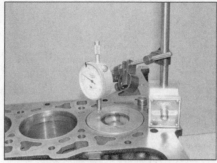

11.24 Using a dial test indicator to measure the piston protrusion

11.37 Locate the new cylinder head gasket over the dowels correctly

be of the same type as the old one. Purchase the required gasket, and proceed to paragraph 28.

23 If the head has been machined, or if new pistons have been fitted, it is likely that a head gasket of different thickness to the original will be needed. Gasket selection is made on the basis of the measured piston protrusion above the cylinder head gasket surface (the protrusion must fall within the range specified at the start of this Chapter).

24 To measure the piston protrusion, anchor a dial test indicator (DTI) to the top face (cylinder head gasket mating face) of the cylinder block, and zero the gauge on the gasket mating face **(see illustration)**.

25 Rest the gauge probe above No 1 piston crown, and turn the crankshaft slowly by hand until the piston reaches TDC (its maximum height). Measure and record the maximum piston projection at TDC.

26 Repeat the measurement for the remaining pistons, and record the results.

27 If the measurements differ from piston to piston, take the highest figure, and use this to determine the thickness of the head gasket required (see the Specifications at the start of this Chapter).

Preparation for refitting

28 The mating faces of the cylinder head and cylinder block must be perfectly clean before refitting the head. Use a hard plastic or wooden scraper to remove all traces of gasket and carbon; also clean the piston crowns. **Note:** *The new head gasket has rubber coated surfaces, which could be damaged from sharp edges or debris left by a metal scraper.*

29 Take particular care when cleaning the piston crowns, as the soft aluminium alloy is easily damaged.

30 Make sure that the carbon is not allowed

to enter the oil and water passages – this is particularly important for the lubrication system, as carbon could block the oil supply to the engine's components. Using adhesive tape and paper, seal the water, oil and bolt holes in the cylinder block.

31 To prevent carbon entering the gap between the pistons and bores, smear a little grease in the gap. After cleaning each piston, use a small brush to remove all traces of grease and carbon from the gap, then wipe away the remainder with a clean rag. Clean all the pistons in the same way.

32 Check the mating surfaces of the cylinder block and the cylinder head for nicks, deep scratches and other damage (refer to the Note in paragraph 28). If slight, they may be removed carefully with a file, but if excessive, machining may be the only alternative to renewal.

33 If warpage of the cylinder head gasket surface is suspected, use a straight-edge to check it for distortion. Refer to Part C of this Chapter if necessary.

34 Ensure that the cylinder head bolt holes in the crankcase are clean and free of oil. Syringe or soak up any oil left in the bolt holes. This is most important in order that the correct bolt tightening torque can be applied, and to prevent the possibility of the block being cracked by hydraulic pressure when the bolts are tightened.

Refitting

35 Make sure the timing is still set at 50° BTDC (see Section 3). This will eliminate any risk of piston-to-valve contact as the cylinder head is refitted.

36 To guide the cylinder head into position, screw two long studs into the end cylinder head bolt locations on the manifold side of the cylinder block. As an alternative to the studs, use old cylinder head bolts with their heads cut off, and slots cut in the ends to enable the bolts to be unscrewed.

37 Ensure that the cylinder head locating dowels are in place in the cylinder block, then fit the new cylinder head gasket over the dowels **(see illustration)**. The gasket can only be fitted one way, with the teeth to determine the gasket thickness at the front **(see illustration 11.21)**. Take care to avoid damaging the gasket's rubber coating.

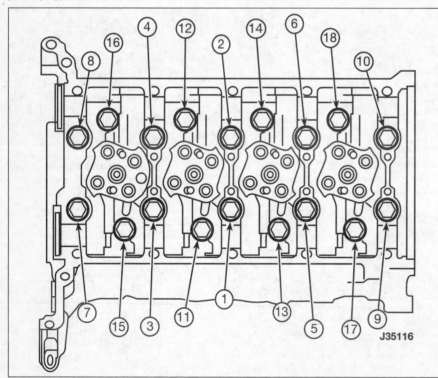

11.41 Tightening sequence for the cylinder head bolts

38 Lower the cylinder head into position on the gasket, ensuring that it engages correctly over the guide studs and dowels.

39 Fit the new cylinder head bolts to the remaining bolt locations and screw them in as far as possible by hand.

40 Unscrew the two guide studs from the cylinder block, then screw in the two remaining new cylinder head bolts as far as possible by hand.

41 Working in the sequence shown **(see illustration)**, tighten the cylinder head bolts to the specified Stage 1 and Stage 2 torque settings.

42 Again working in the sequence shown, tighten all the cylinder head bolts through the specified Stages as given in the Specifications at the beginning of this Chapter.

43 The last Stages involve tightening the bolts through an angle, rather than to a torque. Each bolt in sequence must be rotated through the specified angle – special angle gauges are available from tool outlets. As a guide, a 90° angle is equivalent to a quarter-turn, and this is easily judged by assessing the start and end positions of the socket handle.

44 The remainder of the refitting procedure is a reversal of the removal procedure, bearing in mind the following points:

a) Refit the timing chain with reference to Section 7.

b) Refit the camshafts and hydraulic rockers with reference to Section 9.

c) Refit the fuel injectors with reference to Chapter 4A.

d) Reconnect the exhaust manifold with reference to Section 20.

e) Refit the camshaft cover with reference to Section 4.

f) Refill the cooling system with reference to Chapter 1.

g) Check and if necessary top-up the engine oil level and power steering fluid level as described in 'Weekly checks'.

h) Before starting the engine, read through the section on engine restarting after overhaul, at the end of Chapter 2C.

12 Sump –
removal and refitting

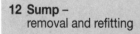

Removal

1 Firmly apply the handbrake, then jack up the front of the vehicle and support it securely on axle stands (see *Jacking and vehicle support*).

2 Drain the engine oil, then clean and refit the engine oil drain plug. Inspect the seal for damage, and fit a new drain plug and seal if required. Tighten the drain plug to the specified torque. Although not strictly necessary as part of the dismantling procedure, owners are advised to remove and discard the oil filter, so that it can be renewed with the oil. Refer to Chapter 1 if necessary.

3 Release the clips, undo the retaining nuts/ bolts and remove the intercooler charge air pipe from under the engine.

4 A conventional sump gasket is not used, and sealant is used instead.

5 Progressively unscrew and remove the sump retaining bolts and nuts.

6 Unfortunately, the use of sealant can make removal of the sump more difficult. If care is taken not to damage the surfaces, the sealant can be cut around using a scraper or a sharp knife. On no account lever between the mating faces, as this will almost certainly damage them, resulting in leaks when finished.

> **HAYNES HiNT**
> *If the sump is particularly difficult to remove, extracting the studs may prove useful – if a Torx socket is not available, thread two nuts onto the stud, tightening them against each other, then use a spanner on the inner nut to unscrew the stud. Note the locations of the studs for refitting.*

Refitting

7 On reassembly, thoroughly clean and degrease the mating surfaces of the cylinder block/crankcase and sump, removing all traces of sealant, then use a clean rag to wipe out the sump and the engine's interior.

8 If the studs have been removed, they must be refitted before the sump is offered up, to ensure that it is aligned correctly. If this is not

12.9 Apply a 3 mm bead of sealant (arrowed) to the lower casing

done, some of the sealant may enter the blind holes for the sump bolts, preventing the bolts from being fully fitted.

9 Apply a 3 mm bead of sealant (Loctite 510, or equivalent) to the sump flange, making sure the bead is around the inside edge of the bolt holes **(see illustration)**. **Note:** *The sump must be refitted within 5 minutes of applying the sealant.*

10 Fit the sump over the studs, and insert the sump bolts and nuts, tightening them by hand only at this stage.

11 Tighten all the bolts and nuts to the specified torques in the sequence shown **(see illustration)**.

12 Refit the intercooler charge air pipe.

13 Lower the vehicle to the ground, and refill the engine with oil. If removed, fit a new oil filter with reference to Chapter 1.

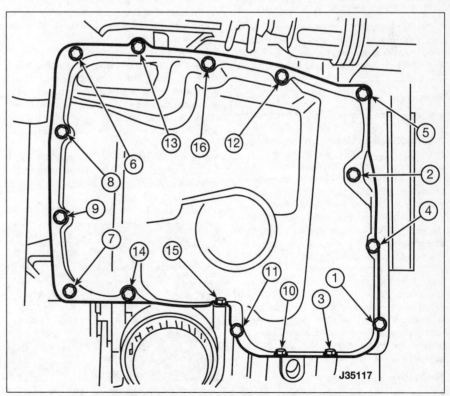

12.11 Tightening sequence for the sump retaining bolts

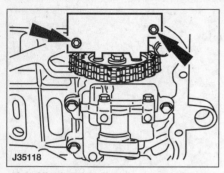

13.3 Aligning the oil pump sprocket using a plate bolted to the lower crankcase

13.4 Removing the oil pick-up pipe from the oil pump

13.10a Mount the DTI gauge on the cylinder block . . .

13.10b . . . with the probe against the inner teeth of the crankshaft sprocket, then zero the gauge

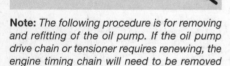

13 Oil pump – removal and refitting

Note: *The following procedure is for removing and refitting of the oil pump. If the oil pump drive chain or tensioner requires renewing, the engine timing chain will need to be removed (see Section 7).*

Removal

1 Remove the sump as described in Section 12.
2 Carefully pull on the oil pump drive chain, to push the oil out of the chain tensioner.
3 Ford special tool (303-705) is used to align the oil pump sprocket – bolt the tool/plate to the sump flange so that it sits flush with oil pump drive sprocket **(see illustration)**.
4 Undo the retaining bolts and remove the pick-up pipe from the oil pump **(see illustration)**.
5 Undo the retaining bolts and remove the oil pump from the lower crankcase, withdraw the chain from the sprocket on removal.
Caution: The oil pump sprocket and crankshaft sprocket must be kept in line with each other, so that the chain runs straight. Use Ford's special tool or a DTI gauge to make sure they are aligned correctly.

Refitting

6 Refit the oil pump to the lower crankcase, installing the drive chain to the sprocket on

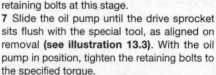

13.11 Move the probe to the oil pump sprocket and move the pump as necessary until the two gauge readings are the same

the oil pump. Only finger-tighten the oil pump retaining bolts at this stage.
7 Slide the oil pump until the drive sprocket sits flush with the special tool, as aligned on removal **(see illustration 13.3)**. With the oil pump in position, tighten the retaining bolts to the specified torque.
8 Ensuring that the alignment of the pump is correct, undo the retaining bolts and remove the special tool from the sump flange.
9 If the oil pump has been removed as part of an engine overhaul procedure, and the timing chain cover has been removed, the oil pump sprocket alignment can be checked with a DTI gauge.
10 Mount the gauge on the cylinder block with the probe against the inner teeth of the crankshaft sprocket **(see illustrations)**. Zero the gauge in this position.
11 Without moving the gauge body, move

14.1 The oil pressure switch (arrowed) is screwed into the oil filter housing

the probe to the oil pump sprocket **(see illustration)**. Move the oil pump as necessary until the two gauge readings are the same, then tighten the pump retaining bolts to the specified torque.
12 Refit the pick-up pipe to the oil pump.
13 Refit the sump with reference to Section 12.

14 Oil pressure warning light switch – removal and refitting

Removal

1 The switch is screwed into the upper part of the oil filter housing **(see illustration)**.
2 To improve access to the switch, it may be necessary to apply the handbrake, then jack up the front of the vehicle and support it on axle stands (see *Jacking and vehicle support*).
3 Unplug the wiring from the switch and unscrew it from the filter housing. Be prepared for some oil loss.

Refitting

4 Refitting is the reverse of the removal procedure. Apply a thin smear of suitable sealant to the switch threads, and tighten it securely.
5 Check the engine oil level and top-up as necessary (see *Weekly checks*).
6 Check for correct warning light operation and for signs of oil leaks, once the engine has been restarted and warmed-up to normal operating temperature.

15 Oil cooler – removal and refitting

Removal

1 The oil cooler is mounted next to the oil filter on the front of the cylinder block **(see illustration)**. Access to the oil cooler is best obtained from below – apply the handbrake, then jack up the front of the vehicle and support it on axle stands (see *Jacking and vehicle support*).
2 Position a container beneath the oil filter to catch escaping oil and coolant.

15.1 The oil cooler (arrowed) is mounted next to the oil filter

3 Clamp the oil cooler coolant hoses to minimise spillage, then remove the clips, and disconnect the hoses from the oil cooler. Be prepared for coolant spillage.

4 Unscrew the four securing bolts and withdraw the oil cooler from the oil filter housing, recover the gasket (a new gasket must be used on refitting) **(see illustration)**.

Refitting

5 Refitting is a reversal of removal, bearing in mind the following points:

a) Use a new gasket.
b) Fit the oil cooler mounting bolts, and tighten them securely.
c) On completion, lower the vehicle to the ground. Check and if necessary top-up the oil and coolant levels, then start the engine and check for signs of oil or coolant leakage.

16 Crankshaft oil seals – renewal

Timing chain end seal

1 Remove the crankshaft pulley with reference to Section 6.

2 Ford technicians use a special seal-removing and refitting tool (303-679), but an adequate substitute can be achieved using a three-legged puller and three bolts **(see illustrations)**. Turn the seal anticlockwise, using the tool, to remove the crankshaft oil seal from the timing chain cover.

3 Wipe clean the oil seal contact surfaces and seating, and clean up any sharp edges or burrs which might damage the new seal as it is fitted, or which might cause the seal to leak once in place.

4 The new oil seal may be supplied fitted with a locating sleeve, which must **not** be removed prior to fitting.

5 Locate the new seal (lips facing inwards) over the end of the crankshaft, and press the seal squarely and fully into position in the cover, remove the locating sleeve **(see illustrations)**.

6 Using the special tool used on removal, turn the seal clockwise until it is located securely into the timing chain cover.

7 Refit the crankshaft pulley with reference to Section 6.

Flywheel end seal

8 Remove the transmission as described

15.4 Unscrew the four bolts and withdraw the oil cooler from the oil filter housing (shown removed for clarity)

in Chapter 7A, and the clutch assembly as described in Chapter 6.

9 Remove the flywheel as described in Section 17.

10 Unbolt and remove the oil seal carrier. The seal is renewed complete with the carrier, and is not available separately. A complete set of new carrier retaining bolts should also be obtained for reassembly.

11 Clean the end of the crankshaft, polishing off any burrs or raised edges, which may have caused the seal to fail in the first place. Clean also the seal carrier mating face on the engine block, using a suitable solvent for degreasing if necessary.

12 The new oil seal is supplied fitted with a locating sleeve, which must **not** be removed prior to fitting **(see illustration)**. A centring sleeve is also supplied with the seal.

16.2a Tool for removing the oil seal, using a three-legged puller and three bolts . . .

16.5a Locate the new seal over the end of the crankshaft using the locating sleeve . . .

16.2b . . . insert the bolts into the recesses (arrowed) in the seal . . .

16.5b . . . remove the locating sleeve

16.2c . . . and rotate the seal anticlockwise to remove

16.12 A locating/centring sleeve (arrowed) is supplied with the new oil seal

16.13a Locate the new seal over the end of the crankshaft using the locating sleeve . . .

16.13b . . . remove the locating sleeve

16.14 Use the centring sleeve to centre the oil seal carrier

16.15 With the oil seal carrier centred around the crankshaft, tighten the retaining bolts

4 Remove each bolt in turn and ensure that new replacements are obtained for reassembly. These bolts are subjected to severe stresses and so must be renewed regardless of their apparent condition, whenever they are disturbed.

5 Withdraw the flywheel, remembering that it is very heavy – do not drop it.

Inspection

6 Clean the flywheel to remove grease and oil. Inspect the surface for cracks, rivet grooves, burned areas and score marks. Light scoring can be removed with emery cloth. Check for cracked and broken ring gear teeth. Lay the flywheel on a flat surface and use a straight-edge to check for warpage.

7 Clean and inspect the mating surfaces of the flywheel and the crankshaft. If the crankshaft seal is leaking, renew it (see Section 16) before refitting the flywheel. If the engine has covered a high mileage, it may be worth fitting a new seal as a matter if course, given the amount of work needed to access it.

8 While the flywheel is removed, clean carefully its inboard (right-hand) face, particularly the recesses which serve as the reference points for the crankshaft speed/position sensor. Clean the sensor's tip and check that the sensor is securely fastened.

9 Thoroughly clean the threaded bolt holes in the crankshaft, removing all traces of locking compound.

Refitting

10 Fit the flywheel to the crankshaft so that all bolt holes align (it will fit only one way), and also check that the dowel is located correctly. Apply suitable locking compound to the threads of the new bolts, then insert them.

11 Lock the flywheel by the method used on dismantling. Working in a diagonal sequence, tighten the bolts to the specified Stage 1 torque wrench setting.

12 Working in the same diagonal sequence, tighten them to the specified Stage 2 torque wrench setting followed by the Stage 3 setting.

13 Stage 4 involves tightening the bolts though an angle, rather than to a torque. Each bolt must be rotated through the specified angle – special angle gauges are available from tool outlets.

14 The remainder of reassembly is the reverse of the removal procedure, referring to the relevant text for details where required.

13 Offer up the carrier into position, feeding the locating sleeve over the end of the crankshaft **(see illustrations)**. Insert the new seal carrier retaining bolts, and tighten them all by hand. Remove the locating sleeve.

14 Using the special centring sleeve supplied with the seal, centre the oil seal carrier around the end of the crankshaft **(see illustration)**.

15 Ensuring that the correct alignment of the carrier is maintained, work in a diagonal sequence, tightening the retaining bolts to the specified torque **(see illustration)**. Remove the seal centring sleeve.

16 The remainder of the reassembly procedure is the reverse of dismantling, referring to the relevant text for details where required. Check for signs of oil leakage when the engine is restarted.

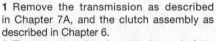

17 Flywheel – removal, inspection and refitting

Removal

1 Remove the transmission as described in Chapter 7A, and the clutch assembly as described in Chapter 6.

2 There is a locating dowel in the end of the crankshaft, to ensure correct alignment during refitting **(see illustration)**.

3 Prevent the flywheel from turning by locking the ring gear teeth, or by bolting a strap between the flywheel and the cylinder block/crankcase **(see illustration)**. Slacken the bolts evenly until all are free.

18 Engine/transmission mountings – inspection and renewal

General

1 The engine/transmission mountings seldom require attention, but broken or deteriorated mountings should be renewed immediately, or the added strain placed on the driveline components may cause damage or wear.

17.2 Locating dowel (arrowed) to align the flywheel when refitting

17.3 Special tool (arrowed) used to lock the flywheel, while the retaining bolts are slackened

2 While separate mountings may be removed and refitted individually, if more than one is disturbed at a time (such as if the engine/transmission unit is removed from its mountings) they must be reassembled and their fasteners tightened in the position marked on removal.

3 On reassembly, the complete weight of the engine/transmission unit must not be taken by the mountings until all are correctly aligned with the marks made on removal. Tighten the engine/transmission mounting nuts/bolts to their specified torque settings.

Inspection

4 During the check, the engine/transmission unit must be raised slightly, to remove its weight from the mountings.

5 Firmly apply the handbrake, then jack up the front of the vehicle and support it securely on axle stands (see *Jacking and vehicle support*). Position a jack under the sump, or under the transmission, with a large block of wood between the jack head and the sump/transmission, then carefully raise the engine/transmission just enough to take the weight off the mountings.

Warning: Do not place any part of your body under the engine when it is supported only by the jack.

6 Check the mountings to see if the rubber is cracked, hardened or separated from the metal components. Sometimes the rubber will split right down the centre.

7 Check for relative movement between each mounting's brackets and the engine/transmission or body (use a large screwdriver or lever to attempt to move the mountings). If movement is noted, lower the engine and check the tightness of the mounting fasteners.

Renewal

Note: *The following paragraphs assume the engine is supported beneath the sump as described earlier.*

Right-hand mounting

8 Mark the position of the mounting on the right-hand inner wing panel.

9 With the engine/transmission supported, unscrew the nut and two bolts securing the mounting to the bracket on the engine **(see illustration)**. Note that new bolts and a new nut will be required for refitting.

10 Unscrew the four bolts securing the mounting to the inner wing panel and withdraw the mounting from the vehicle.

11 On refitting, tighten the nut and bolts to the specified torque. Tighten the new nut and bolts securing the mounting to the engine bracket first, then release the jack to allow the mounting bracket to rest on the inner wing panel. Re-align the marks made on removal then tighten the mounting bracket bolts to the specified torque.

Left-hand mounting

12 With the engine/transmission supported,

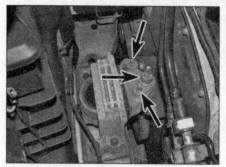

18.9 Right-hand engine/transmission mounting retaining bolts/nut (arrowed)

mark the position of the mounting on the left-hand inner wing panel.

13 On vehicles manufactured up to July 2003, undo the central bolt securing the mounting to the transmission mounting bracket.

14 On vehicles manufactured from July 2003 onward, undo the nut securing the mounting to the transmission mounting bracket **(see illustration)**.

15 On all vehicles, undo the two bolts from below, securing the mounting to the transmission mounting bracket.

16 Unscrew the four bolts securing the mounting to the inner wing panel and withdraw the mounting from the vehicle. Note that new bolts will be required for refitting.

17 On refitting, tighten the nut and bolts to the specified torque. Tighten the nut and bolts securing the mounting to the transmission bracket first, then release the jack to allow the mounting bracket to rest on the inner wing panel. Re-align the marks made on removal then tighten the new mounting bracket bolts to the specified torque.

Rear mounting

18 Undo the four bolts securing the engine/transmission rear mounting to the front subframe. Undo the through-bolt securing the mounting to the transmission and remove the mounting from under the vehicle **(see illustrations)**. Note that a new through-bolt will be required for refitting.

19 On refitting, use a new through-bolt, and tighten all bolts to the specified torque.

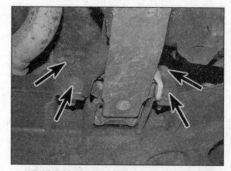

18.18a Undo the four bolts (arrowed) securing the engine/transmission rear mounting to the subframe . . .

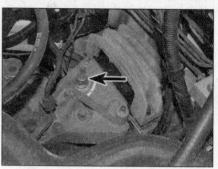

18.14 Left-hand engine/transmission mounting retaining nut (arrowed)

19 Inlet manifold –
removal, inspection and refitting

Removal

1 Move the driver's seat fully forward, open the battery box cover and disconnect the battery negative terminal (refer to *Disconnecting the battery* in the Reference Chapter).

2 Refer to Chapter 4A and remove the intake air resonator and air ducts, then remove the engine upper cover.

3 Release the securing clip and detach the turbocharger outlet pipe from the end of the inlet manifold.

4 Where applicable, detach any wiring or vacuum hoses from across the inlet manifold (releasing it from any relevant connectors and retaining clips, marking or labelling them as they are unplugged), then move the wiring loom to one side of the engine bay.

5 Unscrew the bolts securing the inlet manifold to the cylinder head and withdraw it. Take care not to damage vulnerable components as the manifold is being removed.

Inspection

6 If using a scraper or solvent to remove any traces of old gasket material and sealant from the manifold and cylinder head, be careful to ensure that you do not scratch or damage the material of either. The cylinder head is

18.18b . . . then undo the through-bolt (arrowed) securing the mounting to the transmission

19.8 Fit new gaskets to the inlet ports in the manifold

20.4 Release the securing clip (arrowed) and detach the intake duct from the turbocharger

20.6 Disconnect the oil supply tube from the turbocharger

of aluminium alloy, while the manifold is a plastic moulding – any solvents used must be suitable for this application. If the gasket was leaking, have the mating surfaces checked for warpage at an automotive machine shop. While it may be possible to have the cylinder head gasket surface skimmed if necessary, to remove any distortion, the manifold must be renewed if it is found to be warped or cracked – check with special care around the mounting points.

7 Provided the relevant mating surfaces are clean and flat, a new gasket will be sufficient to ensure the joint is gas-tight. Do not use any kind of silicone-based sealant on any part of the fuel system or inlet manifold.

Refitting

8 Refitting is the reverse of the removal procedure, noting the following points:

a) *Fit new gaskets to the inlet ports in the manifold (see illustration), then locate the manifold on the head and install the retaining bolts.*

b) *Tighten the bolts evenly to the specified torque. Work from the centre outwards, to avoid warping the manifold.*

c) *Refit the remaining parts in the reverse order of removal, and tighten all nuts/ bolts to the torque settings specified.*

d) *If removed, make sure any vacuum hoses and wiring are routed correctly and the connections fitted as labelled up on removal.*

e) *When the engine is fully warmed-up, check for signs of fuel, intake and/or vacuum leaks.*

f) *Road test the vehicle, and check for proper operation of all disturbed components.*

20 Exhaust manifold – removal, inspection and refitting

Warning: The engine must be completely cool before beginning this procedure.

Removal

1 Move the driver's seat fully forward, open the battery box cover and disconnect the battery negative terminal (refer to *Disconnecting the battery* in the Reference Chapter).

2 Firmly apply the handbrake, then jack up the front of the vehicle and support it securely on axle stands (see *Jacking and vehicle support*).

3 Remove the catalytic converter as described in Chapter 4B.

4 Release the securing clip and detach the turbocharger intake duct from the turbocharger **(see illustration)**.

5 Undo the retaining bolts and remove the catalytic converter support bracket.

6 Undo the retaining bolt and disconnect the oil supply tube from the turbocharger **(see illustration)**. Discard the sealing washers.

7 Undo the two retaining bolts and disconnect the oil return tube from under the turbocharger **(see illustration)**. Discard the gasket.

8 Remove the oil return tube lower retaining bolt and withdraw it from the engine **(see illustration)**. Discard the O-ring.

9 Release the securing clip and detach the intercooler intake pipe or the EGR valve tube (as applicable) from the turbocharger **(see illustration)**.

10 Undo the two retaining bolts and disconnect the EGR cooler from the exhaust manifold **(see illustration)**. Discard the gasket.

11 Slacken and remove the retaining nut and bolt to disconnect the other end of the EGR cooler from the exhaust manifold.

12 Where applicable, disconnect the vacuum pipe from the vacuum diaphragm unit **(see illustration)**.

13 Undo the bolts and detach the heat shield from the manifold. **Note:** *The heat shield cannot be completely removed until the manifold is withdrawn.*

20.7 Undo the retaining bolts (arrowed) and disconnect the oil return tube

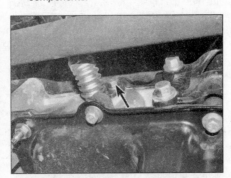

20.8 Remove the oil return tube lower retaining bolt (arrowed)

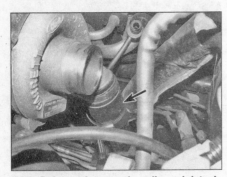

20.9 Release the securing clip and detach the intercooler intake pipe (arrowed)

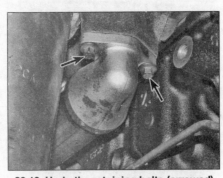

20.10 Undo the retaining bolts (arrowed) and disconnect the EGR cooler

14 Remove the retaining nuts and bolts from the exhaust manifold. Discard the nuts and bolts as new ones will be required for refitting.
15 Withdraw the manifold off the studs, then remove it from the engine compartment and collect the gasket. Remove the heat shield from the manifold.
16 Unscrew the studs from the cylinder head (a female Torx-type socket will be required). Discard the studs as new ones will be required for refitting.

Inspection

17 If using a scraper to remove all traces of old gasket material and carbon deposits from the manifold and cylinder head mating surfaces, be careful to ensure that you do not scratch or damage the material of either component – any solvents used must be suitable for this application. If the gasket was leaking, check the manifold and cylinder head for warpage – this may need to be done at an automotive machine shop, resurface if necessary.
Caution: When scraping, be very careful not to gouge or scratch the delicate aluminium alloy cylinder head.
18 Provided both mating surfaces are clean and flat, a new gasket will be sufficient to ensure the joint is gas-tight. Do not use any kind of exhaust sealant upstream of the catalytic converter.

Refitting

19 Refitting is the reverse of the removal procedure, noting the following points:
a) *Fit a new manifold gasket and cylinder head studs, nuts and bolts.*
b) *Refit the manifold, and tighten the nuts to the specified torque.*
c) *Fit new gaskets, O-rings and sealing washers where required.*

20.12 Disconnecting the vacuum pipe from the vacuum diaphragm unit

d) *Refit the catalytic converter with reference to Chapter 4B.*
e) *Run the engine, and check for exhaust leaks.*

Chapter 2 Part B:
2.4 litre engine in-vehicle repair procedures

Contents

Degrees of difficulty

Easy, suitable for novice with little experience	**Fairly easy,** suitable for beginner with some experience	**Fairly difficult,** suitable for competent DIY mechanic	**Difficult,** suitable for experienced DIY mechanic	**Very difficult,** suitable for expert DIY or professional

Specifications

General

Engine type.	Four-cylinder, in-line, double overhead camshaft
Designation	DuraTorq-Di and TDCi
Engine codes:	
DuraTorq-Di (75 PS – direct injection)	F4FA
DuraTorq-Di (90 PS – direct injection)	D2FA, D2FB and HEFA
DuraTorq-Di (115 PS – direct injection)	FXFA
DuraTorq-Di (120 PS – direct injection)	D4FA and DFFA
DuraTorq-Di (125 PS – direct injection)	DOFA
DuraTorq-TDCi (135 PS – common rail injection).	H9FA
Capacity.	2402 cc
Bore	89.9 mm
Stroke.	94.6 mm
Compression ratio	19 : 1
Power output:	
F4FA.	55 kW (75 PS) at 3500 rpm
D2FA, D2FB and HEFA.	66 kW (90 PS) at 4000 rpm
FXFA.	85 kW (115 PS) at 4000 rpm
D4FA and DFFA	88 kW (120 PS) at 4000 rpm
DOFA.	92 kW (125 PS) at 4000 rpm
H9FA.	101 kW (135 PS) at 4000 rpm
Firing order.	1-3-4-2 (No 1 cylinder at timing chain end)
Direction of crankshaft rotation	Clockwise (seen from right-hand side of vehicle)

Cylinder head

Piston protrusion:	**Thickness of cylinder head gasket**
0.310 to 0.400 mm	1.10 mm (1 hole/tooth)
0.401 to 0.450 mm	1.15 mm (2 holes/teeth)
0.451 to 0.500 mm	1.20 mm (3 holes/teeth)
Maximum permissible gasket surface distortion	0.10 mm

Lubrication

Engine oil capacity.	See Chapter 1
Oil pressure – maximum (engine at operating temperature):	
At idle	1.25 bars
At 2000 rpm	2.00 bars

Torque wrench settings

	Nm	lbf ft
Auxiliary drivebelt idler pulley bolt	53	39
Big-end bearing cap bolts:*		
Stage 1	25	18
Stage 2	60	44
Stage 3	Angle-tighten a further 90°	
Camshaft carrier bolts		
Stage 1 – bolts 1 to 22	23	17
Stage 2 – bolts 23 to 25	10	7
Camshaft cover	10	7
Camshaft position sensor	10	7
Camshaft sprocket bolts	33	24
Coolant outlet elbow bolts	23	17
Coolant pump bolts	23	17
Cooling fan pulley bracket bolts	53	39
Crankshaft oil seal carrier bolts	10	7
Crankshaft position sensor	7	5
Crankshaft position sensor mounting bracket bolts	23	17
Crankshaft pulley bolts:*		
Stage 1	45	33
Stage 2	Angle-tighten a further 90°	
Cylinder head bolts:		
Stage 1 – bolts 1 to 10	10	7
Stage 2 – bolts 11 to 18	10	7
Stage 3 – bolts 1 to 10	20	15
Stage 4 – bolts 11 to 18	20	15
Stage 5 – bolts 1 to 10	35	26
Stage 6 – bolts 11 to 18	26	19
Stage 7 – bolts 1 to 10	45	33
Stage 8 – bolts 1 to 10	Angle-tighten a further 90°	
Stage 9 – bolts 11 to 18	Angle-tighten a further 90°	
Stage 10 – bolts 1 to 10	Angle-tighten a further 90°	
Stage 11 – bolts 11 to 18	Angle-tighten a further 90°	
Engine crossmember bolts	70	52
Engine/transmission mountings:		
Engine mounting-to-engine bracket:		
All engines except H9FA	103	76
H9FA engines	80	59
Engine mounting-to-engine crossmember:		
All engines except H9FA	40	30
H9FA engines	63	46
Transmission mounting support bracket-to-transmission (5-speed transmissions)	63	46
Transmission mounting-to-subframe	40	30
Transmission mounting-to-transmission (6-speed transmissions)	70	52
Exhaust manifold and turbocharger nuts and bolts	40	30
Exhaust manifold to catalytic converter	40	30
Flywheel bolts:		
Stage 1	15	11
Stage 2	30	22
Stage 3	75	55
Stage 4	Angle-tighten a further 45°	
Fuel injection pump sprocket	32	24
Fuel injectors	52	38
Fuel pressure pipe union nuts	40	30
Fuel rail-to-camshaft carrier	23	17
Fuel return line unions	8	6
Glow plugs	12	9
Inlet manifold bolts	16	12
Lower crankcase/ladder to cylinder block	23	17
Main bearing cap bolts:*		
Stage 1	15	11
Stage 2	20	15
Stage 3	35	26
Stage 4	80	59
Stage 5	Angle-tighten a further 90°	
Oil filter housing bolts	23	17
Oil pump bolts	10	7

Torque wrench settings (continued)

	Nm	lbf ft
Oil pump chain tensioner	16	12
Oil pump pick-up pipe	10	7
Power steering pump and alternater mounting bracket bolts	22	16
Power steering pump bolts	23	17
Roadwheel nuts	200	148
Rocker shaft bolts:*		
Stage 1	13	10
Stage 2	Angle-tighten a further 45°	
Starter motor	25	18
Sump bolts:		
Stage 1	7	5
Stage 2	14	10
Sump oil drain plug	23	17
Timing chain cover:		
Nuts	10	7
Bolts	14	10
Timing chain guide retaining bolts	15	11
Timing chain tensioner	15	11
Transmission-to-engine bolts	40	30
Turbocharger oil feed pipe union	10	7
Turbocharger oil return pipe bolts	10	7

* Use new nuts/bolts

---

1 General information

How to use this Chapter

This Part of Chapter 2 is devoted to repair procedures possible while the engine is still installed in the vehicle. Since these procedures are based on the assumption that the engine is installed in the vehicle, if the engine has been removed and mounted on a stand, some of the preliminary dismantling steps outlined will not apply.

Information concerning engine/transmission removal and refitting and engine overhaul can be found in Part C of this Chapter.

Engine description

The 2.4 litre diesel engines covered in this Part of Chapter 2 are all in-line four-cylinder, turbocharged units, with a 16-valve, double overhead camshaft (DOHC) arrangement. The DI engines are of the direct fuel injection type, with the TDCI engine being a common rail design. The engine and transmission are mounted in-line at the front of the vehicle, driving the rear wheels via a propeller shaft to the rear axle.

The engine cylinder block casting is of cast-iron and has a lower aluminium crankcase which is bolted to the underside of the cylinder block, with a pressed steel sump bolted under that.

The crankshaft runs in five main bearings, the centre main bearing's upper half incorporating thrust washers to control crankshaft endfloat. The connecting rods rotate on horizontally split bearing shells at their big-ends. The pistons are attached to the connecting rods by gudgeon pins which are

a floating fit in the connecting rod small-end eyes, secured by circlips. The aluminium alloy pistons are fitted with three piston rings – two compression rings and an oil control ring.

The inlet and exhaust valves are each closed by coil springs. They operate in guides which are shrink-fitted into the cylinder head, as are the valve seat inserts.

The double overhead camshaft sprockets and the fuel injection pump are driven by a chain from a sprocket on the crankshaft. The camshafts operate the sixteen valves via rockers which are mounted on rocker shafts that run parallel with the camshafts. Each camshaft rotates in five bearings that are machined directly in the cylinder head and the (bolted on) bearing caps. This means that the bearing caps are not available separately from the cylinder head, and must not be interchanged with caps from another engine.

Lubrication is by means of a chain driven oil pump driven from a sprocket on the crankshaft. The oil pump is mounted below the lower crankcase, and draws oil through a strainer located in the sump. The pump forces oil through an externally-mounted full-flow cartridge-type filter. From the filter, the oil is pumped into a main gallery in the cylinder block/crankcase, from where it is distributed to the crankshaft (main bearings) and cylinder head. An oil cooler is fitted next to the oil filter, at the side of the block. The cooler is supplied with coolant from the engine cooling system.

While the crankshaft and camshaft bearings receive a pressurised supply, the camshaft lobes and valves are lubricated by splash, as are all other engine components. The undersides of the pistons are cooled by oil, sprayed from nozzles fitted above the upper main bearing shells. The turbocharger receives its own pressurised oil supply.

Repairs with the engine in the vehicle

The following major repair operations can be accomplished without removing the engine from the vehicle. However, owners should note that any operation involving the removal of the timing chain, camshafts or cylinder head require careful forethought, depending on the level of skill and the tools and facilities available. Refer to the relevant text for details.

a) Compression pressure – testing.
b) Camshaft cover – removal and refitting.
c) Timing chain cover – removal and refitting.
d) Timing chain – renewal.
e) Timing chain tensioner and sprockets – removal and refitting.
f) Camshafts and hydraulic rockers – removal and refitting.
g) Cylinder head – removal, overhaul and refitting.
h) Crankshaft pulley – removal and refitting.
i) Sump – removal and refitting.
j) Pistons, connecting rods and big-end bearings – removal and refitting*.
k) Oil filter housing and oil cooler – removal and refitting.
l) Crankshaft oil seals – renewal.
m) Oil pump – removal and refitting.
n) Flywheel – removal and refitting.
o) Engine/transmission mountings – removal and refitting.
p) Inlet manifold – removal and refitting.
q) Exhaust manifold – removal and refitting.

*Although the operation marked with an asterisk can be carried out with the engine in the vehicle (after removal of the sump), it is preferable for the engine to be removed, in the interests of cleanliness and improved access. For this reason, the procedure is described in Chapter 2C.

2 Compression and leakdown tests – description and interpretation

Compression test

Note 1: *A compression tester suitable for use with diesel engines will be required for this test.*

Note 2: *The following procedure is likely to log a fault code in the powertrain control module memory. If the engine management warning light is illuminated after the test, it will be necessary to have the fault code cleared by a Ford dealer or suitably equipped garage using specialist diagnostic equipment.*

1 When engine performance is down, or if misfiring occurs which cannot be attributed to the fuel or emissions systems, a compression test can provide diagnostic clues as to the engine's condition. If the test is performed regularly, it can give warning of trouble before any other symptoms become apparent.

2 The engine must be fully warmed-up to normal operating temperature and the battery must be fully-charged. The aid of an assistant will also be required.

3 Remove the glow plugs as described in Chapter 5.

4 Open the engine compartment fuse/relay box and remove the glow plug relay (R2). The relay is located at the rear of the fuse/relay box on the right-hand side (engine side).

5 On direct injection engines, disconnect the wiring connector at the rear of the fuel injection pump. On engines with common rail injection, disconnect the wiring connectors from the fuel injectors.

6 Fit a compression tester to the No 1 cylinder glow plug hole. The type of tester which screws into the plug thread is preferred.

7 Crank the engine for several seconds on the starter motor. After one or two revolutions, the compression pressure should build up to a maximum figure and then stabilise. Record the highest reading obtained.

8 Repeat the test on the remaining cylinders, recording the pressure in each.

9 The cause of poor compression is less easy to establish on a diesel engine than on a petrol engine. The effect of introducing oil into

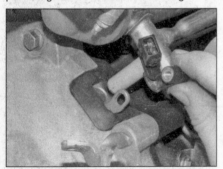

3.8 Undo the retaining bolt and withdraw the crankshaft position sensor

3.7 Unclip and remove the crankshaft position sensor heat shield

the cylinders (wet testing) is not conclusive, because there is a risk that the oil will sit in the recess on the piston crown, instead of passing to the rings. However, the following can be used as a rough guide to diagnosis.

10 An actual compression pressure value is not stated by Ford, however all cylinders should produce very similar pressures. Any significant difference indicates the existence of a fault. Note that the compression should build-up quickly in a healthy engine. Low compression on the first stroke, followed by gradually increasing pressure on successive strokes, indicates worn piston rings. A low compression reading on the first stroke, which does not build-up during successive strokes, indicates leaking valves or a blown head gasket (a cracked head could also be the cause).

11 A low reading from two adjacent cylinders is almost certainly due to the head gasket having blown between them and the presence of coolant in the engine oil will confirm this.

12 On completion, remove the compression tester, and refit the glow plugs as described in Chapter 5.

13 On direct injection engines, reconnect the wiring connector to the fuel injection pump. On engines with common rail injection, reconnect the wiring connectors to the fuel injectors.

14 Refit the glow plug relay to the fuse/relay box.

Leakdown test

15 A leakdown test measures the rate at which compressed air fed into the cylinder is lost. It is an alternative to a compression

3.9 Ford timing tool inserted into the crankshaft sensor bracket (transmission removed for clarity)

test, and in many ways it is better, since the escaping air provides easy identification of where pressure loss is occurring (piston rings, valves or head gasket).

16 The equipment required for leakdown testing is unlikely to be available to the home mechanic. If poor compression is suspected, have the test performed by a suitably equipped garage.

3 Engine timing – setting
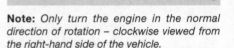

Note: *Only turn the engine in the normal direction of rotation – clockwise viewed from the right-hand side of the vehicle.*

General information

1 Top Dead Centre (TDC) is the highest point in the cylinder that each piston reaches as it travels up and down when the crankshaft turns. Each piston reaches TDC at the end of the compression stroke and again at the end of the exhaust stroke, but TDC generally refers to piston position on the compression stroke. No 1 piston is at the timing chain end of the engine.

2 Setting No 1 piston at 50° before top dead centre (BTDC) is an essential part of many procedures, such as timing chain removal, cylinder head removal and camshaft removal.

3 The design of the engines covered in this Chapter is such that piston-to-valve contact may occur if the camshaft or crankshaft is turned with the timing chain removed. For this reason, it is important to ensure that the camshaft and crankshaft do not move in relation to each other once the timing chain has been removed from the engine.

Setting

Note 1: *Ford service tool 303-675 (for engines with direct injection) or 303-698 (for engines with common rail injection), obtainable from Ford dealers or a tool supplier, will be required to set the timing at 50° BTDC.*

Note 2: *A new crankshaft position sensor will be required for refitting.*

4 Move the driver's seat fully forward, open the battery box cover and disconnect the battery negative terminal (refer to *Disconnecting the battery* in the Reference Chapter).

5 Firmly apply the handbrake then jack up the front of the vehicle and support it securely on axle stands (see *Jacking and vehicle support*).

6 A timing hole is provided on the top of the transmission, to permit the crankshaft position sensor to be located.

7 Unclip and remove the crankshaft position sensor heat shield from the top of the transmission **(see illustration)**.

8 Disconnect the wiring connector from the crankshaft position sensor, undo the retaining bolt and withdraw the sensor from the bellhousing **(see illustration)**. Note that a new sensor will be required for refitting.

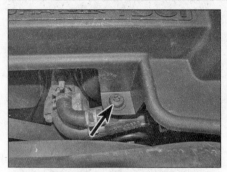

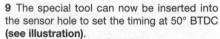

4.2a Undo the auxiliary drivebelt cover right-hand retaining bolt (arrowed) . . .

4.2b . . . and centre retaining bolt (arrowed) . . .

4.2c . . . then release the wiring harness and/or hoses and lift the cover off the engine

9 The special tool can now be inserted into the sensor hole to set the timing at 50° BTDC (see illustration).

10 Turn the crankshaft (by means of the crankshaft pulley) in the direction of engine rotation, until the end of the tool drops into a recess in the outer toothed part of the flywheel. This is the 50° BTDC position.

11 If the engine is being set to 50° BTDC as part of the timing chain removal/renewal procedure, further confirmation of the position can be gained once the timing chain outer cover has been removed. At 50° BTDC, 6 mm timing pins are inserted into the camshaft and fuel pump sprockets, see Section 7.

12 If the holes in the camshaft sprockets do not align, remove the timing pin from the crankshaft and rotate the engine one full turn, then re-install the timing pin.

13 Before rotating the crankshaft again, make sure that the timing pin and where fitted the camshaft sprocket timing pins are removed. When operations are complete, Fit the new crankshaft position sensor as described in Chapter 4A. Refit all other components removed for access. **Do not** use the crankshaft timing setting tool to prevent the crankshaft from rotating.

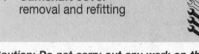

4 Camshaft cover – removal and refitting

Caution: Do not carry out any work on the fuel system with the engine running. Wait for at least 2 minutes after the engine has been stopped before any work is carried out on the fuel system, to make sure the fuel pressure and temperature has dropped sufficiently. Make sure that all the fuel lines are kept clean. Fit blanking plugs to the end of the fuel lines when they are disconnected, to prevent foreign matter entering the components.

Removal

All engines except H9FA

1 Move the driver's seat fully forward, open the battery box cover and disconnect the battery negative terminal (refer to *Disconnecting the battery* in the Reference Chapter).

2 Undo the two bolts securing the auxiliary drivebelt cover to the top of the engine. The centre bolt may be located under a plastic cover on certain models. There may also be an additional bolt at the left-hand side of the cover; if so, undo this bolt also. Release the wiring harness and/or hoses at the rear of the cover and lift the cover off the engine (see illustrations).

3 On 120 PS engines, remove the EGR valve as described in Chapter 4B.

4 Disconnect the cylinder head temperature sensor wiring connector.

5 Remove the engine oil filler pipe.

6 Remove the inlet manifold as described in Section 18.

7 Using a spanner to hold the injectors in position, slacken the fuel supply pipe unions. Note the position of the fuel supply pipes before removal.

8 Slacken the fuel supply pipe unions at the fuel injection pump, then undo the nuts and bolt securing the fuel pipe support bracket to the camshaft cover. Disconnect the fuel supply pipes from the pump and injectors and discard them. New supply pipes will be required on refitting. Fit blanking caps to the injectors and fuel pump unions, to prevent dirt ingress.

9 Disconnect the fuel injector return pipe at the quick-release connector.

10 Release the retaining clips and disconnect the fuel return pipe from the injectors. Discard the return pipe and sealing washers, new ones will be required on refitting.

11 Carefully prise out the four fuel injector

seals from the camshaft cover (see illustration). Discard the seals as new ones will be required for refitting.

12 Disconnect the crankcase ventilation hose from the rear of the camshaft cover.

13 Unscrew the retaining bolts and lift the camshaft cover off the cylinder head. Recover the gasket and discard it – a new gasket and seals will be required for refitting.

H9FA engine

14 Move the driver's seat fully forward, open the battery box cover and disconnect the battery negative terminal (refer to *Disconnecting the battery* in the Reference Chapter).

15 Undo the two bolts securing the auxiliary drivebelt cover to the top of the engine. The centre bolt may be located under a plastic cover on certain models. There may also be an additional bolt at the left-hand side of the cover; if so undo this bolt also. Release the wiring harness and/or hoses at the rear of cover and lift the cover off the engine (see illustrations 4.2a to 4.2c).

16 Disconnect the cylinder head temperature sensor wiring connector.

17 Remove the engine oil filler pipe.

18 Before proceeding further, use a brush and suitable solvent to clean the area around the injector high-pressure fuel pipe unions. It is essential that no dirt enters the system. Allow time for any solvent used to dry.

19 Disconnect the electrical connectors from the fuel injectors (see illustration), and make sure the wiring connectors are kept clean.

4.11 Prise out the four camshaft cover fuel injector seals

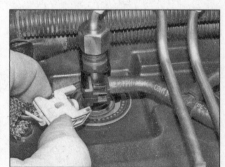

4.19 Disconnecting the electrical connectors from the fuel injectors

4.20a Release the retaining clips and pull the fuel return lines from the injectors

4.20b On later models, release the collar around the injector . . .

4.20c . . . and withdraw the return pipe

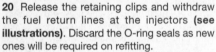

4.21 Using a spanner to hold the injectors in position, slacken the fuel supply pipe unions

4.22 Slacken the fuel supply pipes at the fuel rail

4.25 Where applicable, withdraw the fuel return pipe collars

20 Release the retaining clips and withdraw the fuel return lines at the injectors **(see illustrations)**. Discard the O-ring seals as new ones will be required on refitting.
21 Using a spanner to hold the injectors in position, slacken the fuel supply pipe unions **(see illustration)**. Note the position of the fuel supply pipes before removal.
22 Slacken the fuel supply pipe unions at fuel rail **(see illustration)**.
23 Once the unions are loose, wrap clean absorbent tissue or rag around them briefly, to soak away any dirt which may otherwise enter. If available, Ford recommend using a vacuum line to suck any dirt away from the opening union – do not use an airline, as this may blast dirt inwards, rather than cleaning it away.
24 Disconnect the fuel supply pipes and discard them. New supply pipes will be required for refitting. Fit blanking caps to the injectors and fuel rail unions, to prevent dirt ingress.

25 Temporarily remove the blanking caps from the injectors and withdraw the fuel return pipe collars (where fitted) from the injectors **(see illustration)**. Refit the blanking plugs.
26 Carefully prise out the four fuel injector seals from the camshaft cover **(see illustration 4.11)**. Discard the seals as new ones will be required for refitting.
27 Disconnect the crankcase ventilation hose from the rear of the camshaft cover.
28 Unscrew the retaining bolts and lift the camshaft cover off the cylinder head. Recover the gasket and discard it – a new gasket and seals will be required for refitting.

Refitting

All engines except H9FA

29 Clean the sealing surfaces of the cover and the head, and check the condition of the rubber seals fitted to the cover bolts.
30 Fit the new rubber gasket to the camshaft

cover, ensuring it seats fully in the cover groove **(see illustration)**.
31 Place the new injector seals in the camshaft cover and press them fully into the cover by hand **(see illustration)**.
32 Lubricate the sealing lips of the injector seals with a smear of clean engine oil then place the camshaft cover in position on the engine.
33 Screw in the cover retaining bolts and progressively and evenly tighten them to the specified torque.
34 Reconnect the crankshaft ventilation hose to the camshaft cover.
35 Connect the new injector return line to the fuel injectors and to the quick-release connector.
36 Remove the blanking caps and place the new fuel supply pipes in position over the fuel injection pump and injectors. Screw on the union nuts at the pump and injectors finger tight only at this stage.
37 Tighten the fuel supply pipe unions at the fuel injection pump to the specified torque. Note that it may be necessary to remove the starter motor (see Chapter 5) to provide sufficient clearance for the torque wrench. Refit the starter motor once all four unions have been tightened.
38 Tighten the fuel supply pipe unions at the fuel injectors to the specified torque, while using a spanner to hold the injectors in position.
39 Slacken the bolt securing the two halves of the fuel supply pipe support bracket just sufficiently to allow the two halves to slide relative to each other. Attach the support

4.30 Fit the new rubber gasket to the camshaft cover

4.31 Press the new injector seals fully into the camshaft cover by hand

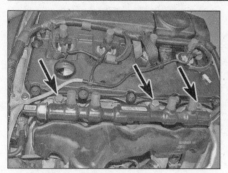

4.57 Slacken the three bolts (arrowed) securing the fuel rail to the camshaft carrier

4.60a Tighten the fuel supply pipe-to-fuel rail unions to the specified torque . . .

4.60b . . . then similarly tighten the pipe unions at the fuel injectors

bracket to the fuel pipes and screw on the two retaining nuts finger tight only at this stage.

40 Refit the fuel supply pipe support bracket retaining bolt, but only tighten the bolt finger tight at this stage.

41 Securely tighten the two nuts securing the support bracket to the fuel pipes then tighten the bracket retaining bolt. With the bracket in position, securely tighten the bolt securing the two halves of the bracket.

42 Refit the inlet manifold as described in Section 18.

43 Refit the engine oil filler pipe and reconnect the cylinder head temperature sensor wiring connector.

44 On 120 PS engines, refit the EGR valve as described in Chapter 4B.

45 Refit the auxiliary drivebelt cover to the top of the engine then reconnect the battery negative lead.

46 On completion, prime and bleed the fuel system as described in Chapter 4A.

47 When the engine has been run for some time, check for signs of oil leakage from the gasket joint.

H9FA engine

48 Clean the sealing surfaces of the cover and the head, and check the condition of the rubber seals fitted to the cover bolts.

49 Fit the new rubber gasket to the camshaft cover, ensuring it seats fully in the cover groove **(see illustration 4.30)**.

50 Place the new injector seals in the camshaft cover and press them fully into the cover by hand **(see illustration 4.31)**.

51 Lubricate the sealing lips of the injector seals with a smear of clean engine oil then place the camshaft cover in position on the engine.

52 Screw in the cover retaining bolts and progressively and evenly tighten them to the specified torque.

53 Reconnect the crankshaft ventilation hose to the camshaft cover.

54 Refit the fuel return pipe collars (where fitted) to the fuel injectors.

55 Using new O-ring seals reconnect the fuel return lines to the injectors.

56 Reconnect the electrical connectors to the fuel injectors.

57 Slacken the three bolts securing the fuel rail to the camshaft carrier **(see illustration)**.

58 Working on one fuel supply pipe at a time, remove the blanking caps from the fuel rail and injectors and place the new fuel supply pipe in position. Keep the pipe ends pushed in to the injector and fuel rail and screw on the union nuts. Tighten the nuts finger tight only at this stage.

59 When all the fuel supply pipes are in place, tighten the three fuel rail retaining bolts to the specified torque.

60 Tighten the fuel supply pipe-to-fuel rail unions to the specified torque then similarly tighten the pipe unions at the fuel injectors **(see illustrations)**.

61 Refit the engine oil filler pipe and reconnect the cylinder head temperature sensor wiring connector.

62 Refit the auxiliary drivebelt cover to the top of the engine then reconnect the battery negative lead.

63 On completion, prime and bleed the fuel system as described in Chapter 4A.

64 When the engine has been run for some time, check for signs of oil leakage from the gasket joint.

5 Timing chain cover – removal and refitting

Note: *Ford technicians use special tools for removing the oil seal and aligning the timing chain cover – see text. A new timing chain cover will be required for refitting, as the cover will be irreparably distorted during removal.*

5.6 Undo the bolts (arrowed) securing the coolant pump and brake vacuum pump assembly to the cylinder block

Removal

1 Move the driver's seat fully forward, open the battery box cover and disconnect the battery negative terminal (refer to *Disconnecting the battery* in the Reference Chapter).

2 Firmly apply the handbrake then jack up the front of the vehicle and support it securely on axle stands (see *Jacking and vehicle support*). Remove the right-hand roadwheel.

3 Drain the cooling system as described in Chapter 1.

4 Remove the radiator cooling fan shroud as described in Chapter 3.

5 Remove the auxiliary drivebelt as described in Chapter 1.

6 Undo the four bolts securing the coolant pump and brake vacuum pump assembly to the cylinder block **(see illustration)**. Move the coolant pump and vacuum pump assembly to one side and collect the gasket. Discard the gasket as a new one must be used for refitting.

7 Undo the two bolts securing the thermostat housing support bracket to the cylinder head **(see illustration)**. Release the clip and disconnect the radiator upper hose from the thermostat housing.

8 Undo the nut and two bolts securing the coolant outlet elbow to the cylinder head. Release the clip securing the degas hose to the pipe stub and withdraw the assembly from the cylinder head. Remove and discard the outlet elbow O-ring seal as a new seal must be used for refitting **(see illustrations)**.

9 Undo the retaining bolt and remove

5.7 Undo the two bolts (arrowed) securing the thermostat housing support bracket to the cylinder head

5.8a Undo the nut and two bolts (arrowed) securing the coolant outlet elbow to the cylinder head

5.8b Release the degas hose clip and withdraw the assembly from the cylinder head

5.8c Remove and discard the outlet elbow O-ring seal

the auxiliary drivebelt idler pulley **(see illustration)**.

10 Undo the three bolts and remove the cooling fan pulley bracket **(see illustration)**.

11 Remove the crankshaft pulley as described in Section 6.

12 Remove the crankshaft timing chain end oil seal as described in Section 15.

13 Undo the retaining bolts and nuts securing the timing chain cover to the cylinder block and cylinder head.

14 Using a couple of well lubricated scrapers or similar, carefully work your way around the timing chain cover and prise it away from the engine. The cover will become distorted on removal, so discard it as a new cover must be used on refitting. Recover the coolant outlet elbow gasket.

15 Measure the length of the timing chain cover retaining bolts. On early engines M6 x 14 mm

bolts were used, whereas M6 x 16 mm bolts were fitted to later engines. If M6 x 14 mm bolts are currently fitted, these must be discarded and a new set of the longer bolts must be obtained.

Refitting

16 To aid installation of the timing chain cover, screw in two M10 x 60 mm locating studs into the holes on the centre of the cylinder block. Locate a new coolant outlet elbow gasket over the studs **(see illustration)**.

17 Make sure that the mating surfaces of the cover and the engine casing are clean. Apply a 3 mm bead of sealant (Loctite 510, or equivalent) around the mating surface of the cylinder block and cylinder head, ensuring that the sealant bead passes around the inside of the retaining bolt holes **(see illustration)**.

Caution: Install the timing chain cover within 5 minutes of applying the sealer to

the engine casing. Make sure the cover does not come into contact with the engine casing, until the correct position for fitting is obtained.

18 Fit the new timing chain cover remove the locating studs and install the retaining nuts and bolts hand tight **(see illustration)**.

19 Using a cover aligning tool (Ford special tool 303-682), insert the tool over the end of the crankshaft to align the cover **(see illustration)**, then tighten all the timing chain cover retaining nuts and bolts to the specified torque. Remove the tool once the cover is in position.

20 Further refitting is a reversal of removal. Noting the following points:

a) *Fit a new crankshaft oil seal as described in Section 15.*

b) *Refit the crankshaft pulley as described in Section 6.*

5.9 Undo the retaining bolt (arrowed) and remove the auxiliary drivebelt idler pulley

5.10 Undo the three bolts (arrowed) and remove the cooling fan pulley bracket

5.16 Locate a new coolant outlet elbow gasket over the studs

5.17 Apply a 3 mm bead of sealant around the mating surface of the cylinder block and cylinder head

5.18 Fit the new timing chain cover . . .

5.19 . . . then insert the aligning tool over the end of the crankshaft before tightening the retaining bolts

c) Use a new O-ring seal when refitting the coolant outlet elbow.

d) Use a new gasket when refitting the coolant pump and vacuum pump assembly.

e) Refit the cooling fan shroud as described in Chapter 3.

f) Refit the auxiliary drivebelt and refill the cooling system as described in Chapter 1.

6 Crankshaft pulley – removal and refitting

Removal

Note: *New crankshaft pulley retaining bolts will be required for refitting.*

1 Move the driver's seat fully forward, open the battery box cover and disconnect the battery negative terminal (refer to *Disconnecting the battery* in the Reference Chapter).

2 Firmly apply the handbrake then jack up the front of the vehicle and support it securely on axle stands (see *Jacking and vehicle support*).

3 Remove the auxiliary drivebelt, as described in Chapter 1.

4 The three bolts which secure the crankshaft pulley must now be slackened. Ensure that the vehicle is adequately supported, as considerable effort may be needed to slacken the bolts.

5 Ford technicians use a special holding tool (303-1310) which locates in the pulley and prevents it from turning. If this or a suitable alternative is not available, select a gear, and have an assistant firmly apply the handbrake and footbrake as the bolts are loosened. If this method is unsuccessful, remove the starter motor as described in Chapter 5, and jam the flywheel ring gear, using a suitable tool, to prevent the crankshaft from rotating.

6 Unscrew the bolts securing the pulley to the crankshaft, and remove the pulley **(see illustration)**. Discard the bolts and obtain new bolts for refitting.

7 With the pulley removed, it is advisable to check the crankshaft oil seal for signs of oil leakage. If necessary, fit a new seal as described in Section 15.

Refitting

8 Refit the pulley to the end of the crankshaft, then fit the new pulley securing bolts and tighten them as far as possible before the crankshaft starts to rotate.

9 Holding the pulley against rotation as for removal, first tighten the bolts to the specified Stage 1 torque.

10 Stage 2 involves tightening the bolts through an angle, rather than to a torque. The bolts must be rotated through the specified angle (special angle gauges are available from tool outlets). As a guide, a 90° angle is equivalent to a quarter-turn, and this is easily judged by assessing the start and end positions of the socket handle or torque wrench.

11 Refit and tension the auxiliary drivebelt as described in Chapter 1.

12 Refit the roadwheel, lower the vehicle to the ground, and reconnect the battery negative lead. Tighten the wheel nuts to the specified torque.

7 Timing chain – removal, inspection and refitting

Note: *Only turn the engine in the normal direction of rotation – clockwise from the right-hand side of the vehicle.*

Removal

1 Remove the timing chain cover, as described in Section 5.

2 Referring to the information in Section 3, set the engine to 50° BTDC on No 1 cylinder. In this position, insert a 6 mm timing pin (6 mm drill bit) in each camshaft sprocket and one in the fuel pump sprocket **(see illustration)**. Note that on the H9FA engine (common rail injection) there may be a timing hole in the sprocket but no corresponding hole in the pump for the pin to engage. As the injection pump on engines with common rail injection does not need to be timed, the use of a timing pin is not strictly necessary.

3 Slacken the timing chain tensioner by inserting a small screwdriver into the access hole in the tensioner and releasing the pawl mechanism. Press against the timing chain guide to depress the piston into the tensioner housing, when fully depressed, insert a locking

6.6 Crankshaft pulley retaining bolts (arrowed)

pin (approximately 1.5 mm) to lock the piston in its compressed position **(see illustration)**.

4 To remove the tensioner, undo the two retaining bolts and remove the timing chain tensioner from the cylinder block, taking care not to remove the locking pin **(see illustration)**.

5 Undo the retaining bolts and remove the tensioner timing chain guide and the fixed timing chain guides from the cylinder block **(see illustrations)**.

6 Holding the fuel injection pump sprocket in position slacken the retaining bolts and remove the sprocket **(see illustration)**. **Note:** *Do not rely on the timing pin (6 mm drill bit) to hold the sprocket in position.*

7 With the camshafts held in position, undo the camshaft sprocket retaining bolts and remove the camshaft sprockets and timing chain **(see illustration)**. Do not rotate the crankshaft until the timing chain is refitted.

7.2 Insert 6 mm timing pins (6 mm drill bits), to align the camshaft sprockets

7.3 Insert a pin to lock the tensioner piston in its compressed position

7.4 Remove the timing chain tensioner from the cylinder block, taking care not to remove the locking pin

7.5a Undo the retaining bolts and remove the tensioner timing chain guide . . .

7.5b . . . then remove the upper fixed chain guide bolts (arrowed) . . .

7.5c . . . the middle fixed chain guide bolts (arrowed) . . .

7.5d . . . and the lower fixed timing chain guide bolts (arrowed)

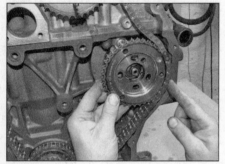

7.6 Remove the fuel pump sprocket

7.7 Undo the sprocket retaining bolts and remove the camshaft sprockets and timing chain

7.9 Insert a locking pin (drill bit) to lock the piston in its compressed position

Note: *Do not rely on the timing pins (6 mm drill bit) to hold the sprockets in position.*

8 Check the condition of the timing chain, tensioner and guides before refitting them. When fitting a new timing chain, a new tensioner should be fitted as a matter of course, especially if the engine has completed a large mileage.

9 To remove the timing chain sprocket from the crankshaft, the oil pump drive chain will need to be removed first, push the tensioner in and insert a locking pin (approximately 1.5 mm) to lock the piston in its compressed position **(see illustration)**. If a hydraulic drive chain tensioner is fitted, undo the two retaining bolts and remove the tensioner from the engine. If a mechanical drive chain tensioner is fitted, slide the tensioner off the mounting stud. The chain can now be removed from the sprocket. Undo the retaining bolt and withdraw the sprocket from the crankshaft.

Inspection

Note: *Keep all components identified for position to ensure correct refitting.*

10 Clean all components thoroughly and wipe dry.

11 Examine the chain tensioner and tensioner guide for excessive wear or other damage. Check the guides for deep grooves made by the timing chain.

12 Examine the timing chain for excessive wear. Hold it horizontally and check how much movement exists in the chain links. If there is any doubt, compare it to a new chain. Renew as necessary.

13 Examine the teeth of the camshaft, crankshaft and fuel injection pump sprockets for excessive wear and damage.

14 Before refitting the timing chain tensioner, the piston must be compressed and locked until refitted (if not already done on removal). To do this, insert a small screwdriver into

the access hole in the tensioner and release the pawl mechanism. Now lightly clamp the tensioner in a soft-jawed vice and slowly compress the piston. Do not apply excessive force and make sure that the piston remains aligned with its cylinder. When completely compressed, insert a locking pin/1.5 mm diameter wire rod into the special hole to lock the piston in its compressed position.

Refitting

15 Ensure that the crankshaft and camshaft are still set to 50° BTDC on No 1 cylinder, as described in Section 3.

16 If not already fitted, refit the crankshaft drive sprocket onto the crankshaft and securely tighten the retaining bolt. Refit the oil pump drive chain and tensioner, then hold pressure against the tensioner guide and withdraw the tensioner locking pin (see Section 12, for further information on refitting the oil pump).

17 Refit the fuel pump sprocket and the exhaust camshaft sprocket, however DO NOT tighten the retaining bolts at this stage.

18 With the timing chain around the inlet camshaft sprocket, and with the coloured link on the chain aligned with the timing mark on the sprocket, refit the timing chain and sprocket. Feed the timing chain around the crankshaft drive sprocket, fuel pump sprocket and exhaust camshaft sprocket.

19 With the timing pins (6 mm drill bits) inserted into the sprockets to re-align them, the coloured links on the timing chain must line up with the timing marks on the sprockets **(see illustrations)**.

7.19a The coloured links on the timing chain must line up with the timing marks (arrowed) on the camshaft sprockets . . .

7.19b . . . and fuel injection pump sprocket

20 Refit the tensioner to the cylinder block and tighten the retaining bolts to the specified torque. Take care not to remove the locking pin.

21 Refit the timing chain tensioner guide on the upper pivot pin and tighten the retaining bolt to the specified torque setting. Hold pressure against the bottom of the tensioner guide and withdraw the tensioner locking pin. This will then tension the timing chain.

22 Refit the three fixed timing chain guides and tighten the retaining bolts to the specified torque setting.

23 Tighten the camshaft sprocket retaining bolts, and the fuel injection pump sprocket retaining bolts, to the specified torque setting shown at the beginning of this Chapter. **Note:** *Do not rely on the timing pins (6 mm drill bits) to hold the sprockets in position.*

24 Check that the engine is still set to 50° BTDC (as described in Section 3), and remove the timing pins (6 mm drill bits) from the sprockets and the timing peg from the crankshaft sensor hole.

25 Turn the engine (in the direction of engine rotation) two full turns. Refit the timing pins and crankshaft timing peg to make sure the engine timing is still set at 50° BTDC (see Section 3 for further information).

26 Check the tension of the chain then remove the timing pins (6 mm drill bits) from the sprockets and the timing peg from the crankshaft sensor hole. Fit the new crankshaft position sensor as described in Chapter 4A.

27 Refit the timing chain cover as described in Section 5.

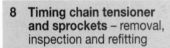

8 Timing chain tensioner and sprockets – removal, inspection and refitting

Timing chain tensioner

1 The timing chain tensioner is removed as part of the timing chain renewal procedure, in Section 7.

Camshaft sprockets

2 The camshaft sprockets are removed as part of the timing chain renewal procedure, in Section 7.

9.4 The rocker shafts are marked at the timing chain end of each shaft: EX for exhaust shaft

Crankshaft sprocket

3 The crankshaft sprocket is removed as part of the timing chain renewal procedure, in Section 7.

Fuel injection pump sprocket

4 Removal of the injection pump sprocket is described as part of the timing chain renewal procedure, in Section 7

9 Camshafts and hydraulic rockers – removal and refitting

Note 1: *New rocker shaft retaining bolts will be required for refitting.*
Note 2: *Only turn the engine in the normal direction of rotation – clockwise from the right-hand side of the vehicle.*

Removal

1 Remove the timing chain cover, as described in Section 5.

2 Referring to the information in Section 3, set the engine to 50° BTDC on No 1 cylinder. In this position, insert a 6 mm timing pin (6 mm drill bit) in each camshaft sprocket and one in the fuel injection pump sprocket (see Section 7).

3 Remove the camshaft cover, as described in Section 4.

4 Slacken and remove the rocker shaft retaining bolts, discard them as new ones will be required on refitting. Lift out the rocker shafts, complete with rocker arms and store them in a clean and safe area. **Note:** *They are*

9.7 Carefully lift the camshafts out of the cylinder head

marked at the timing chain end of the shaft, IN for inlet shaft and EX for exhaust shaft **(see illustration)**.

5 Slacken the timing chain tensioner and remove the tensioner timing chain guide, the upper timing chain guide and the camshaft sprockets as described in Section 7.

6 Slacken the camshaft carrier retaining bolts in the **reverse** of the sequence shown **(see illustration 9.12)** then lift the camshaft carrier from the cylinder head.

7 Carefully lift out the camshafts, and place them somewhere clean and safe, taking care not to scratch the lobes **(see illustration)**.

8 Before removing the hydraulic rocker arms from the rocker shaft, first mark the rockers so that they are fitted in the same position on reassembly. The rocker arms can then be withdrawn from the rocker shaft along with the springs on the inlet shaft **(see illustrations)**.

Refitting

9 Make sure that the top surfaces of the cylinder head, and in particular the camshaft bearing surfaces and the mating surfaces for the camshaft carrier, are completely clean.

10 Lubricate the camshafts and cylinder head bearing journals with clean engine oil then carefully lower the camshafts into position in the cylinder head **(see illustrations)**.

11 Apply a 2.5 mm bead of sealant (Loctite 510, or equivalent) around the outer mating surface of the camshaft carrier **(see illustration)**.

Note: *Install the timing camshaft carrier within*

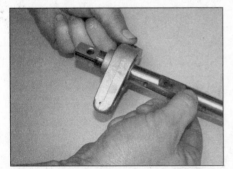

9.8a Withdraw the rocker arms from the rocker shaft . . .

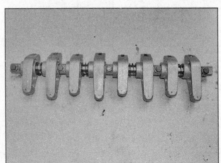

9.8b . . . along with the springs on the inlet shaft

9.10a Lubricate the cylinder head bearing journals with clean engine oil . . .

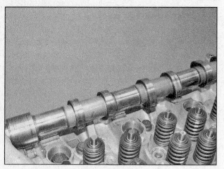

9.10b . . . then carefully lower the camshafts into position

9.11 Apply a 2.5 mm bead of sealant around the outer mating surface of the camshaft carrier

5 minutes of applying the sealer to the mating surface. Make sure the carrier does not come into contact with the cylinder head, until the correct position for fitting is obtained.

12 Install the camshaft carrier retaining bolts and tighten them to the specified torque in the sequence shown **(see illustration)**.

13 Refit the timing chain, sprockets, guides and tensioner as described in Section 7.

14 Install the rocker shafts using new retaining bolts, making sure the oil bores point downwards and that they are fitted in the correct position as noted on removal (see paragraph 4). Tighten the retaining bolts to the specified torque.

15 Refit the camshaft cover, as described in Section 4.

16 Refit the timing chain cover, as described in Section 5.

10 Cylinder head – removal, inspection and refitting

Removal

1 Move the driver's seat fully forward, open the battery box cover and disconnect the battery negative terminal (refer to *Disconnecting the battery* in the Reference Chapter).

2 Release the clips and remove the air outlet duct from the air cleaner and turbocharger.

3 Drain the cooling system as described in Chapter 1.

4 Remove the alternator as described in Chapter 5.

5 Remove the camshafts and hydraulic rockers as described in Section 9.

6 Remove the exhaust manifold as described in Section 19.

7 Remove the inlet manifold as described in Section 18.

8 Remove the glow plugs as described in Chapter 5.

9 On the H9FA (common rail injection) engine, remove the fuel rail as described in Chapter 4A.

10 Slacken the fuel injector locking sleeves and remove the fuel injectors, for further information see Chapter 4A.

11 Release the clips and disconnect the coolant expansion tank hose and the radiator top hose.

12 Undo the four bolts securing the power steering pump to the mounting bracket and move the pump aside.

13 Detach the alternator wiring harness from the engine lifting eye and the power steering pump and alternator mounting bracket.

14 Undo the bolts securing the power steering pump and alternator mounting bracket to the cylinder block and cylinder head and remove the bracket **(see illustration)**.

15 On engines equipped with an EGR cooler, release the clip and disconnect the coolant hose from the cooler. Undo the retaining bolt and detach the cooler from the cylinder head. On engines without an EGR cooler, undo the bolt(s) securing the EGR pipe to the cylinder head.

16 Undo the bolt(s) and release the coolant pipes from the cylinder head.

17 Check around the head and the engine bay that there is nothing still attached to the cylinder head, or anything which would prevent it from being lifted away.

18 Working in the reverse order of the tightening sequence **(see illustration 10.42a)**, loosen the cylinder head bolts by half a turn at a time, until they are all loose. Remove the head bolts, and discard them (Ford state that they must not be re-used, even if they appear to be serviceable).

19 Lift the cylinder head away, and use assistance if possible, as it is a heavy assembly. Do not, under any circumstances, lever the head between the mating surfaces, as this will certainly damage the sealing surfaces for the gasket, leading to leaks.

20 Once the head has been removed, recover the gasket from the two dowels. Discard

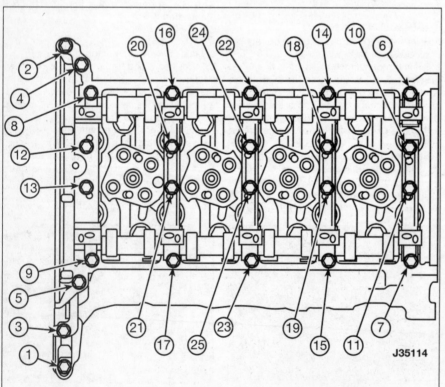

9.12 Tightening sequence for the camshaft carrier retaining bolts

10.14 Remove the power steering pump and alternator mounting bracket

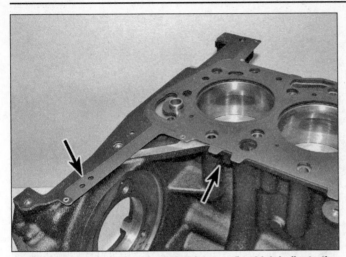

10.22 Teeth and holes in the gasket (arrowed), which indicate the gasket's thickness

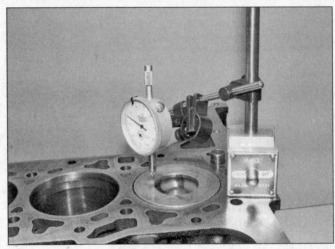

10.25 Using a dial test indicator to measure the piston protrusion

the gasket as a new one will be required on refitting (see paragraph 22).

Inspection

21 If required, dismantling and inspection of the cylinder head is covered in Part C of this Chapter.

Cylinder head gasket selection

22 Examine the old cylinder head gasket for manufacturer's identification markings. These will be in the form of teeth (one, two or three) on the front edge of the gasket and/or holes in the gasket, which indicate the gasket's thickness **(see illustration)**.

23 Unless new components have been fitted, or the cylinder head has been machined (skimmed), the new cylinder head gasket must be of the same type as the old one. Purchase the required gasket, and proceed to paragraph 29.

24 If the head has been machined, or if new pistons have been fitted, it is likely that a head gasket of different thickness to the original will be needed. Gasket selection is made on the basis of the measured piston protrusion above the cylinder head gasket surface (the protrusion must fall within the range specified at the start of this Chapter).

25 To measure the piston protrusion, anchor a dial test indicator (DTI) to the top face (cylinder head gasket mating face) of the cylinder block, and zero the gauge on the gasket mating face **(see illustration)**.

26 Rest the gauge probe above No 1 piston crown, and turn the crankshaft slowly by hand until the piston reaches TDC (its maximum height). Measure and record the maximum piston projection at TDC.

27 Repeat the measurement for the remaining pistons, and record the results.

28 If the measurements differ from piston to piston, take the highest figure, and use this to determine the thickness of the head gasket required. See Specifications at the start of this Chapter.

Preparation for refitting

29 The mating faces of the cylinder head and cylinder block must be perfectly clean before refitting the head. Use a hard plastic or wooden scraper to remove all traces of gasket and carbon; also clean the piston crowns. **Note:** *The new head gasket has rubber-coated surfaces, which could be damaged from sharp edges or debris left by a metal scraper.*

30 Take particular care when cleaning the piston crowns, as the soft aluminium alloy is easily damaged.

31 Make sure that the carbon is not allowed to enter the oil and water passages. This is particularly important for the lubrication system, as carbon could block the oil supply to the engine's components. Using adhesive tape and paper, seal the water, oil and bolt holes in the cylinder block.

32 To prevent carbon entering the gap between the pistons and bores, smear a little grease in the gap. After cleaning each piston, use a small brush to remove all traces of grease and carbon from the gap, then wipe away the remainder with a clean rag. Clean all the pistons in the same way.

33 Check the mating surfaces of the cylinder block and the cylinder head for nicks, deep scratches and other damage (refer to the Note in paragraph 29). If slight, they may be

10.38 Locate the new cylinder head gasket over the dowels correctly

removed carefully with a file, but if excessive, machining may be the only alternative to renewal.

34 If warpage of the cylinder head gasket surface is suspected, use a straight-edge to check it for distortion (refer to Part C of this Chapter if necessary).

35 Ensure that the cylinder head bolt holes in the crankcase are clean and free of oil. Syringe or soak up any oil left in the bolt holes. This is most important in order that the correct bolt tightening torque can be applied, and to prevent the possibility of the block being cracked by hydraulic pressure when the bolts are tightened.

Refitting

36 Make sure the timing is still set at 50° BTDC (see Section 3). This will eliminate any risk of piston-to-valve contact as the cylinder head is refitted.

37 To guide the cylinder head into position, screw two long studs (or old cylinder head bolts with the heads cut off, and slots cut in the ends to enable the bolts to be unscrewed) into the end cylinder head bolt locations on the manifold side of the cylinder block.

38 Ensure that the cylinder head locating dowels are in place in the cylinder block, then fit the new cylinder head gasket over the dowels **(see illustration)**. The gasket can only be fitted one way, with the teeth to determine the gasket thickness at the front **(see illustration 10.22)**. Take care to avoid damaging the gasket's rubber coating.

39 Lower the cylinder head into position on the gasket, ensuring that it engages correctly over the guide studs and dowels.

40 Fit the new cylinder head bolts to the remaining bolt locations and screw them in as far as possible by hand.

41 Unscrew the two guide studs from the cylinder block, then screw in the two remaining new cylinder head bolts as far as possible by hand.

42 Working in the sequence shown, tighten

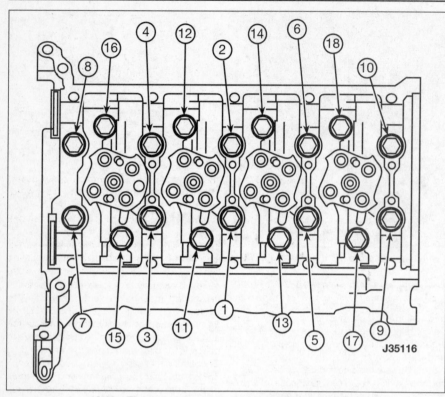

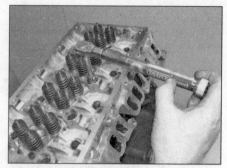

10.42b Tighten the cylinder head bolts in the initial stages using a torque wrench

10.44 Using an angle tightening gauge to tighten the cylinder head bolts through the final stages

10.42a Tightening sequence for the cylinder head bolts

the cylinder head bolts to the specified Stage 1 and Stage 2 torque settings **(see illustrations)**.

43 Again working in the sequence shown, tighten all the cylinder head bolts through the specified Stages as given in the Specifications at the beginning of this Chapter.

44 The last Stages involve tightening the bolts through an angle, rather than to a torque. Each bolt in sequence must be rotated through the specified angle – special angle gauges are available from tool outlets **(see illustration)**. As a guide, a 90° angle is equivalent to a quarter-turn, and this is easily judged by assessing the start and end positions of the socket handle.

45 The remainder of the refitting procedure is a reversal of the removal procedure, bearing in mind the following points:

a) *Refit the fuel injectors as described in Chapter 4A.*

b) *On the H9FA (common rail injection) engine, refit the fuel rail as described in Chapter 4A.*

c) *Refit the glow plugs as described in Chapter 5.*

d) *Refit the fuel injectors with reference to Chapter 4A.*

e) *Refit the inlet manifold as described in Section 18.*

f) *Reconnect the exhaust manifold with reference to Section 19.*

g) *Refit the camshafts and hydraulic rockers with reference to Section 9.*

h) *Refit the alternator as described in Chapter 5.*

i) *Refit the camshaft cover with reference to Section 4.*

j) *Refill the cooling system with reference to Chapter 1.*

k) *Check and if necessary top-up the engine oil level and power steering fluid level as described in 'Weekly checks'.*

l) *Before starting the engine, read through the section on engine restarting after overhaul, at the end of Chapter 2C.*

11 Sump – removal and refitting

Removal

1 Firmly apply the handbrake, then jack up the front of the vehicle and support it securely on axle stands (see *Jacking and vehicle support*).

2 Drain the engine oil, then clean and refit the engine oil drain plug. Inspect the seal for damage, fit a new drain plug and seal if required. Tighten the drain plug to the specified torque. Although not strictly necessary as part of the dismantling procedure, owners are advised to remove and discard the oil filter, so that it can be renewed with the oil (refer to Chapter 1 if necessary).

3 Progressively unscrew and remove the sump retaining bolts.

4 A conventional sump gasket is not used, and sealant is used instead. Unfortunately, the use of sealant can make removal of the sump more difficult. If care is taken not to

damage the surfaces, the sealant can be cut around using a scraper or a sharp knife. On no account lever between the mating faces, as this will almost certainly damage them, resulting in leaks when finished.

5 Once the sump is free, lower it down and rest it on the engine crossmember.

6 Undo the retaining bolts and remove the pick-up pipe from the oil pump. Remove and discard the O-ring seal and obtain a new O-ring for refitting.

7 Slide the sump off the crossmember and remove it from under the vehicle.

Refitting

8 On reassembly, thoroughly clean and degrease the mating surfaces of the lower crankcase and sump, removing all traces of sealant, then use a clean rag to wipe out the sump and the engine's interior.

9 To aid installation of the sump, screw in two M6 x 20 mm locating studs into two diagonally opposite bolt holes in the lower crankcase.

10 Fit the new O-ring to the oil pump pick-up pipe.

11 Apply a 3 mm bead of sealant (Loctite 510, or equivalent) to the sump flange, making sure the bead is around the inside edge of the bolt holes **(see illustration)**. **Note:** *The sump must be refitted within 5 minutes of applying the sealant.*

12 Place the sump under the engine and lay it on the engine crossmember.

13 Refit the oil pump pick-up pipe and tighten the bolts to the specified torque.

14 Fit the sump over the two locating studs,

and insert the sump retaining bolts. Remove the locating studs and insert the remaining two bolts. Tighten all the bolts hand tight only at this stage.

15 Working in a progressive diagonal sequence, tighten all the bolts to the specified torque, in the two Stages given in the Specifications.

16 Lower the vehicle to the ground, and refill the engine with oil. If removed, fit a new oil filter with reference to Chapter 1.

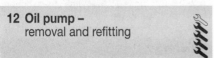

12 Oil pump – removal and refitting

Note: *The following procedure is for removing and refitting of the oil pump. If the oil pump drive chain or tensioner requires renewing, the engine timing chain will need to be removed (see Section 7).*

Removal

1 Remove the sump as described in Section 11.

2 Ford special tool (303-705) is used to align the oil pump sprocket. Bolt the tool/plate to the sump flange so that it sits flush with the oil pump drive sprocket **(see illustration)**.

3 Undo the retaining bolts and remove the pick-up pipe from the oil pump **(see illustration)**. Remove and discard the O-ring seal and obtain a new O-ring for refitting.

4 Undo the retaining bolts and release the oil pump from the lower crankcase. Push or pull on the oil pump drive chain to compress

11.11 Apply a 3 mm bead of sealant to the sump flange

the tensioner, then disengage the oil pump sprocket from the chain and remove the oil pump **(see illustration)**.

Refitting

Caution: The oil pump sprocket and crankshaft sprocket must be kept in line with each other, so that the chain runs straight. Use Ford's special tool or a DTI gauge to make sure they are aligned correctly.

5 Refit the oil pump to the lower crankcase, installing the drive chain to the sprocket on the oil pump. Only finger-tighten the oil pump retaining bolts at this stage.

6 Slide the oil pump until the drive sprocket sits flush with the special tool, as aligned on removal **(see illustration 12.2)**. With the oil pump in position, tighten the retaining bolts to the specified torque.

7 Ensuring that the alignment of the pump is

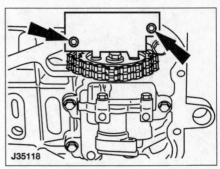

12.2 Aligning the oil pump sprocket using the Ford special tool bolted to the lower crankcase

correct, undo the retaining bolts and remove the special tool from the sump flange.

8 If the oil pump has been removed as part of an engine overhaul procedure, and the timing chain cover has been removed, the oil pump sprocket alignment can be checked with a DTI gauge.

9 Mount the gauge on the cylinder block with the probe against the inner teeth of the crankshaft sprocket **(see illustrations)**. Zero the gauge in this position.

10 Without moving the gauge body, move the probe to the oil pump sprocket **(see illustration)**. Move the oil pump as necessary until the two gauge readings are the same, then tighten the pump retaining bolts to the specified torque.

11 Fit a new O-ring seal to the pick-up pipe, then refit the pick-up pipe to the oil pump **(see illustration)**.

12 Refit the sump with reference to Section 11.

12.3 Undo the retaining bolts and remove the pick-up pipe from the oil pump

12.4 Disengage the oil pump sprocket from the chain and remove the oil pump

12.9a Mount the DTI gauge on the cylinder block . . .

12.9b . . . with the probe against the inner teeth of the crankshaft sprocket, then zero the gauge

12.10 Move the probe to the oil pump sprocket and move the pump as necessary until the two gauge readings are the same

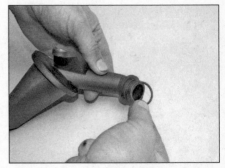

12.11 Fit a new O-ring seal to the pick-up pipe

13.1 Oil pressure warning light switch location (arrowed)

14.6a Unscrew the bolts (arrowed) . . .

4 Clamp the oil cooler coolant hoses to minimise spillage, then remove the clips, and disconnect the hoses from the oil cooler. Be prepared for coolant spillage.

5 Disconnect the oil pressure warning light switch wiring connector.

6 Unscrew the six bolts and withdraw the oil filter housing from the cylinder block. Collect the rubber gasket and note a new gasket must be used on refitting (**see illustrations**).

7 With the filter housing removed, if required, undo the four bolts and separate the oil cooler from the filter housing. Collect the gasket noting a new gasket must be used on refitting.

Refitting

8 Refitting is a reversal of removal, bearing in mind the following points:
   a) *Use new gaskets.*
   b) *Fit the oil cooler mounting bolts, and tighten them securely.*
   c) *Tighten the oil filter housing retaining bolts to the specified torque.*
   d) *On completion, lower the vehicle to the ground. Check and if necessary top-up the oil and coolant levels, then start the engine and check for signs of oil or coolant leakage.*

14.6b . . . withdraw the oil filter housing from the cylinder block . . .

14.6c . . . and collect the rubber gasket

13 Oil pressure warning light switch – removal and refitting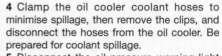

Removal

1 The switch is screwed into the side of the oil filter housing (**see illustration**).
2 To improve access to the switch, it may be necessary to apply the handbrake, then jack up the front of the vehicle and support it on axle stands (see *Jacking and vehicle support*).
3 Unplug the wiring from the switch and unscrew it from the filter housing. Be prepared for some oil loss.

Refitting

4 Refitting is the reverse of the removal procedure. Apply a thin smear of suitable sealant to the switch threads, and tighten it securely.

5 Check the engine oil level and top-up as necessary (see *Weekly checks*).
6 Check for correct warning light operation and for signs of oil leaks, once the engine has been restarted and warmed-up to normal operating temperature.

14 Oil filter housing and cooler – removal and refitting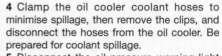

Removal

1 The oil filter housing is mounted on the left-hand side of the cylinder block, with the oil cooler bolted to its upper face.
2 Firmly apply the handbrake, then jack up the front of the vehicle and support it securely on axle stands (see *Jacking and vehicle support*).
3 Position a container beneath the oil filter to catch escaping oil and coolant.

15 Crankshaft oil seals – renewal

Timing chain end seal

1 Remove the crankshaft pulley with reference to Section 6.
2 Ford technicians use a special seal-removing and refitting tool (303-679), but an adequate substitute can be achieved using a three-legged puller and three bolts. Turn the seal anticlockwise, using the tool, to remove the crankshaft oil seal from the timing chain cover (**see illustrations**).
3 Wipe clean the oil seal contact surfaces and seating, and clean up any sharp edges or burrs which might damage the new seal as it is fitted, or which might cause the seal to leak once in place.
4 The new oil seal will be supplied fitted with a locating sleeve, which must **not** be removed prior to fitting.

15.2a Tool for removing the oil seal, using a three-legged puller and three bolts . . .

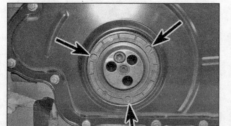

15.2b . . . insert the bolts into the recesses (arrowed) in the seal . . .

15.2c . . . and rotate the seal anticlockwise to remove

15.5a Locate the new seal over the end of the crankshaft using the locating sleeve . . .

15.5b . . . press the seal into position and remove the locating sleeve

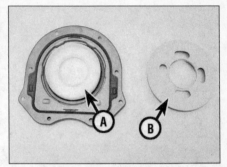

15.12 Flywheel end oil seal locating sleeve (A) and centering sleeve (B)

15.13 Apply sealant to the oil seal carrier, at the cylinder block-to-lower crankcase jointing point

15.14 Offer up the oil seal carrier, feeding the locating sleeve over the end of the crankshaft

15.15 Using the centering sleeve, centre the oil seal carrier around the end of the crankshaft

5 Locate the new seal (lips facing inwards) over the end of the crankshaft, press the seal squarely and fully into position in the cover, then remove the locating sleeve **(see illustrations)**.
6 Using the special tool used on removal, turn the seal clockwise until it is located securely into the timing chain cover.
7 Refit the crankshaft pulley with reference to Section 6.

Flywheel end seal

8 Remove the transmission as described in Chapter 7B, and the clutch assembly as described in Chapter 6.
9 Remove the flywheel as described in Section 16.
10 Unbolt and remove the oil seal carrier, noting that the seal is renewed complete with the carrier, and is not available separately. A complete set of new carrier retaining bolts should also be obtained for reassembly.
11 Clean the end of the crankshaft, polishing off any burrs or raised edges, which may have caused the seal to fail in the first place. Clean also the seal carrier mating face on the engine block, using a suitable solvent for degreasing if necessary.
12 The new oil seal is supplied fitted with a locating sleeve, which must **not** be removed prior to fitting. It should also have a centring sleeve supplied with the seal **(see illustration)**.
13 Apply suitable sealant (Loctite 510, or equivalent) to the oil seal carrier, at the cylinder

block-to-lower crankcase jointing point **(see illustration)**.
14 Offer up the carrier into position, feeding the locating sleeve over the end of the crankshaft **(see illustration)**. Insert the new seal carrier retaining bolts, and tighten them all by hand. Remove the locating sleeve.
15 Using the special centring sleeve supplied with the seal, centre the oil seal carrier around the end of the crankshaft **(see illustration)**.
16 Ensuring that the correct alignment of the carrier is maintained, work in a diagonal sequence, tightening the retaining bolts to the specified torque. Remove the seal centring sleeve.
17 The remainder of the reassembly procedure is the reverse of dismantling, referring to the relevant text for details where required. Check for signs of oil leakage when the engine is restarted.

16 Flywheel – removal, inspection and refitting

Removal

1 Remove the transmission as described in Chapter 7B, and the clutch assembly as described in Chapter 6.
2 There is a locating dowel in the end of the crankshaft, to ensure correct alignment during refitting **(see illustration)**.
3 Prevent the flywheel from turning by locking the ring gear teeth, or by bolting a strap between the flywheel and the cylinder block/crankcase. Slacken the bolts evenly until all are free **(see illustrations)**.
4 Remove each bolt in turn and ensure that new replacements are obtained for reassembly.

16.2 Locating dowel (arrowed) to align the flywheel when refitting

16.3a Use a tool like this (arrowed) to lock the flywheel . . .

16.3b . . . while the retaining bolts (arrowed) are slackened

16.11 Use a torque wrench to tighten the flywheel retaining bolts to the initial settings

These bolts are subjected to severe stresses and so must be renewed, regardless of their apparent condition, whenever they are disturbed.

5 Withdraw the flywheel, remembering that it is very heavy – do not drop it.

Inspection

6 Clean the flywheel to remove grease and oil. Inspect the surface for cracks, rivet grooves, burned areas and score marks. Light scoring can be removed with emery cloth. Check for cracked and broken ring gear teeth. Lay the flywheel on a flat surface and use a straight-edge to check for warpage.

7 Clean and inspect the mating surfaces of the flywheel and the crankshaft. If the crankshaft seal is leaking, renew it (see Section 15) before refitting the flywheel. If the engine has covered a high mileage, it may be worth fitting a new seal as a matter if course, given the amount of work needed to access it.

8 While the flywheel is removed, clean carefully its inboard (right-hand) face, particularly the recesses which serve as the reference points for the crankshaft speed/position sensor. Clean the sensor's tip and check that the sensor is securely fastened.

9 Thoroughly clean the threaded bolt holes in the crankshaft, removing all traces of locking compound.

16.13 Using an angle tightening gauge to tighten the flywheel retaining bolts through the final stage

Refitting

10 Fit the flywheel to the crankshaft so that all bolt holes align (it will fit only one way) check the dowel is located correctly. Apply suitable locking compound to the threads of the new bolts, then insert them.

11 Lock the flywheel by the method used on dismantling. Working in a diagonal sequence, tighten the bolts to the specified Stage 1 torque wrench setting **(see illustration)**.

12 Then working in the same diagonal sequence, tighten them to the specified Stage 2 torque wrench setting followed by the Stage 3 setting.

13 Stage 4 involves tightening the bolts though an angle, rather than to a torque. Each bolt must be rotated through the specified angle – special angle gauges are available from tool outlets **(see illustration)**.

14 The remainder of reassembly is the reverse of the removal procedure, referring to the relevant text for details where required.

17 Engine/transmission mountings – inspection and renewal

General

1 The engine/transmission mountings seldom require attention, but broken or deteriorated mountings should be renewed immediately, or the added strain placed on the driveline components may cause damage or wear.

2 While separate mountings may be removed and refitted individually, if more than one is disturbed at a time (such as if the engine/transmission unit is removed from its mountings), they must be reassembled and their nuts/bolts tightened in the position marked on removal.

3 On reassembly, the complete weight of the engine/transmission unit must not be taken by the mountings until all are correctly aligned with the marks made on removal. Tighten the

engine/transmission mounting nuts and bolts to their specified torque settings.

Inspection

4 During the check, the engine/transmission unit must be raised slightly, to remove its weight from the mountings.

5 Firmly apply the handbrake, then jack up the front of the vehicle and support it securely on axle stands (see *Jacking and vehicle support*). Position a jack under the sump, or under the transmission, with a large block of wood between the jack head and the sump/transmission, then carefully raise the engine/transmission just enough to take the weight off the mountings.

> **Warning: Do not place any part of your body under the engine when it is supported only by the jack.**

6 Check the mountings to see if the rubber is cracked, hardened or separated from the metal components. Sometimes the rubber will split right down the centre.

7 Check for relative movement between each mounting bracket and the engine/transmission or body (use a large screwdriver or lever to attempt to move the mountings). If movement is noted, lower the engine and check the tightness of the mounting nuts/bolts.

Renewal

Engine mountings

8 If not already done, firmly apply the handbrake, then jack up the front of the vehicle and support it securely on axle stands (see *Jacking and vehicle support*).

9 To renew the engine mountings it is necessary to remove the engine crossmember to provide the sufficient clearance. Before doing this the weight of the engine must be supported by one of the following methods.

10 Either support the weight of the assembly from underneath, using a trolley jack and a suitable piece of wood between the jack head and the sump or, preferably, from above by attaching a suitable hoist to the engine.

17.12 Working under the wheel arch, undo the two side bolts securing the engine crossmember to the underbody

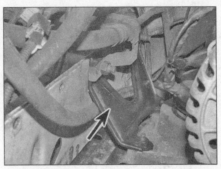

17.13 Undo the two bolts each side and remove the crossmember side brace plates (arrowed)

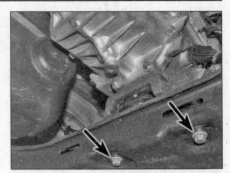

17.18 Undo the two bolts (arrowed) securing the transmission mounting to the subframe

11 With the engine securely supported, undo the nut (or bolts) securing both engine mountings to the brackets on the engine.

12 Working under one front wheel arch, undo the two side bolts securing the crossmember to the underbody **(see illustration)**. Repeat this procedure on the other side.

13 Undo the two bolts each side and remove the crossmember side brace plates (where fitted) **(see illustration)**.

14 Support the engine crossmember on a jack and undo the two lower bolts each side securing the crossmember to the underbody. Lower the jack and remove the engine crossmember from under the vehicle.

15 With the crossmember removed, undo the remaining bolts and remove the mountings from the crossmember.

16 Refitting is a reversal of removal, tightening all nuts and bolts to the specified torque. Tighten the nut (or bolts) securing the mounting to the engine bracket finger tight initially, then finally tighten them once the weight of the engine is again taken by the mounting.

Transmission mounting

17 If not already done, firmly apply the handbrake, then jack up the front of the vehicle and support it securely on axle stands (see *Jacking and vehicle support*).

18 Undo the two bolts securing the transmission mounting to the subframe **(see illustration)**.

19 Position a trolley jack under the transmission with a suitable piece of wood between the jack head and transmission casing. Raise the jack just sufficiently to gain access to the mounting-to-transmission bolts. Take great care not to place undue strain on surrounding components.

20 On 5-speed transmissions, undo the two bolts securing the mounting support bracket to the transmission casing and remove the support bracket and mounting assembly from under the vehicle. The individual mountings can now be unbolted from the support bracket.

21 On 6-speed transmissions, undo the bolt securing the mounting to the transmission casing and remove the mounting from under the vehicle **(see illustrations)**.

17.21a On 6-speed transmissions, undo the bolt securing the mounting to the transmission casing . . .

22 Refitting is a reversal of removal, tightening all bolts to the specified torque, where given.

18 Inlet manifold –
removal, inspection
and refitting

Removal

1 Move the driver's seat fully forward, open the battery box cover and disconnect the battery negative terminal (refer to *Disconnecting the battery* in the Reference Chapter).

2 Undo the two bolts securing the auxiliary drivebelt cover to the top of the engine. The centre bolt may be located under a plastic cover on certain models. There may also be an additional bolt at the left-hand side of the

18.3a Undo the bolts/nuts and detach the EGR valve from the inlet manifold . . .

17.21b . . . and remove the mounting from under the vehicle

cover; if so, undo this bolt also. Release the wiring harness and/or hoses at the rear of the cover and lift the cover off the engine **(see illustrations 4.2a to 4.2c)**.

3 Undo the two bolts (or nuts) and detach the EGR valve from the inlet manifold. Collect and discard the seal as a new one must be used for refitting **(see illustrations)**.

4 Unscrew the bolts securing the inlet manifold to the cylinder head and withdraw it. Take care not to damage vulnerable components as the manifold is being removed.

Inspection

5 If using a scraper or solvent to remove any traces of old gasket material and sealant from the manifold and cylinder head, be careful to ensure that you do not scratch or damage the material of either. The cylinder head is of aluminium alloy, while the manifold is a plastic

18.3b . . . then collect the seal EGR valve seal

moulding, therefore any solvents used must be suitable for this application. If the gasket was leaking, have the mating surfaces checked for warpage at an automotive machine shop. Whilst it may be possible to have the cylinder head gasket surface skimmed if necessary to remove any distortion, the manifold must be renewed if it is found to be warped or cracked. Thoroughly check the inlet manifold around the mounting points.

6 Provided the relevant mating surfaces are clean and flat, a new gasket will be sufficient to ensure the joint is gas-tight. Do not use any kind of silicone-based sealant on any part of the fuel system or inlet manifold.

Refitting

7 Refitting is the reverse of the removal procedure, noting the following points:
  a) Fit new gaskets to the inlet ports in the manifold (see illustration), then locate the manifold on the head and install the retaining bolts.
  b) Tighten the bolts evenly to the specified torque. Work from the centre outwards, to avoid warping the manifold.
  c) Refit the remaining parts in the reverse order of removal, and tighten all nuts/bolts to the torque settings specified.
  d) When the engine is fully warmed-up, check for signs of fuel, intake and/or vacuum leaks.
  e) Road test the vehicle, and check for proper operation of all disturbed components.

18.7 Fit new gaskets to the inlet ports in the manifold

19 Exhaust manifold – removal, inspection and refitting

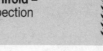

⚠ **Warning: The engine must be completely cool before beginning this procedure.**

Removal

1 Move the driver's seat fully forward, open the battery box cover and disconnect the battery negative terminal (refer to *Disconnecting the battery* in the Reference Chapter).

2 Firmly apply the handbrake, then jack up the front of the vehicle and support it securely on axle stands (see *Jacking and vehicle support*).

3 Refer to Chapter 4A and remove the air intake duct from the air cleaner and turbocharger.

4 Release the clip and disconnect the intercooler charge air intake pipe from the turbocharger.

5 Release the clip and disconnect the crankcase ventilation hose from the turbocharger intake duct (see illustration).

6 Undo the bolt securing the oil level dipstick tube to the cylinder head (see illustration). Pull the tube out of the cylinder block lower casting and collect and discard the O-ring.

7 Disconnect the catalytic converter from the manifold as described in Chapter 4B.

8 Undo the two retaining bolts and disconnect the oil return tube from under the turbocharger (see illustration). Discard the gasket.

9 Remove the oil return tube lower retaining bolt and withdraw it from the engine (see illustration). Discard the O-ring.

10 Undo the retaining bolt and disconnect the oil supply tube from the turbocharger (see illustration). Discard the sealing washers.

11 Note the fitted direction of the retaining clamp, then release the clamp and detach the EGR valve tube or EGR cooler (as applicable) from the manifold (see illustration).

12 Remove the retaining nuts and bolts from the exhaust manifold. Discard the nuts and bolts as new ones will be required for refitting.

13 Withdraw the manifold and turbocharger off the studs, remove it from the engine compartment, and collect the gasket (see illustrations). Discard the gasket as a new one will be required for refitting.

14 Unscrew the studs from the cylinder head (a female Torx-type socket will be required).

19.5 Disconnect the crankcase ventilation hose from the turbocharger intake duct

19.6 Undo the bolt (arrowed) securing the oil level dipstick tube to the cylinder head

19.8 Undo the two bolts (arrowed) and disconnect the oil return tube from under the turbocharger

19.9 Remove the oil return tube lower retaining bolt (arrowed) and withdraw the tube from the engine

19.10 Undo the retaining bolt and disconnect the oil supply tube from the turbocharger

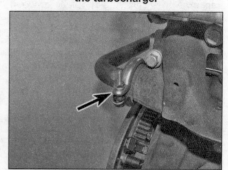

19.11 Release the clamp (arrowed) and detach the EGR valve tube or EGR cooler from the manifold

Discard the studs as new ones will be required for refitting.

Inspection

15 If using a scraper to remove all traces of old gasket material and carbon deposits from the manifold and cylinder head mating surfaces, be careful to ensure that you do not scratch or damage the material of either component, and note that any solvents used must be suitable for this application. If the gasket was leaking, check the manifold and cylinder head for warping. If necessary, resurfacing can be carried out by an automotive machine shop.
Caution: When scraping, be very careful not to gouge or scratch the delicate aluminium alloy cylinder head.
16 Provided both mating surfaces are clean and flat, a new gasket will be sufficient to ensure the joint is gas-tight. Do not use any kind of exhaust sealant upstream of the catalytic converter.

19.13a Withdraw the manifold and turbocharger off the studs . . .

Refitting

17 Refitting is the reverse of the removal procedure, noting the following points:
a) *Fit a new manifold gasket and cylinder head studs, nuts and bolts.*
b) *Refit the manifold, and tighten the nuts/bolts to the specified torque.*

19.13b . . . and collect the gasket

c) *Fit new gaskets, O-rings and sealing washers where required.*
d) *Refit the catalytic converter with reference to Chapter 4B.*
e) *Run the engine, and check for exhaust leaks.*

Chapter 2 Part C:
Engine removal and overhaul procedures

Contents

Degrees of difficulty

Easy, suitable for novice with little experience	**Fairly easy,** suitable for beginner with some experience 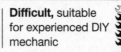	**Fairly difficult,** suitable for competent DIY mechanic 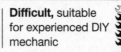	**Difficult,** suitable for experienced DIY mechanic 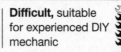	**Very difficult,** suitable for expert DIY or professional

Specifications

Engine identification

Engine type	Manufacturer's engine code
2.0 litre engines:	
DuraTorq-Di (75 PS – direct injection)	D3FA
DuraTorq-Di (85 PS – direct injection)	F3FA
DuraTorq-Di (100 PS – direct injection)	ABFA
DuraTorq-TDCi (125 PS – common rail injection)	FIFA
2.4 litre engines:	
DuraTorq-Di (75 PS – direct injection)	F4FA
DuraTorq-Di (90 PS – direct injection)	D2FA, D2FB and HEFA
DuraTorq-Di (115 PS – direct injection)	FXFA
DuraTorq-Di (120 PS – direct injection)	D4FA and DFFA
DuraTorq-Di (125 PS – direct injection)	DOFA
DuraTorq-TDCi (135 PS – common rail injection)	H9FA

2.0 litre engines

Valves – general

Valve stem-to-guide clearance:	
Inlet	0.045 mm
Exhaust	0.055 mm

Cylinder block

Cylinder bore diameter:	
Class 1	86.000 to 86.010 mm
Class 2	86.010 to 86.020 mm
Class 3	86.020 to 86.030 mm

Pistons and piston rings

Piston diameter:	
Class A	85.94 to 85.95 mm
Class B	85.95 to 85.96 mm
Class C	85.96 to 85.97 mm
Piston-to-cylinder bore clearance	0.05 to 0.07 mm
Piston ring end gaps*:	
Top compression ring	0.25 to 0.50 mm
Second compression ring	0.50 to 0.75 mm
Oil scraper ring	0.25 to 0.50 mm

*Note: Piston ring end gaps should be offset at 120° to each other when fitted

2.0 litre engines (continued)

Gudgeon pin
Length . . . . 66.700 mm
Diameter . . . . 30.000 mm
Clearance in piston . . . . 0.002 to 0.012 mm
Small-end bore (inside connecting rod) diameter . . . . 30.010 to 30.018 mm

Crankshaft and bearings
Crankshaft endfloat . . . . 0.090 to 0.305 mm
Big-end bearing journal standard diameter . . . . 52.980 to 53.000 mm
Big-end bearing shell running clearance . . . . 0.034 mm to 0.100 mm
Main bearing journals standard diameter:
    1 to 4 . . . . 64.950 to 64.970 mm
    5 . . . . 69.950 to 69.970 mm
Main bearing shell running clearance:
    1 to 4 . . . . 0.033 to 0.080 mm
    5 . . . . 0.034 to 0.083 mm

2.4 litre engines

Valves – general
Valve stem-to-guide clearance:
    Inlet . . . . 0.045 mm
    Exhaust . . . . 0.055 mm

Cylinder block
Cylinder bore diameter:
    Class 1 . . . . 89.900 to 89.910 mm
    Class 2 . . . . 89.910 to 89.920 mm
    Class 3 . . . . 89.920 to 89.930 mm

Pistons and piston rings
Piston diameter:
    Class A . . . . 89.84 to 89.85 mm
    Class B . . . . 89.85 to 89.86 mm
    Class C . . . . 89.86 to 89.87 mm
Piston-to-cylinder bore clearance . . . . 0.05 to 0.07 mm
Piston ring end gaps*:
    Top compression ring . . . . 0.25 to 0.50 mm
    Second compression ring . . . . 0.50 to 0.75 mm
    Oil scraper ring . . . . 0.25 to 0.50 mm
*Note: *Piston ring end gaps should be offset at 120° to one another when fitted*

Gudgeon pin
Length . . . . 65.850 to 66.150 mm
Diameter . . . . 31.966 to 32.000 mm
Clearance in piston . . . . 0.002 to 0.012 mm
Small-end bore (inside connecting rod) diameter . . . . 30.010 to 30.018 mm

Crankshaft and bearings
Crankshaft endfloat . . . . 0.090 to 0.305 mm
Big-end bearing journal standard diameter . . . . 52.980 to 53.000 mm
Big-end bearing shell running clearance . . . . 0.034 mm to 0.100 mm
Main bearing journals standard diameter:
    1 to 4 . . . . 64.950 to 64.970 mm
    5 . . . . 69.950 to 69.970 mm
Main bearing shell running clearance:
    1 to 4 . . . . 0.005 to 0.051 mm
    5 . . . . 0.004 to 0.054 mm

Torque wrench settings
Refer to Chapter 2A or 2B Specifications

1 General information

This Part of Chapter 2 is devoted to engine/transmission removal and refitting, to those repair procedures requiring the removal of the engine/transmission from the vehicle, and to the overhaul of engine components. It includes only the Specifications relevant to those procedures. Refer to Part A or B (depending on engine type) for additional Specifications and for all torque wrench settings.

The information ranges from advice concerning preparation for an overhaul and the purchase of new parts, to detailed step-by-step procedures covering removal and installation of internal engine components and the inspection of parts.

The following Sections have been written based on the assumption that the engine has been removed from the vehicle. For information concerning in-vehicle engine repair, as well as removal and installation of the external components necessary for the overhaul, see Part A or B of this Chapter.

2 Engine overhaul – general information

It's not always easy to determine when, or if, an engine should be completely overhauled, as a number of factors must be considered.

High mileage is not necessarily an indication that an overhaul is needed, while low mileage doesn't preclude the need for an overhaul. Frequency of servicing is probably the most important consideration. An engine that has had regular and frequent oil and filter changes, as well as other required maintenance, will most likely give many thousands of miles of reliable service. Conversely, a neglected engine may require an overhaul very early in its life.

Excessive oil consumption is an indication that piston rings, valve seals and/or valve guides are in need of attention. Make sure that oil leaks are not responsible before deciding that the rings and/or guides are worn. Perform a cylinder compression test (refer to Part A or B of this Chapter) to determine the likely cause of the problem.

Check the oil pressure with a gauge fitted in place of the oil pressure switch, and compare it with that specified in Chapter 2A or 2B as applicable. If it is extremely low, the main and big-end bearings, and/or the oil pump, are probably worn out.

Loss of power, rough running, knocking or metallic engine noises, excessive valve gear noise, and high fuel consumption may also point to the need for an overhaul, especially if they are all present at the same time. If a complete service does not cure the situation, major mechanical work is the only solution.

A full engine overhaul involves restoring all internal parts to the specification of a new engine. During a complete overhaul, the pistons and the piston rings are renewed, and the cylinder bores are reconditioned. New main and big-end bearings are generally fitted. If necessary, the crankshaft may be reground, to compensate for wear in the journals. The valves are also serviced as well, since they are usually in less-than-perfect condition at this point. Always pay careful attention to the condition of the oil pump when overhauling the engine, and renew it if there is any doubt as to its serviceability. The end result should be an as-new engine that will give many trouble-free miles.

Critical cooling system components such as the hoses, thermostat and coolant pump should be renewed when an engine is overhauled. The radiator should also be checked carefully, to ensure that it is not clogged or leaking.

Before beginning the engine overhaul, read the entire procedure, to familiarise yourself with the scope and requirements of the job. Check on the availability of parts and make sure that any necessary special tools and equipment are obtained in advance. Most work can be done with typical hand tools, although a number of precision measuring tools are required for inspecting parts to determine if they must be renewed.

The services provided by an engineering machine shop or engine reconditioning specialist will almost certainly be required, particularly if major repairs such as crankshaft regrinding or cylinder reboring are necessary. Apart from carrying out machining operations, these establishments will normally handle the inspection of parts, offer advice concerning reconditioning or renewal and supply new components such as pistons, piston rings and bearing shells. It is recommended that the establishment used is a member of the Federation of Engine Re-Manufacturers, or a similar society.

Always wait until the engine has been completely dismantled, and until all components (especially the cylinder block/crankcase and the crankshaft) have been inspected before deciding what service and repair operations must be performed by an engineering works. The condition of these components will be the major factor to consider when determining whether to overhaul the original engine, or to buy a reconditioned unit. Do not, therefore, purchase parts or have overhaul work done on other components until they have been thoroughly inspected. As a general rule, time is the primary cost of an overhaul, so it does not pay to fit worn or sub-standard parts.

As a final note, to ensure maximum life and minimum trouble from a reconditioned engine, everything must be assembled with care, in a spotlessly clean environment.

3 Engine/transmission removal – methods and precautions

If you have decided that the engine must be removed for overhaul or major repair work, several preliminary steps should be taken.

Locating a suitable place to work is extremely important. Adequate work space, along with storage space for the vehicle, will be needed. If a workshop or garage isn't available, at the very least, a flat, level, clean work surface made of concrete or asphalt is required.

Cleaning the engine compartment and engine/transmission before beginning the removal procedure will help keep tools clean and organised.

The help of an assistant is essential. Apart from the safety aspects involved, there are many instances when one person cannot simultaneously perform all of the operations required during engine/transmission removal.

Plan the operation ahead of time. Arrange for (or obtain) all of the tools and equipment you'll need prior to beginning the job. Some of the equipment necessary to perform engine/transmission removal and installation safely and with relative ease, and which may have to be hired or borrowed, includes:

a) An engine dolly (a low, wheeled platform capable of taking the weight of the engine/transmission, so that it can be removed and then moved easily when on the ground).
b) Heavy duty trolley jacks.
c) A strong pair of axle stands.
d) Ford special tool 204-606 (subframe spacers) to allow the front subframe to be lowered and secured (rear wheel drive models).
e) An assortment of wooden blocks and assorted woden strips.
f) A complete set of spanners and sockets.
g) Rags and cleaning solvent for mopping-up spilled oil, coolant and fuel.

Plan for the vehicle to be out of use for quite a while. An engineering machine shop or engine reconditioning specialist will be required to perform some of the work which cannot be accomplished without special equipment. These places often have a busy schedule, so it would be a good idea to consult them before removing the engine, in order to accurately estimate the amount of time required to rebuild or repair components that may need work.

During the engine/transmission removal procedure, it is advisable to make notes of the locations of all brackets, cable ties, earthing points, etc, as well as how the wiring harnesses, hoses and electrical connections are attached and routed around the engine and engine compartment. An effective way of doing this is to take a series of photographs of the various components before they are disconnected or removed. The resulting

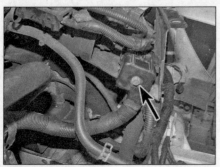

4.13a Undo the retaining bolt (arrowed) . . .

4.13b . . . and disconnect the engine wiring harness connector

4.14a Release the protective cover on the positive (+) cable terminal box . . .

4.14b . . . then undo the retaining nut (arrowed) and disconnect the starter motor positive cable from the terminal stud

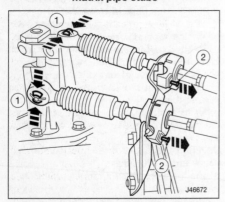

4.16 Release the quick-release fittings and disconnect the heater hoses at the heater matrix pipe stubs

4.18 Press the locking tabs (1) together to release the inner cable end fittings, then pull out the locking pins (2) and withdraw the outer cable end fittings from the transmission abutment bracket

photographs will prove invaluable when the engine/transmission is refitted.

Always be extremely careful when removing and refitting the engine/transmission. Serious injury can result from careless actions. Plan ahead and take your time, and a job of this nature, although major, can be accomplished successfully.

On all models, the engine/transmission is removed as an assembly from the front of the vehicle, after removal of the radiator grille opening panel. The engine is then separated from the transmission after removal.

4 Engine/transmission (front wheel drive models) – removal, separation and refitting

Note: *Read through the entire Section, as well as reading the advice in Section 3, before beginning this procedure. The engine and transmission are removed as a unit, from the front of the vehicle, then separated after removal.*

Removal

1 Move the driver's seat fully forward, open the battery box cover and disconnect the battery negative terminal (refer to *Disconnecting the battery* in the Reference Chapter).
2 Firmly apply the handbrake, then jack up the front of the vehicle and support it securely on axle stands (see *Jacking and vehicle support*).
3 Drain the cooling system as described in Chapter 1.

4 Remove the radiator grille opening panel as described in Chapter 11.
5 Refer to Chapter 4A and remove the intake air resonator and air ducts.
6 Remove the engine upper cover (where fitted).
7 Remove the auxiliary drivebelt as described in Chapter 1.
8 On vehicles fitted with air conditioning, unplug the compressor electrical connector, and unbolt the compressor from the engine. Secure it as far as possible (without disconnecting the system's hoses) clear of the engine/transmission.

⚠️ **Warning: Do not disconnect the refrigerant hoses.**

9 Disconnect the vacuum hoses from the solenoid valves on the right-hand side of the engine compartment.

> **HAYNES HINT** *Whenever any wiring is disconnected, mark or label it, to ensure correct reconnection. Vacuum hoses and pipes should also be similarly marked. Masking tape and/ or a touch-up paint applicator work well for marking items. Take photos, or sketch the locations of components and brackets.*

10 Remove the radiator cooling fan shroud as described in Chapter 3. On vehicles fitted with air conditioning, slide the condenser sideways out of the mounting brackets and position it to one side.

⚠️ **Warning: Do not disconnect the refrigerant hoses.**

11 Release the retaining clips and disconnect the coolant hoses from the coolant pump and thermostat housing.
12 Release the retaining clips and disconnect the radiator top hose, the coolant expansion tank hose and the radiator bottom hose.
13 Undo the retaining bolt and disconnect the engine wiring harness connector located at the left-hand side of the engine compartment **(see illustrations)**.
14 Using a small screwdriver, release the protective cover on the positive (+) cable terminal box . Undo the retaining nut and disconnect the starter motor positive cable from the terminal stud **(see illustrations)**.
15 Disconnect the fuel supply and return lines at the fuel filter quick-release connections. Plug or cap all open fittings.
16 Release the quick-release fittings and disconnect the heater hoses at the heater matrix pipe stubs **(see illustration)**.
17 Disconnect the vacuum hoses at the connection above the heater matrix pipe stubs.
18 Press the locking tabs together and slide the gearchange inner cable end fittings off the transmission selector levers **(see illustration)**.

Pull out the locking pins and withdraw the outer cable end fittings from the transmission abutment bracket.

19 Undo the two nuts and two bolts and remove the heater pipe retaining bracket from the transmission casing.

20 Using a small screwdriver, prise out the retaining clip and disconnect the clutch hydraulic pipe from the transmission (use a suitable clamp on the hydraulic flexible hose to prevent leakage) **(see illustrations)**. Cover both the union and the pipe ends to minimise fluid loss and prevent the entry of dirt into the hydraulic system. **Note:** *Whilst the hydraulic hose/pipe is disconnected, DO NOT depress the clutch pedal.*

21 Position a suitable container beneath the power steering pump, then slacken the clip and disconnect the return hose from the bottom of the pump. Allow the fluid to drain into the container.

22 Hold the power steering pump high pressure pipe adaptor on the pump with a suitable spanner, then unscrew the high pressure pipe union from the adaptor. Discard the pipe union seal as a new seal must be used for refitting. Cover both the adaptor and the pipe end to prevent the entry of dirt into the system.

23 Disconnect the wiring connector at the reversing light switch on top of the transmission.

24 Remove the catalytic converter as described in Chapter 4B.

25 Remove the intercooler as described in Chapter 4A.

26 Remove the radiator as described in Chapter 3.

27 Remove the driveshafts as described in Chapter 8.

28 Remove the engine/transmission rear mounting as described in Chapter 2A.

29 Position an engine dolly (a low, wheeled platform capable of taking the weight of the engine/transmission) under the engine transmission/assembly. Lower the vehicle until the sump is resting on the dolly, then use suitable wooden blocks to securely support the engine/transmission assembly on the dolly.

30 Remove the engine/transmission left-hand and right-hand mountings as described in Chapter 2A.

31 Make a final check to ensure that nothing else remains connected to the engine/transmission. Ensure that the engine/transmission is securely supported on the dolly, then wheel the dolly out through the front of the vehicle. Enlist the help of an assistant during this procedure, as it may be necessary to tilt the assembly slightly to clear the underbody. Great care must be taken to ensure that no components are trapped or damaged during the removal procedure.

Separation

32 With the engine/transmission assembly removed, support the assembly on suitable

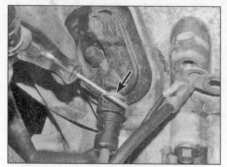

4.20a Prise out the retaining clip . . .

blocks of wood, on a work bench (or failing that, on a clean area of the workshop floor).

33 Ensure that engine and transmission are adequately supported, then slacken and remove the remaining bolts securing the transmission housing to the engine. Note the correct fitted positions of each bolt (and relevant brackets) as they are removed, to use as a reference on refitting.

34 Carefully withdraw the transmission from the engine, ensuring that the weight of the transmission is not allowed to hang on the input shaft while it is engaged with the clutch friction disc (see Chapter 7A).

35 While the engine/transmission is removed, check the mountings and renew them if they are worn or damaged. Similarly, check the condition of all coolant and vacuum hoses and pipes (see Chapter 1). Components that are normally hidden can now be checked properly, and should be renewed if there is any doubt at all about their condition. Also take the opportunity to overhaul the clutch components (see Chapter 6). It is regarded by many as good working practice to renew the clutch assembly as a matter of course, whenever major engine overhaul work is carried out. Check also the condition of all components (such as the transmission oil seals) disturbed on removal, and renew any that are damaged or worn.

Refitting

36 Refitting is the reverse of the removal procedure, noting the following points.

a) *Tighten all nuts/bolts to the torque settings given in the Specifications Sections of Chapter 2A, and in the other applicable Chapters of this manual.*

b) *In addition to the points noted in paragraph 35 above, always renew any circlips and self-locking nuts disturbed on removal.*

c) *Where wiring was secured by cable ties which had to be cut on removal, ensure that it is secured with new ties on refitting.*

d) *With all overhaul operations completed, refit the transmission to the engine as described in Chapter 7A.*

e) *Manoeuvre the engine/transmission unit into the engine compartment, then raise or lower the vehicle as necessary, and refit the engine mountings as described in Chapter 2A.*

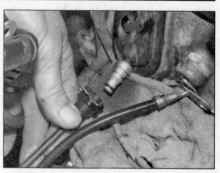

4.20b . . . and disconnect the clutch hydraulic pipe

f) *Refit (and where applicable adjust) all engine related components and systems with reference to the Chapters concerned.*

g) *Add coolant, engine oil, and brake and transmission fluids as needed (see 'Weekly checks' and Chapter 1).*

h) *When installation is complete, prime and bleed the fuel system and power steering system as described in Chapters 4A and 10.*

i) *Run the engine, and check for proper operation and the absence of leaks. Shut off the engine and recheck the fluid levels.*

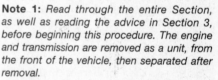

5 Engine/transmission (rear wheel drive models) – removal, separation and refitting

Note 1: *Read through the entire Section, as well as reading the advice in Section 3, before beginning this procedure. The engine and transmission are removed as a unit, from the front of the vehicle, then separated after removal.*

Note 2: *Ford special tool 204-606 (subframe spacers) will be required for this procedure.*

Removal

1 Move the driver's seat fully forward, open the battery box cover and disconnect the battery negative terminal (refer to *Disconnecting the battery* in the Reference Chapter).

2 Firmly apply the handbrake, then jack up the front of the vehicle and support it securely on axle stands (see *Jacking and vehicle support*).

3 Drain the cooling system as described in Chapter 1.

4 Remove the auxiliary drivebelt as described in Chapter 1.

5 Release the retaining clips and disconnect the air duct at the air cleaner and turbocharger.

6 Remove the radiator grille opening panel as described in Chapter 11.

7 Remove the catalytic converter as described in Chapter 4B.

8 Remove the windscreen cowl panel as described in Chapter 11.

9 Release the retaining clips and disconnect the coolant hoses from the coolant pump and thermostat housing.

10 Disconnect the vacuum hoses and wiring

5.15 Radiator mounting bracket-to-underbody retaining bolts (arrowed) – right-hand side shown

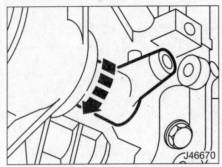

5.17 Rotate the clutch slave cylinder anticlockwise, then remove it from the transmission housing – vehicles with 5-speed transmissions

5.18 Prise out the retaining clip and disconnect the clutch hydraulic hose from the transmission union – vehicles with 6-speed transmissions

connectors from the solenoid valves on the right-hand side of the engine compartment.

 Whenever any wiring is disconnected, mark or label it to ensure correct reconnection. Vacuum hoses and pipes should be similarly marked. Masking tape and/or a touch-up paint applicator work well for marking items. Take photos or sketch the locations of components and brackets.

11 Release the retaining clips and disconnect the coolant expansion tank hose and the radiator bottom hose.
12 Release the retaining clip and disconnect the intercooler outlet duct from the EGR valve. Disconnect the wiring connector from the temperature and manifold absolute pressure sensor located at the other end of the intercooler outlet duct. Release the retaining clip and disconnect the intercooler outlet duct from the intercooler. Remove the duct.
13 Release the retaining clips and disconnect the intercooler intake duct from the turbocharger and intercooler. Remove the duct.
14 Remove the radiator cooling fan shroud as described in Chapter 3. On vehicles fitted with air conditioning, slide the condenser sideways out of the mounting brackets and position it to one side.

⚠ *Warning: Do not disconnect the refrigerant hoses.*

15 Undo the two bolts each side securing the radiator mounting bracket to the underbody **(see illustration)**. Remove the mounting bracket complete with radiator and intercooler from the vehicle.
16 On vehicles fitted with air conditioning, unplug the compressor electrical connector, and unbolt the compressor from the engine. Secure it as far as possible (without disconnecting the system's hoses) clear of the engine/transmission.

⚠ *Warning: Do not disconnect the refrigerant hoses.*

17 On vehicles with a 5-speed transmission, rotate the clutch slave cylinder anticlockwise to release it, then remove the cylinder from the left-hand side of the transmission **(see illustration)**.
18 On vehicles with a 6-speed transmission, using a small screwdriver, prise out the retaining clip and disconnect the clutch hydraulic hose from the transmission union (use a suitable clamp on the flexible hose to prevent leakage) **(see illustration)**. Cover both the union and the hose ends to minimise fluid loss and prevent the entry of dirt into the hydraulic system. **Note:** *Whilst the hydraulic hose is disconnected DO NOT depress the clutch pedal.*
19 Disconnect the wiring connectors from the vehicle speed sensor and reversing light switch on the side of the transmission.
20 On vehicles with a tachograph, disconnect the tachograph wiring connector.

21 Slacken the two bolts securing the propeller shaft front centre bearing to the underbody **(see illustration)**. Do not remove the bolts completely at this stage.
22 If the propeller shaft incorporates a universal joint at its forward end, mark the relative positions of the propeller shaft universal joint flange and transmission output shaft flange. Undo the four bolts securing the universal joint flange to the output shaft flange, then remove the two previously slackened centre bearing retaining bolts. Separate the flanges and position the propeller shaft to one side. Note that new flange retaining bolts and new centre bearing retaining bolts will be required for refitting.
23 If the propeller shaft incorporates a flexible rubber coupling at its forward end, mark the relative positions of the rubber coupling and transmission output shaft flange. Undo the three bolts securing the rubber coupling to the output shaft flange, then remove the two previously slackened centre bearing retaining bolts. Detach the rubber coupling from the output shaft flange and position the propeller shaft to one side. Note that new rubber coupling retaining bolts and new centre bearing retaining bolts will be required for refitting.
24 Turn the steering wheel to set the roadwheels in the straight-ahead position, then remove the ignition key to lock the column.
25 Undo the nut and remove the lower pinch bolt securing the steering column intermediate shaft flexible coupling to the steering gear pinion shaft **(see illustration)**. Note that a new pinch bolt and nut will be required for refitting. Where fitted, extract the circlip from the base of the flexible coupling. Slide the flexible coupling up and off the steering gear pinion shaft.
26 Undo the retaining clamp bolt and release the power steering fluid pipes from the front subframe.
27 Undo the two bolts securing the transmission mounting (or mounting support bracket) to the front subframe **(see illustration)**.
28 Position a trolley jack beneath the centre of the front subframe and just take the weight of the subframe.
29 Undo the bolt and nut each side securing

5.21 Propeller shaft centre bearing and retaining bolts

5.25 Steering column intermediate shaft flexible coupling pinch bolt (arrowed)

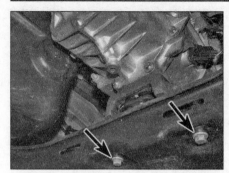

5.27 Undo the two bolts (arrowed) securing the transmission mounting (or mounting support bracket) to the front subframe

5.29a Front subframe right-hand side retaining bolt (arrowed) . . .

5.29b . . . and retaining nut (arrowed)

the front subframe to the underbody **(see illustrations)**. Lower the jack and front subframe approximately 100 mm. Insert the spacers (Ford special tool 204-606) between the subframe and the underbody at the mounting bolt locations. Fit the subframe mounting nuts and the long bolts included in the special tool kit and tighten the nuts and bolts securely to retain the subframe.

30 On vehicles with a 6-speed transmission, reach up over the top of the transmission and undo the four bolts securing the gearchange lever bracket to the transmission. Manipulate the bracket sideways, then twist it through 90° and slide it out down the right-hand side of the transmission **(see illustrations)**.

31 Undo the four bolts securing the power steering pump to the mounting bracket on the engine. Move the pump to one side and suitably secure it with cable ties.

32 Undo the retaining bolt and disconnect the engine wiring harness connector located at the left-hand side of the engine compartment **(see illustrations 4.13a and 4.13b)**.

33 Using a small screwdriver, release the protective cover on the positive (+) cable terminal box . Undo the retaining nut and disconnect the starter motor positive cable from the terminal stud **(see illustrations 4.14a and 4.14b)**.

34 Disconnect the fuel supply and return lines at the fuel filter quick-release connections. Plug or cap all open fittings.

35 Release the quick-release fittings and disconnect the heater hoses at the heater matrix pipe stubs **(see illustration 4.16)**.

36 Disconnect the vacuum hoses at the connection above the heater matrix pipe stubs.

37 Undo the retaining bolt and disconnect the earth cable from the chassis side member **(see illustration)**.

38 Carefully prise out the vacuum hose end fitting from the grommet on the vacuum servo unit **(see illustration)**.

39 The engine/transmission assembly is removed complete with the engine cross-member, and a suitable method for removal must now be established. One method is to use an engine dolly (a low, wheeled platform capable of taking the weight of the engine/transmission) placed under the

5.30a Undo the four bolts securing the gearchange lever bracket to the transmission . . .

5.30b . . . then manipulate the bracket sideways and slide it out down the right-hand side of the transmission – vehicles with 6-speed transmissions

engine crossmember. With a trolley jack positioned on each side of the crossmember, the crossmember is then unbolted from the vehicle and the assembly is lowered onto the dolly. A trolley jack is then positioned under the transmission and the whole assembly is wheeled out from the front of the vehicle. An alternative method is to use three trolley jacks, one under each side of the engine crossmember and one under the transmission. With the help of an assistant, the crossmember is then unbolted and lowered on the jacks and the whole assembly is wheeled out from the front of the vehicle. This was the method used in the Haynes workshop during the preparation of this manual, but it must be stressed that this is slightly precarious method and it is all

too easy for the crossmember to slip off the jacks if great care is not taken. The method chosen is therefore very much dependant on the equipment available and the workplace.

40 Once a removal method has been established, suitably support the engine crossmember and the transmission, then proceed as follows.

Caution: Ensure that the engine/transmission is securely supported by whatever method has been chosen. Keep well clear of the assembly once the engine crossmember is released and have at least one assistant available to help with the removal operation. Do not take any risks.

41 On vehicles with a 6-speed transmission, undo the bolt securing the transmission

5.37 Undo the retaining bolt (arrowed) and disconnect the earth cable from the chassis side member

5.38 Carefully prise out the vacuum hose end fitting (arrowed) from the grommet on the vacuum servo unit

5.41a Undo the bolt securing the transmission mounting to the transmission casing . . .

5.41b . . . and remove the mounting from under the vehicle – vehicles with 6-speed transmissions

5.42 Working under the wheel arch, undo the two side bolts securing the engine crossmember to the underbody

mounting to the transmission casing and remove the mounting from under the vehicle **(see illustrations)**.

42 Working under one front wheel arch, undo the two side bolts securing the crossmember to the underbody **(see illustration)**. Repeat this procedure on the other side.

43 Undo the two bolts each side and remove the crossmember side brace plates (where fitted) **(see illustration)**.

44 Undo the two lower bolts each side securing the crossmember to the underbody **(see illustration)**. Lower the engine and crossmember.

45 Make a final check to ensure that nothing else remains connected to the engine/transmission. Ensure that the engine/transmission is securely supported, then wheel the assembly out through the front of the vehicle. Great care must be taken to ensure that no components are trapped or damaged during the removal procedure and that the engine/transmission remains securely supported and stable.

46 Once the engine/transmission assembly has been removed, connect a suitable hoist to the engine lifting bracket and lift the unit slightly. Undo the nut (or bolts) securing both engine mountings to the brackets on the engine, and remove the engine crossmember.

Separation

47 Support the engine/transmission assembly on suitable blocks of wood, on a work bench (or failing that, on a clean area of the workshop floor).

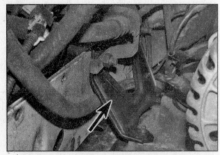

5.43 Undo the two bolts each side and remove the crossmember side brace plates (arrowed)

48 Ensure that engine and transmission are adequately supported, then slacken and remove the remaining bolts securing the transmission housing to the engine. Note the correct fitted positions of each bolt (and relevant brackets) as they are removed, to use as a reference on refitting.

49 Carefully withdraw the transmission from the engine, ensuring that the weight of the transmission is not allowed to hang on the input shaft while it is engaged with the clutch friction disc (see Chapter 7B).

50 While the engine/transmission is removed, check the mountings and renew them if they are worn or damaged. Similarly, check the condition of all coolant and vacuum hoses and pipes (see Chapter 1). Components that are normally hidden can now be checked properly, and should be renewed if there is any doubt at all about their condition. Also take the opportunity to overhaul the clutch components (see Chapter 6). It is regarded by many as good working practice to renew the clutch assembly as a matter of course, whenever major engine overhaul work is carried out. Check also the condition of all components (such as the transmission oil seals) disturbed on removal, and renew any that are damaged or worn.

Refitting

51 Refitting is the reverse of the removal procedure, noting the following points.
a) On vehicles with a 6-speed transmission, before refitting the engine/transmission assembly ensure that the transmission is in 3rd-gear.

5.44 Undo the two lower bolts each side (arrowed) securing the engine crossmember to the underbody

b) Tighten all nuts/bolts to the torque settings given in the Specifications Sections of Chapter 2B, and in the other applicable Chapters of this manual.
c) In addition to the points noted in paragraph 50 above, always renew any circlips and self-locking nuts disturbed on removal.
d) Where wiring was secured by cable ties which had to be cut on removal, ensure that it is secured with new ties on refitting.
e) With all overhaul operations completed refit the transmission to the engine as described in Chapter 7B.
f) On vehicles with a 6-speed transmission, refit and adjust the gearchange lever bracket as described in Chapter 7B, Section 7.
g) Refit (and where applicable adjust) all engine related components and systems with reference to the Chapters concerned.
h) Add coolant, engine oil and transmission fluids as needed (see 'Weekly checks', Chapter 1 and Chapter 7B).
i) When installation is complete, prime and bleed the fuel system as described in Chapter 4A.
j) Run the engine, and check for proper operation and the absence of leaks. Shut off the engine and recheck the fluid levels.

6 Engine overhaul – dismantling sequence

1 It is much easier to dismantle and work on the engine if it is mounted on a portable engine stand. These stands can often be hired from a tool hire shop. Before the engine is mounted on a stand, the flywheel should be removed so that the stand bolts can be tightened into the end of the cylinder block/crankcase.

2 If a stand is not available it is possible to dismantle the engine with it mounted on blocks, on a sturdy workbench or on the floor. Be extra careful not to tip or drop the engine when working without a stand.

3 If you are going to obtain a reconditioned engine, all external components must be removed first to be transferred to the new engine (just as they will if you are doing a complete engine overhaul yourself). **Note:** *When removing the external components from the engine, pay close attention to details that may be helpful or important during refitting. Note the fitted position of gaskets, seals, spacers, pins, washers, bolts and other small items. These external components include the following:*

a) *Alternator, starter and mounting brackets (Chapter 5).*

b) *Glow plug/preheating system components (Chapter 5).*

c) *Cooling system/thermostat housings (Chapter 3).*

d) *Oil level dipstick and dipstick tube.*

e) *All fuel injection system components (Chapter 4A).*

f) *Brake vacuum pump (Chapter 9).*

g) *All electrical switches and sensors and engine wiring harness (Chapters 4A, 4B and 5).*

h) *Inlet and exhaust manifolds (Part A or B of this Chapter).*

i) *Engine/transmission mounting brackets (Part A or B of this Chapter).*

j) *Flywheel (Part A or B of this Chapter).*

4 If you are obtaining a 'short' engine (which consists of the engine cylinder block/crankcase, crankshaft, pistons and connecting rods all assembled), then the cylinder head, sump, oil pump, oil filter cooler/housing and timing chains will have to be removed also.

5 If you are planning a complete overhaul, the engine can be dismantled and the internal components removed in the following order.

a) *Inlet and exhaust manifolds (Part A or B of this Chapter).*

b) *Timing chains tensioners and sprockets (Part A or B of this Chapter).*

c) *Cylinder head (Part A or B of this Chapter).*

d) *Flywheel (Part A or B of this Chapter).*

e) *Sump (Part A or B of this Chapter).*

f) *Oil pump (Part A or B of this Chapter).*

g) *Piston/connecting rod assemblies (Section 10).*

h) *Crankshaft (Section 11).*

6 Before beginning the dismantling and overhaul procedures, make sure that you have all of the correct tools necessary. Refer to *Tools and working facilities* for further information.

7 Cylinder head – dismantling

Note: *New and reconditioned cylinder heads are available from the manufacturers and from engine overhaul specialists. Due to the fact that some specialist tools are required for the dismantling and inspection procedures and new components may not be readily available, it may be more practical and economical for the home mechanic to purchase a reconditioned head, rather than to dismantle, inspect and recondition the original head.*

1 With the cylinder head removed as described in the relevant Part of this Chapter, clean away all external dirt, and remove the following components as applicable, if not already done:

a) *Manifolds (see Chapter 2A or 2B).*

b) *Cooling system components (see Chapter 3).*

c) *Glow plugs (see Chapter 5).*

d) *Fuel injectors (see Chapter 4A).*

e) *Engine lifting brackets.*

2 With the cylinder head resting on one side, using a valve spring compressor compress each valve spring in turn until the split collets can be removed. A special valve spring compressor will be required to reach into the deep wells in the cylinder head without risk of damaging the tappet bores. Such compressors are widely available from most good motor accessory shops. Release the compressor and lift off the spring upper seat and spring **(see illustrations)**.

3 If, when the valve spring compressor is screwed down, the spring upper seat refuses to free and expose the split collets, gently tap the top of the tool, directly over the upper seat, with a light hammer. This will free the seat to remove the collets.

4 Withdraw the valve through the combustion chamber. If it binds in the guide (will not pull through), push it back in and deburr the area around the collet groove with a fine file or whetstone.

5 Use a pair of pliers or a special tool to extract the valve spring lower seat/stem oil seal from the valve guides **(see illustration)**.

6 It is essential that the valves are kept together with their collets, spring seats and springs, and in their correct sequence (unless they are so badly worn that they are to be renewed). If they are going to be kept and used again, place them in a labelled polythene bag or similar small container **(see illustration)**.

7.2a Compress the valve springs using a spring compressor tool . . .

7.2b . . . and remove the split collets

7.2c Release the tool and remove the upper spring seat . . .

7.2d . . . and the valve spring

7.5 Use a removal tool to extract the valve stem oil seal

7.6 Use clearly marked containers to identify components and to keep matched assemblies together

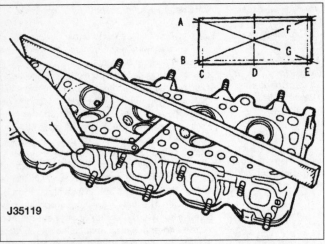

8.7 Check the cylinder head surface for warping in the planes indicated. Using feeler blades under the straight-edge

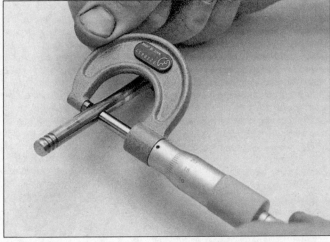

8.13 Measure the diameter of the valve stems with a micrometer

8 Cylinder head and valve components – cleaning and inspection

1 Thorough cleaning of the cylinder head and valve components followed by a detailed inspection, will enable you to decide how much valve service work must be carried out during the engine overhaul. **Note:** *If the engine has been severely overheated, it is best to assume that the cylinder head is warped, and to check carefully for signs of this.*

Cleaning

2 Using a suitable degreasing agent, remove all traces of oil deposits from the cylinder head, paying particular attention to the journal bearings, camshaft bores, valve guides and oilways.
3 Scrape away all traces of old gasket material and sealing compound from the cylinder head, taking great care not to score or gouge the surfaces.
4 Scrape away the carbon from the combustion chambers and ports, then wash the cylinder head thoroughly with paraffin or a suitable solvent to remove the remaining debris.
5 Scrape off any heavy carbon deposits that may have formed on the valves, then

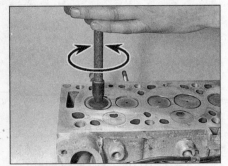

8.16 Grind-in the valves with a reciprocating rotary motion

use a power-operated wire brush to remove deposits from the valve heads and stems.

Inspection

Note: *Be sure to perform all the following inspection procedures before concluding that the services of a machine shop or engine overhaul specialist are required. Make a list of all items that require attention.*

Cylinder head

6 Inspect the head very carefully for cracks, evidence of coolant leakage, and other damage. If cracks are found, a new cylinder head should be obtained.
7 Use a straight-edge and feeler blade to check that the cylinder head gasket surface is not distorted, check the head across a number of different ways to find any distortion **(see illustration)**. If it is, it may be possible to resurface it.
8 Examine the valve seats in each of the combustion chambers. If they are severely pitted, cracked or burned, then they will need to be renewed or recut by an engine overhaul specialist. If they are only slightly pitted, this can be removed by grinding-in the valve heads and seats with fine valve-grinding compound as described below.
9 If the valve guides are worn, indicated by a side-to-side motion of the valve, new guides must be fitted. Measure the diameter of the existing valve stems (see below) and the bore of the guides, then calculate the clearance, and compare the result with the specified value. If the clearance is excessive, renew the valves or guides as necessary.
10 The renewal of valve guides is best carried out by an engine overhaul specialist.
11 If the valve seats are to be recut, this must be done only after the guides have been renewed.

Valves

12 Examine the head of each valve for pitting, burning, cracks and general wear, and check the valve stem for scoring and wear ridges.

Rotate the valve, and check for any obvious indication that it is bent. Look for pits and excessive wear on the tip of each valve stem. Renew any valve that shows any such signs of wear or damage.
13 If the valve appears satisfactory at this stage, measure the valve stem diameter at several points using a micrometer **(see illustration)**. Any significant difference in the readings obtained indicates wear of the valve stem. Should any of these conditions be apparent, the valve(s) must be renewed.
14 If the valves are in satisfactory condition, they should be ground (lapped) into their respective seats to ensure a smooth gas-tight seal. If the seat is only lightly pitted, or if it has been recut, fine grinding compound only should be used to produce the required finish. Coarse valve-grinding compound should not be used unless a seat is badly burned or deeply pitted. If this is the case, the cylinder head and valves should be inspected by an expert to decide whether seat recutting, or even the renewal of the valve or seat insert, is required.
15 Valve grinding is carried out as follows. Place the cylinder head upside-down on a bench, with a block of wood at each end to give clearance for the valve stems.
16 Smear a trace of the appropriate grade of valve-grinding compound on the seat face, and press a suction grinding tool onto the valve head. With a semi-rotary action, grind the valve head to its seat, lifting the valve occasionally to redistribute the grinding compound **(see illustration)**. A light spring placed under the valve head will greatly ease this operation.
17 If coarse grinding compound is being used, work only until a dull, matt even surface is produced on both the valve seat and the valve, then wipe off the used compound and repeat the process with fine compound. When a smooth unbroken ring of light grey matt finish is produced on both the valve and seat, the grinding operation is complete. Do not

9.2a Fit the new valve spring lower seat/ stem oil seal . . .

9.2b . . . then use a suitable socket or metal tube to press the seal firmly onto the guide

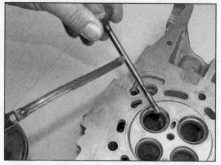

9.3 Apply clean engine oil to the valve stem, and refit the valve

9.4a Refit the valve spring . . .

9.4b . . . and the upper spring seat

9.5 Compress the spring and install the collets. Use grease to hold the two halves of the split collet in the groove

grind in the valves any further than absolutely necessary, or the seat will be prematurely sunk into the cylinder head.
18 When all the valves have been ground-in, carefully wash off all traces of grinding compound, using paraffin or a suitable solvent, before reassembly of the cylinder head.

Valve components

19 Examine the valve springs for signs of damage and discolouration, and also measure their free length by comparing each of the existing springs with a new component.
20 Stand each spring on a flat surface and check it for squareness. If any of the springs are damaged, distorted, or have lost their tension, obtain a complete set of new springs.
21 Check the spring upper seats and collets for obvious wear and cracks. Any questionable parts should be renewed, as extensive damage will occur if they fail during engine operation. Any damaged or excessively-worn parts must be renewed. The valve spring lower seat/ stem oil seals must be renewed as a matter of course whenever they are disturbed.

9 Cylinder head – reassembly

1 Regardless of whether or not the head was sent away for repair work of any sort, make sure that it is clean before beginning reassembly. Be sure to remove any metal particles and abrasive grit that may still be present from operations such as valve

grinding or head resurfacing. Use compressed air, if available, to blow out all the oil holes and passages.

⚠️ *Warning: Wear eye protection when using compressed air.*

2 Beginning at one end of the head, fit the new valve spring lower seat/stem oil seal. Use a suitable socket or metal tube to press the seal firmly onto the guide **(see illustrations)**.
3 Apply clean engine oil to the valve stem, and refit the valve **(see illustration)**. Where the original valves are being re-used, ensure that each is refitted in its original guide. If new valves are being fitted, insert them into the locations to which they have been ground.
4 Refit the valve spring and upper seat **(see illustrations)**.
5 Compress the spring with the valve spring compressor, and carefully install the collets in the stem groove. Apply a small dab of

10.2 Undo the retaining bolts and remove the pick-up pipe from the oil pump

grease to each collet to hold it in place if necessary **(see illustration)**. Slowly release the compressor and make sure the collets seat properly.
6 When the valves are installed, use a hammer and interposed block of wood (to prevent the end of the valve stem being damaged), to tap the end of the valve stem gently in order to settle the components.
7 Repeat the procedure for the remaining valves. Be sure to return the valve assembly components to their original locations – don't mix them up!
8 Refit the components removed in Section 7, paragraph 1.

10 Piston/connecting rod assemblies – removal and inspection

Note: *While this task is theoretically possible when the engine is in place in the vehicle, in practice it requires so much preliminary dismantling and is so difficult to carry out due to the restricted access, that owners are advised to remove the engine from the vehicle first. The following paragraphs assume that the engine has been removed.*

Removal

1 Remove the cylinder head and sump with reference to Part A or B of this Chapter.
2 Undo the retaining bolts and remove the pick-up pipe from the oil pump **(see illustration)**. Remove and discard the O-ring seal and obtain a new O-ring for refitting.

10.3 Disengage the oil pump sprocket from the chain and remove the oil pump

10.5 If necessary, make your own marks (arrowed) to correspond with the connecting rod location

10.6 A ridge reamer may be required, to remove the ridge from the top of each cylinder

3 Undo the retaining bolts and release the oil pump from the lower crankcase. Push or pull on the oil pump drive chain to compress the tensioner, then disengage the oil pump sprocket from the chain and remove the oil pump **(see illustration)**.

4 Unscrew the bolts securing the lower crankcase to the cylinder block. Loosen the bolts gradually and evenly, then separate the lower crankcase from the cylinder block. Remove the gasket.

5 Temporarily refit the crankshaft pulley so that the crankshaft can be rotated. Note that each piston/connecting rod assembly can be identified by its cylinder number (counting from the timing chain end of the engine) etched into the flat-machined surface of both the connecting rod and its cap. Furthermore, each piston has an arrow stamped into its crown, pointing towards the timing chain end of the engine. If no marks can be seen, make your own before disturbing any of the components so that you can be certain of refitting each piston/connecting rod assembly the right way round, and to its correct (original) bore, with the cap also the right way round **(see illustration)**.

6 Use your fingernail to feel if a ridge has formed at the upper limit of ring travel (about 6 mm down from the top of each cylinder). If carbon deposits or cylinder wear have produced ridges, they must be completely removed with a special tool called a ridge reamer **(see illustration)**. Follow the manufacturer's instructions provided with the tool.

Caution: Failure to remove the ridges before attempting to remove the piston/connecting rod assemblies may result in piston ring breakage.

7 Slacken each of the big-end bearing cap bolts half a turn at a time, until they can be removed by hand. Remove the No 1 cap and bearing shell. Don't drop the shell out of the cap.

Caution: The connecting rod/bearing cap mating surfaces are not machined flat, since the big-end bearing caps are 'cracked' off from the rod during production and left untouched to ensure the cap and rod mate perfectly. Great care must be taken to ensure the mating surfaces of the cap and rod are not marked or damaged in anyway. Any damage to the mating surfaces will adversely affect the strength of the connecting rod and could lead to premature failure.

8 Remove the upper bearing shell, and push the connecting rod/piston assembly out through the top of the cylinder block. Use a wooden hammer handle to push on the connecting rod's bearing recess. If resistance is felt, double-check that all of the ridge was removed from the cylinder. Repeat the procedure for the remaining cylinders.

9 After removal, reassemble the big-end bearing caps and shells on their respective connecting rods, and refit the bolts finger-tight. Leaving the old shells in place until reassembly will help prevent the bearing recesses from being accidentally nicked or gouged. New shells should be used on reassembly.

10 Remove the retaining screws and withdraw the piston cooling jets from the bottom of the cylinder bores **(see illustrations)**.

Inspection

11 Before the inspection process can be carried out, the piston/connecting rod assemblies must be cleaned and the original piston rings removed from the pistons. The rings should have smooth, polished working surfaces, with no dull or carbon-coated sections and no traces of wear on their top and bottom surfaces. Any discoloured sections will show that the ring is not sealing correctly against the bore wall, so allowing combustion gases to blow by. The end gaps should be clear of carbon but not polished (indicating a too-small end gap), and all the rings (including the elements of the oil control ring) should be free to rotate in their grooves, but without excessive up-and-down movement. If the rings appear to be in good condition, they are probably fit for further use; if so, check the end gaps (in an unworn part of the bore) as described in Section 15. If any of the rings appears to be worn or damaged, or has an end gap significantly different from the specified value, the usual course of action is to renew all of them as a set. **Note:** *While it is usual to renew piston rings when an engine is overhauled, they may be re-used if in acceptable condition. If re-using the rings, make sure that each ring is marked during removal to ensure that it is refitted correctly.*

12 Using a piston ring removal tool, carefully remove the rings from the pistons. Be careful not to nick or gouge the pistons in the process, and mark or label each ring as it is removed, so that its original top surface can be identified on reassembly, and so that it can be returned to its original groove. Take care also with your hands – piston rings are sharp! **(see Tool Tip).**

10.10a Remove the piston cooling jet-retaining screws . . .

10.10b . . . and remove the jets from their mounting holes

> **TOOL TiP** *If a piston ring removal tool is not available, the rings can be removed by hand, expanding them over the top of the pistons. The use of two or three old feeler blades will be helpful in preventing the rings dropping into empty grooves*

13 Scrape all traces of carbon from the top of the piston. A hand-held wire brush or a piece of fine emery cloth can be used once the majority of the deposits have been scraped away. Do not under any circumstances use a wire brush mounted in a drill motor to remove deposits from the pistons as the piston material is soft, and may be eroded away by the wire brush.

14 Use a piston ring groove-cleaning tool to remove carbon deposits from the ring grooves. If a tool isn't available, but replacement rings have been found, a piece broken off the old ring will do the job. Be very careful to remove only the carbon deposits (don't remove any metal) and do not nick or scratch the sides of the ring grooves **(see illustrations)**. Protect your fingers as piston rings are sharp.

15 Once the deposits have been removed, clean the piston/rod assemblies with solvent and dry them with compressed air if available. Make sure the oil return holes in the back sides of the ring grooves and the oil hole in the lower end of each rod are clear.

16 If the pistons and cylinder walls are not damaged or worn excessively and if the cylinder block/crankcase is not rebored, new pistons will not be necessary. Normal piston wear appears as even vertical wear on the piston thrust surfaces, and slight looseness of the top ring in its groove.

17 Carefully inspect each piston for cracks around the skirt, at the pin bosses, and at the ring lands (between the ring grooves).

18 Look for scoring and scuffing on the thrust faces of the piston skirt, holes in the piston crown, and burned areas at the edge of the crown. If the skirt is scored or scuffed, the engine may have been suffering from overheating and/or abnormal combustion which caused excessively high operating temperatures. The cooling and lubrication systems should be checked thoroughly. A hole in the piston crown, or burned areas at the edge of the piston crown indicates that abnormal combustion (knocking or detonation) has been occurring. If any of the above problems exist, the causes must be investigated and corrected or the damage will occur again. The causes may include intake air leaks, incorrect fuel/air mixture, or EGR system malfunctions.

10.14a The piston ring grooves can be cleaned with a special tool as shown here . . .

19 Corrosion of the piston in the form of small pits, indicates that coolant is leaking into the combustion chamber and/or the crankcase. Again, the cause must be corrected or the problem may persist in the rebuilt engine.

20 Check the piston-to-rod clearance by twisting the piston and rod in opposite directions. Any noticeable play indicates excessive wear which must be corrected. The piston/connecting rod assemblies should be taken to a Ford dealer or engine reconditioning specialist to have the pistons, gudgeon pins and rods checked, and new components fitted as required.

21 Check the connecting rods for cracks and other damage. Temporarily remove the big-end bearing caps and the old bearing shells, wipe clean the rod and cap bearing recesses, and inspect them for nicks, gouges and scratches. After checking the rods, refit the old shells, slip the caps into place, and tighten the bolts finger-tight.

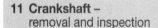

11 Crankshaft – removal and inspection

Removal

Note: *The crankshaft can be removed only after the engine/transmission has been removed from the vehicle. It is assumed that the transmission, flywheel, timing chain, lower crankcase, cylinder head, sump, oil pump, and piston/connecting rod assemblies, have*

10.14b . . . or alternatively a section of a broken piston ring may be used, if available

already been removed. The crankshaft oil seal carrier must be unbolted from the cylinder block/crankcase before proceeding with crankshaft removal.

1 Before the crankshaft is removed, check the endfloat. Mount a DTI (Dial Test Indicator, or dial gauge) with the probe in line with the crankshaft and just touching the crankshaft **(see illustration)**.

2 Push the crankshaft fully away from the gauge, and zero the gauge. Next, lever the crankshaft towards the gauge as far as possible, and check the reading obtained. The distance that the crankshaft moved is its endfloat. If it is greater than specified, check the crankshaft thrust surfaces for wear. If no wear is evident, new thrustwashers (integral with No 3 main bearing upper shell) should correct the end-float.

3 If a dial gauge is not available, feeler gauges can be used. Gently lever or push the crankshaft all the way towards the right-hand end of the engine. Slip feeler gauges between the crankshaft and the right-hand face of No 3 (centre) main bearing to determine the clearance **(see illustration)**.

4 The main bearing caps are numbered consecutively from the timing chain end of the engine. The caps also have an embossed arrow pointing to the timing chain end of the engine **(see illustrations)**. Slacken the cap bolts a quarter-turn at a time each, starting with the end caps and working toward the centre, until they can be removed by hand.

5 Gently tap the caps with a soft-faced hammer, then separate them from the cylinder

11.1 Measure the crankshaft endfloat using a DTI gauge

11.3 If a DTI gauge is not available, measure the endfloat using feeler gauges

11.4a Note the main bearing caps are numbered to indicate their locations . . .

11.4b ... and the caps have an embossed arrow pointing to the timing chain end of the engine

block/crankcase. If necessary, use the bolts as levers to remove the caps. Take care not to drop the bearing shells as the bearing caps are removed.

6 Carefully lift the crankshaft out of the engine **(see illustration)**. It may be a good idea to have an assistant available since the crankshaft is quite heavy. With the bearing shells in place in the cylinder block/crankcase and main bearing caps, return the caps to their respective locations on the block and tighten the bolts finger-tight. Leaving the old shells in place until reassembly will help prevent the bearing recesses from being accidentally nicked or gouged. New shells should be used on reassembly.

Inspection

7 Clean the crankshaft, and dry it with compressed air if available. Be sure to clean the oil holes with a pipe cleaner or similar probe.

 Warning: Wear eye protection when using compressed air.

8 Check the main and crankpin (big-end) bearing journals carefully. If uneven wear, scoring, pitting and cracking are evident then the crankshaft should be reground (where possible) by an engineering workshop, and refitted to the engine with new undersize bearings.

9 Rather than attempt to determine the crankshaft journal sizes and the bearing clearances, take the crankshaft to an

12.2 Felt marker pens can be used as shown to identify bearing shells without damaging them

automotive engineering workshop. Have them perform the necessary measurements, grind the journals if necessary, and supply the appropriate new shell bearings.

10 Check the oil seal journals at each end of the crankshaft for wear and damage. If either seal has worn an excessive groove in its journal, it may cause the new seals to leak when the engine is reassembled. Consult an engine overhaul specialist, who will be able to advise whether a repair is possible or whether a new crankshaft is necessary.

12 Cylinder block/crankcase – cleaning and inspection

Cleaning

1 For complete cleaning, make sure that all the external components have been removed, including mounting brackets, oil cooler and filter housing, piston cooling jets, fuel injection pump mounting bracket (where applicable) and all electrical switches/sensors. **Note:** *If the crankshaft position sensor mounting bracket is removed, its new fitted position will have to be established on reassembly (see Section 17).*

2 Remove the main bearing caps, and separate the bearing shells from the caps and the cylinder block. Mark or label the shells, indicating which bearing they were removed from, and whether they were in the cap or the block, then set them aside **(see illustration)**. Wipe clean the block and cap bearing

12.8 All bolt holes in the block, particularly the main bearing cap and head bolt holes, should be cleaned and restored with a tap

11.6 Carefully remove the crankshaft from the cylinder block

recesses and inspect them for nicks, gouges and scratches.

3 Scrape all traces of gasket from the cylinder block, taking care not to damage the sealing surfaces.

4 Remove all oil gallery plugs (where fitted). The plugs are usually very tight and they may have to be drilled out and the holes retapped. Use new plugs when the engine is reassembled.

5 If any of the castings are extremely dirty, they should be steam-cleaned.

6 After the castings are returned from steam-cleaning, clean all oil holes and oil galleries one more time. Flush all internal passages with warm water until the water runs clear, then dry thoroughly and apply a light film of oil to all machined surfaces, to prevent rusting. If you have access to compressed air, use it to speed the drying process, and to blow out all the oil holes and galleries.

 Warning: Wear eye protection when using compressed air.

7 If the castings are not very dirty, you can do an adequate cleaning job with hot soapy water and a stiff brush. Take plenty of time, and do a thorough job. Regardless of the cleaning method used, be sure to clean all oil holes and galleries very thoroughly, and to dry all components completely. Protect the machined surfaces as described above to prevent rusting.

8 The threaded holes in the cylinder block must be clean to ensure accurate torque readings when tightening nuts/bolts during reassembly. Run the correct-size tap (which can be determined from the size of the relevant bolt) into each of the holes to remove rust, corrosion, thread sealant or other contamination, and to restore damaged threads **(see illustration)**. If possible, use compressed air to clear the holes of debris produced by this operation. Do not forget to clean the threads of all bolts and nuts which are to be re-used, as well.

9 Where applicable, apply suitable sealant to the new oil gallery plugs, and insert them into the relevant holes in the cylinder block. Tighten the plugs securely. Refit the piston cooling jets into the block and secure with the retaining bolts tightened securely.

10 Refit the main bearing caps and tighten the bolts finger-tight. If the engine is not going to be reassembled right away, cover it with a large plastic bag to keep it clean. Apply a thin coat of engine oil to all machined surfaces to prevent rusting.

Inspection

11 Visually check the castings for cracks and corrosion. Look for stripped threads in the threaded holes. If there has been any history of internal coolant leakage, it may be worthwhile having an engine overhaul specialist check the cylinder block/crankcase for cracks with special equipment. If defects are found, have them repaired, if possible, or renew the assembly.

12 Check each cylinder bore for scuffing and scoring. Any evidence of this kind of damage should be double-checked with an inspection of the pistons (see Section 10). If the damage is in its early stages, it may be possible to repair the block by reboring it. Seek the advice of an engineering workshop.

13 Place the cylinder block on a level surface, crankcase downwards. Use a straight-edge and set of feeler blades to measure the distortion of the cylinder head mating surface in both planes. A maximum figure is not quoted by the manufacturer, but use the figure 0.05 mm as a rough guide. If the measurement exceeds this figure, repair may be possible by machining (consult an engineering workshop for advice).

14 To allow an accurate assessment of the wear in the cylinder bores to be made, take the cylinder block to an automotive engineering workshop, and have them carry out the measurement procedures. If necessary, they will be able to rebore the cylinders, and supply the appropriate piston kits.

15 Even if the cylinder bores are not excessively worn, the cylinder bores must be honed. This process involves using an abrasive tool to produce a fine, cross-hatch pattern on the inner surface of the bore. This has the effect of seating the piston rings, resulting in a good seal between the piston and cylinder. Again, an engineering workshop will be able to carry out the job for you at a reasonable cost.

16 Refit all the components removed in paragraph 1.

13 Main and big-end bearings – inspection

1 Even though the main and big-end bearing shells should be renewed during the engine overhaul, the old shells should be retained for close examination, as they may reveal valuable information about the condition of the engine **(see illustration)**.

2 Bearing failure occurs because of lack of lubrication, the presence of dirt or other foreign particles, overloading the engine, and corrosion. Regardless of the cause of bearing failure, it must be corrected before the engine is reassembled, to prevent it from happening again.

3 When examining the bearing shells, remove them from the cylinder block/crankcase and main bearing caps, and from the connecting rods and the big-end bearing caps, then lay them out on a clean surface in the same general position as their location in the engine. This will enable you to match any bearing problems with the corresponding crankshaft journal.

4 Dirt or other foreign matter gets into the engine in a variety of ways. It may be left in the engine during assembly, or it may pass through filters or the crankcase ventilation

system. It may get into the oil and from there into the bearings. Metal chips from machining operations and normal engine wear are often present. Abrasives are sometimes left in engine components after reconditioning, especially when parts are not thoroughly cleaned using the proper cleaning methods. Whatever the source, these foreign objects often end up embedded in the soft bearing material and are easily recognized. Large particles will not embed in the material, and will score or gouge the shell and journal. The best prevention for this cause of bearing failure is to clean all parts thoroughly and to keep everything spotlessly clean during engine assembly. Frequent and regular engine oil and filter changes are also recommended.

5 Lack of lubrication (or lubrication breakdown) has a number of inter-related causes. Excessive heat which thins the oil, overloading which squeezes the oil from the bearing face and oil leakage (from excessive bearing clearances, worn oil pump or high engine speeds) all contribute to lubrication breakdown. Blocked oil passages which usually are the result of misaligned oil holes in a bearing shell, will also starve a bearing of oil and destroy it. When lack of lubrication is the cause of bearing failure, the bearing material is wiped or extruded from the steel backing of the shell. Temperatures may increase to the point where the steel backing turns blue from overheating.

6 Driving habits can have a definite effect on bearing life. Full-throttle, low-speed operation (labouring the engine) puts very high loads on bearings, which tends to squeeze out the oil film. These loads cause the shells to flex, which produces fine cracks in the bearing face (fatigue failure). Eventually, the bearing material will loosen in pieces, and tear away from the steel backing.

7 Short-distance driving leads to corrosion of bearings, because insufficient engine heat is produced to drive off condensed water and corrosive gases. These products collect in the engine oil forming acid and sludge. As the oil is carried to the engine bearings, the acid attacks and corrodes the bearing material.

8 Incorrect shell refitting during engine assembly will lead to bearing failure as well. Tight-fitting shells leave insufficient bearing running clearance and will result in oil starvation. Dirt or foreign particles trapped behind a bearing shell result in high spots on the bearing which lead to failure.

9 Do not touch the internal bearing surface of any shell with your fingers during reassembly, as there is a risk of scratching the delicate surface or of depositing particles of dirt on it.

10 As mentioned at the beginning of this Section, the bearing shells should be renewed as a matter of course during an engine overhaul. To do otherwise is false economy.

14 Engine overhaul – reassembly sequence

1 Before reassembly begins, ensure that all new parts have been obtained, and that all necessary tools are available. Read the entire procedure to familiarise yourself with the work involved, and to ensure that all items necessary for reassembly of the engine are at hand. In addition to all normal tools and materials, thread-locking compound will be needed. A suitable tube of sealant will also be required for certain joint faces that are without gaskets. It is recommended that the manufacturers own products are used, as these are specially formulated for the purpose.

2 In order to save time and avoid problems, engine reassembly can be carried out in the following order:
  a) Crankshaft (Section 16).
  b) Piston/connecting rod assemblies (Section 17).
  c) Oil pump (Part A or B of this Chapter).
  d) Sump (Part A or B of this Chapter).
  e) Flywheel (Part A or B of this Chapter).
  f) Cylinder head (Part A or B of this Chapter).
  g) Timing chains, tensioners and sprockets (Part A or B of this Chapter).
  h) Inlet and exhaust manifolds (Part A or B of this Chapter).
  i) Engine external components and ancillaries.

3 At this stage, all engine components should be absolutely clean and dry with all faults repaired. All components should be neatly arranged on a completely clean work surface or in individual containers.

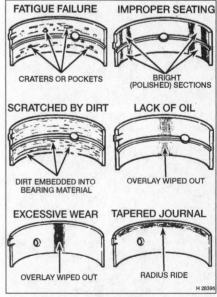

13.1 When inspecting the main and big end bearings, look for any of these problems

15.2 When checking the piston ring end gap, the ring must be square in the cylinder bore. Push the ring down with the top of the piston

15 Piston rings – refitting

1 Before installing new piston rings, check their end gaps. Lay out each piston set with a piston/connecting rod assembly, and keep them together as a matched set from now on.
2 Insert the top compression ring into the first cylinder, and square it up with the cylinder walls by pushing it in with the top of the piston **(see illustration)**. The ring should be near the bottom of the cylinder, at the lower limit of ring travel.
3 To measure the end gap, slip feeler gauges between the ends of the ring until a gauge equal to the gap width is found **(see illustration)**. The feeler gauge should slide between the ring ends with a slight amount of drag. Compare the measurement to the value given in the Specifications. If the gap is larger or smaller than specified, double-check to make sure you have the correct rings before proceeding. If you are assessing the condition of used rings, have the cylinder bores checked and measured by a Ford dealer or similar engine reconditioning specialist, so that you can be sure of exactly which component is worn, and seek advice as to the best course of action to take.
4 If the end gap is still too small, it must be opened up by careful filing of the ring ends using a fine file. If it is too large, this is not as serious, unless the specified limit is exceeded, in which case very careful checking is required of the dimensions of all components, as well as of the new parts.
5 Repeat the procedure for each ring that will be installed in the first cylinder, and for each ring in the remaining cylinders. Remember to keep rings, pistons and cylinders matched up.
6 Refit the piston rings as follows. Where the original rings are being refitted, use the marks or notes made on removal, to ensure that each ring is refitted to its original groove and the same way up. New rings generally have their top surfaces identified by markings, often an indication of size (such as STD or the word TOP). The rings must be fitted with such markings uppermost **(see illustration)**. **Note:** *Always follow the instructions printed on the ring package or box as different manufacturers may require different approaches. Do not mix up the top and second compression rings as they usually have different cross-sections.*
7 The oil control ring (lowest one on the piston) is usually installed first. It is usually composed of three separate elements. Slip the spacer/expander into the groove. Next, install the lower side rail. Do not use a piston ring installation tool on the oil ring side rails, as they may be damaged. Instead, place one end of the side rail into the groove between the spacer/expander and the ring land, hold it firmly in place, then slide a finger around the piston while pushing the rail into the groove. Next, install the upper side rail in the same manner.
8 After all the oil ring components have been installed, check that both the upper and lower side rails can be turned smoothly in the ring groove.
9 The second compression (middle) ring is installed next, followed by the top compression ring. Make sure their marks are uppermost. Do not expand either ring any more than necessary to slide it over the top of the piston.
10 With all the rings in position, space the ring gaps (including the elements of the oil control ring) uniformly around the piston at 120° intervals. Repeat the procedure for the remaining pistons and rings.

16 Crankshaft – refitting

Note: *New main bearing cap retaining bolts must be used when refitting the crankshaft.*
1 Crankshaft refitting is the first major step in engine reassembly. It is assumed at this point that the cylinder block/crankcase and crankshaft have been cleaned, inspected and repaired or reconditioned as necessary. Where removed, the oil jets must be refitted at this stage and their mounting bolts tightened securely.
2 Place the cylinder block on a clean, level work surface, with the crankcase facing upwards. Wipe out the inner surfaces of the main bearing caps and crankcase with a clean cloth as they must be kept spotlessly clean.
3 Clean the rear surface of the new main bearing shells with a lint free cloth. Fit the shells with an oil groove in each main bearing location in the block. Note the thrustwashers integral with the No 3 (centre) upper main bearing shell **(see illustrations)**. Fit the other shell from each bearing set in the corresponding main bearing cap. The oil holes in the block must line up with one of the oil holes in the bearing shell. Don't hammer the shells into place, and don't nick or gouge the bearing faces. It is critically important that the surfaces of the bearings are kept free from damage and contamination.
4 Clean the bearing surfaces of the shells in the block and the crankshaft main bearing journals with a clean, lint-free cloth. Check or

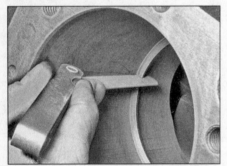

15.3 With the ring square in the bore, measure the end gap with a feeler gauge

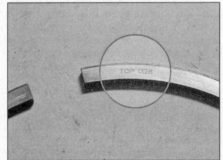

15.6 Piston ring TOP markings

16.3a Fitting the shells in each main bearing location

16.3b Note the thrustwashers integral with the No 3 (centre) upper main bearing shell

16.5 Ensure the bearing shells are absolutely clean and lubricate liberally

16.10 Tighten the main bearing cap bolts in the initial Stages using a torque wrench

16.12 Using an angle-tightening gauge to tighten the main bearing cap bolts to the final Stage

clean the oil holes in the crankshaft, as any dirt will become embedded in the new bearings when the engine is first started.

5 Apply a thin, uniform layer of clean molybdenum disulphide-based grease, engine assembly lubricant, or clean engine oil to each surface **(see illustration)**. Coat the thrustwasher surfaces as well.

6 Making sure the crankshaft journals are clean, lay the crankshaft back in place in the block.

7 Lubricate the crankshaft oil seal journals with molybdenum disulphide-based grease, engine assembly lubricant, or clean engine oil.

8 Clean the bearing surfaces of the shells in the caps then lubricate them. Refit the caps in their respective positions, with the arrows pointing to the timing chain end of the engine.

9 Apply a smear of clean engine oil to the threads and underneath the heads of the new main bearing cap bolts. Fit the bolts tightening them all by hand.

10 Working on one cap at a time, from the centre main bearing outwards (and ensuring that each cap is tightened down squarely and evenly onto the block), tighten the main bearing cap bolts to the specified Stage 1 torque setting given in Chapter 2A or 2B **(see illustration)**.

11 When all the bolts have been tightened to the Stage 1 setting, go around again and tighten them to the Stage 2 setting, then Stage 3 and Stage 4.

12 Stage 5 involves tightening the bolts though an angle, rather than to a torque. The bolts must be rotated through the specified

angle – special angle gauges are available from tool outlets **(see illustration)**. As a guide, a 90° angle is equivalent to a quarter-turn, and this is easily judged by assessing the start and end positions of the socket handle.

13 Rotate the crankshaft a number of times by hand, to check for any obvious binding.

14 Check the crankshaft endfloat (see Section 11). It should be correct if the crankshaft thrust faces are not worn or damaged, and if the thrust control bearings have been renewed.

15 Referring to Part A or B of this Chapter, fit a new crankshaft oil seal, then refit the flywheel.

16 Refit the piston connecting rod assemblies as described in Section 17.

17 Piston/connecting rod assemblies – refitting

Note 1: *At this point, it is assumed that the crankshaft has been measured, renewed/reground as necessary, and has been fitted to the engine as described in Section 16.*

Note 2: *New retaining bolts must be used when refitting the big-end bearing caps.*

1 Before refitting the piston/connecting rod assemblies, the cylinder bores must be perfectly clean, the top edge of each cylinder must be chamfered, and the crankshaft must be in place.

2 Remove the big-end bearing cap from No 1 cylinder connecting rod (refer to the marks noted or made on removal). Remove the original bearing shells, and wipe the bearing

recesses of the connecting rod and cap with a clean, lint-free cloth. They must be kept spotlessly clean.

3 Ensure that all traces of the protective grease on the new bearing shells are cleaned off using paraffin, then wipe the shells dry with a lint-free cloth. Press the bearing shells into the connecting rods and caps ensuring they sit centrally within the rods and caps **(see illustration)**.

4 Lubricate the cylinder bores, the pistons, piston rings and upper bearing shells with clean engine oil. Lay out each piston/connecting rod assembly in order on a clean work surface. Take care not to scratch the crankpins and cylinder bores when the pistons are refitted.

5 Start with piston/connecting rod assembly No 1. Make sure that the piston rings are still spaced as described in Section 15, then clamp them in position with a piston ring compressor.

6 Insert the piston/connecting rod assembly into the top of cylinder No 1 **(see illustration)**. Lower the big-end in first, guiding it to protect the cylinder bores. Take particular care not to damage or break off the oil spray jets when guiding the connecting rods onto the crankpins.

7 Ensure that the orientation of the piston in its cylinder is correct. The piston crown, connecting rod and big-end bearing caps should have markings which must be aligned in the position noted on removal (see Section 10).

8 Using a block of wood or hammer handle against the piston crown, tap the assembly into the cylinder until the piston crown is flush with the top of the cylinder **(see illustration)**.

17.3 Press the bearing shells into the connecting rods and caps ensuring they sit centrally

17.6 Insert the piston/connecting rod assembly into the top of the cylinder

17.8 Using a hammer handle to tap the piston into its bore

17.9 Note the markings on the bearing cap with respect to the connecting rod on refitting

17.10a Tighten the big-end bearing cap bolts to the Stage 1 and Stage 2 torque settings using a torque wrench . . .

17.10b . . . then tighten the bolts to the Stage 3 setting using an angle-tightening gauge

17.13a Fit the new lower crankcase-to-cylinder block gasket . . .

17.13b . . . then refit the lower crankcase to the cylinder block

9 Ensure that the bearing shell is still correctly installed. Liberally lubricate the crankpin and both bearing shells with clean engine oil. Taking care not to mark the cylinder bores, tap the piston/connecting rod assembly down the bore and onto the crankpin. Oil the threads and underside of the new retaining bolt heads, then fit the big-end bearing cap, tightening its retaining bolts finger tight at first. Note that the orientation of the bearing cap with respect to the connecting rod must be correct when the two components are reassembled **(see illustration)**.

10 Tighten the retaining bolts to the specified Stage 1 torque setting, then to the Stage 2 setting. Stage 3 involves tightening the bolts though an angle rather than to a torque. The bolts must be rotated through the specified angle (special angle gauges are available from tool outlets). As a guide, a 90° angle

is equivalent to a quarter-turn, and this is easily judged by assessing the start and end positions of the socket handle **(see illustrations)**.

11 Repeat the entire procedure for the remaining piston/connecting rod assemblies.

12 After all the piston/connecting rod assemblies have been properly installed, rotate the crankshaft a number of times by hand to check for any obvious binding or tight spots.

13 Fit the new lower crankcase-to-cylinder block gasket. Refit the lower crankcase to the cylinder block, then insert the bolts and hand-tighten **(see illustrations)**.

14 Place a straight-edge across the transmission mating surface of the cylinder block and the lower crankcase to check the lower crankcase-to-cylinder block alignment. The lower crankcase should be flush with the

cylinder block. If not flush, the alignment should be within −0.01 mm overlap to a +0.2 mm gap at the rear of the cylinder block. Repeat this check by placing the straight-edge against the two projecting bosses on the fuel injection pump side of the cylinder block **(see illustrations)**. In this instance the alignment should be −0.05 mm overlap to a +0.05 mm gap

15 Once the alignment is within tolerance, tighten the lower crankcase bolts to the specified torque.

16 Where applicable, set the position of the crankshaft position sensor mounting bracket, then refer to Part A or B of this Chapter (as applicable) and refit the relevant assemblies.

Setting the crankshaft position sensor mounting bracket

Note: *Ford service tool 303-675 (for engines with direct injection) or 303-698 (for engines with common rail injection) obtainable from Ford dealers or a tool supplier, will be required for this procedure.*

17 If the crankshaft position sensor mounting bracket was removed from the cylinder block during the cleaning and reconditioning procedures described previously, its position in relation to the flywheel will need to be reset as follows.

18 Refit the crankshaft position sensor mounting bracket and install the bolts, tightened finger tight.

19 Make up an arrow pointer out of stiff tin plate or similar. Drill a hole in the plate and bolt it to the cylinder block using the upper left-hand transmission mounting bolt hole. Use suitable washers as necessary so that the pointer lies just flush with the flywheel periphery **(see illustration)**. Once the pointer is in place, do not move it during the setting procedure.

20 Mount a DTI (Dial Test Indicator, or dial gauge) on the cylinder head mating face of the cylinder block, with the probe in line with No 1 cylinder piston.

21 Rotate the crankshaft until No 1 piston is approximately 10 mm before top dead centre (TDC). Zero the dial gauge and mark the position of the flywheel using a white marker pen or similar, in relation to the arrow pointer **(see illustrations)**.

22 Turn the flywheel anticlockwise until the

17.14a Place a straight-edge across the transmission mating surface of the cylinder block . . .

17.14b . . . and against the two projecting bosses on the fuel injection pump side of the cylinder block

17.19 Make up an arrow pointer out of stiff tin plate and bolt it to the cylinder block using suitable washers as necessary

17.21a Rotate the crankshaft until No 1 piston is approximately 10 mm before top dead centre, then zero the dial gauge

17.21b Mark the position of the flywheel using a white marker pen (or similar) in relation to the arrow pointer

17.24 Measure the distance between the two marks made on the flywheel

17.26 Arrangement of the flywheel markings

A First mark
B Second mark
C Established TDC position
D Established 50° BTDC position

dial gauge indicates 'O'. Again, mark the position of the flywheel, using a white marker pen or similar, in relation to the arrow pointer.

23 Repeat paragraphs 21 and 22 to make sure that the markings on the flywheel are correct.

24 Using a dressmaker's tape measure (or a suitable length of string) measure the distance between the two marks on the flywheel **(see illustration)**. Divide this measurement by 2 and mark that measurement on the flywheel. This will be the TDC position.

25 Again, using a tape measure or a suitable length of string, wrap it around the flywheel outer periphery to measure the flywheel circumference. Record this measurement.

26 Multiply the circumference measurement by 0.1388 and mark this new figure on the flywheel by measuring anticlockwise from the previously marked TDC position. This new figure will be the 50° BTDC position **(see illustration)**.

27 Turn the flywheel to align the newly

established 50° BTDC position with the arrow pointer **(see illustration)**.

28 Insert the Ford special tool into the crankshaft position sensor mounting bracket, and move the bracket within the limit of the elongated bolt holes until the tool drops into position in the flywheel **(see illustrations)**. Now tighten the crankshaft position sensor mounting bracket retaining bolts to the specified torque. Remove the special tool on completion.

17.27 Turn the flywheel to align the newly established 50° BTDC position with the arrow pointer

17.28a Insert the Ford special tool into the crankshaft position sensor mounting bracket ...

17.28b ... and move the bracket until the tool drops into position in the flywheel

18 Engine –
initial start-up after overhaul

1 With the engine refitted in the vehicle, double-check the engine oil and coolant levels. Make a final check that everything has been reconnected, and that there are no tools or rags left in the engine compartment.

2 Turn the engine on the starter until the oil pressure warning light goes out. If the lamp fails to extinguish after several seconds of cranking, check the engine oil level and oil filter security. Assuming these are correct, check the security of the oil pressure switch wiring. **Do not** progress any further until you are satisfied that oil is being pumped around the engine at sufficient pressure.

3 Prime and bleed the fuel system as described in Chapter 4A, then start the engine, noting that this may take a little longer than usual.

4 While the engine is idling, check for fuel, water and oil leaks. Don't be alarmed if there are some odd smells and smoke from parts getting hot and burning off oil deposits.

5 Assuming all is well, run the engine until it reaches normal operating temperature, then switch off the engine.

6 After a few minutes, recheck the oil and coolant levels as described in *Weekly checks*, and top-up as necessary.

7 Note that there is no need to retighten the cylinder head bolts once the engine has first run after reassembly.

8 If new pistons, rings or crankshaft bearings have been fitted, the engine must be treated as new and run-in for the first 600 miles (1000 km). Do not operate the engine at full-throttle or allow it to labour at low engine speeds in any gear. It is recommended that the oil and filter be changed at the end of this period.

Chapter 3
Cooling, heating and ventilation systems

Contents

Degrees of difficulty

Easy, suitable for novice with little experience	Fairly easy, suitable for beginner with some experience	Fairly difficult, suitable for competent DIY mechanic	Difficult, suitable for experienced DIY mechanic	Very difficult, suitable for expert DIY or professional

Specifications

Coolant
Mixture type .... See Lubricants and fluids on page 0•18
Cooling system capacity .... See Chapter 1

Expansion tank filler cap
Pressure rating .... 13 to 18 psi (0.9 to 1.2 bar)

Air conditioning system
Refrigerant R134a

Torque wrench settings

	Nm	lbf ft
Air conditioning compressor bolts	25	19
Air conditioning low pressure cut-off switch	8	6
Coolant hose support bracket (2.0 litre engines)	22	16
Coolant pipe block-to-coolant pump (2.0 litre engines)	10	7
Coolant pump bolts:		
2.0 litre engines	24	18
2.4 litre engines	22	16
Oil temperature control thermostat (2.0 litre engines)	10	7
Power steering pump-to-coolant pump (2.0 litre engines)	22	16
Radiator support bracket bolts	10	7
Radiator thermo-viscous cooling fan (2.4 litre engines)	45	33
Refrigerant union to accumulator	8	6
Refrigerant union to air conditioning compressor	20	15
Thermostat housing bolt	22	16
Thermostat housing cover bolts	10	7

1 General information and precautions

Engine cooling system

2.0 litre engines

The cooling system is of pressurised type, comprising a coolant pump, a crossflow radiator, electric cooling fan, and thermostat. The coolant pump is bolted to the left-hand front of the engine cylinder block, and is driven by a drivebelt off the left-hand end of the inlet camshaft, via the power steering pump which is bolted to the coolant pump. The drivebelt drives the power steering pump pulley, and the power steering pump drives the coolant pump by splines.

The thermostat is located in a housing on the left-hand end of the cylinder block, beneath the brake vacuum pump.

The system functions as follows. Cold coolant from the radiator passes to the coolant pump, where it is pumped around the cylinder block, head passages and heater matrix. After cooling the cylinder bores, combustion surfaces and valve seats, the coolant reaches the underside of the thermostat which is initially closed. The coolant passes through the heater and is returned to the coolant pump.

When the engine is cold, the coolant circulates only through the cylinder block, cylinder head and heater. When the coolant reaches a predetermined temperature, the thermostat opens and the coolant also passes through to the radiator. As the coolant circulates through the radiator, it is cooled by the inrush of air when the vehicle is in forward motion. Airflow is supplemented by the action of the electric cooling fan when necessary. Once the coolant has passed through the radiator and has cooled, the cycle is repeated.

The electric cooling fan, mounted on the rear of the radiator, is controlled by the engine management system powertrain control module. At a predetermined coolant temperature, the fan is actuated.

An expansion tank is fitted to the left-hand side of the engine compartment to accommodate expansion of the coolant when hot. The expansion tank is connected to the top of the radiator.

2.4 litre engines

The cooling system is of pressurised type, comprising a coolant pump, a crossflow radiator, temperature-conscious thermo-viscous cooling fan, and thermostat. The coolant pump is bolted to the left-hand side of the engine cylinder block, and is driven by the auxiliary drivebelt off the crankshaft pulley. The thermo-viscous cooling fan is attached to a pulley bolted to the front of the engine cylinder block, and is also driven by the auxiliary drivebelt off the crankshaft pulley.

The thermostat is located in a housing bolted to the cylinder head at the front of the cylinder block, above the brake vacuum pump.

The system functions as follows. Cold coolant from the radiator passes to the coolant pump, where it is pumped around the cylinder block, head passages and heater matrix. After cooling the cylinder bores, combustion surfaces and valve seats, the coolant reaches the underside of the thermostat, which is initially closed. The coolant passes through the heater, and is returned to the coolant pump.

When the engine is cold, the coolant circulates only through the cylinder block, cylinder head and heater. When the coolant reaches a predetermined temperature, the thermostat opens and the coolant also passes through to the radiator. As the coolant circulates through the radiator, it is cooled by the inrush of air when the vehicle is in forward motion. Airflow is supplemented by the action of the cooling fan when necessary. Once the coolant has passed through the radiator, and has cooled, the cycle is repeated.

An expansion tank is fitted to the left-hand side of the engine compartment to accommodate expansion of the coolant when hot. The expansion tank is connected to the top of the radiator.

The thermo-viscous cooling fan is controlled by the temperature of air behind the radiator. When the air temperature reaches a predetermined level, a bi-metallic coil opens a valve within the unit, and silicon fluid is fed through a system of vanes. Half of the vanes are driven directly by the coolant pump pulley by the auxiliary drivebelt, and the remaining half are connected to the fan blades. The vanes are arranged so that drive is transmitted to the fan blades in relation to the drag, or viscosity of the fluid, and this in turn depends on ambient temperature and engine speed. The fan is therefore only operated when required.

On models with air conditioning, a supplementary electric cooling fan is also fitted and is mounted on the rear of the radiator. The electric fan is controlled by the engine management system powertrain control module according to air conditioning system demand.

Heating/ventilation system

The heating system consists of a blower fan and heater matrix (radiator) located in the heater unit, with hoses connecting the heater matrix to the engine cooling system. Hot engine coolant is circulated through the heater matrix. Incoming fresh air for the ventilation system enters the vehicle through the windscreen cowl panel grille. The ventilation system air distribution is controlled by a number of flap doors in the heater housing. When the heater controls are operated, the flap doors open to direct the air to the chosen areas of the passenger compartment. When the blower control is operated, the blower fan forces air through the unit according to the setting selected.

Air conditioning system

See Section 11.

Precautions

 Warning: DO NOT attempt to remove the expansion tank filler cap, or to disturb any part of the cooling system, while it or the engine is hot, as there is a very great risk of scalding. If the expansion tank filler cap must be removed before the engine and radiator have fully cooled down (even though this is not recommended) the pressure in the cooling system must first be released. Cover the cap with a thick layer of cloth, to avoid scalding, and slowly unscrew the filler cap until a hissing sound can be heard. When the hissing has stopped, showing that pressure is released, slowly unscrew the filler cap further until it can be removed, however, if more hissing sounds are heard, wait until they have stopped before unscrewing the cap completely. At all times, keep well away from the filler opening.

Warning: Do not allow antifreeze to come in contact with your skin, or with the painted surfaces of the vehicle. Rinse off spills immediately with plenty of water. Never leave antifreeze lying around in an open container, or in a puddle in the driveway or on the garage floor. Children and pets are attracted by its sweet smell, but antifreeze is fatal if ingested.

Warning: If the engine is hot, the electric cooling fan may start rotating even if the engine is not running, so be careful to keep hands, hair and loose clothing well clear when working in the engine compartment.

Warning: Refer to Section 11 for precautions to be observed when working on models equipped with air conditioning.

2 Cooling system hoses – disconnection and renewal

Note: Refer to the warnings given in Section 1 of this Chapter before starting work.

1 If the checks described in Chapter 1 reveal a faulty hose, it must be renewed as follows.

2 First drain the cooling system (see Chapter 1). If the antifreeze is not due for renewal, the drained coolant may be re-used if it is collected in a clean container.

3 To disconnect any hose, use a pair of pliers to release the spring clamps (or a screwdriver to slacken screw-type clamps),

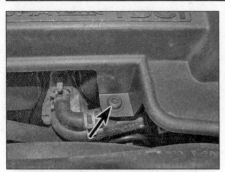

3.2a Undo the auxiliary drivebelt cover right-hand retaining bolt (arrowed) . . .

3.2b . . . and centre retaining bolt (arrowed) . . .

3.2c . . . then release the wiring harness and/or hoses and lift the cover off the engine

then move them along the hose clear of the union. Carefully work the hose off its stubs. The hoses can be removed with relative ease when new, however, on an older vehicle they may have stuck.

4 If a hose proves stubborn, try to release it by rotating it on its unions before attempting to work it off. Gently prise the end of the hose with a blunt instrument (such as a flat-bladed screwdriver), but do not apply too much force, and take care not to damage the pipe stubs or hoses. Note in particular that the radiator hose unions are fragile, therefore do not use excessive force when attempting to remove the hoses. If all else fails, cut the hose with a sharp knife, then slit it so that it can be peeled off in two pieces. While expensive, this is preferable to buying a new radiator. Check first, however, that a new hose is readily available.

5 When refitting a hose, first slide the clamps onto the hose, then work the hose onto its stubs. If the hose is stiff, use soap or washing-up liquid as a lubricant, or soften it by soaking it in boiling water (take care to prevent scalding).

6 Work each hose end fully onto its stub, then check that the hose is settled correctly and is properly routed. Slide each clip along the hose until it is behind the stub flared end, before tightening it securely.

7 Refill the system with coolant (see Chapter 1).

8 Check carefully for leaks as soon as possible after disturbing any part of the cooling system.

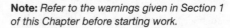

3 Thermostat –
removal, testing and refitting

Note: *Refer to the warnings given in Section 1 of this Chapter before starting work.*

Removal

1 Drain the cooling system as described in Chapter 1. If the coolant is relatively new or in good condition, drain it into a clean container and re-use it.

2 On 2.4 litre engines, undo the two bolts securing the auxiliary drivebelt cover to the top of the engine. The centre bolt may be located under a plastic cover on certain models. There may also be an additional bolt at the left-hand side of the cover; if so, undo this bolt also. Release the wiring harness and/or hoses at

the rear of the cover and lift the cover off the engine **(see illustrations)**.

3 Release the clips and disconnect the coolant hoses from the thermostat housing cover.

4 Unscrew the three bolts and separate the cover from the thermostat housing **(see illustrations)**.

5 Note how the thermostat is fitted and withdraw it from the housing. Recover the O-ring seal and discard it, then obtain a new one for refitting **(see illustrations)**.

6 If necessary, the thermostat housing may be removed from the cylinder head outlet elbow. To do this, disconnect the remaining coolant hoses(s) from the housing, then unscrew the single bolt and remove the housing. On 2.0 litre engines, recover the O-ring seal and discard it, then obtain a new one for refitting **(see illustrations)**. Withdraw the housing from the engine compartment.

3.4a Unscrew the bolts . . .

3.4b . . . and separate the cover from the thermostat housing

3.5a Remove the thermostat from the housing . . .

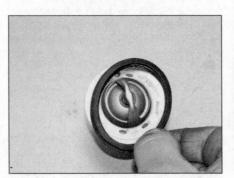

3.5b . . . then remove the O-ring seal

3.6a Unscrew the single bolt . . .

3.6b . . . remove the housing . . .

3.6c . . . and recover the O-ring seal – 2.0 litre engines

Testing

7 A rough test of the thermostat may be made by suspending it with a piece of string in a container full of water, so that it is immersed in the water but not touching the sides or bottom of the container **(see illustration)**. Heat the water to bring it to the boil, and check that the thermostat opens by the time the water boils. If not, renew it.

8 If a thermometer is available, the precise opening temperature of the thermostat may be determined. Compare the figures with the opening temperature marked on the thermostat.

9 A thermostat which fails to close as the water cools must also be renewed.

Refitting

10 Refitting is a reversal of removal, but clean all sealing surfaces, fit new O-ring seals, and tighten the bolts to the specified torque. Refill the cooling system as described in Chapter 1.

---

4 Radiator electric cooling fan assembly – testing, removal and refitting

Note: *Refer to the warnings given in Section 1 of this Chapter before starting work.*

Testing

1 The radiator cooling fan is controlled by the engine management system's powertrain

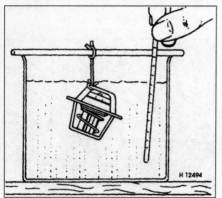

3.7 Method of checking thermostat opening temperature

control module, acting on the information received from the cylinder head temperature sensor.

2 First, check the relevant fuses and relays (see Chapter 12).

3 To test the fan motor, unplug the electrical connector and use fused jumper wires to connect the fan directly to the battery. If the fan still does not work, renew the motor.

4 If the motor tested good, the fault lies in the cylinder head temperature sensor (see Chapter 4A), in the wiring loom (see Chapter 12) or in the engine management system (see Chapter 4A).

Removal

2.0 litre engines without air conditioning

5 Move the driver's seat fully forward, slide open the battery box cover and disconnect the battery negative terminal (refer to *Disconnecting the battery* in the Reference Chapter).

6 Firmly apply the handbrake, then jack up the front of the vehicle and support it securely on axle stands (see *Jacking and vehicle support*).

7 Unscrew the two nuts securing the cooling fan shroud to the radiator.

8 From under the vehicle, slacken the retaining clips and disconnect the intake and outlet air ducts from the intercooler.

9 Disconnect the cooling fan wiring connector, then carefully slide the electric cooling fan and shroud assembly upwards then forward and remove it from the vehicle.

2.0 litre engines with air conditioning

10 Move the driver's seat fully forward, slide open the battery box cover and disconnect the battery negative terminal (refer to *Disconnecting the battery* in the Reference Chapter).

11 Firmly apply the handbrake, then jack up the front of the vehicle and support it securely on axle stands (see *Jacking and vehicle support*).

12 Detach the wiring harness connector from the cooling fan shroud.

13 Unscrew the two nuts securing the cooling fan shroud to the radiator.

14 From under the vehicle, slacken the retaining clips and disconnect the intake and outlet air ducts from the intercooler.

15 Disconnect the wiring connector from the

temperature and manifold absolute pressure sensor on the intercooler .

16 Release the retaining studs and remove the left-hand and right-hand air deflectors from the bumper.

17 Using string or plastic cable ties, support the weight of the radiator, then unscrew the radiator support bracket lower bolt. Unscrew the two remaining bolts each side and remove the radiator support bracket.

18 Disconnect the cooling fan wiring connector, then carefully slide the electric cooling fan and shroud assembly upwards then forward and remove it from the vehicle.

2.4 litre engines

Note: *An electric cooling fan is fitted in addition to the mechanical thermo-viscous cooling fan on models equipped with air conditioning. The electric cooling fan provides supplementary air-flow through the air conditioning system condenser. On models without air conditioning, only the mechanical thermo-viscous cooling fan is used.*

19 Move the driver's seat fully forward, slide open the battery box cover and disconnect the battery negative terminal (refer to *Disconnecting the battery* in the Reference Chapter).

20 Remove the thermo-viscous cooling fan assembly as described in Section 6.

21 Disconnect the wiring connector and the vacuum hoses at the EGR valve solenoid, then undo the retaining nuts and remove the solenoid from the fan shroud.

22 Detach the vacuum hose from the fan shroud, then disconnect the cooling fan wiring connector.

23 Unscrew the two nuts securing the cooling fan shroud to the radiator.

24 Remove the intercooler as described in Chapter 4A.

25 Carefully slide the electric cooling fan and shroud assembly upwards from the side brackets, then remove it from the engine compartment.

Refitting

26 Refitting is a reversal of removal.

---

5 Radiator cooling fan shroud (2.4 litre engines) – removal and refitting

Removal

Note: *The following procedure applies to models without air conditioning. Where air conditioning is fitted, remove the radiator electric cooling fan assembly as described in Section 4.*

1 Remove the radiator thermo-viscous cooling fan as described in Section 6.

2 Disconnect the wiring connector and the vacuum hoses at the EGR valve solenoid, then undo the retaining nuts and remove the solenoid from the fan shroud.

3 Detach the vacuum hose from the fan shroud.

4 Unscrew the two nuts securing the cooling fan shroud to the radiator **(see illustration)**.
5 Lift the shroud upwards from the side brackets, then remove it from the engine compartment.

Refitting

6 Refitting is a reversal of removal.

6 Radiator thermo-viscous cooling fan assembly – removal and refitting

Note: *The mechanical thermo-viscous cooling fan is only fitted to 2.4 litre engines.*

Removal

1 Undo the two bolts securing the auxiliary drivebelt cover to the top of the engine. The centre bolt may be located under a plastic cover on certain models. There may also be an additional bolt at the left-hand side of the cover; if so, undo this bolt also. Release the wiring harness and/or hoses at the rear of the cover and lift the cover off the engine **(see illustrations 3.2a to 3.2c)**.
2 Unscrew the nut securing the fan unit to the pulley shaft and remove the fan **(see illustration)**. Note that unlike the thermo-viscous fan clutch unit fitted to many Ford vehicles, the unit fitted to the Transit has a conventional right-hand thread, and is unscrewed in the normal way. To stop the pulley from rotating as the fan clutch is loosened, hold it with the aid of a strap wrench, a forked tool, or similar. If necessary, tap the spanner to free the clutch unit.
3 On removal, the fan blades can be separated from the clutch unit by unscrewing the four retaining bolts.

Refitting

4 Refitting is a reversal of removal.

7 Radiator – removal, inspection and refitting

Note 1: *Refer to the warnings given in Section 1 of this Chapter before starting work.*
Note 2: *If leakage is the reason for removing the radiator, bear in mind that minor leaks can often be cured using a radiator sealant added to the coolant without removing the radiator.*

Removal

2.0 litre engines without air conditioning

1 Drain the cooling system as described in Chapter 1. If the coolant is relatively new or in good condition, drain it into a clean container and re-use it.
2 Release the retaining clip and disconnect the top hose from the radiator.
3 Release the clip and disconnect the expansion tank hose, then detach it from the electric cooling fan motor and shroud.

5.4 Radiator cooling fan shroud right-hand retaining nut (arrowed)

4 Remove the radiator electric cooling fan assembly as described in Section 4.
5 Release the retaining clip and disconnect the bottom hose from the radiator.
6 Disconnect the wiring connector from the temperature and manifold absolute pressure sensor on the intercooler .
7 Release the retaining studs and remove the left-hand and right-hand air deflectors from the bumper.
8 Using string or plastic cable ties, support the weight of the radiator, then unscrew the radiator support bracket lower bolt. Unscrew the two remaining bolts each side and remove the radiator support bracket **(see illustrations)**.
9 Release the string or cable ties used to support the radiator, then lower the radiator and remove it from under the vehicle.
10 Remove the rubber radiator mounting bushes from the top and bottom brackets, and inspect them for wear and damage. If worn excessively, obtain and fit new ones before refitting the radiator.

2.0 litre engines with air conditioning

11 Drain the cooling system as described in Chapter 1. If the coolant is relatively new or in good condition, drain it into a clean container and re-use it.
12 Release the retaining clip and disconnect the top hose from the radiator.
13 Release the clip and disconnect the expansion tank hose, then detach it from the electric cooling fan motor and shroud.

6.2 Unscrew the nut (arrowed) securing the fan unit to the pulley shaft

14 Remove the radiator electric cooling fan assembly as described in Section 4.
15 Release the retaining clip and disconnect the bottom hose from the radiator.
16 Slide the condenser sideways out of the mounting brackets and position it to one side.

> ⚠ **Warning: Do not disconnect the refrigerant hoses.**

17 Release the string or cable ties used to support the radiator, then lower the radiator and remove it from under the vehicle.
18 Remove the rubber radiator mounting bushes from the top and bottom brackets, and inspect them for wear and damage. If worn excessively, obtain and fit new ones before refitting the radiator.

2.4 litre engines

19 Drain the cooling system as described in Chapter 1. If the coolant is relatively new or in good condition, drain it into a clean container and re-use it.
20 Release the clips and disconnect the expansion tank hose, and the top and bottom hoses from the radiator.
21 On models without air conditioning, remove the radiator cooling fan shroud as described in Section 5, then remove the intercooler as described in Chapter 4A.
22 On models with air conditioning, remove the radiator electric cooling fan assembly as described in Section 4, then slide the condenser sideways out of the mounting brackets and position it to one side.

7.8a Unscrew the radiator support bracket lower bolt . . .

7.8b . . . then unscrew the two remaining bolts each side (arrowed) and remove the radiator support bracket

8.6 Power steering pump-to-coolant pump mounting bolts (arrowed) – 2.0 litre engines

8.8a Unscrew the coolant pump housing-to-block bolts . . .

Inspection

25 With the radiator removed, it can be inspected for leaks and damage. If it needs repair, have a radiator specialist or dealer service department perform the work, as special techniques are required.
26 Insects and dirt can be removed from the radiator with a garden hose or a soft brush. Take care not to bend the cooling fins.

Refitting

27 Refitting is the reverse of the removal procedure, but refill the cooling system as described in Chapter 1.

8.8b . . . withdraw the assembly . . .

8.8c . . . and remove the gasket – 2.0 litre engines

23 On all models, release the string or cable ties used to support the radiator, then lower the radiator and remove it from under the vehicle.
24 Remove the rubber radiator mounting bushes from the top and bottom brackets, and inspect them for wear and damage. If worn excessively, obtain and fit new ones before refitting the radiator.

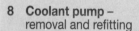

| 8 | Coolant pump – removal and refitting |

Note: *Refer to the warnings given in Section 1 of this Chapter before starting work.*

Removal

2.0 litre engines

1 Drain the cooling system as described in Chapter 1. If the coolant is relatively new or in good condition, drain it into a clean container and re-use it.
2 Remove the power steering pump drivebelt as described in Chapter 1.
3 Remove the inlet manifold as described in Chapter 2A.
4 Release the clips and remove the intake air hose.
5 Undo the four bolts and remove the coolant hose support bracket.
6 Unscrew the bolts securing the power steering pump to the coolant pump, and position it to one side (see illustration).
7 Release the retaining clips and disconnect the accessible coolant hoses from the coolant pump.
8 Unscrew and remove the coolant pump housing-to-cylinder block retaining bolts, noting the location of the wiring harness on the lower bolts. Withdraw the pump sufficiently to disconnect the remaining hose. Remove the gasket and discard it (see illustrations). Obtain a new gasket for refitting.
9 Unbolt the engine oil temperature control thermostat from the coolant pump housing and discard the O-ring seal (see illustrations). Obtain a new O-ring for refitting.

2.4 litre engines

10 Drain the cooling system as described in Chapter 1. If the coolant is relatively new or in good condition, drain it into a clean container and re-use it.
11 Remove the braking system vacuum pump as described in Chapter 9.
12 Release the clip and disconnect the coolant hose from the rear of the coolant pump.
13 Undo the four bolts and detach the coolant pump from the cylinder block. Release the clips and disconnect the remaining coolant hoses, then remove the pump from the engine

8.9a Unscrew the bolt . . .

8.9b . . . and remove the oil temperature control thermostat from the coolant pump housing – 2.0 litre engines

8.13a Undo the four bolts (arrowed) and detach the coolant pump from the cylinder block . . .

8.13b . . . release the clips and disconnect the remaining coolant hoses, then remove the pump from the engine

9.2 Disconnect the wiring from the heater blower motor

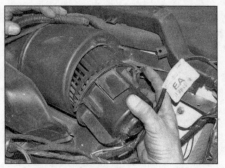

9.3 Pull up the tab on the side of the blower motor, then rotate the motor housing anticlockwise to remove

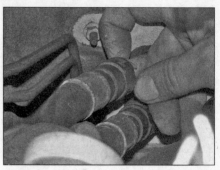

9.7 Release the quick-release fittings and disconnect the heater hoses at the heater matrix pipe stubs

(see illustrations). Remove the gasket and discard it. Obtain a new gasket for refitting.

14 If required, undo the three bolts and remove the coolant pipe block from the rear of the pump. Discard the O-ring seal and obtain a new O-ring for refitting.

Refitting

15 Refitting is a reversal of removal, but tighten the mounting bolts/nuts to the specified torque. Refill the cooling system as described in Chapter 1.

9 Heater/ventilation components – removal and refitting

Heater blower motor

Removal

1 Remove the complete facia as described in Chapter 11.
2 Disconnect the wiring from the heater blower motor (see illustration).
3 Pull up the tab on the side of the blower motor, then rotate the motor housing anti-clockwise and remove it from the heater casing (see illustration).

Refitting

4 Refitting is a reversal of removal.

Heater matrix

Removal

5 Remove the complete facia as described in Chapter 11.
6 Drain the cooling system as described in Chapter 1. If the coolant is relatively new or in good condition, drain it into a clean container and re-use it.
7 On the engine side of the bulkhead, release the quick-release fittings and disconnect the heater hoses at the heater matrix pipe stubs (see illustration).
8 Disconnect the vacuum hoses at the connection above the heater matrix pipe stubs.
9 From inside the vehicle, release the three clips each side and remove the heater housing lower cover (where fitted).
10 Undo the three screws and remove the

heater matrix pipe cover from the side of the heater housing (see illustration).
11 If still in place, remove the remaining air ducts from the heater housing.
12 Disconnect the wiring connectors at the heater blower motor and heater blower motor resistor (see illustration).
13 Undo the two bolts each side securing the heater housing to the bulkhead (see illustrations).
14 Withdraw the heater housing from inside the vehicle. Be prepared for some spillage of coolant by placing cloth rags on the floor of the vehicle.
15 With the heater housing removed, the heater core can be withdrawn from the side of the housing.

Refitting

16 Refitting is a reversal of removal. Refill the cooling system with reference to Chapter 1.

9.10 Undo the three screws and remove the heater matrix pipe cover from the side of the heater housing

9.13a Heater housing right-hand retaining bolts (arrowed) . . .

10 Heater/air conditioning controls – removal and refitting

Removal

1 Move the driver's seat fully forward, open the battery box cover and disconnect the battery negative terminal (refer to *Disconnecting the battery* in the Reference Chapter).
2 Remove the radio/CD player as described in Chapter 12.
3 Remove the facia centre panel as described in Chapter 11.
4 Undo the four screws securing the heater control panel to the facia (see illustration).
5 Push the panel forward (into the facia) and tip it upwards at the rear. Disconnect the

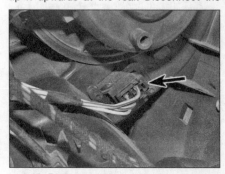

9.12 Disconnect the wiring connector (arrowed) at the heater blower motor resistor

9.13b . . . and left-hand retaining bolts (arrowed)

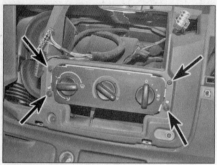

10.4 Undo the four screws (arrowed) securing the heater control panel to the facia

10.5 Disconnect the wiring connectors from the rear of the panel

wiring connectors from the rear of the panel **(see illustration)**.

6 Depress the retaining tangs and release the heater control outer cables from the supports on the rear of the panel, then slip the inner cable ends off the actuator arms **(see illustrations)**.

7 Remove the control panel through the opening in the facia.

Refitting

8 Refitting is a reversal of removal.

---

11 Air conditioning system – general information and precautions

General information

The air conditioning system consists of a condenser mounted in front of the radiator, an evaporator mounted adjacent to the heater matrix, a compressor driven by the auxiliary drivebelt, an accumulator/dehydrator, and the pipes connecting all of the above components.

The cooling side of the system works in the same way as a domestic refrigerator. Refrigerant gas at low pressure is drawn into a belt-driven compressor and passes into a condenser mounted on the front of the radiator, where it loses heat and becomes liquid. The liquid passes through an expansion valve to an evaporator, where it changes from liquid under high pressure to gas under

low pressure. This change is accompanied by a drop in temperature, which cools the evaporator. The refrigerant returns to the compressor, and the cycle begins again.

Air blown through the evaporator passes to the air distribution unit, where it is mixed with hot air blown through the heater matrix to achieve the desired temperature in the passenger compartment.

The heating side of the system works in the same way as on models without air conditioning.

Precautions

⚠️ **Warning: The air conditioning system is under high pressure. Do not loosen any fittings or remove any components until after the system has been discharged. Air conditioning refrigerant should be properly discharged into an approved type of container, at a dealer service department or an automotive air conditioning repair facility capable of handling R134a refrigerant. Always wear eye protection when disconnecting air conditioning system fittings.**

When an air conditioning system is fitted, it is necessary to observe the following special precautions whenever dealing with any part of the system, its associated components, and any items which necessitate disconnection of the system:

a) *While the refrigerant used (R134a) is less damaging to the environment than*

the previously-used R12, it is still a very dangerous substance. It must not be allowed into contact with the skin or eyes, or there is a risk of frostbite. It must also not be discharged in an enclosed space since, while it is not toxic, there is a risk of suffocation. The refrigerant is heavier than air, and so must never be discharged over a pit.

b) *The refrigerant must not be allowed to come in contact with a naked flame, otherwise a poisonous gas will be created and under certain circumstances, this can form an explosive mixture with air. For similar reasons, smoking in the presence of refrigerant is highly dangerous, particularly if the vapour is inhaled through a lighted cigarette.*

c) *Never discharge the system to the atmosphere. R134a is not an ozone-depleting ChloroFluoroCarbon (CFC) like R12, but is instead a hydrofluorocarbon, which causes environmental damage by contributing to the 'greenhouse effect' if released into the atmosphere.*

d) *R134a refrigerant must not be mixed with R12. The system uses different seals (now green-coloured, previously black) and has different fittings requiring different tools, so that there is no chance of the two types of refrigerant becoming mixed accidentally.*

e) *If for any reason the system must be disconnected, entrust this task to your Ford dealer or a refrigeration engineer.*

f) *It is essential that the system be professionally discharged prior to using any form of heat (welding, soldering, brazing, etc) in the vicinity of the system, before having the vehicle oven-dried at a temperature exceeding 70°C after repainting, and before disconnecting any part of the system.*

---

12 Air conditioning system components – removal and refitting

⚠️ **Warning: The air conditioning system is under high pressure. Do not loosen any fittings or remove any components until after the system has been discharged. Air conditioning refrigerant should be properly discharged into an approved type of container, at a dealer service department or an automotive air conditioning repair facility capable of handling R134a refrigerant. Cap or plug the pipe lines as soon as they are disconnected, to prevent the entry of moisture. Always wear eye protection when disconnecting air conditioning system fittings.**

Note: *This Section refers to the components of the air conditioning system itself. Refer to Sections 9 and 10 for details of components common to the heating/ventilation system.*

10.6a Depress the retaining tangs and release the heater control outer cables from the supports on the panel . . .

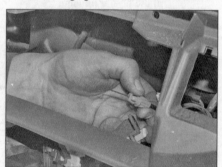

10.6b . . . then slip the inner cable ends off the actuator arms

Condenser

Removal

1 Have the refrigerant discharged at a dealer service department or an automotive air conditioning repair facility.

2 Remove the intercooler as described in Chapter 4A.

3 Release the retaining studs and remove the left-hand and right-hand air deflectors from the bumper.

4 Disconnect the refrigerant lines from the condenser, and immediately cap the openings to prevent the entry of dirt and moisture. Discard the O-ring seals and obtain new ones for refitting.

5 Slide the condenser sideways out of the mounting brackets and remove it from under the vehicle.

Refitting

6 Refitting is a reversal of removal, but fit new O-ring seals. The O-ring seals must be coated with clean refrigerant oil before refitting them. Have the system evacuated, charged and leak-tested by the specialist who discharged it.

Heater/evaporator housing

Note: *Ford special tools 412-038 and 412-027 will be required for this work.*

Removal

7 Have the refrigerant discharged at a dealer service department or an automotive air conditioning repair facility.

8 Remove the complete facia as described in Chapter 11.

9 Drain the cooling system as described in Chapter 1. If the coolant is relatively new or in good condition, drain it into a clean container and re-use it.

10 On the engine side of the bulkhead, release the quick-release fittings and disconnect the heater hoses at the heater matrix pipe stubs **(see illustration 9.7)**.

11 Disconnect the vacuum hoses at the connection above the heater matrix pipe stubs.

12 Using the Ford special tools 412-038 and 412-027, disconnect the refrigerant lines from the evaporator matrix. Discard the O-ring seals and suitably plug or cover the disconnected unions.

13 From inside the vehicle, release the three clips each side and remove the heater/evaporator housing lower cover (where fitted).

14 Undo the three screws and remove the heater matrix pipe cover from the side of the heater/evaporator housing **(see illustration 9.10)**.

15 Disconnect the vacuum hose from the air inlet blend door actuator.

16 If still in place, remove the remaining air ducts from the heater/evaporator housing.

17 Disconnect the wiring connectors at the heater blower motor and heater blower motor resistor **(see illustration 9.2 and 9.12)**.

18 Undo the two bolts each side securing the heater/evaporator housing to the bulkhead **(see illustrations 9.13a and 9.13b)**.

19 Check that all wiring has been disconnected and positioned to one side, then withdraw the heater/evaporator housing from inside the vehicle. Be prepared for some spillage of coolant by placing cloth rags on the floor of the vehicle.

20 Release the wiring harness from the top of the heater/evaporator housing.

21 Undo the support bracket screw and release the refrigerant piped from the housing.

22 Remove the six retaining clips and two clamps and lift off the heater/evaporator housing cover.

23 Withdraw the evaporator from the housing.

Refitting

24 Refitting is a reversal of removal, but fit new O-ring seals. The O-ring seals must be coated with clean refrigerant oil before refitting them. Have the system evacuated, charged and leak-tested by the specialist who discharged it.

Compressor

Removal

25 Have the refrigerant discharged at a dealer service department or an automotive air conditioning repair facility.

26 Firmly apply the handbrake, then jack up the front of the vehicle and support it securely on axle stands (see *Jacking and vehicle support*).

27 Remove the auxiliary drivebelt as described in Chapter 1.

28 Disconnect the wiring from the air conditioning compressor.

29 Support the air conditioning compressor, then unscrew the mounting bolts. Withdraw the compressor from the engine then unscrew the bolt and disconnect the pipe union block from the compressor. Discard the O-ring seals and obtain new ones for the refitting procedure. Tape over or plug the compressor apertures and line ends to prevent entry of dust and dirt.

Refitting

30 Refitting is a reversal of removal, but fit new O-ring seals after coating them with clean refrigerant oil, and tighten the mounting bolts to the specified torque. Have the system evacuated, charged and leak-tested by the specialist that discharged it.

Accumulator/dehydrator

Removal

31 Have the refrigerant discharged at a dealer service department or an automotive air conditioning repair facility.

32 On 2.4 litre engines, undo the retaining bolt and move the power steering reservoir to one side.

33 Release the retaining clips and remove the air cleaner air outlet duct.

34 Disconnect the refrigerant lines from the accumulator. Discard the O-ring seals and obtain new ones for refitting. Tape over or plug the accumulator apertures and line ends to prevent entry of dust and dirt.

35 Disconnect the wiring connector from the low-pressure cut-off switch on the side of the accumulator.

36 Unscrew the mounting bolts and remove the accumulator/dehydrator from the engine compartment.

Refitting

37 Refitting is a reversal of removal, but fit new O-ring seals after coating them with clean refrigerant oil. Have the system evacuated, charged and leak-tested by the specialist who discharged it.

Low pressure cut-off switch

 Warning: This work is best carried out by a dealer service department or an automotive air conditioning repair facility.

Removal

38 On 2.4 litre engines, undo the retaining bolt and move the power steering reservoir to one side.

39 Release the retaining clips and remove the air cleaner air outlet duct.

40 Disconnect the wiring connector from the low-pressure cut-off switch on the side of the accumulator.

41 Connect a 20 amp fuse rated jumper wire between Pin 1 and Pin 4 of the switch wiring, then start the engine and turn the air conditioning switch to ON.

Caution: The air conditioning compressor MUST run during removal of the lower pressure cut-off switch.

42 Unscrew and remove the switch and discard the O-ring seals. **Note:** *Check that the low pressure cut-off switch valve closes completely after removal of the switch, to prevent loss of refrigerant. Obtain new seals for refitting.*

Refitting

43 Refitting is a reversal of removal, but fit new O-ring seals after coating them with clean refrigerant oil, and tighten the switch **only** to the specified torque.

Chapter 4 Part A:
Fuel and exhaust systems

Contents

Degrees of difficulty

Easy, suitable for novice with little experience	Fairly easy, suitable for beginner with some experience	Fairly difficult, suitable for competent DIY mechanic	Difficult, suitable for experienced DIY mechanic	Very difficult, suitable for expert DIY or professional

Specifications

General

System type	Electronic fuel injection, controlled by powertrain control module (PCM)
Firing order.	1 – 3 – 4 – 2 (No 1 at timing chain end)
Idle speed.	900 rpm (regulated by engine management system – no adjustment possible)

Fuel

Fuel type.	Commercial diesel fuel for road vehicles (DERV)

Injection pump

Make and type:
  2.0 litre engines:

DuraTorq-Di (75 PS – direct injection) – engine code D3FA	Bosch VP30
DuraTorq-Di (85 PS – direct injection) – engine code F3FA	Bosch VP30
DuraTorq-Di (100 PS – direct injection) – engine code ABFA.	Bosch VP44
DuraTorq-TDCi (125 PS – common rail injection) – engine code FIFA	Delphi

  2.4 litre engines:

DuraTorq-Di (75 PS – direct injection) – engine code F4FA	Bosch VP30
DuraTorq-Di (90 PS – direct injection) – engine code D2FA, D2FB and HEFA	Bosch VP30
DuraTorq-Di (115 PS – direct injection) – engine code FXFA	Bosch VP30
DuraTorq-Di (120 PS – direct injection) – engine code D4FA and DFFA	Bosch VP30
DuraTorq-Di (125 PS – direct injection) – engine code DOFA.	Bosch VP44
DuraTorq-TDCi (135 PS – common rail injection) – engine code H9FA	Bosch EDC
Rotation (viewed from crankshaft pulley end)	Clockwise
Drive.	Twin chain via crankshaft and camshaft sprockets

Turbocharger

Type	Fixed or variable vane turbocharger, integral with exhaust manifold

Torque wrench settings

	Nm	lbf ft
Crankshaft position sensor bolt	7	5
Cylinder head temperature sensor	11	8
Fuel gauge sender unit retaining ring	65	48
Fuel injection pump mounting bolts	22	16
Fuel injection pump sprocket retaining bolts	33	24
Fuel injection pump support bracket bolts:		
DuraTorq-Di engines	22	16
DuraTorq-TDCi engines	33	24
Fuel injector locking sleeves	52	38
DuraTorq-Di engines	52	38
DuraTorq-TDCi engines	47	35
Fuel rail bolts	23	17
Fuel rail support bracket bolts	14	10
Fuel supply pipe union nuts	40	30
Fuel tank strap	35	26
Fuel temperature sensor	15	11
Knock sensor	20	15
Radiator support bracket lower centre bolt	15	11
Radiator support bracket side bolts	10	7

1 General information and precautions

General information

DuraTorq-Di engines

The fuel system consists of a side-mounted fuel tank, fuel filter, electronic fuel injection pump with pump control unit, injectors, fuel lines and hoses, fuel gauge sender unit mounted in the fuel tank, and powertrain control module (PCM).

Fuel is drawn from the tank and then passes through the fuel filter located in the engine compartment, where foreign matter and water are removed. The injection pump is driven from the crankshaft (via a twin-row chain which also drives the camshafts), and supplies fuel under high pressure to each injector in turn as it is needed.

The DuraTorq-Di engine features a full electronic engine management system. An extensive array of sensors are fitted, which supply information on many different parameters to the PCM.

Information on crankshaft position and engine speed is generated by a crankshaft position sensor. The inductive head of the sensor runs just above the engine flywheel, and scans a series of 36 protrusions on the flywheel periphery. As the crankshaft rotates, the sensor transmits a pulse every time a protrusion passes it. There is one missing protrusion in the flywheel periphery at a point corresponding to 50° BTDC. The PCM recognises the absence of a pulse from the crankshaft position sensor at this point to establish a reference mark for crankshaft position. Similarly, the time interval between absent pulses is used to determine engine speed.

On 2.0 litre engines, information on the quantity and temperature of the intake air is derived from the temperature and manifold absolute pressure (T-MAP) sensor. The T-MAP sensor is located on the intercooler, below the radiator. It measures the temperature and the pressure of the air in the intake system. The temperature and quantity of air has a direct bearing on the quantity of fuel to be injected for optimum efficiency. On 2.4 litre engines, information on the quantity and temperature of the intake air is obtained from two individual sensors. A manifold absolute pressure (MAP) sensor is mounted on the engine compartment bulkhead, and an intake air temperature (IAT) sensor is mounted on the EGR valve, attached to the inlet manifold.

The traditional coolant temperature sensor has been superseded by a cylinder head temperature (CHT) sensor. The new sensor is seated in a blind hole in the cylinder head, and measures the temperature of the metal directly. Information on engine temperature is critical for accurate fuelling calculations, and is also used to control the preheating system for cold starts.

The clutch pedal sensor informs the PCM whether the clutch is engaged or disengaged. When the clutch pedal is depressed, the quantity of fuel injected is momentarily reduced, to make gearchanging smoother.

The stop-light switch informs the PCM when the brakes are applied – when this signal is received, the PCM puts the engine into idle mode until a signal is received from the accelerator pedal position sensor.

Vehicle speed information is provided by the vehicle speed sensor, and is vital to the engine management calculations performed by the PCM.

The amount of fuel delivered is determined by the pump's internal quantity and timing solenoid valves, which are controlled by the pump control unit (PCU), mounted on top of the pump. The pump is internally equipped with a pulse ring fitted to the main rotor, and an angle sensor determines the pump rotor's position and speed, in much the same way as the crankshaft position sensor and engine flywheel, except that there are four gaps in the pump rotor 'teeth' – one for each cylinder. The pump control unit is supplied with information from the PCM, and from this is able to calculate the most appropriate values for injection timing and quantity (injection duration). The electronically-controlled pump internals enable these calculated values to be delivered with great accuracy, for improved efficiency and reduced emissions.

No accelerator cable is fitted on the DuraTorq engines – instead, a sensor located next to the accelerator pedal informs the PCM of the accelerator position, and this information is used to determine the most appropriate fuelling requirements from the injection pump. The engine idle speed is also controlled by the PCM, and cannot be adjusted. From the signals it receives from the various sensors, the PCM can control the idle speed very accurately, compensating automatically for additional engine loads or unfavourable ambient/engine temperatures.

Rigid pipes connect the pump to the four injectors. Each injector disperses the fuel evenly, and sprays fuel directly into the combustion chamber as its piston approaches TDC on the compression stroke. This system is known as direct injection. The pistons have a recess machined into their crowns, the shape of which has been calculated to improve 'swirl' (fuel/air mixing). Lubrication is provided by allowing a small quantity of fuel to leak back past the injector internal components. The leaked-back fuel is returned to the pump and then to the fuel tank.

Cold-starting performance is automatically controlled by the PCM. Under cold start conditions, the cylinder head temperature sensor informs the PCM of the engine temperature, this determines the preheat time. The glow plugs are located in the side of the cylinder head, one for each cylinder, and are electrically-heated. A warning light illuminates when the ignition is switched on, showing that the glow plugs are in operation. When the light goes out, preheating is complete and the engine can be started.

The fuel system has a built-in 'strategy' to prevent it from drawing in air should the vehicle run low on fuel. The PCM monitors the level of fuel in the tank, via the gauge sender unit. After switching on the low fuel level warning light, it will eventually induce a misfire as a further warning to the driver, and lower the engine's maximum speed until the engine stops.

The fuel system on diesel engines is normally very reliable. Provided that clean fuel is used and the specified maintenance is conscientiously carried out, no problems should be experienced. The injection pump and injectors may require overhaul after a high mileage has been covered, but this cannot be done on a DIY basis.

DuraTorq-TDCi engines

The fuel system consists of a side-mounted fuel tank, fuel gauge sender unit mounted in the fuel tank, fuel filter, high-pressure fuel injection pump, fuel rail, fuel pipes, injectors, injector driver module (early 2.0 litre engines), and powertrain control module (PCM).

Fuel is drawn from the tank via a transfer pump, built into and driven from the high-pressure pump, and it then passes through the fuel filter located in the engine compartment, where foreign matter and water are removed. The high-pressure injection pump is driven from the crankshaft via the twin-row timing chain which also drives the camshafts.

The pump supplies fuel at very high pressure to a common rail (fuel rail) supplying all four injectors, which are then opened as signalled by the PCM (in conjunction with the injector driver module on early 2.0 litre engines). On reaching the high-pressure pump, the fuel is pressurised according to demand, and accumulates in the fuel rail, which acts as a fuel reservoir. The pressure in the rail is accurately maintained using a pressure sensor in the end of the rail and the pump's metering valve, with fuel return being controlled according to fuel temperature. The PCM determines the exact timing and duration of the injection period according to engine operating conditions. The four fuel injectors operate sequentially according to the firing order of the cylinders.

There are four pipes from the fuel rail (one for each of the injectors), and one from the fuel pump to the fuel rail. Each injector disperses the fuel evenly, and sprays fuel directly into the combustion chamber as its piston approaches TDC on the compression stroke.

The DuraTorq TDCi engine is very much a 'state-of-the-art' unit, in that it features a full electronic engine management system. An extensive array of sensors are fitted, which supply information on many different parameters to the PCM.

In addition to the crankshaft position sensor, T-MAP sensor, IAT sensor, MAP sensor, CHT sensor, clutch pedal sensor, vehicle speed sensor, accelerator pedal position sensor, and stop-light switch, described previously, the following additional sensors are used on the TDCi engine.

The mass air flow (MAF) sensor is used to provide the PCM with information on the quantity (mass) of air entering the intake system. The MAF sensor is located in the air cleaner cover in the air outlet duct.

A camshaft sensor is located in the camshaft carrier adjacent to the inlet camshaft. The camshaft sensor provides information on camshaft position to enable the PCM to determine the injector sequence.

To enable the PCM to further refine injector duration according to engine loads, a knock sensor is fitted to the cylinder block to detect the onset of detonation (knock).

Cold-starting performance is automatically controlled by the PCM. Under cold start conditions, the cylinder head temperature (CHT) sensor informs the PCM on the engine temperature, this determines the preheat time. The glow plugs are located in the side of the cylinder head, one for each cylinder, and are electrically-heated. A warning light illuminates when the ignition is switched on, showing that the glow plugs are in operation. When the light goes out, preheating is complete and the engine can be started.

The fuel system has a built-in 'strategy' to prevent it from drawing in air should the vehicle run low on fuel. The PCM monitors the level of fuel in the tank, via the gauge sender unit. After switching on the low fuel level warning light, it will eventually induce a misfire as a further warning to the driver, and lower the engine's maximum speed until the engine stops.

The fuel system on common rail diesel engines is normally very reliable. Provided that clean fuel is used, that the specified maintenance is conscientiously carried out, and absolute cleanliness is observed during any maintenance or repair operation, no problems should be experienced. The injection pump and injectors may require overhaul after a high mileage has been covered, but this cannot be done on a DIY basis.

Precautions

⚠️ **Warning: It is necessary to take certain precautions when working on the fuel system components, particularly the high-pressure side of the system. Before carrying out any operations on the fuel system, refer to the precautions given in 'Safety first!' at the beginning of this manual, and to any additional warning notes at the start of the relevant Sections. On common rail systems, also refer to the additional information contained in Section 2.**

Caution: Do not operate the engine if any of air intake ducts are disconnected or the filter element is removed. Any debris entering the engine will cause severe damage to the turbocharger.

Caution: To prevent damage to the turbocharger, do not race the engine immediately after start-up, especially if it is cold. Allow it to idle smoothly to give the oil a few seconds to circulate around the turbocharger bearings. Always allow the engine to return to idle speed before switching it off – do not blip the throttle and switch off, as this will leave the turbo spinning without lubrication.

Caution: Observe the recommended intervals for oil and filter changing, and use a reputable oil of the specified quality. Neglect of oil changing, or use of inferior oil, can cause carbon formation on the turbo shaft, leading to subsequent failure.

2 Common rail diesel injection system – special information

Warnings and precautions

1 It is essential to observe strict precautions when working on the fuel system components, particularly the high-pressure side of the system. Before carrying out any operations on the fuel system, refer to the precautions given in Safety first! at the beginning of this manual, and to the following additional information.

- *Do not carry out any repair work on the high-pressure fuel system unless you are competent to do so, have all the necessary tools and equipment required, and are aware of the safety implications involved.*
- *Before starting any repair work on the fuel system, wait at least 30 seconds after switching off the engine to allow the fuel circuit to return to atmospheric pressure.*
- *Never work on the high-pressure fuel system with the engine running.*
- *Keep well clear of any possible source of fuel leakage, particularly when starting the engine after carrying out repair work. A leak in the system could cause an extremely high-pressure jet of fuel to escape, which could result in severe personal injury.*
- *Never place your hands or any part of your body near to a leak in the high-pressure fuel system.*
- *Do not use steam cleaning equipment or compressed air to clean the engine or any of the fuel system components.*

Repair procedures and general information

2 Strict cleanliness must be observed at all times when working on any part of the fuel system. This applies to the working area in general, the person doing the work, and the components being worked on.

3 Before working on the fuel system components, they must be thoroughly cleaned with a suitable degreasing fluid. Cleanliness is particularly important when working on the fuel system connections at the following components:

a) *Fuel filter.*
b) *Fuel injection pump.*
c) *Fuel rail.*
d) *Fuel injectors.*
e) *High-pressure fuel pipes.*

4 After disconnecting any fuel pipes or components, the open union or orifice must be immediately sealed to prevent the entry of dirt or foreign material. Plastic plugs and caps in various sizes are available in packs from motor factors and accessory outlets, and are particularly suitable for this application **(see illustration)**. Fingers cut from disposable rubber gloves should be used to protect components such as fuel pipes, fuel injectors and wiring connectors, and can be secured in place using elastic bands. Suitable gloves of this type are available at no cost from most petrol station forecourts.

5 Whenever any of the high-pressure fuel pipes are disconnected or removed, a new pipe(s) must be obtained for refitting.

6 The torque wrench settings given in the Specifications must be strictly observed when tightening component mountings and connections. This is particularly important when tightening the high-pressure fuel pipe unions.

3 Fuel system – priming and bleeding

Note 1: *Ford special tool 310-110A (hand-priming pump) or a suitable alternative will be required for this procedure.*

Note 2: *Be aware of the information contained in paragraph 9, before proceeding.*

Note 3: *Some early 2.4 litre vehicles with 120 PS engines, had an electric lift pump fitted to the fuel filter. The fuel filter on vehicles with an electric lift pump is primed after installation by turning the ignition key to position II and allowing the electric lift pump to operate for 20 seconds. The ignition key is then turned to position 0 and back to position II for a further 20 seconds.*

1 After disconnecting part of the fuel supply system or running out of fuel, it is necessary

2.4 Typical plastic plug and cap set for sealing disconnected fuel pipes and components

to prime the fuel system and bleed off any air which may have entered the system components.

2 The priming and bleeding operation is carried out by connecting a hand-priming pump (Ford special tool 310-110A) between the fuel supply pipe from the fuel tank and the fuel supply connection on the fuel filter. The priming pump consists of a hose with a rubber 'bulb' or squeezable part, contained in the hose assembly. The 'bulb' is squeezed to pump fuel from the tank to the filter and pump, and a one-way valve, incorporated in the unit, prevents the fuel from returning to the tank. This type of hand-priming pump is common to many makes of diesel engines and suitable alternatives to the Ford special tool are available from motor factors. To carry out the priming and bleeding operation, proceed as follows.

3 Disconnect the quick-release connector at the fuel supply pipe connection on the fuel filter **(see illustration)**.

4 Connect one end of the hand-priming pump to the fuel supply pipe, and connect the other end to the fuel filter. Be sure to follow the direction of flow arrow on the hand-priming pump to be sure it is connected the correct way round.

5 Squeeze the priming pump bulb until the fuel filter is full and the priming bulb becomes firm. Continue squeezing the priming bulb during engine cranking.

6 With the aid of an assistant, crank the engine on the starter motor for 10 seconds at a time, allowing the starter motor to

cool for 30 seconds between each starting attempt.

7 Once the engine starts, allow it to idle until it reaches normal operating temperature.

8 Once normal operating temperature has been reached, switch the engine off and disconnect the hand-priming pump. Reconnect the fuel supply pipe to the filter.

9 The above procedure is based on the Ford recommendations for priming and bleeding the fuel system. In practise, the common rail fuel system is notoriously difficult to bleed, and some problems may be encountered. If the fuel system components have been disconnected and removed according to the procedures described in this manual, the system should prime and bleed satisfactorily as described above. Be aware, however, that this might not always be the case. It has been known, in exceptional circumstances, that the only way to start common rail fuel injection engines, is to tow the vehicle behind another vehicle until it starts. If this proves to be the case, observe all the precautions described in 'Towing' at the start of this manual, and proceed accordingly.

4 Air cleaner assembly and air intake ducts – removal and refitting

2.0 litre engines

Air cleaner assembly

1 Release the hose clips and disconnect the air outlet duct at the air cleaner cover **(see illustration)**. Note that the hose clip may not be of the screw type, and will have to be separated by prising the crimped section with a small screwdriver. The clip can be re-used if care is taken, but it may be preferable to fit a screw-drive clip when refitting.

2 Where applicable, disconnect the wiring connector from the mass airflow (MAF) sensor **(see illustration)**.

3 Where fitted, disconnect the vacuum hose from the air cleaner cover **(see illustration)**.

4 Pull the water drain pipe down to release it from the water drain channel in the windscreen cowl panel **(see illustration)**.

5 On vehicles with air conditioning, undo the

3.3 Fuel supply pipe quick-release connector (arrowed) on the fuel filter

4.1 Release the hose clip and disconnect the air outlet duct at the air cleaner cover

4.2 Where applicable, disconnect the wiring connector from the mass airflow (MAF) sensor

4.3 Where fitted, disconnect the vacuum hose from the air cleaner cover

4.4 Pull the water drain pipe down to release it from the water drain channel

4.6a Undo the retaining bolt (arrowed) securing the air intake duct to the radiator grille opening panel

4.6b Detach the intake duct (arrowed) from the front of the air cleaner housing and remove the duct

4.7a Release the two clips securing the air cleaner cover to the air cleaner housing

4.7b Move the water drain pipe to one side, then lift the air cleaner cover up and manipulate it out from the engine compartment

retaining bolts and move the accumulator/dehydrator to one side.

6 Undo the retaining bolt securing the air intake duct to the radiator grille opening panel. Detach the intake duct from the front of the air cleaner housing and remove the duct **(see illustrations)**.

7 Release the two clips securing the air cleaner cover to the air cleaner housing. Move the water drain pipe to one side, then lift the air cleaner cover up at the front, disengage it at the rear and manipulate it out from the engine compartment **(see illustrations)**.

8 Lift the air cleaner body up to release it from the retaining grommets and remove it from the engine compartment **(see illustration)**.

9 Refitting is the reverse of the removal procedure. Ensure that the air cleaner pegs seat fully in their rubber grommets.

Intake air resonator and air ducts

10 Extract the retaining peg on the side of the oil filler neck, then rotate the filler neck clockwise and remove it from the camshaft cover **(see illustrations)**.

11 Where applicable, undo the two bolts and release the oil level dipstick tube from the intake air resonator.

12 Refer to paragraph 1 and disconnect the air outlet duct at the air cleaner cover. Similarly disconnect the turbocharger intake air duct at the resonator **(see illustration)**.

13 Undo the two intake air resonator retaining bolts and lift the resonator and air outlet duct off the engine **(see illustration)**.

14 Release the hose clips at the turbocharger and camshaft cover, disconnect the intake duct from the turbocharger and camshaft cover and remove the intake duct.

4.8 Lift the air cleaner body up to release it from the retaining grommets, and remove it from the engine compartment

4.10a Extract the retaining peg on the side of the oil filler neck . . .

4.10b . . . then rotate the filler neck clockwise and remove it from the camshaft cover

4.12 Disconnect the turbocharger intake air duct at the resonator

4.13 Intake air resonator retaining bolt locations (arrowed)

4.17 Release the hose clip and disconnect the air outlet duct at the air cleaner cover

4.22a Undo the three screws (arrowed) . . .

4.22b . . . and detach the vacuum solenoid mounting bracket from the side of the air cleaner housing

15 The remaining ducts between the turbocharger and intercooler, and between the intercooler and inlet manifold can be removed after releasing the hose clips and, where applicable, detaching the ducts from the support brackets.

16 Refitting is the reverse of the removal procedure.

2.4 litre engines

Air cleaner assembly

17 Release the hose clip and disconnect the air outlet duct at the air cleaner cover **(see illustration)**. Note that the hose clip may not be of the screw type, and will have to be separated by prising the crimped section with a small screwdriver. The clip can be re-used if care is taken, but it may be preferable to fit a screw-drive clip when refitting.

18 Where applicable, disconnect the wiring

5.1 Accelerator pedal position sensor wiring connector (arrowed)

from the mass airflow (MAF) sensor **(see illustration 4.2)**.

19 Where fitted, disconnect the vacuum hose from the air cleaner cover **(see illustration 4.3)**.

20 Pull the water drain pipe down to release it from the water drain channel **(see illustration 4.4)**.

21 On vehicles with air conditioning, undo the retaining bolts and move the accumulator/ dehydrator to one side.

22 Undo the three screws and detach the vacuum solenoid mounting bracket from the side of the air cleaner housing **(see illustrations)**.

23 Undo the retaining bolt securing the air intake duct to the radiator grille opening panel. Detach the intake duct from the front of the air cleaner housing and remove the duct **(see illustrations 4.6a and 4.6b)**.

24 Release the two clips securing the air

6.4 Using a brake hose clamp or similar tool, clamp the fuel tank filler hose (arrowed)

cleaner cover to the air cleaner housing. Move the water drain pipe to one side, then lift the air cleaner cover up at the front, disengage it at the rear and manipulate it out from the engine compartment **(see illustrations 4.7a and 4.7b)**.

25 Lift the air cleaner body up to release it from the retaining grommets and remove it from the engine compartment **(see illustration 4.8)**.

26 Refitting is the reverse of the removal procedure. Ensure that the air cleaner pegs seat fully in their rubber grommets.

Air ducts

27 The air ducts between the air cleaner and turbocharger, between the turbocharger and intercooler, and between the intercooler and inlet manifold can be removed after releasing the hose clips and, where applicable, detaching the ducts from the support brackets.

28 Refitting is the reverse of the removal procedure.

5 Accelerator pedal – removal and refitting

Removal

1 Disconnect the wiring connector from the accelerator pedal position sensor, then unscrew the nuts and remove the accelerator pedal assembly **(see illustration)**.

Refitting

2 Refit in the reverse order of removal. On completion, check the action of the pedal with the engine running.

6 Fuel tank – removal and refitting

Note: *Refer to the warning note in Section 1 before proceeding.*

Removal

1 Before removing the fuel tank, all fuel must be drained from the tank. Since a fuel tank drain plug is not provided, it is therefore preferable to carry out the removal operation when the tank is nearly empty. The remaining fuel can then be syphoned or hand-pumped from the tank.

2 Move the driver's seat fully forward, open the battery box cover and disconnect the battery negative terminal (refer to *Disconnecting the battery* in the Reference Chapter).

3 Firmly apply the handbrake, then jack up the front of the vehicle and support it securely on axle stands (see *Jacking and vehicle support*).

4 Using a brake hose clamp or similar tool, clamp the fuel tank filler hose **(see illustration)**.

5 Slacken the retaining clips and disconnect the fuel tank filler hose and the ventilation hose from the fuel tank filler pipe.

6 Support the weight of the fuel tank on a jack with interposed block of wood.

7 Undo the fuel tank front support strap inner and outer retaining bolts and remove the strap **(see illustration)**.

8 Undo the fuel tank rear support strap inner and outer retaining bolts and remove the strap **(see illustration)**.

9 Taking care not to strain the fuel lines and wiring, partially lower the tank until access can be gained to the connections on the top of the tank.

10 Detach the fuel tank ventilation hose from the tank.

11 Disconnect the fuel lines at the quick-release connectors on the fuel gauge sender unit. Release the fuel lines from the clip on the top of the tank.

12 Trace the wiring back from the fuel gauge sender unit and disconnect the wiring at the connector.

13 Lower the tank to the ground and remove it from under the vehicle.

14 If the tank contains sediment or water, it may cleaned out with two or three rinses of clean fuel. Remove the fuel gauge sender unit as described in Section 7. Shake the tank vigorously, and change the fuel as necessary to remove all contamination from the tank.

15 Any repairs to the fuel tank should be carried out by a professional. Do not under any circumstances attempt any form of DIY repair to a fuel tank.

Refitting

16 Refitting is the reverse of the removal procedure, noting the following points:

a) *When raising the tank back into position, take care to ensure that none of the fuel lines become trapped between the tank and vehicle body. Refit the retaining straps and tighten the bolts to the specified torque.*

b) *Ensure all pipes and hoses are correctly routed and all hose unions are securely joined.*

c) *On completion, refill the tank with a small amount of fuel, and check for signs of leakage prior to taking the vehicle out on the road.*

7 Fuel gauge sender unit – removal and refitting

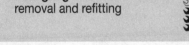

Note 1: *Refer to the warning note in Section 1 before proceeding.*
Note 2: *Ford special tool 23-055 (or a suitable alternative) will be required to unscrew the sender unit retaining ring.*

Removal

1 Remove the fuel tank as described in Section 6.

2 Using the special tool, unscrew and remove the sender unit retaining ring **(see illustration)**.

3 Lift the sender unit out of the fuel tank,

6.7 Fuel tank front support strap inner retaining bolt (arrowed)

taking care not to damage the float or bend the float arm. Remove and discard the O-ring seal, a new seal will be required for refitting.

Refitting

4 Refitting is the reverse of the removal procedure, using a new O-ring seal, and tightening the sender unit retaining ring to the specified torque.

8 Diesel injection system – checking

Note: *Refer to the warning note in Section 1 before proceeding.*

1 If a fault appears in the diesel injection system, first ensure that all the system wiring connectors are securely connected and free of corrosion. Then ensure that the fault is not due to poor maintenance; ie, check that the air cleaner filter element is clean, the cylinder compression pressures are correct, the fuel filter has been drained (or changed) and the engine breather hoses are clear and undamaged, referring to Chapter 1 or the relevant Part of Chapter 2.

2 If these checks fail to reveal the cause of the problem, the vehicle should be taken to a suitably-equipped Ford dealer for testing. A diagnostic connector is incorporated in the engine management system wiring harness, into which dedicated electronic test equipment can be plugged (the connector is located under facia on the driver's side). The test equipment is capable of 'interrogating'

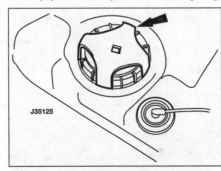

7.2 Ford special tool (arrowed) used to release the fuel gauge sender unit retaining ring

6.8 Fuel tank rear support strap inner retaining bolt (arrowed)

the powertrain control module (PCM) electronically and accessing its internal fault log (reading fault codes).

3 Fault codes can only be extracted from the PCM using a dedicated fault code reader. A Ford dealer will obviously have such a reader, but they are also available from other suppliers. It is unlikely to be cost-effective for the private owner to purchase a fault code reader, but a well-equipped local garage or auto-electrical specialist will have one.

4 Using this equipment, faults can be pinpointed quickly and simply, even if their occurrence is intermittent. Testing all the system components individually in an attempt to locate the fault by elimination is a time-consuming operation that is unlikely to be fruitful (particularly if the fault occurs dynamically), and carries a high risk of damage to the PCM's internal components.

5 Experienced home mechanics equipped with a diesel tachometer or other diagnostic equipment may be able to check the engine idle speed; if found to be out of specification, the vehicle must be taken to a suitably-equipped Ford dealer for assessment. The engine idle speed is not manually adjustable; incorrect test results indicate the need for maintenance (possibly, injector cleaning or recalibration) or a fault within the injection system.

6 If excessive smoking or knocking is evident, it may be due to a problem with the fuel injectors. Proprietary treatments are available which can be added to the fuel, in order to clean the injectors. Injectors deteriorate with prolonged use, however, and it is reasonable to expect them to need reconditioning or renewal after 60 000 miles or so. Accurate testing, overhaul and calibration of the injectors must be left to a specialist.

9 Injection system electronic components (2.0 litre engines) – removal and refitting

DuraTorq-Di engines

Crankshaft position sensor

Note: *Ford stipulate that a new crankshaft position sensor must be fitted if the fitted position of the original sensor is disturbed.*

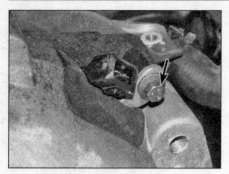

9.4a Unscrew the mounting bolt (arrowed) . . .

9.4b . . . and withdraw the crankshaft position sensor from the mounting bracket

9.10 Cylinder head temperature sensor location (arrowed)

1 Move the driver's seat fully forward, open the battery box cover and disconnect the battery negative terminal (refer to *Disconnecting the battery* in the Reference Chapter).

2 The sensor is located in the top of the bellhousing to the rear.

3 Firmly apply the handbrake, then jack up the front of the vehicle and support it securely on axle stands (see *Jacking and vehicle support*).

4 Disconnect the wiring connector, then unscrew the mounting bolt and withdraw the sensor from the mounting bracket **(see illustrations)**.

5 Look down through the centre of the crankshaft position sensor mounting bracket and make sure that one of the trigger teeth on the flywheel is directly below the centre of the mounting bracket. If necessary turn the engine crankshaft, by means of the crankshaft pulley, to align the trigger tooth.

6 Insert the new sensor into the mounting bracket and push it down until the pip on the underside of the sensor rests on the flywheel trigger tooth. Refit the retaining bolt and tighten it securely.

7 Reconnect the sensor wiring connector.

8 Lower the vehicle to the ground and reconnect the battery.

Cylinder head temperature sensor

Note: *Ford stipulate that a new cylinder head temperature sensor must be fitted if the original sensor is disturbed.*

9 Move the driver's seat fully forward, open the battery box cover and disconnect the battery negative terminal (refer to *Disconnecting the battery* in the Reference Chapter).

10 The switch is screwed into the left-hand (flywheel) end of the cylinder head, behind the power steering pump pulley **(see illustration)**.

11 Refer to Section 4 if necessary and disconnect the air duct between the intake air resonator and turbocharger.

12 Remove the plastic cover over the power steering pump pulley.

13 Trace the wiring from the sensor, and disconnect it at the connector on top of the engine.

14 The sensor can now be unscrewed and removed. Due to the length of the wiring it may prove difficult to gain access with a ring spanner. If necessary, cut the sensor wiring.

15 Refitting is a reversal of removal, using a new sensor tightened securely.

Vehicle speed sensor

16 Refer to Chapter 7A.

Temperature and manifold absolute pressure sensor

17 Move the driver's seat fully forward, open the battery box cover and disconnect the battery negative terminal (refer to *Disconnecting the battery* in the Reference Chapter).

18 Firmly apply the handbrake, then jack up the front of the vehicle and support it securely on axle stands (see *Jacking and vehicle support*).

19 Disconnect the wiring connector from the sensor which is located on the right-hand side of the intercooler **(see illustration)**.

20 Unscrew and remove the two retaining screws, and withdraw the sensor from the intercooler.

21 Refitting is a reversal of removal.

EGR valve

22 Refer to Chapter 4B.

Clutch pedal position switch

23 Move the driver's seat fully forward, open the battery box cover and disconnect the battery negative terminal (refer to *Disconnecting the battery* in the Reference Chapter).

24 Move the driver's seat fully rearward, then reach up and disconnect the wiring from the clutch pedal position switch at the top of the pedal bracket **(see illustration)**.

25 Turn the switch anti-clockwise and remove it from the pedal mounting bracket **(see illustration)**.

26 To refit the switch, hold the clutch pedal in the raised position and insert the clutch switch into the hole in the pedal mounting bracket.

27 Push the switch down to depress the plunger, then turn the switch clockwise to lock it in position.

28 Reconnect the switch wiring connector, then reconnect the battery.

Brake stop-light switch

29 Move the driver's seat fully forward, open the battery box cover and disconnect the battery negative terminal (refer to *Disconnecting the battery* in the Reference Chapter).

30 Move the driver's seat fully rearward, then reach up and disconnect the wiring from the brake stop-light switch at the top of the pedal bracket **(see illustration)**.

9.19 Temperature and manifold absolute pressure sensor location (arrowed) on the side of the intercooler

9.24 Disconnect the wiring connector from the clutch pedal position switch . . .

9.25 . . . then turn the switch anti-clockwise and remove it from the pedal mounting bracket

9.30 Disconnect the wiring connector from the brake stop-light switch at the top of the pedal bracket

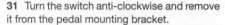

9.38a Drill out the rivets (arrowed) . . .

9.38b . . . and remove the PCM security shield from the engine compartment bulkhead

31 Turn the switch anti-clockwise and remove it from the pedal mounting bracket.

32 To refit the switch, hold the brake pedal in the raised position and insert the stop-light switch into the hole in the pedal mounting bracket. Push the switch down to depress the plunger, then turn the switch clockwise to lock it in position.

33 Reconnect the switch wiring connector, then reconnect the battery.

Accelerator pedal position sensor

34 The accelerator pedal sensor is integral with the pedal assembly, which is removed as described in Section 5.

Injection pump control unit

35 The pump control unit is integral with the injection pump, and cannot be separated from it. If a new injection pump is fitted, the PCU must be electronically 'matched' to the

powertrain control module (PCM), otherwise the pump will not function correctly (or even at all, if the immobiliser function is not correctly set up) – this is a task for a Ford dealer, as specialised electronic equipment is required.

Powertrain Control Module

Caution: The PCM is fragile. Take care not to drop it or subject it to any other kind of impact, and do not subject it to extremes of temperature, or allow it to get wet. Do not touch the PCM terminals as there is a chance that static electricity may damage the internal electronic components.

Note: *If renewing the powertrain control module, note that it must be reprogrammed for the specific model by a Ford dealer using Ford diagnostic equipment. Failure to do so will result in the PCM assuming its 'limited operating strategy' (LOS) settings giving poor performance and economy.*

36 Move the driver's seat fully forward, open the battery box cover and disconnect the battery negative terminal (refer to *Disconnecting the battery* in the Reference Chapter).

37 Remove the windscreen cowl panel as described in Chapter 11.

38 Drill out the rivets and remove the PCM security shield from the engine compartment bulkhead **(see illustration)**.

39 Undo the retaining bolt and disconnect the PCM multiplug **(see illustrations)**.

40 Undo the two PCM retaining plate nuts, and remove the retaining plate **(see illustrations)**.

41 Remove the intermediate plate, then withdraw the PCM from its location **(see illustrations)**.

42 Refitting is a reversal of removal, bearing in mind the following points:

a) *Ensure that the intermediate plate is refitted with the direction arrow pointing upward* **(see illustration)**.

9.39a Undo the retaining bolt (arrowed) . . .

9.39b . . . and disconnect the PCM multiplug

9.40a Undo the two PCM retaining plate nuts (arrowed) . . .

9.40b . . . and remove the retaining plate

9.41a Remove the intermediate plate . . .

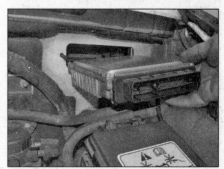

9.41b . . . then withdraw the PCM from its location

9.42 Ensure that the intermediate plate is refitted with the direction arrow pointing upward

b) Use new rivets to secure the security shield in position.

c) Refit the windscreen cowl panel as described in Chapter 11.

DuraTorq-TDCi (common rail) engines

Crankshaft position sensor

43 Proceed as described in paragraphs 1 to 8.

Cylinder head temperature sensor

44 Proceed as described in paragraphs 9 to 15, noting that the sensor is screwed into the rear of the cylinder head adjacent to the engine compartment bulkhead, and references to removal of the plastic cover over the power steering pump pulley can be ignored.

Vehicle speed sensor

45 Refer to Chapter 7A.

Temperature and manifold absolute pressure sensor

46 Proceed as described in paragraphs 17 to 21.

EGR valve

47 Refer to Chapter 4B.

Clutch pedal position switch

48 Proceed as described in paragraphs 23 to 28.

Brake stop-light switch

49 Proceed as described in paragraphs 29 to 33.

Accelerator pedal position sensor

50 Proceed as described in paragraph 34.

Powertrain Control Module

51 Proceed as described in paragraphs 36 to 42.

Mass airflow sensor

52 Move the driver's seat fully forward, open the battery box cover and disconnect the battery negative terminal (refer to *Disconnecting the battery* in the Reference Chapter).

53 Remove the air cleaner cover from the air cleaner housing as described in Section 4. Unscrew and remove the sensor mounting bolts and withdraw the sensor from the air cleaner cover (see illustration).

54 Refitting is the reverse of the removal pro-

9.53 Mass airflow sensor mounting bolts (arrowed)

cedure. Ensure that the sensor and air cleaner cover are seated correctly and securely fastened, so that there are no air leaks.

Injector driver module

Note: *On later models, the injector driver module has been integrated into the PCM and a separate unit is not fitted.*

55 Remove the complete facia as described in Chapter 11.

56 Detach the injector driver module wiring harness from the support bracket.

57 Undo the retaining nuts and withdraw the injector driver module from the bulkhead.

58 Drill out the rivets and remove the security shield from the module.

59 Release the locking clamps and disconnect the three wiring harness connectors from the module.

60 Drill out the rivets and remove the module from the mounting bracket.

61 Refitting is a reversal of removal, using new rivets to secure the module and the security shield.

Fuel temperature sensor

Note: *Refer to the warning note in Section 1 before proceeding.*

62 Move the driver's seat fully forward, open the battery box cover and disconnect the battery negative terminal (refer to *Disconnecting the battery* in the Reference Chapter).

63 Remove the intake air resonator and air ducts as described in Section 4.

64 Cover the alternator with a plastic bag or similar, to protect it from any fuel which may be lost when the sensor is removed.

9.80 Disconnect the wiring connector from the camshaft sensor

65 Clean the area around the sensor using a brush and suitable solvent – it is vital that no dirt enters the pump.

66 Disconnect the wiring connector from the fuel temperature sensor, then unscrew and withdraw the sensor from the pump. If the sensor will be removed for some time, cover over or plug the opening in the pump to stop dirt getting in.

67 Fit a new O-ring to the sensor, and lubricate it lightly with a general-purpose spray lubricant (such as WD-40).

68 Screw the sensor into position, and tighten it to the specified torque. Reconnect the wiring connector, then refit the intake air resonator and air ducts as described in Section 4.

69 Reconnect the battery on completion.

Fuel metering valve

Note: *Refer to the warning note in Section 1 before proceeding.*

70 Move the driver's seat fully forward, open the battery box cover and disconnect the battery negative terminal (refer to *Disconnecting the battery* in the Reference Chapter).

71 Remove the intake air resonator and air ducts as described in Section 4.

72 Cover the alternator with a plastic bag or similar, to protect it from any fuel which may be lost when the metering valve is removed.

73 Clean the area around the metering valve using a brush and suitable solvent – it is vital that no dirt enters the pump.

74 Disconnect the wiring connector from the fuel temperature sensor and from the metering valve, then remove the two mounting screws and withdraw the valve from the pump. Recover the valve's O-ring seal – a new one must be used when refitting. If the valve will be removed for some time, cover over or plug the valve opening in the pump, to stop dirt getting in.

75 Fit a new O-ring to the valve, and lubricate it lightly with a general-purpose spray lubricant (such as WD-40).

76 Fit the valve in position, and insert the bolts. Tighten them evenly and gently until the valve is secure. Reconnect the wiring connectors, then refit the intake air resonator and air ducts as described in Section 4.

77 Reconnect the battery on completion.

Camshaft sensor

78 Move the driver's seat fully forward, open the battery box cover and disconnect the battery negative terminal (refer to *Disconnecting the battery* in the Reference Chapter).

79 Remove the intake air resonator and air ducts as described in Section 4.

80 Disconnect the wiring connector from the camshaft sensor, located just below the fuel rail (see illustration).

81 Undo the sensor retaining bolt and remove the sensor from the camshaft carrier.

82 Fit a new O-ring to the sensor, and lubricate it lightly with a general-purpose spray lubricant (such as WD-40).

83 Refit the sensor, and tighten the retaining bolt securely. Reconnect the wiring connector, then refit the intake air resonator and air ducts as described in Section 4.

84 Reconnect the battery on completion.

Knock sensor

85 Move the driver's seat fully forward, open the battery box cover and disconnect the battery negative terminal (refer to *Disconnecting the battery* in the Reference Chapter).

86 Remove the inlet manifold as described in Chapter 2A.

87 Trace the knock sensor wiring back to the connector located behind the fuel injection pump **(see illustration)**. Disconnect the wiring and release the connector.

88 Note and record the fitted position of the knock sensor, then undo the retaining bolt **(see illustration)**. Remove the sensor from the cylinder block.

89 Refitting is a reversal of removal, bearing in mind the following points:

a) *Thoroughly clean the mating faces of the cylinder block and knock sensor.*
b) *Ensure the sensor is fitted in the same position as noted during removal.*
c) *Tighten the sensor retaining bolt to the specified torque.*
d) *Refit the inlet manifold as described in Chapter 2A.*

---

10 Injection system electronic components (2.4 litre engines) – removal and refitting

---

DuraTorq-Di engines

Crankshaft position sensor

Note: *Ford stipulate that a new crankshaft position sensor must be fitted if the fitted position of the original sensor is disturbed.*

1 Move the driver's seat fully forward, open the battery box cover and disconnect the battery negative terminal (refer to *Disconnecting the battery* in the Reference Chapter).

2 The sensor is located in the top of the bellhousing to the rear.

3 Firmly apply the handbrake, then jack up the front of the vehicle and support it securely on axle stands (see *Jacking and vehicle support*).

9.87 Knock sensor wiring connector (arrowed) located behind the fuel injection pump

4 Lift off the heat shield fitted over the top of the sensor **(see illustration)**.

5 Disconnect the wiring connector, then unscrew the mounting bolt and withdraw the sensor from the mounting bracket **(see illustrations 9.4a and 9.4b)**.

6 Look down through the centre of the crankshaft position sensor mounting bracket and make sure that one of the trigger teeth on the flywheel is directly below the centre of the mounting bracket. If necessary turn the engine crankshaft, by means of the crankshaft pulley, to align the trigger tooth.

7 Insert the new sensor into the mounting bracket and push it down until the pip on the underside of the sensor rests on the flywheel trigger tooth. Refit the retaining bolt and tighten it securely.

8 Reconnect the sensor wiring connector.

9 Lower the vehicle to the ground and reconnect the battery.

Cylinder head temperature sensor

Note: *Ford stipulate that a new cylinder head temperature sensor must be fitted if the original sensor is disturbed.*

10 Move the driver's seat fully forward, open the battery box cover and disconnect the battery negative terminal (refer to *Disconnecting the battery* in the Reference Chapter).

11 The sensor is screwed into a blind hole at the rear of the cylinder head.

12 Remove the inlet manifold as described in Chapter 2B.

13 Trace the wiring from the sensor, and

9.88 Note and record the fitted position of the knock sensor, then undo the retaining bolt (arrowed)

disconnect it at the connector on top of the engine.

14 The sensor can now be unscrewed and removed **(see illustration)**. Due to the length of the wiring it may prove difficult to gain access with a ring spanner. If necessary, cut the sensor wiring.

15 Refitting is a reversal of removal, using a new sensor tightened securely.

Vehicle speed sensor

16 Refer to Chapter 7A.

Intake air temperature sensor

17 Move the driver's seat fully forward, open the battery box cover and disconnect the battery negative terminal (refer to *Disconnecting the battery* in the Reference Chapter).

18 The sensor is screwed into the side of the EGR valve which is attached to the inlet manifold.

19 Undo the two bolts securing the auxiliary drivebelt cover to the top of the engine. The centre bolt may be located under a plastic cover on certain models. There may also be an additional bolt at the left-hand side of the cover; if so undo this bolt also. Release the wiring harness and/or hoses at the rear of the cover and lift the cover off the engine **(see illustrations)**.

20 Disconnect the wiring connector at the intake air temperature sensor.

21 Unscrew the sensor and remove it from the EGR valve.

22 Refitting is a reversal of removal, ensuring the sensor is tightened securely.

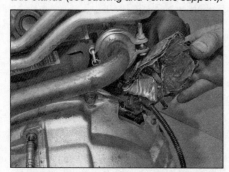

10.4 Lift off the heat shield fitted over the top of the crankshaft position sensor

10.14 Unscrew and remove the cylinder head temperature sensor from the rear of the cylinder head

10.19a Undo the auxiliary drivebelt cover right-hand retaining bolt (arrowed) . . .

10.19b . . . and centre retaining bolt (arrowed) . . .

EGR valve

23 Refer to Chapter 4B.

Clutch pedal position switch

24 Proceed as described in Section 9, paragraphs 23 to 28.

Brake stop-light switch

25 Proceed as described in Section 9, paragraphs 29 to 33.

Accelerator pedal position sensor

26 The accelerator pedal sensor is integral with the pedal assembly, which is removed as described in Section 5.

Powertrain Control Module

27 Proceed as described in Section 9, paragraphs 36 to 42.

Manifold absolute pressure sensor

28 Move the driver's seat fully forward, open the battery box cover and disconnect the battery negative terminal (refer to *Disconnecting the battery* in the Reference Chapter).
29 The sensor is located on a bracket attached to the bulkhead at the rear of the engine compartment.
30 Disconnect the wiring connector and vacuum hose from the sensor.
31 Undo the retaining screws and remove the sensor from the mounting bracket.
32 Refitting is a reversal of removal.

DuraTorq-TDCi (common rail) engines

Crankshaft position sensor

33 Proceed as described in paragraphs 1 to 9.

Cylinder head temperature sensor

34 Proceed as described in paragraphs 10 to 15.

Vehicle speed sensor

35 Refer to Chapter 7A.

Temperature and manifold absolute pressure sensor

36 Move the driver's seat fully forward, open the battery box cover and disconnect the battery negative terminal (refer to *Disconnecting the battery* in the Reference Chapter).
37 Firmly apply the handbrake, then jack up the front of the vehicle and support it securely

10.19c . . . then release the wiring harness and/or hoses and lift the cover off the engine

on axle stands (see *Jacking and vehicle support*).
38 Disconnect the wiring connector from the sensor which is located in the air duct on the left-hand side of the intercooler **(see illustration)**.
39 Slacken the retaining clip and disconnect the intake air duct from the sensor.
40 Slacken the remaining retaining clip and withdraw the sensor from the intercooler duct.
41 Refitting is a reversal of removal.

EGR valve

42 Refer to Chapter 4B.

Clutch pedal position switch

43 Proceed as described in Section 9, paragraphs 23 to 28.

Brake stop-light switch

44 Proceed as described in Section 9, paragraphs 29 to 33.

Accelerator pedal position sensor

45 The accelerator pedal sensor is integral with the pedal assembly, which is removed as described in Section 5.

Powertrain Control Module

46 Proceed as described in Section 9, paragraphs 36 to 42.

Mass airflow sensor

47 Proceed as described in Section 9, paragraphs 52 to 54.

Fuel temperature sensor

Note: *Refer to the warning note in Section 1 before proceeding.*

10.38 Temperature and manifold absolute pressure sensor wiring connector (arrowed)

48 Move the driver's seat fully forward, open the battery box cover and disconnect the battery negative terminal (refer to *Disconnecting the battery* in the Reference Chapter).
49 Remove the inlet manifold as described in Chapter 2B.
50 Clean the area around the sensor using a brush and suitable solvent – it is vital that no dirt enters the pump.
51 Disconnect the wiring connector from the fuel temperature sensor, then unscrew and withdraw the sensor from the fuel injection pump. If the sensor will be removed for some time, cover over or plug the opening in the pump, to stop dirt getting in.
52 Fit a new O-ring to the sensor, and lubricate it lightly with a general-purpose spray lubricant (such as WD-40).
53 Screw the sensor into position, and tighten it to the specified torque. Reconnect the wiring connector.
54 Refit the inlet manifold as described in Chapter 2B.
55 Reconnect the battery on completion.

Fuel metering valve

Note: *Refer to the warning note in Section 1 before proceeding.*
56 Move the driver's seat fully forward, open the battery box cover and disconnect the battery negative terminal (refer to *Disconnecting the battery* in the Reference Chapter).
57 Remove the inlet manifold as described in Chapter 2B.
58 Clean the area around the metering valve using a brush and suitable solvent – it is vital that no dirt enters the pump.
59 Disconnect the wiring connector from the fuel temperature sensor and from the metering valve, then remove the two mounting screws and withdraw the valve from the pump. Recover the valve's O-ring seal – a new one must be used when refitting. If the valve will be removed for some time, cover over or plug the valve opening in the pump, to stop dirt getting in.
60 Fit a new O-ring to the valve, and lubricate it lightly with a general-purpose spray lubricant (such as WD-40).
61 Fit the valve in position, and insert the bolts. Tighten them evenly and gently until the valve is secure. Reconnect the wiring connectors.
62 Refit the inlet manifold as described in Chapter 2B.
63 Reconnect the battery on completion.

Camshaft sensor

64 Move the driver's seat fully forward, open the battery box cover and disconnect the battery negative terminal (refer to *Disconnecting the battery* in the Reference Chapter).
65 Undo the two bolts securing the auxiliary drivebelt cover to the top of the engine. The centre bolt may be located under a plastic cover on certain models. There may also be an additional bolt at the left-hand side of the

cover; if so undo this bolt also. Release the wiring harness and/or hoses at the rear of the cover and lift the cover off the engine (see illustrations 10.19a to 10.19c).

66 Disconnect the wiring connector from the camshaft sensor, located just below the fuel rail (see illustration 9.80).

67 Undo the sensor retaining bolt and remove the sensor from the camshaft carrier.

68 Fit a new O-ring to the sensor, and lubricate it lightly with a general-purpose spray lubricant (such as WD-40).

69 Refit the sensor, and tighten the retaining bolt securely. Reconnect the wiring connector, then refit the auxiliary drivebelt cover.

70 Reconnect the battery on completion.

Knock sensor

71 Move the driver's seat fully forward, open the battery box cover and disconnect the battery negative terminal (refer to *Disconnecting the battery* in the Reference Chapter).

72 Remove the inlet manifold as described in Chapter 2B.

73 Trace the knock sensor wiring back to the connector located behind the fuel injection pump (see illustration 9.87). Disconnect the wiring and release the connector.

74 Note and record the fitted position of the knock sensor, then undo the retaining bolt (see illustration 9.88). Remove the sensor from the cylinder block.

75 Refitting is a reversal of removal, bearing in mind the following points:

a) *Thoroughly clean the mating faces of the cylinder block and knock sensor.*

b) *Ensure the sensor is fitted in the same position as noted during removal.*

c) *Tighten the sensor retaining bolt to the specified torque.*

d) *Refit the inlet manifold as described in Chapter 2B.*

11 Fuel injection pump (2.0 litre engines) – removal and refitting

Caution: Be careful not to allow dirt into the injection pump or injector pipes during this procedure.

DuraTorq-Di engines

Note 1: *If a new injection pump is fitted, there is a possibility that the engine may not run properly (or even at all) until both the powertrain control module (PCM) and the new pump control unit have been electronically 'configured' using Ford diagnostic equipment. In particular, the immobiliser may not function correctly, leading to the engine not starting.*

Note 2: *Ford special tools will be required for the removal and refitting procedure of the fuel injection pump – see text.*

Removal

1 Move the driver's seat fully forward, open the battery box cover and disconnect the battery

11.3 Using a home-made tool to remove the access cover from the timing chain cover

negative terminal (refer to *Disconnecting the battery* in the Reference Chapter).

2 Remove the inlet manifold as described in Chapter 2A.

3 Using the Ford special tool (303-679), remove the access cover from the timing chain cover. A suitable alternative tool was made up using a three-legged puller and three bolts (see illustration). Note that a new access cover will be required for refitting.

4 Remove the crankshaft position sensor as described in Section 9.

5 Firmly apply the handbrake, then jack up the front of the vehicle and support it securely on axle stands (see *Jacking and vehicle support*).

6 Remove the auxiliary drivebelt cover (two fasteners) from under the wheel arch.

7 Turn the engine crankshaft, by means of the crankshaft pulley, until the timing hole in the fuel injection pump sprocket is in approximately the 12 o'clock position.

8 Refer to the procedures contained in Chapter 2A, Section 3, and set the crankshaft at the 50° BTDC position, then insert the setting tool to lock the crankshaft in this position.

9 Using a spanner to hold the injectors in position, slacken the fuel supply pipe unions. Note the position of the fuel supply pipes before removal.

10 Remove the starter motor as described in Chapter 5 to gain access to the fuel supply pipe unions on the fuel injection pump.

11 Slacken the fuel supply pipe unions at the fuel injection pump, then disconnect the fuel supply pipes from the pump.

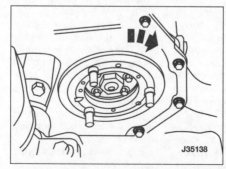

11.17 Special tool used to lock the pump sprocket in place

11.16 Disconnect the fuel lines at the quick-release connectors (arrowed) on the timing chain cover

12 Detach the engine wiring harness from the fuel supply line support bracket.

13 Undo the retaining nuts and remove the fuel supply line support bracket.

14 Remove the fuel supply pipes and discard them. New supply pipes will be required on refitting. Fit blanking caps to the injectors and fuel pump unions to prevent dirt ingress.

15 Slide out the locking tang and disconnect the wiring connector from the fuel injection pump.

16 Disconnect the fuel lines at the quick-release connectors on the timing chain cover (see illustration).

17 Fit Ford special tool 303-1151 to the timing chain cover, and turn it clockwise to lock the sprocket to the timing chain cover (see illustration). Make sure this tool does not slip as the pump mounting bolts and sprocket bolts are loosened.

18 Using Ford tool 310-083 (which appears to be a slim box spanner), loosen the three pump mounting bolts, accessible through the holes in the special tool and fuel pump sprocket (see illustration). **Note:** *The bolts cannot be completely removed.*

19 Undo the four sprocket retaining bolts, making sure the tool stays in place to lock the sprocket to the timing chain cover.

20 Unbolt and remove the injection pump rear support bracket from the cylinder block.

21 Remove the fuel injection pump from the cylinder block, discard the gasket, a new one will be required on refitting.

22 Unbolt and remove the injection pump rear support bracket from the pump.

11.18 Access holes (arrowed) to fuel pump retaining bolts (timing chain cover removed for clarity)

Refitting

23 Ensure that the engine timing setting is still set at 50° BTDC, using the information in Chapter 2A, Section 3, if necessary.

24 Refit the injection pump rear support bracket to the cylinder block, but do not tighten the retaining bolts at this stage.

25 Using a 6 mm pin (drill bit), align the hole in the pump drive pulley with the cut-out provided in the pump rotor mounting face. With the cut-out aligned, remove the 6 mm pin.

26 Offer the pump into position, with a new gasket **(see illustration)**, and fit the support bracket mounting bolts, do not tighten them at this stage.

27 Install the four sprocket retaining bolts, do not tighten them at this stage.

28 Gain access to the fuel pump retaining bolts, through the holes provided in the special tool and fuel pump sprocket, and tighten them to their specified torque setting.

29 With the fuel pump in position remove the Ford special tool (303-681) used to lock the fuel injection pump sprocket in place.

30 With the hole in the fuel pump sprocket aligned with the cut-out in the pump mounting face **(see illustration 11.26)**, insert the 6 mm pin (drill bit).

31 The four sprocket retaining bolts can now be tightened to their specified torque setting.

32 Tighten the bolts securing the rear support bracket to the pump and to the cylinder block to their specified torque settings.

33 Remove the 6 mm pin (drill bit) from the fuel injection pump sprocket.

34 Using a suitable paint, mark the position of the crankshaft pulley in relation to the timing chain cover, then remove the special tool from the crankshaft position sensor hole.

35 Rotate the engine in the normal direction of rotation, turning it two complete revolutions.

 Warning: Do not turn the engine while any of the special tools are in the fitted position.

36 The engine timing setting should still be set at 50° BTDC, using the information in Chapter 2A, Section 3, if necessary.

37 Insert the Ford special tool (303-675) back into the crankshaft position sensor hole to locate in the flywheel.

11.26 Fitting a new gasket to the fuel injection pump – note the cut-out (arrowed)

38 The hole in the fuel pump sprocket should be aligned with the cut-out in the pump mounting face, insert the 6 mm pin (drill bit).

39 With the timing re-aligned, remove the special tool from the crankshaft position sensor hole and refit the crankshaft position sensor as described in Section 9.

40 Remove the 6 mm pin (drill bit) from the fuel injection pump sprocket.

41 Using the Ford special tool (303-679) or the home-made tool, fit the new access cover to the timing chain cover.

42 Reconnect the wiring connector to the pump control unit, and secure it in position with the locking catch.

43 Reconnect the fuel lines at the quick-release connectors on the timing cover.

44 Fit the new fuel supply pipes to injectors No 1 and No 2. Screw on the fuel supply pipe union nuts at the injectors and fuel injection pump. Tighten the union nuts at the injection pump to their specified torque setting, but only tighten the union nuts at the injectors finger tight at this stage.

45 Fit the new fuel supply pipes to injectors No 3 and No 4. Screw on the fuel supply pipe union nuts at the injectors and fuel injection pump. Tighten the union nuts at the injection pump to their specified torque setting, but only tighten the union nuts at the injectors finger tight at this stage.

46 Refit the starter motor as described in Chapter 5.

47 Fit a new fuel filter as described in Chapter 1.

48 Refer to the procedures contained in Section 3 and connect a hand-priming pump (Ford special tool 310-110A or a suitable equivalent) between the fuel supply pipe from the fuel tank, and the fuel supply connection on the fuel filter.

49 Refer to the previously-made paint marks on the crankshaft pulley and timing chain cover and make sure that the crankshaft is still set at the 50° BTDC position.

50 Squeeze the hand-priming pump bulb until the fuel filter is full and fuel can be seen escaping from one of the fuel injector fuel supply pipe unions. **Note:** *Only one fuel supply pipe union will show signs of fuel escaping.*

51 Once escaping fuel is visible, hold the injector with a spanner to prevent it turning, and tighten the fuel supply pipe union to its specified torque setting.

52 Using the paint marks as a reference, turn the crankshaft, in the normal direction of rotation 180°. Repeat the procedures contained in paragraphs 50 and 51, to bleed the next injector. Continue this procedure to bleed the remaining two injectors, turning the crankshaft 180° each time.

53 Refit the fuel supply line support bracket and securely tighten the two outer retaining nuts, followed by the centre nut.

54 Reattach the engine wiring harness to the fuel supply line support bracket.

55 Refit the inlet manifold as described in Chapter 2A.

56 Refit the auxiliary drivebelt cover under the wheel arch, then lower the vehicle to the ground.

57 Reconnect the battery negative terminal.

58 With the aid of an assistant, crank the engine on the starter motor for 10 seconds at a time, allowing the starter motor to cool for 30 seconds between each starting attempt. Continue squeezing the hand-priming pump bulb during engine cranking.

59 Once the engine starts, allow it to idle until it reaches normal operating temperature. Note that it may take a while before a stable idle speed is achieved, as the powertrain control module (PCM) may have to relearn some of the 'adaptive' values. As the engine warms-up, check for signs of leakage from the fuel unions.

60 Once normal operating temperature has been reached, switch the engine off and disconnect the hand-priming pump. Reconnect the fuel supply pipe to the filter. Take the vehicle for a short journey (of at least 5 miles) to allow the PCM to complete its 'learning' process.

DuraTorq-TDCi (common rail) engines

Note 1: *Refer to the warnings contained in Sections 1 and 2 before proceeding.*

Note 2: *Ford special tools will be required for the removal and refitting procedure of the fuel injection pump – see text.*

Removal

61 Move the driver's seat fully forward, open the battery box cover and disconnect the battery negative terminal (refer to *Disconnecting the battery* in the Reference Chapter).

62 Remove the intake air resonator and air ducts as described in Section 4. On early models, undo the two bolts and remove the engine upper cover.

63 Refit the engine oil filler cap to the camshaft cover.

64 Using the Ford special tool (303-679), remove the access cover from the timing chain cover. A suitable alternative tool was made up using a three-legged puller and three bolts **(see illustration 11.3)**. Note that a new access cover will be required for refitting.

65 Firmly apply the handbrake, then jack up the front of the vehicle and support it securely on axle stands (see *Jacking and vehicle support*).

66 Remove the auxiliary drivebelt cover (two fasteners) from under the wheel arch.

67 Turn the engine crankshaft, by means of the crankshaft pulley, until the timing hole in the fuel injection pump sprocket is in approximately the 1 o'clock position.

68 Release the clips and disconnect the intake air duct from the EGR valve and inlet manifold.

69 Undo the retaining nut and disconnect the glow plug supply cable from the terminal stud.

70 Remove the inlet manifold as described in Chapter 2A.

71 Disconnect the wiring connectors from the fuel temperature sensor and from the metering valve on the rear of the fuel injection pump **(see illustration)**. Suitably cover the connectors on the pump to prevent the entry of dirt and cleaning solvent.

72 At the rear of the injection pump, undo the nut and release the pump-to-fuel rail fuel supply pipe clamp bracket.

73 Before proceeding further, use a brush and suitable solvent to clean the area around the pump's fuel supply pipe union and surrounding areas. It is essential that no dirt enters the pump. Allow time for any solvent used to dry.

74 Carefully loosen the fuel supply pipe union at the fuel pump and the one to the fuel rail. Ford recommend (if possible) that the tool used to loosen these unions is fitted at the **top** of the union, to reduce the chance of damaging the union as it is loosened.

75 Once the unions are loose, wrap clean absorbent tissue or rag around them briefly, to soak away any dirt which may otherwise enter. If available, Ford recommend using a vacuum line to suck any dirt away from the opening union – do not use an airline, as this may blast dirt inwards, rather than cleaning it away.

76 Remove the fuel supply pipe, and discard it – a new one should be used when refitting. Plug or suitably cover the open connections.

77 Release the quick-release fitting and disconnect the fuel return hose at the fuel injection pump. Plug or suitably cover the open connections. Detach the return hose from the retaining clip.

78 Disconnect the fuel supply and return pipes at the quick-release connectors on the timing chain cover. Plug or suitably cover the open connections. Slacken the nut, undo the bolt and slide the fuel supply and return pipe support bracket upwards from its location. Position the pipes and bracket to one side.

79 Fit Ford special tool 303-1151 to the timing chain cover, and turn it clockwise to lock the sprocket to the timing chain cover **(see illustration 11.17)**. Make sure this tool does not slip as the pump mounting bolts and sprocket bolts are loosened.

80 Using Ford tool 310-083 (which appears to be a slim box spanner), loosen the three pump mounting bolts, accessible through the holes in the special tool and fuel pump sprocket **(see illustration 11.18)**. **Note:** *The bolts cannot be completely removed.*

81 Undo the four fuel pump sprocket retaining bolts, making sure the tool stays in place to lock the sprocket to the timing chain cover.

82 Unbolt the injection pump rear support bracket from the cylinder block **(see illustration)**.

83 Remove the fuel injection pump from the cylinder block. Recover and discard the gasket – a new one will be required on refitting.

84 If a new pump is being fitted, unbolt and remove the support bracket and shield from the old unit, and transfer them to the new one

11.71 Disconnect the wiring connectors (arrowed) from the fuel temperature sensor and from the metering valve

– tighten the support bracket bolts by hand only at this stage. If the original pump is to be refitted, slacken the support bracket retaining bolts.

Refitting

85 Offer the pump into position, with a new gasket. Apply a little thread-locking fluid to the threads of the support bracket bolts, then fit them hand-tight only at this stage.

86 Install the four sprocket retaining bolts, but tighten them hand-tight only at this stage.

87 Gain access to the fuel pump retaining bolts, through the holes provided in the special tool and fuel pump sprocket and tighten them to their specified torque setting.

88 With the fuel pump in position remove the Ford special tool (303-1151) used to lock the fuel injection pump sprocket in place.

89 Tighten the fuel injection pump rear support bracket-to-cylinder block retaining bolts to their specified torque setting. Now tighten the support bracket-to-pump retaining bolts to their specified torque setting.

90 Reconnect the fuel return hose to the fuel injection pump quick-release fitting. Attach the return hose to the retaining clip.

91 Place the fuel supply and return pipe support bracket back in position, then refit and tighten the retaining nut and bolt. Reconnect the pipes at the quick-release connectors on the timing chain cover.

92 Place the new fuel supply pipe in position and screw on the union nuts at the fuel injection pump and fuel rail. Tighten the unions by hand until the pipe clamp bracket has been

11.82 Unbolt the rear support bracket (arrowed) from the cylinder block

refitted and tightened. When refitting, do not bend or strain the pipe, and make sure it is kept clean. Also, do not allow the union nuts to hit the olive-shaped ends of the pipe during fitting, as this may result in damage.

93 Refit the fuel pump-to-fuel rail fuel supply pipe clamp bracket and tighten the nut securely.

94 Tighten the fuel supply pipe unions at the fuel injection pump and fuel rail to their specified torque setting.

95 Reconnect the wiring connectors to the fuel temperature sensor and metering valve on the rear of the pump.

96 Using the Ford special tool (303-679) or the home-made tool, fit the new access cover to the timing chain cover.

97 Refit the inlet manifold as described in Chapter 2A.

98 Reconnect the glow plug supply cable to the terminal stud and secure with the retaining nut.

99 Reconnect the intake air duct to the EGR valve and inlet manifold.

100 Refit the auxiliary drivebelt cover under the wheel arch, then lower the vehicle to the ground.

101 Remove the engine oil filler cap from the camshaft cover, and where applicable, refit the engine upper cover.

102 Refit the intake air resonator and air ducts as described in Section 4.

103 Fit a new fuel filter as described in Chapter 1.

104 Reconnect the battery negative terminal, then prime and bleed the fuel system as described in Section 3.

105 Once the engine starts, allow it to idle until it reaches normal operating temperature. As the engine warms-up, check for signs of leakage from the fuel unions.

12 Fuel injection pump (2.4 litre engines) – removal and refitting

Caution: Be careful not to allow dirt into the injection pump or injector pipes during this procedure.

DuraTorq-Di engines

Note 1: *If a new injection pump is fitted, there is a possibility that the engine may not run properly (or even at all) until both the powertrain control module (PCM) and the new pump control unit have been electronically 'configured' using Ford diagnostic equipment. In particular, the immobiliser may not function correctly, leading to the engine not starting.*

Note 2: *Ford special tools will be required for the removal and refitting procedure of the fuel injection pump – see text.*

Removal

1 Move the driver's seat fully forward, open the battery box cover and disconnect the battery negative terminal (refer to *Disconnecting the battery* in the Reference Chapter).

2 Undo the two bolts securing the auxiliary drivebelt cover to the top of the engine. The centre bolt may be located under a plastic cover on certain models. There may also be an additional bolt at the left-hand side of the cover; if so undo this bolt also. Release the wiring harness and/or hoses at the rear of the cover and lift the cover off the engine **(see illustrations 10.19a to 10.19c)**.

3 Firmly apply the handbrake, then jack up the front of the vehicle and support it securely on axle stands (see *Jacking and vehicle support*).

4 Remove the auxiliary drivebelt as described in Chapter 1.

5 Remove the exhaust gas recirculation (EGR) valve as described in Chapter 4B.

6 Disconnect the cylinder head temperature sensor wiring at the connector located on the camshaft cover.

7 Remove the engine oil filler pipe from the camshaft cover.

8 Remove the inlet manifold as described in Chapter 2B.

9 Using a spanner to hold the injectors in position, slacken the fuel supply pipe unions. Note the position of the fuel supply pipes before removal.

10 Remove the starter motor as described in Chapter 5 to gain access to the fuel supply pipe unions on the fuel injection pump.

11 Slacken the fuel supply pipe unions at the fuel injection pump, then disconnect the fuel supply pipes from the pump.

12 Where fitted, undo the EGR cooler to EGR valve pipe retaining bolts. Remove the EGR valve pipe. Note that a new pipe will be required for refitting.

13 Undo the retaining nuts and bolt and remove the fuel supply line support bracket.

14 Remove the fuel supply pipes and discard them. New supply pipes will be required on refitting. Fit blanking caps to the injectors and fuel pump unions to prevent dirt ingress.

15 Disconnect the fuel return line at the quick-release connector.

16 Using the Ford special tool (303-679), remove the access cover from the timing chain cover. A suitable alternative tool was made up using a three-legged puller and three bolts **(see illustration 11.3)**. Note that a new access cover will be required for refitting.

17 Turn the engine crankshaft, by means of the crankshaft pulley, until the timing hole in the fuel injection pump sprocket is in approximately the 12 o'clock position.

18 Remove the crankshaft position sensor as described in Section 10.

19 Refer to the procedures contained in Chapter 2B, Section 3, and set the crankshaft at the 50° BTDC position, then insert the setting tool to lock the crankshaft in this position.

20 Fit Ford special tool 303-1151 to the timing chain cover, and turn it clockwise to lock the sprocket to the timing chain cover **(see illustration 11.17)**. Make sure this tool does not slip as the pump mounting bolts and sprocket bolts are loosened.

21 Using Ford tool 310-083 (which appears to be a slim box spanner), loosen the three pump mounting bolts, accessible through the holes in the special tool and fuel pump sprocket **(see illustration 11.18)**. Note: *The bolts cannot be completely removed.*

22 Undo the four sprocket retaining bolts, making sure the tool stays in place to lock the sprocket to the timing chain cover.

23 Slide out the locking tang and disconnect the wiring connector from the fuel injection pump.

24 Release the quick-release connectors and disconnect the fuel supply and return pipes at the fuel injection pump,

25 Unbolt and remove the injection pump rear support bracket from the cylinder block.

26 Remove the fuel injection pump from the cylinder block, discard the gasket, a new one will be required on refitting.

27 Unbolt and remove the injection pump rear support bracket from the pump.

Refitting

28 Ensure that the engine timing setting is still set at 50° BTDC, using the information in Chapter 2B, Section 3, if necessary.

29 Refit the injection pump rear support bracket to the cylinder block, but do not tighten the retaining bolts at this stage.

30 Using a 6 mm pin (drill bit), align the hole in the pump drive pulley with the cut-out provided in the pump rotor mounting face. With the cut-out aligned, remove the 6 mm pin.

31 Offer the pump into position, with a new gasket **(see illustration 11.26)**, and fit the support bracket mounting bolts, do not tighten them at this stage.

32 Install the four sprocket retaining bolts, do not tighten them at this stage.

33 Gain access to the fuel pump retaining bolts, through the holes provided in the special tool and fuel pump sprocket, and tighten them to their specified torque setting.

34 With the fuel pump in position remove the Ford special tool (303-1151) used to lock the fuel injection pump sprocket in place.

35 With the hole in the fuel pump sprocket aligned with the cut-out in the pump mounting face **(see illustration 11.26)**, insert the 6 mm pin (drill bit).

36 The four sprocket retaining bolts can now be tightened to their specified torque setting.

37 Tighten the bolts securing the rear support bracket to the pump and to the cylinder block to their specified torque settings.

38 Attach the quick-release connectors to the fuel supply and return pipes at the fuel injection pump,

39 Remove the 6 mm pin (drill bit) from the fuel injection pump sprocket.

40 Using a suitable paint, mark the position of the crankshaft pulley in relation to the timing chain cover, then remove the special tool from the crankshaft position sensor hole.

41 Rotate the engine in the normal direction of rotation, turning it two complete revolutions.

Warning: Do not turn the engine while any of the special tools are in the fitted position.

42 The engine timing setting should still be set at 50° BTDC, using the information in Chapter 2B, Section 3, if necessary.

43 Insert the Ford special tool (303-675) back into the crankshaft position sensor hole to locate in the flywheel.

44 The hole in the fuel pump sprocket should be aligned with the cut-out in the pump mounting face, insert the 6 mm pin (drill bit).

45 With the timing re-aligned, remove the special tool from the crankshaft position sensor hole and refit the crankshaft position sensor as described in Section 10.

46 Remove the 6 mm pin (drill bit) from the fuel injection pump sprocket.

47 Using the Ford special tool (303-679) or the home-made tool, fit the new access cover to the timing chain cover.

48 Reconnect the wiring connector to the pump control unit, and secure it in position with the locking catch.

49 Reconnect the fuel return line at the quick-release connector.

50 Fit the new fuel supply pipes to injectors No 1 and No 2. Screw on the fuel supply pipe union nuts at the injectors and fuel injection pump. Tighten the union nuts at the injection pump to their specified torque setting, but only tighten the union nuts at the injectors finger tight at this stage.

51 Fit the new fuel supply pipes to injectors No 3 and No 4. Screw on the fuel supply pipe union nuts at the injectors and fuel injection pump. Tighten the union nuts at the injection pump to their specified torque setting, but only tighten the union nuts at the injectors finger tight at this stage.

52 Refit the starter motor as described in Chapter 5.

53 Where applicable, fit the new EGR valve pipe and refit the retaining bolts, finger tight at this stage.

54 Refit the inlet manifold as described in Chapter 2B.

55 Refit the engine oil filler pipe to the camshaft cover.

56 Reconnect the cylinder head temperature sensor wiring at the connector located on the camshaft cover.

57 Refit the auxiliary drivebelt as described in Chapter 1.

58 Refit the exhaust gas recirculation (EGR) valve as described in Chapter 4B.

59 Securely tighten the EGR valve pipe retaining bolts.

60 Fit a new fuel filter as described in Chapter 1.

61 Refer to the procedures contained in Section 3 and connect a hand-priming pump (Ford special tool 310-110A or a suitable equivalent) between the fuel supply pipe from the fuel tank, and the fuel supply connection on the fuel filter.

62 Refer to the previously-made paint marks on the crankshaft pulley and timing chain cover and make sure that the crankshaft is still set at the 50° BTDC position.

63 Squeeze the hand-priming pump bulb until the fuel filter is full and fuel can be seen escaping from one of the fuel injector fuel supply pipe unions. **Note:** *Only one fuel supply pipe union will show signs of fuel escaping.*

64 Once escaping fuel is visible, hold the injector with a spanner to prevent it turning, and tighten the fuel supply pipe union to its specified torque setting.

65 Using the paint marks as a reference, turn the crankshaft, in the normal direction of rotation 180°. Repeat the procedures contained in paragraphs 63 and 64, to bleed the next injector. Continue this procedure to bleed the remaining two injectors, turning the crankshaft 180° each time.

66 Slacken the bolt securing the two halves of the fuel supply pipe support bracket just sufficiently to allow the two halves to slide relative to each other. Attach the support bracket to the fuel pipes and screw on the two retaining nuts finger tight only at this stage.

67 Refit the fuel supply pipe support bracket retaining bolt, but only tighten the bolt finger tight at this stage.

68 Securely tighten the two nuts securing the support bracket to the fuel pipes, then tighten the bracket retaining bolt. With the bracket in position, securely tighten the bolt securing the two halves of the bracket.

69 Refit the inlet manifold as described in Chapter 2B.

70 Refit the auxiliary drivebelt cover under the wheel arch, then lower the vehicle to the ground.

71 Reconnect the battery negative terminal.

72 With the aid of an assistant, crank the engine on the starter motor for 10 seconds at a time, allowing the starter motor to cool for 30 seconds between each starting attempt. Continue squeezing the hand-priming pump bulb during engine cranking.

73 Once the engine starts, allow it to idle until it reaches normal operating temperature. Note that it may take a while before a stable idle speed is achieved, as the powertrain control module (PCM) may have to relearn some of the 'adaptive' values. As the engine warms-up, check for signs of leakage from the fuel unions.

74 Once normal operating temperature has been reached, switch the engine off and disconnect the hand-priming pump. Reconnect the fuel supply pipe to the filter. Take the vehicle for a short journey (of at least 5 miles) to allow the PCM to complete its 'learning' process.

DuraTorq-TDCi (common rail) engines

Note 1: *Refer to the warnings contained in Sections 1 and 2 before proceeding.*
Note 2: *Ford special tools will be required for the removal and refitting procedure of the fuel injection pump – see text.*

Removal

75 Remove the windscreen cowl panel as described in Chapter 11.

76 Move the driver's seat fully forward, open the battery box cover and disconnect the battery negative terminal (refer to *Disconnecting the battery* in the Reference Chapter).

77 Undo the two bolts securing the auxiliary drivebelt cover to the top of the engine. The centre bolt may be located under a plastic cover on certain models. There may also be an additional bolt at the left-hand side of the cover; if so undo this bolt also. Release the wiring harness and/or hoses at the rear of the cover and lift the cover off the engine **(see illustrations 10.19a to 10.19c)**.

78 Remove the auxiliary drivebelt as described in Chapter 1.

79 Remove the exhaust gas recirculation (EGR) valve as described in Chapter 4B.

80 Using the Ford special tool (303-679), remove the access cover from the timing chain cover. A suitable alternative tool was made up using a three-legged puller and three bolts **(see illustration 11.3)**. Note that a new access cover will be required for refitting.

81 Turn the engine crankshaft, by means of the crankshaft pulley, until the timing hole in the fuel injection pump sprocket is in approximately the 1 o'clock position.

82 Fit Ford special tool 303-1151 to the timing chain cover, and turn it clockwise to lock the sprocket to the timing chain cover **(see illustration 11.17)**. Make sure this tool does not slip as the pump mounting bolts and sprocket bolts are loosened.

83 Using Ford tool 310-083 (which appears to be a slim box spanner), loosen the three pump mounting bolts, accessible through the holes in the special tool and fuel pump sprocket **(see illustration 11.18)**. **Note:** *The bolts cannot be completely removed.*

84 Undo the four fuel pump sprocket retaining bolts, making sure the tool stays in place to lock the sprocket to the timing chain cover.

85 Detach the camshaft position sensor wiring harness from the retaining clip on the inlet manifold.

86 Remove the inlet manifold as described in Chapter 2B.

87 Disconnect the wiring connectors from the fuel temperature sensor and from the metering valve on the rear of the fuel injection pump **(see illustration 11.71)**. Suitably cover the connectors on the pump to prevent the entry of dirt and cleaning solvent.

88 Before proceeding further, use a brush and suitable solvent to clean the area around the pump's fuel supply pipe union and surrounding areas. It is essential that no dirt enters the pump. Allow time for any solvent used to dry.

89 Disconnect the quick-release connectors and disconnect the two fuel return hoses and the fuel supply hose from the fuel injection pump. Plug or suitably cover the open connections – dirt must not be allowed to

12.90 Undo the nut (arrowed) and release the pump-to-fuel rail fuel supply pipe clamp bracket

enter the pump. Noting how they are routed, unclip the hoses and move them aside.

90 At the rear of the fuel injection pump, undo the nut and release the pump-to-fuel rail fuel supply pipe clamp bracket **(see illustration)**.

91 Carefully loosen the fuel supply pipe union at the fuel pump and the one to the fuel rail. Ford recommend (if possible) that the tool used to loosen these unions is fitted at the **top** of the union, to reduce the chance of damaging the union as it is loosened.

92 Once the unions are loose, wrap clean absorbent tissue or rag around them briefly, to soak away any dirt which may otherwise enter. If available, Ford recommend using a vacuum line to suck any dirt away from the opening union – do not use an airline, as this may blast dirt inwards, rather than cleaning it away.

93 Remove the fuel supply pipe, and discard it – a new one should be used when refitting. Plug or suitably cover the open connections.

94 Detach the knock sensor wiring connector from the fuel injection pump support bracket **(see illustration)**.

95 Undo the four bolts securing the fuel injection pump support bracket to the pump and cylinder block and remove the bracket **(see illustration)**.

96 Remove the fuel injection pump from the cylinder block. Recover and discard the gasket – a new one will be required on refitting.

Refitting

97 Offer the pump into position, with a new gasket. Apply a little thread-locking fluid to

12.94 Detach the knock sensor wiring connector (arrowed) from the pump support bracket

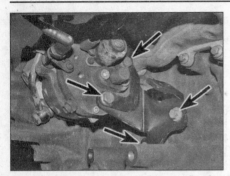

12.95 Undo the four bolts (arrowed) and remove the pump support bracket

the threads of the support bracket bolts, then fit them hand-tight only at this stage.

98 Install the four sprocket retaining bolts, but tighten them hand-tight only at this stage.

99 Gain access to the fuel pump retaining bolts, through the holes provided in the special tool and fuel pump sprocket and tighten them to their specified torque setting.

100 With the fuel pump in position remove the Ford special tool (303-1151) used to lock the fuel injection pump sprocket in place.

101 Tighten the fuel injection pump rear support bracket-to-cylinder block retaining bolts to their specified torque setting. Now tighten the support bracket-to-pump retaining bolts to their specified torque setting.

102 Reattach the knock sensor electrical connector to the fuel injection pump support bracket.

103 Using the Ford special tool (303-679) or the home-made tool, fit the new access cover to the timing chain cover.

104 Place the new fuel supply pipe in position and screw on the union nuts at the fuel injection pump and fuel rail. Tighten the unions by hand until the pipe clamp bracket has been refitted and tightened. When refitting, do not bend or strain the pipe, and make sure it is kept clean. Also, do not allow the union nuts to hit the olive-shaped ends of the pipe during fitting, as this may result in damage.

105 Refit the fuel pump-to-fuel rail fuel supply pipe clamp bracket and tighten the nut securely.

106 Tighten the fuel supply pipe unions at the fuel injection pump and fuel rail to their specified torque setting.

107 Reconnect all the disturbed fuel return hoses and the fuel supply hose, routed as noted prior to removal.

108 Reconnect the wiring connectors to the fuel temperature sensor and metering valve on the rear of the pump.

109 Refit the inlet manifold as described in Chapter 2B.

110 Attach the camshaft position sensor wiring harness to the retaining clip on the inlet manifold.

111 Refit the exhaust gas recirculation (EGR) valve as described in Chapter 4B.

112 Refit the auxiliary drivebelt as described in Chapter 1, then refit the auxiliary drivebelt cover.

113 Reconnect the battery negative terminal, then refer to Chapter 11 and refit the windscreen cowl panel.

114 Fit a new fuel filter as described in Chapter 1, then prime and bleed the fuel system as described in Section 3.

115 Once the engine starts, allow it to idle until it reaches normal operating temperature. As the engine warms-up, check for signs of leakage from the fuel unions.

---

13 Fuel injectors –
removal, testing and refitting

> **Warning: Exercise extreme caution when working on the fuel injectors. Never expose the hands or any part of the body to injector spray, as the high working pressure can cause the fuel to penetrate the skin, with possibly fatal results. You are strongly advised to have any work which involves testing the injectors under pressure carried out by a dealer or fuel injection specialist.**
> **Caution: Be careful not to allow dirt into the injection system during this procedure.**
> **Note 1:** *Ford special tools will be required for the refitting procedure of the fuel injectors – see text.*
> **Note 2:** *If new injectors are being fitted on common rail engines, there is a possibility that the engine may not run properly (or even at all) until the powertrain control module (PCM) has been electronically 'configured' to recognise the new injector codes, using Ford diagnostic equipment.*

Removal

1 Move the driver's seat fully forward, open the battery box cover and disconnect the battery negative terminal (refer to *Disconnecting the battery* in the Reference Chapter).

2 Thoroughly clean the area around the injectors and the injection pipe unions.

3 Remove the camshaft cover as described in Chapter 2A or 2B.

4 Slacken the fuel injector locking sleeves until they are all the way off, then remove the fuel injectors from the cylinder head **(see illustration)**. Note: *The injectors may be tight, carefully work them free until they can be withdrawn.*

5 Recover the sealing washers and O-rings from each injector **(see illustration)**, and discard them – new washers/O-rings must be used on reassembly.

6 Suitably cap the injector fuel pipe union connection and the injector base to protect against dirt ingress and damage.

7 On common rail injection engines, it is advisable to mount the injectors in a suitable stand, the right way up. This will help to prevent difficulties when priming and bleeding after refitting **(see illustration)**.

Testing

8 On DuraTorq-Di engines, testing of the injectors requires a special high-pressure test rig, and is best left to a professional. If the skin is exposed to spray from the injectors, the pressure is high enough for diesel fuel to penetrate the skin, with potentially fatal results. Defective injectors should be renewed or professionally repaired. DIY repair is not a practical proposition.

9 On DuraTorq-TDCi (common rail) engines, no effective repairs are possible on the injectors, and if confirmed to be defective, they must be renewed.

Refitting

Note: *If new injectors are being fitted on common rail engines, record the injector identification code stamped on the side of the injector body prior to fitting.*

10 Commence refitting by inserting new washers to the injector bores and fitting O-ring seals to the injectors.

11 Insert the injectors, using the Ford Special

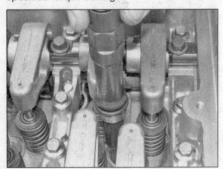

13.4 Slacken the locking sleeve and remove the fuel injectors

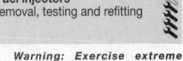
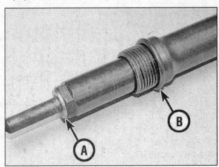

13.5 Recover the sealing washers (A) and O-rings (B) from each injector

13.7 It is advisable to mount the injectors the right way up in a suitable stand after removal

tool (303-711) to align the injectors in the cylinder head **(see illustration)**.

12 With the injectors held in position with the special tool, tighten the locking sleeve to the specified torque setting, using Ford special socket (303-677).

13 Refit the camshaft cover (Chapter 2A or 2B).

14 Check the position of the injectors using the Ford Special tool (303-711) when refitting the fuel pipes.

15 On completion, reconnect the battery negative terminal, then prime and bleed the fuel system as described in Section 3.

16 On common rail engines, have the injector codes programmed into the powertrain control module (PCM) using Ford diagnostic equipment.

14 Fuel rail (common rail engines) – removal and refitting

Note: *Refer to the warnings contained in Sections 1 and 2 before proceeding.*

2.0 litre engines

Removal

1 Move the driver's seat fully forward, open the battery box cover and disconnect the battery negative terminal (refer to *Disconnecting the battery* in the Reference Chapter).

2 Refer to Section 4 and remove the intake air resonator and air ducts, then remove the engine upper cover (where fitted).

3 Undo the retaining nut and disconnect the glow plug supply cable from the terminal stud.

4 Disconnect the wiring connector from the fuel pressure sensor on the end of the fuel rail.

5 Remove the inlet manifold as described in Chapter 2A.

6 Disconnect the wiring connectors from the fuel temperature sensor and from the metering valve on the rear of the fuel injection pump. Suitably cover the connectors on the pump to prevent the entry of dirt and cleaning solvent.

7 Before proceeding further, use a brush and suitable solvent to clean the area around the fuel pipe unions on the injectors and fuel rail. It is essential that no dirt enters the system. Allow time for any solvent used to dry.

8 At the rear of the injection pump, undo

the nut and release the pump-to-fuel rail fuel supply pipe clamp bracket.

9 Carefully loosen the fuel supply pipe union at the fuel pump and the one to the fuel rail. Ford recommend (if possible) that the tool used to loosen these unions is fitted at the **top** of the union, to reduce the chance of damaging the union as it is loosened.

10 Once the unions are loose, wrap clean absorbent tissue or rag around them briefly, to soak away any dirt which may otherwise enter. If available, Ford recommend using a vacuum line to suck any dirt away from the opening union – do not use an airline, as this may blast dirt inwards, rather than cleaning it away.

11 Remove the fuel supply pipe, and discard it – a new one must be used when refitting **(see illustration)**. Plug or suitably cover the open connections.

12 Using a spanner to hold the injectors and prevent them turning, slacken the fuel pipe union at each injector **(see illustration)**.

13 Slacken the four injector fuel pipe unions at the fuel rail **(see illustration)**.

14 Once the unions are loose, wrap clean absorbent tissue or rag around them briefly, to soak away any dirt which may otherwise enter. If available, Ford recommend using a vacuum line to suck any dirt away from the opening union – do not use an airline, as this may blast dirt inwards, rather than cleaning it away.

15 With all the unions slackened, the fuel pipes can now be completely disconnected and removed. Fit blanking plugs to the injectors and fuel rail.

16 Discard the fuel pipes – new ones must be used when refitting.

13.11 Using the Ford special tool to align the injectors in the cylinder head

17 Remove a total of three fuel rail mounting bolts, then remove two further bolts at each end from the rail mounting brackets. Lift off the fuel rail.

Refitting

18 Offer the fuel rail into position, then fit the mounting and support bracket bolts, hand-tight only.

19 Fit new fuel pipes to the fuel rail, injectors and fuel pump, leaving the union nuts hand-tight only at this stage. Do not bend or strain the pipes, and make sure they are kept clean. Also, do not allow the union nuts to hit the olive-shaped ends of the pipes during fitting, as this may result in damage.

20 Tighten the four fuel rail support bracket bolts to the specified torque, then tighten the three fuel rail mounting bolts.

21 With all the fuel injection pipes in place, fully tighten the union nuts to the specified torque **(see illustrations)**.

14.11 Disconnect the fuel supply pipe from the fuel rail

14.12 Hold the injector with one spanner, while slackening the pipe union with another

14.13 Slacken the four injector fuel pipe unions at the fuel rail

14.21a Tighten the fuel pipe unions at the fuel injectors . . .

14.21b . . . and fuel rail to the specified torque

Caution: The injectors are not to turn from their position in the cylinder head – a special tool is used to align the injectors (see Section 13)

22 Further refitting is a reversal of removal. On completion, prime and bleed the fuel system as described in Section 3.

2.4 litre engines

Removal

23 Move the driver's seat fully forward, open the battery box cover and disconnect the battery negative terminal (refer to *Disconnecting the battery* in the Reference Chapter).

24 Undo the two bolts securing the auxiliary drivebelt cover to the top of the engine. The centre bolt may be located under a plastic cover on certain models. There may also be an additional bolt at the left-hand side of the cover; if so undo this bolt also. Release the wiring harness and/or hoses at the rear of the cover and lift the cover off the engine (see illustrations 10.19a to 10.19c).

25 Remove the engine oil filler pipe from the camshaft cover.

26 Remove the exhaust gas recirculation (EGR) valve as described in Chapter 4B.

27 Undo the retaining nut and disconnect the glow plug supply cable from the terminal stud.

28 Disconnect the wiring connector from the fuel pressure sensor on the end of the fuel rail.

29 Remove the inlet manifold as described in Chapter 2B.

30 Disconnect the fuel injection pump fuel return line at the quick-release connector.

31 Disconnect the wiring connectors from the fuel temperature sensor and from the metering valve on the rear of the fuel injection pump. Suitably cover the connectors on the pump to prevent the entry of dirt and cleaning solvent.

32 Before proceeding further, use a brush and suitable solvent to clean the area around the fuel pipe unions on the injectors and fuel rail. It is essential that no dirt enters the system. Allow time for any solvent used to dry.

33 At the rear of the injection pump, undo the nut and release the pump-to-fuel rail fuel supply pipe clamp bracket.

34 Carefully loosen the fuel supply pipe union at the fuel pump and the one to the fuel rail. Ford recommend (if possible) that the tool used to loosen these unions is fitted at the **top** of the union, to reduce the chance of damaging the union as it is loosened.

35 Once the unions are loose, wrap clean absorbent tissue or rag around them briefly, to soak away any dirt which may otherwise enter. If available, Ford recommend using a vacuum line to suck any dirt away from the opening union – do not use an airline, as this may blast dirt inwards, rather than cleaning it away.

36 Remove the fuel supply pipe, and discard it – a new one must be used when refitting (see illustration 14.11). Plug or suitably cover the open connections.

37 Using a spanner to hold the injectors and prevent them turning, slacken the fuel pipe union at each injector (see illustration 14.12).

38 Slacken the four injector fuel pipe unions at the fuel rail (see illustration 14.13).

39 Once the unions are loose, wrap clean absorbent tissue or rag around them briefly, to soak away any dirt which may otherwise enter. If available, Ford recommend using a vacuum line to suck any dirt away from the opening union – do not use an airline, as this may blast dirt inwards, rather than cleaning it away.

40 With all the unions slackened, the fuel pipes can now be completely disconnected and removed. Fit blanking plugs to the injectors and fuel rail.

41 Discard the fuel pipes – new ones must be used when refitting.

42 Undo the three fuel rail mounting bolts, then lift off the fuel rail (see illustration).

Refitting

43 Offer the fuel rail into position, then fit the mounting bolts, hand-tight only.

44 Fit new fuel pipes to the fuel rail, injectors and fuel pump, leaving the union nuts hand-tight only at this stage. Do not bend or strain the pipes, and make sure they are kept clean. Also, do not allow the union nuts to hit the olive-shaped ends of the pipes during fitting, as this may result in damage.

45 Tighten the three fuel rail mounting bolts to the specified torque.

46 With all the fuel injection pipes in place, fully tighten the union nuts to the specified torque (see illustrations 14.21a and 14.21b).

Caution: The injectors are not to turn from their position in the cylinder head – a special tool is used to align the injectors (see Section 13)

47 Further refitting is a reversal of removal. On completion, prime and bleed the fuel system as described in Section 3.

---

15 Turbocharger – general information, removal and refitting

General information

1 The turbocharger increases engine efficiency by raising the pressure in the intake manifold above atmospheric pressure. Instead of the

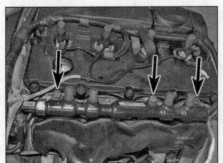

14.42 Fuel rail mounting bolts (arrowed)

air simply being sucked into the cylinders, it is forced in. Additional fuel is supplied by the injection pump, in proportion to the increased amount of air.

2 Energy for the operation of the turbocharger comes from the exhaust gas. The gas flows through a specially-shaped housing (the turbine housing) and in so doing, spins the turbine wheel. The turbine wheel is attached to a shaft, at the end of which is another vaned wheel, known as the compressor wheel. The compressor wheel spins in its own housing, and compresses the inducted air on the way to the intake manifold.

3 Between the turbocharger and the inlet manifold, the compressed air passes through an intercooler (see Section 16 for details). The purpose of the intercooler is to remove from the inducted air some of the heat gained in being compressed. Because cooler air is denser, removal of this heat further increases engine efficiency.

4 Boost pressure (the pressure in the intake manifold) is limited by a wastegate, which diverts the exhaust gas away from the turbine wheel in response to a pressure-sensitive actuator.

5 The turbo shaft is pressure-lubricated by its own dedicated oil feed pipe. The shaft 'floats' on a cushion of oil. Oil is returned to the sump via a return pipe that connects to the sump.

6 On all engines, the turbocharger is integral with the exhaust manifold, and is not available separately. The turbocharger is either of fixed vane type, or variable vane type according to engine type. On the fixed vane type there is a wastegate control valve, which opens a flap at high engine speeds. On the variable vane type, as the engine speed increases the guide vanes in the turbine housing are progressively opened.

Removal and refitting

7 Removal and refitting of the exhaust manifold/turbocharger is covered in Chapter 2A (2.0 litre engines), or 2B (2.4 litre engines).

---

16 Intercooler – general information, removal and refitting

General information

1 The intercooler is effectively an 'air radiator', used to cool the pressurised intake air before it enters the engine.

2 When the turbocharger compresses the intake air, one side-effect is that the air is heated, causing the air to expand. If the intake air can be cooled, a greater effective volume of air will be inducted, and the engine will produce more power.

3 The compressed air from the turbocharger, which would normally be fed straight into the inlet manifold, is instead ducted forwards around the side of the engine to the base of the intercooler. The intercooler is mounted

at the front of the vehicle, in the airflow. The heated air entering the base of the unit rises upwards, and is cooled by the airflow over the intercooler fins, much as with the radiator. When it reaches the top of the intercooler, the cooled air is then ducted rearwards into the inlet manifold.

Removal

4 Move the driver's seat fully forward, open the battery box cover and disconnect the battery negative terminal (refer to *Disconnecting the battery* in the Reference Chapter).

5 Using suitable pieces of wire, support the radiator at the upper mounting rubber bushes, to prevent it dropping down when the support bracket is removed.

6 Firmly apply the handbrake, then jack up the front of the vehicle and support it securely on axle stands (see *Jacking and vehicle support*).

7 From under the vehicle, slacken the retaining clips and disconnect the intake and outlet air ducts from the intercooler **(see illustrations)**.

8 Where fitted, disconnect the wiring connector from the temperature and manifold absolute pressure sensor on the right-hand end of the intercooler.

9 Disconnect the wiring connector at the horn, then undo the retaining bolt and remove the horn and bracket.

10 Undo the radiator support bracket lower centre bolt, and the two bolts each side **(see illustration)**. Lower the radiator support bracket complete with intercooler and remove it from under the vehicle.

11 Undo the two bolts each side and remove the intercooler from the radiator support bracket **(see illustration)**.

Refitting

12 Refitting is a reversal of removal. Check the intake and outlet air ducts for signs of damage, and make sure that the clips are securely tightened.

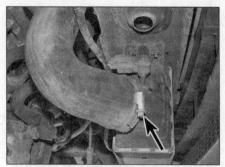

16.7a Slacken the retaining clip (arrowed) and disconnect the intake . . .

16.7b . . . and outlet air ducts from the intercooler

16.10 Undo the two bolts each side (arrowed) securing the radiator support bracket to the underbody

16.11 Undo the two bolts each side (arrowed) and remove the intercooler from the radiator support bracket

---

17 Exhaust system –
general information and component renewal

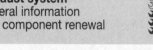

⚠ *Warning: Inspection and repair of exhaust system components should be done only after the system has cooled completely. This applies particularly to the catalytic converter, which runs at very high temperatures.*

General information

1 The exhaust system consists of three main sections; a front pipe incorporating a catalytic converter, an intermediate pipe incorporating the silencers, and a tailpipe.

2 The front pipe is fitted with a flexible section to allow for exhaust system movement and the system is suspended throughout its entire length by rubber mountings.

3 To remove a part of the system, first jack up the front or rear of the vehicle, and support it on axle stands (see *Jacking and vehicle support*). Alternatively, position the vehicle over an inspection pit, or on car ramps.

4 Ford recommend that all nuts (such as flange joint nuts, clamp joint nuts, or converter-to-manifold nuts) are renewed on reassembly – given that they may be in less-than-perfect condition as a result of corrosion, this seems a good idea, especially as it will make subsequent removal easier.

Component renewal

Note: *Refer to Chapter 4B for details of catalytic converter renewal.*

5 If any section of the exhaust is damaged or deteriorated, excessive noise and vibration will occur.

6 Carry out regular inspections of the exhaust system, to check security and condition. Look for any damaged or bent parts, open seams, holes, loose connections, excessive corrosion, or other defects which could allow exhaust fumes to enter the vehicle. Deteriorated sections of the exhaust system should be renewed.

7 If the exhaust system components are extremely corroded or rusted together, it may not be possible to separate them. In this case, simply cut off the old components with a hacksaw, and remove any remaining corroded pipe with a cold chisel. Be sure to wear safety glasses to protect your eyes, and wear gloves to protect your hands.

8 Here are some simple guidelines to follow when repairing the exhaust system:

a) *Work from the back to the front when removing exhaust system components.*

b) *Apply penetrating fluid to the flange nuts before unscrewing them.*

c) *Use new gaskets and rubber mountings when installing exhaust system components.*

d) *Apply anti-seize compound to the threads of all exhaust system studs during reassembly.*

e) *Be sure to allow sufficient clearance between newly-installed parts and all points on the underbody, to avoid overheating the floorpan.*

Notes

Chapter 4 Part B:
Emissions control systems

Contents

Degrees of difficulty

Easy, suitable for novice with little experience	Fairly easy, suitable for beginner with some experience	Fairly difficult, suitable for competent DIY mechanic	Difficult, suitable for experienced DIY mechanic	Very difficult, suitable for expert DIY or professional

Specifications

Torque wrench settings	Nm	lbf ft
Catalytic converter to support bracket (2.0 litre engines)	25	18
Exhaust clamp retaining bolt nuts	55	41
Exhaust front pipe (catalytic converter) to manifold	40	30

1 General information

1 All models are designed to meet strict emission requirements. The engines are fitted with a crankcase emission control system and a catalytic converter to keep exhaust emissions down to a minimum. An exhaust gas recirculation (EGR) system is also fitted to further decrease exhaust emissions.

2 The emissions control systems function as follows.

Crankcase emission control

3 To reduce the emission of unburned hydrocarbons from the crankcase into the atmosphere, the engine is sealed and the blow-by gases and oil vapour are drawn from inside the crankcase, through an oil separator, into the inlet tract to be burned by the engine during normal combustion.

4 Under all conditions the gases are forced out of the crankcase by the (relatively) higher crankcase pressure; if the engine is worn, the raised crankcase pressure (due to increased blow-by) will cause some of the flow to return under all manifold conditions.

5 The components of this system require no attention other than to check that the hose(s) are clear and undamaged at regular intervals.

Exhaust emission control

6 To minimise the level of exhaust pollutants released into the atmosphere, an unregulated catalytic converter is fitted in the exhaust system.

7 The catalytic converter consists of a canister containing a fine mesh impregnated with a catalyst material, over which the hot exhaust gases pass. The catalyst speeds up the oxidation of harmful carbon monoxide, unburned hydrocarbons and soot, effectively reducing the quantity of harmful products released into the atmosphere via the exhaust gases.

Exhaust gas recirculation (EGR) system

8 This system is designed to recirculate small quantities of exhaust gas into the inlet tract, and therefore into the combustion process. This process reduces the level of unburnt hydrocarbons present in the exhaust gas before it reaches the catalytic converter. The system is controlled by the powertrain control module (PCM), using the information from its various sensors, via the EGR valve.

2.10a Undo the auxiliary drivebelt cover right-hand retaining bolt (arrowed) . . .

2.10b . . . and centre retaining bolt (arrowed) . . .

2.10c . . . then release the wiring harness and/or hoses and lift the cover off the engine

2 Exhaust Gas Recirculation (EGR) system – testing and component renewal

Testing

EGR valve

1 Start the engine and allow it to idle.

2 Detach the vacuum hose from the EGR valve, and attach a hand vacuum pump in its place.

3 Apply vacuum to the EGR valve. Vacuum should remain steady, and the engine should run poorly or stall.

 a) If the vacuum doesn't remain steady and the engine doesn't run poorly, renew the EGR valve and recheck it.

 b) If the vacuum remains steady but the engine doesn't run poorly, remove the EGR valve, and check the valve and the inlet manifold for blockage. Clean or renew parts as necessary, and recheck.

EGR system

4 Any further checking of the system requires special tools and test equipment. Take the vehicle to a dealer service department for checking.

EGR valve renewal

2.0 litre engines

5 Remove the intake air resonator and air ducts as described in Chapter 4A.

6 Disconnect the vacuum pipe and wiring connector from the EGR valve.

7 Undo the bolts securing the EGR tube to the EGR valve, renew the gasket on refitting.

8 Undo the two bolts and remove the EGR valve from its location, renew the gasket on refitting.

9 Refitting is a reversal of removal.

2.4 litre DuraTorq-Di engines

10 Undo the two bolts securing the auxiliary drivebelt cover to the top of the engine. The centre bolt may be located under a plastic cover on certain models. There may also be an additional bolt at the left-hand side of the cover; if so undo this bolt also. Release the wiring harness and/or hoses at the rear of the cover and lift the cover off the engine **(see illustrations)**.

11 Release the retaining clip and disconnect the intercooler outlet duct from the EGR valve.

12 Disconnect the wiring connectors from the EGR valve and intake air temperature sensor.

13 Disconnect the vacuum pipes from the EGR valve.

14 Undo the EGR cooler to EGR tube bolts from the EGR valve.

15 Firmly apply the handbrake, then jack up the front of the vehicle and support it securely on axle stands (see Jacking and vehicle support).

16 From under the vehicle, undo the two bolts and remove the EGR cooler-to-EGR valve tube. Note that a new tube must be used on refitting.

17 Detach the wiring harness from the EGR valve.

18 Undo the two nuts and remove the EGR valve from the manifold, renew the gasket on refitting.

19 Refitting is a reversal of removal.

2.4 litre DuraTorq-TDCi engines

20 Undo the two bolts securing the auxiliary drivebelt cover to the top of the engine. The centre bolt may be located under a plastic cover on certain models. There may also be an additional bolt at the left-hand side of the cover; if so undo this bolt also. Release the wiring harness and/or hoses at the rear of the cover and lift the cover off the engine **(see illustrations 2.10a to 2.10c)**.

21 Release the retaining clip and disconnect the intercooler outlet duct from the EGR valve.

22 Disconnect the vacuum pipe from the EGR valve.

23 Undo the EGR tube nuts from the EGR valve and position the wiring harness support bracket to one side **(see illustration)**.

24 Undo the two nuts and remove the EGR valve from the manifold, renew the gasket on refitting **(see illustration)**.

25 Refitting is a reversal of removal.

EGR tube/cooler renewal

26 The EGR systems on certain models are fitted with a cooler (supplied from the cooling system), which reduces the temperature of the exhaust gas being recycled; the cooler is effectively a water jacket around the pipe connecting the exhaust manifold and the EGR valve.

27 If the cooler is to be removed, drain the cooling system as described in Chapter 1.

28 Depending on engine and power output, the EGR tube/cooler routing will vary. Follow the tube and undo the retaining nuts/bolts and release any retaining clips and coolant hoses to remove the tube/cooler.

29 Refitting is a reversal of removal, making sure that the hoses are correctly refitted. **Note:** Check the condition of the hoses and renew them if necessary, refill the cooling system as required (see Chapter 1).

2.23 Undo the EGR tube nuts (arrowed) from the EGR valve and position the wiring harness support bracket to one side

2.24 Undo the two nuts and remove the EGR valve from the manifold

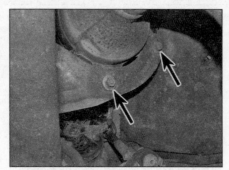

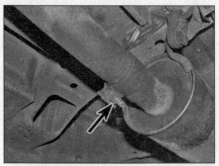

3.6 Undo the four nuts (arrowed) securing the catalytic converter to the exhaust manifold – 2.0 litre engine shown

3.8 On 2.0 litre engines, undo the two nuts (arrowed) and disconnect the catalytic converter from the support bracket

3.9 Undo the clamp bolt and nut (arrowed) securing the exhaust front pipe to the intermediate pipe

3 Catalytic converter –
general information,
removal and refitting

General information

1 The catalytic converter reduces harmful exhaust emissions by chemically converting the more poisonous gases to ones which (in theory at least) are less harmful. The chemical reaction is known as an 'oxidising' reaction, or one where oxygen is 'added'.

2 Inside the converter is a honeycomb structure, made of ceramic material and coated with the precious metals palladium, platinum and rhodium (the 'catalyst' which promotes the chemical reaction). The chemical reaction generates heat, which itself promotes the reaction – therefore, once the vehicle has been driven several miles, the body of the converter will be very hot.

3 The ceramic structure contained within the converter is understandably fragile, and will not withstand rough treatment. Since the converter runs at a high temperature, driving through deep standing water (in flood conditions, for example) is to be avoided, since the thermal stresses imposed when plunging the hot converter into cold water may well cause the ceramic internals to fracture, resulting in a 'blocked' converter – a common cause of failure. A converter which has been damaged in this way can be checked by shaking it (do not strike it) – if a rattling noise is heard, this indicates probable failure. **Note:** *Checking the operation of a*

catalytic converter requires expensive and sophisticated diagnostic equipment, starting with a high-quality exhaust gas analyser. If the level of CO in the exhaust gases is too high, a full check of the engine management system must be carried out to eliminate all other possibilities before the converter is suspected of being faulty. The vehicle should be taken to a Ford dealer for this work to be carried out using the correct diagnostic equipment. Do not waste time trying to test the system without such facilities.

Precautions

4 The catalytic converter is a reliable and simple device which needs no maintenance in itself, but there are some facts of which an owner should be aware if the converter is to function properly for its full service life.

a) *DO NOT use fuel or engine oil additives – these may contain substances harmful to the catalytic converter.*

b) *DO NOT continue to use the vehicle if the engine burns oil to the extent of leaving a visible trail of blue smoke.*

c) *Remember that the catalytic converter operates at very high temperatures. DO NOT, therefore, park the vehicle in dry undergrowth, over long grass or piles of dead leaves after a long run.*

d) *Remember that the catalytic converter is FRAGILE – do not strike it with tools during servicing work.*

e) *The catalytic converter, used on a well-maintained and well-driven vehicle, should last for between 50 000 and 100 000 miles – if the converter is no longer effective it must be renewed.*

Removal and refitting

Note: *Do not over bend the front exhaust flexible pipe as it is removed or damage will occur. Support the flexible pipe with a support wrap or a splint.*

5 Move the driver's seat fully forward, open the battery box cover and disconnect the battery negative terminal (refer to *Disconnecting the battery* in the Reference Chapter).

6 Undo the four nuts securing the top of the catalytic converter to the exhaust manifold **(see illustration)**.

7 Firmly apply the handbrake, then jack up the front of the vehicle and support it securely on axle stands (see *Jacking and vehicle support*).

8 On 2.0 litre engines, undo the two retaining nuts and disconnect the catalytic converter from the support bracket **(see illustration)**.

9 Undo the clamp bolt and nut securing the exhaust front pipe to the intermediate pipe **(see illustration)**.

10 Lower the catalytic converter and front pipe, and collect the converter-to-manifold gasket. Apply liberal amounts of penetrating oil to the front pipe-to-intermediate pipe joint, then twist it back-and-forth to detach the front pipe from the intermediate pipe.

11 Refitting is a reversal of removal. Use new nuts, bolts and gaskets as necessary, and tighten all fasteners to the specified torque. **Note:** *Exhaust sealant paste should not be used on any part of the exhaust system upstream of the catalytic converter (between the engine and the converter) – even if the sealant does not contain additives harmful to the converter, pieces of it may break off and foul the element, causing local overheating.*

Chapter 5
Starting and charging systems

Contents

Degrees of difficulty

Easy, suitable for novice with little experience	**Fairly easy,** suitable for beginner with some experience	**Fairly difficult,** suitable for competent DIY mechanic	**Difficult,** suitable for experienced DIY mechanic	**Very difficult,** suitable for expert DIY or professional

Specifications

General
Electrical system type . . . . 12 volt negative earth

Battery
Type . . . . Lead-calcium
Charge condition:
  Poor . . . . 12.5 volts
  Normal . . . . 12.6 volts
  Good. . . . . 12.7 volts

Torque wrench settings

	Nm	lbf ft
Alternator mounting bolts.	48	35
Glow plugs	12	9
Roadwheel nuts	200	148
Starter motor mounting bolts	25	18
Steering column flexible coupling pinch bolt*	23	17

* Use new nuts/bolts

1 General information, precautions and battery disconnection

General information

The engine electrical system consists mainly of the charging and starting systems, and the engine pre/post-heating system. Because of their engine-related functions, these components are covered separately from the body electrical devices such as the lights, instruments, etc (which are covered in Chapter 12).

The electrical system is of 12-volt negative earth type.

The battery is of the low-maintenance type, and is charged by the alternator, which is belt-driven from the crankshaft pulley.

The starter motor is of pre-engaged type incorporating an integral solenoid. On starting, the solenoid moves the drive pinion into engagement with the flywheel ring gear before the starter motor is energised. Once the engine has started, a one-way clutch prevents the motor armature being driven by the engine until the pinion disengages.

Further details of the various systems are given in the relevant Sections of this Chapter. While some repair procedures are given, the usual course of action is to renew the component concerned. The owner whose interest extends beyond mere component renewal should obtain a copy of the *Automobile Electrical & Electronic Systems Manual*, available from the publishers of this manual.

Precautions

It is necessary to take extra care when working on the electrical system to avoid damage to semi-conductor devices (diodes and transistors), and to avoid the risk of personal injury. In addition to the precautions given in *Safety first!* at the beginning of this manual, observe the following when working on the system:

• *Always remove rings, watches, etc before working on the electrical system. Even with the battery disconnected, capacitive discharge could occur if a component's live terminal is earthed through a metal object. This could cause a shock or nasty burn.*

• *Do not reverse the battery connections. Components such as the alternator, electronic control units, or any other components having semi-conductor circuitry could be irreparably damaged.*

• *If the engine is being started using jump leads and a slave battery, connect the batteries positive-to-positive and negative-to-negative (see 'Jump starting'). This also applies when connecting a battery charger but in this case both of the battery terminals should first be disconnected.*

• *Never disconnect the battery terminals, the alternator, any electrical wiring or*

any test instruments when the engine is running.

• *Do not allow the engine to turn the alternator when the alternator is not connected.*

• *Never test for alternator output by flashing the output lead to earth.*

• *Never use an ohmmeter of the type incorporating a hand-cranked generator for circuit or continuity testing.*

• *Always ensure that the battery negative lead is disconnected when working on the electrical system.*

• *Before using electric arc welding equipment on the car, disconnect the battery, alternator and components such as the engine powertrain control module to protect them from the risk of damage.*

Battery disconnection

Refer to the precautions listed in *Disconnecting the battery* in the Reference Chapter.

2 Electrical fault finding – general information

Refer to Chapter 12.

3 Battery – testing and charging

Testing

Low maintenance battery

1 If the vehicle covers a small annual mileage, it is worthwhile checking the specific gravity of the electrolyte every three months to determine the state of charge of the battery. Use a hydrometer to make the check and compare the results with the following table. Note that the specific gravity readings assume an electrolyte temperature of 15°C. For every 10°C below 15°C subtract 0.007. For every 10°C above 15°C add 0.007.

	Ambient temperature	
	Above 25°C	Below 25°C
Fully-charged	1.210 to 1.230	1.270 to 1.290
70% charged	1.170 to 1.190	1.230 to 1.250
Discharged	1.050 to 1.070	1.110 to 1.130

2 If the battery condition is suspect, first check the specific gravity of electrolyte in each cell. A variation of 0.040 or more between any cells indicates loss of electrolyte or deterioration of the internal plates.

3 If the specific gravity variation is 0.040 or more, the battery should be renewed. If the cell variation is satisfactory but the battery is discharged, it should be charged as described later in this Section.

Maintenance-free battery

4 Where a 'sealed for life' maintenance-free battery is fitted, topping-up and testing of the electrolyte in each cell is not possible. The

condition of the battery can therefore only be tested using a battery condition indicator or a voltmeter.

All battery types

5 If testing the battery using a voltmeter, connect the voltmeter across the battery and compare the result with those given in the Specifications under 'charge condition'. The test is only accurate if the battery has not been subjected to any kind of charge for the previous six hours. If this is not the case, switch on the headlights for 30 seconds, then wait four to five minutes before testing the battery after switching off the headlights. All other electrical circuits must be switched off, so check that the doors and, where applicable, the tailgate are fully shut when making the test.

6 If the voltage reading is less than 12.2 volts, then the battery is discharged, whilst a reading of 12.2 to 12.4 volts indicates a partially discharged condition.

7 If the battery is to be charged, remove it from the vehicle (Section 4) and charge it as described later in this Section.

Charging

Note: *The following is intended as a guide only. Always refer to the manufacturer's recommendations (often printed on a label attached to the battery) before charging a battery.*

Low maintenance battery

8 Charge the battery at a rate of 3.5 to 4 amps and continue to charge the battery at this rate until no further rise in specific gravity is noted over a four hour period.

9 Alternatively, a trickle charger charging at the rate of 1.5 amps can safely be used overnight.

10 Specially rapid 'boost' charges which are claimed to restore the power of the battery in 1 to 2 hours are not recommended, as they can cause serious damage to the battery plates through overheating.

11 While charging the battery, note that the temperature of the electrolyte should never exceed 38°C.

Maintenance-free battery

12 This battery type takes considerably longer to fully recharge than the standard type, the time taken being dependent on the extent of discharge, but it will take anything up to three days.

13 A constant voltage type charger is required, to be set, when connected, to 13.9 to 14.9 volts with a charger current below 25 amps. Using this method, the battery should be usable within three hours, giving a voltage reading of 12.5 volts, but this is for a partially-discharged battery and, as mentioned, full charging can take considerably longer.

14 If the battery is to be charged from a fully discharged state (condition reading less than 12.2 volts), have it recharged by your dealer or local automotive electrician, as the charge rate is higher and constant supervision during charging is necessary.

4 Battery –
removal and refitting

Note 1: *Refer to 'Disconnecting the battery' in the Reference Chapter before proceeding.*
Note 2: *If a new battery is to be fitted, it must be of the type capable of venting to the outside of the vehicle.*

Removal

1 The battery is located inside the vehicle beneath the driver's seat. Two batteries may be fitted on certain models.
2 Move the driver's seat fully forward, then open the battery box cover **(see illustration)**.
3 Disconnect the lead at the negative (–) terminal by unscrewing the retaining nut and removing the terminal clamp **(see illustration)**. Where two batteries are fitted, disconnect the lead at the negative (–) terminal on the second battery in the same way. Note that the battery negative (–) and positive (+) terminal connections are stamped on the battery case.
4 Disconnect the lead at the positive (+) terminal by lifting the plastic terminal cover, unscrewing the retaining nut and removing the terminal clamp. Where two batteries are fitted, disconnect the lead at the positive (+) terminal on the second battery in the same way.
5 Unscrew the three retaining bolts and remove the battery retaining clamp **(see illustration)**.
6 Disconnect the battery breather hose and carefully lift the battery from its location and remove it from the vehicle. Make sure the battery is kept upright at all times.

Refitting

Note: *As a precaution, before refitting the battery check that all doors are unlocked.*
7 Refitting is a reversal of removal, but smear petroleum jelly on the terminals after reconnecting the leads to reduce corrosion, and always reconnect the positive lead(s) first, followed by the negative lead(s).

5 Charging system –
testing

Note: *Refer to the precautions given in 'Safety first!' and in Section 1 of this Chapter before starting work.*
1 If the ignition no-charge warning light fails to illuminate when the ignition is switched on, first check the alternator wiring connections for security. If satisfactory, check the condition of all related fuses, fusible links, wiring connections and earthing points. If this fails to reveal the fault, the vehicle should be taken to a Ford dealer or auto electrician, as further testing entails the use of specialist diagnostic equipment.
2 If the ignition warning light illuminates when the engine is running, stop the engine and

4.2 Move the driver's seat fully forward, then open the battery box cover

check the condition of the auxiliary drivebelt (see Chapter 1) and the security of the alternator wiring connections. If satisfactory, have the alternator checked by a Ford dealer or auto electrician.
3 If the alternator output is suspect even though the warning light functions correctly, the regulated voltage may be checked as follows.
4 Connect a voltmeter across the battery terminals, and start the engine.
5 Increase the engine speed until the voltmeter reading remains steady. The reading should be approximately 12 to 13 volts, and no more than 14 volts.
6 Switch on as many electrical accessories (eg, the headlights and heater blower) as possible, and check that the alternator maintains the regulated voltage at around 13.5 to 14.5 volts.
7 If the regulated voltage is not as stated, the fault may be due to worn brushes, weak brush springs, a faulty voltage regulator, a faulty diode, a severed phase winding, or worn or damaged slip rings. The alternator should be renewed or taken to a Ford dealer or auto electrician for testing and repair.

6 Auxiliary drivebelt –
removal and refitting

Refer to Chapter 1.

7 Alternator –
removal and refitting

Removal

2.0 litre engines

Note: *A new steering column flexible coupling lower pinch bolt and nut will be required for refitting. A new auxiliary drivebelt will also be required on models without air conditioning.*
1 Move the driver's seat fully forward, open the battery box cover and disconnect the battery negative terminal (refer to *Disconnecting the battery* in the Reference Chapter).
2 Firmly apply the handbrake, then jack up the

4.3 Disconnect the lead at the battery negative (–) terminal by unscrewing the retaining nut and removing the clamp

4.5 Unscrew the bolts and remove the battery retaining clamp (one of three arrowed)

front of the vehicle and support it securely on axle stands (see *Jacking and vehicle support*).
3 Turn the steering wheel to set the roadwheels in the straight-ahead position, then remove the ignition key to lock the column.
4 Undo the two fasteners and remove the splash shield around the crankshaft pulley.
5 On models with air conditioning, working as described in Chapter 1, release the tension on the auxiliary drivebelt, and slip the belt off the alternator pulley. On models without air conditioning, remove the auxiliary drivebelt by cutting through it with a sharp knife.
6 Undo the nut and remove the lower pinch bolt securing the steering column intermediate shaft flexible coupling to the steering gear pinion shaft **(see illustration)**. Note that a new pinch bolt and nut will be required for refitting. Where fitted, extract the circlip from the base of the flexible coupling.

7.6 Undo the nut and remove the pinch bolt (arrowed) securing the flexible coupling to the steering gear pinion shaft

7.13 Alternator upper mounting bolt (arrowed) . . .

7 Slide the flexible coupling up and off the steering gear pinion shaft and move the intermediate shaft to one side.

8 Unplug the wiring connector from the rear of the alternator, then undo the nut to disconnect the wiring terminal from the alternator.

9 Unscrew the upper mounting bolt and the two lower mounting bolts, then withdraw the alternator downwards from the block.

2.4 litre engines

10 Move the driver's seat fully forward, open the battery box cover and disconnect the battery negative terminal (refer to *Disconnecting the battery* in the Reference Chapter).

11 Firmly apply the handbrake, then jack up the front of the vehicle and support it securely on axle stands (see *Jacking and vehicle support*).

12 Remove the auxiliary drivebelt as described in Chapter 1.

13 Unscrew the alternator upper mounting bolt **(see illustration)**.

14 Unscrew the alternator lower, front mounting bolt and, where fitted, lift off the splash shield **(see illustration)**.

15 Unplug the wiring connector from the rear of the alternator, then undo the nut to disconnect the wiring terminal from the alternator.

16 Unscrew the remaining lower mounting bolt, then withdraw the alternator downwards from the block.

Refitting

2.0 litre engines

17 Manoeuvre the alternator into position and refit the upper and lower mounting bolts.

7.14 . . . and lower mounting bolts (arrowed)

Progressively tighten the bolts to the specified torque.

18 Reconnect the wiring to the alternator and tighten the terminal retaining nut securely.

19 Reconnect the steering column flexible coupling using a new pinch bolt and nut tightened to the specified torque. Where applicable, refit the circlip to the base of the flexible coupling.

20 Refit or renew the auxiliary drivebelt as described in Chapter 1, then refit the splash shield around the crankshaft pulley.

21 On completion, reconnect the battery negative terminal.

2.4 litre engines

22 Manoeuvre the alternator into position and refit the lower, rear mounting bolt. Tighten the bolt finger tight only at this stage.

23 Reconnect the wiring to the alternator and tighten the terminal retaining nut securely.

24 Place the splash shield (where fitted) in position and refit the lower front retaining bolt finger tight only. Refit the upper retaining bolt, then progressively tighten all three retaining bolts to the specified torque.

25 Refit the auxiliary drivebelt as described in Chapter 1.

26 On completion, reconnect the battery negative terminal.

8 Alternator – testing and overhaul

If the alternator is thought to be suspect, it should be removed from the vehicle and taken to an auto electrician for testing. Most auto electricians will be able to supply and fit brushes at a reasonable cost. However, check on the cost of repairs before proceeding as it may prove more economical to obtain a new or exchange alternator.

9 Starting system – testing

Note: *Refer to the precautions given in 'Safety first!' and in Section 1 of this Chapter before starting work.*

1 If the starter motor fails to operate during the normal starting procedure, the possible causes are as follows:
   a) The engine immobiliser is faulty.
   b) The battery is faulty.
   c) The electrical connections between the switch, solenoid, battery and starter motor are somewhere failing to pass the necessary current from the battery through the starter to earth.
   d) The solenoid is faulty.
   e) The starter motor is mechanically or electrically defective.

2 To check the battery, switch on the headlights. If they dim after a few seconds, this indicates that the battery is discharged –

recharge (see Section 3) or renew the battery. If the headlights glow brightly, operate the starter switch while watching the headlights. If they dim, then this indicates that current is reaching the starter motor, therefore the fault must lie in the starter motor. If the lights continue to glow brightly (and no clicking sound can be heard from the starter motor solenoid), this indicates that there is a fault in the circuit or solenoid – see the following paragraphs. If the starter motor turns slowly when operated, but the battery is in good condition, then this indicates either that the starter motor is faulty, or there is considerable resistance somewhere in the circuit.

3 If a fault in the circuit is suspected, disconnect the battery leads (including the earth connection to the body), the starter/solenoid wiring and the engine/transmission earth strap. Thoroughly clean the connections, and reconnect the leads and wiring. Use a voltmeter or test light to check that full battery voltage is available at the battery positive lead connection to the solenoid. Smear petroleum jelly around the battery terminals to prevent corrosion – corroded connections are among the most frequent causes of electrical system faults.

4 If the battery and all connections are in good condition, check the circuit by disconnecting the ignition switch supply wire from the solenoid terminal. Connect a voltmeter or test lamp between the wire end and a good earth (such as the battery negative terminal), and check that the wire is live when the ignition switch is turned to the 'start' position. If it is, then the circuit is sound – if not the circuit wiring can be checked as described in Chapter 12.

5 The solenoid contacts can be checked by connecting a voltmeter or test light between the battery positive feed connection on the starter side of the solenoid and earth. When the ignition switch is turned to the 'start' position, there should be a reading or lighted bulb, as applicable. If there is no reading or lighted bulb, the solenoid is faulty.

6 If the circuit and solenoid are proved sound, the fault must lie in the starter motor. In this event, it may be possible to have the starter motor overhauled by a specialist, but check on the cost of spares before proceeding, as it may prove more economical to obtain a new or exchange motor.

10 Starter motor – removal and refitting

Removal

2.0 litre engines

1 Move the driver's seat fully forward, open the battery box cover and disconnect the battery negative terminal (refer to *Disconnecting the battery* in the Reference Chapter).

2 Firmly apply the handbrake, then jack up the

front of the vehicle and support it securely on axle stands (see *Jacking and vehicle support*).

3 Undo the nut and disconnect the earth lead from the starter motor lower stud bolt.

4 Slacken and remove the two retaining nuts and disconnect the wiring from the starter motor solenoid. Recover the washers under the nuts.

5 Unscrew the starter motor lower stud bolt and upper mounting bolt, then manoeuvre the starter motor downwards and out from under the vehicle.

2.4 litre engines

6 Move the driver's seat fully forward, open the battery box cover and disconnect the battery negative terminal (refer to *Disconnecting the battery* in the Reference Chapter).

7 Firmly apply the handbrake, then jack up the front of the vehicle and support it securely on axle stands (see *Jacking and vehicle support*).

8 Unscrew the starter motor upper and lower mounting bolts, noting the location of the earth lead on the lower bolt **(see illustration)**.

9 Taking care not to strain the wiring harness, lower the starter sufficiently to gain access to the wiring connections on the solenoid. Recover the gasket as the starter is removed from the transmission housing.

10 Slacken and remove the two retaining nuts and disconnect the wiring from the starter motor solenoid. Recover the washers under the nuts.

11 Manoeuvre the starter motor downwards and out from under the vehicle.

Refitting

12 Refitting is a reversal of removal, tightening the mounting bolts to the specified torque. Ensure all wiring is correctly routed and the retaining nuts are securely tightened.

---

11 Starter motor – testing and overhaul

If the starter motor is thought to be suspect, it should be removed from the vehicle and taken to an auto electrician for testing. Most auto electricians will be able to supply and fit brushes at a reasonable cost. However, check on the cost of repairs before proceeding as it may prove more economical to obtain a new or exchange motor.

---

12 Pre/post-heating system – general information

System description

1 Cold-starting performance is automatically controlled by the powertrain control module (PCM). Under cold start conditions, the cylinder head temperature (CHT) sensor informs the PCM of the engine temperature and this determines the pre/post-heat time.

2 Each cylinder of the engine is fitted with a heater plug (commonly called a glow plug) screwed into it. The plugs are electrically operated before and during start-up when the engine is cold. Electrical feed to the glow plugs is controlled by the PCM via the glow plug relay.

3 A warning light in the instrument panel tells the driver that pre/post-heating is taking place. When the light goes out, the engine is ready to be started. The voltage supply to the glow plugs continues for several seconds after the light goes out. If no attempt is made to start, the PCM then cuts off the supply, in order to avoid draining the battery and overheating the glow plugs.

4 The glow plugs also provide a post-heating function, whereby the glow plugs remain switched on after the engine has started. The post-heating function only operates at below 2500 rpm, and below temperatures of 50ºC. This helps the engine to run more smoothly during idling and reduces exhaust emissions through more efficient combustion just after starting.

Component locations

5 The pre/post-heating is controlled by the powertrain control module which is located in the engine compartment bulkhead on the left-hand side. Refer to Chapter 4A for removal and refitting details.

6 The cylinder head temperature sensor is screwed into the transmission end of the cylinder head. Refer to Chapter 4A for removal and refitting details.

7 The glow plug relay is located in the fuse/relay box situated in the engine compartment on the left-hand side. Refer to Chapter 12 for further details.

---

13 Glow plugs – testing, removal and refitting

Testing

1 If the system malfunctions, testing is ultimately by substitution of known good units, but some preliminary checks may be made as follows.

2 Connect a voltmeter or 12 volt test lamp between the glow plug supply cable and earth (engine or vehicle metal). Make sure that the live connection is kept clear of the engine and bodywork.

3 Have an assistant switch on the ignition, and check that voltage is applied to the glow plugs. Note the time for which the warning light is lit, and the total time for which voltage is applied before the system cuts out. Switch off the ignition.

4 If an ammeter of suitable range (0 to 50 amp) is available, connect it between the glow plug feed wire and the busbar (the wire that connects the four plugs together). During the pre-heating period, the ammeter should show

10.8 Starter motor mounting bolts (arrowed). Note the location of the earth lead on the lower bolt

a current draw of approximately 8 amps per working plug, ie, 32 amps if all four plugs are working. If one or more plugs appear not to be drawing current, remove the busbar and check each plug separately with a continuity tester or self-powered test light.

5 If there is no supply at all to the glow plugs, the relay or associated wiring may be at fault. Otherwise this points to a defective cylinder head temperature sensor (see Chapter 4A), or to a problem with the powertrain control module.

6 To locate a defective glow plug, disconnect the main feed wire and the interconnecting busbar from the top of the glow plugs. Be careful not to drop the nuts and washers.

7 Use a continuity tester, or a 12 volt test lamp connected to the battery positive terminal, to check for continuity between each glow plug terminal and earth. The resistance of a glow plug in good condition is very low (less than 1 ohm), so if the test lamp does not light or the continuity tester shows a high resistance, the glow plug is certainly defective.

8 If an ammeter is available, the current draw of each glow plug can be checked. After an initial surge of 15 to 20 amps, each plug should draw 10 amps. Any plug which draws much more or less than this is probably defective.

9 As a final check, the glow plugs can be removed and inspected as described below.

Removal

Caution: If the pre/post-heating system has just been energised, or if the engine has been running, the glow plugs will be very hot.

2.0 litre engines

10 Move the driver's seat fully forward, open the battery box cover and disconnect the battery negative terminal (refer to *Disconnecting the battery* in the Reference Chapter).

11 Remove the intake air resonator as described in Chapter 4A.

12 On engines with common rail fuel injection, remove the inlet manifold as described in Chapter 4A.

13 Unscrew the nut and remove the washer securing each glow plug connector, then lift the wiring away from the plugs **(see**

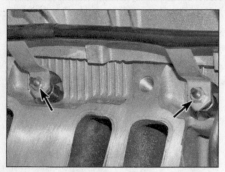

13.13 Unscrew the retaining nut (two of four arrowed) from each glow plug

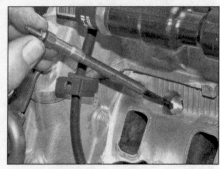

13.14 Remove the glow plug from the cylinder head

illustration). Note that the wiring need not be removed completely for access to the plugs.

14 Unscrew the glow plugs and remove them from the engine for inspection **(see illustration)**.

15 Inspect the glow plug stems for signs of damage. A badly burned or charred stem may be an indication of a faulty fuel injector – consult a diesel specialist for advice if necessary. Otherwise, if one plug is found to be faulty and the engine has completed a high mileage, it is probably worth renewing all four plugs as a set.

2.4 litre engines

16 Move the driver's seat fully forward, open the battery box cover and disconnect the battery negative terminal (refer to *Disconnecting the battery* in the Reference Chapter).

17 Remove the exhaust gas recirculation (EGR) valve as described in Chapter 4B.

18 Remove the inlet manifold as described in Chapter 4A.

19 Unscrew the nut and remove the washer securing each glow plug connector, then lift the wiring away from the plugs **(see illustration 13.13)**. Note that the wiring need

not be removed completely for access to the plugs.

20 Unscrew the glow plugs and remove them from the engine for inspection **(see illustration 13.14)**.

21 Inspect the glow plug stems for signs of damage. A badly burned or charred stem may be an indication of a faulty fuel injector – consult a diesel specialist for advice if necessary. Otherwise, if one plug is found to be faulty and the engine has completed a high mileage, it is probably worth renewing all four plugs as a set.

Refitting

22 Refitting is a reversal of removal, noting the following points:

a) *Apply a little anti-seize compound (or copper brake grease) to the glow plug threads.*

b) *Tighten the glow plugs to the specified torque.*

c) *Make sure when remaking the glow plug wiring connections that the contact surfaces are clean.*

d) *Where applicable, refit the inlet manifold and EGR valve as described in Chapters 4A and 4B respectively.*

Chapter 6
Clutch

Contents

Degrees of difficulty

Easy, suitable for novice with little experience	**Fairly easy,** suitable for beginner with some experience	**Fairly difficult,** suitable for competent DIY mechanic	**Difficult,** suitable for experienced DIY mechanic	**Very difficult,** suitable for expert DIY or professional

Specifications

General

Type	Single dry plate, hydraulically-operated with automatic adjustment
Disc diameter:	
2.0 litre engines	240 mm
2.4 litre engines with 5-speed transmission	240 mm
2.4 litre engines with 6-speed transmission	258 mm
Lining thickness:	
New	6.8 mm
Minimum (worn)	6.0 mm

Torque wrench settings

	Nm	lbf ft
Clutch pressure plate-to-flywheel:		
2.0 litre engines	23	17
2.4 litre engines	29	21
Clutch release cylinder retaining bolts	10	7

1 General information

The clutch consists of a friction disc, a pressure plate assembly, and the release mechanism; all of these components are contained in the large cast-aluminium alloy bellhousing, sandwiched between the engine and the transmission.

The friction disc is fitted between the engine flywheel and the clutch pressure plate, and is allowed to slide on the transmission input shaft splines.

The pressure plate assembly is bolted to the engine flywheel. When the engine is running, drive is transmitted from the crankshaft, via the flywheel, to the friction disc (these components being clamped securely together by the pressure plate assembly) and from the friction disc to the transmission input shaft.

To interrupt the drive, the pressure plate spring pressure must be relaxed. This is achieved using a hydraulic release mechanism which consists of a master cylinder, and a slave cylinder and release bearing, or a release cylinder. On 2.4 litre engines with 5-speed transmissions, the clutch release bearing is fitted concentrically around the transmission input shaft and the slave cylinder is mounted externally on the side of the transmission. The bearing is pushed onto the pressure plate assembly by means of a release lever actuated by the slave cylinder. On 2.4 litre engines with 6-speed transmissions, and all 2.0 litre engines, the release bearing is integral with the slave cylinder to form a single release cylinder assembly fitted concentrically around the transmission input shaft.

The clutch pedal is connected to the clutch master cylinder by a short pushrod. The master cylinder is mounted behind the clutch pedal and receives its hydraulic fluid supply from a separate chamber in the brake master cylinder reservoir. Depressing the clutch pedal moves the piston in the master cylinder forwards, so forcing hydraulic fluid through the clutch hydraulic pipe to the slave cylinder or release cylinder. On models with an externally mounted slave cylinder, the piston in the slave cylinder moves forward on the entry of the fluid and actuates the clutch release lever by means of a short pushrod. The release lever pivots on its mounting stud and presses the release bearing against the pressure plate spring fingers. This causes the springs to deform and releases the clamping force on the pressure plate. On models with a release cylinder, the piston in the release cylinder moves forward on the entry of the fluid and presses the integral release bearing directly against the pressure plate spring fingers.

On all models, the clutch operating mechanism is self-adjusting and no manual adjustment is required.

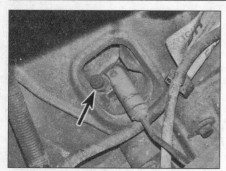

2.9 Clutch release cylinder bleed screw (arrowed) – 2.0 litre engines

2 Clutch hydraulic system – bleeding

⚠️ **Warning: Hydraulic fluid is poisonous. Wash off immediately and thoroughly in the case of skin contact, and seek immediate medical advice if any fluid is swallowed or gets into the eyes. Certain types of hydraulic fluid are inflammable, and may ignite when allowed into contact with hot components. When servicing any hydraulic system, it is safest to assume that the fluid IS inflammable, and to take precautions against the risk of fire as though it is petrol that is being handled. Hydraulic fluid is also an effective paint stripper, and will attack plastics. If any is spilt, it should be washed off immediately, using copious quantities of clean water. When topping-up or renewing the fluid, always use the recommended type, and ensure that it comes from a freshly-opened sealed container.**

1 The clutch hydraulic system will not normally require bleeding, and this task should only be

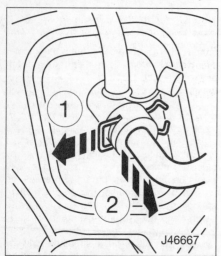

2.14 On vehicles up to April 2002, pull out the retaining spring clip (1) to the first stage, then pull the hydraulic hose (2) out of the union slightly to open the bleed screw orifice – 2.0 litre engines

necessary when the system has been opened for repair work. However, as with the brake pedal, if the clutch pedal feels at all soggy or unresponsive in operation, this may indicate the need for bleeding.

2 The manufacturer recommends that the system should be bled by the 'back-bleeding' method using a hand pump kit – Ford tool – 416-D001 (23-036A), or equivalent. This entails connecting the hand pump kit, containing fresh brake fluid, to the slave cylinder or release cylinder bleed screw. After syphoning some of the fluid out of the master cylinder reservoir, the bleed screw is opened, the pump is operated, and hydraulic fluid is delivered under pressure, backwards, to the reservoir.

3 In practice, this method would normally only be required if new hydraulic components have been fitted, or if the system has been completely drained of hydraulic fluid. If the system has only been disconnected to allow component removal and refitting procedures to be carried out, such as removal and refitting of the transmission (for example for clutch replacement) or engine removal and refitting, then it is quite likely that normal bleeding will be sufficient.

4 Our advice would therefore be as follows:
   a) *If the hydraulic system has only been partially disconnected, and suitable precautions were taken to minimise fluid loss, try bleeding by the conventional method described in the relevant paragraphs below.*
   b) *If conventional bleeding fails to produce a firm pedal on completion, it will be necessary to 'back-bleed' the system using the Ford hand-pump kit or suitable alternative equipment as described in the relevant paragraphs below.*

5 During the bleeding procedure, add only clean, unused hydraulic fluid of the recommended type; never re-use fluid that has already been bled from the system. Ensure that sufficient fluid is available before starting work.

6 If there is any possibility of incorrect fluid being already in the system, the hydraulic circuit must be flushed completely with uncontaminated fluid of the specified type (see *Lubricants and fluids*).

7 If hydraulic fluid has been lost from the system, or air has entered because of a leak, ensure that the fault is cured before continuing further.

8 The bleeding procedure varies slightly according to engine/transmission type. Proceed as described in the relevant sub-Section below.

2.0 litre engines

9 The system bleed screw is located on top of the transmission bellhousing **(see illustration)**.

10 Obtain a clean jar, a suitable length of rubber or clear plastic tubing, which is a tight fit over the bleed screw on the clutch release cylinder, and a tin of the specified hydraulic

fluid (see *Lubricants and fluids*). The help of an assistant will also be required.

11 Remove the filler cap from the brake master cylinder reservoir, and if necessary top-up the fluid. Keep the reservoir topped-up during subsequent operations.

12 Remove the bleed screw dust cap.

13 Connect one end of the bleed tube to the bleed screw, and insert the other end of the tube in the jar containing sufficient clean hydraulic fluid to keep the end of the tube submerged.

14 On vehicles manufactured up to April 2002, using a small screwdriver pull out the retaining spring clip securing the hydraulic hose to the release cylinder union. Only pull the clip out to the first stage – do not remove it completely. Now pull the hydraulic hose out of the union slightly to open the bleed screw orifice **(see illustration)**.

15 On vehicles manufactured from April 2002 onwards, open the bleed screw approximately half a turn.

16 On all vehicles, have your assistant depress the clutch pedal and then slowly release it. Continue this procedure until clean hydraulic fluid, free from air bubbles, emerges from the tube. Make sure that the brake master cylinder reservoir is checked frequently to ensure that the level does not drop too far, allowing air into the system. At the end of a downstroke, push the hydraulic hose back into the union and push the retaining clip back in to secure, or tighten the bleed screw, as applicable.

17 Check the operation of the clutch pedal. After a few strokes, it should feel normal. Any sponginess would indicate air still present in the system.

18 On completion remove the bleed tube and refit the dust cap. Top-up the master cylinder reservoir if necessary and refit the cap. Fluid expelled from the hydraulic system should now be discarded as it will be contaminated with moisture, air and dirt, making it unsuitable for further use.

19 If conventional bleeding does not work, it may be necessary to 'back-bleed' the system using the hand pump kit described previously. Syphon some of the fluid out of the master cylinder reservoir until the level is at the MIN mark, remove the bleed screw dust cap and connect the hose from the hand pump to the bleed screw. Fill the hand pump reservoir with new hydraulic fluid, open the bleed screw as previously described, and pump the fluid backwards through the system and up to the reservoir until it reaches its MAX mark.

20 On completion, push the hydraulic hose back into the union and push the retaining clip back in to secure, or tighten the bleed screw, as applicable.

21 Remove the hand pump hose and refit the bleed screw dust cap. Top-up the master cylinder reservoir if necessary and refit the cap.

22 Depress the clutch pedal five to ten times to dispel any residual air still remaining in the system.

2.4 litre engines with 5-speed transmissions

23 Firmly apply the handbrake, then jack up the front of the vehicle and support it securely on axle stands (see *Jacking and vehicle support*).

24 The system bleed screw is located on the clutch slave cylinder, fitted to the left-hand side of the transmission.

25 Obtain a clean jar, a suitable length of rubber or clear plastic tubing, which is a tight fit over the bleed screw on the clutch slave cylinder, and a tin of the specified hydraulic fluid (see *Lubricants and fluids*). The help of an assistant will also be required.

26 Remove the filler cap from the brake master cylinder reservoir, and if necessary top-up the fluid. Keep the reservoir topped-up during subsequent operations.

27 Remove the bleed screw dust cap.

28 Connect one end of the bleed tube to the bleed screw, and insert the other end of the tube in the jar containing sufficient clean hydraulic fluid to keep the end of the tube submerged.

29 On vehicles manufactured up to April 2002, using a small screwdriver pull out the retaining spring clip securing the hydraulic hose to the slave cylinder. Only pull the clip out to the first stage – do not remove it completely. Now pull the hydraulic hose out of the slave cylinder slightly to open the bleed screw orifice **(see illustration)**.

30 On vehicles manufactured from April 2002 onwards, open the bleed screw approximately half a turn.

31 On all vehicles, have your assistant depress the clutch pedal and then slowly release it. Continue this procedure until clean hydraulic fluid, free from air bubbles, emerges from the tube. Make sure that the brake master cylinder reservoir is checked frequently to ensure that the level does not drop too far, allowing air into the system. At the end of a downstroke, push the hydraulic hose back into the slave cylinder and push the retaining clip back in to secure, or tighten the bleed screw, as applicable.

32 Check the operation of the clutch pedal. After a few strokes it should feel normal. Any sponginess would indicate air still present in the system.

33 On completion remove the bleed tube, refit the dust cap then lower the vehicle to the ground. Top-up the master cylinder reservoir if necessary and refit the cap. Fluid expelled from the hydraulic system should now be discarded as it will be contaminated with moisture, air and dirt, making it unsuitable for further use.

34 If conventional bleeding does not work, it may be necessary to 'back-bleed' the system as described in paragraphs 19 to 22.

2.4 litre engines with 6-speed transmissions

35 Firmly apply the handbrake, then jack up the front of the vehicle and support it securely

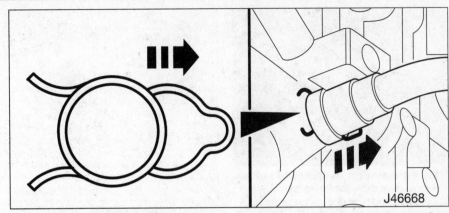

2.29 On vehicles up to April 2002, pull out the retaining spring clip to the first stage, then pull the hydraulic hose out of the slave cylinder slightly to open the bleed screw orifice – 2.4 litre engines with 5-speed transmissions

on axle stands (see *Jacking and vehicle support*).

36 The system bleed screw is located on the release cylinder hydraulic fluid hose union, situated at the upper left-hand side of the transmission **(see illustration)**.

37 Obtain a clean jar, a suitable length of rubber or clear plastic tubing, which is a tight fit over the bleed screw on the clutch release cylinder, and a tin of the specified hydraulic fluid (see *Lubricants and fluids*). The help of an assistant will also be required.

38 Remove the filler cap from the brake master cylinder reservoir, and if necessary top-up the fluid. Keep the reservoir topped-up during subsequent operations.

39 Remove the bleed screw dust cap.

40 Connect one end of the bleed tube to the bleed screw, and insert the other end of the tube in the jar containing sufficient clean hydraulic fluid to keep the end of the tube submerged.

41 Open the bleed screw approximately half a turn.

42 Have your assistant depress the clutch pedal and then slowly release it. Continue this procedure until clean hydraulic fluid, free from air bubbles, emerges from the tube, then tighten the bleed screw at the end of a downstroke. Make sure that the brake master

2.36 Clutch release cylinder bleed screw (arrowed) located on the hydraulic fluid hose union – 2.4 litre engines with 6-speed transmissions

cylinder reservoir is checked frequently to ensure that the level does not drop too far, allowing air into the system.

43 Check the operation of the clutch pedal. After a few strokes it should feel normal. Any sponginess would indicate air still present in the system.

44 On completion remove the bleed tube, refit the dust cap then lower the vehicle to the ground. Top-up the master cylinder reservoir if necessary and refit the cap. Fluid expelled from the hydraulic system should now be discarded as it will be contaminated with moisture, air and dirt, making it unsuitable for further use.

45 If conventional bleeding does not work, it may be necessary to 'back-bleed' the system as described in paragraphs 19 to 22.

3 Clutch master cylinder – removal and refitting

Note: *Refer to the warning in Section 2 concerning the dangers of hydraulic fluid before proceeding.*

Removal

1 Before proceeding, anticipate some spillage of hydraulic (brake) fluid in the engine compartment. Place a good quantity of clean rags below the clutch master cylinder.

2 Remove the brake fluid reservoir cap, and then tighten it down over a piece of polythene, to obtain an airtight seal. This may help to reduce the spillage of fluid when the hydraulic lines are disconnected.

3 Working in the driver's footwell, extract the retaining clip and washer and detach the master cylinder pushrod from the clutch pedal **(see illustration)**.

4 Working in the engine compartment, release the hose clip and disconnect the fluid supply hose from the clutch master cylinder. Plug or clamp the hose end if possible, to reduce fluid loss and to prevent dirt entry.

5 Pull out the spring clip, then pull the hydraulic pipe fitting out of the master cylinder

3.3 Extract the retaining clip and washer (arrowed) and detach the master cylinder pushrod from the clutch pedal

(see illustration). Again, plug or tape over the pipe end, to avoid losing fluid, and to prevent dirt entry.

6 Rotate the master cylinder 90° clockwise and release it from the bulkhead mounting plate.

Refitting

7 Refitting is a reversal of removal, noting the following points:

a) Remove the polythene from under the fluid reservoir cap, and top-up the fluid level (see 'Weekly checks').

b) Refer to Section 2 and bleed the clutch hydraulic system.

4 Clutch release cylinder – removal, inspection and refitting

Note 1: *The following procedure is applicable*

4.3a Remove the bleed screw dust cap . . .

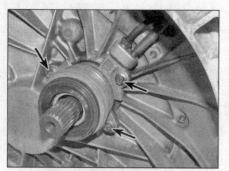

4.4a Remove the three mounting bolts (arrowed) . . .

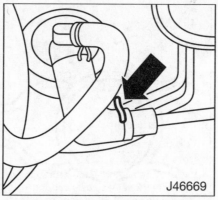

J46669

3.5 Pull out the spring clip (arrowed), then pull the hydraulic pipe fitting out of the master cylinder

to 2.0 litre engines, and 2.4 litre engines with 6-speed transmissions.
Note 2: *Refer to the warning in Section 2 concerning the dangers of hydraulic fluid before proceeding.*

2.0 litre engines

Removal

Note: *The manufacturers stipulate that whenever the release cylinder is removed, a new unit must always be fitted.*

1 The release bearing and slave cylinder are combined to form a release cylinder unit, which is located in the bellhousing of the transmission.
2 Remove the transmission as described in Chapter 7A. Wrap some adhesive tape around the splines of the transmission input shaft to

4.3b . . . then prise out the grommet from the transmission housing – 2.0 litre engines

4.4b . . . and withdraw the release cylinder from the transmission input shaft – 2.0 litre engines

protect the input shaft oil seal in the release cylinder.
3 Remove the bleed screw dust cap, and prise out the grommet from the top of the transmission housing **(see illustrations)**.
4 Remove the three mounting bolts, and withdraw the release cylinder from over the transmission input shaft **(see illustrations)**.

Refitting

5 Thoroughly clean the mating surfaces of the transmission and the new release cylinder.
6 Make sure there is sufficient adhesive tape around the splines of the transmission input shaft to protect the input shaft oil seal located in the release cylinder.
7 Apply suitable sealant (Ford specification WSK-M2G348-A5) to the rear mating surface of the release cylinder and locate the cylinder in position. Refit the three mounting bolts and tighten them to the specified torque.
8 Remove the adhesive tape from the transmission input shaft splines and refit the grommet to the top of the transmission housing. Refit the bleed screw dust cap.
9 Refit the transmission as described in Chapter 7A.

2.4 litre engines with 6-speed transmissions

Removal

10 The release bearing and slave cylinder are combined to form a release cylinder unit, which is located in the bellhousing of the transmission.
11 Remove the transmission as described in Chapter 7B.
12 Extract the retaining clip and withdraw the hydraulic pipe from the release cylinder and bellhousing **(see illustrations)**.
13 Remove the three mounting bolts, and withdraw the release cylinder from the transmission **(see illustration)**.

Inspection

14 Check the release bearing for smoothness of operation, and renew it if there is any sign of harshness or roughness as the bearing is spun. Do not attempt to dismantle, clean or lubricate the bearing.
15 Repair kits are not available from Ford. If a fault develops, the complete release cylinder must be renewed.

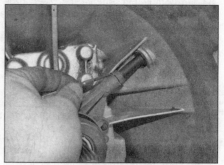

4.12a Extract the retaining clip . . .

Refitting

16 Refitting is a reversal of the removal procedure, noting the following points:
  a) *Tighten the mounting bolts to the specified torque.*
  b) *Refit the transmission as described in Chapter 7B.*

5 Clutch slave cylinder – removal and refitting

Note 1: *The following procedure is applicable to 2.4 litre engines with 5-speed transmissions.*
Note 2: *Refer to the warning in Section 2 concerning the dangers of hydraulic fluid before proceeding.*

Removal

1 Firmly apply the handbrake, then jack up the front of the vehicle and support it securely on axle stands (see *Jacking and vehicle support*).
2 To minimise hydraulic fluid loss, remove the brake master cylinder reservoir filler cap then tighten it down onto a piece of polythene to obtain an airtight seal.
3 Place absorbent rags under the clutch slave cylinder located on the left-hand side of the transmission. Be prepared for hydraulic fluid loss.
4 Extract the retaining clip, then disconnect the hydraulic hose from the end of the slave cylinder. Suitably plug or cap the hose end to prevent further fluid loss and dirt entry.
5 Rotate the slave cylinder anticlockwise to release it, then remove the cylinder from the transmission housing **(see illustration)**.

Refitting

6 Refitting is a reversal of the removal procedure, noting the following points:
  a) *Ensure that the slave cylinder pushrod correctly engages with the clutch release lever.*
  b) *Remove the polythene from under the fluid*

4.12b **. . . and withdraw the hydraulic pipe from the release cylinder and bellhousing – 2.4 litre engines with 6-speed transmissions**

reservoir cap and bleed the clutch hydraulic system as described in Section 2.

6 Clutch release mechanism – removal, inspection and refitting

Note: *The following procedure is applicable to 2.4 litre engines with 5-speed transmissions.*

Removal

1 Unless the complete engine/transmission unit is to be removed from the car and separated for major overhaul (see Chapter 2C), the clutch release mechanism can be reached by removing the transmission only, as described in Chapter 7B.
2 Free the release bearing from the release lever and withdraw it from the input shaft guide sleeve.
3 Pull the release lever off its mounting stud, then withdraw the lever over the guide sleeve and input shaft.

Inspection

4 Check that the release bearing contact surface rotates smoothly and easily, with no sign of noise or roughness, and that the surface itself is smooth and unworn, with no

signs of cracks, pitting or scoring. If there is any doubt about its condition, the bearing must be renewed.
5 Check the bearing surfaces and points of contact on the release lever and mounting stud, renewing any component which is worn or damaged.

Refitting

6 Refitting is a reversal of the removal procedure, noting the following points:
  a) *Apply a thin smear of high-melting-point grease to the guide sleeve and release lever mounting stud.*
  b) *Ensure that the release bearing is correctly located in the release lever.*

7 Clutch pedal – removal and refitting

The clutch pedal is removed and refitted together with the brake pedal and pedal mounting bracket. Refer to the brake pedal removal and refitting procedures contained in Chapter 9.

8 Clutch assembly – removal, inspection and refitting

> ⚠ *Warning: Dust created by clutch wear and deposited on the clutch components may contain asbestos, which is a health hazard. DO NOT blow it out with compressed air, and do not inhale any of it. DO NOT use petrol or petroleum-based solvents to clean off the dust. Brake system cleaner or methylated spirit should be used to flush the dust into a suitable receptacle. After the clutch components are wiped clean with rags, dispose of the contaminated rags and cleaner in a sealed, marked container.*

4.13 Remove the three mounting bolts, and withdraw the release cylinder from the transmission – 2.4 litre engines with 6-speed transmissions

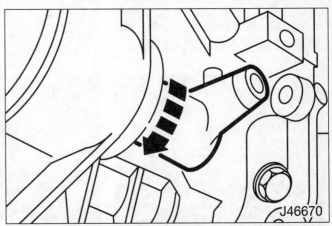

5.5 Rotate the slave cylinder anticlockwise, then remove it from the transmission housing – 2.4 litre engines with 5-speed transmissions

8.3a Unscrew the clutch pressure plate retaining bolts . . .

8.3b . . . using a home-made locking tool to hold the flywheel

8.12 Mount a large bolt and washer into a vice, then fit the pressure plate over it

Removal

1 Unless the complete engine/transmission unit is to be removed from the vehicle and separated for major overhaul (see Chapter 2C), the clutch can be reached by removing the transmission as described in Chapter 7A or 7B, as applicable.

2 Before disturbing the clutch, use a marker pen to mark the relationship of the pressure plate assembly to the flywheel.

3 Unscrew and remove the clutch pressure plate retaining bolts, working in a diagonal sequence, and slackening the bolts only a turn at a time. If necessary, the flywheel may be held stationary using a home-made locking tool **(see illustrations)** or a wide-bladed screwdriver, inserted in the teeth of the starter ring gear and resting against part of the cylinder block.

4 Ease the pressure plate off its locating dowels. Be prepared to catch the friction disc, which will drop out as the plate is removed. Note which way round the disc is fitted.

Inspection

5 The most common problem which occurs in the clutch is wear of the friction disc. However, all the clutch components should be inspected at this time, particularly if the engine has covered a high mileage. Unless the clutch components are known to be virtually new, it is worth renewing them all as a set (disc, pressure plate and release bearing/cylinder). Renewing a worn friction disc by itself is not always satisfactory, especially if the old disc was slipping and causing the pressure plate to overheat.

6 Examine the linings of the friction disc for wear, and the disc hub and rim for distortion, cracks, broken torsion springs, and worn splines. The surface of the friction linings may be highly glazed, but as long as the friction material pattern can be clearly seen (and the thickness of the lining is within the specifications at the beginning of this Chapter), this is satisfactory. The disc must be renewed if the lining thickness has worn down to the minimum thickness given in the specifications.

7 If there is any sign of oil contamination, indicated by shiny black discoloration, the disc must be renewed, and the source of the contamination traced and rectified. This will be a leaking crankshaft oil seal or transmission input shaft oil seal. The renewal procedure for the former is given in the relevant Part of Chapter 2. Renewal of the transmission input shaft oil seal is given in the relevant Part of Chapter 7.

8 Check the machined faces of the flywheel and pressure plate. If either is grooved, or heavily scored, renewal is necessary. The pressure plate must also be renewed if any cracks are apparent, or if the diaphragm spring is damaged or its pressure suspect. Pay particular attention to the tips of the spring fingers, where the release bearing acts upon them.

9 With the transmission removed, it is also advisable to check the condition of the release bearing/release cylinder, as described in Sections 4 and 6. Having got this far, it is almost certainly worth renewing it.

Refitting

10 On 2.4 litre engines fitted with a 6-speed transmission, the clutch pressure plate is unusual, as it incorporates a pre-adjustment mechanism to compensate for wear in the friction disc. This mechanism must be reset before refitting the pressure plate. A new plate may be supplied preset, in which case this procedure can be ignored.

11 A large diameter bolt (M14 at least) long enough to pass through the pressure plate, a matching nut, and several large diameter washers, will be needed for this procedure. Mount the bolt head in the jaws of a sturdy bench vice, with one large washer fitted.

12 Offer the plate over the bolt, friction disc surface facing down, and locate it centrally over the bolt and washer – the washer should bear on the centre hub **(see illustration)**.

13 Fit several further large washers over the bolt, so that they bear on the ends of the spring fingers, then add the nut and tighten by hand to locate the washers **(see illustration)**.

14 The purpose of the procedure is to turn the plate's internal adjuster disc so that the three small coil springs visible on the plate's outer surface are fully compressed. Tighten the nut just fitted until the adjuster disc is free to turn. Using a pair of thin-nosed, or circlip pliers, in one of the three windows in the top surface, open the jaws of the pliers to turn the adjuster disc anticlockwise, so that the springs are fully compressed **(see illustrations)**.

15 Hold the pliers in this position, then unscrew the centre nut. Once the nut is released, the adjuster disc will be gripped in

8.13 Fit large washers and a nut to the bolt and hand-tighten

8.14a Tighten the nut until the spring adjuster is free to turn . . .

8.14b . . . then open up the jaws of suitable pliers to compress the springs

position, and the pliers can be removed. Take the pressure plate from the vice, and it is ready to fit.

16 It is important that no oil or grease is allowed to come into contact with the friction material of the clutch disc or the pressure plate and flywheel faces. To ensure this, it is advisable to refit the clutch assembly with clean hands, and to wipe down the pressure plate and flywheel faces with a clean dry rag before assembly begins.

17 Ford technicians use a special tool for centralising the friction disc at this stage. The tool holds the disc centrally on the pressure plate, and locates in the middle of the diaphragm spring fingers. If the tool is not available, it will be necessary to centralise the disc after assembling the pressure plate loosely on the flywheel, as described in the following paragraphs.

18 Place the friction disc against the flywheel, ensuring that it is the right way round. It should be marked TRANS – SIDE, but if not, position it so that the raised hub with the cushion springs is facing away from the flywheel **(see illustration)**.

19 Place the clutch pressure plate over the dowels. Refit the retaining bolts, and tighten them finger-tight so that the friction disc is gripped lightly, but can still be moved.

20 If the Ford tool is not being used, the

8.18 Transmission side TRANS-SIDE marking on the clutch friction disc

friction disc must now be centralised so that, when the engine and transmission are mated, the splines of the transmission input shaft will pass through the splines in the centre of the disc hub.

21 Centralisation can be carried out by inserting a round bar through the hole in the centre of the friction disc, so that the end of the bar rests in the spigot bearing in the rear end of the crankshaft. Move the bar sideways or up-and-down, to move the disc in whichever direction is necessary to achieve centralisation. Centralisation can then be checked by removing the bar and viewing the friction disc hub in relation to the diaphragm spring fingers, and checking that the disc is

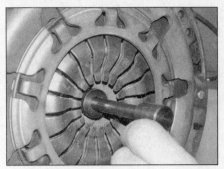

8.22 Using a clutch alignment tool to centralise the clutch friction disc

central in relation to the outer edge of the pressure plate.

22 An alternative and more accurate method of centralisation is to use a commercially-available clutch-alignment tool, obtainable from most accessory shops **(see illustration)**.

23 Once the clutch is centralised, progressively tighten the cover bolts in a diagonal sequence to the torque setting given in the Specifications.

24 Ensure that the input shaft splines, clutch disc splines and release bearing guide sleeve are clean. Apply a thin smear of high-melting-point grease to the input shaft splines.

25 Refit the transmission to the engine as described in the relevant Part of Chapter 7.

Chapter 7 Part A:
Manual transmission – front-wheel drive models

Contents

Degrees of difficulty

Easy, suitable for novice with little experience	Fairly easy, suitable for beginner with some experience	Fairly difficult, suitable for competent DIY mechanic	Difficult, suitable for experienced DIY mechanic	Very difficult, suitable for expert DIY or professional

Specifications

General
Type . . . . 5 forward speeds and reverse. Synchromesh on all forward speeds and on reverse
Identification code VXT-75

Lubrication
Lubricant type . . . . See *Lubricants and fluids* on page 0•18
Lubricant capacity . . . . See Chapter 1

Torque wrench settings

	Nm	lbf ft
Engine/transmission rear mounting through-bolt*	103	76
Engine/transmission rear mounting-to-subframe.	23	17
Transmission-to-engine	40	30

* Use a new bolt

1 General information

The transmission is contained in a cast-aluminium alloy casing bolted to the engine's left-hand end, and consists of the gearbox and final drive differential.

Drive is transmitted from the crankshaft via the clutch to the input shaft, which has a splined extension to accept the clutch friction disc, and rotates in roller bearings at each end. From the input shaft, drive is transmitted to the output shaft, which also rotates in roller bearings at each end. From the output shaft, the drive is transmitted to the differential crown-wheel, which rotates with the differential case and planetary gears, thus driving the sun gears and driveshafts. The rotation of the planetary gears on their shaft allows the inner roadwheel to rotate at a slower speed than the outer roadwheel when the vehicle is cornering.

The input and output shafts are arranged side-by-side, parallel to the crankshaft and driveshafts, so that their gear pinion teeth are in constant mesh. In the neutral position, the output shaft gear pinions rotate freely, so that drive cannot be transmitted to the crownwheel.

Gear selection is via a floor-mounted lever and cable-operated selector linkage mechanism. The selector linkage causes the appropriate selector fork to move its respective synchro-sleeve along the shaft,

to lock the gear pinion to the synchro-hub. Since the synchro-hubs are splined to the output shaft, this locks the pinion to the shaft, so that drive can be transmitted. To ensure that gearchanging can be made quickly and quietly, a synchromesh system is fitted to all gears, consisting of baulk rings and spring-loaded fingers, as well as the gear pinions and synchro-hubs. The synchromesh cones are formed on the mating faces of the baulk rings and gear pinions.

Because of the complexity, possible unavailability of parts and special tools necessary, internal repair procedures for the transmission are not recommended for the home mechanic. The bulk of the information in this Chapter is therefore devoted to removal and refitting procedures.

2.3a Release the retaining clips securing the cover to the base of the gearchange lever housing . . .

2.3b . . . then lower the right-hand side of the cover and slide it to the rear to disengage the locating lugs

2.4 Retain the gearchange lever in neutral by inserting a 10 mm bolt, 30 mm long (arrowed) through the locking hole

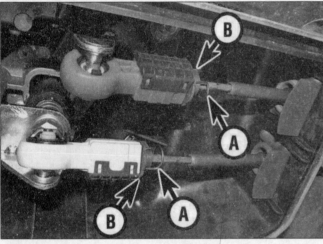

2.5 Remove the wire retaining clips (A) on the cable end fittings, then pull out the locking sliders (B)

3.4 Extract the retaining clips (arrowed) securing each outer cable to the gearchange lever housing

2 Gearchange cables – adjustment

1 Move the driver's seat fully forward, open the battery box cover and disconnect the battery negative terminal (refer to *Disconnecting the battery* in the Reference Chapter).
2 Firmly apply the handbrake, then jack up the front of the vehicle and support it securely on axle stands (see *Jacking and vehicle support*).
3 From under the vehicle, release the four

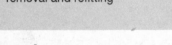

3.5 Press the locking tabs (arrowed) together and slide the inner cable end fittings off the gearchange housing linkage arms

retaining clips securing the cover to the base of the gearchange lever housing. Lower the right-hand side of the cover and slide it to the rear to disengage the locating lugs **(see illustrations)**.
4 Move the gearchange lever to the neutral position and retain it in neutral by inserting a 10 mm bolt, 30 mm long through the locking hole at the base of the gearchange lever **(see illustration)**. Screw the bolt into the corresponding hole in the lever housing to lock the lever in position.
5 Remove the wire retaining clips on the cable end fittings, then pull out the locking sliders **(see illustration)**. Note that on vehicles manufactured after September 2003, only the selector cable is adjustable, no adjustment is possible on the shift cable.
6 Make sure that the selector levers on the transmission are both in the neutral position, then push the locking slider(s) back into the cable end fittings. Refit the retaining clips to secure the locking sliders.
7 Remove the bolt securing the gearchange lever in the neutral position and check the operation of the gearchange mechanism.
8 Refit the cover to the base of the gearchange lever housing.
9 Lower the vehicle to the ground and reconnect the battery negative terminal.

3 Gearchange lever – removal and refitting

Removal

1 Move the driver's seat fully forward, open the battery box cover and disconnect the battery negative terminal (refer to *Disconnecting the battery* in the Reference Chapter).
2 Firmly apply the handbrake, then jack up the front of the vehicle and support it securely on axle stands (see *Jacking and vehicle support*).
3 From under the vehicle, release the four retaining clips securing the cover to the base of the gearchange lever housing. Lower the right-hand side of the cover and slide it to the rear to disengage the locating lugs **(see illustrations 2.3a and 2.3b)**.
4 Extract the retaining clip securing each outer cable to the gearchange lever housing **(see illustration)**.
5 Press the locking tabs together and slide the inner cable end fittings off the gearchange housing linkage arms **(see illustration)**.
6 Undo the four nuts securing the gearchange housing to the underbody **(see illustration)**.
7 From inside the vehicle, pull up the gearchange lever rubber boot and pull out the

3.6 Gearchange housing retaining nuts (arrowed)

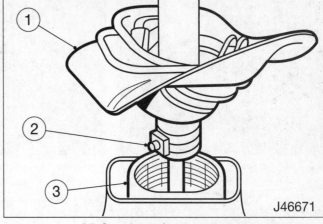

3.7 Gearchange lever components

1 *Rubber boot*   2 *Locking plunger*   3 *Insulator*

locking plunger securing the lever to the lever base **(see illustration)**.

8 Lift out the insulator and remove the gearchange lever housing from the vehicle.

Refitting

9 Refitting is a reversal of removal. On completion, check the gearchange cable adjustment as described in Section 2.

| 4 | Gearchange cables –
removal and refitting |
|---|---|

Removal

1 Move the driver's seat fully forward, open the battery box cover and disconnect the battery negative terminal (refer to *Disconnecting the battery* in the Reference Chapter).

2 Firmly apply the handbrake, then jack up the front of the vehicle and support it securely on axle stands (see *Jacking and vehicle support*).

3 From under the vehicle, release the four retaining clips securing the cover to the base of the gearchange lever housing. Lower the right-hand side of the cover and slide it to the rear to disengage the locating lugs **(see illustrations 2.3a and 2.3b)**.

4 Extract the retaining clip securing each outer cable to the gearchange lever housing **(see illustration 3.4)**.

5 Press the locking tabs together and slide the inner cable end fittings off the gearchange lever linkage arms **(see illustration 3.5)**.

6 At the transmission end of the cables, press the locking tabs together and slide the inner cable end fittings off the transmission selector levers **(see illustration)**.

7 Pull out the locking pins and withdraw the

outer cable end fittings from the transmission abutment bracket.

8 Note the correct routing of the cables and remove them from under the vehicle.

Refitting

9 Refitting is a reversal of removal. On completion, check the gearchange cable adjustment as described in Section 2.

| 5 | Vehicle speed sensor –
removal and refitting |
|---|---|

Removal

1 Move the driver's seat fully forward, open the battery box cover and disconnect the battery negative terminal (refer to *Disconnecting the battery* in the Reference Chapter).

2 Firmly apply the handbrake, then jack up the front of the vehicle and support it securely on axle stands (see *Jacking and vehicle support*).

3 Disconnect the wiring connector from the vehicle speed sensor.

4 Unscrew the retaining bolt and remove the sensor from the transmission **(see illustration)**.

Refitting

5 Refitting is a reversal of the removal procedure. Where applicable, fit a new O-ring to the speed sensor.

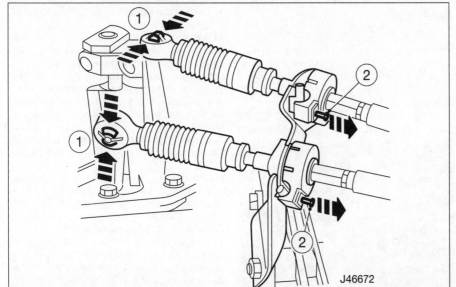

4.6 Press the locking tabs (1) together to release the inner cable end fittings, then pull out the locking pins (2) and withdraw the outer cable end fittings from the transmission abutment bracket

5.4 Vehicle speed sensor retaining bolt (arrowed)

6.3 Prise out the oil seal with a suitable lever

6.6 Using a socket to drive in the new seal

6 Oil seals – renewal

Differential oil seals

1 The differential oil seals are located at the sides of the transmission, where the driveshafts enter the transmission. If leakage at the seal is suspected, firmly apply the handbrake, then jack up the front of the vehicle and support it securely on axle stands (see *Jacking and vehicle support*). If the seal is leaking, oil will be found on the side of the transmission below the driveshaft.

2 Refer to Chapter 8 and remove the appropriate driveshaft.

3 Using a large screwdriver or lever, carefully prise the oil seal out of the transmission casing, taking care not to damage the casing **(see illustration)**.

4 Wipe clean the oil seal seating area in the transmission casing.

5 Apply a smear of grease to the outer lip of the new oil seal. Ensure the seal is correctly positioned, then press it a little way into the casing by hand, making sure that it is square to its seating.

6 Using suitable tubing or a large socket, carefully drive the oil seal into the casing until it contacts the seating **(see illustration)**.

7 Refit the driveshaft with reference to Chapter 8.

8 Check the oil level in the transmission as described in Chapter 1.

Input shaft oil seal

9 The input shaft oil seal is an integral part of the clutch release cylinder. If the seal is leaking it will be necessary to renew the complete release cylinder assembly as described in Chapter 6.

Vehicle speed sensor O-ring

10 This procedure is covered in Section 5 of this Chapter.

7 Reversing light switch – removal and refitting

Removal

1 The reversing light circuit is controlled by a switch mounted on the gearchange selector lever bracket located on the top of the transmission casing.

2 Disconnect the wiring connector from the reversing light switch.

3 Unscrew the switch from the selector lever bracket on the transmission.

Refitting

4 Refitting is a reversal of the removal procedure.

8 Transmission – removal and refitting

Note: *Read through this procedure before*

starting work to see what is involved, particularly in terms of lifting equipment. Depending on the facilities available, the home mechanic may prefer to remove the engine and transmission together, then separate them on the bench, as described in Chapter 2C.

Removal

1 Move the driver's seat fully forward, open the battery box cover and disconnect the battery negative terminal (refer to *Disconnecting the battery* in the Reference Chapter).

2 Firmly apply the handbrake, then jack up the front of the vehicle and support it securely on axle stands (see *Jacking and vehicle support*). There must be sufficient clearance below the vehicle for the transmission to be lowered and removed. Remove both front roadwheels.

3 Disconnect the wiring connector from the vehicle speed sensor located above the right-hand driveshaft intermediate shaft.

4 Disconnect the wiring connector from the crankshaft position sensor, located at the top of the bellhousing, to the rear.

5 Undo the four bolts securing the engine/transmission rear mounting to the front subframe. Undo the through-bolt securing the mounting to the transmission and remove the mounting from under the vehicle **(see illustrations)**. Note that a new through-bolt will be required for refitting.

6 Remove the driveshafts as described in Chapter 8.

7 Undo the two nuts and two bolts and remove the heater pipe retaining bracket from the transmission casing.

8 Press the locking tabs together and slide the gearchange inner cable end fittings off the transmission selector levers (see Section 4). Pull out the locking pins and withdraw the outer cable end fittings from the transmission abutment bracket.

9 Remove the starter motor as described in Chapter 5.

10 Using a small screwdriver, prise out the retaining clip and disconnect the clutch hydraulic pipe from the transmission (use a suitable clamp on the hydraulic flexible hose to prevent leakage) **(see illustrations)**. Cover both the union and the pipe ends to minimise fluid loss and prevent the entry of dirt into the hydraulic system.

Caution: Whilst the hydraulic hose/pipe is disconnected, DO NOT depress the clutch pedal.

11 Disconnect the wiring from the reversing light switch on the top of the transmission.

12 Detach the engine wiring harness from the support bracket.

13 Release the exhaust system rubber mountings from the underbody brackets and lower the system onto the rear axle.

14 The engine and transmission must now be supported, as the left-hand mounting must be disconnected. This can be done using a support bar which locates in the tops of the inner wing panels, and connected to the engine lifting eye at the left-hand end of the

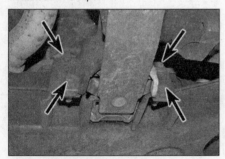

8.5a Undo the four bolts (arrowed) securing the engine/transmission rear mounting to the subframe . . .

8.5b . . . then undo the through-bolt (arrowed) securing the mounting to the transmission

cylinder head – proprietary engine support bars are available from tool outlets.

15 If a support bar is not available, an engine hoist should be used. With an engine hoist, the engine/transmission can be manoeuvred more easily and safely; balancing the engine on a jack is not recommended.

16 Support the transmission with a trolley jack from below, then remove the engine/ transmission left-hand mounting as described in Chapter 2A.

17 Lower the engine/transmission assembly slightly on the left-hand side to provide sufficient clearance for removal of the transmission.

18 Working your way around the transmission casing, slacken and remove the transmission-to-engine securing bolts. Disconnect any wiring loom brackets, where applicable.

19 With the help of an assistant, withdraw the transmission squarely from the engine, taking care not to allow its weight to hang on the clutch friction disc. Once the transmission is free, lower the transmission on the jack and manoeuvre the unit out from under the vehicle.

20 The clutch components can now be inspected with reference to Chapter 6, and renewed if necessary. Unless they are virtually new, it is worth renewing the clutch components as a matter of course, even if the transmission has been removed for some other reason.

Refitting

21 With the transmission secured on the trolley jack as on removal, raise it into position, and then carefully slide it onto the engine, at the same time engaging the input shaft with the clutch friction disc splines. Do not use excessive force to refit the transmission – if the input shaft does not slide into place easily, readjust the angle of the transmission so that it is level, and/or turn the input shaft so that the splines engage properly with the disc. If problems are still experienced, check that the clutch friction disc is correctly centred (Chapter 6).

22 The remainder of refitting is a reversal of the removal procedure, bearing in mind the following points:

a) Use a new through-bolt when refitting the engine/transmission rear mounting.

b) Tighten all nuts and bolts to the specified torque (where given).

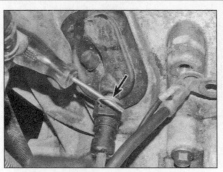

8.10a Prise out the retaining clip . . .

c) If required, renew the differential oil seals as described in Section 6.

d) Refit the driveshafts as described in Chapter 8.

e) Check and if necessary top-up the oil level in the transmission as described in Chapter 1.

f) If required, adjust the gearchange cables as described in Section 2.

23 Make a final check that all connections have been made, and all bolts tightened fully. Road test the vehicle to check for proper transmission operation, then check the transmission visually for leakage of oil.

9 Transmission overhaul – general information

Overhauling a manual transmission unit is a difficult and involved job for the DIY home mechanic. In addition to dismantling and reassembling many small parts, clearances must be precisely measured and, if necessary, changed by selecting shims and spacers. Internal transmission components are also often difficult to obtain, and in many instances, extremely expensive. Because of this, if the transmission develops a fault or becomes noisy, the best course of action is to have the unit overhauled by a specialist repairer, or to obtain an exchange reconditioned unit.

Nevertheless, it is not impossible for the more experienced mechanic to overhaul the transmission, provided the special tools are available, and the job is done in a deliberate step-by-step manner, so that nothing is overlooked.

The tools necessary for an overhaul include

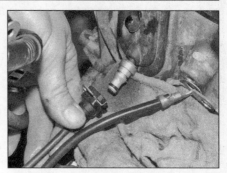

8.10b . . . and disconnect the clutch hydraulic pipe

internal and external circlip pliers, bearing pullers, a slide hammer, a set of pin punches, a dial test indicator, and possibly a hydraulic press. In addition, a large, sturdy workbench and a vice will be required.

During dismantling of the transmission, make careful notes of how each component is fitted, to make reassembly easier and more accurate.

Before dismantling the transmission, it will help if you have some idea what area is malfunctioning. Certain problems can be closely related to specific areas in the transmission, which can make component examination and replacement easier. Refer to the *Fault finding* Section of this manual for more information.

10 Transmission oil draining and refilling – general information

The VXT-75 transmission is essentially a 'sealed for life' unit and renewal of the transmission oil is not required in service. No provision is made for transmission oil draining and a drain plug is not fitted.

If for any reason it is felt necessary to renew the transmission oil, this can only be done by removing the transmission from the vehicle, tipping it on its side, and allowing the oil to drain from the driveshaft apertures in the differential.

Refilling and/or topping up of the transmission oil is carried out through the filler/level plug aperture on the front face of the transmission. Refer to the *Transmission oil level check* procedures contained in Chapter 1 for details.

Notes

Chapter 7 Part B:
Manual transmission – rear-wheel drive models

Contents

Degrees of difficulty

Easy, suitable for novice with little experience	**Fairly easy,** suitable for beginner with some experience	**Fairly difficult,** suitable for competent DIY mechanic	**Difficult,** suitable for experienced DIY mechanic	**Very difficult,** suitable for expert DIY or professional

Specifications

General

Type	5 or 6 forward speeds and reverse. Synchromesh on all forward speeds and on reverse
Designation:	
5-speed transmission	MT-75
6-speed transmission	MT-82

Lubrication

Lubricant type	See *Lubricants and fluids* on page 0•18
Lubricant capacity	See Chapter 1

Torque wrench settings

	Nm	lbf ft

5-speed transmissions

	Nm	lbf ft
Front subframe mountings:		
Bolts	250	185
Nuts	175	129
Gearchange lever base-to-transmission bracket	12	9
Input shaft guide sleeve-to-transmission	250	185
Oil filler and drain plugs	35	26
Output shaft flange locknut*	200	148
Propeller shaft centre bearing retaining bolts*	22	16
Propeller shaft rubber coupling-to-output shaft flange*	115	85
Propeller shaft universal joint flange-to-output shaft flange*	80	59
Reversing light switch	12	9
Steering column intermediate shaft flexible coupling pinch bolt nut*	23	17
Transmission mounting-to-subframe	40	30
Transmission-to-engine	40	30

6-speed transmissions

	Nm	lbf ft
Front subframe mountings:		
Bolts	250	185
Nuts	175	129
Gearchange lever bracket-to-transmission	25	19
Output shaft flange retaining bolt:		
Stage 1	210	155
Stage 2	Slacken the bolt completely	
Stage 3	180	133
Propeller shaft centre bearing retaining bolts*	22	16
Propeller shaft rubber coupling-to-output shaft flange*	175	129
Oil drain plug	50	37
Oil filler plug	35	26
Steering column intermediate shaft flexible coupling pinch bolt nut*	23	17
Transmission mounting-to-subframe	40	30
Transmission-to-engine	40	30

* Use new nuts/bolts

1 General information

Rear wheel drive models covered by this manual are fitted with either a 5- or 6-speed manual transmission. The transmission is mounted in-line, and to the rear of the engine. A propeller shaft transfers the drive to the rear axle.

The MT-75 (5-speed) and MT-82 (6-speed) transmissions are of similar design and construction, both being of constant-mesh type, with five (or six) forward speeds and one reverse. The input shaft and mainshaft are in-line, and rotate on ball and roller bearings in the front and rear transmission housings. Caged needle-roller bearings are used to support the mainshaft spigot, the countershaft gear assembly and the gears on the mainshaft.

The synchronisers are of baulk ring type, and operate in conjunction with tapered cones machined onto the gears. When engaging a gear, the synchroniser sleeve pushes the baulk ring against the tapered gear cone by means of synchroniser rings. The drag of the baulk ring causes the gear to rotate at the same speed as the synchroniser unit, and at this point, further movement of the sleeve locks the sleeve, baulk ring and gear dog teeth together.

Reverse gear is obtained by moving the reverse idler gear into mesh with the countershaft gear and the spur teeth of the 1st/2nd synchroniser.

The gearchange lever is mounted on a support bracket attached to the rear of the transmission, and engages directly with the transmission selector shaft.

Because of the complexity, possible unavailability of parts and special tools necessary, internal repair procedures for the transmission are not recommended for the home mechanic. The bulk of the information in this Chapter is therefore devoted to removal and refitting procedures.

2 Gearchange lever – removal and refitting

5-speed transmissions

Removal

1 From inside the vehicle, move the gearchange lever into the 3rd gear position, then disengage the rubber gaiter from the floor locating flange, and slide it up the gearchange lever **(see illustration)**.
2 Pull out the locking plunger on the gearchange lever and remove the lever extension from the primary lever.
3 Remove the insulator and insulation pad from the lever base.
4 Undo the four bolts securing the lever base to the transmission bracket, and withdraw the lever base from the vehicle.

Refitting

5 Refitting is a reversal of removal, but tighten the gear lever base retaining bolts to the specified torque.

6-speed transmissions

Removal

6 From inside the vehicle, move the gearchange lever into the 3rd gear position, then disengage the rubber gaiter from the floor locating flange, and slide it up the gearchange lever **(see illustration)**.
7 Lift the locking tabs securing the gearchange lever extension to the primary lever and remove the lever extension **(see illustration)**.
8 Lift out the rubber insulator fitted around the gearchange lever base **(see illustration)**.
9 Undo the four bolts securing the lever

2.1 Gearchange lever components – 5-speed transmissions

1 *Lever extension*	5 *Locking collar*	9 *Bush*
2 *Floor locating flange*	6 *Insulation pad*	10 *Transmission bracket*
3 *Insulator*	7 *Locking plunger*	11 *Selector shaft*
4 *Primary lever*	8 *Lever base*	*coupling*

J46673

2.6 Disengage the rubber gaiter from the floor locating flange – 6-speed transmissions

2.7 Lift the locking tabs and remove the lever extension from the primary lever – 6-speed transmissions

2.8 Lift out the rubber insulator fitted around the gearchange lever base – 6-speed transmissions

base to the transmission bracket, and withdraw the lever base from the vehicle **(see illustrations)**.

Refitting

10 Refitting is a reversal of removal.

---

3 Vehicle speed sensor – removal and refitting

Removal

1 On 5-speed transmissions the vehicle speed sensor is located on the left-hand side of the transmission, adjacent to the output shaft flange. On 6-speed transmissions, the sensor is located on the lower right-hand side of the transmission **(see illustration)**.

2 Firmly apply the handbrake, then jack up the front of the vehicle and support it securely on axle stands (see *Jacking and vehicle support*).

3 Drain the transmission oil as described in Section 10, or be prepared for oil spillage when the sensor is removed.

4 Disconnect the vehicle speed sensor wiring connector.

5 Unscrew the retaining bolt and remove the sensor from the transmission.

Refitting

6 Refitting is a reversal of the removal procedure. On completion refill or top-up the transmission oil as described in Section 10, or Chapter 1, as applicable.

---

4 Oil seals – renewal

Front (input shaft) oil seal

5-speed transmissions

Note: *The following procedure entails the use of Ford special tool 308-109 to remove and refit the input shaft guide sleeve. Ensure that this tool, or a suitable alternative, is available before proceeding.*

1 Remove the transmission from the vehicle as described in Section 6.

2.9a Undo the four bolts securing the lever base to the transmission bracket . . .

2.9b . . . and withdraw the lever base from the vehicle – 6-speed transmissions

2 Thoroughly clean the transmission assembly, paying particular attention to the area inside the clutch housing.

3 Free the clutch release bearing from the release lever and withdraw it from the input shaft guide sleeve.

4 Pull the release lever off its mounting stud, then withdraw the lever over the guide sleeve and input shaft.

5 Using Ford special tool 308-109 or a suitable alternative, unscrew the input shaft guide sleeve, and withdraw it from the transmission **(see illustration)**. Take care not to lose the thrustwasher located behind the guide sleeve.

6 Using a screwdriver, prise out the old oil seal from the guide sleeve bore. Fit the new oil seal using a large socket or tube of suitable diameter to drive it home. Ensure that the seal is fitted so that the sealing lip faces the transmission case when installed. Also renew the large O-ring on the periphery of the guide sleeve **(see illustration)**.

7 Lubricate the oil seal lip and the O-ring with a smear of multi-purpose grease.

8 Refit the guide sleeve and thrustwasher, and tighten it to the specified torque using the special tool or an alternative.

9 Apply a thin smear of high-melting-point grease to the guide sleeve and release lever mounting stud, then refit the clutch release bearing and lever.

10 Refit the transmission as described in Section 6.

6-speed transmissions

11 Remove the transmission from the vehicle as described in Section 7.

12 Thoroughly clean the transmission assembly, paying particular attention to the area inside the clutch housing.

13 Remove the clutch release cylinder as described in Chapter 6.

14 Carefully punch or drill two small holes opposite each other in the oil seal. Screw a self-tapping screw into each and pull on the screws with pliers to extract the seal.

15 Clean the seal housing and polish off any burrs or raised edges which may have caused the seal to fail in the first place.

16 Lubricate the lip of the new oil seal with a smear of multi-purpose grease, then ease the seal into position on the end of the input shaft. Press the seal a little way into the housing by hand, making sure that it is square to its seating then, using suitable tubing, carefully drive the oil seal fully into the housing. Take great care not to damage the seal lips during fitting and ensure that the seal lips face inwards.

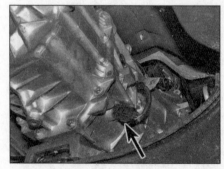

3.1 Vehicle speed sensor location – 6-speed transmissions

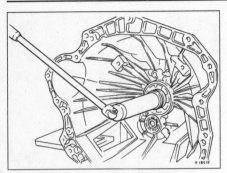

4.5 Using Ford special tool 308-109 to unscrew the input shaft guide sleeve – 5-speed transmissions

4.6 Input shaft guide sleeve showing oil seal location and O-ring – 5-speed transmissions

4.20 Propeller shaft centre bearing and retaining bolts

17 Refit the clutch release cylinder as described in Chapter 6, then refit the transmission as described in Section 7.

Rear (output shaft) oil seal

Note: *A new output shaft flange retaining nut, new propeller shaft universal joint/rubber coupling retaining bolts, and new propeller shaft centre bearing retaining bolts will be required for refitting.*

18 Firmly apply the handbrake, then jack up the front of the vehicle and support it securely on axle stands (see *Jacking and vehicle support*).

19 Drain the transmission oil as described in Section 10.

20 Slacken the two bolts securing the propeller shaft front centre bearing to the underbody **(see illustration)**. Do not remove the bolts completely at this stage.

21 If the propeller shaft incorporates a universal

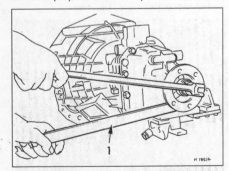

4.23 Using a bar (1) bolted to the output shaft flange to hold it stationary while unscrewing the retaining nut/bolt

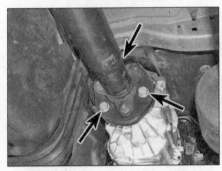

4.22 Propeller shaft flexible rubber coupling retaining bolts (arrowed)

joint at its forward end, mark the relative positions of the propeller shaft universal joint flange and transmission output shaft flange. Undo the four bolts securing the universal joint flange to the output shaft flange, then remove the two previously slackened centre bearing retaining bolts. Separate the flanges and position the propeller shaft to one side. Note that new flange retaining bolts and new centre bearing retaining bolts will be required for refitting.

22 If the propeller shaft incorporates a flexible rubber coupling at its forward end, mark the relative positions of the rubber coupling and transmission output shaft flange. Undo the three bolts securing the rubber coupling to the output shaft flange, then remove the two previously slackened centre bearing retaining bolts **(see illustration)**. Detach the rubber coupling from the output shaft flange and position the propeller shaft to one side. Note

4.32 Fit a clamp (arrowed) consisting of two worm-drive hose clips joined together to compress the rubber coupling when refitting

that new rubber coupling retaining bolts and new centre bearing retaining bolts will be required for refitting.

23 Using a bar or suitable forked tool bolted to the output shaft flange holes, hold the flange stationary and unscrew the retaining nut (5-speed transmissions) or retaining bolt (6-speed transmissions) **(see illustration)**. Note that on 5-speed transmissions, a new nut will be required when refitting.

24 Withdraw the output shaft flange using a two- or three-legged puller.

25 Using a screwdriver, prise the old oil seal out of its location in the transmission housing. Alternatively, screw two self-tapping screws into the face of the oil seal, 180° apart. Using pliers, pull or lever on each screw alternately to withdraw the oil seal.

26 Wipe clean the oil seal seating in the housing.

27 Press the new seal a little way into the housing by hand, making sure that it is square to its seating.

28 Using suitable tubing or a large socket, carefully drive the oil seal fully into the housing.

29 Lubricate the oil seal lip and the running surface of the output shaft flange, then refit the flange to the output shaft.

30 Fit a new nut/bolt, and tighten it to the specified torque. Whilst tightening, prevent the output shaft flange from turning by holding it as described for removal.

31 If the propeller shaft incorporates a universal joint at its forward end, align the flange marks made on removal and fit the new flange retaining bolts. Refit the propeller shaft centre bearing using two new bolts then tighten the universal joint flange bolts, followed by the centre bearing bolts, to the specified torque.

32 If the propeller shaft incorporates a flexible rubber coupling at its forward end, fit a clamp, comprising of two worm-drive hose clips joined together, around the circumference of the coupling, and tighten it until it just begins to compress the rubber. Align the marks made on the rubber coupling and transmission output shaft flange, then fit the new rubber coupling retaining bolts **(see illustration)**. Refit the propeller shaft centre bearing using two new bolts then tighten the rubber coupling bolts, followed by the centre bearing bolts, to the specified torque. Remove the clamp from the coupling.

33 Refill the transmission with oil as described in Section 10, then lower the vehicle to the ground.

5	Reversing light switch – removal and refitting

5-speed transmissions

Removal

1 The reversing light circuit is controlled by a plunger-type switch screwed into the upper left-hand side of the transmission casing.

2 Firmly apply the handbrake, then jack up the front of the vehicle and support it securely on axle stands (see *Jacking and vehicle support*).
3 Disconnect the wiring from the reversing light switch, then unscrew the two bolts and remove the switch from the side of the transmission.

Refitting

4 Refitting is a reversal of the removal procedure, ensuring that the two retaining bolts are tightened securely. On completion, check and if necessary, top-up the transmission oil level with reference to Chapter 1.

6-speed transmissions

Removal

5 The reversing light circuit is controlled by a plunger-type switch screwed into the upper left-hand side of the transmission casing, at the rear.
6 Firmly apply the handbrake, then jack up the front of the vehicle and support it securely on axle stands (see *Jacking and vehicle support*).
7 Disconnect the wiring from the reversing light switch, then unscrew the switch from the side of the transmission.

Refitting

8 Refitting is a reversal of the removal procedure, ensuring that the switch is tightened securely. On completion, check and if necessary, top-up the transmission oil level with reference to Chapter 1.

---

6   Transmission (5-speed) –
    removal and refitting

Note 1: *The transmission can be removed as a unit with the engine as described in Chapter 2C, then separated from the engine on the bench. However, if work is only necessary on the transmission or clutch unit, it is better to remove the transmission on its own from underneath the vehicle. The latter method is described in this Section. The aid of an assistant will be required during the actual removal and refitting procedures.*
Note 2: *New propeller shaft universal joint/ rubber coupling retaining bolts, new propeller shaft centre bearing retaining bolts and a new steering column flexible coupling lower pinch bolt and nut will be required for refitting.*

Removal

1 Move the driver's seat fully forward, open the battery box cover and disconnect the battery negative terminal (refer to *Disconnecting the battery* in the Reference Chapter).
2 Remove the gearchange lever as described in Section 2.
3 Firmly apply the handbrake, then jack up the front of the vehicle and support it securely on axle stands (see *Jacking and vehicle support*). There must be sufficient clearance below the vehicle for the transmission to be lowered and removed.

6.9 Steering column intermediate shaft flexible coupling pinch bolt (arrowed)

4 If any work is to be carried out on the transmission after removal, it is advisable, at this stage, to drain the transmission oil as described in Section 10.
5 Slacken the two bolts securing the propeller shaft front centre bearing to the underbody **(see illustration 4.20)**. Do not remove the bolts completely at this stage.
6 If the propeller shaft incorporates a universal joint at its forward end, mark the relative positions of the propeller shaft universal joint flange and transmission output shaft flange. Undo the four bolts securing the universal joint flange to the output shaft flange, then remove the two previously slackened centre bearing retaining bolts. Separate the flanges and position the propeller shaft to one side. Note that new flange retaining bolts and new centre bearing retaining bolts will be required for refitting.
7 If the propeller shaft incorporates a flexible rubber coupling at its forward end, mark the relative positions of the rubber coupling and transmission output shaft flange. Undo the three bolts securing the rubber coupling to the output shaft flange, then remove the two previously slackened centre bearing retaining bolts. Detach the rubber coupling from the output shaft flange and position the propeller shaft to one side. Note that new rubber coupling retaining bolts and new centre bearing retaining bolts will be required for refitting.
8 Turn the steering wheel to set the roadwheels in the straight-ahead position, then remove the ignition key to lock the column.

6.18a Front subframe right-hand side retaining bolt (arrowed) . . .

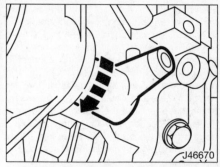

6.12 Rotate the clutch slave cylinder anticlockwise, then remove it from the transmission housing

9 Undo the nut and remove the lower pinch bolt securing the steering column intermediate shaft flexible coupling to the steering gear pinion shaft **(see illustration)**. Note that a new pinch bolt and nut will be required for refitting. Where fitted, extract the circlip from the base of the flexible coupling. Slide the flexible coupling up and off the steering gear pinion shaft.
10 Where applicable, undo the retaining clamp bolt and release the power steering fluid pipes from the front subframe.
11 Undo the two bolts securing the transmission mounting support bracket to the front subframe.
12 Rotate the clutch slave cylinder anticlockwise to release it, then remove the cylinder from the left-hand side of the transmission **(see illustration)**.
13 Disconnect the wiring connectors from the vehicle speed sensor and reversing light switch.
14 Detach the heat shield and disconnect the wiring connector from the crankshaft position sensor.
15 Remove the starter motor as described in Chapter 5.
16 Support the engine by positioning a wooden block of suitable thickness between the sump and the engine crossmember.
17 Position a trolley jack beneath the centre of the front subframe and just take the weight of the subframe.
18 Undo the bolt and nut each side securing the front subframe to the underbody **(see illustrations)**. Lower the jack and front subframe approximately 100 mm.

6.18b . . . and retaining nut (arrowed)

19 Enlist the aid of an assistant to help steady the transmission, then work around the transmission casing and slacken and remove the transmission-to-engine securing bolts.

20 Check that all fixings are fully disconnected and positioned out of the way, then pull the transmission rearwards and detach it from the engine. Where applicable, it may be necessary to initially prise free the clutch housing from the engine location dowels. At no time during its removal (and subsequent refitting), allow the weight of the transmission to rest on the input shaft.

21 When the unit is fully clear of the engine, lower it, and withdraw it from underneath the vehicle.

22 The clutch components can now be inspected with reference to Chapter 6, and renewed if necessary. Unless they are virtually new, it is worth renewing the clutch components as a matter of course, even if the transmission has been removed for some other reason.

Refitting

23 Before lifting the unit into position, check that the clutch release bearing is correctly positioned, and apply a thin smear of high-melting-point grease to the transmission input shaft.

24 Lift the transmission into position, and then carefully slide it onto the rear of the engine, at the same time engaging the input shaft with the clutch friction disc splines. Do not use excessive force to refit the transmission – if the input shaft does not slide into place easily, turn the input shaft so that the splines engage properly with the disc. If problems are still experienced, check that the clutch friction disc is correctly centred (Chapter 6).

25 Once the transmission is fully engaged with the engine, insert the retaining bolts and tighten them to the specified torque.

26 Raise the trolley jack and front subframe back into position and refit the retaining nut and bolt each side. Tighten the nuts/bolts to the specified torque, then remove the trolley jack and the wooden block positioned under the sump.

27 Refit the two bolts securing the transmission mounting/support bracket to the subframe and tighten the bolts to the specified torque.

28 Refit the starter motor as described in Chapter 5.

29 Reconnect the crankshaft position sensor wiring connector, then locate the sensor heat shield back in position.

30 Reconnect the wiring connectors at the vehicle speed sensor and reversing light switch.

31 Ensuring that the clutch slave cylinder pushrod correctly engages with the release lever, place the slave cylinder in position and turn it clockwise to secure.

32 Where applicable, refit the power steering fluid pipe clamp to the subframe and tighten the clamp bolt securely.

33 Refit the steering column intermediate shaft flexible coupling to the steering gear pinion shaft. Fit the new pinch bolt and nut, then tighten the nut to the specified torque.

34 If the propeller shaft incorporates a universal joint at its forward end, align the flange marks made on removal and fit the new flange retaining bolts. Refit the propeller shaft centre bearing using two new bolts then tighten the universal joint flange bolts, followed by the centre bearing bolts, to the specified torque.

35 If the propeller shaft incorporates a flexible rubber coupling at its forward end, fit a clamp, comprising of two worm-drive hose clips joined together, around the circumference of the coupling, and tighten it until it just begins to compress the rubber. Align the marks made on the rubber coupling and transmission output shaft flange, then fit the new rubber coupling retaining bolts **(see illustration 4.32)**. Refit the propeller shaft centre bearing using two new bolts then tighten the rubber coupling bolts, followed by the centre bearing bolts, to the specified torque. Remove the clamp from the coupling.

36 Refit the gearchange lever as described in Section 2.

37 Refill/top-up the transmission oil with reference to Section 10 and/or Chapter 1, then lower the vehicle to the ground and reconnect the battery negative terminal.

7 Transmission (6-speed) – removal and refitting

Note 1: *The transmission can be removed as a unit with the engine as described in Chapter 2C, then separated from the engine on the bench. However, if work is only necessary on the transmission or clutch unit, it is better to remove the transmission on its own from underneath the vehicle. The latter method is described in this Section. The aid of an assistant will be required during the actual removal and refitting procedures.*

Note 2: *New propeller shaft rubber coupling retaining bolts, new propeller shaft centre bearing retaining bolts and a new steering column flexible coupling lower pinch bolt and nut will be required for refitting.*

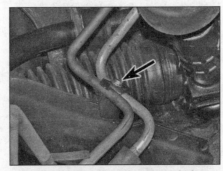

7.9 Undo the retaining clamp bolt (arrowed) and release the power steering fluid pipes from the subframe

Note 3: *Ford special tool 308-561 will be required to accurately align the gearchange lever bracket when refitting the transmission.*

Removal

1 Move the driver's seat fully forward, open the battery box cover and disconnect the battery negative terminal (refer to *Disconnecting the battery* in the Reference Chapter).

2 Remove the gearchange lever as described in Section 2.

3 Firmly apply the handbrake, then jack up the front of the vehicle and support it securely on axle stands (see *Jacking and vehicle support*). There must be sufficient clearance below the vehicle for the transmission to be lowered and removed.

4 If any work is to be carried out on the transmission after removal, it is advisable, at this stage, to drain the transmission oil as described in Section 10.

5 Slacken the two bolts securing the propeller shaft front centre bearing to the underbody **(see illustration 4.20)**. Do not remove the bolts completely at this stage.

6 Mark the relative positions of the propeller shaft rubber coupling and transmission output shaft flange. Undo the three bolts securing the rubber coupling to the output shaft flange, then remove the two previously slackened centre bearing retaining bolts. Detach the rubber coupling from the output shaft flange and position the propeller shaft to one side. Note that new rubber coupling retaining bolts and new centre bearing retaining bolts will be required for refitting.

7 Turn the steering wheel to set the roadwheels in the straight-ahead position, then remove the ignition key to lock the column.

8 Undo the nut and remove the lower pinch bolt securing the steering column intermediate shaft flexible coupling to the steering gear pinion shaft **(see illustration 6.9)**. Note that a new pinch bolt and nut will be required for refitting. Slide the flexible coupling up and off the steering gear pinion shaft.

9 Undo the retaining clamp bolt and release the power steering fluid pipes from the front subframe **(see illustration)**.

10 Using a small screwdriver, prise out the retaining clip and disconnect the clutch hydraulic hose from the transmission union (use a suitable clamp on the flexible hose to prevent leakage) **(see illustration)**. Cover both the union and the hose ends to minimise fluid loss and prevent the entry of dirt into the hydraulic system.

Caution: Whilst the hydraulic hose is disconnected, DO NOT depress the clutch pedal.

11 Disconnect the wiring connectors from the vehicle speed sensor and reversing light switch.

12 Detach the heat shield and disconnect the wiring connector from the crankshaft position sensor.

13 Remove the starter motor as described in Chapter 5.

14 Undo the two bolts securing the transmission mounting to the front subframe **(see illustration)**.

15 Support the engine by positioning a wooden block of suitable thickness between the sump and the engine crossmember.

16 Position a trolley jack beneath the centre of the front subframe and just take the weight of the subframe.

17 Undo the bolt and nut each side securing the front subframe to the underbody **(see illustrations 6.18a and 6.18b)**. Lower the jack and front subframe approximately 100 mm.

18 Reach up over the top of the transmission and undo the four bolts securing the gearchange lever bracket to the transmission. Manipulate the bracket sideways, twist it through 90° and slide it out down the right-hand side of the transmission **(see illustrations)**.

19 Enlist the aid of an assistant to help steady the transmission, then work around the transmission casing and slacken and remove the transmission-to-engine securing bolts.

20 Check that all fixings are fully disconnected and positioned out of the way, then pull the transmission rearwards and detach it from the engine. Where applicable, it may be necessary to initially prise free the clutch housing from the engine location dowels. At no time during its removal (and subsequent refitting), allow the weight of the transmission to rest on the input shaft.

21 When the unit is fully clear of the engine, lower it, and withdraw it from underneath the vehicle.

22 The clutch components can now be inspected with reference to Chapter 6, and renewed if necessary. Unless they are virtually new, it is worth renewing the clutch components as a matter of course, even if the transmission has been removed for some other reason.

Refitting

23 Before lifting the unit into position, apply a thin smear of high-melting-point grease to the transmission input shaft. Ensure that the transmission is in 3rd gear.

24 Lift the transmission into position, and then carefully slide it onto the rear of the engine, at the same time engaging the input shaft with the clutch friction disc splines. Do not use excessive force to refit the transmission – if the input shaft does not slide into place easily, turn the input shaft so that the splines engage properly with the disc. If problems are still experienced, check that the clutch friction disc is correctly centred (Chapter 6).

25 Once the transmission is fully engaged with the engine, insert the retaining bolts and tighten them to the specified torque.

26 Manipulate the gearchange lever bracket into position on the top of the transmission and insert the four retaining bolts. Only tighten the bolts finger-tight at this stage.

27 From inside the vehicle, refit the gearchange lever base to the lever bracket, ensuring that the lever correctly engages in

7.10 Prise out the retaining clip and disconnect the clutch hydraulic hose from the transmission union

7.18a Undo the four bolts securing the gearchange lever bracket to the transmission . . .

the transmission selector shaft. Insert the four bolts and tighten them securely.

28 With the transmission in 3rd gear, place the aligning tool (Ford special tool 308-561) over the gearchange lever base **(see illustration)**. Move the gearchange lever bracket as necessary until the special tool is fully seated in position. With the gearchange lever bracket now correctly positioned and held in place by the special tool, tighten the four retaining bolts to the specified torque. Remove the special tool.

29 Raise the trolley jack and front subframe back into position and refit the retaining nut and bolt each side. Tighten the nuts/bolts to the specified torque, then remove the trolley jack and the wooden block positioned under the sump.

30 Refit the two bolts securing the transmission mounting to the subframe and tighten the bolts to the specified torque.

31 Refit the starter motor as described in Chapter 5.

32 Reconnect the crankshaft position sensor wiring connector, then locate the sensor heat shield back in position.

33 Reconnect the wiring connectors at the vehicle speed sensor and reversing light switch.

34 Engage the clutch hydraulic hose with the transmission union and refit the hose retaining clip. Remove the hose clamp used to prevent fluid leakage.

35 Refit the power steering fluid pipe clamp to the subframe and tighten the clamp bolt securely.

7.14 Undo the two bolts (arrowed) securing the transmission mounting to the front subframe

7.18b . . . then manipulate the bracket sideways and slide it out down the right-hand side of the transmission

36 Refit the steering column intermediate shaft flexible coupling to the steering gear pinion shaft. Fit the new pinch bolt and nut, then tighten the nut to the specified torque.

37 Fit a clamp, comprising of two worm-drive hose clips joined together, around the circumference of the propeller shaft rubber coupling, and tighten it until it just begins to compress the rubber. Align the marks made on the rubber coupling and transmission output shaft flange, then fit the new rubber coupling retaining bolts **(see illustration 4.32)**. Refit the propeller shaft centre bearing using two new bolts then tighten the rubber coupling bolts, followed by the centre bearing bolts, to the specified torque. Remove the clamp from the coupling.

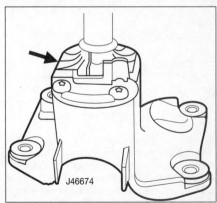

7.28 Ford special tool 308-561 (arrowed) in position on the gearchange lever base

38 From inside the vehicle, refit the rubber insulator to the gearchange lever base. Engage the gearchange lever extension with the lever base, ensuring that it is correctly secured by the two locking tabs. Slide the rubber gaiter down the gearchange lever and into position over the floor locating flange.

39 Refill/top-up the transmission oil with reference to Section 10 and/or Chapter 1.

40 Bleed the clutch hydraulic system as described in Chapter 6.

41 On completion, lower the vehicle to the ground and reconnect the battery negative terminal.

8 Transmission mounting – checking and renewal

This procedure is covered in Chapter 2B.

9 Transmission overhaul – general information

Overhauling a manual transmission unit is a difficult and involved job for the DIY home mechanic. In addition to dismantling and reassembling many small parts, clearances must be precisely measured and, if necessary, changed by selecting shims and spacers. Internal transmission components are also often difficult to obtain, and in many instances, extremely expensive. Because of this, if the transmission develops a fault or becomes noisy, the best course of action is to have the unit overhauled by a specialist repairer, or to obtain an exchange reconditioned unit.

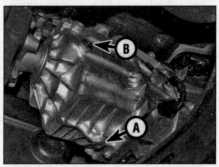

10.2 Transmission oil drain plug (A) and filler/level plug (B) – 6-speed transmissions

Nevertheless, it is not impossible for the more experienced mechanic to overhaul the transmission, provided the special tools are available, and the job is done in a deliberate step-by-step manner, so that nothing is overlooked.

The tools necessary for an overhaul include internal and external circlip pliers, bearing pullers, a slide hammer, a set of pin punches, a dial test indicator, and possibly a hydraulic press. In addition, a large, sturdy workbench and a vice will be required.

During dismantling of the transmission, make careful notes of how each component is fitted, to make reassembly easier and more accurate.

Before dismantling the transmission, it will help if you have some idea what area is malfunctioning. Certain problems can be closely related to specific areas in the transmission, which can make component examination and replacement easier. Refer to the *Fault finding* Section of this manual for more information.

10 Transmission oil – draining and refilling

Caution: If this procedure is to be carried out on a hot transmission unit, take care not to burn yourself on the hot exhaust or the transmission/engine unit.

1 Firmly apply the handbrake, then jack up the front of the vehicle and support it securely on axle stands (see *Jacking and vehicle support*).

2 Wipe clean the area around the drain plug at the base of the transmission and position a suitable container underneath **(see illustration)**.

3 Unscrew the drain plug and allow the transmission oil to drain completely into the container. If the oil is hot, take precautions against scalding.

4 Once the oil has finished draining, ensure the drain plug is clean and refit it to the transmission with a new washer. Tighten the drain plug to the specified torque. Lower the vehicle to the ground.

5 The transmission is refilled through the filler/level plug hole on the side of the transmission casing **(see illustration 10.2)**. Wipe clean the area around the filler/level plug and unscrew it from the casing. Refill the transmission with the specified type and amount of oil given in the specifications, until the oil begins to trickle out of the level hole. Refit the plug and tighten it to the specified torque.

6 Take the vehicle on a short journey so that the new oil is distributed fully around the transmission components.

7 On your return, park on level ground and check the transmission oil level as described in Chapter 1.

Chapter 8
Driveshafts, propeller shaft and rear axle

Contents

Degrees of difficulty

Easy, suitable for novice with little experience	Fairly easy, suitable for beginner with some experience	Fairly difficult, suitable for competent DIY mechanic	Difficult, suitable for experienced DIY mechanic	Very difficult, suitable for expert DIY or professional

Specifications

Driveshafts

Type . . . .   Solid steel shafts with inner and outer constant velocity (CV) joints. Right-hand driveshaft incorporating intermediate shaft

Inner CV joint grease quantity:
  75/85 PS engines . . . .   155 grams
  100/125 PS engines . . . .   250 grams
Outer CV joint grease quantity:
  75/85 PS engines . . . .   155 grams
  100/125 PS engines . . . .   240 grams

Propeller shaft

Type . . . .   Two- or three-piece with centre support bearing(s), centre and rear universal joints, and front universal joint or rubber coupling according to model

Rear axle (front wheel drive models)

Type . . . .   Beam axle supported on semi-eliptic single leaf springs

Rear axle (rear wheel drive models)

Type . . . .   Semi-floating or fully-floating hypoid axle supported on semi-eliptic multi-leaf springs

Rear hub bearing play (twin wheel axles with oil filler plug on the
  drive pinion housing) . . . .   0.05 to 0.20 mm
Lubricant type . . . .   See *Lubricants and fluids* on page 0•18
Lubricant capacity . . . .   See Chapter 1

Torque wrench settings

	Nm	lbf ft
Driveshaft		
Driveshaft retaining nut:*		
Stage 1	Rotate the wheel hub 5 times	
Stage 2	250	185
Stage 3	Rotate the wheel hub 5 times	
Stage 4	420	310
Stage 5	Rotate the wheel hub 5 times	
Intermediate shaft support bearing retaining plate nuts*	25	19
Steering knuckle balljoint-to-lower suspension arm nut*	150	111

Torque wrench settings (continued)

	Nm	lbf ft
Propeller shaft		
Centre bearing housing-to-underbody bolts*	22	16
Flexible rubber coupling-to-transmission output shaft flange bolts:*		
5-speed transmissions	115	85
6-speed transmissions	175	129
Propeller shaft-to-rear axle final drive coupling flange bolts*	80	59
Propeller shaft-to-transmission output shaft flange bolts*	80	59
Rear axle (front wheel drive models)		
Rear hub retaining nut:*		
44 mm flange diameter nut:		
Stage 1	Rotate the wheel hub 5 times	
Stage 2	200	148
Stage 3	Rotate the wheel hub 5 times	
Stage 4	300	221
Stage 5	Rotate the wheel hub 5 times	
51 mm flange diameter nut:		
Stage 1	Rotate the wheel hub 5 times	
Stage 2	200	148
Stage 3	Rotate the wheel hub 5 times	
Stage 4	450	332
Stage 5	Rotate the wheel hub 5 times	
Rear spring-to-axle U-bolt nuts:*		
Stage 1	25	19
Stage 2	50	37
Stage 3	75	55
Stage 4	100	74
Stage 5	125	92
Stage 6	150	111
Stage 7	175	129
Shock absorber lower mounting bolt nuts	80	59
Rear axle (rear wheel drive models)		
ABS wheel speed sensor retaining bolts	8	6
Differential housing cover bolts:		
Axles with oil filler plug on the differential housing cover	61	45
Axles with oil filler plug on the drive pinion housing	45	33
Differential pinion shaft retaining bolt*	30	22
Drive pinion flange locknut (axles with oil filler plug on the differential housing cover)	365	269
Rear anti-roll bar clamp bolts	40	30
Rear axle halfshaft bolts (twin wheel axles):*		
Axles with oil filler plug on the differential housing cover	134	99
Axles with oil filler plug on the drive pinion housing	117	86
Rear hub retaining nut (single wheel axles)*	425	314
Rear hub retaining nut locknut (twin wheel axles with oil filler plug on the drive pinion housing)	75	55
Rear hub retaining nut (twin wheel axles):*		
Axles with oil filler plug on the differential housing cover	425	314
Axles with oil filler plug on the drive pinion housing	85	63
Rear spring-to-axle U-bolt nuts:*		
Stage 1	25	19
Stage 2	50	37
Stage 3	75	55
Stage 4	100	74
Stage 5	125	92
Stage 6	150	111
Stage 7	175	129
Shock absorber lower mounting bolt nuts	90	66
Roadwheels		
Roadwheel nuts	200	148

* Use new nuts/bolts

1 General information

Driveshafts

On front wheel drive models, drive is transmitted from the transmission differential to the front wheels by means of two, solid steel driveshafts, each incorporating two constant velocity (CV) joints. The right-hand driveshaft is in two sections, and incorporates a support bearing **(see illustration)**.

Each driveshaft consists of three main components: the sliding (tripod type) inner joint, the actual driveshaft, and the outer (fixed ball) joint. The inner (male) end of the left-hand tripod joint is secured in the differential side gear by the engagement of a circlip. The inner (female) end of the right-hand driveshaft is held on the intermediate shaft by the engagement of a circlip. The intermediate shaft is held in the transmission by the support bearing, which in turn is supported by a bracket bolted to the rear of the cylinder block. The outer CV joint on both driveshafts is of fixed ball-bearing type, and is secured in the front hub by the hub nut. The outer CV joint must not be dismantled from the driveshaft, as it is a press-fit.

Propeller shaft

On rear wheel drive models, drive is transmitted from the transmission to the rear axle by a finely-balanced two- or three-piece tubular propeller shaft, supported at the centre by one or two rubber-mounted bearings.

Fitted at the front, centre and rear of the propeller shaft assembly are universal joints, which cater for movement of the rear axle with suspension travel, and slight movement of the power unit on its mountings. On vehicles manufactured from October 2001 onwards, a flexible rubber coupling is used in place of the front universal joint.

Rear axle
(front wheel drive models)

On front wheel drive models, the rear axle is a tubular steel beam axle supported on semi-elliptic single leaf springs. Stub axles are bolted to the ends of the axle beam on each side and these carry the rear hub and bearing assemblies. Telescopic shock absorbers provide the damping for the axle assembly.

Rear axle
(rear wheel drive models)

On rear wheel drive models, the rear axle is a live axle suspended on semi-elliptic multi-leaf springs and utilising telescopic shock absorbers to provide the damping for the axle assembly.

Two different axle designs are used, according to model, with two different versions of each design available. All axle types are visually similar, and the easiest way of identifying each individual type is by the location of the oil filler plug, and whether the axle is a single or twin wheel type. The differences in terms of repair and overhaul procedures between these axle types centre mainly on the design of the rear hub assemblies.

On axles with the oil filler plug on the drive pinion housing, a semi-floating axle is used on vehicles with single rear wheels and a fully-floating axle is used on vehicles with twin rear wheels. On vehicles with single rear wheels, drive to the wheels is by two solid steel halfshafts supported on ball bearings at their outer ends. On vehicles with twin rear wheels, drive to the wheels is by two solid steel halfshafts bolted to the rear hubs. The rear hubs each contain two taper-roller bearings, the free play of which is set by an adjuster nut which is secured by a locktab and locknuts. The rear brake drums are separate components on both axle types, and are fitted over the rear roadwheel studs.

On axles with the oil filler plug on the differential housing cover, a fully-floating axle is used on both single and twin wheel vehicles. Drive to the wheels is by two solid steel halfshafts bolted to the rear hubs.

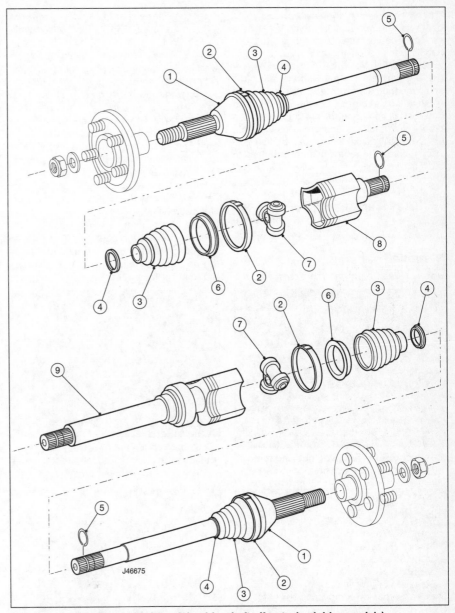

1.1 Exploded view of the driveshafts (front wheel drive models)

1 Driveshaft with fixed outer CV joint	3 Gaiter	6 Collar
	4 Small gaiter retaining clamp	7 Inner joint tripod
2 Large gaiter retaining clamp	5 Circlip	8 Inner joint housing
		9 Intermediate shaft

2.2a Bend up the split pin legs . . .

2.2b . . . then extract the split pin . . .

2.2c . . . and remove the retaining nut locking ring

The rear hubs each contain two taper-roller bearings, the free play of which is set by a spacer located between the bearings. The hub is retained on the axle by a large nut which is staked into the axle casing. The rear brake drums are integral with the rear hubs and cannot be removed separately.

On all axle types, the final drive and differential components are supported on taper-roller bearings and are housed within the axle casing itself. Access to the differential is by means of a removable cover bolted to the rear of the axle.

2 Driveshafts – removal and refitting

Removal

Note 1: *When removing the driveshafts, the inner CV joint must not be bent by more than 21° and the outer CV joint must not be bent by more than 45°.*

Note 2: *A new driveshaft retaining nut and washer, split pin and steering knuckle balljoint retaining nut will be required for refitting. If working on the right-hand driveshaft, a new intermediate shaft support bearing retaining plate and nuts will also be required.*

1 Firmly apply the handbrake, then jack up the front of the vehicle and support it securely on axle stands (see *Jacking and vehicle support*). Remove the relevant front roadwheel.

2 Extract the split pin from the driveshaft and remove the retaining nut locking ring **(see illustrations)**.

3 Have an assistant firmly depress the brake pedal to prevent the front hub from rotating, then using a socket and extension bar, slacken the driveshaft retaining nut. Alternatively, a tool can be fabricated from two lengths of

steel strip (one long, one short) and a nut and bolt (the nut and bolt forming the pivot of a forked tool). Bolt the tool to the hub using two wheel nuts, and hold the tool to prevent the hub from rotating as the driveshaft retaining nut is undone.

4 Unscrew the driveshaft retaining nut, and remove the washer **(see illustration)**. Discard the nut and washer as new components must be used on refitting.

5 Slacken the nut securing the steering knuckle balljoint to the lower suspension arm **(see illustration)**. Attach a two-legged puller to the lower suspension arm and tighten the puller to apply tension to the balljoint shank. Strike the end of the lower suspension arm with a hammer a few times to release the balljoint shank taper.

6 Remove the puller and unscrew the balljoint retaining nut. Discard the nut as a new one must be used for refitting.

7 Push down on the lower suspension arm and disengage the steering knuckle balljoint from the arm.

Left-hand driveshaft

8 Insert a lever between the inner driveshaft joint and the transmission case, with a thin piece of wood against the case. Prise free the inner joint from the differential **(see illustration)**. If it proves reluctant to move, strike the lever firmly with the palm of the hand. Be careful not to damage adjacent components, and in particular, make sure that the driveshaft oil seal in the differential is not damaged. Be prepared for some oil spillage from the transmission. Support the inner end of the driveshaft on an axle stand.

9 Press the outer end of the driveshaft through the front hub and steering knuckle. If necessary, use a universal puller located on the hub flange.

10 Withdraw the driveshaft from under the vehicle.

11 Extract the circlip from the groove on the inner end of the driveshaft, and obtain a new one **(see illustration)**.

12 Check the condition of the differential oil seals, and if necessary renew them as described in Chapter 7A.

Right-hand driveshaft

13 Unscrew the nuts and remove the retaining

2.4 Unscrew the retaining nut, and remove the washer

2.5 Slacken the nut (arrowed) securing the steering knuckle balljoint to the lower suspension arm

2.8 Using a lever to remove the left-hand driveshaft from the transmission

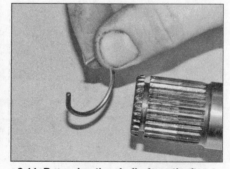

2.11 Removing the circlip from the inner end of the left-hand driveshaft

plate securing the intermediate shaft support bearing to the cylinder block **(see illustration)**. Note that new nuts and a new retaining plate will be required for refitting.

14 Pull the intermediate shaft out of the transmission and support on an axle stand. Be prepared for some oil spillage from the transmission.

15 Press the outer end of the driveshaft through the front hub and steering knuckle. if necessary, use a universal puller located on the hub flange. Withdraw the driveshaft from under the vehicle.

16 Check the condition of the differential oil seals, and if necessary renew them as described in Chapter 7A. Check the support bearing, and if necessary renew it as described in Section 5.

Refitting

Left-hand driveshaft

17 Fit the new circlip to the groove on the inner end of the driveshaft, making sure it is correctly seated.

18 Keeping the driveshaft level, insert the splined inner end into the transmission and engage with the splines in the differential sun gear. Take care not to damage the transmission oil seal. Press in the driveshaft until the circlip is fully engaged.

19 Pull the knuckle outwards, and insert the outer end of the driveshaft through the hub. Turn the driveshaft as necessary to engage the splines in the hub, and fully push on the hub. If necessary, use a wooden mallet to tap the hub fully onto the driveshaft splines.

Right-hand driveshaft

20 Pull the knuckle outwards, and insert the outer end of the driveshaft through the hub. Turn the driveshaft as necessary to engage the splines in the hub, and fully push on the hub. If necessary, use a wooden mallet to tap the hub fully onto the driveshaft splines.

21 Insert the inner end of the intermediate shaft into the transmission and engage it with the splines on the differential sun gear, taking care not to damage the oil seal. Locate the intermediate shaft support bearing in position, fit the new retaining plate, and tighten the new retaining nuts to the specified torque.

2.13 Unscrew the nuts (arrowed) and remove the intermediate shaft support bearing retaining plate

Both driveshafts

22 Push down on the lower suspension arm and engage the steering knuckle balljoint with the arm. Fit the new balljoint retaining nut and tighten the nut to the specified torque.

23 Place the new washer over the end of the driveshaft and screw on the new retaining nut. Tighten the driveshaft retaining nut to the specified torque in the five stages given in the Specifications. Prevent the driveshaft from rotating as the nut is tightened, using the method employed for removal.

24 Refit the driveshaft retaining nut locking ring, aligning the slots with the split pin hole in the driveshaft. Insert a new split pin and bend over the split pin legs to secure.

25 Refit the roadwheel and tighten the wheel nuts to the specified torque.

26 Top-up the transmission oil as described in Chapter 1, then lower the vehicle to the ground.

3 Driveshaft inner CV joint gaiter – renewal

Note: *If both the inner and outer gaiters are being renewed at the same time, the outer gaiter is removed from the inner end of the driveshaft.*

1 Remove the driveshaft as described in Section 2, and mount it in a vice.

2 Mark the driveshaft in relation to the joint housing, to ensure correct refitting.

3 Release the retaining clips from the gaiter, and slide the gaiter back along the driveshaft a little way **(see illustrations)**.

4 Withdraw the inner joint housing from the tripod and scoop out the grease from the joint and gaiter **(see illustration)**.

5 Check that the inner end of the driveshaft is marked in relation to the splined tripod hub. If not, carefully centre-punch the two items, to ensure correct refitting. Alternatively, use dabs of paint on the driveshaft and one end of the tripod.

6 Extract the circlip retaining the tripod on the driveshaft **(see illustration)**.

7 Using a puller, remove the tripod from the end of the driveshaft, and slide off the gaiter **(see illustration)**.

8 If the outer gaiter is also to be renewed, remove it and fit the new one with reference to Section 4.

9 Clean the driveshaft, and obtain a new joint retaining circlip. The gaiter retaining clips must also be renewed.

3.3a Remove the inner joint gaiter large clip . . .

3.3b . . . and small clip

3.4 Withdraw the inner joint housing from the tripod and scoop out the grease

3.6 Extract the circlip retaining the tripod on the driveshaft

3.7 Using a puller, remove the tripod from the end of the driveshaft

3.10a Slide on the small clip . . .

3.10b . . . followed by the gaiter

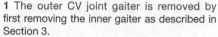

3.12 Pack the specified amount of CV joint grease into the tripod and joint housing

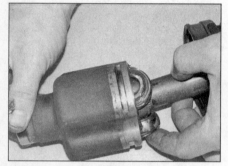

3.13a Guide the joint housing onto the tripod fully . . .

3.13b . . . and locate the gaiter in position

1 The outer CV joint gaiter is removed by first removing the inner gaiter as described in Section 3.
2 Clean the exposed part of the driveshaft to facilitate removal of the outer gaiter.
3 Release the outer gaiter retaining clips. Slip the gaiter off the outer CV joint, then slide it off the inner end of the driveshaft together with the clips **(see illustrations)**. Scoop out the grease from the outer CV joint.
4 Slide the new gaiter, together with the new clips, onto the driveshaft until it is near the outer CV joint.
5 Pack the outer CV joint with the specified amount of CV joint grease, then slide the gaiter fully into position on the driveshaft and CV joint housing. Ensure the gaiter is not twisted or distorted.
6 Make sure that the gaiter is located in the special groove in the driveshaft, then fit and tighten the new small diameter retaining clip. If possible, use a gaiter retaining clip tightening tool to tighten the clip, otherwise, use pincers.
7 Insert a small screwdriver under the lip of the gaiter at the housing end. This will allow trapped air to escape, then position the joint housing so that the distance from the inner end of the gaiter to the outer end is 102.0 mm for 75 and 85 PS engines or 118 mm for 100 and 125 PS engines.
8 Fit and tighten the new large diameter retaining clip. If possible, use the special tool to tighten the clip, otherwise, use pincers.
9 Refit the inner gaiter with reference to Section 3.

10 Slide the new gaiter on the driveshaft, together with the new small diameter clip **(see illustrations)**. Make sure that the gaiter is located in the special groove in the driveshaft, then tighten the retaining clip. If possible, use a gaiter retaining clip tightening tool to tighten the clip, otherwise, use pincers.
11 Refit the tripod on the driveshaft splines, if necessary using a soft-faced mallet and a suitable metal tube to drive it fully onto the splines. It must be fitted with the chamfered edge leading (towards the driveshaft), and with the previously-made marks aligned. Secure it in position using a new circlip. Ensure that the circlip is fully engaged in its groove.
12 Pack the specified amount of CV joint grease into the tripod and joint housing **(see illustration)**.
13 Guide the joint housing onto the tripod fully, and locate the gaiter in position,

ensuring it is not twisted or distorted **(see illustrations)**.
14 Insert a small screwdriver under the lip of the gaiter at the housing end. This will allow trapped air to escape, then position the joint housing so that the distance from the inner end of the gaiter to the outer end is 90.0 mm.
15 Fit and tighten the new large diameter retaining clip. If possible, use the special tool to tighten the clip, otherwise, use pincers.
16 Refit the driveshaft with reference to Section 2.

4 Driveshaft outer CV joint gaiter – renewal

Note: *The outer CV joint is pressed onto the driveshaft and must not be removed.*

4.3a Remove the small clip . . .

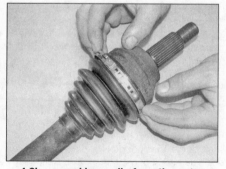

4.3b . . . and large clip from the outer joint . . .

4.3c . . . then slide the gaiter off the inner end of the driveshaft

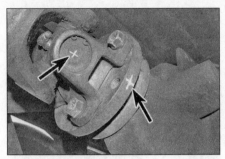

7.2 Make alignment marks (arrowed) on the rear universal joint and final drive coupling flanges

7.4a Make alignment marks (arrowed) between the propeller shaft rear section and the centre section . . .

7.4b . . . and remove the rear section

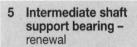

5 Intermediate shaft support bearing – renewal

1 Remove the right-hand driveshaft as described in Section 2, then remove the inner CV joint gaiter as described in Section 3.
2 Using a press or suitable puller, draw the bearing off the end of the intermediate shaft.
3 Drive or press on the new bearing, applying the pressure to the inner race only.
4 Refit (or renew) the inner CV joint gaiter as described in Section 3, then refit the driveshaft as described in Section 2.

6 Driveshafts – inspection and joint renewal

1 Road test the vehicle, and listen for a metallic clicking from the front as the vehicle is driven slowly in a circle on full-lock. If a clicking noise is heard, this indicates wear in the outer constant velocity joint, which means that the driveshaft and outer joint must be renewed. It is not possible to renew the joint separately.
2 If vibration, consistent with road speed, is felt through the car when accelerating, there is a possibility of wear in the inner constant velocity joints. To renew an inner joint, remove the driveshaft as described in Section 2, then separate the joint from the driveshaft with reference to Section 3.
3 Continual noise from the right-hand driveshaft, increasing with road speed, may indicate wear in the intermediate shaft support bearing. Renewal procedures for the support bearing are contained in Section 5.

7 Propeller shaft – removal and refitting

Removal

Note: *New propeller shaft universal joint/ rubber coupling retaining bolts, and new centre bearing retaining bolts will be required for refitting.*

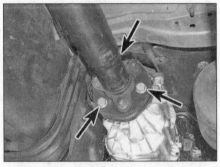

7.6 Propeller shaft flexible rubber coupling retaining bolts (arrowed)

1 Chock the front wheels then jack up the rear of the vehicle and securely support it on axle stands (see *Jacking and vehicle support*).
2 Mark the rear universal joint and final drive coupling flanges in relation to each other **(see illustration)**.
3 Unscrew the four bolts securing the propeller shaft to the final drive coupling flange. Hold the shaft stationary with a long screwdriver inserted between the joint spider. Support the shaft on an axle stand after disconnecting the flanges. Note that new flange retaining bolts will be required for refitting.
4 If the propeller shaft is not fitted with a rubber gaiter over the rear section sliding spline connection, make alignment marks between the rear section and the centre section and remove the rear section **(see illustrations)**.
5 If the propeller shaft incorporates a universal joint at its forward end, mark the relative positions of the propeller shaft universal joint flange and transmission output shaft flange. Undo the four bolts securing the universal joint flange to the output shaft flange, then separate the flanges and support the shaft on an axle stand. Note that new flange retaining bolts will be required for refitting.
6 If the propeller shaft incorporates a flexible rubber coupling at its forward end, mark the relative positions of the rubber coupling and transmission output shaft flange. Undo the three bolts securing the rubber coupling to the output shaft flange, then position the propeller shaft to one side and support it on an axle stand **(see illustration)**. Note that new rubber coupling retaining bolts will be required for refitting.

7.7 Propeller shaft centre bearing and retaining bolts

7 Undo the two bolts securing the propeller shaft front centre bearing to the underbody **(see illustration)**. Note that new bolts will be required for refitting.
8 Enlist the aid of an assistant to support the propeller shaft then undo the two bolts securing the propeller shaft rear centre bearing to the underbody. Lower the propeller shaft assembly to the ground and remove it from under the vehicle. Note that new centre bearing retaining bolts will be required for refitting.

Refitting

9 If the propeller shaft incorporates a universal joint at its forward end, align the flange marks made on removal and fit the new flange retaining bolts. Do not fully tighten the bolts at this stage.
10 If the propeller shaft incorporates a flexible

7.10 Fit a clamp (arrowed) consisting of two worm-drive hose clips joined together to compress the rubber coupling when refitting

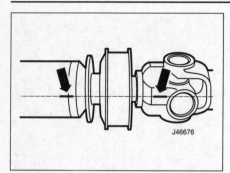

8.5 Make alignment marks on the propeller shaft tube and the universal joint yoke

8.6a Prise up the locktab (arrowed) from the universal joint retaining bolt . . .

8.6b . . . then loosen off the bolt using a suitable flat ring spanner

rubber coupling at its forward end, fit a clamp, comprising of two worm-drive hose clips joined together, around the circumference of the coupling, and tighten it until it just begins to compress the rubber. Align the marks made on the rubber coupling and transmission output shaft flange, then fit the new rubber coupling retaining bolts **(see illustration)**. Do not fully tighten the bolts at this stage.

11 Raise the propeller shaft centre section, and fit the new retaining bolts to both centre bearings. Do not fully tighten the bolts at this stage.

12 If the propeller shaft rear section was separated from the centre section, align the marks made on removal and re-engage the sliding spline connection.

13 Raise the propeller shaft rear section, align the coupling flange marks made on removal, and fit the new flange retaining bolts. Do not fully tighten the bolts at this stage.

14 With the propeller shaft in position, tighten all the retaining bolts to the specified torque in the following sequence:
a) *Front universal joint/rubber coupling flange bolts.*
b) *Front centre bearing retaining bolts.*
c) *Rear centre bearing retaining bolts.*
d) *Final drive coupling flange bolts.*
15 Where applicable, remove the clamp from the flexible rubber coupling, then lower the vehicle to the ground.

8 Propeller shaft centre bearing – renewal

Note: *New propeller shaft universal joint/rubber coupling retaining bolts, and new centre bearing retaining bolts will be required for refitting.*

Front centre bearing

1 Firmly apply the handbrake, then jack up the front of the vehicle and support it securely on axle stands (see *Jacking and vehicle support*).
2 If the propeller shaft incorporates a universal joint at its forward end, mark the relative positions of the propeller shaft universal joint flange and transmission output shaft flange. Undo the four bolts securing the universal joint flange to the output shaft flange, then separate the flanges and support the shaft on an axle stand. Note that new flange retaining bolts will be required for refitting.
3 If the propeller shaft incorporates a flexible rubber coupling at its forward end, mark the relative positions of the rubber coupling and transmission output shaft flange.
4 Undo the three bolts securing the rubber coupling to the output shaft flange, then position the propeller shaft to one side and support it on an axle stand. Note that new rubber coupling retaining bolts will be required for refitting.
5 Make alignment marks on the propeller shaft tube and the universal joint yoke **(see illustration)**.
6 Prise up the locktab from the universal joint retaining bolt, then loosen off the bolt using a suitable flat ring spanner **(see illustrations)**.
7 Extract the U-shaped washer from the bolt head, then insert a screwdriver or metal bar between the bolt head and the universal joint, and lever the two propeller shaft sections apart **(see illustrations)**. Remove the retaining bolt and locktab. Note that a new locktab will be required for refitting.
8 Undo the two bolts securing the propeller shaft centre bearing to the underbody **(see illustration)**. Note that new bolts will be required for refitting.
9 The centre bearing can now be removed from the propeller shaft using a suitable puller **(see illustration)**.
10 Locate the new centre bearing on the propeller shaft and drive it fully into position, using a hammer and tubular sleeve, as far as the stop **(see illustration)**.
11 Refit the bolt, together with a new locktab, but don't tighten the bolt at this stage.
12 Reassemble the universal joint yoke to the shaft, aligning the marks made on removal, and press them together.

8.7a Extract the U-shaped washer from the bolt head . . .

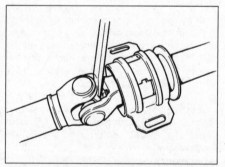

8.7b . . . then lever the two propeller shaft sections apart

8.8 Undo the two bolts (arrowed) securing the propeller shaft centre bearing to the underbody

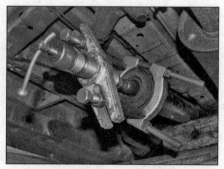

8.9 Remove the centre bearing from the propeller shaft using a suitable puller

13 Slide the U-shaped washer into position with the pegged side towards the bearing, then tighten the universal joint retaining bolt securely.

14 Use a length of rod or a suitable drift to tap up the locktab and secure the bolt.

15 If the propeller shaft incorporates a universal joint at its forward end, align the flange marks made on removal and fit the new flange retaining bolts. Do not fully tighten the bolts at this stage.

16 If the propeller shaft incorporates a flexible rubber coupling at its forward end, fit a clamp, comprising of two worm-drive hose clips joined together, around the circumference of the coupling, and tighten it until it just begins to compress the rubber. Align the marks made on the rubber coupling and transmission output shaft flange, then fit the new rubber coupling retaining bolts **(see illustration 7.10)**. Do not fully tighten the bolts at this stage.

17 Raise the propeller shaft, and fit the new retaining bolts to the centre bearing. Do not fully tighten the bolts at this stage.

18 Tighten the universal joint flange/rubber coupling retaining bolts, followed by the centre bearing retaining bolts, to the specified torque.

19 Where applicable, remove the clamp from the flexible rubber coupling, then lower the vehicle to the ground.

Rear centre bearing

20 Chock the front wheels then jack up the rear of the vehicle and securely support it on axle stands (see *Jacking and vehicle support*).

21 Mark the rear universal joint and final drive coupling flanges in relation to each other **(see illustration 7.2)**.

22 Unscrew the four bolts securing the propeller shaft to the final drive coupling flange. Hold the shaft stationary with a long screwdriver inserted between the joint spider. Support the shaft on an axle stand after disconnecting the flanges. Note that new flange retaining bolts will be required for refitting.

23 If the propeller shaft is not fitted with a rubber gaiter over the rear section sliding spline connection, make alignment marks between the rear section and the centre section and remove the rear section **(see illustrations 7.4a and 7.4b)**.

24 Carry out the operations described above in paragraphs 6 to 14 to remove the old centre bearing and fit the new one.

25 Raise the propeller shaft centre section, and fit the new retaining bolts to the centre bearing. Do not fully tighten the bolts at this stage.

26 If the propeller shaft rear section was separated from the centre section, align the marks made on removal and re-engage the sliding spline connection.

27 Raise the propeller shaft rear section, align the coupling flange marks made on removal, and fit the new flange retaining bolts. Do not fully tighten the bolts at this stage.

8.10 Locate the new centre bearing on the propeller shaft and drive it fully into position, using a hammer and tubular sleeve

28 With the propeller shaft in position, tighten the final drive coupling flange retaining bolts, followed by the centre bearing retaining bolts, to the specified torque, then lower the vehicle to the ground.

9 Propeller shaft flexible rubber coupling – removal and refitting

Removal

Note: *New rubber coupling retaining bolts and nuts will be required for refitting.*

1 Firmly apply the handbrake, then jack up the front of the vehicle and support it securely on axle stands (see *Jacking and vehicle support*).

2 Mark the relative positions of the propeller shaft and transmission output shaft flange. Undo the three bolts securing the rubber coupling to the output shaft flange, then position the propeller shaft to one side and support it on an axle stand. Note that new rubber coupling retaining bolts will be required for refitting.

3 Undo the three nuts, withdraw the bolts and remove the rubber coupling from the propeller shaft. Note that new nuts and bolts will be required for refitting.

4 Carefully inspect the rubber coupling for signs of deterioration, and renew if necessary.

Refitting

5 If the original rubber coupling is being refitted, fit a clamp, comprising of two worm-drive hose clips joined together, around

10.7 Tap the uppermost bearing cup to release the bottom cup

the circumference of the coupling, and tighten it until it just begins to compress the rubber **(see illustration 7.10)**. New rubber couplings are supplied with a retaining band already fitted and this band should be left in place until the coupling is installed.

6 Position the coupling on the propeller shaft, and fit the new retaining bolts and nuts. Tighten the nuts securely.

7 Align the previously-made marks on the propeller shaft and transmission output shaft flange, locate the rubber coupling in position on the flange and fit the new retaining bolts. Tighten the bolts to the specified torque.

8 If the original rubber coupling has been refitted, remove the clamp. If a new coupling has been fitted, cut off and discard the metal retaining band.

9 On completion, lower the vehicle to the ground.

10 Propeller shaft universal joints – renewal

1 If the inspection procedures described in Chapter 1 indicate wear in the universal joint(s), the joint spider and bearings can be renewed as follows.

2 Remove the propeller shaft as described in Section 7.

3 Make alignment marks on the propeller shaft on each side of the joint to be renewed. This is vital to ensure correct reassembly, and to ensure that the shaft balance is maintained.

4 Clean away all traces of dirt and grease from the circlips located on the ends of the joint spiders, and from the grease nipple.

5 Unscrew and remove the grease nipple.

6 Using a suitable pair of circlip pliers, remove the four joint circlips. If a circlip proves difficult to remove, as a last resort, place a drift on the bearing cup, in the centre of the circlip, and tap the top of the bearing cup to ease the pressure on the circlip.

7 Carefully support the propeller shaft in a vice with the yoke in a vertical plane. Using a hammer and a suitable drift (a socket of appropriate size, for example), tap the uppermost bearing cup until the bottom bearing cup protrudes from the yoke **(see illustration)**.

8 Remove the propeller shaft from the vice, then securely grip the protruding bearing cup in the vice jaws. Turn the propeller shaft from side-to-side while at the same time lifting the shaft until the bearing cup comes free.

9 Refit the propeller shaft to the vice with the exposed spider uppermost. Tap the spider with the hammer and drift until the lower bearing cup protrudes, then remove the cup as described previously.

10 The spider can now be removed from the propeller shaft and the remaining two bearing cups can be removed as described previously.

11 Where applicable, repeat the previous

10.12 Universal joint bearing components

10.19 Press the bearing cups into place using a vice and socket

10.20 Fit the new circlips to retain the bearing cups

operations to remove the remaining joint(s) from the shaft.

12 With the universal joint dismantled, carefully examine the needle rollers, bearing cups and spider for wear, scoring and pitting of the surface finish. If any wear is detected, the joint must be renewed **(see illustration)**.

13 If a new joint is being fitted, remove the bearing cups from the new spider. Check that all the needle rollers are present, and correctly positioned in the bearing cups.

14 Ensure that the bearing cups are one-third full of fresh grease (multi-purpose lithium based grease).

15 Fit the new spider, complete with seals into the coupling flange, or propeller shaft yoke.

16 Partially insert one of the bearing cups into the yoke, and enter the spider trunnion into the bearing cup, taking care not to dislodge the needle rollers.

17 Similarly, insert a bearing cup into the opposite yoke.

18 Using the vice, carefully press both bearing cups into place, ensuring that the spider trunnions do not dislodge any of the needle rollers.

19 Using a suitable tube or socket of a slightly smaller diameter than the bearing cups, press each cup into its respective yoke, until the top of the cup just reaches the lower land of the circlip groove **(see illustration)**. Do not press the cups below this point, as damage may be caused to the cups and seals.

20 Fit the new circlips to retain the bearing cups **(see illustration)**.

21 Engage the spider with the yokes on the relevant propeller shaft section, ensuring that the marks made during removal are aligned. Partially fit both bearing cups to the yokes, taking care not to dislodge any of the needle rollers.

22 Press the bearing cups into position, and fit the new circlips, as described in paragraphs 18 to 20.

23 Screw the grease nipple into position in the joint spider.

24 Where applicable, repeat the operations described in paragraphs 13 to 23, to fit the remaining joint(s) to the shaft.

25 Refit the propeller shaft as described in Section 7, then lubricate the joints using a grease gun applied to the grease nipples (see Chapter 1).

11 Rear axle (front wheel drive models) – removal and refitting

Note 1: *The rear axle removal/refitting details described below are for the removal of the unit on its own. If required, it can be removed together with the roadwheels and rear leaf springs as a combined unit, although this method requires the vehicle to be raised and supported at a greater height (to allow the roadwheels to clear the body during withdrawal of the unit). If the latter method is used, follow the instructions given, but ignore the references to removal of the roadwheels*

and detaching the springs from the axle. Refer to Chapter 10 for details on detaching the springs from the underbody.

Note 2: *New spring-to-axle U-bolt retaining nuts will be required for refitting.*

Removal

1 Chock the front wheels then jack up the rear of the vehicle and securely support it on axle stands positioned beneath the underframe side members in front of the rear springs (see *Jacking and vehicle support*). Remove the rear roadwheels on both sides.

2 Support the weight of the rear axle with a trolley jack positioned beneath the centre of the axle beam.

3 Using two brake hose clamps, clamp the flexible hydraulic hoses leading to the rear axle.

4 Unscrew the union nuts and disconnect the rear brake hydraulic pipes from the flexible hoses at the support bracket on the rear axle. Be prepared for some loss of brake fluid, and plug or tape over the ends of the pipes and hoses to prevent entry of dust and dirt.

5 Undo the retaining bolt and lift the flexible hydraulic hose support bracket off the rear axle.

6 Slacken the handbrake cable adjustment nut until there is sufficient slack to enable the handbrake inner cable ends to be slipped out of the slots in the equaliser **(see illustration)**.

7 Depress the tabs on the end fittings, and withdraw the handbrake cables from the abutment bracket.

8 Undo the bolt each side securing the handbrake cable supports to the underbody **(see illustration)**. Release the cables from any additional clips so that both cables are free to be removed with the axle.

9 On vehicles equipped with a load apportioning valve in the brake hydraulic circuit, undo the retaining bolt and detach the load apportioning valve operating rod from the rear axle bracket.

10 On vehicles equipped with ABS, disconnect the wheel speed sensor wiring at the chassis side member **(see illustration)**.

11 Undo the retaining nuts and bolts, and detach the rear shock absorbers from the axle **(see illustration)**.

12 Check that the axle unit is securely

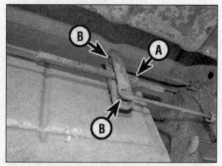

11.6 Slacken the handbrake cable adjustment nut (A), then slip the handbrake inner cable ends (B) out of the slots in the equaliser

11.8 Undo the retaining bolt (arrowed) on each side and release the handbrake cable supports from the underbody

11.10 Disconnect the wheel speed sensor wiring (arrowed) at the chassis side member

11.11 Undo the nuts (arrowed), remove the bolts and detach the rear shock absorbers from the axle

11.13 Undo the retaining nuts (two of four arrowed), and remove the spring-to-axle U-bolts and fittings each side

supported in the centre by the jack. Have an assistant available, to steady the axle each side as it is lowered from the vehicle.

13 Undo the retaining nuts, and remove the spring-to-axle U-bolts and fittings each side **(see illustration)**. Check that the various axle fittings and attachments are disconnected and out of the way, then carefully lower the axle unit and withdraw it from under the vehicle.

Refitting

14 Refitting is a reversal of the removal procedure, noting the following points:
  a) *Tighten all retaining nuts and bolts to the specified torque (where given).*
  b) *Use new retaining nuts on the spring-to-axle U-bolts.*
  c) *Final tightening of the rear axle U-bolt nuts, and shock absorber mounting nuts should be carried out with the weight of the vehicle resting on the roadwheels.*
  d) *Referring to the procedures contained in Chapter 9, top-up and bleed the brake hydraulic system, then adjust the handbrake as described in Chapter 1.*

---

12 Rear axle (rear wheel drive models) – removal and refitting

Note 1: *The rear axle removal/refitting details described below are for the removal of the unit on its own. If required, it can be removed together with the roadwheels and rear leaf springs as a combined unit, although this method requires the vehicle to be raised and supported at a greater height (to allow the roadwheels to clear the body during withdrawal of the unit). If the latter method is used, follow the instructions given, but ignore the references to removal of the roadwheels and detaching the springs from the axle. Refer to Chapter 10 for details on detaching the springs from the underbody.*
Note 2: *New spring-to-axle U-bolt retaining nuts, and new propeller shaft final drive coupling flange retaining bolts will be required for refitting.*

Removal

1 Chock the front wheels then jack up the rear

of the vehicle and securely support it on axle stands positioned beneath the underframe side members in front of the rear springs (see *Jacking and vehicle support*). Remove the rear roadwheels on both sides.

2 Mark the propeller shaft rear universal joint and final drive coupling flanges in relation to each other **(see illustration 7.2)**.

3 Unscrew the four bolts securing the propeller shaft to the final drive coupling flange. Hold the shaft stationary with a long screwdriver inserted between the joint spider. Support the shaft on an axle stand after disconnecting the flanges. Note that new flange retaining bolts will be required for refitting.

4 If the propeller shaft is not fitted with a rubber gaiter over the rear section sliding spline connection, make alignment marks between the rear section and the centre section and remove the rear section **(see illustrations 7.4a and 7.4b)**.

5 Support the weight of the rear axle with a trolley jack positioned beneath the final drive housing.

6 Using two brake hose clamps, clamp the flexible hydraulic hoses leading to the rear axle **(see illustration)**.

7 Unscrew the union nuts and disconnect the rear brake hydraulic pipes from the flexible hoses at the support bracket on the rear axle. Be prepared for some loss of brake fluid, and plug or tape over the ends of the pipes and hoses to prevent entry of dust and dirt.

8 Undo the retaining bolt and lift the flexible

12.6 Using brake hose clamps, clamp the flexible hydraulic hoses (arrowed) leading to the rear axle

hydraulic hose support bracket off the rear axle.

9 Slacken the handbrake cable adjuster nut at the cable compensator plate until there is sufficient slack to enable the handbrake inner cable ends to be slipped out of the slots in the compensator **(see illustration)**.

10 Depress the tabs on the end fittings, and withdraw the handbrake cables from the abutment bracket.

11 Undo the bolt each side securing the handbrake cable supports to the underbody **(see illustration 11.8)**. Release the cables from any additional clips so that both cables are free to be removed with the axle.

12 On vehicles equipped with a load apportioning valve in the brake hydraulic circuit, undo the retaining bolts and detach the load apportioning valve operating rod bracket from the rear axle.

13 On vehicles equipped with ABS, disconnect the wheel speed sensor wiring at the chassis side member.

14 Undo the retaining nuts and bolts, and detach the rear shock absorbers from the axle **(see illustration)**.

15 On vehicles fitted with a rear anti-roll bar, undo the two bolts each side and release the anti-roll bar clamps from the axle.

16 Check that the axle unit is securely supported in the centre by the jack. Have an assistant available, to steady the axle each side as it is lowered from the vehicle.

17 Undo the retaining nuts, and remove the

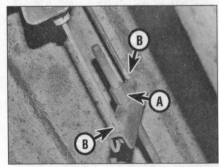

12.9 Slacken the handbrake cable adjustment nut (A), then slip the handbrake inner cable ends (B) out of the slots in the equaliser

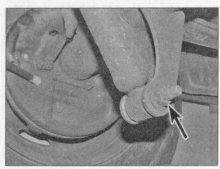

12.14 Undo the nuts (arrowed), remove the bolts and detach the rear shock absorbers from the axle

spring-to-axle U-bolts and fittings each side **(see illustration)**. Check that the various axle fittings and attachments are disconnected and out of the way, then carefully lower the axle unit and withdraw it from under the vehicle.

Refitting

18 Refitting is a reversal of the removal procedure, noting the following points:
a) Tighten all retaining nuts and bolts to the specified torque (where given).
b) Use new retaining nuts on the spring-to-axle U-bolts.
c) If the propeller shaft rear section was separated from the centre section, align the marks made on removal and re-engage the sliding spline connection.
d) Align the marks made on removal when refitting the propeller shaft coupling flange, and use new retaining bolts.

13.5 Wheel speed sensor retaining bolt (arrowed)

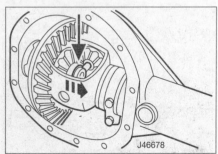

13.7 Push the halfshaft towards the centre of the axle and extract the snap ring from the differential end of the halfshaft

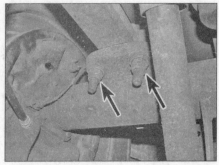

12.17 Undo the retaining nuts (two of four arrowed), and remove the spring-to-axle U-bolts and fittings each side

e) Final tightening of the rear axle U-bolt nuts, and shock absorber mounting nuts should be carried out with the weight of the vehicle resting on the roadwheels.
f) Referring to the procedures contained in Chapter 9, top-up and bleed the brake hydraulic system, then adjust the handbrake as described in Chapter 1.
g) If the axle has been dismantled during removal, top-up the oil level as described in Chapter 1.

13 Rear axle halfshaft (single wheel axles) – removal and refitting

Removal

1 Chock the front wheels then jack up the rear of the vehicle and securely support it on

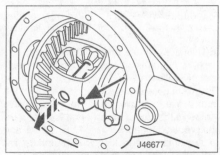

13.6 Undo the differential pinion shaft retaining bolt and slide the pinion shaft out through the hole in the differential case

13.9 Unscrew the three bolts (arrowed) securing the halfshaft to the hub/drum

axle stands (see *Jacking and vehicle support*). Remove the appropriate rear wheel.
2 Two different axles types may be fitted according to model, and it is necessary to identify the axle being worked on before proceeding. To do this, locate the axle oil filler plug which will be either on the front left-hand side of the drive pinion housing, or on the differential housing cover. Proceed as described in the appropriate following sub-sections according to axle type.

Axles with oil filler plug on the drive pinion housing

3 Release the handbrake, then withdraw the brake drum from the halfshaft by tapping the rear of the drum with a soft-faced mallet to free it from the shaft flange.
4 Place a large container beneath the differential, then unbolt and remove the differential housing cover and collect the gasket. Allow the oil to drain into the container.
5 On models with ABS, undo the retaining bolt and withdraw the ABS wheel speed sensor from the rear of the brake backplate **(see illustration)**.
6 From within the differential assembly, undo the differential pinion shaft retaining bolt and slide the pinion shaft out through the hole in the side of the differential case **(see illustration)**. Note that a new pinion shaft retaining bolt will be required for refitting.
7 Push the halfshaft towards the centre of the axle and extract the snap ring from the differential end of the halfshaft **(see illustration)**.
8 Taking care not to damage the oil seal, withdraw the halfshaft from the axle housing.

Axles with oil filler plug on the differential housing cover

9 Mark the position of the halfshaft relative to the brake drum, then unscrew the three bolts securing the halfshaft to the drum **(see illustration)**.
10 Release the halfshaft by tapping the flange or carefully easing the flange away from the brake drum with a screwdriver. Withdraw the halfshaft from the axle housing and recover the gasket **(see illustrations)**. Be prepared for some oil spillage.

13.10a Withdraw the halfshaft from the axle housing . . .

11 Check the condition of the halfshaft flange gasket and obtain a new gasket if necessary.

Refitting

Axles with oil filler plug on the drive pinion housing

12 Lubricate the oil seal with multi-purpose grease, then carefully insert the halfshaft into the axle housing.

13 Push the halfshaft towards the centre of the axle and refit the snap ring to the differential end of the halfshaft.

14 Refit the differential pinion shaft and secure with a new retaining bolt tightened to the specified torque.

15 Before refitting the rear cover, clean the cover and axle housing mating surfaces, and remove the remains of the old gasket. Also clean the threads of the retaining bolts with a wire brush, and the threaded holes in the casing with a suitable cleaning solvent.

16 Locate the new gasket and the rear cover, smear the retaining bolt threads with thread locking compound, and fit them. Tighten the bolts in an alternate and progressive sequence to the specified torque.

17 On models with ABS, refit the wheel speed sensor to the brake backplate. Refit and tighten the retaining bolt to the specified torque.

18 Referring to Chapter 1, fill the rear axle with the correct grade of oil until the level is 6 to 14 mm below the filler plug hole, then refit and tighten the plug.

19 Refit the brake drum and roadwheel, then tighten the wheel nuts to the specified torque, and lower the vehicle to the ground.

Axles with oil filler plug on the differential housing cover

20 Clean the mating surfaces of the halfshaft flange and the brake drum, then place the gasket in position.

21 Insert the halfshaft into the axle housing, aligning the marks made on removal on the halfshaft and drum.

22 Refit the three halfshaft retaining bolts and tighten them securely.

23 Check and if necessary, top-up the rear axle oil level as described in Chapter 1, then refit the roadwheel, tighten the wheel nuts to the specified torque, and lower the vehicle to the ground.

13.10b . . . and recover the gasket

14 Rear axle halfshaft (twin wheel axles) – removal and refitting

Removal

1 Chock the front wheels then jack up the rear of the vehicle and securely support it on axle stands (see *Jacking and vehicle support*). Remove the appropriate rear wheels.

2 Mark the position of the halfshaft relative to the rear hub, then unscrew the bolts securing the halfshaft to the hub. Note that new bolts will be required for refitting.

3 Release the halfshaft by tapping the flange or carefully easing the flange away from the hub with a screwdriver. Withdraw the halfshaft from the axle housing and recover the gasket (where fitted). Be prepared for some oil spillage.

4 Check the condition of the halfshaft flange gasket (where fitted) and obtain a new gasket if necessary.

Refitting

5 Clean the mating surfaces of the halfshaft flange and the rear hub then (where applicable) place the gasket in position.

6 Insert the halfshaft into the axle housing, aligning the marks made on removal on the halfshaft and hub.

7 Apply thread locking compound to the threads of the new halfshaft retaining bolts, then refit the bolts and progressively tighten them to the specified torque.

8 Check and if necessary, top-up the rear

axle oil level as described in Chapter 1, then refit the roadwheels, tighten the wheel nuts to the specified torque, and lower the vehicle to the ground.

15 Rear hub and bearing (front wheel drive models) – removal, overhaul and refitting

Removal

Caution: Due to the extremely high tightening torque of the rear hub retaining nut take great care when removing and refitting the nut. Use only the correct sockets and make sure you have a suitable extension bar for removal, and a torque wrench capable of tightening the nut to the correct setting (see Specifications) for refitting. Entrust this work to a dealer or suitably-equipped garage if in doubt about the procedure, or if the required tools are not available.

Note: *A new rear hub retaining nut will be required for refitting.*

1 Chock the front wheels then jack up the rear of the vehicle and securely support it on axle stands (see *Jacking and vehicle support*).

2 Remove the appropriate rear wheel and release the handbrake.

3 Unscrew the rear hub retaining nut, collect the washer, then withdraw the brake drum and rear hub as an assembly, off the stub axle **(see illustrations)**.

4 Measure the diameter of the hub retaining nut flange. The diameter will be either 44 mm, or 51 mm. Obtain a new hub retaining nut of the appropriate size for refitting.

5 If necessary, separate the brake drum from the hub. Note, however, that due to the likely build-up of corrosion on the mating surfaces of the drum and hub, it may be necessary to use a hydraulic press to separate the two components.

Overhaul

6 Wipe clean all the components, then carefully examine each item for damage and deterioration. Check the bearing for wear by spinning the inner track and checking for any roughness. Similarly, attempt to move the inner track laterally. Excessive movement is an indication of wear.

15.3a Unscrew the rear hub retaining nut . . .

15.3b . . . collect the washer . . .

15.3c . . . then withdraw the brake drum and rear hub as an assembly, off the stub axle

16.8a Unscrew the hub nut from the axle . . .

16.8b . . . and remove the washer

Note: *A new rear hub retaining nut will be required for refitting.*

6 Remove the rear axle halfshaft on the side concerned as described in Section 13.

7 Lever up the hub nut staking using a thin chisel to prise it clear of the slot, but take care not to damage the threads.

8 Using a 65 mm socket, a sturdy, long extension bar, unscrew the hub nut from the axle and remove the washer **(see illustrations)**.

9 Withdraw the outer taper-roller bearing race and the spacer, then remove the hub and brake drum assembly from the axle **(see illustrations)**. On vehicles equipped with ABS, take care to avoid damaging the wheel speed sensor ring.

7 At the time of writing, it would appear that the hub bearing is not available separately. If the bearing is worn or damaged, it will be necessary to obtain a complete rear hub and bearing assembly. Seek the advice of a Ford dealer regarding parts availability.

Refitting

8 Slide the hub and drum assembly into position over the stub axle. Fit the washer and a new hub retaining nut, then tighten the nut to the specified torque in the five stages given in the Specifications.

9 With the handbrake fully released, adjust the lining-to-drum clearance by repeatedly depressing the brake pedal. Whilst depressing the pedal, have an assistant listen to the rear drums, to check that the adjuster strut is functioning correctly; if so, a clicking sound will be emitted by the strut as the pedal is depressed.

10 With the lining-to-drum clearance set, check and, if necessary, adjust the handbrake as described in Chapter 1.

11 Refit the roadwheel, then lower the vehicle to the ground and tighten the roadwheel nuts to the specified torque.

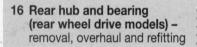

16 Rear hub and bearing (rear wheel drive models) – removal, overhaul and refitting

Removal (single wheel axles)

1 Chock the front wheels then jack up the rear of the vehicle and securely support it on

axle stands (see *Jacking and vehicle support*). Remove the appropriate rear wheel.

2 Two different axles types may be fitted according to model, and it is necessary to identify the axle being worked on before proceeding. To do this, locate the axle oil filler plug which will be either on the front left-hand side of the drive pinion housing, or on the differential housing cover. Proceed as described in the appropriate following sub-sections according to axle type.

Axles with oil filler plug on the drive pinion housing

3 Remove the rear axle halfshaft on the side concerned as described in Section 13.

4 Using a large screwdriver or lever, carefully prise the oil seal out of the rear axle, taking care not to damage the casing.

5 Using a two-legged puller and a 40 to 50 mm internal extractor, draw the hub bearing out of the axle. Obtain a new oil seal and bearing for refitting as the original components will have been damaged during removal.

Axles with oil filler plug on the differential housing cover

Caution: Due to the extremely high tightening torque of the rear hub retaining nut take great care when removing and refitting the nut. Use only the correct sockets and make sure you have a suitable extension bar for removal, and a torque wrench capable of tightening the nut to the correct setting (see Specifications) for refitting. Entrust this work to a dealer or suitably-equipped garage if in doubt about the procedure, or if the required tools are not available.

Overhaul (single wheel axles)

10 Wipe clean all the components, then carefully examine each item for damage and deterioration. Check the bearings for wear by spinning the inner track and checking for any roughness. Similarly, attempt to move the inner track laterally. Excessive movement is an indication of wear; any component which is unserviceable must be renewed.

11 To dismantle the hub (where applicable), support it on its inner and outer flange faces, not on the brake drum or wheel studs, and take care not to damage the sensor ring on vehicles fitted with ABS.

12 Before removing the old oil seal, note and record the position and fitted depth in the hub, as a guide to reassembly. Ford special shouldered tools are available to fit the new seal accurately, but suitable sockets or tubes can be used, provided the correct final fitted position of the seal is known.

13 Using a screwdriver, prise out the inner oil seal and lift out the inner taper-roller bearing race **(see illustrations)**.

14 Using a soft metal drift or tube of suitable diameter, drive out the inner and outer taper-roller bearing cups **(see illustration)**.

15 Thoroughly clean the hub, using a fine file to remove any nicks or burrs caused by removal of the bearing cups.

16 To reassemble the hub, support it on its inner face inside the brake drum (not on the drum itself) with the wheel studs uppermost.

17 Press the new outer taper-roller bearing

16.9a Withdraw the outer taper-roller bearing race . . .

16.9b . . . and the spacer . . .

16.9c . . . then remove the hub and brake drum assembly from the axle

16.13a Using a screwdriver, prise out the inner oil seal . . .

16.13b . . . and lift out the inner taper-roller bearing race

16.14 Drive out the inner and outer taper-roller bearing cups

cup into the hub, until it contacts the shoulder in the hub.

18 Turn the hub and drum assembly over, and support it on the hub face with the studs facing down.

19 Press the new inner taper-roller bearing cup into the hub, until it contacts the shoulder in the hub.

20 Liberally grease the inner taper-roller bearing, and place it in position in the bearing cup.

21 With the sealing lip facing downwards, press the outer oil seal into the bearing cup, to the fitted position noted during removal.

Refitting (single wheel axles)

Axles with oil filler plug on the drive pinion housing

22 Place the new bearing in position in the axle and tap it fully into place using a socket or tube of suitable diameter, in contact with the bearing outer race.

23 Grease the lips of the new oil seal, then using a socket or tube of suitable diameter, carefully drive the oil seal into the axle until it contacts the seating

24 Refit the halfshaft as described in Section 13.

Axles with oil filler plug on the differential housing cover

25 Prior to refitting the hub, dress the hub nut threads on the rear axle with a suitable thread chaser.

26 With the hub reassembled, lubricate the inner and outer oil seals and the inner taper-roller bearing with grease, and refit the hub assembly to the axle.

27 Refit the spacer, then grease the outer taper-roller bearing, and locate it in the outer bearing cup in the hub.

28 Screw on the new hub nut, and tighten it to the specified torque while rotating the hub/drum assembly in both directions to settle the bearing.

29 Secure the hub nut by staking it into the axle groove using a suitable punch **(see illustration)**.

30 Refit the halfshaft as described in Section 13.

Removal (twin wheel axles)

31 Chock the front wheels then jack up the

rear of the vehicle and securely support it on axle stands (see *Jacking and vehicle support*). Remove the appropriate rear wheels.

32 Two different axles types may be fitted according to model, and it is necessary to identify the axle being worked on before proceeding. To do this, locate the axle oil filler plug which will be either on the front left-hand side of the drive pinion housing, or on the differential housing cover. Proceed as described in the appropriate following sub-sections according to axle type.

Axles with oil filler plug on the drive pinion housing

33 Remove the rear axle halfshaft on the side concerned as described in Section 14.

34 If necessary, withdraw the brake drum from the rear hub by tapping the rear of the drum with a soft-faced mallet to free it from the hub flange.

35 Prise up the tab over the hub locknut, and unscrew the locknut using a 65 mm socket **(see illustration)**. Remove the tab washer and unscrew the hub nut. Note that a new tab washer will be required for refitting.

36 Remove the hub assembly from the axle, collecting the outer taper-roller bearing as the hub assembly is withdrawn. On vehicles equipped with ABS, take care to avoid damaging the wheel speed sensor ring.

Axles with oil filler plug on the differential housing cover

37 Refer to the procedures contained in paragraphs 6 to 9.

Overhaul (twin wheel axles)

38 Refer to the procedures contained in paragraphs 10 to 21, but note that on axles with the oil filler plug on the drive pinion housing, there are two oil seals in the hub assembly. Before removing the old oil seals, note and record their position and fitted depth in the hub, as a guide to reassembly.

Refitting (twin wheel axles)

Axles with oil filler plug on the drive pinion housing

39 With the hub reassembled, lubricate the inner and outer oil seals and the inner taper-roller bearing with grease, and refit the hub assembly to the axle.

40 Grease the outer taper-roller bearing, and locate it in the outer bearing cup in the hub.

41 Screw on the hub nut, and tighten it to the specified torque while rotating the hub assembly in both directions to settle the bearing.

42 Back off the hub nut by approximately 120°, then fit the tab washer, locating the tab in the groove in the axle.

43 Screw on the hub locknut, and tighten it to the specified torque.

44 Where applicable, refit the brake drum to the hub.

45 Check the hub bearing play using a suitable dial gauge **(see illustration)**. If necessary, further adjust the hub bearings to comply with the specified play. When the bearing play is satisfactory, bend the tab washer tabs inwards over the hub nut, and outwards over the locknut to secure.

16.29 Secure the hub nut by staking it into the axle groove using a suitable punch

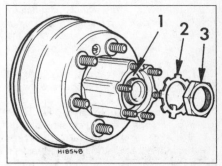

16.35 Rear hub nut (1), tab washer (2) and hub locknut (3)

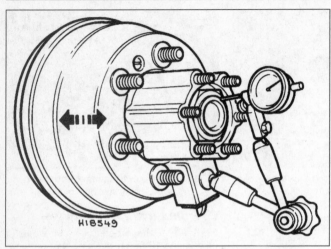

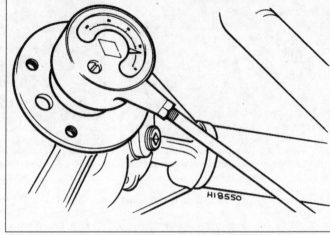

16.45 Checking the hub bearing play using a dial gauge

17.6 Using a pre-load gauge to determine the torque required to turn the drive pinion

46 Refit the halfshaft as described in Section 14.

Axles with oil filler plug on the differential housing cover

47 Refer to the procedures contained in paragraphs 25 to 30.

17 Drive pinion oil seal (rear axle) – renewal

1 Two different axles types may be fitted according to model, and it is necessary to identify the axle being worked on before proceeding. To do this, locate the axle oil filler plug which will be either on the front left-hand side of the drive pinion housing, or on the differential housing cover. Proceed as described in the appropriate following sub-sections according to axle type.

Axles with oil filler plug on the drive pinion housing

Note 1: *The axle is fitted with a collapsible spacer sleeve between the pinion shaft taper-roller bearings. Renewal of the drive pinion oil seal should only be attempted by the more experienced DIY mechanic. A pre-load gauge will be needed to measure the pinion turning torque, and a new pinion flange locknut must be fitted on reassembly. No difficulty should be encountered unless the pinion nut is overtightened, in which case removal of the taper-roller bearing to renew the collapsible spacer may present problems.*

Note 2: *New propeller shaft universal joint flange retaining bolts will also be required for refitting.*

2 Chock the front wheels then jack up the rear of the vehicle and securely support it on axle stands (see *Jacking and vehicle support*).

3 Remove the rear roadwheels then release the handbrake. Remove both rear brake drums by tapping the rear of the drum with a soft-faced mallet to free it.

4 Mark the propeller shaft rear universal joint and rear axle drive pinion flanges in relation to each other.

5 Unscrew the four bolts securing the propeller shaft to the drive pinion flange. Hold the shaft stationary with a long screwdriver inserted between the joint spider. Support the shaft on an axle stand after disconnecting the flanges. Note that new flange retaining bolts will be required for refitting.

6 Using a pre-load gauge, determine the torque required to turn the drive pinion, and note it down **(see illustration)**.

7 Using a bar or suitable forked tool bolted to the pinion flange holes, hold the flange stationary and unscrew the locknut **(see illustration)**. Note that a new locknut will be required when refitting.

8 Mark the position of the pinion flange in relation to the pinion shaft, then remove the flange, using a puller if necessary.

9 Carefully prise free the old oil seal using a blunt screwdriver or similar implement, then clean out the oil seal location in the pinion housing.

10 Locate the new oil seal in the pinion housing, having first greased the mating surfaces of the seal and the housing. The lips of the oil seal must face inwards.

11 Using a soft metal tube of suitable

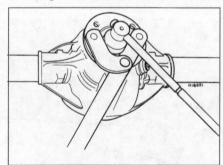

17.7 Using a forked tool bolted to the pinion flange to hold the flange and unscrew the locknut

diameter, carefully drive the new oil seal into the housing recess, until the face of the seal is flush with the housing. Make sure that the end of the pinion shaft is not knocked during this operation.

12 Lubricate the oil seal lip and the running surface of the drive pinion flange, then refit the flange to its original position on the pinion splines.

13 Fit a new locknut, and progressively tighten it in small increments. Check the pinion turning torque, using the pre-load gauge, at regular intervals during tightening. Whilst tightening the nut, prevent the pinion flange from turning as described in paragraph 5.

14 When the nut is tightened to the previously-recorded torque value, rotate the pinion to settle the bearing, then further tighten the nut by an additional torque of 0.3 Nm, this being the added value required to compensate for the additional friction of the new oil seal. For example, if the original value noted during removal (paragraph 6) was 2.2 Nm, and the compensating value for the new oil seal of 0.3 Nm is added to it, the total turning torque requirement in this instance will be 2.5 Nm. It is most important that the required torque is not exceeded for the reasons outlined in the introductory paragraph at the start of this Section.

15 Reconnect the propeller shaft, ensuring that the alignment marks correspond. Tighten the new retaining bolts to the specified torque.

16 Check and if necessary, top-up the rear axle oil level as described in Chapter 1, then refit the brake drums and roadwheels. Tighten the wheel nuts to the specified torque, and lower the vehicle to the ground.

Axles with oil filler plug on the differential housing cover

Note: *New propeller shaft universal joint flange retaining bolts, and a new pinion flange locknut will be required for refitting.*

17 Chock the front wheels then jack up the

rear of the vehicle and securely support it on axle stands (see *Jacking and vehicle support*).

18 Mark the propeller shaft rear universal joint and rear axle drive pinion flanges in relation to each other.

19 Unscrew the four bolts securing the propeller shaft to the drive pinion flange. Hold the shaft stationary with a long screwdriver inserted between the joint spider. Support the shaft on an axle stand after disconnecting the flanges. Note that new flange retaining bolts will be required for refitting.

20 Using a bar or suitable forked tool bolted to the pinion flange holes, hold the flange stationary and unscrew the locknut. Note that a new locknut will be required when refitting.

21 Mark the position of the pinion flange in relation to the pinion shaft, then remove the flange, using a puller if necessary.

22 Carefully prise free the old oil seal using a blunt screwdriver or similar implement, then clean out the oil seal location in the pinion housing.

23 Locate the new oil seal in the pinion housing, having first greased the mating surfaces of the seal and the housing. The lips of the oil seal must face inwards.

24 Using a soft metal tube of suitable diameter, carefully drive the new oil seal into the housing recess, until the face of the seal is flush with the housing. Make sure that the end of the pinion shaft is not knocked during this operation.

25 Lubricate the oil seal lip and the running surface of the drive pinion flange, then refit the flange to its original position on the pinion splines.

26 Fit a new locknut, and tighten it to the specified torque. Whilst tightening the nut, prevent the pinion flange from turning as described in paragraph 20.

27 Reconnect the propeller shaft, ensuring that the alignment marks correspond. Tighten the new retaining bolts to the specified torque.

28 Check and if necessary, top-up the rear axle oil level as described in Chapter 1, then and lower the vehicle to the ground.

18 Differential unit (rear axle) – overhaul

1 The design and layout of the axle is such that any attempt to remove the differential unit or pinion assembly from the axle housing will upset their preset meshing.

2 Since special tools and skills are required to set up the crownwheel and pinion mesh, the removal, overhaul and assembly of these differential types is not recommended, and should be entrusted to a dealer.

3 In any case, the current trend is for rear axle components not to be supplied individually, but the complete factory-built unit only to be supplied as a replacement.

4 If required, an inspection of the differential unit can be made to assess for excessive wear or damage to its component parts. To do this, place a large container beneath the differential to catch the oil which will drain out. Unbolt and remove the differential housing cover, and allow the oil to drain into the container.

5 Before refitting the rear cover, clean the cover and axle case mating surfaces, and remove the remains of the old gasket. Also clean the threads of the retaining bolts with a wire brush, and the threaded holes in the casing with a suitable cleaning solvent.

6 Locate the new gasket and the cover, smear the retaining bolt threads with sealant, and fit them. Tighten the bolts in an alternate and progressive sequence to the specified torque setting.

7 Referring to Chapter 1, fill the rear axle with the correct grade of oil, then refit and tighten the plug.

Chapter 9
Braking system

Contents

Degrees of difficulty

Easy, suitable for novice with little experience	**Fairly easy,** suitable for beginner with some experience	**Fairly difficult,** suitable for competent DIY mechanic	**Difficult,** suitable for experienced DIY mechanic	**Very difficult,** suitable for expert DIY or professional

Specifications

Front brakes

Type . . . .   Ventilated disc, with twin-piston sliding caliper
Brake pad friction material minimum thickness . . . .   1.5 mm
Disc diameter . . . .   294.0 mm
Disc thickness:
   New . . . .   24.3 mm
   Minimum. . . . .   22.1 mm
Maximum disc run-out . . . .   0.10 mm
Maximum disc thickness variation . . . .   0.02 mm

Rear Brakes

Type . . . .   Drum with leading and trailing shoes and automatic adjusters
Brake shoe friction material minimum thickness . . . .   1.0 mm
Drum diameter (inner):
   Front wheel drive models:
      New. . . . .   254.0 mm
      Maximum . . . .   256.0 mm
   Rear wheel drive models:
      New. . . . .   280.0 mm
      Maximum . . . .   282.0 mm

Torque wrench settings

	Nm	lbf ft
ABS hydraulic modulator mounting bracket bolt	20	15
ABS hydraulic modulator-to-mounting bracket	15	11
ABS wheel speed sensor retaining bolts	8	6
Brake caliper guide pin bolts*	32	24
Brake caliper mounting bracket bolts	175	129
Brake disc-to-hub flange bolts*	69	51
Brake fluid pipe unions	15	11
Brake hydraulic hose banjo union bolts	30	22
Brake pedal mounting bracket bolts/nuts	20	15
Driveshaft retaining nut:*		
Stage 1	Rotate the wheel hub 5 times	
Stage 2	250	185
Stage 3	Rotate the wheel hub 5 times	
Stage 4	420	310
Stage 5	Rotate the wheel hub 5 times	
Front wheel spindle retaining nut:*		
Stage 1	Rotate the wheel hub 5 times	
Stage 2	250	185
Stage 3	Rotate the wheel hub 5 times	
Stage 4	420	310
Stage 5	Rotate the wheel hub 5 times	
Handbrake lever retaining nuts	22	16
Hub assembly-to-steering knuckle bolts*	53	39
Master cylinder retaining nuts	20	15
Rear hub retaining nut – front wheel drive models:*		
44 mm flange diameter nut:		
Stage 1	Rotate the wheel hub 5 times	
Stage 2	200	148
Stage 3	Rotate the wheel hub 5 times	
Stage 4	300	221
Stage 5	Rotate the wheel hub 5 times	
51 mm flange diameter nut:		
Stage 1	Rotate the wheel hub 5 times	
Stage 2	200	148
Stage 3	Rotate the wheel hub 5 times	
Stage 4	450	332
Stage 5	Rotate the wheel hub 5 times	
Roadwheel nuts	200	148
Steering column retaining nuts*	20	15
Thermostat housing-to-vacuum pump bolt (2.0 litre engines)	22	16
Vacuum pump-to-coolant pump bolts (2.4 litre engines)	20	15
Vacuum pump-to-cylinder head bolts (2.0 litre engines)	22	16
Vacuum servo unit mounting nuts	20	15
Wheel cylinder retaining bolts	16	12

* Use new nuts/bolts

1 General information

The braking system is of servo-assisted, dual-circuit hydraulic type split diagonally. The arrangement of the hydraulic system is such that each circuit operates one front and one rear brake from a tandem master cylinder. Under normal circumstances, both circuits operate in unison. However, in the event of hydraulic failure in one circuit, full braking force will still be available at two wheels.

All models are fitted with front disc brakes and rear drum brakes. An Anti-lock Braking System (ABS) is fitted as standard or an optional extra to all vehicles covered in this manual. Refer to Section 19 for further information on ABS operation.

The front brake discs are of the ventilated type and are fitted with twin-piston sliding pin type brake calipers.

The rear drum brakes incorporate leading and trailing shoes, which are actuated by twin-piston wheel cylinders. A self-adjust mechanism is incorporated to automatically compensate for brake shoe wear. As the brake shoe linings wear, the footbrake operation automatically operates the adjuster mechanism, which effectively lengthens the shoe strut, and repositions the brake shoes to maintain the lining-to-drum clearance.

The cable-operated handbrake provides an independent mechanical means of rear brake application.

A vacuum servo unit is fitted between the master cylinder and the bulkhead, its function being to reduce the amount of pedal pressure required to operate the brakes. Since there is

no throttling as such of the inlet manifold on diesel engines, the manifold is not a suitable source of vacuum to operate the vacuum servo unit. The servo unit is therefore connected to a separate engine-mounted vacuum pump. On 2.0 litre engines, the pump is bolted to the left-hand end of the cylinder head and driven by the exhaust camshaft. On 2.4 litre engines, the pump is attached to the coolant pump and driven by the auxiliary drivebelt.

On models without ABS, a load-apportioning valve (LAV) is incorporated in the rear brake hydraulic circuit. The valve function is to regulate the braking force available at each rear wheel, to reduce the possibility of the rear wheels locking up under heavy braking. On models equipped with ABS, the braking force available at the rear wheels is controlled by the ABS hydraulic modulator under all driving conditions.

⚠️ *Warning: When servicing any part of the system, work carefully and methodically; also observe scrupulous cleanliness when overhauling any part of the hydraulic system. Always renew components (in axle sets, where applicable) if in doubt about their condition, and use only genuine Ford replacement parts, or at least those of known good quality. Note the warnings given in 'Safety first!' and at relevant points in this Chapter concerning the dangers of asbestos dust and hydraulic fluid.*

2 Hydraulic system – bleeding

⚠️ *Warning: Hydraulic fluid is poisonous. Wash off immediately and thoroughly in the case of skin contact, and seek immediate medical advice if any fluid is swallowed or gets into the eyes. Certain types of hydraulic fluid are inflammable, and may ignite when allowed into contact with hot components. When servicing any hydraulic system, it is safest to assume that the fluid is inflammable, and to take precautions against the risk of fire as though it is petrol that is being handled. Hydraulic fluid is also an effective paint stripper, and will attack plastics; if any is spilt, it should be washed off immediately, using copious quantities of fresh water. Finally, it is hygroscopic (it absorbs moisture from the air) therefore old fluid may be contaminated and unfit for further use. When topping-up or renewing the fluid, always use the recommended type, and ensure that it comes from a freshly-opened sealed container.*

General

1 The correct operation of any hydraulic system is only possible after removing all air from the components and circuit; this is achieved by bleeding the system.

2 During the bleeding procedure, add only clean, unused hydraulic fluid of the recommended type; never re-use fluid that has already been bled from the system. Ensure that sufficient fluid is available before starting work.

3 If there is any possibility of incorrect fluid being already in the system, the brake components and circuit must be flushed completely with uncontaminated, correct fluid, and new seals should be fitted to the various components.

4 If hydraulic fluid has been lost from the system, or air has entered because of a leak, ensure that the fault is cured before proceeding further.

5 When bleeding the brakes on vehicles with a load-apportioning valve in the rear brake hydraulic circuit, it is important to note that the vehicle must be standing on its wheels. If the

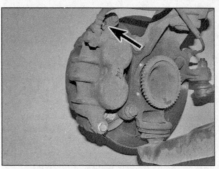

2.12a Front caliper bleed screw (arrowed) . . .

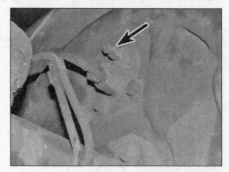

2.12b . . . and rear wheel cylinder bleed screw (arrowed)

rear of the vehicle is jacked up and the axle is in a 'wheel free' state, the load-apportioning valve will prevent complete bleeding of the system.

6 Check that all pipes and hoses are secure, unions tight and bleed screws closed. Clean any dirt from around the bleed screws.

7 Unscrew the master cylinder reservoir cap, and top-up the master cylinder reservoir to the MAX level line. Refit the cap loosely, and remember to maintain the fluid level at least above the MIN level line throughout the procedure, otherwise there is a risk of further air entering the system.

8 There are a number of one-man, do-it-yourself brake bleeding kits currently available from motor accessory shops. It is recommended that one of these kits is used whenever possible, as they greatly simplify the bleeding operation, and also reduce the risk of expelled air and fluid being drawn back into the system. If such a kit is not available, the basic (two-man) method must be used, which is described in detail below.

9 If a kit is to be used, prepare the vehicle as described previously, and follow the kit manufacturer's instructions, as the procedure may vary slightly according to the type being used, Generally, they are as outlined below in the relevant sub-Section.

10 If the system has been only partially disconnected, and suitable precautions were taken to minimise fluid loss, it should only be necessary to bleed that part of the system (ie, the primary or secondary circuit). If the master cylinder or main brake lines have been disconnected, then the complete system must be bled.

Bleeding

Basic (two-man) method

11 Collect together a clean glass jar, a suitable length of plastic or rubber tubing which is a tight fit over the bleed screw, and a ring spanner to fit the screw. The help of an assistant will also be required.

12 Remove the dust cap from the bleed screw at the wheel to be bled **(see illustrations)**. Fit the spanner and tube to the screw, place the other end of the tube in the jar, and pour in sufficient fluid to cover the end of the tube.

13 Ensure that the master cylinder reservoir

fluid level is maintained at least above the MIN level line throughout the procedure.

14 Have the assistant fully depress the brake pedal several times to build-up pressure, then maintain it on the final downstroke.

15 While pedal pressure is maintained, unscrew the bleed screw (approximately one turn) and allow the compressed fluid and air to flow into the jar. The assistant should maintain pedal pressure, following it down to the floor if necessary, and should not release it until instructed to do so. When the flow stops, tighten the bleed screw again, have the assistant release the pedal slowly, and recheck the reservoir fluid level.

16 Repeat the steps given in paragraphs 14 and 15 until the fluid emerging from the bleed screw is free from air bubbles. If the master cylinder has been drained and refilled, and air is being bled from the first bleed screw, allow approximately five seconds between cycles for the master cylinder passages to refill.

17 When no more air bubbles appear, securely tighten the bleed screw, remove the tube and spanner, and refit the dust cap. Do not overtighten the bleed screw.

18 Repeat the procedure on the remaining bleed screws, until all air is removed from the system and the brake pedal feels firm again.

Using a one-way valve kit

19 As the name implies, these kits consist of a length of tubing with a one-way valve fitted, to prevent expelled air and fluid being drawn back into the system. Some kits include a translucent container, which can be positioned so that the air bubbles can be more easily seen flowing from the end of the tube.

20 The kit is connected to the bleed screw, which is then opened. The user returns to the driver's seat, depresses the brake pedal with a smooth, steady stroke, and slowly releases it; this is repeated until the expelled fluid is clear of air bubbles.

21 Note that these kits simplify work so much that it is easy to forget the master cylinder reservoir fluid level, therefore ensure that this is maintained at least above the MIN level line at all times.

Using a pressure-bleeding kit

22 These kits are usually operated by a reservoir of pressurised air contained in the spare tyre. However, note that it will probably be necessary to reduce the pressure to a lower level than normal. Refer to the instructions supplied with the kit.

23 By connecting a pressurised, fluid-filled container to the master cylinder reservoir, bleeding can be carried out simply by opening each bleed screw in turn, and allowing the fluid to flow out until no more air bubbles can be seen in the expelled fluid.

24 This method has the advantage that the large reservoir of fluid provides an additional safeguard against air being drawn into the system during bleeding.

25 Pressure-bleeding is particularly effective when bleeding 'difficult' systems, or when bleeding the complete system at the time of routine fluid renewal.

All methods

26 When bleeding is complete, and firm pedal feel is restored, wash off any spilt fluid, securely tighten the bleed screws, and refit the dust caps.

27 Check the hydraulic fluid level in the master cylinder reservoir, and top-up if necessary (see *Weekly checks*).

28 Discard any hydraulic fluid that has been bled from the system as it will not be fit for re-use.

29 Check the feel of the brake pedal. If it feels at all spongy, air must still be present in the system, and further bleeding is required. Failure to bleed satisfactorily after a reasonable repetition of the bleeding procedure may be due to worn master cylinder seals.

3 Hydraulic pipes and hoses – renewal

Note: Before starting work, refer to the note at the beginning of Section 2 concerning the dangers of hydraulic fluid.

1 If any pipe or hose is to be renewed, minimise fluid loss by first removing the master cylinder reservoir cap and screwing it down onto a piece of polythene. Alternatively, flexible hoses can be sealed, if required, using a proprietary brake hose clamp. Metal brake pipe unions can be plugged (if care is taken not to allow dirt into the system) or capped immediately they are disconnected. Place a wad of rag under any union that is to be disconnected, to catch any spilt fluid.

2 If a flexible hose is to be disconnected, unscrew the brake pipe union nut(s) before removing the spring clip or retaining bolt which secures the hose to its mounting bracket. Where applicable, unscrew the banjo union bolt securing the hose to the caliper and recover the copper washers. When removing the front flexible hose, undo the retaining bolt and release the hose support bracket from the suspension strut.

3 To unscrew union nuts, it is preferable to obtain a brake pipe spanner of the correct size; these are available from most motor accessory shops. Failing this, a close-fitting open-ended spanner will be required, though if the nuts are tight or corroded, their flats may be rounded-off if the spanner slips. In such a

case, a self-locking wrench is often the only way to unscrew a stubborn union, but it follows that the pipe and the damaged nuts must be renewed on reassembly. Always clean a union and surrounding area before disconnecting it. If disconnecting a component with more than one union, make a careful note of the connections before disturbing any of them.

4 If a brake pipe is to be renewed, it can be obtained, cut to length and with the union nuts and end flares in place, from Ford dealers. All that is then necessary is to bend it to shape, following the line of the original, before fitting it to the vehicle. Alternatively, most motor accessory shops can make up brake pipes from kits, but this requires very careful measurement of the original, to ensure that the replacement is of the correct length. The safest answer is usually to take the original to the shop as a pattern.

5 On refitting, do not overtighten the union nuts.

6 When refitting hoses to the front calipers, always use new copper washers and tighten the banjo union bolts to the specified torque. Make sure that the hoses are positioned so that they will not touch surrounding bodywork or the roadwheels.

7 Ensure that the pipes and hoses are correctly routed, with no kinks, and that they are secured in the clips or brackets provided. After fitting, remove the polythene from the reservoir, and bleed the hydraulic system as described in Section 2. Wash off any spilt fluid, and check carefully for fluid leaks.

4 Front brake pads – renewal

⚠ *Warning: Renew BOTH sets of front brake pads at the same time – NEVER renew the pads on only one wheel, as uneven braking may result. Note that the dust created by wear of the pads may contain asbestos, which is a health hazard. Never blow it out with compressed air, and do not inhale any of it. An approved filtering mask should be worn when working on the brakes. DO NOT use petroleum-based solvents to clean brake parts – use brake cleaner or methylated spirit only.*

Note: A new caliper lower guide pin bolt will be required for refitting.

1 Apply the handbrake, then jack up the front of the vehicle and support it on axle stands (see *Jacking and vehicle support*). Remove the front roadwheels.

2 Follow the accompanying photos (**illustrations 4.2a to 4.2k**) for the actual pad renewal procedure, bearing in mind the additional points given in the following paragraphs. Be sure to stay in order and read the caption under each illustration. Note that if the old pads are to be refitted, ensure that they are identified so that they can be returned to their original positions.

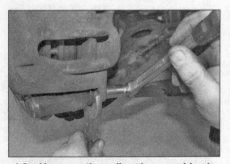

4.2a Unscrew the caliper lower guide pin bolt while counterholding the guide pin with a spanner

4.2b Pivot the brake caliper upwards . . .

4.2c . . . and secure it in the raised position using a cable tie

4.2d Lift the inner and outer brake pads off the caliper mounting bracket

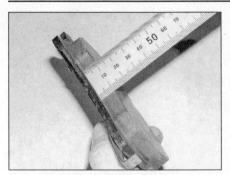

4.2e Measure the thickness of the pad friction material. If any are worn down to the specified minimum, or fouled with oil or grease, all four pads must be renewed

4.2f Apply a little high-melting-point copper brake grease to the pad backing plate contact areas

4.2g If new pads are to be fitted, before refitting the caliper, push back the caliper pistons whilst temporarily opening the bleed screw. This is to prevent any dirt/debris being forced back up the hydraulic circuit in the ABS modulator

4.2h Fit the new brake pads to the caliper, ensuring that the friction material is facing the brake disc. Note that the inner pad is the one fitted with the wear indicator strip

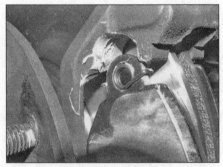

4.2i As the pads are fitted, ensure that the anti-rattle spring correctly engages with the mounting bracket

4.2j Pivot the caliper down over the pads and fit the new guide pin bolt

3 If the original brake pads are still serviceable, carefully clean them using a clean, fine wire brush or similar, paying particular attention to the sides and back of the metal backing plate. Clean out the grooves in the friction material, and pick out any large embedded particles of dirt or debris. Carefully clean the pad locations in the caliper mounting bracket.

4 Prior to fitting the pads, check that the guide pins are a snug fit in the caliper mounting bracket. Inspect the dust seals around the pistons for damage, and the pistons for evidence of fluid leaks, corrosion or damage. If attention to any of these components is necessary, refer to Section 6.

5 If new brake pads are to be fitted, the caliper pistons must be pushed back into the cylinder to allow for the extra pad thickness. Either use a G-clamp or similar tool, or use suitable pieces of wood as levers. Clamp off the flexible brake hose leading to the caliper then connect a brake bleeding kit to the caliper bleed screw. Open the bleed screw as the pistons are retracted, the surplus brake fluid will then be collected in the bleed kit vessel. Close the bleed screw just before the caliper pistons are pushed fully into the caliper. This should ensure no air enters the hydraulic system.

Note: *The ABS unit contains hydraulic components that are very sensitive to impurities in the brake fluid. Even the smallest particles can cause the system to fail through blockage. The pad retraction method described here prevents any debris in the brake fluid expelled from the caliper from being passed back to the ABS hydraulic unit, as well as preventing any chance of damage to the master cylinder seals.*

6 With the brake pads installed, depress the brake pedal repeatedly, until normal (non-assisted) pedal pressure is restored, and the pads are pressed into firm contact with the brake disc.

7 Repeat the above procedure on the remaining front brake caliper.

8 Refit the roadwheels, then lower the vehicle to the ground and tighten the roadwheel nuts to the specified torque setting.

9 Check the hydraulic fluid level as described in *Weekly checks*.

Caution: New pads will not give full braking efficiency until they have bedded-in. Be prepared for this, and avoid hard braking as far as possible for the first hundred miles or so after pad renewal.

4.2k Tighten the guide pin bolt to the specified torque while counterholding the guide pin

5 Front brake disc –
inspection, removal and refitting

Note: *Before starting work, refer to the warning at the beginning of Section 4 concerning the dangers of asbestos dust. If either disc requires renewal, both should be renewed at the same time together with new pads, to ensure even and consistent braking.*

5.8a Bend up the split pin legs . . .

5.8b . . . then extract the split pin . . .

5.8c . . . and remove the retaining nut locking ring

Inspection

1 Firmly apply the handbrake, then jack up the front of the vehicle and support it securely on axle stands (see *Jacking and vehicle support*). Remove the roadwheel.

2 Rotate the brake disc, and examine it for deep scoring or grooving. Light scoring is normal, but if excessive, the disc should be removed and either renewed or machined (within the specified limits) by an engineering works. The minimum thickness is given in the Specifications at the start of this Chapter.

3 Using a dial gauge, or a flat metal block and feeler blades, check that the disc run-out does not exceed the figure given in the Specifications. Measure the run-out 10.0 mm in from the outer edge of the disc.

4 If the disc run-out is excessive, remove the disc as described later, and check that the disc-to-hub surfaces are perfectly clean. Refit the disc and check the run-out again.

5 If the run-out is still excessive, the disc should be renewed.

6 To remove a disc, proceed as follows.

Front wheel drive models

Removal

Caution: Due to the extremely high tightening torque of the driveshaft retaining nut, take great care when removing and refitting the nut. Use only the correct sockets and make sure you have a suitable extension bar for removal, and a torque wrench capable of tightening the nut to the correct setting (see Specifications) for refitting. Entrust this work to a dealer or suitably-equipped garage if in doubt about the procedure, or if the required tools are not available.

Note: *A new driveshaft retaining nut, washer and split pin, together with new brake disc and hub assembly retaining bolts will be required for refitting.*

7 Firmly apply the handbrake, then jack up the front of the vehicle and support it securely on axle stands (see *Jacking and vehicle support*). Remove the relevant front roadwheel.

8 Extract the split pin from the driveshaft and remove the retaining nut locking ring **(see illustrations)**.

9 Have an assistant firmly depress the brake pedal to prevent the front hub from rotating, then using a socket and extension bar, slacken the driveshaft retaining nut. Alternatively, a tool can be fabricated from two lengths of steel strip (one long, one short) and a nut and bolt, the nut and bolt forming the pivot of a forked tool. Bolt the tool to the hub using two wheel nuts, and hold the tool to prevent the hub from rotating as the driveshaft retaining nut is undone.

10 Unscrew the driveshaft retaining nut, and remove the washer **(see illustration)**. Discard the nut and washer as new components must be used on refitting.

11 Undo the two bolts securing the brake caliper mounting bracket to the steering knuckle. Slide the caliper and mounting bracket, complete with brake pads, off the disc and suspend the assembly from the coil spring using a cable tie **(see illustration)**.

12 Using a long socket bit inserted through the holes in the hub flange, undo the five bolts securing the hub assembly to the steering knuckle **(see illustration)**. Note that new bolts will be required for refitting.

13 Withdraw the hub assembly and brake disc from the steering knuckle and driveshaft. If necessary, tap the rear of the brake disc with a soft faced mallet to free the hub assembly from the knuckle.

5.10 Unscrew the retaining nut, and remove the washer

5.11 Slide the caliper and mounting bracket, complete with brake pads, off the disc

5.12 Hub assembly-to-steering knuckle retaining bolts (arrowed)

5.14a Undo the bolts (arrowed) securing the brake disc to the hub flange . . .

5.14b . . . then turn the assembly over and lift off the disc

14 With the hub assembly on the bench, undo the five bolts securing the brake disc to the hub flange, then turn the assembly over and lift off the disc **(see illustrations)**. Note that new bolts will be required for refitting. If the original disc is to be refitted, make alignment marks on the hub flange and disc prior to separation to ensure correct reassembly.

Refitting

15 Thoroughly clean the mating surfaces of the brake disc and hub flange ensuring that all traces of dirt and corrosion are removed.

16 Place the disc in position on the hub flange, aligning the marks made on removal if the original disc is being refitted. Fit the five new disc retaining bolts and tighten them in a progressive diagonal sequence to the specified torque.

17 Clean the mating faces of the hub assembly and steering knuckle, then locate the hub assembly over the end of the driveshaft and into position on the knuckle. Fit the five new hub assembly retaining bolts and tighten them in a progressive diagonal sequence to the specified torque.

18 Slide the brake caliper assembly over the disc and into position on the steering knuckle. Refit the two mounting bracket retaining bolts and tighten them to the specified torque.

19 Place the new washer over the end of the driveshaft and screw on the new retaining nut. Tighten the driveshaft retaining nut to the specified torque in the five stages given in the Specifications. Prevent the driveshaft from rotating as the nut is tightened, using the method employed for removal.

20 Refit the driveshaft retaining nut locking ring, aligning the slots with the split pin hole in the driveshaft. Insert a new split pin and bend over the split pin legs to secure.

21 Refit the roadwheel, tighten the wheel nuts to the specified torque, then lower the vehicle to the ground.

Rear wheel drive models

Removal

Caution: Due to the extremely high tightening torque of the wheel spindle retaining nut, take great care when removing and refitting the nut. Use only the correct sockets and make sure you have a suitable extension bar for removal, and a torque wrench capable of tightening the nut to the correct setting (see Specifications) for refitting. Entrust this work to a dealer or suitably-equipped garage if in doubt about the procedure, or if the required tools are not available.

Note: *A new wheel spindle retaining nut, washer and split pin, together with new brake disc and hub assembly retaining bolts will be required for refitting.*

22 Firmly apply the handbrake, then jack up the front of the vehicle and support it securely on axle stands (see *Jacking and vehicle support*). Remove the relevant front roadwheel.

23 Extract the split pin from the wheel spindle and remove the retaining nut locking ring **(see illustrations 5.8a 5.8b and 5.8c)**.

24 Have an assistant firmly depress the brake pedal to prevent the front hub from rotating, then using a socket and extension bar, slacken the wheel spindle retaining nut. Alternatively, a tool can be fabricated from two lengths of steel strip (one long, one short) and a nut and bolt, the nut and bolt forming the pivot of a forked tool. Bolt the tool to the hub using two wheel nuts, and hold the tool to prevent the hub from rotating as the wheel spindle retaining nut is undone.

25 Fully unscrew the wheel spindle retaining nut, and remove the washer **(see illustration 5.10)**. Discard the nut and washer as new components must be used on refitting.

26 Undo the two bolts securing the brake caliper mounting bracket to the steering knuckle. Slide the caliper and mounting bracket, complete with brake pads, off the disc and suspend the assembly from the coil spring using a cable tie **(see illustration 5.11)**.

27 Withdraw the wheel spindle from the rear of the steering knuckle **(see illustration)**.

28 Using a long socket bit inserted through the holes in the hub flange, undo the five bolts securing the hub assembly to the steering knuckle **(see illustration 5.12)**. Note that new bolts will be required for refitting.

29 Withdraw the hub assembly and brake disc from the steering knuckle. If necessary, tap the rear of the brake disc with a soft faced mallet to free the hub assembly from the knuckle.

30 With the hub assembly on the bench, undo the five bolts securing the brake disc to the hub flange, then turn the assembly over and lift off the disc **(see illustrations 5.14a and 5.14b)**. Note that new bolts will be required for refitting. If the original disc is to be refitted, make alignment marks on the hub flange and disc prior to separation to ensure correct reassembly.

Refitting

31 Thoroughly clean the mating surfaces of the brake disc and hub flange ensuring that all traces of dirt and corrosion are removed.

32 Place the disc in position on the hub flange, aligning the marks made on removal if the original disc is being refitted. Fit the five new disc retaining bolts and tighten them in a progressive diagonal sequence to the specified torque.

33 Clean the mating faces of the hub assembly and steering knuckle, then locate the hub assembly in position on the knuckle. Fit the five new hub assembly retaining bolts and tighten them in a progressive diagonal sequence to the specified torque.

34 Insert the wheel spindle through the rear of the steering knuckle and into the hub flange. Place the new washer over the end of the spindle and screw on the new retaining nut. Only tighten the nut finger tight at this stage.

35 Slide the brake caliper assembly over the

5.27 Withdraw the wheel spindle from the rear of the steering knuckle

disc and into position on the steering knuckle. Refit the two mounting bracket retaining bolts and tighten them to the specified torque.

36 Tighten the wheel spindle retaining nut to the specified torque in the five stages given in the Specifications. Prevent the hub from rotating as the nut is tightened, using the method employed for removal.

37 Refit the wheel spindle retaining nut locking ring, aligning the slots with the split pin hole in the spindle. Insert a new split pin and bend over the split pin legs to secure.

38 Refit the roadwheel, tighten the wheel nuts to the specified torque, then lower the vehicle to the ground.

6 Front brake caliper – removal, overhaul and refitting

Note: *New brake hose copper washers and a new caliper upper guide pin bolt will be required when refitting. Before starting work, refer to the note at the beginning of Section 2 concerning the dangers of hydraulic fluid, and to the warning at the beginning of Section 4 concerning the dangers of asbestos dust.*

Removal

1 Apply the handbrake, then jack up the front of the vehicle and support it on axle stands (see *Jacking and vehicle support*). Remove the roadwheel.

2 Minimise fluid loss by first removing the master cylinder reservoir cap and screwing it down onto a piece of polythene. Alternatively, use a brake hose clamp to clamp the flexible hose leading to the brake caliper.

3 Clean the area around the caliper brake hose union. Unscrew and remove the union bolt, and recover the copper sealing washer from each side of the hose union. Discard the washers as new ones must be used on refitting. Plug the hose end and caliper hole, to minimise fluid loss and prevent the ingress of dust and dirt into the hydraulic system.

4 Remove the brake pads as described in Section 4.

5 Unscrew the caliper upper guide pin bolt while counterholding the guide pin with a spanner, then lift the caliper off the mounting bracket.

Overhaul

6 With the caliper on the bench, wipe it clean with a cloth rag.

7 Carefully remove the dust seals from the two pistons and the caliper body.

8 Using a G-clamp or similar tool, or suitable pieces of wood, retain one of the pistons in the fully retracted position.

9 Apply compressed air to the brake hose union hole to push out the remaining piston approximately half way out of its bore. Only low pressure should be required, such as is generated by a foot pump.

10 Retain the partially ejected piston in position using the G-clamp or similar tool, or suitable pieces of wood. Again, using compressed air, push out the other piston approximately half way out of its bore. The two partially ejected pistons can now be removed by hand from the caliper body. Suitably identify the two pistons so that they can be refitted to their original bores in the caliper.

11 Using a small screwdriver, carefully remove the piston seals from the grooves in the caliper, taking care not to mark the bore.

12 Thoroughly clean all components, using only methylated spirit or clean hydraulic fluid. Never use mineral-based solvents such as petrol or paraffin, which will attack the rubber components of the hydraulic system. Dry the components using compressed air or a clean, lint-free cloth. If available, use compressed air to blow clear the fluid passages.

 Warning: Wear eye protection when using compressed air.

13 Check all components, and renew any that are worn or damaged. If the pistons and/or caliper bore are scratched excessively, renew the complete caliper body. Similarly check the condition of the guide pin bushes in the caliper mounting bracket. Both bushes and guide pins should be undamaged and (when cleaned) a reasonably tight sliding fit. If there is any doubt about the condition of any component, renew it.

14 If the caliper is fit for further use, obtain the necessary components from your Ford dealer. Renew the caliper seals and dust covers as a matter of course since these should never be re-used.

15 On reassembly, ensure that all components are absolutely clean and dry.

16 Dip the first piston and the new piston seal in clean hydraulic fluid, and smear clean fluid on the caliper bore surface.

17 Locate the new seal in the caliper bore groove, using only the fingers to manipulate it into position.

18 Fit the new dust seal to the piston, then insert the piston into the cylinder bore using a twisting motion to ensure it enters the seal correctly. Locate the dust seal in the body groove, and push the piston fully into the caliper bore.

19 Repeat paragraphs 16 to 18 to reassemble the remaining piston.

Refitting

20 Place the caliper in position on the mounting bracket and fit the new upper guide pin bolt. Tighten the upper guide pin bolt to

the specified torque while counterholding the guide pin with a spanner.

21 Refit the brake pads as described in Section 4.

22 Position a new copper sealing washer on each side of the hose union, and connect the brake hose to the caliper. Ensure that the hose is correctly positioned against the caliper body lug, then install the union bolt and tighten it to the specified torque.

23 Remove the brake hose clamp or polythene, and bleed the hydraulic system as described in Section 2. Note that, providing the precautions described were taken to minimise brake fluid loss, it should only be necessary to bleed the relevant front brake circuit.

24 Refit the roadwheel, then lower the vehicle to the ground and tighten the roadwheel nuts to the specified torque.

---

7 Rear brake drum – removal, inspection and refitting

Note: *Before starting work, refer to the warning at the beginning of Section 8 concerning the dangers of asbestos dust.*

Front wheel drive models

Removal

Caution: It may be necessary to remove the brake drum and rear hub as an assembly if the drum is severely corroded in position. Due to the extremely high tightening torque of the hub retaining nut, take great care when removing and refitting the nut. Use only the correct sockets and make sure you have a suitable extension bar for removal, and a torque wrench capable of tightening the nut to the correct setting (see Specifications) for refitting. Entrust this work to a dealer or suitably-equipped garage if in doubt about the procedure, or if the required tools are not available.

Note: *A new rear hub retaining nut may be required for refitting.*

1 Chock the front wheels then jack up the rear of the vehicle and securely support it on axle stands (see *Jacking and vehicle support*). Remove the appropriate rear wheel and release the handbrake.

2 Where fitted, remove the brake drum retaining clip from the roadwheel stud.

3 It should now be possible to withdraw the brake drum from the wheel hub by tapping the rear of the drum with a soft-faced mallet to free it from the hub. In practice, the build-up of corrosion on the mating surfaces of the drum and hub often make it impossible to remove the drum in this way. If so, unscrew the rear hub retaining nut, collect the washer, then withdraw the brake drum and rear hub as an assembly, off the stub axle **(see illustrations)**.

4 If the drum and hub were removed together as an assembly, measure the diameter of the hub retaining nut flange. The diameter will be

7.3a Withdraw the brake drum from the wheel hub

7.3b If the drum is corroded to the hub, unscrew the hub retaining nut . . .

7.3c . . . collect the washer . . .

7.3d . . . then withdraw the brake drum and rear hub, as an assembly, off the stub axle

either 44 mm, or 51 mm. Obtain a new hub retaining nut of the appropriate size for refitting.

5 If necessary, separate the brake drum from the hub using a hydraulic press.

Inspection

Note: *If either drum requires renewal, BOTH should be renewed at the same time, to ensure even and consistent braking.*

6 Working carefully, remove all traces of brake dust from the drum, but *avoid inhaling the dust, as it is a health hazard.*

7 Scrub clean the outside of the drum, and check it for obvious signs of wear or damage (such as cracks around the roadwheel stud holes) and renew the drum if necessary.

8 Examine the inside of the drum carefully. Light scoring of the friction surface is normal, but if heavy scoring is found, the drum must be renewed. It is usual to find a lip on the drum's inboard edge which consists of a mixture of rust and brake dust. This should be scraped away to leave a smooth surface which can be polished with fine (120- to 150-grade) emery paper. If, however, the lip is due to the friction surface being recessed by excessive wear, then the drum must be renewed.

9 If the drum is thought to be excessively worn, or oval, its internal diameter must be measured at several points using an internal micrometer. Take measurements in pairs, the second at right-angles to the first, and compare the two to check for signs of ovality. Provided that it does not enlarge the drum to beyond the specified maximum diameter, it may be possible to have the drum refinished by skimming or grinding; if this is not possible, the drums on both sides must be renewed. Note that if the drum is to be skimmed, both drums must be refinished, to maintain a consistent internal diameter on both sides.

Refitting

10 If a new brake drum is to be installed, use a suitable solvent to remove any preservative coating that may have been applied to its interior. Note that it may also be necessary to shorten the brake shoe adjuster strut length to allow the new drum to pass over the brake shoes (see Section 8).

11 If the drum was removed leaving the rear hub in position, slide the drum over the roadwheel studs and onto the hub. Where applicable, refit the brake drum retaining clip to the roadwheel stud.

12 If the drum was removed complete with the rear hub, slide the hub and drum assembly into position over the stub axle. Fit the washer and a new hub retaining nut, then tighten the nut to the specified torque in the five stages given in the Specifications.

13 With the handbrake fully released, adjust the lining-to-drum clearance by repeatedly depressing the brake pedal. Whilst depressing the pedal, have an assistant listen to the rear drums, to check that the adjuster strut is functioning correctly; if so, a clicking sound will be emitted by the strut as the pedal is depressed.

14 With the lining-to-drum clearance set, check and, if necessary, adjust the handbrake as described in Chapter 1.

15 Refit the roadwheel, then lower the vehicle to the ground and tighten the roadwheel nuts to the specified torque setting.

Rear wheel drive models

Removal (single wheel axles)

16 Chock the front wheels then jack up the rear of the vehicle and securely support it on axle stands (see *Jacking and vehicle support*). Remove the appropriate rear wheel and release the handbrake.

17 On models with the brake drum mounted over the roadwheel studs on the axle halfshaft, withdraw the brake drum from the halfshaft by tapping the rear of the drum with a soft-faced mallet to free it from the shaft flange.

18 On models with the rear axle halfshaft mounted over the roadwheel studs on the brake drum, the brake drum and rear hub are an integral assembly. Refer to the procedures contained in Chapter 8 and remove the rear hub and bearing assembly.

Inspection (single wheel axles)

19 Refer to paragraphs 6 to 9.

Refitting (single wheel axles)

20 If a new brake drum/hub is to be installed, use a suitable solvent to remove any preservative coating that may have been applied to its interior. Note that it may also be necessary to shorten the brake shoe adjuster strut length to allow the new drum to pass over the brake shoes (see Section 8).

21 If the drum was removed leaving the axle halfshaft in position, slide the drum over the roadwheel studs and into position on the halfshaft flange.

22 If the drum and rear hub were removed as an assembly, refer to the procedures contained in Chapter 8 and refit the rear hub and bearing assembly.

23 With the handbrake fully released, adjust the lining-to-drum clearance by repeatedly depressing the brake pedal. Whilst depressing the pedal, have an assistant listen to the rear drums, to check that the adjuster strut is functioning correctly; if so, a clicking sound will be emitted by the strut as the pedal is depressed.

24 With the lining-to-drum clearance set, check and, if necessary, adjust the handbrake as described in Chapter 1.

25 Refit the roadwheel, then lower the vehicle to the ground and tighten the roadwheel nuts to the specified torque setting.

Removal (twin wheel axles)

26 Chock the front wheels then jack up the rear of the vehicle and securely support it on axle stands (see *Jacking and vehicle support*). Remove the appropriate rear wheels and release the handbrake.

27 Depending on axle type, the brake drum and rear hub will be either an integral assembly, or the brake drum will be a separate

component that can be individually removed. To identify the axle being worked on locate the axle oil filler plug which will be either on the front left-hand side of the drive pinion housing, or on the differential housing cover.

28 If the oil filler plug is located on the front left-hand side of the drive pinion housing, the brake drum is a separate component. Withdraw the brake drum from the rear hub by tapping the rear of the drum with a soft-faced mallet to free it from the hub flange.

29 If the oil filler plug is located on the differential housing cover, the brake drum and rear hub are an integral assembly. Refer to the procedures contained in Chapter 8 and remove the rear hub and bearing assembly.

Inspection (twin wheel axles)

30 Refer to paragraphs 6 to 9.

Refitting (twin wheel axles)

31 If a new brake drum/hub is to be installed, use a suitable solvent to remove any preservative coating that may have been applied to its interior. Note that it may also be necessary to shorten the brake shoe adjuster strut length to allow the new drum to pass over the brake shoes (see Section 8).

32 If the drum was removed leaving the rear hub in position, slide the drum over the roadwheel studs and into position on the hub flange.

33 If the drum and rear hub were removed as an assembly, refer to the procedures contained in Chapter 8 and refit the rear hub and bearing assembly.

34 With the handbrake fully released, adjust the lining-to-drum clearance by repeatedly depressing the brake pedal. Whilst depressing the pedal, have an assistant listen to the rear drums, to check that the adjuster strut is functioning correctly; if so, a clicking sound will be emitted by the strut as the pedal is depressed.

35 With the lining-to-drum clearance set, check and, if necessary, adjust the handbrake as described in Chapter 1.

36 Refit the roadwheels, then lower the vehicle to the ground and tighten the roadwheel nuts to the specified torque setting.

8 Rear brake shoes – renewal

⚠ *Warning: Brake shoes must be renewed on BOTH rear wheels at the same time – NEVER renew the shoes on only one wheel, as uneven braking may result. The dust created as the shoes wear may contain asbestos, which is a health hazard. Never blow it out with compressed air, and don't inhale any of it. An approved filtering mask should be worn when working on the brakes. DO NOT use petroleum-based solvents to clean brake parts – use brake cleaner or methylated spirit only.*

1 Remove the brake drum as described in Section 7.

2 Working carefully and taking the necessary precautions, remove all traces of brake dust from the brake drum, backplate and shoes.

3 Measure the thickness of the brake shoe friction material at several points. If any are worn down to the specified minimum, or fouled with oil or grease, all four shoes must be renewed

4 Follow the accompanying photos (illustrations 8.4a to 8.4w) for the actual brake shoe renewal procedure, bearing in mind the additional points given in the following paragraphs. Be sure to stay in order and read the caption under each illustration.

8.4a Prior to disturbing the brake shoes, note the correct fitted locations of all components, paying particular attention to the adjuster strut components

8.4b Remove the brake shoe retainer spring cups by depressing and turning them through 90°. With the cup removed, lift off the spring and withdraw the retainer pin

8.4c Prise the upper ends of the brake shoes apart and ease them away from the wheel cylinder pistons

8.4d Similarly spread the lower ends of the brake shoes apart and release them from the abutment bracket on the backplate

8.4e Turn the assembly over, compress the spring and unhook the handbrake cable from the lever on the trailing shoe

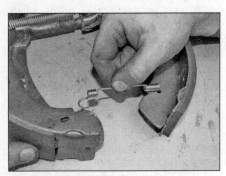

8.4f With the assembly on the bench, remove the lower return spring . . .

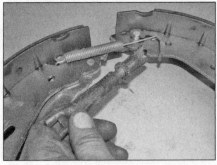

8.4g . . . adjuster strut . . .

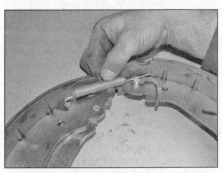

8.4h . . . upper return spring . . .

8.4i . . . and the adjuster lever

8.4j Thoroughly clean the backplate, then apply a smear of high-melting-point brake grease to the contact surfaces

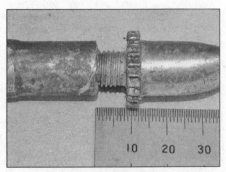

8.4k Dismantle and clean the adjuster strut then set the adjuster position according to model (see text)

8.4l Locate the adjuster lever in the slot in the leading shoe peg . . .

8.4m . . . then engage the adjuster strut with leading shoe and adjuster lever

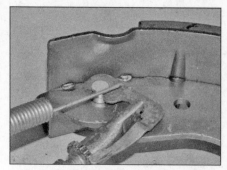

8.4n Fit the straight end of the upper return spring to the adjuster lever . . .

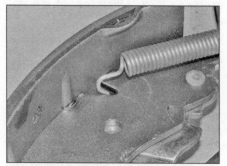

8.4o . . . then insert the coiled end of the spring in the trailing shoe slot

8.4p Spread the shoes apart and locate the adjuster strut in the cut-out in the handbrake lever

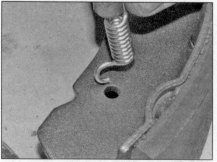

8.4q Fit the end of the lower return spring with the most coils to the leading shoe . . .

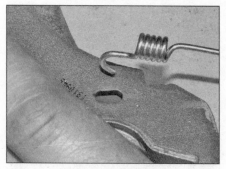

8.4r . . . and the end with the least coils to the trailing shoe

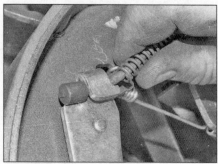

8.4s Pull back the spring and connect the handbrake cable to the lever on the trailing shoe

8.4t Position the assembled brake shoes on the backplate and engage the lower end of the leading shoe with the abutment bracket

8.4u Spread the shoes apart and engage the lower end of the trailing shoe with the abutment bracket

8.4v Pull the upper ends of the brake shoes apart and engage them with the wheel cylinder pistons

8.4w Insert the brake shoe retainer spring pins, then refit the retainer springs and cups

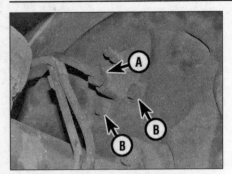

9.4 Rear wheel cylinder brake pipe union nut (A) and retaining bolts (B)

5 Prior to refitting the adjuster strut, turn the forked end of the adjuster, so that the distance between the end of the strut and the adjuster wheel is 7 to 7.5 mm for front wheel drive models, and 9.5 to 10 mm for rear wheel drive models.

6 On completion, refit the brake drum as described in Section 7.

7 Repeat the above procedure on the remaining rear brake.

8 Once both sets of rear shoes have been renewed, with the handbrake fully released, adjust the lining-to-drum clearance by repeatedly depressing the brake pedal. Whilst depressing the pedal, have an assistant listen to the rear drums, to check that the adjuster strut is functioning correctly; if so, a clicking sound will be emitted by the strut as the pedal is depressed.

9 Check and, if necessary, adjust the handbrake as described in Chapter 1.

10 Refit the roadwheels, then lower the vehicle to the ground and tighten the roadwheel nuts to the specified torque setting.

Caution: New brake shoes will not give full braking efficiency until they have bedded-in. Be prepared for this, and avoid hard braking as far as possible for the first hundred miles or so after shoe renewal.

9 Rear wheel cylinder – removal, overhaul and refitting

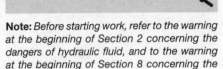

Note: *Before starting work, refer to the warning at the beginning of Section 2 concerning the dangers of hydraulic fluid, and to the warning at the beginning of Section 8 concerning the dangers of asbestos dust.*

Removal

1 Remove the brake drum as described in Section 7.

2 Pull the upper ends of the brake shoes away from the wheel cylinder to disengage them from the pistons.

3 Minimise fluid loss by first removing the master cylinder reservoir cap, then tightening it down onto a piece of polythene to obtain an airtight seal. Alternatively, use a brake hose clamp or a similar tool to clamp the relevant flexible hose leading to the rear axle.

4 Wipe away all traces of dirt around the brake pipe union at the rear of the wheel cylinder, and unscrew the union nut **(see illustration)**. Carefully ease the pipe out of the wheel cylinder, and plug or tape over its end to prevent dirt entry. Wipe off any spilt fluid immediately.

5 Unscrew and remove the bleed screw from the rear of the wheel cylinder.

6 Unscrew the two wheel cylinder retaining bolts from the rear of the backplate, and remove the cylinder, taking great care not to allow surplus hydraulic fluid to contaminate the brake shoe linings.

Overhaul

Note: *Before starting work, check with your local dealer for the availability of parts to overhaul the wheel cylinder.*

7 Brush the dirt and dust from the wheel cylinder, but take care not to inhale it.

8 Pull the rubber dust seals from the ends of the cylinder body **(see illustration)**.

9 The pistons will normally be ejected by the

pressure of the coil spring, but if they are not, tap the end of the cylinder body on a piece of wood. Alternatively, refit the bleed screw and apply low air pressure (eg, from a foot pump) to the hydraulic fluid union hole to eject the pistons from their bores.

10 Inspect the surfaces of the pistons and their bores in the cylinder body for scoring, or evidence of metal-to-metal contact. If evident, renew the complete wheel cylinder assembly.

11 If the pistons and bores are in good condition, discard the seals and obtain a repair kit, which will contain all the necessary renewable items.

12 Lubricate the new piston seals with clean brake fluid, and carefully fit them to the pistons so that their larger diameter is toward the spring end of the piston.

13 Dip the pistons in clean brake fluid, and insert them into the cylinder bores, together with the spring.

14 Fit the dust seals, and check that the pistons can move freely in their bores.

Refitting

15 Ensure that the backplate and wheel cylinder mating surfaces are clean, then spread the brake shoes and manoeuvre the wheel cylinder into position.

16 Engage the brake pipe, and screw in the union nut two or three turns to ensure that the thread has started.

17 Insert the wheel cylinder retaining bolts, and tighten them to the specified torque, then securely tighten the brake pipe union nut.

18 Refit the bleed screw to the wheel cylinder.

19 Remove the clamp from the flexible brake hose, or the polythene from the master cylinder reservoir (as applicable).

20 Ensure that the brake shoes are correctly located against the cylinder pistons, then refit the brake drum as described in Section 7.

21 Bleed the brake hydraulic system as described in Section 2. Providing suitable precautions were taken to minimise loss of fluid, it should only be necessary to bleed the relevant rear brake.

10 Master cylinder – removal, overhaul and refitting

Note: *Before starting work, refer to the warning at the beginning of Section 2 concerning the dangers of hydraulic fluid.*

Removal

1 Remove the master cylinder reservoir cap, and syphon the hydraulic fluid from the reservoir. **Note:** *Do not syphon the fluid by mouth, as it is poisonous therefore use a syringe or an old hydrometer.* Alternatively, open the front brake caliper bleed screws, one at a time, and gently pump the brake pedal to expel the fluid through a plastic tube connected to the screw (see Section 2).

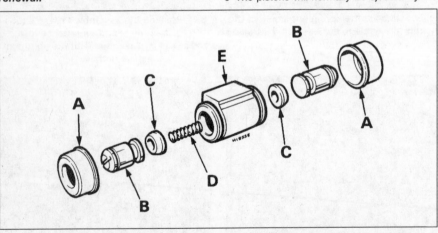

9.8 Exploded view of the rear wheel cylinder assembly

A Dust seals
B Pistons
C Piston seals
D Spring
E Cylinder body

2 For improved access, refer to Chapter 4A and remove the intake air resonator and air ducts (2.0 litre engines), or the air intake duct from the air cleaner and turbocharger (2.4 litre engines).

3 Pull the tab, depress the clips and disconnect the wiring connector from the brake fluid level sensor on the reservoir **(see illustration)**.

4 Release the clip and disconnect the clutch hydraulic hose from the fluid reservoir. Tape over or plug the outlet.

5 Place cloth rags beneath the master cylinder to collect escaping brake fluid. Identify the brake pipes for position, then unscrew the union nuts and move the pipes to one side. Plug or tape over the pipe ends to prevent dirt entry.

6 Unscrew the two mounting nuts and withdraw the master cylinder from the vacuum servo unit. Take care not to spill fluid on the vehicle paintwork. Recover the master cylinder-to-servo unit seal.

7 If required, the fluid reservoir can be removed from the master cylinder by releasing the retaining tabs and pulling the reservoir up and off the mounting seals.

Overhaul

8 At the time of writing, master cylinder overhaul is not possible as no spares are available.

9 The only parts available individually are the fluid reservoir and its mounting seals, and the filler cap.

10 If the master cylinder is worn excessively, it must be renewed.

11 If new reservoir seals are to be fitted, extract the old seals from the cylinder body, lubricate the new seals with clean brake hydraulic fluid and push the seals into position.

Refitting

12 Where applicable, refit the fluid reservoir to the master cylinder body, ensuring that the retaining tabs lock into position.

13 Place the master cylinder-to-servo unit seal in position, then fit the master cylinder to the servo unit. Ensure that the servo unit pushrod enters the master cylinder piston

centrally. Fit the retaining nuts and tighten them to the specified torque.

14 Refit the brake pipes and tighten the union nuts securely.

15 Reconnect the clutch hydraulic hose to the fluid reservoir.

16 Reconnect the wiring connector to the brake fluid level sensor.

17 Where applicable, refit the air intake ducts and resonator, with reference to Chapter 4A.

18 Remove the reservoir filler cap and polythene, then top-up the reservoir with fresh hydraulic fluid to the MAX mark (see *Weekly checks*).

19 Bleed the brake and clutch hydraulic systems as described in Section 2 and Chapter 6 then refit the filler cap. Thoroughly check the operation of the brakes and clutch before using the vehicle on the road.

11 Brake pedal – removal and refitting

Note: *This Section includes the removal and refitting of the brake pedal **and** clutch pedal as an assembly.*

Removal

1 Move the driver's seat fully forward, open the battery box cover and disconnect the battery negative terminal (refer to *Disconnecting the battery* in the Reference Chapter).

2 Move the driver's seat fully rearward,

10.3 Disconnect the wiring connector (arrowed) from the brake fluid level sensor on the master cylinder reservoir

then disconnect the wiring connector at the stop-light switch located above the brake pedal **(see illustration)**. Release the wiring harness from the support clips, then turn the stop-light switch anticlockwise and remove it from the pedal mounting bracket.

3 Disconnect the wiring connector at the clutch pedal position switch (where fitted) located above the clutch pedal. Release the wiring harness from the support clips, then turn the switch anticlockwise and remove it from the pedal mounting bracket **(see illustrations)**.

4 Detach the direction indicator relay from the pedal mounting bracket.

5 Extract the locking plate and retaining clip, then slide the servo unit pushrod off the stud on the brake pedal **(see illustrations)**.

11.2 Disconnect the wiring connector at the stop-light switch, then turn the switch anticlockwise to remove

11.3a Disconnect the wiring connector at the clutch pedal position switch . . .

11.3b . . . then turn the switch anticlockwise to remove

11.5a Extract the locking plate . . .

11.5b . . . and retaining clip (arrowed), then slide the servo unit pushrod off the brake pedal stud

11.6 Extract the retaining clip and washer (arrowed) and detach the clutch master cylinder pushrod from the clutch pedal

11.10a Steering column upper retaining bolts (arrowed) . . .

11.10b . . . and lower retaining bolts (arrowed)

6 Extract the retaining clip and washer and detach the clutch master cylinder pushrod from the clutch pedal **(see illustration)**.

7 Working in the engine compartment, rotate the clutch master cylinder 90° clockwise and release it from the bulkhead mounting plate.

8 Set the roadwheels in the straight-ahead position, then remove the ignition key to engage the steering column lock.

9 Remove the steering column upper and lower shrouds as described in Chapter 11.

10 Undo the four steering column retaining nuts and lower the column from its location **(see illustrations)**. Note that new nuts will be required for refitting.

11 Undo the eight mounting bracket retaining nuts/bolts and remove the pedals and mounting bracket assembly from the vehicle **(see illustration)**.

12 Check the pedals and mounting bracket for excessive wear and damage. It is not possible to renew the pedal pivot bushes separately, so if they are worn, the complete assembly must be renewed.

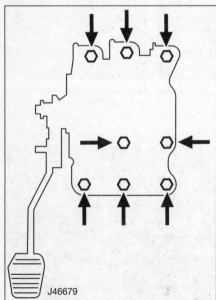

11.11 Brake pedal mounting bracket retaining nuts/bolts (arrowed)

Refitting

13 Manoeuvre the pedal and mounting bracket assembly into place making sure the brake servo pushrod fits correctly over the brake pedal.

14 Refit the pedal mounting bracket nuts/bolts and tighten to the specified torque.

15 Lift the steering column back into position and fit the four new retaining nuts. Tighten the nuts to the specified torque.

16 Refit the steering column upper and lower shrouds as described in Chapter 11.

17 Refit the clutch master cylinder to the bulkhead and rotate it 90° anticlockwise to lock it in position.

18 Engage the clutch master cylinder pushrod with the clutch pedal, then refit the washer and retaining clip.

19 With the servo unit pushrod engaged with the stud on the brake pedal, refit the retaining clip and locking plate.

20 Re-attach the direction indicator relay to the pedal mounting bracket.

21 Hold the brake pedal in the raised position and insert the stop-light switch into the hole in the pedal mounting bracket. Push the switch down to depress the plunger, then turn the switch clockwise to lock it in position. Where applicable, refit the clutch pedal position switch in the same way, then reconnect the wiring connectors to the switches.

22 Reconnect the battery negative terminal on completion.

12 Vacuum servo unit – testing, removal and refitting

Testing

1 To test the operation of the servo unit, with the engine off, depress the footbrake pedal several times to exhaust the vacuum. Now start the engine, keeping the pedal firmly depressed. As the engine starts, there should be a noticeable 'give' in the brake pedal as the vacuum builds-up. Allow the engine to run for at least two minutes, then switch it off. The brake pedal should now feel normal, but further applications should result in the pedal

feeling firmer, the pedal stroke decreasing with each application.

2 If the servo does not operate as described, first inspect the servo unit check valve as described in Section 13.

3 If the servo unit still fails to operate satisfactorily, the fault lies within the unit itself. Repairs to the unit are not possible; if faulty, the servo unit must be renewed.

Removal

4 Remove the brake master cylinder as described in Section 10.

5 If not already done, refer to Chapter 4A and remove the intake air resonator and air ducts (2.0 litre engines), or the air intake duct from the air cleaner and turbocharger (2.4 litre engines).

6 Carefully ease the vacuum hose out of the servo unit, taking care not to displace the sealing grommet.

7 Working in the driver's footwell, extract the locking plate and retaining clip, then slide the servo unit pushrod off the stud on the brake pedal **(see illustrations 11.5a and 11.5b)**.

8 Undo the four nuts securing the servo unit to the pedal mounting bracket and bulkhead.

9 Return to the engine compartment, and lift the servo unit out of position. Recover the servo unit-to-bulkhead gasket.

Refitting

10 Refit the gasket, then locate the vacuum servo unit in position on the bulkhead. Refit the four nuts and tighten them to the specified torque.

11 With the servo unit pushrod engaged with the stud on the brake pedal, refit the retaining clip and locking plate.

12 Refit the vacuum hose to the servo grommet, ensuring that the hose is correctly seated.

13 Refit the brake master cylinder as described in Section 10.

13 Vacuum servo unit check valve and hose – removal, testing and refitting

Removal

1 Refer to Chapter 4A and remove the intake

14.8 Vacuum pump mounting bolts (arrowed) – 2.0 litre engines

14.10a Fit a new vacuum pump housing gasket on the cylinder head – 2.0 litre engines

14.10b Vacuum pump drive dogs (arrowed) on the end of the camshaft – 2.0 litre engines

air resonator and air ducts (2.0 litre engines), or the air intake duct from the air cleaner and turbocharger (2.4 litre engines)

2 Carefully ease the vacuum hose out of the servo unit, taking care not to displace the sealing grommet.

3 Unscrew the union nut, or disconnect the quick-release fitting (as applicable) and remove the vacuum hose from the vacuum pump.

4 Unclip the vacuum hose from its supports, then remove the hose and check valve from the vehicle.

Testing

5 Examine the check valve and hose for signs of damage, and renew if necessary. The valve may be tested by blowing through it in both directions. Air should flow through the valve in one direction only – when blown through from the servo unit end. If air flows in both directions, or not at all, renew the valve and hose as an assembly.

6 Examine the check valve rubber sealing grommet for signs of damage or deterioration, and renew as necessary.

Refitting

7 Refitting is a reversal of removal ensuring that the hose is correctly seated in the servo grommet.

8 On completion, start the engine and check that there are no air leaks.

---

14 Vacuum pump – removal and refitting

2.0 litre engines

Removal

1 Drain the cooling system as described in Chapter 1.

2 Refer to Chapter 4A and remove the intake air resonator and air ducts.

3 Remove the power steering pump drivebelt cover from the top of the engine.

4 Release the clip and disconnect the coolant expansion tank hose from the vacuum pump.

5 Release the clips and disconnect the two coolant hoses from the thermostat housing.

6 Unbolt the thermostat housing from the vacuum pump and recover the O-ring seal. Note that a new O-ring seal will be required for refitting.

7 Disconnect the vacuum hose from the rear of the vacuum pump.

8 Unscrew the mounting bolts, withdraw the vacuum pump from the end of the cylinder head and recover the gasket **(see illustration)**. Note that a new gasket will be required for refitting.

9 Thoroughly clean the mating surfaces of the vacuum pump, cylinder head and thermostat housing.

Refitting

10 Locate a new gasket on the vacuum

pump, then refit the pump to the cylinder head, making sure that the drive dog engages correctly with the end of the camshaft **(see illustrations)**. Insert the mounting bolts and tighten them to the specified torque.

11 Refit the thermostat housing to the vacuum pump using a new O-ring seal and tighten the mounting bolts to the specified torque.

12 Reconnect the vacuum hose to the rear of the vacuum pump.

13 Reconnect the two coolant hoses to the thermostat housing and the expansion tank hose to the vacuum pump.

14 Refit the power steering drivebelt cover.

15 Refit the intake air resonator and air ducts with reference to Chapter 4A.

16 Refill the cooling system as described in Chapter 1.

2.4 litre engines

Removal

17 Remove the auxiliary drivebelt as described in Chapter 1.

18 Release the clip and disconnect the intercooler charge air duct from the exhaust gas recirculation valve.

19 Unscrew the union nut and disconnect the vacuum hose from the vacuum pump.

20 Unscrew the three mounting bolts, withdraw the vacuum pump from the top of the coolant pump and recover the gasket **(see illustrations)**. Note that a new gasket will be required for refitting.

14.20a Unscrew the vacuum pump mounting bolts (arrowed) . . .

14.20b . . . withdraw the vacuum pump from the top of the coolant pump . . .

14.20c . . . and recover the gasket – 2.4 litre engines

16.3 Handbrake cable adjuster nut (arrowed)

Refitting

21 Locate a new gasket on the coolant pump, then refit the vacuum pump to the coolant pump. Insert the mounting bolts and tighten them to the specified torque.

22 Refit the vacuum hose to the vacuum pump and tighten the union nut securely.

23 Reconnect the intercooler charge air duct to the exhaust gas recirculation valve, then refill the cooling system as described in Chapter 1.

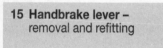

15 Handbrake lever – removal and refitting

Removal

1 Chock the front wheels then jack up the rear of the vehicle and securely support it on axle stands (see *Jacking and vehicle support*). Ensure that the handbrake lever is released (off).

2 From under the vehicle, slacken the handbrake cable adjuster nut at the cable compensator plate.

3 Release the handbrake lever rubber gaiter from the floor and slide it up and off the lever.

4 Disconnect the wiring connector from the handbrake lever warning light switch.

5 Detach the handbrake inner cable from the lever, then release the outer cable from the bracket on the side of the lever base.

6 Move the driver's seat fully forward and open the battery box cover.

16.15 Compress the tabs on the handbrake cable end fitting and withdraw the cable from the brake backplate

16.6 Disconnect the front handbrake cable at the cable connector (arrowed)

7 Undo the three nuts securing the handbrake lever assembly to the side of the battery box and remove the lever assembly from the vehicle.

Refitting

8 Refitting is the reverse of removal, bearing in mind the following points:

a) Lubricate the exposed end of the handbrake cable and the cable attachment on the lever with molybdenum disulphide grease.

b) Adjust the handbrake as described in Chapter 1 on completion.

16 Handbrake cables – removal and refitting

Removal

1 The handbrake cable consists of three sections, a front cable which connects the handbrake lever to the intermediate cable, an intermediate cable which links the front cable to the compensator plate, and the rear cables which link the compensator plate to the rear brake shoes. Each section can be removed individually as follows.

Front cable

2 Chock the front wheels then jack up the rear of the vehicle and securely support it on axle stands (see *Jacking and vehicle support*). Ensure that the handbrake lever is released (off).

16.16 Undo the retaining bolt (arrowed) and release the handbrake cable support from the underbody

3 From under the vehicle, slacken the handbrake cable adjuster nut at the cable compensator plate **(see illustration)**.

4 Release the handbrake lever rubber gaiter from the floor and slide it up and off the lever.

5 Detach the handbrake inner cable from the lever, then release the outer cable from the bracket on the side of the lever base.

6 Disconnect the front cable from the connector joining the front cable to the intermediate cable **(see illustration)**.

7 Detach the front cable from the abutment bracket on the underbody.

8 From inside the vehicle, lift up the floor covering below the handbrake lever and prise out the handbrake cable grommet from the floor.

9 Pull the cable up and remove it from inside the vehicle.

Intermediate cable

10 Chock the front wheels then jack up the rear of the vehicle and securely support it on axle stands (see *Jacking and vehicle support*). Ensure that the handbrake lever is released (off).

11 From under the vehicle, unscrew and remove the handbrake cable adjuster nut at the cable compensator plate and withdraw the intermediate cable from the compensator **(see illustration 16.3)**.

12 Disconnect the intermediate cable from the connector joining the intermediate cable to the front cable, then remove the cable from under the vehicle **(see illustration 16.6)**.

Rear cables

Note: *There is a separate cable for each rear brake.*

13 Chock the front wheels then jack up the rear of the vehicle and securely support it on axle stands (see *Jacking and vehicle support*). Ensure that the handbrake lever is released (off).

14 Remove the brake shoes on the relevant side as described in Section 8.

15 Using pliers, compress the tabs on the outer cable end fitting and withdraw the cable from the brake backplate **(see illustration)**.

16 Undo the retaining bolt and release the cable support bracket from the underbody **(see illustration)**.

16.18 Compress the tabs (arrowed) on the handbrake cable end fitting and withdraw the cable from the abutment bracket

17 Slacken the handbrake cable adjuster nut at the cable compensator plate, then slip the inner cable end out of the slot in the compensator **(see illustration 16.3)**.

18 Compress the tabs on the outer cable end fitting and withdraw the cable from the abutment bracket on the underbody **(see illustration)**. Remove the cable from under the vehicle.

Refitting

19 Refitting is a reversal of the removal procedure, but adjust the handbrake as described in Chapter 1.

17 Stop-light switch –
removal, refitting and adjustment

Removal

1 The stop-light switch is located on the brake pedal mounting bracket in the driver's footwell.

2 Disconnect the wiring connector at the stop-light switch then turn the switch anticlockwise and remove it from the pedal mounting bracket.

Refitting and adjustment

3 Hold the brake pedal in the raised position and insert the stop-light switch into the hole in the pedal mounting bracket. Push the switch down to depress the plunger and automatically adjust the switch, then turn the switch clockwise to lock it in position.

4 Reconnect the switch wiring connector on completion.

18 Handbrake
warning light switch –
removal and refitting

Removal

1 Release the handbrake lever rubber gaiter from the floor and slide it up and off the lever.

2 Disconnect the wiring connector from the warning light switch on the side of the handbrake lever.

3 Undo the screws and remove the switch from the handbrake lever bracket.

Refitting

4 Refitting is a reversal of removal.

19 Anti-lock Braking and
Traction Control systems –
general information

ABS is fitted as standard or optional equipment on all models. On higher specification models, the ABS may also incorporate traction control as additional safety features.

The ABS system comprises a hydraulic modulator and electronic control unit together with four wheel speed sensors. The hydraulic modulator contains the electronic control unit (ECU), the hydraulic solenoid valves (one set for each brake) and the electrically-driven pump. The purpose of the system is to prevent the wheel(s) locking during heavy braking. This is achieved by automatic release of the brake on the relevant wheel, followed by re-application of the brake.

The solenoid valves are controlled by the ECU, which itself receives signals from the four wheel speed sensors which monitor the speed of rotation of each wheel. By comparing these signals, the ECU can determine the speed at which the vehicle is travelling. It can then use this speed to determine when a wheel is decelerating at an abnormal rate, compared to the speed of the vehicle, and therefore predicts when a wheel is about to lock. During normal operation, the system functions in the same way as a conventional braking system.

If the ECU senses that a wheel is about to lock, it operates the relevant solenoid valve(s) in the hydraulic unit, which then isolates from the master cylinder the relevant brake(s) on the wheel(s) which is/are about to lock, effectively sealing-in the hydraulic pressure.

If the speed of rotation of the wheel continues to decrease at an abnormal rate, the ECU operates the electrically-driven pump which pumps the hydraulic fluid back into the master cylinder, releasing the brake. Once the speed of rotation of the wheel returns to an acceptable rate, the pump stops, and the solenoid valves switch again, allowing the hydraulic master cylinder pressure to return to the caliper or wheel cylinder, which then re-applies the brake. This cycle can be carried out many times a second.

The action of the solenoid valves and return pump creates pulses in the hydraulic circuit. When the ABS system is functioning, these pulses can be felt through the brake pedal.

On models with traction control, the ABS hydraulic modulator incorporates an additional set of solenoid valves which operate the traction control system. The system operates at speeds up to approximately 30 mph (60 km/h) using the signals supplied by the wheel speed sensors. If the ECU senses that a driving wheel is about to lose traction, it prevents this by momentarily applying the relevant front brake.

The operation of the ABS and traction control programs is entirely dependent on electrical signals. To prevent the system responding to any inaccurate signals, a built-in safety circuit monitors all signals received by the ECU. If an inaccurate signal or low battery voltage is detected, the system is automatically shut down, and the relevant warning light on the instrument panel is illuminated, to inform the driver that the system is not operational. Normal braking is still available, however.

If a fault develops in the ABS/traction control system, the vehicle must be taken to a Ford dealer for fault diagnosis and repair.

20 Anti-lock Braking and
Traction Control components
– removal and refitting

Note 1: *Faults on the ABS system can only be diagnosed using Ford diagnostic equipment or compatible alternative equipment.*

Note 2: *Before starting work, refer to the note at the beginning of Section 2 concerning the dangers of hydraulic fluid.*

Hydraulic modulator and ECU

Removal

1 Remove the master cylinder reservoir cap, and syphon the hydraulic fluid from the reservoir. Alternatively, open the front brake caliper bleed screws, one at a time, and gently pump the brake pedal to expel the fluid through a plastic tube connected to the screw (see Section 2).

Caution: Do not syphon the fluid by mouth, as it is poisonous. Use a syringe or an old hydrometer.

2 Undo the bolt securing the rear right-hand side of the coolant expansion tank to the engine compartment fuse/relay box.

3 Undo the two bolts at the front and one bolt on the left-hand side, then lift the fuse/relay box and bracket from its location and position it to one side **(see illustration)**.

4 Undo the two bolts and remove the fuse/relay box mounting bracket.

5 Note and record the fitted position of the brake pipes at the modulator, then unscrew the union nuts and release the pipes. As a precaution, place absorbent rags beneath the brake pipe unions when unscrewing them. Suitably plug or cap the disconnected unions to prevent dirt entry and fluid loss.

6 Pull out the locking bar and disconnect the wiring harness plug from the ECU on the front of the modulator.

7 Undo the retaining nut and bolt securing the modulator mounting bracket to the engine compartment side panel. Note that access to the nut is gained from under the wheel arch.

8 Move the modulator and mounting bracket sideways, then manipulate the assembly out from its location in the engine compartment.

20.3 Fuse/relay box bracket front retaining bolts (arrowed)

20.24 Front wheel speed sensor retaining bolt (arrowed)

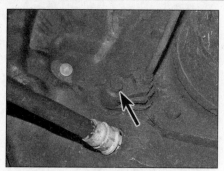

20.29 Rear wheel speed sensor retaining bolt (arrowed)

20.30 Disconnect the wheel speed sensor wiring at the connector (arrowed) on the underbody

Refitting

9 Refitting is the reverse of the removal procedure, noting the following points:

a) Refit the brake pipes to their respective locations, and tighten the union nuts securely.

b) Ensure that the wiring is correctly routed, and that the ECU wiring harness plug is firmly pressed into position and secured locked.

c) On completion, bleed the complete hydraulic system as described in Section 2.

Electronic control unit (ECU)

Removal

10 Move the driver's seat fully forward, open the battery box cover and disconnect the battery negative terminal (refer to *Disconnecting the battery* in the Reference Chapter).

11 Remove the left-hand headlight as described in Chapter 12.

12 Detach the wheel speed sensor wiring harness connector from the body panel.

13 Pull out the locking bar and disconnect the wiring harness plug from the ECU on the front of the hydraulic modulator.

14 Thoroughly clean the area around the ECU and hydraulic modulator and exercise extreme cleanliness during the following operations.

15 Disconnect the return pump wiring connector from the front of the ECU.

16 Undo the six bolts and carefully withdraw the ECU from the hydraulic modulator. Recover the ECU to modulator seal.

Refitting

17 Ensure that the mating faces of the modulator and ECU are clean, then carefully position the seal and ECU on the modulator. Take great care not to damage the contact pins.

18 Refit the retaining bolts and tighten them progressively in a diagonal sequence.

19 Reconnect the return pump wiring connector to the ECU.

20 Reconnect the ECU wiring harness plug ensuring it is securely locked in position.

21 Refit the wheel speed sensor wiring harness connector to the body panel.

22 Refit the left-hand headlight as described in Chapter 12, then reconnect the battery negative terminal.

Front wheel speed sensors

Removal

23 Firmly apply the handbrake, then jack up the front of the vehicle and support it securely on axle stands (see *Jacking and vehicle support*). Remove the roadwheel.

24 Undo the retaining bolt and withdraw the sensor from the steering knuckle **(see illustration)**.

25 Release the sensor wiring from the suspension strut and from the support bracket and clips under the wheel arch, then trace the wiring back to the connector located in the engine compartment.

26 Disconnect the sensor wiring at the engine compartment connector, release the grommet, then remove the sensor and wiring from under the wheel arch.

Refitting

27 Refitting is the reverse of the removal procedure, tightening the sensor retaining bolt to the specified torque.

Rear wheel speed sensors

Removal

28 Chock the front wheels then jack up the rear of the vehicle and securely support it on axle stands (see *Jacking and vehicle support*).

29 Undo the retaining bolt and withdraw the sensor from the brake backplate **(see illustration)**.

30 Release the sensor wiring from the clips on the rear axle, then disconnect the wiring at the connector on the underbody **(see illustration)**. Remove the sensor and wiring from under the vehicle.

Refitting

31 Refitting is the reverse of the removal procedure, tightening the sensor retaining bolt to the specified torque.

21 Load-apportioning valve – general information

A load apportioning valve is fitted to vehicles not equipped with ABS. The purpose of the valve is to regulate the hydraulic pressure applied to the rear brakes according to vehicle loading. This prevents the rear brakes locking up under heavy braking when the vehicle is in a lightly loaded condition.

The valve is mounted on the chassis in front of the rear axle and is operated by a lever inter- connected between the valve and rear axle.

If the valve position is disturbed, it will require readjustment which entails the use of specialised equipment and reference to several graphs depending on the vehicle body type. Any work on the load-apportioning valve should therefore be entrusted to a Ford dealer.

Chapter 10
Suspension and steering

Contents

Degrees of difficulty

| Easy, suitable for novice with little experience | | Fairly easy, suitable for beginner with some experience | | Fairly difficult, suitable for competent DIY mechanic | | Difficult, suitable for experienced DIY mechanic | | Very difficult, suitable for expert DIY or professional | |

Specifications

Front suspension

Type . . . .   Independent with MacPherson struts, gas-filled shock absorbers and anti-roll bar

Rear suspension

Type:
   Front wheel drive models . . . .   Beam axle supported on semi-elliptic single leaf springs
   Rear wheel drive models . . . .   Semi-floating or fully-floating hypoid axle supported on semi-elliptic multi-leaf springs

Steering

Type . . . .   Rack-and-pinion with power steering available on all models
Fluid type . . . .   See *Lubricants and fluids* on page 0•18

Torque wrench settings

	Nm	lbf ft
Front suspension		
ABS wheel speed sensor retaining bolts	8	6
Anti-roll bar clamp bolts.	30	22
Anti-roll bar connecting link-to-lower suspension arm	25	18
Anti-roll bar connecting link-to-suspension strut.	56	41
Brake caliper mounting bracket bolts	175	129
Brake disc-to-hub flange bolts*	69	51
Driveshaft retaining nut:*		
Stage 1.	Rotate the wheel hub 5 times	
Stage 2.	250	185
Stage 3.	Rotate the wheel hub 5 times	
Stage 4.	420	310
Stage 5.	Rotate the wheel hub 5 times	
Front subframe mountings:		
Bolts	250	185
Nuts	175	129
Front wheel spindle retaining nut:*		
Stage 1.	Rotate the wheel hub 5 times	
Stage 2.	250	185
Stage 3.	Rotate the wheel hub 5 times	
Stage 4.	420	310
Stage 5.	Rotate the wheel hub 5 times	
Hub assembly-to-steering knuckle bolts*	53	39
Steering knuckle balljoint-to-lower suspension arm nut*.	150	111
Suspension lower arm front mounting bolt/nut	175	129
Suspension lower arm rear mounting bolt/nut.	250	185
Suspension strut piston rod retaining nut	70	52
Suspension strut-to-steering knuckle pinch-bolt.	90	66
Suspension strut upper mounting retaining nuts.	30	22
Rear suspension		
Anti-roll bar connecting link nuts*	103	76
Anti-roll bar clamp bolts.	40	30
Leaf spring front mounting bolt nuts	225	166
Leaf spring rear mounting bolt nuts.	115	85
Spring-to-axle U-bolt nuts:*		
Stage 1.	25	18
Stage 2.	50	37
Stage 3.	75	55
Stage 4.	100	74
Stage 5.	125	92
Stage 6.	150	111
Stage 7.	175	129
Shock absorber lower mounting bolt nuts.	90	66
Shock absorber upper mounting bolt nuts	150	111
Steering		
Power steering fluid pipe locking plate bolt	25	18
Power steering pump attachments (2.0 litre engines):		
High-pressure pipe union.	57	42
Mounting bolts	18	13
Pulley retaining bolts	10	7
Support bracket bolts.	18	13
Power steering pump attachments (2.4 litre engines):		
High-pressure pipe union.	65	48
Mounting bolts	23	17
Pipe support bracket bolt.	23	17
Steering column flexible coupling-to-steering gear pinion shaft pinch bolt nut*	23	17
Steering column intermediate shaft-to-flexible coupling pinch-bolt nut*	28	21
Steering column lower bearing-to-bulkhead	12	9
Steering column retaining nuts*.	20	15
Steering gear-to-front subframe.	115	85
Steering wheel retaining bolt	47	35
Track rod end balljoint nut*.	80	59
Roadwheels		
Roadwheel nuts	200	148

Use new nuts/bolts

2.2a Bend up the split pin legs . . .

2.2b . . . then extract the split pin . . .

2.2c . . . and remove the retaining nut locking ring

1 General information

The independent front suspension is of the MacPherson strut type, incorporating coil springs and integral telescopic shock absorbers. The MacPherson struts are located by transverse lower suspension arms, connected to the front subframe by rubber mounting bushes, and to the steering knuckles via a balljoint. The front steering knuckles, which carry the hub bearings, brake calipers and disc assemblies, are bolted to the MacPherson struts, and connected to the lower arms via the balljoints. A front anti-roll bar is fitted, which has link rods at each end to connect it to the strut or lower suspension arms.

On front wheel drive models, the rear axle is a tubular steel beam axle supported on semi-elliptic single leaf springs. Stub axles are bolted to the ends of the axle beam on each side and these carry the rear hub and bearing assemblies. Telescopic shock absorbers provide the damping for the axle assembly.

On rear wheel drive models, the rear axle is a live axle suspended on semi-elliptic multi-leaf springs and utilising telescopic shock absorbers to provide the damping for the axle assembly.

On all models, further information and procedures relating to the rear axle assembly are contained in Chapter 8.

The steering column incorporates an intermediate shaft with a universal joint at the upper end. The lower end of the shaft is connected to the steering gear pinion shaft by means of a flexible coupling.

The steering gear is mounted on the front subframe. It is connected by two track rods and track rod ends to the steering arms projecting rearwards from the steering knuckles. The track rod ends are threaded to enable wheel alignment adjustment.

Power steering is fitted to all models. The power steering pump is belt-driven from the crankshaft pulley or from a pulley on the rear of the inlet camshaft, according to engine type.

2 Front hub assembly – removal and refitting

Caution: Due to the extremely high tightening torque of the driveshaft retaining nut, take great care when removing and refitting the nut. Use only the correct sockets and make sure you have a suitable extension bar for removal, and a torque wrench capable of tightening the nut to the correct setting (see Specifications) for refitting. Entrust this work to a dealer or suitably-equipped garage if in doubt about the procedure, or if the required tools are not available.

Front wheel drive models

Removal

Note: *A new driveshaft retaining nut, washer and split pin, together with new brake disc and*

hub assembly retaining bolts will be required for refitting.

1 Firmly apply the handbrake, then jack up the front of the vehicle and support it securely on axle stands (see *Jacking and vehicle support*). Remove the relevant front roadwheel.

2 Extract the split pin from the driveshaft and remove the retaining nut locking ring **(see illustrations)**.

3 Have an assistant firmly depress the brake pedal to prevent the front hub from rotating, then using a socket and extension bar, slacken the driveshaft retaining nut. Alternatively, a tool can be fabricated from two lengths of steel strip (one long, one short) and a nut and bolt; the nut and bolt forming the pivot of a forked tool. Bolt the tool to the hub using two wheel nuts, and hold the tool to prevent the hub from rotating as the driveshaft retaining nut is undone.

4 Unscrew the driveshaft retaining nut, and remove the washer **(see illustration)**. Discard the nut and washer; new components must be used on refitting.

5 Undo the two bolts securing the brake caliper mounting bracket to the steering knuckle. Slide the caliper and mounting bracket, complete with brake pads, off the disc and suspend the assembly from the coil spring using a cable tie **(see illustration)**.

6 Using a long socket bit inserted through the holes in the hub flange, undo the five bolts securing the hub assembly to the steering knuckle **(see illustration)**. Note that new bolts will be required for refitting.

7 Withdraw the hub assembly and brake disc from the steering knuckle and driveshaft. If

2.4 Unscrew the retaining nut, and remove the washer

2.5 Slide the caliper and mounting bracket, complete with brake pads, off the disc

2.6 Hub assembly-to-steering knuckle retaining bolts (arrowed)

2.8a Undo the bolts (arrowed) securing the brake disc to the hub flange . . .

necessary, tap the rear of the brake disc with a soft faced mallet to free the hub assembly from the knuckle.

8 With the hub assembly on the bench, undo the five bolts securing the brake disc to the hub flange, then turn the assembly over and lift off the disc **(see illustrations)**. Note that new bolts will be required for refitting. Make alignment marks on the hub flange and disc prior to separation to ensure correct reassembly.

Refitting

9 Thoroughly clean the mating surfaces of the brake disc and hub flange ensuring that all traces of dirt and corrosion are removed.

10 Place the disc in position on the hub flange, aligning the marks made on removal. Fit the five new disc retaining bolts and tighten them in a progressive diagonal sequence to the specified torque.

11 Clean the mating faces of the hub assembly and steering knuckle, then locate the hub assembly over the end of the driveshaft and into position on the knuckle. Fit the five new hub assembly retaining bolts and tighten them in a progressive diagonal sequence to the specified torque.

12 Slide the brake caliper assembly over the disc and into position on the steering knuckle. Refit the two mounting bracket retaining bolts and tighten them to the specified torque.

13 Place the new washer over the end of the driveshaft and screw on the new retaining nut. Tighten the driveshaft retaining nut to the specified torque in the five stages given in the Specifications. Prevent the driveshaft

2.21 Withdraw the wheel spindle from the rear of the steering knuckle

2.8b . . . then turn the assembly over and lift off the disc

from rotating as the nut is tightened, using the method employed for removal.

14 Refit the driveshaft retaining nut locking ring, aligning the slots with the split pin hole in the driveshaft. Insert a new split pin and bend over the split pin legs to secure.

15 Refit the roadwheel, tighten the wheel nuts to the specified torque, then lower the vehicle to the ground.

Rear wheel drive models

Removal

Note: *A new wheel spindle retaining nut, washer and split pin, together with new brake disc and hub assembly retaining bolts will be required for refitting.*

16 Firmly apply the handbrake, then jack up the front of the vehicle and support it securely on axle stands (see *Jacking and vehicle support*). Remove the relevant front roadwheel.

17 Extract the split pin from the wheel spindle and remove the retaining nut locking ring **(see illustrations 2.2a to 2.2c)**.

18 Have an assistant firmly depress the brake pedal to prevent the front hub from rotating, then using a socket and extension bar, slacken the wheel spindle retaining nut. Alternatively, a tool can be fabricated from two lengths of steel strip (one long, one short) and a nut an bolt; the nut and bolt forming the pivot of a forked tool. Bolt the tool to the hub using two wheel nuts, and hold the tool to prevent the hub from rotating as the wheel spindle retaining nut is undone.

19 Unscrew the wheel spindle retaining nut, and remove the washer **(see illustration 2.4)**. Discard the nut and washer; new components must be used on refitting.

20 Undo the two bolts securing the brake caliper mounting bracket to the steering knuckle. Slide the caliper and mounting bracket, complete with brake pads, off the disc and suspend the assembly from the coil spring using a cable tie **(see illustration 2.5)**.

21 Withdraw the wheel spindle from the rear of the steering knuckle **(see illustration)**.

22 Using a long socket bit inserted through the holes in the hub flange, undo the five bolts securing the hub assembly to the steering knuckle **(see illustration 2.6)**. Note that new bolts will be required for refitting.

23 Withdraw the hub assembly and brake disc from the steering knuckle. If necessary, tap the rear of the brake disc with a soft faced mallet to free the hub assembly from the knuckle.

24 With the hub assembly on the bench, undo the five bolts securing the brake disc to the hub flange, then turn the assembly over and lift off the disc **(see illustrations 2.8a and 2.8b)**. Note that new bolts will be required for refitting. Make alignment marks on the hub flange and disc prior to separation to ensure correct reassembly.

Refitting

25 Thoroughly clean the mating surfaces of the brake disc and hub flange ensuring that all traces of dirt and corrosion are removed.

26 Place the disc in position on the hub flange, aligning the marks made on removal. Fit the five new disc retaining bolts and tighten them in a progressive diagonal sequence to the specified torque.

27 Clean the mating faces of the hub assembly and steering knuckle, then locate the hub assembly in position on the knuckle. Fit the five new hub assembly retaining bolts and tighten them in a progressive diagonal sequence to the specified torque.

28 Insert the wheel spindle through the rear of the steering knuckle and into the hub flange. Place the new washer over the end of the spindle and screw on the new retaining nut. Only tighten the nut finger tight at this stage.

29 Slide the brake caliper assembly over the disc and into position on the steering knuckle. Refit the two mounting bracket retaining bolts and tighten them to the specified torque.

30 Tighten the wheel spindle retaining nut to the specified torque in the five stages given in the Specifications. Prevent the hub from rotating as the nut is tightened, using the method employed for removal.

31 Refit the wheel spindle retaining nut locking ring, aligning the slots with the split pin hole in the spindle. Insert a new split pin and bend over the split pin legs to secure.

32 Refit the roadwheel, tighten the wheel nuts to the specified torque, then lower the vehicle to the ground.

---

3 Front hub bearings – inspection and renewal

Inspection

1 The front hub bearings are of sealed, pre-adjusted and prelubricated, double-row roller type, and are intended to last the vehicle's entire service life without maintenance or attention. The bearings are integral with the front hub assembly and if renewal is necessary a complete hub assembly must be obtained. The actual bearings are not available separately.

2 To check the bearings for excessive wear, firmly apply the handbrake, then jack up the

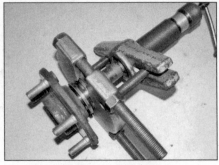

3.5 Using a tubular spacer which bears only on the inner end of the hub flange (arrowed) press the flange out of the hub assembly

3.6a Using a bearing puller . . .

3.6b . . . to remove the outer bearing inner race from the hub flange

front of the vehicle and support it securely on axle stands (see *Jacking and vehicle support*).
3 Grip the front wheel at the top and bottom and attempt to rock it. If excessive movement is noted, it may be that the hub bearings are worn. Do not confuse wear in the front suspension lower arm balljoint with wear in the bearings. Hub bearing wear will show up as roughness or vibration when the wheel is spun; it will also be noticeable as a rumbling or growling noise when driving.

Renewal

Note: *A press will be required to dismantle and rebuild the assembly. The bearing's inner races are an interference fit on the hub flange and the outer bearing inner race will remain on the hub flange when the flange is pressed out of the hub assembly. A knife-edged bearing puller will be required to remove it.*

4 Remove the front hub assembly as described in Section 2.
5 Support the outer face of the hub assembly on the press bed, with the hub flange facing downward. Using a tubular spacer (or suitable socket) which bears only on the inner end of the hub flange, press the hub flange out of the hub assembly **(see illustration)**.
6 With the hub flange removed from hub assembly, lift off the outer bearing rollers. Remove the outer bearing inner race by supporting the race and pressing the hub flange down through it. Alternatively, use a bearing puller to remove it **(see illustrations)**.

7 Thoroughly clean the hub flange, removing all traces of dirt and grease, and polish away any burrs or raised edges which might hinder reassembly. Obtain a new hub assembly (complete with new bearings) for reassembly.
8 Support the hub flange on the press bed with the wheel studs facing downwards, and place the new hub assembly on the hub flange. Using a tubular spacer (or suitable socket) which bears only on the inner bearing inner race, press the hub assembly onto the hub flange approximately one third of the way. Make sure that the hub assembly remains square when pressing it on and doesn't bind on the hub flange.
9 Rotate the hub assembly a minimum of five turns, then continue to press it onto the hub flange approximately half way. Rotate the hub assembly a minimum of five turns again, then continue to press it onto the hub flange until it is fully home. Finally, rotate the hub assembly a minimum of five turns again then remove it from the press bed.
10 Refit the brake disc, then refit the hub assembly to the steering knuckle as described in Section 2.

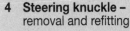

4 Steering knuckle –
    removal and refitting

Removal

1 Remove the front hub assembly as described in Section 2.

2 On vehicles with ABS, undo the retaining bolt and withdraw the wheel speed sensor from the steering knuckle **(see illustration)**.
3 Slacken the track rod end balljoint nut several turns, then use a balljoint separator tool to release the balljoint shank from the steering arm. With the balljoint released, unscrew the nut and disconnect the balljoint from the steering arm. Discard the nut as a new one must be used for refitting.
4 On vehicles with a solid anti-roll bar connecting link, undo the nut securing the link through-bolt to the lower suspension arm.
5 Slacken the nut securing the steering knuckle balljoint to the lower suspension arm **(see illustration)**. Attach a two-legged puller to the lower suspension arm and tighten the puller to apply tension to the balljoint shank. Strike the end of the lower suspension arm with a hammer a few times to shock-free the balljoint shank taper.
6 Remove the puller and unscrew the balljoint retaining nut. Discard the nut as a new one must be used for refitting.
7 Push down on the lower suspension arm and disengage the steering knuckle balljoint from the arm.
8 Unscrew and remove the pinch-bolt securing the steering knuckle assembly to the front suspension strut **(see illustration)**. Prise open the clamp using a wedge-shaped tool and release the knuckle from the strut. If necessary, tap the knuckle downwards with a soft-headed mallet to separate the two components. Remove the knuckle from the vehicle.

4.2 Front wheel speed sensor retaining bolt (arrowed)

4.5 Slacken the nut (arrowed) securing the steering knuckle balljoint to the lower suspension arm

4.8 Unscrew the pinch-bolt (arrowed) securing the steering knuckle to the front suspension strut

Refitting

9 Thoroughly clean the bottom end of the suspension strut and its location in the steering knuckle. Locate the knuckle onto the strut and over the tab, then insert the pinch-bolt and tighten it to the specified torque.

10 Push down on the lower suspension arm and engage the steering knuckle balljoint with the arm. Fit the new balljoint retaining nut and tighten the nut to the specified torque.

11 On vehicles with a solid anti-roll bar connecting link, refit the nut securing the link through-bolt to the lower suspension arm and tighten it to the specified torque.

12 Locate the track rod end balljoint on the steering arm. Screw on a new nut and tighten it to the specified torque. If the balljoint shank is hollow, a 5 mm Allen key can be used to prevent the balljoint from rotating as the nut is tightened. If the shank is solid, use a stout bar to lever up on the underside of the track rod end. This will lock the balljoint shank taper in the steering arm and prevent rotation as the nut is tightened.

13 On vehicles with ABS, refit the wheel speed sensor to the steering knuckle and secure with the retaining bolt, tightened to the specified torque.

14 Refit the front hub assembly as described in Section 2.

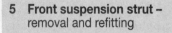

5 Front suspension strut – removal and refitting

Removal

Note: *If removing the left-hand suspension strut, it will be necessary to remove the powertrain control module to gain access to the strut upper mounting nuts. This is an involved process and reference should be made to Chapter 4A, Section 9 or 10 before proceeding.*

1 Firmly apply the handbrake, then jack up the front of the vehicle and support it securely on axle stands (see *Jacking and vehicle support*). Remove the roadwheel.

2 On vehicles with a solid anti-roll bar connecting link, undo the retaining bolt and release the brake hose and ABS wiring

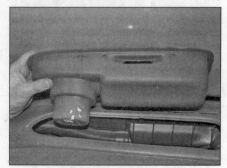

5.7 Remove the storage tray from the top of the facia

5.2 Undo the bolt (arrowed) and release the brake hose and ABS wiring harness support bracket from the strut

harness support bracket from the strut **(see illustration)**.

3 On vehicles with a balljoint anti-roll bar connecting link, undo the retaining nut and bolt and release the ABS wiring harness support bracket from the strut. Unscrew the nut and detach the anti-roll bar connecting link from the strut bracket. If necessary, use a 5 mm Allen key to hold the spindle while the nut is unscrewed.

4 Undo the two bolts securing the brake caliper mounting bracket to the steering knuckle. Slide the caliper and mounting bracket, complete with brake pads, off the disc and suspend the assembly from a suitable place under the wheel arch using a cable tie.

5 Unscrew and remove the pinch-bolt securing the steering knuckle assembly to the front suspension strut **(see illustration 4.8)**. Prise open the clamp using a wedge-shaped tool and release the knuckle from the strut. If necessary, tap the knuckle downwards with a soft-headed mallet to separate the two components.

6 If the right-hand strut is being removed, detach and remove the floor covering at the right-hand side of the footwell.

7 If the left-hand strut is being removed, refer to the procedures contained in Chapter 4A, Section 9 or 10, as applicable, and remove the powertrain control module (PCM). Now lift up and remove the storage tray from the top of the facia **(see illustration)**. Detach and remove the floor covering as necessary

8 Have an assistant support the strut

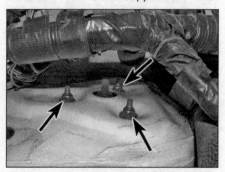

5.8 Front suspension strut upper mounting nuts (arrowed)

from under the wheel arch. Undo the three upper mounting nuts, then lower the strut and remove it from under the vehicle **(see illustration)**. If working on the right-hand strut, access to the nuts is from inside the vehicle in the right-hand side footwell. If working on the left-hand strut, access to mounting nuts is from inside the vehicle, working through the storage tray aperture in the top of the facia.

Refitting

9 Lift the suspension strut into position and insert the upper mounting studs through the holes in the body.

10 Screw on the upper mounting retaining nuts and tighten them to the specified torque.

11 Thoroughly clean the bottom end of the suspension strut and its location in the steering knuckle. Locate the strut onto the knuckle and over the tab, then insert the pinch-bolt and tighten it to the specified torque.

12 If the left-hand strut is being refitted, refer to the procedures contained in Chapter 4A, Section 9 or 10, as applicable, and refit the powertrain control module (PCM), then refit the storage tray to the facia. Reattach the floor covering as necessary.

13 If the right-hand strut is being refitted, reattach the floor covering at the right-hand side of the footwell.

14 Slide the brake caliper assembly over the disc and into position on the steering knuckle. Refit the two mounting bracket retaining bolts and tighten them to the specified torque.

15 On vehicles with a balljoint anti-roll bar connecting link, refit the ABS wiring harness support bracket to the strut and securely tighten the retaining bolt and nut. Attach the anti-roll bar connecting link to the strut bracket and tighten the retaining nut to the specified torque. If necessary, use a 5 mm Allen key to hold the spindle while the nut is tightened.

16 On vehicles with a solid anti-roll bar connecting link, refit the brake hose and ABS wiring harness support bracket to the strut, and securely tighten the retaining bolt.

17 Refit the roadwheel, then lower the vehicle to the ground and tighten the roadwheel nuts to the specified torque.

---

6 Front suspension strut – overhaul

Warning: Before attempting to dismantle the suspension strut, a suitable tool to hold the coil spring in compression must be obtained. Adjustable coil spring compressors which can be positively secured to the spring coils are readily available, and are recommended for this operation. Any attempt to dismantle the strut without such a tool is likely to result in damage or personal injury.

1 If the front suspension struts exhibit signs of wear (leaking fluid, loss of damping capability, sagging or cracked coil springs) then they should be dismantled and overhauled as necessary. The struts themselves cannot be serviced, and should be renewed if faulty, but the springs and related components can be renewed. To maintain balanced characteristics on both sides of the vehicle, the components on both sides should be renewed at the same time.

2 With the strut removed from the vehicle, clean away all external dirt, then carefully mount it in a vice.

3 Fit the coil spring compressor tools (ensuring they are fully engaged) and compress the spring until all tension is relieved from the upper mounting.

4 Hold the strut piston with an Allen key, and unscrew the piston rod retaining nut with a ring spanner **(see illustration)**.

5 Remove the piston rod retaining nut, upper mounting, thrust bearing, bump stop and upper spring seat, gaiter and coil spring **(see illustrations)**.

6 If a new spring is to be fitted, the original spring must now be carefully released from the compressor. If it is to be re-used, it can be left in compression.

7 With the strut assembly now completely dismantled, examine all the components for wear or damage, and check the thrust bearing for smoothness of operation. Renew components as necessary.

8 Examine the strut for signs of fluid leakage. Check the strut piston for signs of pitting along its entire length, and check the strut body for signs of damage.

9 Test the operation of the strut, while holding it in an upright position, by moving the piston rod through a full stroke and then through short strokes of 50 to 100 mm. In both cases the resistance felt should be smooth and continuous. If the resistance is jerky, or uneven, or if there is any visible sign of wear or damage to the strut, renewal is necessary.

10 Reassembly is a reversal of dismantling, noting the following points:

a) Make sure that the coil spring ends are correctly located in the upper and lower seats before releasing the spring compressor **(see illustration)**.

b) Check that the thrust bearing is correctly fitted to the upper mounting.

c) Tighten the piston rod retaining nut to the specified torque.

---

7 Front suspension lower arm
    – removal and refitting

Removal

1 Firmly apply the handbrake, then jack up the front of the vehicle and support it securely on axle stands (see *Jacking and vehicle support*). Remove the roadwheel.

2 On vehicles with a solid anti-roll bar connecting link, undo the nut securing the link

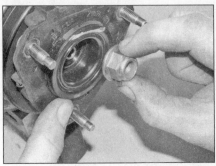

6.4 Hold the strut piston with an Allen key while unscrewing the piston rod retaining nut

6.5a Remove the nut . . .

6.5b . . . followed by the top mounting . . .

6.5c . . . thrust bearing . . .

through-bolt to the lower suspension arm **(see illustration)**.

3 Slacken the nut securing the steering knuckle balljoint to the lower suspension arm **(see illustration 4.5)**. Attach a two-legged puller to the lower suspension arm and tighten the puller to apply tension to the balljoint shank. Strike the end of the lower suspension arm with a hammer a few times to shock-free the balljoint shank taper.

6.5d . . . bump stop and upper spring seat . . .

6.5e . . . gaiter . . .

6.5f . . . and coil spring (with compressor tool)

6.10 Make sure that the coil spring ends are located against the spring seats

7.2 Anti-roll bar connecting link through-bolt (arrowed)

4 Remove the puller and unscrew the balljoint retaining nut. Discard the nut as a new one must be used for refitting.

5 Push down on the lower suspension arm and disengage the steering knuckle balljoint from the arm.

6 Unscrew the lower arm front and rear mounting bolts/nuts and remove the lower arm from the subframe.

Refitting

7 Locate the lower arm in position in the subframe and refit the retaining nuts/bolts. Tighten the mountings to the specified torque.

8 Push down on the lower suspension arm and engage the steering knuckle balljoint with the arm. Fit the new balljoint retaining nut and tighten the nut to the specified torque.

9 On vehicles with a solid anti-roll bar connecting link, refit the nut securing the link through-bolt to the lower suspension arm and tighten it to the specified torque.

10 Refit the roadwheel, then lower the vehicle to the ground and tighten the roadwheel nuts to the specified torque.

8 Front suspension lower arm bushes – renewal

1 Remove the front suspension lower arm as described in Section 7.

2 If the suspension arm bushes are worn or perished, they can be withdrawn from the suspension arm using a simple puller comprising a metal tube of suitable diameter (just less than

11.3 Steering column intermediate shaft flexible coupling pinch-bolt (arrowed)

that of the arm eye inside diameter), washers, and a long bolt and nut. Alternatively (and preferably), if a press is at hand, the bushes can be pushed out using a suitable rod or a length of tube of suitable diameter. If the horizontal bush is being renewed, first cut off the bush lips using a sharp knife or a hacksaw.

3 To ease the fitting of the new bushes into the suspension arm, lubricate the relevant bush and the eye in the arm with multi-purpose grease, then press or draw (as applicable) the bush into the arm so that the bush lips are seated correctly.

4 Wipe off any excess grease, then refit the front suspension lower arm as described in Section 7.

9 Steering knuckle balljoint – renewal

1 Remove the steering knuckle as described in Section 4.

2 Using circlip pliers, extract the circlip securing the balljoint to the steering knuckle.

3 Mount a G-clamp or similar tool over the balljoint, with suitable spacers above, and a tube of a diameter to allow the balljoint to pass through, below.

4 Tighten the G-clamp to press the balljoint down and out of the steering knuckle.

5 Clean the balljoint locating area in the knuckle and remove any burrs that might hinder refitting.

6 Lubricate the balljoint locating area in the knuckle with multi-purpose grease and place the balljoint in position.

7 Using the G-clamp with suitable spacers and a tube of suitable diameter, press the new balljoint back into position in the steering knuckle.

8 Refit the circlip to secure the balljoint in position.

9 Refit the steering knuckle as described in Section 4.

10 Front anti-roll bar – removal and refitting

Removal

1 Firmly apply the handbrake, then jack up the front of the vehicle and support it securely on axle stands (see *Jacking and vehicle support*). Remove the roadwheel.

2 On vehicles with a solid anti-roll bar connecting link, undo the nut securing the link through-bolt to the lower suspension arm **(see illustration 7.2)**. Withdraw the through-bolt and remove the connecting link, noting the orientation of the rubber bushes.

3 On vehicles with a balljoint anti-roll bar connecting link, unscrew the nut and detach the anti-roll bar connecting link from the anti-roll bar. If necessary, use a 5 mm Allen

key to hold the connecting link spindle while the nut is unscrewed.

4 Undo the two bolts each side securing the anti-roll bar clamps to the subframe.

5 Manipulate the anti-roll bar out from the side of the vehicle to remove.

6 With the anti-roll bar removed, check the condition of the mounting bushes and renew as necessary.

Refitting

7 Refitting is a reversal of removal, tightening all fastenings to the specified torque.

11 Front subframe – removal and refitting

Removal

1 Firmly apply the handbrake, then jack up the front of the vehicle and support it securely on axle stands (see *Jacking and vehicle support*). Set the front wheels in the straight-ahead position, then remove the ignition key to lock the column in position.

2 Remove the front anti-roll bar as described in Section 10, then disconnect the steering knuckle balljoint from the lower suspension arm as described in Section 4.

3 Undo the nut and remove the lower pinch-bolt securing the steering column intermediate shaft flexible coupling to the steering gear pinion shaft **(see illustration)**. Note that a new pinch-bolt and nut will be required for refitting. Where fitted, extract the circlip from the base of the flexible coupling. Slide the flexible coupling up and off the steering gear pinion shaft.

4 Undo the retaining clamp bolt and release the power steering fluid pipes from the front subframe.

5 On front wheel drive models, undo the four bolts securing the engine/transmission rear mounting to the subframe. Undo the through-bolt securing the mounting to the transmission and remove the mounting from under the vehicle. Note that a new through-bolt will be required for refitting. On rear wheel drive models, undo the two bolts securing the transmission mounting, or mounting support bracket to the subframe **(see illustration)**.

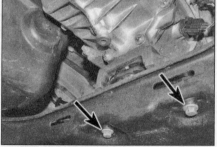

11.5 Undo the two bolts (arrowed) securing the transmission mounting, or mounting support bracket to the front subframe

Suitably support the transmission on a trolley jack.

6 Undo the two bolts securing the steering gear to the front subframe. Using cable ties, support the steering gear clear of the subframe.

7 Undo the bolt and nut each side securing the front subframe to the underbody **(see illustrations)**. Lower the jack and remove the subframe from under the vehicle.

Refitting

8 Refitting is a reversal of removal, using new nuts/bolts where applicable, and tightening all fastenings to the specified torque.

12 Rear axle leaf spring – removal and refitting

Removal

1 Chock the front wheels then jack up the rear of the vehicle and securely support it on axle stands (see *Jacking and vehicle support*). Remove the roadwheel on the side concerned.

2 Support the rear axle with a trolley jack.

3 Undo the retaining nuts, and remove the spring-to-axle U-bolts and fittings each side **(see illustration)**. Discard the nuts as new ones must be used for refitting.

4 Unscrew and remove the front mounting and rear mounting retaining nuts, and drive out the mounting bolts with a soft metal drift **(see illustrations)**. Discard the nuts as new ones must be used for refitting.

5 The rear spring can now be lifted from the rear axle and withdrawn from beneath the vehicle.

6 Examine the front and rear mounting bushes, and check the condition of the U-bolts and spring leaves; renew any faulty components.

Refitting

7 Refitting is a reversal of removal, but note the following additional points:

a) Use new retaining nuts on the spring-to-axle U-bolts and the spring mounting bolts.

b) Tighten all nuts and bolts to the specified torque, noting that the mounting bolt nuts must not be fully tightened until after the vehicle is lowered to the ground.

11.7a Front subframe right-hand side retaining bolt (arrowed) . . .

13 Rear shock absorber – removal and refitting

Removal

1 Chock the front wheels then jack up the rear of the vehicle and securely support it on axle stands (see *Jacking and vehicle support*).

2 Support the rear axle with a trolley jack.

3 Undo the retaining nut, and withdraw the shock absorber lower mounting bolt **(see illustration)**.

4 Unscrew the upper mounting bolt and remove the shock absorber **(see illustration)**.

5 To test the shock absorber for efficiency, grip the upper or lower mounting eye in a vice, and then pump the piston repeatedly through its full stroke. If the resistance is weak or is felt to be uneven, the shock absorber is

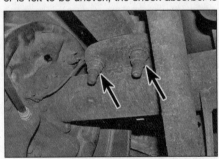

12.3 Undo the retaining nuts (two of four arrowed), and remove the spring-to-axle U-bolts and fittings each side

11.7b . . . and retaining nut (arrowed)

defective and must be renewed. It must also be renewed if it is leaking fluid. It is advisable to renew both rear shock absorbers at the same time, or the handling characteristics of the vehicle could be adversely affected.

Refitting

6 Refitting is a reversal of removal. Ensure that the mounting bolts are tightened to the specified torque.

14 Rear anti-roll bar – removal and refitting

Removal

1 Firmly apply the handbrake, then jack up the front of the vehicle and support it securely on axle stands (see *Jacking and vehicle support*).

2 Support the rear axle with a trolley jack.

12.4a Rear spring front mounting bolt nut . . .

12.4b . . . and rear mounting bolt nut

13.3 Rear shock absorber lower mounting bolt retaining nut (arrowed) . . .

13.4 . . . and upper mounting bolt

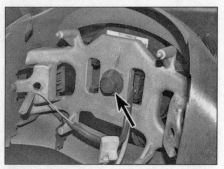

15.3 Unscrew the retaining bolt (arrowed) securing the steering wheel to the column

15.4 If no alignment marks are visible, mark wheel and column shaft with quick-drying paint (arrowed)

Removal

1 Remove the airbag as described in Chapter 12.

2 Set the front wheels in the straight-ahead position, then remove the ignition key to lock the column in position.

3 Unscrew the Torx retaining bolt securing the steering wheel to the column **(see illustration)**.

4 Check that there are alignment marks between the steering column shaft and steering wheel. If no marks are visible, suitably mark the wheel and column shaft with quick-drying paint to ensure correct alignment when refitting **(see illustration)**.

5 Grip the steering wheel with both hands and carefully rock it from side-to-side to release it from the splines on the steering column **(see illustration)**. As the steering wheel is being removed, guide the wiring for the airbag and horn through the aperture in the wheel, taking care not to damage the wiring connectors.

15.5 Rock the steering wheel from side-to-side to release it from the splines on the steering column

3 Unscrew the nut each side and detach the anti-roll bar connecting links from the anti-roll bar. If necessary, use a 5 mm Allen key to hold the spindles while the nuts are unscrewed. Discard the nuts as new ones must be used for refitting.

4 Undo the retaining nuts, and withdraw the shock absorber lower mounting bolts.

5 Undo the two bolts each side and release the anti-roll bar clamps from the rear axle.

Refitting

6 Refitting is a reversal of removal. Tighten all nuts and bolts to the specified torque, and use new nuts to secure the anti-roll bar connecting links.

---

15 Steering wheel – removal and refitting

> ⚠ **Warning: Make sure that the airbag safety recommendations given in Chapter 12 are followed, to prevent personal injury.**

Refitting

6 Refit the steering wheel, aligning the marks made prior to removal. Route the airbag and horn wiring connectors through the steering wheel aperture. **Note:** *Make sure the lugs on the airbag rotary connector locate correctly with the opening on the steering wheel, and that the two arrows on the rotary connector are aligned. If necessary, refer to the procedures contained in Chapter 12 and centralise the rotary connector if there is any doubt about its position.*

7 Clean the threads in the steering column, coat the retaining bolt threads with locking compound, then fit the bolt and tighten to the specified torque.

8 Release the steering lock, and refit the airbag as described in Chapter 12.

---

16 Ignition switch/ steering column lock – removal and refitting

Removal

1 Move the driver's seat fully forward, open the battery box cover and disconnect the battery negative terminal (refer to *Disconnecting the battery* in the Reference Chapter).

2 Remove the steering column shrouds as described in Chapter 11.

3 Disconnect the wiring connector from the Passive Anti-Theft System (PATS) transceiver **(see illustration)**.

4 Undo the screw and remove the PATS transceiver from the ignition switch/steering column lock **(see illustrations)**.

5 Depress the locking tang and disconnect the ignition switch wiring connector **(see illustration)**.

6 Using a screwdriver, release the retaining clips and remove the ignition switch **(see illustrations)**.

16.3 Disconnect the wiring connector from the PATS transceiver

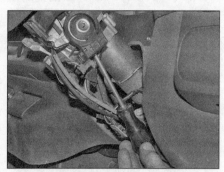

16.4a Undo the retaining screw . . .

16.4b . . . and remove the PATS transceiver from the ignition switch/steering column lock

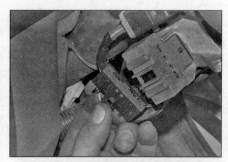

16.5 Depress the locking tang and disconnect the ignition switch wiring connector

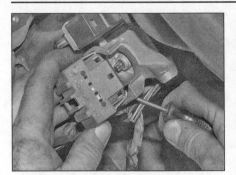

16.6a Using a screwdriver, release the retaining clips . . .

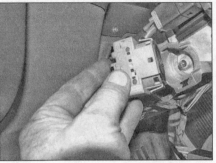

16.6b . . . and remove the ignition switch

16.8 Remove the ignition switch lock cylinder

7 Insert the ignition key into the ignition switch/lock, and turn it to position I.

8 Insert a thin screwdriver into the hole in the lock housing, press the screwdriver to release the detent spring, and pull out the lock cylinder using the key **(see illustration)**.

Refitting

9 Refitting is a reversal of removal.

---

17 Steering column –
removal and refitting

Removal

1 Remove the steering wheel as described in Section 15.

2 Remove the steering column shrouds as described in Chapter 11.

3 Undo the two bolts and detach the steering column lower bearing from the bulkhead **(see illustration)**.

4 Firmly apply the handbrake, then jack up the front of the vehicle and support it securely on axle stands (see *Jacking and vehicle support*).

5 From under the vehicle, undo the nut and remove the upper pinch-bolt securing the steering column intermediate shaft to the flexible coupling **(see illustration)**. Note that a new pinch-bolt and nut will be required for refitting. Slide the intermediate shaft out of the flexible coupling.

6 Release the clips and disconnect the airbag rotary connector wiring connectors on the side of the steering column.

7 Disconnect the wiring connectors for the Passive Anti-Theft System (PATS) transceiver, windscreen wiper/washer switch, horn switch, ignition switch and direction indicator switch.

8 Undo the two bolts and detach the diagnostic socket from the base of the steering column.

9 Undo the four steering column retaining nuts and remove the column from vehicle **(see illustrations)**. Note that new nuts will be required for refitting.

Refitting

10 Refitting is a reversal of removal, but note the following additional points:

a) *Ensure that both the steering column*

and roadwheels are centralised when refitting the intermediate shaft to the flexible coupling, and secure with a new pinch-bolt and nut.

b) *Tighten all fastenings to the specified torque.*

c) *Refit the steering wheel as described in Section 15.*

d) *Ensure that all wiring is securely connected and correctly routed.*

---

18 Steering gear –
removal and refitting

Removal

1 Move the driver's seat fully forward, open the battery box cover and disconnect the battery

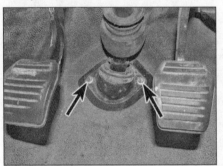

17.3 Undo the two bolts (arrowed) and detach the steering column lower bearing from the bulkhead

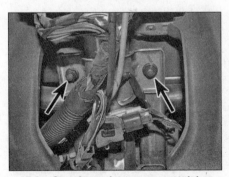

17.9a Steering column upper retaining bolts (arrowed) . . .

negative terminal (refer to *Disconnecting the battery* in the Reference Chapter).

2 Set the front wheels in the straight-ahead position, then remove the ignition key to lock the column in position.

3 Firmly apply the handbrake, then jack up the front of the vehicle and support it securely on axle stands (see *Jacking and vehicle support*). Remove both front roadwheels.

4 Undo the nut and remove the lower pinch-bolt securing the steering column intermediate shaft flexible coupling to the steering gear pinion shaft **(see illustration 11.3)**. Note that a new pinch-bolt and nut will be required for refitting. Where fitted, extract the circlip from the base of the flexible coupling. Slide the flexible coupling up and off the steering gear pinion shaft.

5 Undo the retaining clamp bolt and release the power steering fluid pipes from the front subframe.

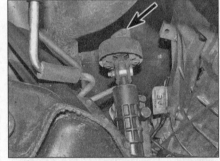

17.5 Undo the nut (arrowed) and remove the upper pinch-bolt securing the intermediate shaft to the flexible coupling

17.9b . . . and lower retaining bolts (arrowed)

20.2 Loosen the track rod end locknut (arrowed) on the track rod a quarter turn

6 Slacken the track rod end balljoint nut several turns, then use a balljoint separator tool to release the balljoint shank from the steering arm. With the balljoint released, unscrew the nut and disconnect the balljoint from the steering arm. Discard the nut as a new one must be used for refitting.

7 On vehicles with a solid anti-roll bar connecting link, undo the nut securing the link through-bolt to the lower suspension arm.

8 Thoroughly clean the area around the fluid pipe connections on the steering gear. Place a suitable container beneath the steering gear, then unscrew the pipe locking plate and withdraw the pipes from the pinion housing. Allow the fluid to drain into the container as the pipes are released. Remove and discard the O-rings from the fluid pipes and obtain new O-rings for refitting. Cover the pipe ends and steering gear orifices after disconnection, to prevent the ingress of foreign matter.

9 Undo the two bolts securing the steering gear to the front subframe and remove the steering gear through the driver's side wheel arch.

Refitting

10 Refitting is a reversal of removal, but note the following additional points:
 a) *Ensure that both the steering wheel and steering gear are centralised when refitting the intermediate shaft flexible coupling to the steering gear pinion.*
 b) *If a new steering gear unit is being fitted, the straight-ahead position can be ascertained by halving the number of*

21.5 High-pressure fluid pipe (arrowed) at the top of the power steering pump – 2.0 litre engines

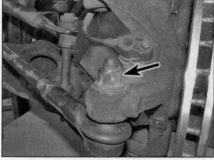

20.3 Track rod end balljoint retaining nut (arrowed)

 turns necessary to move the rack from lock-to-lock.
 c) *Use new nuts/bolts when refitting the intermediate shaft flexible coupling and track rod end balljoints.*
 d) *Fit new O-rings to the fluid pipes.*
 e) *Tighten all fastenings to the specified torque.*
 f) *Fill and bleed the power steering hydraulic system as described in Section 23.*
 g) *Have the front wheel toe-setting checked and adjusted at the earliest opportunity.*

19 Steering gear rubber gaiters – renewal

1 Remove the track rod end as described in Section 20.

2 Note the position of the track rod end locknut by counting the number of threads from the nut face to the end of the track rod. Record this figure, then unscrew and remove the locknut.

3 Remove the clips, and slide the gaiter from the track rod and steering gear housing.

4 Slide the new gaiter over the track rod, and onto the steering gear. Where applicable, make sure that the gaiter locates in the cut-outs provided in the track rod and steering gear housing.

5 Fit and tighten the clips, ensuring that the gaiter is not twisted.

6 Screw the track rod end locknut onto the track rod, and position it with the exact number of threads exposed as noted during removal.

7 Refit the track rod end as described in Section 20.

20 Track rod end – removal and refitting

Removal

1 Firmly apply the handbrake, then jack up the front of the vehicle and support it securely on axle stands (see *Jacking and vehicle support*). Remove the relevant front roadwheel.

2 Loosen the track rod end securing locknut

on the track rod a quarter turn, while holding the track rod stationary with a second spanner on the flats provided **(see illustration)**. If necessary, use a wire brush to remove rust from the nut and threads and lubricate the threads with penetrating oil before unscrewing the nut. As an additional check, measure the visible amount of threads on the track rod using vernier calipers. This will ensure the track rod end is refitted in the same position.

3 Slacken the track rod end balljoint nut several turns, then use a balljoint separator tool to release the balljoint shank from the steering arm **(see illustration)**. With the balljoint released, unscrew the nut and disconnect the balljoint from the steering arm. Discard the nut as a new one must be used for refitting.

4 Unscrew the track rod end from the track rod, counting the number of turns necessary to remove it and taking care not to disturb the locknut.

Refitting

5 Screw the new track rod end onto the track rod the exact number of turns as noted during removal.

6 Engage the track rod end balljoint shank in the steering arm, and screw on the new retaining nut. Tighten the nut to the specified torque.

7 Tighten the track rod end locknut.

8 Refit the roadwheel, then lower the vehicle to the ground, and tighten the roadwheel nuts to the specified torque.

9 Have the front wheel alignment checked and adjusted at the earliest opportunity.

21 Power steering pump – removal and refitting

2.0 litre engines

Removal

1 Move the driver's seat fully forward, open the battery box cover and disconnect the battery negative terminal (refer to *Disconnecting the battery* in the Reference Chapter).

2 Remove the power steering pump drivebelt as described in Chapter 1.

3 Remove the inlet manifold as described in Chapter 2A.

4 Position a suitable container beneath the power steering pump, then slacken the retaining clip and disconnect the fluid return hose from the bottom of the pump. Allow the fluid to drain into the container. Cover the hose end and pump orifice after disconnection, to prevent the ingress of foreign matter.

5 Unscrew the union nut and disconnect the high-pressure pipe from the top of the pump **(see illustration)**. Hold the union adaptor on the pump with a second spanner while unscrewing the union nut. Remove the union O-ring seal and discard it; a new one must be used for refitting. Cover the pipe end and

21.7a Unscrew the mounting bolts (arrowed) . . .

21.7b . . . and remove the power steering pump from the coolant pump housing – 2.0 litre engines

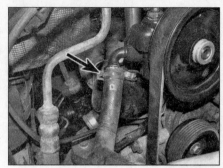

21.21 Fluid return hose connection (arrowed) on the power steering pump – 2.4 litre engines

pump orifice after disconnection, to prevent the ingress of foreign matter.

6 Unscrew and remove the pump support bracket bolts.

7 Unscrew the mounting bolts and remove the pump from the coolant pump housing **(see illustrations)**.

8 If fitting a new pump, unbolt the pulley from the old unit.

Refitting

9 Where applicable, fit the pulley to the new pump and tighten the retaining bolts to the specified torque.

10 Fit a new O-ring to the high-pressure pipe union. Ideally, the special Ford fitting sleeve should be used to prevent damage to the O-ring as it passes over the union threads, however, a suitable alternative can be made out of plastic tubing or by wrapping suitable tape over the threads.

11 At the rear of the pump, apply grease to the splines of the coolant pump drive dog.

12 Refit the power steering pump to the coolant pump housing, then insert the mounting bolts and tighten them to the specified torque.

13 Refit the pump support bracket bolts and tighten them to the specified torque.

14 Reconnect the high-pressure pipe to the pump and tighten the pipe union to the specified torque, while holding the union adaptor.

15 Reconnect the fluid return hose to the pump and tighten the retaining clip.

16 Refit the inlet manifold as described in Chapter 2A.

17 Refit the power steering pump drivebelt as described in Chapter 1.

18 Reconnect the battery, then fill and bleed the power steering hydraulic system as described in Section 23.

2.4 litre engines

Removal

19 Move the driver's seat fully forward, open the battery box cover and disconnect the battery negative terminal (refer to *Disconnecting the battery* in the Reference Chapter).

20 Remove the auxiliary drivebelt as described in Chapter 1.

21 Position a suitable container beneath the

21.22 Unscrew the bolt (arrowed) securing the pipe support bracket to the power steering pump – 2.4 litre engines

power steering pump, then slacken the retaining clip and disconnect the fluid return hose from the side of the pump **(see illustration)**. Allow the fluid to drain into the container. Cover the hose end and pump orifice after disconnection, to prevent the ingress of foreign matter.

22 Unscrew the bolt securing the high-pressure pipe support bracket to the pump **(see illustration)**.

23 Unscrew the union nut and disconnect the high-pressure pipe from the top of the pump **(see illustration)**. Remove the union O-ring seal and discard it; a new one must be used for refitting. Cover the pipe end and pump orifice after disconnection, to prevent the ingress of foreign matter.

24 Unscrew the three mounting bolts and remove the pump from the engine.

Refitting

25 Fit a new O-ring to the high-pressure pipe union. Ideally, the special Ford fitting sleeve should be used to prevent damage to the O-ring as it passes over the union threads, however, a suitable alternative can be made out of plastic tubing or by wrapping suitable tape over the threads.

26 Refit the power steering pump to the engine, then insert the mounting bolts and tighten them to the specified torque.

27 Reconnect the high-pressure pipe to the pump and tighten the pipe union to the specified torque.

28 Refit the bolt securing the high-pressure pipe support bracket to the pump and tighten the bolt to the specified torque.

21.23 Unscrew the union nut and disconnect the high-pressure pipe from the top of the pump – 2.4 litre engines

29 Reconnect the fluid return hose to the pump and tighten the retaining clip.

30 Refit the auxiliary drivebelt as described in Chapter 1.

31 Reconnect the battery, then fill and bleed the power steering hydraulic system as described in Section 23.

22 Power steering fluid cooler – removal and refitting

Removal

1 Remove the front bumper as described in Chapter 11.

2 Undo the two fluid cooler mounting bolts and lower the unit from its location **(see illustration)**.

22.2 Power steering fluid cooler mounting bolts (arrowed)

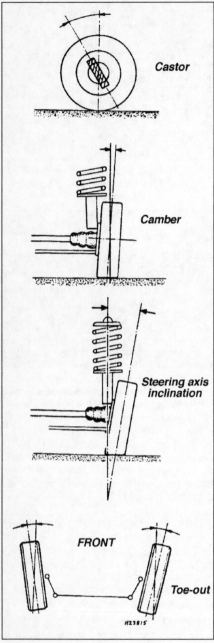

24.1 Wheel alignment and steering angles

3 Position a suitable container beneath the fluid cooler, then clamp the two fluid hoses using brake hose clamps or similar tools.
4 Release the retaining clips and disconnect the fluid hoses from the cooler. Allow the surplus fluid to drain into the container. Cover the hose ends and fluid cooler orifices after disconnection, to prevent the ingress of foreign matter.

Refitting

5 Refitting is a reversal of removal. On completion, fill and bleed the power steering hydraulic system as described in Section 23.

23 Power steering hydraulic system – bleeding

1 This will normally only be required if any part of the hydraulic system has been disconnected.
2 Referring to *Weekly checks*, remove the fluid reservoir filler cap, and top-up with the specified fluid to the maximum level mark.
3 Firmly apply the handbrake, then jack up the front of the vehicle and support it securely on axle stands (see *Jacking and vehicle support*).
4 With the engine switched off, slowly turn the steering wheel from lock-to-lock several times, adding fluid to the reservoir as necessary. Continue turning the steering wheel from lock-to-lock until the fluid level in the reservoir stops dropping.
5 Lower the vehicle to the ground, start the engine and allow it to idle. With the engine idling, turn the steering wheel to full left, or full right lock and hold it there for two or three seconds. Now turn the steering to full lock in the other direction and again hold it there for a few seconds. Repeat this procedure several times, adding fluid to the reservoir as necessary, until the fluid level in the reservoir stops dropping.
6 Stop the engine, lower the vehicle to the ground and re-check the fluid level. Top-up the fluid if necessary.

24 Wheel alignment and steering angles – general information

Definitions

1 A vehicle's steering and suspension geometry is defined in four basic settings **(see illustration)** – all angles are expressed in degrees (toe settings are also expressed as a measurement); the steering axis is defined as an imaginary line drawn through the axis of the suspension strut, extended where necessary to contact the ground.
2 Camber is the angle between each roadwheel and a vertical line drawn through its centre and tyre contact patch, when viewed from the front or rear of the vehicle. Positive camber is when the roadwheels are tilted outwards from the vertical at the top; negative camber is when they are tilted inwards. The camber angle is not adjustable.
3 Castor is the angle between the steering axis and a vertical line drawn through each roadwheel's centre and tyre contact patch, when viewed from the side of the vehicle. Positive castor is when the steering axis is tilted so that it contacts the ground ahead of the vertical; negative castor is when it contacts the ground behind the vertical. The castor angle is not adjustable.
4 Toe is the difference, viewed from above, between lines drawn through the roadwheel centres and the vehicle's centre-line. 'Toe-in' is when the roadwheels point inwards, towards each other at the front, while 'toe-out' is when they splay outwards from each other at the front.
5 The front wheel toe setting is adjusted by screwing the track rod in or out of its track rod ends, to alter the effective length of the track rod assembly.
6 Rear wheel toe setting is not adjustable.

Checking and adjustment

7 Due to the special measuring equipment necessary to check the wheel alignment and steering angles, and the skill required to use it properly, the checking and adjustment of these settings is best left to a Ford dealer or similar expert. Note that most tyre-fitting shops now possess sophisticated checking equipment.

Chapter 11
Bodywork and fittings

Contents

Degrees of difficulty

Easy, suitable for novice with little experience	Fairly easy, suitable for beginner with some experience	Fairly difficult, suitable for competent DIY mechanic	Difficult, suitable for experienced DIY mechanic	Very difficult, suitable for expert DIY or professional

Specifications

Torque wrench settings	Nm	lbf ft
Driver's seat retaining bolts	47	35
Passenger's seat retaining bolts	25	18
Seat belt mounting bolts	40	30
Steering column retaining nuts*	20	15

* Use new nuts

1 General information

The body and chassis on all versions of the Transit is of all-steel construction. Three basic chassis types are available: short-wheelbase, medium-wheelbase and long-wheelbase models.

The three main body types are Van, Bus and Chassis Cab. Twin opening rear doors or a tailgate are fitted and, on some models, side opening door(s) are available. The bodyshell is as aerodynamic in shape as possible, to promote economy and reduce wind noise levels.

Extensive use is made of plastic materials, mainly on the interior, but also in exterior components. The front and rear bumpers are injection-moulded from a synthetic material which is very strong and yet light. Plastic components such as wheel arch liners are fitted to the underside of the vehicle, to improve the body's resistance to corrosion.

Due to the large number of specialist applications of this vehicle range, information contained in this Chapter is given on parts found to be common on the popular factory-produced versions. No information is provided on special body versions.

2 Maintenance –
bodywork and underframe

The general condition of a vehicle's bodywork is the one thing that significantly affects its value. Maintenance is easy, but needs to be regular. Neglect, particularly after minor damage, can lead quickly to further deterioration and costly repair bills. It is important also to keep watch on those parts of the vehicle not immediately visible, for instance the underside, inside all the wheel arches, and the lower part of the engine compartment.

The basic maintenance routine for the bodywork is washing – preferably with a lot of water, from a hose. This will remove all the loose solids which may have stuck to the vehicle. It is important to flush these off in such a way as to prevent grit from scratching the finish. The wheel arches and underframe need washing in the same way, to remove any accumulated mud, which will retain moisture and tend to encourage rust. Paradoxically enough, the best time to clean the underframe and wheel arches is in wet weather, when the mud is thoroughly wet and soft. In very wet weather, the underframe is usually cleaned of large accumulations automatically, and this is a good time for inspection.

Periodically, except on vehicles with a wax-based underbody protective coating, it is a good idea to have the whole of the underframe of the vehicle steam-cleaned, engine compartment included, so that a thorough inspection can be carried out to see what minor repairs and renovations are necessary. Steam-cleaning is available at many garages, and is necessary for the removal of the accumulation of oily grime, which sometimes is allowed to become thick in certain areas. If steam-cleaning facilities are not available, there are some excellent grease solvents available which can be brush-applied; the dirt can then be simply hosed off. Note that these methods should not be used on vehicles with wax-based underbody protective coating, or the coating will be removed. Such vehicles should be inspected annually, preferably just prior to Winter, when the underbody should be washed down, and any damage to the wax coating repaired. Ideally, a completely fresh coat should be applied. It would also be worth considering the use of such wax-based protection for injection into door panels, sills, box sections, etc, as an additional safeguard against rust damage, where such protection is not provided by the vehicle manufacturer.

After washing paintwork, wipe off with a chamois leather to give an unspotted clear finish. A coat of clear protective wax polish will give added protection against chemical pollutants in the air. If the paintwork sheen has dulled or oxidised, use a cleaner/polisher combination to restore the brilliance of the shine. This requires a little effort, but such dulling is usually caused because regular washing has been neglected. Care needs to be taken with metallic paintwork, as special non-abrasive cleaner/polisher is required to avoid damage to the finish. Always check that the door and ventilator opening drain holes and pipes are completely clear, so that water can be drained out. Brightwork should be treated in the same way as paintwork. Windscreens and windows can be kept clear of the smeary film which often appears, by the use of proprietary glass cleaner. Never use any form of wax or other body or chromium polish on glass.

3 Maintenance –
upholstery and carpets

Mats and carpets should be brushed or vacuum-cleaned regularly, to keep them free of grit. If they are badly stained, remove them from the vehicle for scrubbing or sponging, and make quite sure they are dry before refitting. Seats and interior trim panels can be kept clean by wiping with a damp cloth. If they do become stained (which can be more apparent on light-coloured upholstery), use a little liquid detergent and a soft nail brush to scour the grime out of the grain of the material. Do not forget to keep the headlining clean in the same way as the upholstery. When using liquid cleaners inside the vehicle, do not over-wet the surfaces being cleaned. Excessive damp could get into the seams and padded interior, causing stains, offensive odours or even rot.

4 Minor body damage –
repair

Minor scratches

If the scratch is very superficial, and does not penetrate to the metal of the bodywork, repair is very simple. Lightly rub the area of the scratch with a paintwork renovator, or a very fine cutting paste, to remove loose paint from the scratch, and to clear the surrounding bodywork of wax polish. Rinse the area with clean water.

Apply touch-up paint to the scratch using a fine paint brush; continue to apply fine layers of paint until the surface of the paint in the scratch is level with the surrounding paintwork. Allow the new paint at least two weeks to harden, then blend it into the surrounding paintwork by rubbing the scratch area with a paintwork renovator or a very fine cutting paste. Finally, apply wax polish.

Where the scratch has penetrated right through to the metal of the bodywork, causing the metal to rust, a different repair technique is required. Remove any loose rust from the bottom of the scratch with a penknife, then apply rust-inhibiting paint to prevent the formation of rust in the future. Using a rubber or nylon applicator, fill the scratch with bodystopper paste. If required, this paste can be mixed with cellulose thinners to provide a very thin paste which is ideal for filling narrow scratches. Before the stopper-paste in the scratch hardens, wrap a piece of smooth cotton rag around the top of a finger. Dip the finger in cellulose thinners, and quickly sweep it across the surface of the stopper-paste in the scratch; this will ensure that the surface of the stopper-paste is slightly hollowed. The scratch can now be painted over as described earlier in this Section.

Dents

When deep denting of the vehicle's bodywork has taken place, the first task is to pull the dent out, until the affected bodywork almost attains its original shape. There is little point in trying to restore the original shape completely, as the metal in the damaged area will have stretched on impact, and cannot be reshaped fully to its original contour. It is better to bring the level of the dent up to a point which is about 3 mm below the level of the surrounding bodywork. In cases where the dent is very shallow anyway, it is not worth trying to pull it out at all. If the underside of the dent is accessible, it can be hammered out gently from behind, using a mallet with a wooden or plastic head. Whilst doing this, hold a suitable block of wood firmly against the outside of the panel, to absorb the impact from the hammer blows and thus prevent a large area of the bodywork from being 'belled-out'.

Should the dent be in a section of the

bodywork which has a double skin, or some other factor making it inaccessible from behind, a different technique is called for. Drill several small holes through the metal inside the area – particularly in the deeper section. Then screw long self-tapping screws into the holes, just sufficiently for them to gain a good purchase in the metal. Now the dent can be pulled out by pulling on the protruding heads of the screws with a pair of pliers.

The next stage of the repair is the removal of the paint from the damaged area, and from an inch or so of the surrounding 'sound' bodywork. This is accomplished most easily by using a wire brush or abrasive pad on a power drill, although it can be done just as effectively by hand, using sheets of abrasive paper. To complete the preparation for filling, score the surface of the bare metal with a screwdriver or the tang of a file, or alternatively, drill small holes in the affected area. This will provide a really good 'key' for the filler paste.

To complete the repair, see the Section on filling and respraying.

Rust holes or gashes

Remove all paint from the affected area, and from an inch or so of the surrounding 'sound' bodywork, using an abrasive pad or a wire brush on a power drill. If these are not available, a few sheets of abrasive paper will do the job most effectively. With the paint removed, you will be able to judge the severity of the corrosion, and therefore decide whether to renew the whole panel (if this is possible) or to repair the affected area. New body panels are not as expensive as most people think, and it is often quicker and more satisfactory to fit a new panel than to attempt to repair large areas of corrosion.

Remove all fittings from the affected area, except those which will act as a guide to the original shape of the damaged bodywork (eg headlight shells etc). Then, using tin snips or a hacksaw blade, remove all loose metal and any other metal badly affected by corrosion. Hammer the edges of the hole inwards, in order to create a slight depression for the filler paste.

Wire-brush the affected area to remove the powdery rust from the surface of the remaining metal. Paint the affected area with rust-inhibiting paint, if the back of the rusted area is accessible, treat this also.

Before filling can take place, it will be necessary to block the hole in some way. This can be achieved by the use of aluminium or plastic mesh, or aluminium tape.

Aluminium or plastic mesh, or glass-fibre matting, is probably the best material to use for a large hole. Cut a piece to the approximate size and shape of the hole to be filled, then position it in the hole so that its edges are below the level of the surrounding bodywork. It can be retained in position by several blobs of filler paste around its periphery.

Aluminium tape should be used for small or very narrow holes. Pull a piece off the roll,

trim it to the approximate size and shape required, then pull off the backing paper (if used) and stick the tape over the hole; it can be overlapped if the thickness of one piece is insufficient. Burnish down the edges of the tape with the handle of a screwdriver or similar, to ensure that the tape is securely attached to the metal underneath.

Filling and respraying

Before using this Section, see the Sections on dent, deep scratch, rust holes and gash repairs.

Many types of bodyfiller are available, but generally speaking, those proprietary kits which contain a tin of filler paste and a tube of resin hardener are best for this type of repair. A wide, flexible plastic or nylon applicator will be found invaluable for imparting a smooth and well-contoured finish to the surface of the filler.

Mix up a little filler on a clean piece of card or board – measure the hardener carefully (follow the maker's instructions on the pack), otherwise the filler will set too rapidly or too slowly. Using the applicator, apply the filler paste to the prepared area; draw the applicator across the surface of the filler to achieve the correct contour and to level the surface. As soon as a contour that approximates to the correct one is achieved, stop working the paste – if you carry on too long, the paste will become sticky and begin to 'pick-up' on the applicator. Continue to add thin layers of filler paste at 20-minute intervals, until the level of the filler is just proud of the surrounding bodywork.

Once the filler has hardened, the excess can be removed using a metal plane or file. From then on, progressively-finer grades of abrasive paper should be used, starting with a 40-grade production paper, and finishing with a 400-grade wet-and-dry paper. Always wrap the abrasive paper around a flat rubber, cork, or wooden block – otherwise the surface of the filler will not be completely flat. During the smoothing of the filler surface, the wet-and-dry paper should be periodically rinsed in water. This will ensure that a very smooth finish is imparted to the filler at the final stage.

At this stage, the 'dent' should be surrounded by a ring of bare metal, which in turn should be encircled by the finely 'feathered' edge of the good paintwork. Rinse the repair area with clean water, until all of the dust produced by the rubbing-down operation has gone.

Spray the whole area with a light coat of primer – this will show up any imperfections in the surface of the filler. Repair these imperfections with fresh filler paste or bodystopper, and once more smooth the surface with abrasive paper. Repeat this spray-and-repair procedure until you are satisfied that the surface of the filler, and the feathered edge of the paintwork, are perfect. Clean the repair area with clean water, and allow to dry fully.

The repair area is now ready for final spraying. Paint spraying must be carried out in a warm, dry, windless and dust-free atmosphere. This condition can be created artificially if you have access to a large indoor working area, but if you are forced to work in the open, you will have to pick your day very carefully. If you are working indoors, dousing the floor in the work area with water will help to settle the dust which would otherwise be in the atmosphere. If the repair area is confined to one body panel, mask off the surrounding panels; this will help to minimise the effects of a slight mis-match in paint colours. Bodywork fittings (eg chrome strips, door handles etc) will also need to be masked off. Use genuine masking tape, and several thicknesses of newspaper, for the masking operations.

Before commencing to spray, agitate the aerosol can thoroughly, then spray a test area (an old tin, or similar) until the technique is mastered. Cover the repair area with a thick coat of primer; the thickness should be built up using several thin layers of paint, rather than one thick one. Using 400-grade wet-and-dry paper, rub down the surface of the primer until it is really smooth. While doing this, the work area should be thoroughly doused with water, and the wet-and-dry paper periodically rinsed in water. Allow to dry before spraying on more paint.

Spray on the top coat, again building up the thickness by using several thin layers of paint. Start spraying at one edge of the repair area, and then, using a side-to-side motion, work until the whole repair area and about 2 inches of the surrounding original paintwork is covered. Remove all masking material 10 to 15 minutes after spraying on the final coat of paint.

Allow the new paint at least two weeks to harden, then, using a paintwork renovator, or a very fine cutting paste, blend the edges of the paint into the existing paintwork. Finally, apply wax polish.

Plastic components

With the use of more and more plastic body components by the vehicle manufacturers (eg bumpers. spoilers, and in some cases major body panels), rectification of more serious damage to such items has become a matter of either entrusting repair work to a specialist in this field, or renewing complete components. Repair of such damage by the DIY owner is not really feasible, owing to the cost of the equipment and materials required for effecting such repairs. The basic technique involves making a groove along the line of the crack in the plastic, using a rotary burr in a power drill. The damaged part is then welded back together, using a hot-air gun to heat up and fuse a plastic filler rod into the groove. Any excess plastic is then removed, and the area rubbed down to a smooth finish. It is important that a filler rod of the correct plastic is used, as body components can be made of a variety of different types (eg polycarbonate, ABS, polypropylene).

6.2 Mark around the bonnet hinges to show the outline of their fitted positions to aid alignment

Damage of a less serious nature (abrasions, minor cracks etc) can be repaired by the DIY owner using a two-part epoxy filler repair material. Once mixed in equal proportions, this is used in similar fashion to the bodywork filler used on metal panels. The filler is usually cured in twenty to thirty minutes, ready for sanding and painting.

If the owner is renewing a complete component himself, or if he has repaired it with epoxy filler, he will be left with the problem of finding a suitable paint for finishing which is compatible with the type of plastic used. At one time, the use of a universal paint was not possible, owing to the complex range of plastics encountered in body component applications. Standard paints, generally speaking, will not bond to plastic or rubber satisfactorily. However, it is now possible to obtain a plastic body parts finishing kit which

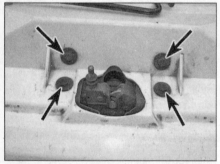

7.2 Bonnet lock retaining bolts (arrowed)

consists of a pre-primer treatment, a primer and coloured top coat. Full instructions are normally supplied with a kit, but basically, the method of use is to first apply the pre-primer to the component concerned, and allow it to dry for up to 30 minutes. Then the primer is applied, and left to dry for about an hour before finally applying the special-coloured top coat. The result is a correctly-coloured component, where the paint will flex with the plastic or rubber, a property that standard paint does not normally possess.

5 Major body damage – repair

With the exception of Chassis Cab versions, the chassis members are spot-welded to the underbody, and in this respect can be termed of being monocoque or unit construction. Major damage repairs to this type of body combination must of necessity be carried out by body shops with welding and hydraulic straightening facilities.

Extensive damage to the body may distort the chassis, and result in unstable and dangerous handling, as well as excessive wear to tyres and suspension or steering components. It is recommended that checking of the chassis alignment be entrusted to a Ford agent or accident repair specialist with special checking jigs.

6 Bonnet – removal, refitting and adjustment

Removal

1 Open the bonnet, and support it with its stay rod.
2 Mark around the bonnet hinges, to show the outline of their fitted positions for correct realignment on assembly **(see illustration)**.
3 Have an assistant support the bonnet whilst you unscrew and remove the hinge retaining bolts, then lift the bonnet clear.

Refitting

4 Refitting is a reversal of removal. Tighten

the hinge bolts fully when bonnet alignment is satisfactory.

Adjustment

5 Further adjustment of the bonnet fit is available by loosening the hinges and the locknuts of the bump stops on the radiator grille opening panel. The bonnet can now be adjusted to give an even clearance between its outer edges and the surrounding panels. Adjust the front bump stops to align the edges of the bonnet with the front wing panels, then retighten the locknuts and hinge bolts.

7 Bonnet lock – removal and refitting

Removal

1 Remove the radiator grille opening panel as described in Section 24.
2 Undo the four bolts and remove the bonnet lock mounting bracket from the radiator grille opening panel **(see illustration)**.
3 Undo the two bolts and remove the bonnet lock from the mounting bracket.

Refitting

4 Refitting is a reversal of removal.

8 Door trim panels – removal and refitting

Front doors

Removal

1 On models with manual window regulators, fully shut the window, note the position of the regulator handle, then release the spring clip and withdraw the handle. The clip can be released by inserting a clean cloth between the handle and the door trim, and pulling the cloth back against the open ends of the clip to release its tension, whilst simultaneously pulling the handle from the regulator shaft splines **(see illustrations)**.
2 Using a small screwdriver, lift off the trim cap, then undo the retaining screw in the door pull aperture **(see illustrations)**.

8.1a Pull a cloth back and forth under the regulator handle spring clip . . .

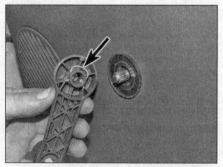

8.1b . . . to release the clip (arrowed) from the regulator shaft

8.2a Lift off the trim cap . . .

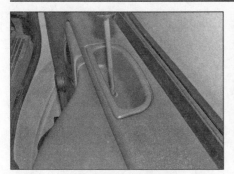

8.2b . . . then undo the retaining screw in the door pull aperture

8.3a Undo the retaining screw . . .

8.3b . . . and remove the interior release handle surround

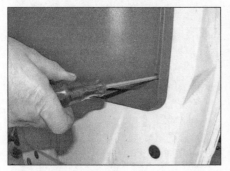

8.4 Undo the four screws securing the trim panel to the door

8.5 Carefully prise free the door trim panel to release the retaining clips and remove the panel

8.7 Cut through the adhesive securing the insulation sheet to the door using a sharp knife and carefully peel back the sheet as necessary

3 Undo the retaining screw, and remove the interior release handle surround **(see illustrations)**.

4 Undo the four screws securing the trim panel to the door **(see illustration)**.

5 Carefully prise free the door trim panel, prising with a suitable tool between the panel around its outer and lower edges, and remove the panel **(see illustration)**.

6 On models with electric window regulators, disconnect the wiring connector at the electric window switch as the panel is removed.

7 If the panel has been removed for access to the door internal components, the plastic insulation sheet will have to be locally removed for access. To do this, cut through the adhesive securing the plastic sheet to the door using a sharp knife. Now carefully peel back the insulation sheet as necessary

(see illustration). Do not attempt to peel back the sheet without first cutting through the adhesive, and take care not to touch the adhesive after the sheet has been removed. If care is taken, the existing adhesive will re-bond the sheet on completion.

Refitting

8 Refitting is a reversal of removal. On models with manual window regulators, refit the spring clip to the regulator handle, then push the handle onto the regulator shaft in the position noted on removal.

Rear doors and tailgate

Removal

9 Remove the interior handle (where applicable) by lifting up the trim covers and undoing the two screws **(see illustrations)**.

10 The rear door and tailgate trim panels are secured by plastic retaining clips, the removal of which requires the use of a suitable forked tool **(see illustration)**. These clips are easily broken, so take care when prising them free. Remove the trim panel.

11 If necessary, remove the plastic insulation sheet with reference to paragraph 7.

Refitting

12 Refitting is a reversal of removal. Align the panel, and press the clips into position.

Sliding side door

Removal

13 Proceed as described in paragraph 10 and 11.

Refitting

14 Refitting is a reversal of removal.

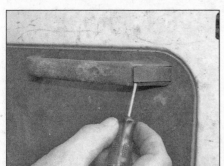

8.9a Lift up the rear door handle trim covers . . .

8.9b . . . and undo the two screws

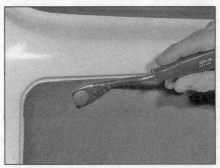

8.10 Using a forked tool to remove the trim panel retaining clips

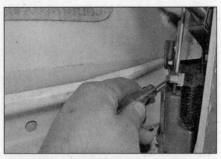

9.2 Open the retaining clip and detach the exterior handle operating rod from the door lock lever

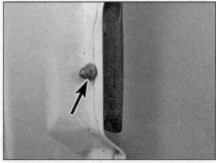

9.3a Undo the retaining nut (arrowed) . . .

9.3b . . . and remove the exterior handle from the door

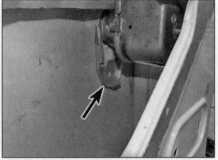

9.6 Extract the door lock cylinder retaining clip (arrowed)

9.8a Depress the tang on the lock cylinder body (arrowed) . . .

9.8b . . . then turn the ignition key anti-clockwise and withdraw the cylinder from the door

9 Front door fittings – removal and refitting

Exterior handle

Removal

1 Remove the front door trim panel as described in Section 8.

2 Using a small screwdriver, open the retaining clip and detach the exterior handle operating rod from the door lock lever (**see illustration**).

3 Undo the retaining nut, and remove the exterior handle from the door (**see illustrations**).

Door lock cylinder

Removal

5 Remove the front door trim panel as described in Section 8.

6 Extract the lock cylinder retaining clip (**see illustration**).

7 Insert the ignition key into the lock cylinder and turn it clockwise.

8 Depress the tang on the cylinder body, turn the key anti-clockwise and withdraw the cylinder from the door (**see illustrations**).

Refitting

4 Refitting is a reversal of removal.

Door lock unit

Removal

10 Remove the front door trim panel as described in Section 8.

11 Where applicable, remove the door lock cylinder as described previously.

12 Using a screwdriver, carefully prise the front of the interior release handle from the door, then slide it forward to disengage the rear locating lug (**see illustrations**).

13 Extract the retaining clip and cut off the

Refitting

9 Refitting is a reversal of removal.

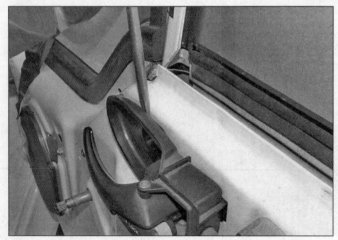

9.12a Carefully prise the front of the interior release handle from the door . . .

9.12b . . . then slide it forward to disengage the rear locating lug

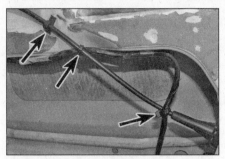

9.13 Extract the retaining clip and cut off the cable ties securing the release cable to the door and wiring harness (arrowed)

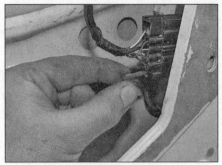

9.14a Pull out the locking clip . . .

9.14b . . . and disconnect the wiring connector from the door lock unit

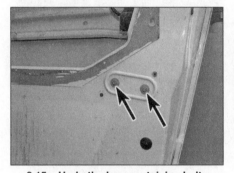

9.15a Undo the lower retaining bolts (arrowed) . . .

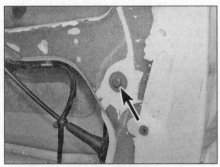

9.15b . . . and upper retaining bolt (arrowed) . . .

9.15c . . . then remove the door window glass guide channel

cable ties securing the release cable to the door and wiring harness **(see illustration)**.

14 Pull out the locking clip and disconnect the wiring connector from the door lock unit **(see illustrations)**.

15 Undo the retaining bolts and remove the door window glass rear upper guide channel **(see illustrations)**.

16 Using a small screwdriver, open the retaining clip and detach the exterior handle operating rod from the door lock lever **(see illustration 9.2)**.

17 Undo the three bolts and remove the door lock unit, complete with interior release handle and cable, from the door **(see illustrations)**.

18 To remove the release cable from the lock unit, depress the locating tab to release the outer cable from the lock bracket **(see illustration)**.

19 Lift the outer cable from the lock bracket, then disengage the inner cable from the lock lever **(see illustration)**.

Refitting

20 Refitting is a reversal of removal.

10 Front door – removal, refitting and adjustment

Removal

1 Move the driver's seat fully forward, open the battery box cover and disconnect the battery negative terminal (refer to *Disconnecting the battery* in the Reference Chapter).

2 Open the door, and position a suitable padded jack or support blocks underneath it; don't lift the door, just take its weight.

3 Undo the two screws and remove the door

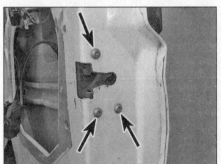

9.17a Undo the three bolts (arrowed) . . .

check strap bracket from the body pillar **(see illustration)**.

4 Disconnect the door wiring harness connector.

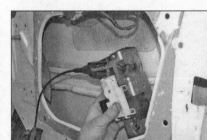

9.17b . . . and remove the door lock unit, complete with interior release handle and cable

9.18 Depress the locating tab to release the outer cable from the lock bracket . . .

9.19 . . . then disengage the inner cable from the lock lever

10.3 Undo the two screws (arrowed) and remove the door check strap bracket from the body pillar

5 Extract the circlips from the upper and lower door hinge pins **(see illustration)**.

6 Have an assistant support the door, then drive out the two hinge pins, and remove the door.

10.5 Extract the circlips (arrowed) from the upper and lower door hinge pins

Refitting and adjustment

7 Refitting is a reversal of removal. Open and shut the door to ensure that it does not bind with the body aperture at any point. Adjust the door striker plate if necessary.

11 Sliding side door fittings – removal and refitting

Exterior handle

Removal

1 Remove the door inner trim panel as described in Section 8.

2 Release the operating cable end fitting from the handle lever, then remove the outer cable from the handle bracket **(see illustrations)**.

3 Undo the handle retaining nut and remove the bracket, then withdraw the handle from the door **(see illustration)**.

Refitting

4 Refitting is a reversal of removal.

Door lock cylinder

Note: *A door lock cylinder is not fitted to vehicles with central locking.*

Removal

5 Remove the door inner trim panel as described in Section 8.

6 Extract the circlip securing the lock cylinder to the door.

7 Insert the ignition key into the lock cylinder and rotate it clockwise.

8 Insert a 2.5 mm drill bit into the hole in the side of the door lock to release the lock cylinder.

9 Rotate the lock cylinder anti-clockwise and remove it from the door.

Refitting

10 Refitting is a reversal of removal.

Door lock unit

Removal

11 Remove the door inner trim panel as described in Section 8.

12 Remove the sliding door lock knob **(see illustration)**.

13 On vehicles without central locking, remove the door lock cylinder as described previously.

14 Make sure the door lock is in the locked position, then undo the three bolts securing the lock to the door **(see illustration)**.

15 Withdraw the lock unit from its location and, on vehicles with central locking, disconnect the wiring connector from the central locking actuator **(see illustrations)**.

16 Note the fitted position of the exterior handle operating cable end fitting, then open the clip and disconnect the end fitting from the lock lever **(see illustration)**. Slip the outer cable out of the lock bracket.

17 Detach the interior release handle operating cable from the lock bracket, then slide the inner cable end fitting out of the bellcrank **(see illustrations)**.

18 Remove the door lock unit and, where applicable, undo the two bolts and remove the central locking actuator from the lock unit.

11.2a Release the operating cable end fitting (arrowed) from the handle lever . . .

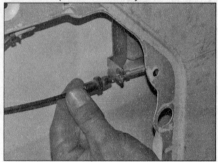

11.2b . . . then remove the outer cable from the handle bracket

11.3a Undo the handle retaining nut and remove the bracket . . .

11.3b . . . then withdraw the handle from the door

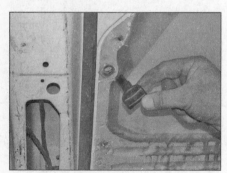

11.12 Remove the sliding door lock knob

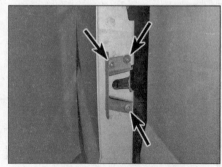

11.14 Undo the three bolts (arrowed) securing the lock to the door

11.15a Withdraw the lock unit from its location . . .

11.15b . . . and, where applicable, disconnect the wiring connector

11.16 Open the clip and disconnect the operating cable end fitting from the lock lever

Refitting

19 Refitting is a reversal of removal.

Interior release handle

Removal

20 Remove the door inner trim panel as described in Section 8.
21 Disconnect the interior release handle operating cable from the door lock unit as described in paragraphs 12 to 17.
22 Remove the trim covers over the interior release handle retaining bolts, then undo the two bolts and remove the handle and operating cable from the door **(see illustrations)**.

Refitting

23 Refitting is a reversal of removal.

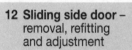

12 Sliding side door –
removal, refitting and adjustment

Removal

Note: *Before slackening any retaining bolts, make alignment marks on the guide supports to aid alignment when refitting.*
1 Undo the retaining nut/bolt, and remove the end stop from the centre rail.
2 Slide the door open, and unscrew the bolts securing the door lower guide support.
3 Enlist the aid of an assistant to support the weight of the door on the centre rail, then remove the bolts securing the upper guide support **(see illustration)**.
4 Support the door at each end, slide it to the rear, and remove it from the vehicle.

Refitting

5 Refitting is a reversal of removal. Align the door and engage it onto the centre track, then reconnect the fittings.

Adjustment

6 Check the door for satisfactory flush-fitting adjustment. Adjust if necessary by loosening off the lower support bolts to reposition the door as required, then tighten them and recheck the fitting.
7 To adjust the height, loosen off the upper support locknut, turn the adjuster bolt

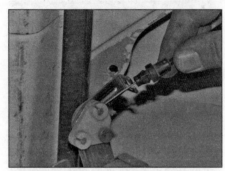

11.17a Detach the interior release handle operating cable from the lock bracket . . .

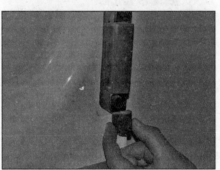

11.22a Remove the trim covers over the interior release handle retaining bolts . . .

as required, then retighten the locknut to secure.
8 When fitted, and in the closed position, the door should be aligned flush to the

12.3 Sliding side door upper guide support retaining bolts (arrowed)

11.17b . . . then slide the inner cable end fitting out of the bellcrank

11.22b . . . then undo the two bolts and remove the handle and operating cable from the door

surrounding body, and should close securely. If required, adjust the striker plate position to suit.

13 Rear door fittings –
removal and refitting

Exterior handle (right-hand door)

Removal

1 Remove the rear door trim panel as described in Section 8.
2 Using a small screwdriver, open the retaining clip and detach the door lock operating rod from the exterior handle **(see illustration)**.
3 Drill out the two pop rivets, and remove

13.2 Open the retaining clip and detach the door lock operating rod from the exterior handle

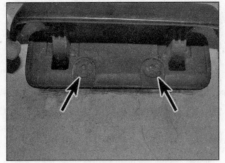

13.3 Right-hand rear door exterior handle pop rivets (arrowed)

13.6 Detach the inner cable end fittings (arrowed) from the handle lever

13.7 Left-hand rear door exterior handle pop rivets (arrowed)

the exterior handle from the door **(see illustration)**.

Refitting

4 Refitting is a reversal of removal, using new pop rivets.

Exterior handle (left-hand door)

Removal

5 Remove the rear door trim panel as described in Section 8.

6 Detach the latch operating cables from the exterior handle bracket, then detach the inner cable end fittings from the handle lever **(see illustration)**.

7 Drill out the two pop rivets, and remove the exterior handle from the door **(see illustration)**.

Refitting

8 Refitting is a reversal of removal, using new pop rivets.

13.22 Undo the two bolts (arrowed) securing the lower latch to the door

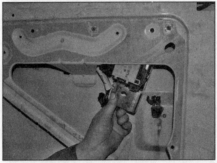

13.16 Undo the four bolts and remove the door lock through the door aperture

Door lock cylinder

Removal and refitting

9 Proceed as described in Section 11, paragraphs 5 to 10.

Door lock unit

Removal

10 Remove the door inner trim panel as described in Section 8.

11 Using a small screwdriver, open the retaining clip and detach the door lock operating rod from the exterior handle **(see illustration 13.2)**.

12 On vehicles without central locking, remove the door lock cylinder as described previously.

13 On vehicles with central locking, disconnect the wiring connector from the central locking actuator.

14 On high-roof vehicles, detach the lock upper latch operating cable from the upper

13.23 Detach the latch operating cable from the latch bracket, then detach the inner cable end fitting from the latch lever

bracket, then detach the inner cable end fitting from the latch lever.

15 Where fitted detach the rear door lock knob.

16 Undo the four bolts securing the lock to the door, lower the lock unit and remove it through the door aperture **(see illustration)**.

Refitting

17 Refitting is a reversal of removal.

Lock upper latch

Removal

18 Detach the latch operating cable from the latch bracket, then detach the inner cable end fitting from the latch lever.

19 Undo the two bolts and remove the latch from the door.

Refitting

20 Refitting is a reversal of removal.

Lock lower latch

Removal

21 Remove the door inner trim panel as described in Section 8.

22 Undo the two bolts securing the latch to the door **(see illustration)**.

23 Detach the latch operating cable from the latch bracket, then detach the inner cable end fitting from the latch lever **(see illustration)**. Remove the lower latch from the door.

Refitting

24 Refitting is a reversal of removal.

14 Rear doors – removal, refitting and adjustment

Removal

1 Open the rear doors. If removing the left-hand rear door, remove its inner trim panel (Section 8).

2 Undo the two bolts and detach the check strap from the body **(see illustration)**. Disconnect the wiring from the appropriate fitting(s) in the door (as applicable), and withdraw the loom from the door.

3 Mark around the periphery of each door hinge with a suitable marker pen, to show

14.2 Undo the two bolts and detach the rear door check strap

14.3a Rear door hinge lower retaining bolts (arrowed) . . .

14.3b . . . and upper retaining bolts (arrowed)

the fitted position of the hinges when refitting the door. Have an assistant support the door, undo the retaining bolts from each hinge, and withdraw the door (see illustrations).

Refitting and adjustment

4 Refitting is a reversal of removal. Align the hinges with the previously-made marks, then tighten the bolts. Ensure that the check strap is central with the door when reconnected.

5 Open and shut the doors, and ensure that they don't bind with the body aperture at any point. Adjust the door hinges and striker plate if necessary, to provide an even clearance all round.

15 Tailgate fittings – removal and refitting

Exterior handle

Removal

1 Remove the tailgate inner trim panel as described in Section 8.

2 Using a small screwdriver, open the retaining clip and detach the lock operating rod from the exterior handle.

3 Disconnect the wiring connectors from the number plate bulb holders.

4 Undo the two nuts and remove the number plate panel.

5 Undo the nuts securing the exterior handle to the tailgate. With the handle in the open position, rotate it to one side and remove it from the tailgate.

Refitting

6 Refitting is a reversal of removal.

Tailgate lock cylinder

Removal

7 Remove the tailgate inner trim panel as described in Section 8.

8 Extract the circlip securing the lock cylinder to the tailgate.

9 Insert the ignition key into the lock cylinder and rotate it clockwise.

10 Insert a thin screwdriver into the hole in the side of the lock to depress the tang and release the lock cylinder.

11 Rotate the lock cylinder anti-clockwise and remove it from the door.

Refitting

12 Refitting is a reversal of removal.

Tailgate lock unit

Removal

13 Remove the tailgate inner trim panel as described in Section 8.

14 On vehicles without central locking, remove the door lock cylinder as described previously.

15 On vehicles with central locking, disconnect the wiring connector from the central locking actuator.

16 Using a small screwdriver, open the retaining clip and detach the lock operating rod from the exterior handle.

17 Undo the three bolts and remove the lock unit from the tailgate.

Refitting

18 Refitting is a reversal of removal.

16 Tailgate – removal, refitting and adjustment

Removal

1 The aid of two assistants will be required to support the tailgate as it is removed. First open the tailgate, then support it in the open position and detach the wiring harness at the multi-plug connectors in the body. Pull the wiring loom through the body, and leave it attached to the tailgate.

2 Where applicable, disconnect the rear window washer hose.

3 Loosen off the tailgate hinge bolts, and have the two assistants support the weight of the tailgate.

4 Prise up the retaining clips securing the tailgate strut balljoints, and detach the balljoint from the stud each side. Take care not to lift the clips by more than 4 mm.

5 Unscrew the hinge bolts and remove the tailgate.

Refitting

6 Refit the tailgate in the reverse order of removal. Press the strut balljoints onto their studs, using hand pressure only. Note that the struts are gas-filled, and therefore cannot be repaired. If renewing them, be sure to obtain the correct replacements.

Adjustment

7 When the tailgate is refitted, check its adjustment and if necessary re-adjust as follows.

Height adjustment

8 Loosen off the hinge retaining bolts, and reset the tailgate at the required height to suit the latch/striker engagement and the body aperture, then fully retighten the bolts.

Side clearance adjustment

9 Loosen off the tailgate side bump guides, the striker plate and the hinge bolts. Centralise the tailgate in its aperture, then retighten the hinge bolts. If required, re-adjust the position of the striker plate so that the tailgate closes securely. Now adjust the position of the side bump guides so that they only just contact the D-pillar bumpers when the tailgate is set at the safety catch position, and only make full contact when the tailgate is closed.

17 Front door window glass – removal and refitting

Removal

1 Remove the door inner trim panel as described in Section 8.

2 On vehicles with electric windows, disconnect the one-touch down relay wiring connector (if fitted).

3 Temporarily refit the window regulator handle, or reconnect the wiring connector at the electric window switch, as applicable.

4 Position the window glass so that the rivets securing the base of the glass to the regulator lifting channel are accessible through the door aperture.

5 Drill out the two pop rivets securing the window glass to the regulator lifting channel. Slide the window glass up and retain it in the closed position using masking tape over the top of the door frame.

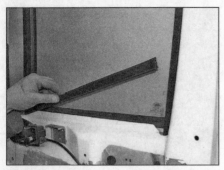

17.8 Remove the inner waist seal from the top edge of the door panel

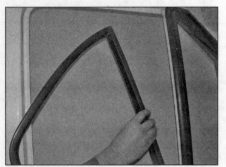

17.9b ... then pull the complete weather-strip from its location, and remove it from the door

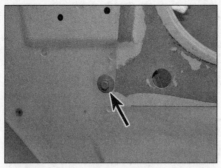

17.9a Undo the window glass inner guide channel retaining bolt (arrowed) ...

17.10 Carefully lift the window glass up and out towards the inside of the door

6 Undo the three bolts and remove the window glass outer guide channel from the door **(see illustrations 9.15a to 9.15c)**.

7 Remove the masking tape and carefully lower the window glass to the base of the door.

8 Remove the inner waist seal from the top edge of the door panel **(see illustration)**.

9 Undo the window glass inner guide channel retaining bolt, then starting from the top centre and working around the window aperture, pull the complete weatherstrip from its location, and remove it from the door **(see illustrations)**.

10 Carefully lift the window glass up and out towards the inside of the door **(see illustration)**.

11 Clean out the remains of the old rivets from inside the door.

18.3 Front door window regulator pop rivets (arrowed)

Refitting

12 Refitting is a reversal of removal using new rivets to secure the window glass to the regulator. When refitting the weatherstrip, engage the front lower corner first, then work round ensuring correct seating. Before refitting the door trim panel, raise and lower the window to ensure that it operates in a satisfactory manner.

18 Front door window regulator – removal and refitting

Removal

1 Remove the front door window glass as described in Section 17.

2 On vehicles with electric windows, disconnect the regulator motor wiring connector.

3 Drill out the four pop rivets (manual windows) or drill out the two pop rivets and undo the two nuts (electric windows) securing the window regulator to the door **(see illustration)**.

4 Manipulate the regulator assembly out through the door aperture.

5 Clean out the remains of the old rivets from inside the door.

Refitting

6 Refitting is a reversal of removal using new rivets to secure the regulator to the door.

19 Front door quarter glass – removal and refitting

Removal

1 Undo the screw, detach the retaining clips and remove the front door exterior trim panel.

2 Press the glass outwards using firm hand pressure, whilst simultaneously pulling free the rubber weatherstrip from the top corner. As the glass is extracted from the door, push it firmly, in a progressive manner, clear along its edges from the inside out until finally it can be removed.

Refitting

3 First loop a length of strong cord into the weatherstrip groove, so that the cord ends are at the lower corners. Passing the cord through the aperture of the window, locate the lower edges of the weatherstrip over the flange of the aperture, then press the glass inwards and simultaneously pull the cord to progressively locate the weatherstrip over the window aperture flange. Apply a progressive and continuous pressure until the window and weatherstrip are fully engaged in the aperture, at which point the cord will pull free.

4 Refit the exterior trim panel to complete.

20 Windscreen/tailgate and fixed/sliding windows – removal and refitting

The windscreen, tailgate and fixed/sliding side window assemblies are direct-glazed to the body, using special adhesive. Purpose-made tools are required to remove the old glass and fit the new glass, and therefore this work is best entrusted to a specialist.

21 Exterior mirrors – removal and refitting

Removal

Note: *The mirror can only be removed and refitted as a complete assembly. Replacement of the mirror glass separately is not possible.*

1 Using a small screwdriver, carefully prise out the direction indicator side repeater from the mirror surround **(see illustration)**. Disconnect the wiring connector and remove the side repeater.

2 Carefully prise off the trim caps over the mirror base retaining bolts **(see illustration)**.

3 Undo the three bolts securing the mirror base to the front door, taking care not to drop the bolts into the inside of the door **(see illustration)**.

4 Remove the mirror assembly from the door and disconnect the wiring connector **(see illustration)**.

Refitting

5 Refitting is a reversal of removal.

22 Front bumper –
removal and refitting

Removal

1 Firmly apply the handbrake, then jack up the front of the vehicle and support it securely on axle stands (see *Jacking and vehicle support*).
2 Where applicable, disconnect the wiring connectors at the front fog lights.
3 From under the wheel arch on each side, remove the side attachments to the front panel and wing by removing the clip (where fitted) and undoing the retaining screw **(see illustration)**.
4 Undo the two bolts each side and remove the bumper cover from the vehicle **(see illustration)**.
5 To remove the bumper brace, undo the two power steering fluid cooler mounting bolts and lower the fluid cooler from its location **(see illustration)**.
6 Undo the two bolts each side and remove the bumper brace from the vehicle **(see illustration)**.

Refitting

7 Refitting is a reversal of removal. Align the bumper correctly before fully tightening the retaining bolts.

23 Rear bumper –
removal and refitting

Removal

1 Drill out the pop rivets securing the upper edge of the bumper centre section to the body **(see illustration)**.
2 Undo the bolts securing the underside of the bumper centre section to the body **(see illustration)**.

21.1 Carefully prise out the direction indicator side repeater from the mirror surround

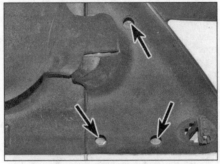

21.3 Undo the three bolts (arrowed) securing the mirror base to the front door

3 Release the retaining clips and pull the bumper centre section rearwards to remove.
4 Drill out the rivets securing the bumper end caps to the body and to the edge of the wheel arch **(see illustrations)**.

22.3 Remove the front attachments by removing the clip (where fitted) and undoing the retaining screw (arrowed)

22.5 Power steering fluid cooler mounting bolts (arrowed)

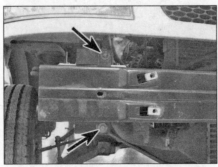

22.6 Undo the two bolts (arrowed) each side and remove the bumper brace

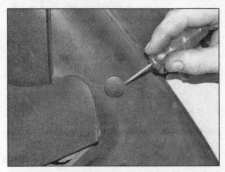

21.2 Prise off the trim caps over the mirror base retaining bolts

21.4 Remove the mirror assembly from the door and disconnect the wiring connector

5 Release the retaining clips and pull the bumper end caps rearwards to remove.
6 If required, undo the two bolts each side and remove the bumper brace from the vehicle.

22.4 Undo the two bolts (arrowed) each side and remove the front bumper cover

23.1 Drill out the pop rivets securing the upper edge of the rear bumper centre section to the body

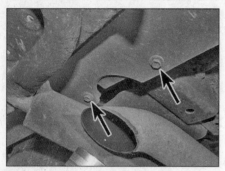

23.2 Undo the bolts (arrowed) securing the underside of the bumper centre section to the body

23.4a Drill out the rivets securing the bumper end caps to the body (arrowed) . . .

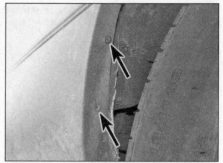

23.4b . . . and to the edge of the wheel arch (arrowed)

Refitting

7 Refitting is a reversal of removal, using new pop rivets.

24 Radiator grille opening panel – removal and refitting

Removal

1 Move the driver's seat fully forward, open the battery box cover and disconnect the battery negative terminal (refer to *Disconnecting the battery* in the Reference Chapter).
2 Remove the front bumper and the bumper brace as described in Section 22.

3 Undo the three retaining bolts each side securing the upper edges of the front wings in position **(see illustration)**.
4 Undo the two bolts each side securing the lower edges of the front wings to the underbody **(see illustration)**.
5 Using a suitable prop, support the bonnet in the open position.
6 Lift the power steering fluid reservoir out of its mounting bracket and position it to one side **(see illustration)**.
7 Undo the bolt securing the air cleaner air intake duct to the radiator grille opening panel and remove the intake duct.
8 Undo the two bolts securing the front of the fuse/relay box to the radiator grille opening panel **(see illustration)**.

9 Undo the bolt securing the bonnet lock brace to the radiator support bracket **(see illustration)**.
10 Undo the two bolts each side securing the radiator grille opening panel to the side members **(see illustration)**.
11 Undo the two bolts each side securing the radiator grille opening panel to the front wing apron panels **(see illustration)**.
12 With the help of an assistant, carefully push the front wings outward slightly and lift the radiator grille opening panel upwards and forwards **(see illustration)**. When sufficient clearance exists, disconnect the wiring connectors at the rear of the headlights, then remove the opening panel from the vehicle.

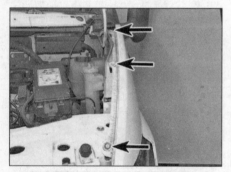

24.3 Undo the three retaining bolts (arrowed) each side securing the upper edges of the front wings in position

24.4 Undo the two bolts (arrowed) each side securing the lower edges of the front wings to the underbody

24.6 Lift the power steering fluid reservoir out of its mounting bracket and position it to one side

24.8 Undo the two bolts (arrowed) securing the front of the fuse/relay box to the radiator grille opening panel

24.9 Undo the bolt (arrowed) securing the bonnet lock brace to the radiator support bracket

24.10 Undo the two bolts (arrowed) each side securing the radiator grille opening panel to the side members

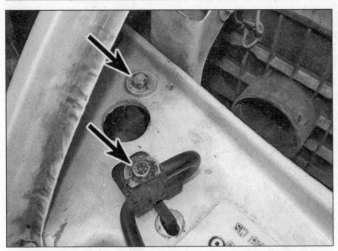

24.11 Undo the two bolts (arrowed) each side securing the radiator grille opening panel to the front wing apron panels

24.12 Carefully push the front wings outward slightly and lift the radiator grille opening panel upwards and forwards

Refitting

13 Refitting is a reversal of removal. Check the alignment of the front wings with the bonnet and surrounding panels when tightening the retaining bolts.

25 Windscreen cowl panel – removal and refitting

Removal

1 Remove the windscreen wiper arms as described in Chapter 12.
2 Extract the screw covers and unscrew the four windscreen cowl panel trim upper retaining screws (see illustrations).
3 Open and support the bonnet, then remove the bonnet weatherstrip from the cowl panel trim. Undo the retaining screw now exposed, at each end of the trim (see illustration).
4 On vehicles with common rail injection, detach the heat shield from the cowl panel.

5 Disconnect the windscreen washer hose, then remove the hose from the cowl panel.
6 Release the retaining clips and remove the cowl panel trim from the cowl panel.
7 Using a forked tool, extract the two retaining clips and detach the water drain tube from the cowl panel (see illustration).

8 Undo the screw each side securing the A-pillar exterior trim to the body (see illustration).
9 Unscrew the windscreen wiper motor mounting bracket retaining bolt from the cowl panel (see illustration).
10 Unscrew the two bolts at each side, and

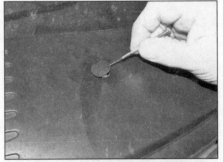

25.2a Extract the screw covers . . .

25.2b . . . and unscrew the windscreen cowl panel trim upper retaining screws (arrowed)

25.3 Remove the bonnet weatherstrip from the cowl panel trim and undo the retaining screw (arrowed) at each end

25.7 Using a forked tool, extract the two retaining clips and detach the water drain tube from the cowl panel

25.8 Undo the screw (arrowed) each side securing the A-pillar exterior trim to the body

25.9 Unscrew the windscreen wiper motor mounting bracket retaining bolt (arrowed) from the cowl panel

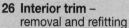

26 Interior trim –
removal and refitting

Door trim panels

1 Refer to the procedures contained in Section 8.

A-pillar trim

Removal

2 Pull the upper edge of the trim away from the pillar to disengage the retaining clips, then lift the trim up to disengage the lower lugs from the facia **(see illustrations)**.

Refitting

3 Refitting is a reversal of removal.

B-pillar trim

Removal

4 Lift the plastic cover off the seat belt upper mounting, then unscrew the upper mounting bolt **(see illustrations)**.

5 Using a small screwdriver, extract the horseshoe-shaped wire retaining clip from the slot on the underside of the seat height adjust levers, then withdraw the levers from the spindles **(see illustrations)**.

6 Undo the two screws and remove the seat base panel **(see illustrations)**.

7 Undo the seat belt lower mounting bolt from the base of the seat **(see illustration)**.

25.10a Unscrew the two bolts (arrowed) at each side . . .

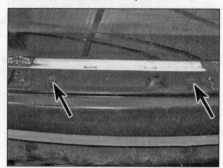

25.10b . . . and the bolts along the top (arrowed) and remove the cowl panel from the body

Refitting

11 Refitting is a reversal of removal.

the bolts along the top and remove the cowl panel from the body **(see illustrations)**.

26.2a Pull the upper edge of the A-pillar trim away from the pillar to disengage the retaining clips . . .

26.2b . . . then lift the trim up to disengage the lower lugs from the facia

26.4a Lift the plastic cover off the seat belt upper mounting . . .

26.4b . . . then unscrew the upper mounting bolt

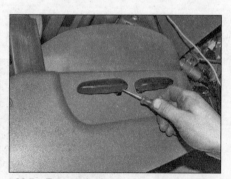

26.5a Extract the horseshoe-shaped wire retaining clip from the slot on the underside of the seat height adjust levers . . .

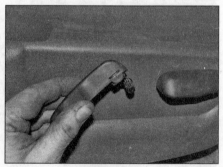

26.5b . . . then withdraw the levers from the spindles

26.6a Undo the two screws (arrowed) . . .

26.6b . . . and remove the seat base panel

26.7 Undo the seat belt lower mounting bolt (arrowed) from the base of the seat

Ensure that the spacer and paper washer remain in place on the mounting bolt when it is removed.

8 Undo the three upper screws and two lower screws and withdraw the trim from the B-pillar **(see illustrations)**. Feed the seat belt through the opening in the trim and remove the trim from the vehicle.

Refitting

9 Refitting is a reversal of removal, ensuring that the seat belt mountings are tightened to the specified torque.

Loadspace trim

Removal

10 The loadspace trim panels are secured by a combination of screws and plastic retaining clips, the removal of which requires the use of a suitable forked tool **(see illustration 8.10)**. These clips are easily broken, so take care when prising them free.

11 Remove the rear seats, where applicable, for access to the panel attachments.

12 Release the panel retaining clips and screws, and withdraw the panel.

Refitting

13 Refitting is a reversal of removal.

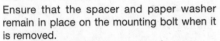

27 Seats –
removal and refitting

Driver's seat

Removal

1 Using a small screwdriver, extract the horseshoe-shaped wire retaining clip from the slot on the underside of the seat height adjust levers, then withdraw the levers from the spindles **(see illustrations 26.5a and 26.5b)**.

2 Undo the two screws and remove the seat base panel **(see illustrations 26.6a and 26.6b)**.

3 Undo the seat belt lower mounting bolt from the base of the seat **(see illustration 26.7)**. Ensure that the spacer and paper washer remain in place on the mounting bolt when it is removed.

4 Disconnect the heated seat wiring connectors (where fitted).

26.8a Undo the B-pillar trim retaining screws (upper screws arrowed) . . .

5 Move the seat fully to the rear and undo the two front seat rail retaining bolts **(see illustration)**.

6 Move the seat fully to the front and undo the three rear seat rail retaining bolts each side, then remove the seat from the vehicle **(see illustration)**.

Refitting

7 Refitting is a reversal of removal.

Front passenger's seat

8 Where fitted, undo the three fasteners and remove the seat lower panel.

9 Undo the seat belt lower mounting bolt from the base of the seat **(see illustration)**. Ensure that the spacer and paper washer remain in place on the mounting bolt when it is removed.

10 Extract the retaining clips above, and

26.8b . . . and withdraw the trim from the B-pillar

undo the two nuts below, and remove the step well **(see illustrations)**.

11 Undo the inner and outer bolts securing

27.5 Driver's seat front seat rail retaining bolt (arrowed)

27.6 Driver's seat rear seat rail retaining bolts (two of three arrowed)

27.9 Undo the seat belt lower mounting bolt from the base of the front passenger's seat

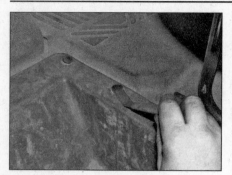

27.10a Extract the retaining clips above . . .

2710b . . . and undo the two nuts below (arrowed – shown with step well removed) and remove the step well

27.11 Front passenger's seat outer retaining bolts (arrowed)

the seat frame to the floor and remove the seat from the vehicle **(see illustration)**.

Refitting

12 Refitting is a reversal of removal.

Rear seats

13 Various combinations of rear seats may be fitted, according to vehicle type and specification. The removal and refitting procedures are essentially the same as those described previously for the front seats.

28 Seat belt components – removal and refitting

Front seat belt

Removal

1 Remove the B-pillar trim as described in Section 26.
2 Undo the retaining bolt and remove the inertia reel from the B-pillar **(see illustration)**.

Refitting

3 Refitting is a reversal of removal, ensuring that the tag on the inertia reel engages correctly in the B-pillar. Tighten the retaining bolts to the specified torque.

Front centre seat belt

4 On vehicles equipped with a double front passenger's seat, the seat belt inertia reel is fitted internally within the seat. To

remove and refit the inertia reel, the seat must be dismantled which entails the use of Ford special tools and equipment. It is recommended that this task is entrusted to a Ford dealer

Rear seat belt

Removal

5 Undo the seat belt lower mounting bolt from the base of the seat. Ensure that the spacer and paper washer remain in place on the mounting bolt when it is removed.
6 Lift the plastic covers off the seat belt upper mountings, then unscrew the upper mounting bolts.
7 Remove the inertia reel cover and feed the seat belt through the opening in the cover.
8 Undo the retaining bolt and remove the inertia reel from the seat.

Refitting

9 Refitting is a reversal of removal, ensuring that the tag on the inertia reel engages correctly in the seat. Tighten the retaining bolts to the specified torque.

Seat belt stalks

10 Various combinations of seat belt stalks may be fitted, according to vehicle type and specification. The removal and refitting procedures are essentially self-explanatory, but it may be necessary in some instances to remove certain interior trim panels for access. Ensure that all attachment bolts are tightened to the specified torque when refitting.

29 Sunroof – general information

An electric sunroof was offered as an optional extra on certain models. Due to the complexity of the sunroof mechanism, considerable expertise is needed to repair, renew or adjust the sunroof components successfully. Removal of the roof first requires the headlining to be removed, which is a complex and tedious operation in itself, and not a task to be undertaken lightly. Therefore, any problems with the sunroof should be referred to a Ford dealer.

30 Facia panel components – removal and refitting

Steering column shrouds

Removal

1 Insert a thin screwdriver through the holes on the front face of the lower shroud and release the two upper shroud retaining clips, one each side. Lift the upper shroud off the lower shroud **(see illustrations)**.
2 Undo the three retaining screws and remove the lower shroud from the steering column **(see illustrations)**.

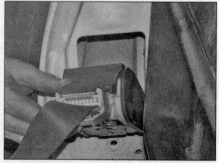

28.2 Undo the retaining bolt and remove the front seat belt inertia reel from the B-pillar

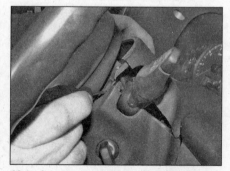

30.1a Insert a screwdriver through the holes on the lower shroud and release the two upper shroud retaining clips, one each side

30.1b Lift the upper shroud off the lower shroud

30.2a Undo the three retaining screws
(arrowed) . . .

30.2b . . . and remove the lower shroud
from the steering column

30.5a Undo the two upper screws
(arrowed) . . .

Refitting

3 Refitting is a reversal of removal.

Instrument panel surround

Removal

4 Remove the steering column shrouds as described previously.
5 Undo the two upper screws and two lower screws securing the surround to the facia **(see illustrations)**.
6 Pull the surround away from the facia to release the retaining clips and remove the surround from the facia **(see illustration)**.

Refitting

7 Refitting is a reversal of removal.

Facia centre panel

Removal

8 Move the driver's seat fully forward, open the battery box cover and disconnect the battery negative terminal (refer to *Disconnecting the battery* in the Reference Chapter).
9 Remove the instrument panel surround as described previously.
10 Remove the radio/cassette/CD player as described in Chapter 12.
11 Undo the two screws securing the lower edge of the centre panel to the facia **(see illustrations)**.
12 Undo the two screws securing the centre panel to the facia on the driver's side **(see illustration)**.
13 On the passenger's side, undo the screw

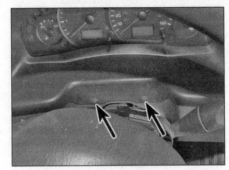

30.5b . . . and the two lower screws
(arrowed) securing the instrument panel
surround to the facia

at the base of the storage tray and remove the tray from the facia **(see illustrations)**.

30.11a Undo the left-hand screw . . .

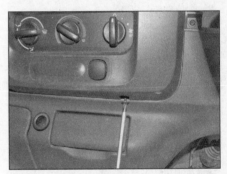

30.6 Pull the surround away from the facia
to release the retaining clips and remove
the surround from the facia

14 Undo the screw now exposed in the storage tray aperture **(see illustration)**.

30.11b . . . and right-hand screw securing
the lower edge of the centre panel to the
facia

30.12 Undo the two screws (arrowed)
securing the centre panel to the facia on
the driver's side

30.13a Undo the screw at the base of the
storage tray . . .

30.13b . . . and remove the tray from the
facia

30.14 Undo the screw now exposed (arrowed) in the storage tray aperture

30.15a Withdraw the centre panel from the facia . . .

30.15b . . . and disconnect the wiring connectors at the rear

30.19a Undo the lower retaining screw . . .

30.19b . . . and the two upper retaining screws (arrowed) securing the switch/vent panel to the facia

30.20 Withdraw the switch/vent panel from the facia and disconnect the switch wiring connectors at the rear

15 Withdraw the centre panel from the facia and disconnect the wiring connectors at the rear **(see illustrations)**.

Refitting

16 Refitting is a reversal of removal.

Driver's side switch/vent panel

Removal

17 Move the driver's seat fully forward, open the battery box cover and disconnect the battery negative terminal (refer to *Disconnecting the battery* in the Reference Chapter).

18 Remove the instrument panel surround as described previously.

19 Undo the lower retaining screw and the two upper retaining screws securing the switch/vent panel to the facia **(see illustrations)**.

20 Withdraw the switch/vent panel from

the facia and disconnect the switch wiring connectors at the rear **(see illustration)**.

Refitting

21 Refitting is a reversal of removal.

Complete facia assembly

Removal

22 Move the driver's seat fully forward, open the battery box cover and disconnect the battery negative terminal (refer to *Disconnecting the battery* in the Reference Chapter).

23 Remove the A-pillar trim panels on both sides as described in Section 26.

24 Remove the following facia panels as described previously in this Section:
 a) *Steering column shrouds.*
 b) *Instrument panel surround.*
 c) *Facia centre panel.*

 d) *Driver's side switch/vent panel.*

25 Remove the following components as described in Chapter 12:
 a) *Instrument panel.*
 b) *Tachograph (where fitted).*
 c) *Radio/cassette/CD player.*

26 Undo the four steering column retaining nuts and lower the steering column from its location **(see illustrations)**. Note that new nuts will be required for refitting.

27 Undo the four screws securing the heater control panel to the facia **(see illustration)**.

28 Remove the ashtray, and disconnect the wiring connector from the cigarette lighter **(see illustrations)**.

29 Lift out the storage tray from the top of the facia **(see illustration)**.

30 On vehicles with a passenger's airbag, disconnect the airbag wiring connector.

30.26a Steering column upper retaining bolts (arrowed) . . .

30.26b . . . and lower retaining bolts (arrowed)

30.27 Undo the four screws (arrowed) securing the heater control panel to the facia

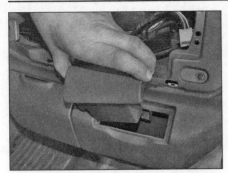

30.28a Remove the ashtray . . .

30.28b . . . and disconnect the wiring
connector from the cigarette lighter

30.29 Lift out the storage tray from the top
of the facia

30.31 Undo the four bolts (arrowed)
securing the fuse/relay box mounting
bracket to the facia

30.32a Release the retaining clips
and detach the fuse relay box and the
additional relay holder from the mounting
bracket . . .

30.32b . . . then remove the bracket

31 Working through the storage tray aperture, undo the four bolts securing the fuse/relay box mounting bracket to the facia (see illustration).
32 Release the retaining clips and detach the fuse relay box and the additional relay holder from the mounting bracket, then remove the bracket (see illustrations).
33 Disconnect the wiring connector from the power socket.
34 Lift off the trim covers and remove the facia upper retaining bolts (see illustrations).
35 Undo the six bolts securing the facia lower support bracket to the bulkhead (see illustration).
36 Release the retaining clips and remove the finisher panels from the facia on both sides (see illustration).
37 Using a small screwdriver, release the

bolt covers from the facia on both sides (see illustration).

38 Undo the two outer mounting bolts from the facia on both sides (see illustration).

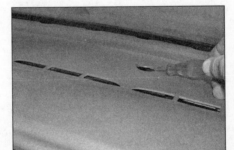

30.34a Lift off the trim covers . . .

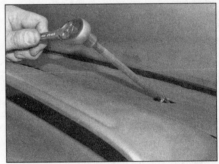

30.34b . . . and remove the facia upper
retaining bolts

30.35 Undo the six bolts (arrowed)
securing the facia lower support bracket
to the bulkhead

30.36 Release the retaining clips and
remove the finisher panels from the facia
on both sides

30.37 Using a small screwdriver, release
the bolt covers from the facia on both
sides

30.38 Undo the two outer mounting bolts (arrowed) from the facia on both sides

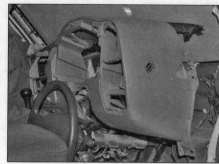

30.39 With the help of an assistant, carefully lift the facia from its location and remove it from the vehicle

39 Detach the ventilation ducts from the heater housing then, with the help of an assistant, carefully lift the facia from its location (**see illustration**). Check that all wiring has been disconnected, then remove the facia from the vehicle.

Refitting

40 Refitting is a reversal of removal ensuring that all wiring is correctly reconnected and all mountings securely tightened. Use new retaining nuts when refitting the steering column and tighten the nuts to the specified torque.

Chapter 12
Body electrical systems

Contents

Degrees of difficulty

Easy, suitable for novice with little experience	**Fairly easy,** suitable for beginner with some experience	**Fairly difficult,** suitable for competent DIY mechanic	**Difficult,** suitable for experienced DIY mechanic	**Very difficult,** suitable for expert DIY or professional

Specifications

Fuses and relays
Refer to the wiring diagrams at the end of this Chapter.

Bulbs
	Wattage
Direction indicator lights	21
Direction indicator side repeater lights	5
Front foglights	55
Headlights	60/55
High-level stop-light (5x)	5
Illuminated stepwell light	5
Interior lights	10
Number plate light (Chassis Cab models)	10
Number plate light (Van and Bus models with rear doors)	5
Number plate light (Van and Bus models with tailgate)	10
Rear foglights	21
Rear reading lights	5
Reversing lights	21
Sidelights	5
Side marker/direction indicator lights (Chassis Cab models)	21/5
Side marker lights (Jumbo Van models)	4
Stop-lights (Chassis Cab models)	21
Stop/tail lights (Van and Bus models)	21/5
Tail lights (Chassis Cab models)	10

Torque wrench settings
	Nm	lbf ft
Tailgate/rear window wiper arm nut	15	11
Windscreen wiper arm nuts	22	16
Windscreen wiper motor crank arm nut	26	19
Windscreen wiper motor-to-bracket bolts	12	9

1 General information and precautions

⚠️ *Warning: Before carrying out any work on the electrical system, read through the precautions given in 'Safety first!' at the beginning of this manual, and in Chapter 5.*

1 The electrical system is of the 12 volt negative earth type. Power for the lights and all electrical accessories is supplied by a lead-calcium type battery, which is charged by the engine-driven alternator.

2 This Chapter covers repair and service procedures for the various electrical components not associated with the engine. Information on the battery, alternator and starter motor can be found in Chapter 5.

3 It should be noted that, prior to working on any component in the electrical system, the battery negative terminal should first be disconnected, to prevent the possibility of electrical short-circuits and/or fires.

Caution: Before proceeding, refer to 'Disconnecting the battery' in the Reference Chapter for further information.

2 Electrical fault finding – general information

Note: *Refer to the precautions given in 'Safety first!' and in Section 1 of this Chapter before starting work. The following tests relate to testing of the main electrical circuits, and should not be used to test delicate electronic circuits, particularly where an electronic control module is used.*

General

1 A typical electrical circuit consists of an electrical component, any switches, relays, motors, fuses, fusible links or circuit breakers related to that component, and the wiring and connectors which link the component to both the battery and the chassis. To help to pinpoint a problem in an electrical circuit, wiring diagrams are included at the end of this Chapter.

2 Before attempting to diagnose an electrical fault, first study the appropriate wiring diagram, to obtain a complete understanding of the components included in the particular circuit concerned. The possible sources of a fault can be narrowed down by noting if other components related to the circuit are operating properly. If several components or circuits fail at one time, the problem is likely to be related to a shared fuse or earth connection.

3 Electrical problems usually stem from simple causes, such as loose or corroded connections, a faulty earth connection, a blown fuse, a melted fusible link, or a faulty relay (refer to Section 3 for details of testing relays). Visually inspect the condition of all fuses, wires and connections in a problem circuit before testing the components. Use the wiring diagrams to determine which terminal connections will need to be checked in order to pinpoint the trouble-spot.

4 The basic tools required for electrical fault-finding include a circuit tester or voltmeter (a 12-volt bulb with a set of test leads can also be used for certain tests); an ohmmeter (to measure resistance and check for continuity); a battery and set of test leads; and a jumper wire, preferably with a circuit breaker or fuse incorporated, which can be used to bypass suspect wires or electrical components. Before attempting to locate a problem with test instruments, use the wiring diagram to determine where to make the connections.

5 To find the source of an intermittent wiring fault (usually due to a poor or dirty connection, or damaged wiring insulation), a 'wiggle' test can be performed on the wiring. This involves wiggling the wiring by hand to see if the fault occurs as the wiring is moved. It should be possible to narrow down the source of the fault to a particular section of wiring. This method of testing can be used in conjunction with any of the tests described in the following sub-Sections.

6 Apart from problems due to poor connections, two basic types of fault can occur in an electrical circuit – open-circuit, or short-circuit.

7 Open-circuit faults are caused by a break somewhere in the circuit, which prevents current from flowing. An open-circuit fault will prevent a component from working.

8 Short-circuit faults are caused by a 'short' somewhere in the circuit, which allows the current flowing in the circuit to 'escape' along an alternative route, usually to earth. Short-circuit faults are normally caused by a breakdown in wiring insulation, which allows a feed wire to touch either another wire, or an earthed component such as the bodyshell. A short-circuit fault will normally cause the relevant circuit fuse to blow.

Finding an open-circuit

9 To check for an open-circuit, connect one lead of a circuit tester or the negative lead of a voltmeter either to the battery negative terminal or to a known good earth.

10 Connect the other lead to a connector in the circuit being tested, preferably nearest to the battery or fuse. At this point, battery voltage should be present, unless the lead from the battery or the fuse itself is faulty (bearing in mind that some circuits are live only when the ignition switch is moved to a particular position).

11 Switch on the circuit, then connect the tester lead to the connector nearest the circuit switch on the component side.

12 If voltage is present (indicated either by the tester bulb lighting or a voltmeter reading, as applicable), this means that the section of the circuit between the relevant connector and the switch is problem-free.

13 Continue to check the remainder of the circuit in the same fashion.

14 When a point is reached at which no voltage is present, the problem must lie between that point and the previous test point with voltage. Most problems can be traced to a broken, corroded or loose connection.

Finding a short-circuit

15 To check for a short-circuit, first disconnect the load(s) from the circuit (loads are the components which draw current from a circuit, such as bulbs, motors, heating elements, etc).

16 Remove the relevant fuse from the circuit, and connect a circuit tester or voltmeter to the fuse connections.

17 Switch on the circuit, bearing in mind that some circuits are live only when the ignition switch is moved to a particular position.

18 If voltage is present (indicated either by the tester bulb lighting or a voltmeter reading, as applicable), this means that there is a short-circuit.

19 If no voltage is present during this test, but the fuse still blows with the load(s) reconnected, this indicates an internal fault in the load(s).

Finding an earth fault

20 The battery negative terminal is connected to 'earth' – the metal of the engine/transmission and the vehicle body – and many systems are wired so that they only receive a positive feed, the current returning via the metal of the car body. This means that the component mounting and the body form part of that circuit. Loose or corroded mountings can therefore cause a range of electrical faults, ranging from total failure of a circuit, to a puzzling partial failure. In particular, lights may shine dimly (especially when another circuit sharing the same earth point is in operation), motors (eg wiper motors or the heater blower motor) may run slowly, and the operation of one circuit may have an apparently-unrelated effect on another. Note that on many vehicles, earth straps are used between certain components, such as the engine/transmission and the body, usually where there is no metal-to-metal contact between components, due to flexible rubber mountings, etc.

21 To check whether a component is properly earthed, disconnect the battery and connect one lead of an ohmmeter to a known good earth point. Connect the other lead to the wire or earth connection being tested. The resistance reading should be zero; if not, check the connection as follows.

22 If an earth connection is thought to be faulty, dismantle the connection, and clean both the bodyshell and the wire terminal (or the component earth connection mating surface) back to bare metal. Be careful to remove all traces of dirt and corrosion, then use a knife to trim away any paint, so that a clean metal-to-metal joint is made.

On reassembly, tighten the joint fasteners securely; if a wire terminal is being refitted, use serrated washers between the terminal and the bodyshell, to ensure a clean and secure connection. When the connection is remade, prevent the onset of corrosion in the future by applying a coat of petroleum jelly or silicone-based grease, or by spraying on (at regular intervals) a proprietary water-dispersant lubricant.

3 Fuses and relays – general information

Fuses

1 The main fuses, relays and timers are located in the fuse/relay box situated below the storage tray in the facia on the passenger's side. To gain access, lift out the storage tray, then release the clips and lift off the fuse/relay box cover **(see illustrations)**.

2 Additional fuses and relays are located in the fuse/relay box on the left-hand side of the engine compartment. To gain access, release the catches at the front and lift up the lid **(see illustration)**.

3 The respective fuses and relays are identified on the diagram on the inside surface of the fuse/relay box cover or lid. Each fuse is also marked with its rating. Plastic tweezers are attached to the inside face of the lid to remove and fit the fuses.

4 To remove a fuse, pull it out of the holder, preferably using the tweezers, then slide the fuse sideways from the tweezers. The wire within the fuse is clearly visible, and it will be broken if the fuse is blown **(see illustration)**.

5 Always renew a fuse with one of an identical rating. Never renew a fuse more than once without tracing the source of the trouble. The fuse rating is stamped on top of the fuse.

6 Fusible links are incorporated in the positive feed from the battery, their function being to protect the main wiring loom in the event of a short-circuit. When the links blow, all of the wiring circuits are disconnected, and will remain so until the cause of the malfunction is repaired and the link renewed.

Relays

7 A relay is an electrically-operated switch, which is used for the following reasons:

a) *A relay can switch a heavy current remotely from the circuit in which the current is flowing, allowing the use of lighter-gauge wiring and switch contacts.*

b) *A relay can receive more than one control input, unlike a mechanical switch.*

c) *A relay can have a timer function – for example an intermittent wiper delay.*

8 The relays and timers are located in the two fuse/relay boxes. The various relays can be removed from their respective locations by carefully pulling them from the sockets.

3.1a Lift out the storage tray . . .

3.1b . . . then release the clips and lift off the fuse/relay box cover

3.2 To gain access to the engine compartment fuse/relay box fuses, release the catches at the front and lift up the lid

9 If a system controlled by a relay becomes inoperative and the relay is suspect, listen to the relay as the circuit is operated. If the relay is functioning, it should be possible to hear it click as it is energised. If the relay proves satisfactory, the fault lies with the components or wiring of the system. If the relay is not being energised, then it is not receiving a main supply voltage or a switching voltage, or the relay is faulty.

4 Switches – removal and refitting

Note: *Disconnect the battery negative terminal (refer to 'Disconnecting the battery' in the Reference Chapter) before removing any switch, and reconnect the terminal after refitting.*

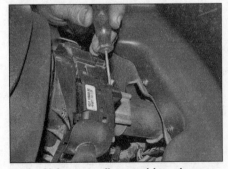

4.4a Using a small screwdriver, depress the locking tangs . . .

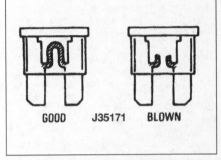

3.4 The fuses can be checked visually to determine if they are blown

Ignition switch/ steering column lock

1 Refer to Chapter 10.

Steering column multi-function switch

2 The steering column multi-function switch consists of left-hand and right-hand assemblies. The left-hand switch assembly comprises the headlight dip/flasher switch and the direction indicator switch; the right-hand switch assembly comprises the wiper/washer switch. The two halves can be removed and refitted independently of each other as follows.

3 Remove the steering column shrouds as described in Chapter 11.

4 Using a small screwdriver, depress the locking tangs and lift the switch upwards, out of the housing **(see illustrations)**.

4.4b . . . and lift the multi-function switch upwards, out of the housing

4.5 Disconnect the wiring connector and remove the switch

4.8 To remove the light control switch, undo the four screws (arrowed) at the rear of the panel, and remove the switch

individually removed. Should a switch become faulty, the complete control unit assembly must be renewed (see Chapter 3).

5 Instrument panel – removal and refitting

Removal

1 Move the driver's seat fully forward, open the battery box cover and disconnect the battery negative terminal (refer to *Disconnecting the battery* in the Reference Chapter).

2 Remove the instrument panel surround as described in Chapter 11.

3 Undo the screws securing the instrument panel to the facia. On pre-July 2003 vehicles there are four screws, and on July 2003 vehicles onward, there are two screws (see illustrations).

4 Withdraw the instrument panel from the facia and disconnect the wiring connector(s) at the rear of the panel (see illustration).

Refitting

5 Refitting is a reversal of removal.

4.12a Depress the retaining tabs at the rear of the relevant switch...

4.12b ... and withdraw the switch from the facia centre panel

5 Disconnect the wiring connector and remove the relevant switch (see illustration).

6 Refitting is a reversal of removal.

Facia side switches

7 Remove the driver's side switch/vent panel as described in Chapter 11.

8 To remove the light control switch, undo the four screws at the rear of the panel, and remove the switch (see illustration).

9 Depending on vehicle specification and equipment fitted, the remaining switches in the panel can be removed by undoing the retaining screws, or releasing the retaining clips.

10 Refitting is a reversal of removal.

Facia centre panel switches

11 Remove the facia centre panel as described in Chapter 11.

12 Depress the retaining tabs at the rear of

the relevant switch, and withdraw the switch from the panel (see illustrations).

13 Refitting is a reversal of removal.

Stop-light switch

14 Refer to Chapter 9.

Handbrake warning light switch

15 Refer to Chapter 9.

Electric window switch

16 Remove the front door trim panel as described in Chapter 11.

17 Depress the switch side catches and carefully remove the switch from the trim panel.

18 Refitting is a reversal of removal.

Heating/ventilation/ air conditioning system switches

19 The switches are all an integral part of the heating/ventilation control unit, and cannot be

6 Instrument panel components (pre-July 2003 vehicles) – removal and refitting

Note: *On vehicles manufactured from July 2003 onward, the instrument panel is a sealed assembly and cannot be dismantled.*

1 Remove the instrument panel as described in Section 5. When handling the instrument panel and removing or refitting its components, take care not to damage the printed circuit. Avoid knocking or dropping the unit, as it can easily be damaged.

Warning and illumination bulbs

2 Untwist the bulbholder, and withdraw it from the rear face of the panel. Remove the bulb from its holder.

3 Refitting is a reversal of removal.

Panel glass

4 Carefully pull off the odometer reset knob.

5 Release the locking tabs and remove the panel glass from the instrument panel.

6 Refitting is a reversal of removal.

5.3a Undo the left-hand (arrowed) ...

5.3b ... and right-hand (arrowed) screws securing the instrument panel to the facia

5.4 Withdraw the instrument panel from the facia and disconnect the wiring connector(s)

Speedometer head

7 Remove the panel glass, then undo the four screws and withdraw the speedometer head from the main panel.
8 Refitting is a reversal of removal.

Fuel and temperature gauges

9 Remove the panel glass, then undo the single screw securing each gauge. Withdraw the fuel or temperature gauge, as applicable, from the main panel.
10 Refitting is a reversal of removal.

Printed circuit

11 Remove the bulbholders, instruments and gauges as previously described.
12 Remove the gauge and instrument pin contacts from the printed circuit.
13 Remove the illumination cards from the printed circuit.
14 Carefully lift the printed circuit off the locating dowels, and remove it from the rear of the instrument panel.
15 Refitting is a reversal of removal.

7 Tachograph – removal and refitting

Removal

Note: *Two special tools, obtainable from most car accessory shops, are required for removal. Alternatively, suitable tools can be fabricated from 3 mm diameter wire, such as welding rod.*
1 Turn the ignition key to position II.
2 Press the eject button, then wait for the two sets of LEDs on the front of the unit to flash alternately.
3 Press the tachograph display, then carefully pull the unit open.
4 Turn the ignition key to position 0.
5 Insert the special tools into the holes on the front of the unit, and push them until they snap into place. The tachograph can then be slid out of the facia.
6 Disconnect the wiring connections at the rear of the unit, and remove the unit from the vehicle.
7 Remove the special tools.

Refitting

8 To refit the tachograph, reconnect the wiring and simply push the unit into the facia until the retaining lugs snap into place, then close the tachograph display.

8 Clock – removal and refitting

Removal

1 Remove the radio/cassette/CD player as described in Section 19.

10.2 Depress the tab and lift off the cover at the rear of the headlight unit

2 Reach up through the radio/cassette/CD player aperture and depress the clock retaining tangs.
3 Withdraw the clock from the facia and disconnect the wiring connector at the rear.

Refitting

4 Refitting is a reversal of removal.

9 Headlight/foglight beam alignment – general information

1 Accurate adjustment of the headlight/foglight beam is only possible using optical beam-setting equipment, and this work should therefore be carried out by a Ford dealer or suitably-equipped workshop.
2 Most models have an electrically-operated headlight beam adjustment system, controlled via a switch in the facia. With the vehicle unladen, the switch should be set in position '0'. With the vehicle partially or fully loaded, set the switch position to provide adequate illumination without dazzling oncoming drivers.

10 Bulbs (exterior lights) – renewal

General

1 Whenever a bulb is renewed, note the following points:
a) Make sure the switch is in the OFF

10.4a Compress the leg of the retaining spring clip and pivot the clip off the bulb . . .

10.3 Disconnect the wiring connector from the rear of the headlight bulb

position, for the respective bulb you are working on.
b) Remember that if the light has just been in use, the bulb may be extremely hot.
c) Always check the bulb contacts and holder, ensuring that there is clean metal-to-metal contact between the bulb and its live(s) and earth. Clean off any corrosion or dirt before fitting a new bulb.
d) Wherever bayonet-type bulbs are fitted, ensure that the live contact(s) bear firmly against the bulb contact.
e) Always ensure that the new bulb is of the correct rating, and that it is completely clean before fitting it; this applies particularly to headlight/foglight bulbs.

Headlight

2 Depress the tab and lift off the cover at the rear of the headlight unit **(see illustration)**.
3 Disconnect the wiring connector from the rear of the bulb **(see illustration)**.
4 Compress the leg of the retaining spring clip and pivot the clip off the bulb. Lift the bulb out of the light unit **(see illustration)**. When handling the new bulb, use a tissue or clean cloth to avoid touching the glass with the fingers; moisture and grease from the skin can cause blackening and rapid failure of this type of bulb. If the glass is accidentally touched, wipe it clean using methylated spirit.
5 Fit the new bulb to the headlight unit and secure with the spring clip. Reconnect the wiring connector.
6 Refit the plastic cover to the rear of the headlight unit. Check for satisfactory operation on completion.

10.4b . . . then lift the bulb out of the light unit

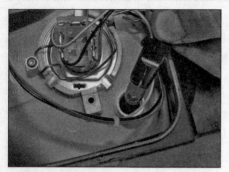

10.7 Untwist the sidelight bulbholder from the rear of the headlight, and withdraw the bulb and holder

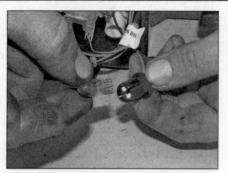

10.8 Remove the sidelight bulb from the bulbholder

10.10 Twist the indicator bulbholder anti-clockwise, and remove it from the rear of the headlight unit

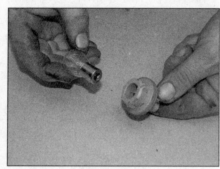

10.11 Remove the bulb from the bulbholder

Front sidelight

7 Untwist the sidelight bulbholder from the rear of the headlight, and withdraw the bulb and holder (see illustration).
8 Remove the bulb from the bulbholder (see illustration).
9 Fit the new bulb using a reversal of the removal procedure. Check for satisfactory operation on completion.

Front direction indicator

10 Twist the indicator bulbholder anti-clockwise, and remove it from the rear of the headlight unit (see illustration).
11 The bulb is a bayonet fit in the holder, and can be removed by pressing it and twisting in an anti-clockwise direction (see illustration).
12 Fit the new bulb using a reversal of the

removal procedure. Check for satisfactory operation on completion.

Front direction indicator side repeater

13 Using a small screwdriver, carefully prise out the direction indicator side repeater from the exterior mirror surround (see illustration). Disconnect the wiring connector and remove the side repeater.
14 Untwist the bulbholder from the rear of the side repeater, and withdraw the bulb and holder (see illustration).
15 Remove the bulb from the bulbholder (see illustration).
16 Fit the new bulb using a reversal of the removal procedure. Check for satisfactory operation on completion.

Front side marker/ direction indicator

Chassis Cab models

17 Insert a small screwdriver into the slot on the front facing side of the light unit. Depress the retaining tab and at the same time turn the lens clockwise to remove.
18 The bulb is a bayonet fit in the holder, and can be removed by pressing it and twisting in an anti-clockwise direction.
19 Fit the new bulb using a reversal of the removal procedure. Check for satisfactory operation on completion.

Jumbo Van models

20 Turn the light unit lens approximately 30° in either direction and remove it from the light unit.
21 Remove the bulb from the light unit.
22 Fit the new bulb using a reversal of the removal procedure. Check for satisfactory operation on completion.

Front foglight

23 From under the front bumper, pull out the cover from the rear of the light unit.
24 Press the clip outwards and withdraw the bulb from the light unit.
25 Disconnect the wiring connector and remove the bulb.
26 Fit the new bulb using a reversal of the removal procedure. Check for satisfactory operation on completion.

Rear light cluster

Van and Bus models

27 Undo the two plastic wing nuts, withdraw the light cluster and disconnect the wiring connector (see illustrations).
28 Compress the lower lugs followed by the upper lugs, and separate the bulbholder from the light cluster. Press and untwist the bulb to remove it from its holder (see illustrations).
29 Fit the new bulb(s) using a reversal of the removal procedure. Check for satisfactory operation on completion.

Chassis Cab models

30 Release the lens retaining clip, and

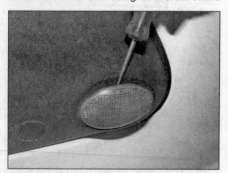

10.13 Carefully prise out the direction indicator side repeater from the exterior mirror surround

10.14 Untwist the bulbholder from the rear of the side repeater, and withdraw the bulb and holder

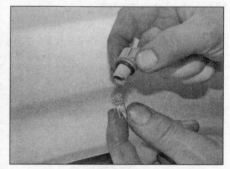

10.15 Remove the bulb from the bulbholder

10.27a Undo the two plastic wing nuts (arrowed) . . .

10.27b . . . withdraw the light cluster . . .

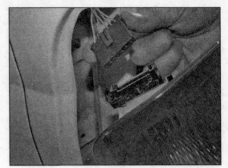

10.27c . . . and disconnect the wiring connector

10.28a Compress the retaining lugs . . .

10.28b . . . and separate the bulbholder from the light cluster

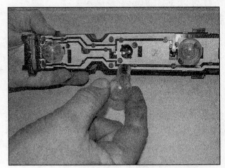

10.28c Press and untwist the bulb to remove it from its holder

move the lens out of the way. Remove the appropriate bulb from the holder in the light unit.

31 Fit the new bulb(s) using a reversal of the removal procedure. Check for satisfactory operation on completion.

Rear number plate light

Double rear door models

32 Prise free the light cap using a suitable screwdriver, then remove the bulb from its holder by pulling it free (see illustrations).

33 Fit the new bulb using a reversal of the removal procedure. Check for satisfactory operation on completion.

Tailgate models

34 Slide the light lens to the left, and pivot it out of the way. Push and untwist the bulb to remove it from its holder (see illustration).

35 Fit the new bulb using a reversal of the removal procedure. Check for satisfactory operation on completion.

Chassis Cab models

36 Pull free the light cap and lens, then press and untwist the bulb to remove it from its holder (see illustration).

37 Fit the new bulb using a reversal of the removal procedure. Check for satisfactory operation on completion.

High-level stop-light

38 Using a coin or wide-blade screwdriver, turn the light unit cover a quarter turn anti-clockwise and lift off the cover.

39 Unclip the bulbholder from the light unit and pull the relevant bulb from the bulb-holder.

40 Fit the new bulb(s) using a reversal of the removal procedure. Check for satisfactory operation on completion.

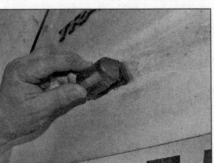

10.32a Prise free the number plate light cap using a suitable screwdriver . . .

10.32b . . . then remove the bulb from its holder by pulling it free

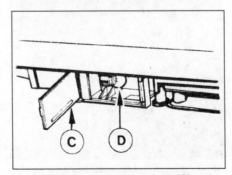

10.34 Rear number plate lens (C) and bulb (D) on tailgate models

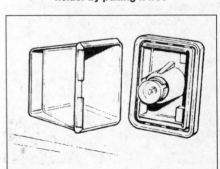

10.36 Rear number plate light assembly on Chassis Cab models

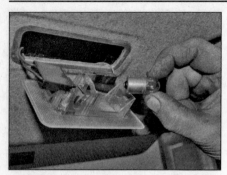

11.3 Press and untwist the courtesy light bulb from its holder

11 Bulbs (interior lights) – renewal

General

1 Refer to Section 10, paragraph 1.

Courtesy lights

2 Insert a small electrical screwdriver blade into the indent in the light unit, and carefully prise it free.
3 Press and untwist the bulb from its holder **(see illustration)**. The rear courtesy light has a festoon-type bulb, and this type is simply prised free from its holder.
4 Fit the new bulb using a reversal of the removal procedure. Check for satisfactory operation on completion.

Instrument panel illumination and warning lights

5 Procedures for renewal of the panel illumination and warning light bulbs are contained in Section 6. **Note:** *On vehicles manufactured from July 2003 onward, the instrument panel is a sealed assembly and cannot be dismantled.*

Stepwell light

6 Carefully prise the light unit from its location and remove the bulbholder from the unit. Pull the bulb from the bulbholder.
7 Fit the new bulb using a reversal of the

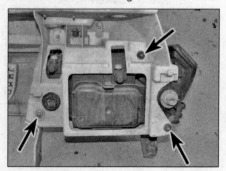

12.2 Undo the three nuts (arrowed) securing the headlight unit to the radiator grille opening panel (panel removed for clarity)

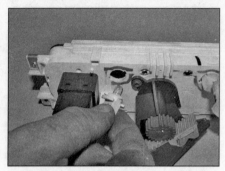

11.9 Twist the bulbholder anti-clockwise and remove it from the rear of the heater control panel

removal procedure. Check for satisfactory operation on completion.

Heater control illumination

8 Remove the heater/air conditioning control panel as described in Chapter 3.
9 Twist the bulbholder anti-clockwise and remove it from the rear of the panel **(see illustration)**. The bulb is integral with the bulbholder and cannot be renewed separately.
10 Fit the new bulbholder using a reversal of the removal procedure.

12 Exterior light units – removal and refitting

Note: *Move the driver's seat fully forward, open the battery box cover and disconnect the battery negative terminal (refer to Disconnecting the battery in the Reference Chapter) before removing any light unit. Reconnect the terminal after refitting.*

Headlight unit

1 For improved access, remove the air cleaner assembly as described in Chapter 4A, if working on the right-hand headlight.
2 From under the vehicle, undo the three nuts securing the headlight unit to the radiator grille opening panel **(see illustration)**.
3 From the front of the vehicle, undo the upper retaining bolt **(see illustration)**.
4 Withdraw the headlight unit from its location,

12.3 From the front of the vehicle, undo the headlight upper retaining bolt (arrowed)

disconnect the wiring connectors and remove the unit from the vehicle.
5 Refit in the reverse order of removal. Refer to Section 9 for details on headlight beam alignment. Check the headlights and indicators for satisfactory operation on completion.

Direction indicator side repeater

6 Removal and refitting of the light unit is part of the bulb renewal procedure. Refer to the procedures contained in Section 10.

Front side marker/ direction indicator

Chassis Cab models

7 Insert a small screwdriver into the slot on the front facing side of the light unit. Depress the retaining tab and at the same time turn the lens clockwise to remove.
8 Carefully release the light unit from its location and disconnect the wiring connector.
9 Refit in the reverse order of removal. Check for satisfactory operation on completion.

Jumbo Van models

10 Turn the light unit lens approximately 30° in either direction and remove it from the light unit.
11 Undo the two retaining screws, remove the light unit and disconnect the wiring connector.
12 Refit in the reverse order of removal. Check for satisfactory operation on completion.

Front foglight

13 From under the front bumper, undo the screws securing the light unit to the bumper brackets. Remove the light unit and disconnect the wiring connector.
14 Refit in the reverse order of removal. Check for satisfactory operation on completion, and refer to Section 9 for details on beam alignment.

Rear light cluster

Van and Bus models

15 Removal and refitting of the light unit is part of the bulb renewal procedure. Refer to the procedures contained in Section 10.

Chassis Cab models

16 Release the light cluster wiring loom from the clip on the rear crossmember, then disconnect the wiring connector from its loom connection.
17 Unscrew the two nuts from the studs at the rear of the light cluster assembly.
18 Withdraw the light cluster assembly sideways and outwards, until the two studs and retaining clip are clear. Pull the wiring loom out of the crossmember, and remove the assembly.
19 Refit in the reverse order of removal. Check for satisfactory operation on completion.

Rear number plate light

Double rear door models

20 Refer to Chapter 11 and remove the rear door interior trim panel.
21 Disconnect the wiring connector from the light unit.
22 Using a small screwdriver, depress the retaining tabs and remove the light unit from the door **(see illustration)**.
23 Refit in the reverse order of removal. Check for satisfactory operation on completion.

Tailgate models

24 Refer to Chapter 11, and remove the rear door interior trim panel.
25 Disconnect the two wiring connectors at the rear of the light unit, and unscrew the four light unit retaining nuts.
26 Remove the light unit from the tailgate.
27 Refit in the reverse order of removal. Check for satisfactory operation on completion.

Chassis Cab models

28 Pull free the light cap and lens from the light unit.
29 Disconnect the wiring connector at the loom connector on the rear crossmember.
30 Withdraw the light unit rubber housing from the crossmember, pull out the wiring loom and remove the unit.
31 Refit in the reverse order of removal. Check for satisfactory operation on completion.

High-level stop-light

32 Using a coin or wide-blade screwdriver, turn the light unit cover a quarter turn anti-clockwise and lift off the cover.
33 Unclip the bulbholder from the light unit.
34 Disconnect the wiring connectors and remove the light unit from the rear door or tailgate.
35 Refit in the reverse order of removal. Check for satisfactory operation on completion.

13 Headlight levelling motor – removal and refitting

Removal

1 Remove the headlight unit as described in Section 12.
2 Depress the tab and lift off the cover at the rear of the headlight unit.
3 Rotate the levelling motor anti-clockwise to the horizontal position, while at the same time lifting the reflector under the headlight bulbholder.
4 Push the motor to disconnect the shaft from the reflector bracket, then disconnect the wiring connector and remove the motor **(see illustrations)**.

Refitting

5 Refit in the reverse order of removal. Check for satisfactory operation on completion.

12.22 Using a small screwdriver, depress the retaining tabs and remove the number plate light unit from the door

14 Horn – removal and refitting

Removal

1 The horn is located under the front of the vehicle on the left-hand side **(see illustration)**.
2 Detach the wiring connectors from the horn, then unscrew the horn mounting bracket bolt and withdraw the horn.
3 If required, the horn can be separated from the mounting bracket by undoing the retaining nut. The horn cannot be adjusted or repaired, and therefore if defective, it must be renewed.

Refitting

4 Refit in the reverse order of removal. Check for satisfactory operation on completion.

13.4a Disconnect the headlight levelling motor shaft from the reflector bracket . . .

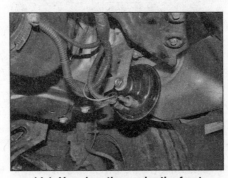

14.1 Horn location under the front left-hand side of the vehicle

15 Wiper arms – removal and refitting

Removal

1 With the wipers 'parked' (ie, in the normal at-rest position), mark the position of the blades on the windscreen/rear window, using a wax crayon or strips of masking tape.
2 Lift up the plastic cap from the bottom of the wiper arm, and loosen the nut one or two turns **(see illustration)**.
3 Lift the wiper arm and release it from the taper on the spindle by easing it from side to side. If necessary, use a puller to release it.
4 Completely remove the nut and withdraw the wiper arm from the spindle. If necessary, remove the blade from the arm as described in *Weekly checks*.

Refitting

5 Refitting is a reversal of removal. Make sure the arm is fitted in its previously noted position before tightening the nut to the specified torque.

16 Windscreen wiper motor and linkage – removal and refitting

Removal

1 Move the driver's seat fully forward, open the battery box cover and disconnect the battery

13.4b . . . then disconnect the wiring connector and remove the motor

15.2 Lift up the plastic cap from the bottom of the wiper arm, and loosen the nut (arrowed) one or two turns

16.4 Disconnect the windscreen wiper motor wiring connector

16.5a Undo the left-hand retaining bolt (arrowed) . . .

16.5b . . . and the right-hand retaining bolt (arrowed) . . .

16.5c . . . and remove the windscreen wiper motor and linkage assembly from the vehicle

16.7 Undo the crank arm retaining nut (arrowed) and withdraw the crank arm from the motor shaft

negative terminal (refer to *Disconnecting the battery* in the Reference Chapter).
2 Remove the wiper arms as described in Section 15.
3 Remove the windscreen cowl panel as described in Chapter 11.
4 Disconnect the wiper motor wiring connector **(see illustration)**.
5 Undo the two bolts securing the wiper motor bracket to the bulkhead, and remove the complete motor and linkage assembly from the vehicle **(see illustrations)**.
6 Mark the position of the motor crank arm in relation to the motor mounting bracket to aid installation.
7 Undo the crank arm retaining nut and withdraw the crank arm from the motor shaft **(see illustration)**.
8 Undo the three retaining bolts and remove the motor from the mounting bracket.

18.1 Wiring connector and washer hose connection at the washer reservoir pump

9 To remove the linkage arms, prise the linkage balljoints off the pivot housing shaft and crank arm ballpins, using an open-ended spanner as a lever. Recover the felt washers, noting their fitted positions.

Refitting

10 Refitting is a reversal of removal, noting the following points:
a) Ensure that the motor crank arm is correctly realigned, as noted during removal, as it is refitted to the motor shaft.
b) Refit the windscreen cowl panel with reference to Chapter 11.
c) On completion, check the wipers for satisfactory operation.

17 Tailgate/rear door wiper motor – removal and refitting

Removal

1 Move the driver's seat fully forward, open the battery box cover and disconnect the battery negative terminal (refer to *Disconnecting the battery* in the Reference Chapter).
2 Remove the wiper arm as described in Section 15.
3 Remove the tailgate/rear door trim panel as described in Chapter 11.
4 Disconnect the wiper motor wiring connector and washer hose.
5 If removing the tailgate wiper motor, undo

the three bolts and remove the wiper motor and mounting bracket from the tailgate.
6 If removing the rear door wiper motor, drill out the three rivets and remove the wiper motor and mounting bracket from the door.
7 Undo the three bolts securing the motor to the mounting bracket. Lift off the motor and recover the spacers, noting their fitted position.

Refitting

8 Refitting is a reversal of removal, using new pop rivets (where applicable). Check for satisfactory operation on completion.

18 Windscreen/tailgate washer reservoir – removal and refitting

Removal

1 Disconnect the wiring connector(s) and washer hose(s) from the reservoir pump(s) **(see illustration)**.
2 Detach the wiring loom and hose(s) from the side of the reservoir.
3 Undo the retaining bolts and remove the reservoir from under the wheel arch.
4 If required, the pumps can be removed from the reservoir by prising them from their location. Recover the seal after removal of the pump.

Refitting

5 Refitting is a reversal of removal. Lubricate the pump seal (if removed) with a little washing-up liquid, to ease fitting.
6 On completion, top-up the reservoir with the required water/washer solution mix, and check for leaks and satisfactory operation.

19 Radio/cassette/CD player – removal and refitting

Removal

Note: *Two special tools, obtainable from most car accessory shops, are required for removal. Alternatively, suitable tools can be fabricated from 3 mm diameter wire, such as welding rod.*

1 Move the driver's seat fully forward, open the battery box cover and disconnect the battery negative terminal (refer to *Disconnecting the battery* in the Reference Chapter).
2 Insert the special tools into the holes on the front of the unit, and push them until they snap into place. The radio/cassette/CD player can then be slid out of the facia **(see illustration)**.
3 Disconnect the aerial and wiring connections at the rear of the unit, and remove the unit from the vehicle **(see illustration)**.
4 Remove the special tools.

Refitting

5 Refitting is a reversal of removal bearing in mind the following points:
   a) *When the leads are reconnected to the rear of the unit, press it into position to the point where the retaining clips are felt to engage.*
   b) *On units with a security code, reactivate the unit in accordance with the code and the instructions given in the Ford Audio Operating Manual supplied with the vehicle.*

20 Loudspeakers – removal and refitting

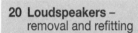

Removal

1 Remove the appropriate trim panel for access to the speaker, as described in Chapter 11.
2 Undo the retaining screws and withdraw the speaker unit. Disconnect the wiring and remove the speaker **(see illustrations)**.

Refitting

3 Refitting is a reversal of removal bearing in mind the following points:

21 Anti-theft alarm system – general information

1 Most models in the range are fitted with an anti-theft alarm system, incorporating an engine immobiliser, as standard equipment. The system is activated when the vehicle is locked, and has both active and passive capabilities. The active section includes the front, side and rear door lock actuators, tailgate lock actuator, bonnet lock, audio unit security and the alarm horn. The passive section includes the ignition key transponder, passive anti-theft system (PATS) transceiver and LED, starter relay, fuel injection pump and the powertrain control module (PCM).
2 When activating the anti-theft alarm system, there is a 20 second delay during which time it is still possible to open the vehicle without triggering the alarm. After the 20 second delay, the system monitors all doors, bonnet and tailgate, provided they are closed. If one of these items is closed later, the system will monitor it after the 20 second delay.

19.2 Insert the special tools into the holes on the front of the radio/cassette/CD player and slide the unit out of the facia

3 If the alarm is triggered, the alarm horn will sound for a period of 30 seconds, and the hazard lights will flash for a period of 5 minutes. An attempt to start the engine or remove the audio unit, automatically triggers the alarm horn.
4 To deactivate the system, one of the front doors must be unlocked with the ignition key or remote control. The rear doors/tailgate may be unlocked with the ignition key or remote control with the alarm still activated, however the alarm is again reactivated when the rear doors/tailgate are locked.
5 The PATS includes a starter inhibitor circuit, which makes it impossible to start the engine with the system armed. The immobiliser is deactivated by a transponder chip built into the ignition key.
6 The PATS transceiver unit is fitted around the ignition switch, and it 'reads' the code from a microchip in the ignition key. This means that any replacement or duplicate keys must be obtained through a Ford dealer – any keys cut locally will not contain the microchip, and will therefore not disarm the immobiliser.
7 If any attempt is made to remove the audio unit while the alarm is active, the alarm will sound.

22 Airbag system – general information and precautions

General information

A driver's airbag is fitted as standard

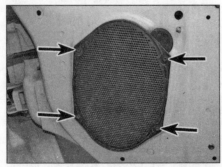

20.2a Undo the retaining screws (arrowed) and withdraw the speaker unit . . .

19.3 Disconnect the aerial and wiring connections at the rear of the unit, and remove the unit from the vehicle

equipment on most models. The airbag is fitted in the steering wheel centre pad. Additionally, a passenger's airbag located in the facia is optionally available.

The system is armed only when the ignition is switched on, however, a reserve power source maintains a power supply to the system in the event of a break in the main electrical supply. The steering wheel and facia airbags are activated by a 'g' sensor (deceleration sensor), and controlled by an electronic control unit located under the facia.

The airbags are inflated by a gas generator, which forces the bag out from its location in the steering wheel or facia.

Precautions

⚠ *Warning: The following precautions must be observed when working on vehicles equipped with an airbag system, to prevent the possibility of personal injury.*

General precautions

The following precautions must be observed when carrying out work on a vehicle equipped with an airbag:
   a) *Do not disconnect the battery with the engine running.*
   b) *Before carrying out any work in the vicinity of the airbag, removal of any of the airbag components, or any welding work on the vehicle, de-activate the system as described in the following sub-Section.*
   c) *Do not attempt to test any of the airbag system circuits using test meters or any other test equipment.*

20.2b . . . then disconnect the wiring and remove the speaker

23.2a Carefully prise off the trim covers . . .

23.2b . . . and undo the airbag retaining bolts

23.4a Disconnect the airbag wiring connector . . .

23.4b . . . and the horn wiring connectors, and remove the airbag

d) If the airbag warning light comes on, or any fault in the system is suspected, consult a Ford dealer without delay. **Do not** attempt to carry out fault diagnosis, or any dismantling of the components.

Precautions when handling an airbag

a) Transport the airbag by itself, bag upward.
b) Do not put your arms around the airbag.
c) Carry the airbag close to the body, bag outward.
d) Do not drop the airbag or expose it to impacts.
e) Do not attempt to dismantle the airbag unit.
f) Do not connect any form of electrical equipment to any part of the airbag circuit.

Precautions when storing an airbag

a) Store the unit in a cupboard with the airbag upward.

23.6 Remove the storage tray from the top of the facia for access to the passenger's airbag

b) Do not expose the airbag to temperatures above 80ºC.
c) Do not expose the airbag to flames.
d) Do not attempt to dispose of the airbag – consult a Ford dealer.
e) Never refit an airbag which is known to be faulty or damaged.

De-activation of airbag system

The system must be de-activated before carrying out any work on the airbag components or surrounding area:
a) Switch on the ignition and check the operation of the airbag warning light on the instrument panel. The light should illuminate when the ignition is switched on, then extinguish.
b) Switch off the ignition.
c) Remove the ignition key.
d) Switch off all electrical equipment.
e) Disconnect the battery negative terminal (refer to 'Disconnecting the battery' in the Reference Chapter).
f) Insulate the battery negative terminal and the end of the battery negative lead to prevent any possibility of contact.
g) Wait for at least two minutes before carrying out any further work. Wait at least ten minutes if the airbag warning light did not operate correctly.

Activation of airbag system

To activate the system on completion of any work, proceed as follows:
a) Ensure that there are no occupants in the vehicle, and that there are no loose objects around the vicinity of the steering wheel.

b) Ensure that the ignition is switched off then reconnect the battery negative terminal.
c) Open the driver's door and switch on the ignition, without reaching in front of the steering wheel. Check that the airbag warning light illuminates briefly then extinguishes.
d) Switch off the ignition.
e) If the airbag warning light does not operate as described in paragraph c), consult a Ford dealer before driving the vehicle.

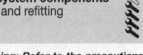

23 Airbag system components – removal and refitting

⚠ **Warning: Refer to the precautions given in Section 22 before attempting to carry out work on any of the airbag components.**

1 De-activate the airbag system as described in the previous Section, then proceed as described under the relevant heading.

Driver's airbag

2 Turn the steering wheel as necessary, so that one of the airbag unit retaining bolts becomes accessible from the rear of the steering wheel. Carefully prise off the trim cover and undo the bolt **(see illustrations)**. Turn the steering wheel again until the second bolt is accessible. Prise off the trim cover and undo this bolt also.
3 Withdraw the airbag unit from the steering wheel, far enough to access the wiring connectors.
4 Disconnect the airbag wiring connector, and the two horn wiring connectors, from the rear of the unit, and remove it from the vehicle **(see illustrations)**.
5 Refitting is a reversal of the removal procedure, with reference to Section 22.

Passenger's airbag

6 Remove the storage tray from the top of the facia **(see illustration)**.
7 Working through the facia aperture, disconnect the airbag wiring connector.
8 Undo the four retaining nuts and remove the airbag from the facia.
9 Refitting is a reversal of the removal procedure, with reference to Section 22.

Airbag control unit

10 The airbag control unit is located beneath the facia and no attempt should be made to remove it. Any suspected problems with the control unit should be referred to a Ford dealer.

Airbag rotary connector

11 Remove the steering column shrouds as described in Chapter 11.
12 Ensure that the front wheels are in the straight-ahead position, then remove the steering wheel as described in Chapter 10.

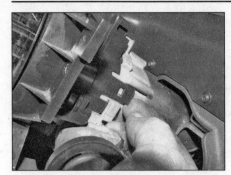

23.15a Release the rotary connector retaining tabs on each side of the steering column . . .

23.15b . . . then remove the rotary connector from the column

23.17 When centralising the rotary connector, align the mark on the centre section with the mark (arrowed) on the connector body

13 Disconnect the rotary connector wiring connectors at the base of the steering column.

14 Remove the steering column multi-function switches as described in Section 4.

15 Release the rotary connector retaining tabs on each side of the steering column, then remove the rotary connector from the column **(see illustrations)**.

16 Prior to refitting the rotary connector, it must be centralised as follows.

17 Rotate the movable centre section of the rotary connector anti-clockwise until resistance is felt. Now turn the centre section clockwise approximately 2.5 turns and align the mark on the centre section with the mark on the rotary connector body **(see illustration)**. Maintain this alignment as the unit is refitted.

18 The remainder of refitting is a reversal of the removal procedure, with reference to Section 22.

Ford Transit wiring diagrams

Diagram 1

 WARNING: *This vehicle is fitted with a supplemental restraint system (SRS) consisting of a combination of driver (and passenger) airbag(s), side impact protection airbags and seatbelt pre-tensioners. The use of electrical test equipment on any SRS wiring systems may cause the seatbelt pre-tensioners to abruptly retract and airbags to explosively deploy, resulting in potentially severe personal injury. Extreme care should be taken to correctly identify any circuits to be tested to avoid choosing any of the SRS wiring in error.*

For further information see airbag system precautions in body electrical systems chapter.
Note: The SRS wiring harness can normally be identified by yellow and/or orange harness or harness connectors.

Key to symbols

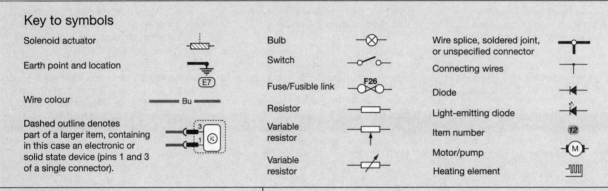

Solenoid actuator

Earth point and location

Wire colour — Bu —

Dashed outline denotes part of a larger item, containing in this case an electronic or solid state device (pins 1 and 3 of a single connector).

Bulb

Switch

Fuse/Fusible link F26

Resistor

Variable resistor

Variable resistor

Wire splice, soldered joint, or unspecified connector

Connecting wires

Diode

Light-emitting diode

Item number

Motor/pump

Heating element

Engine fusebox ⑤

Fuse	Rating	Circuit protected
(F1-F2 not used)		
F3	20A	Daytime running lights, dip beam
F4	5A	Battery voltage sensor
F5	15A	Fuel injection system cut off switch
F6	30A	Towing equipment
F7	15A	Horn
F8	20A	ABS
F9	20A	Main beam
F10	10A	Air conditioning
F11	15A	Screen washer, rear wiper
(F12 not used)		
F13	30A	Multi-function lever, front screen wiper
F14	10A	Reversing light
F15	5A	Engine immobiliser
F16	5A	Auxiliary heater
F17	30A	Towing equipment
(F18-F20 not used)		
F21	20A	Engine management
F22	20A	Fuel pump
F23	10A	RH dip beam
F24	10A	LH dip beam
F25	40A	ABS
F26	40A	LH heated front screen
F27	50A	Electrical system power supply
F28	50A	Electrical system power supply
F29	40A	Engine cooling fan
F30	30A	Ignition
F31	30A	Ignition
F32	40A	Ignition
F33	30A	Engine cooling fan
F34	40A	RH heated front screen
F35	30A	Ignition
(F36-F46 Not used)		

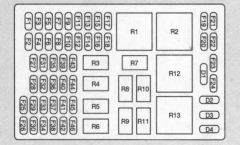

Passenger fusebox ⑦

Fuse	Rating	Circuit protected
F47	15A	Instrument cluster, wash/wipe, central locking
F48	5A	Heated front screen
F49	20A	Fog lights
(F50 not used)		
F51	20A	Ignition
F52	5A	Number plate light
F53	10A	Airbag control unit
F54	10A	Illumination dimmer
F55	15A	Side lights
F56	15A	Tachometer, clock
F57	30A	Rear heater blower
F58	20A	Cigar lighter
F59	10A	Rear air conditioning
F60	15A	Interior lights, electric mirrors
F61	20A	Heated front screen, auxiliary heater, rear screen wiper, battery saver relay
F62	20A	Accessory socket
F63	15A	Heated rear screen, heated door mirrors
(F64 not used)		
F65	30A	Electric windows
F66	20A	Heated rear window
F67	15A	Stop light switch
F68	15A	Audio system
F69	30A	Heater blower motor
F70	20A	Headlight switch
F71	15A	Heated rear window, air con.
F72	20A	Hazard warning lights
F73	5A	Audio system, ABS, instrument cluster

Earth locations

E1	On battery box
E2	LH rear engine compartment
E3	Base of RH 'A' pillar
E4	Behind LH rear light unit
E5	Behind RH rear light unit
E6	LH rear engine compartment
E7	LH kick panel
E8	Base of RH 'A' pillar
E9	Behind dash, centre of bulkhead
E10	Behind dash, centre of bulkhead
E11	Behind dash, centre of bulkhead

H33924

Colour codes

WH	White	**OG**	Orange
BU	Blue	**RD**	Red
GY	Grey	**PK**	Pink
YE	Yellow	**GN**	Green
BN	Brown	**VT**	Violet
BK	Black	**SR**	Silver
NA	Natural	**LG**	Light green

Key to items

1 Battery no.1
2 Battery no.2
3 Starter motor
4 Alternator
5 Engine fusebox
  R1 = starter relay
  R2 = glow plug/
        cooling fan relay
  R3 = horn relay

R5 = generator cut-off relay
R7 = engine management relay
R12 = cooling fan high speed relay
R13 = ignition relay
6 Ignition switch
7 Passenger fusebox
  R15 = battery saver relay
8 Horn
9 Horn switch

10 Steering wheel clock springs
11 Engine cooling fan
12 Glow plugs

Diagram 2

H33925

Typical starting & charging

Earthed via engine management (not shown)

See diagram 8 Instrument cluster (alternator warning light)

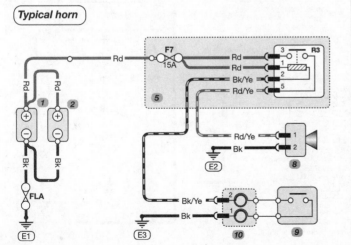

Typical horn

Typical engine cooling fan

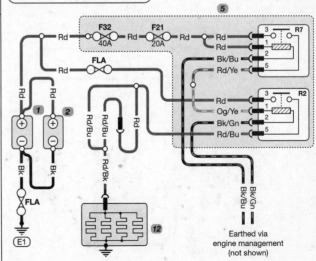

Typical pre-heating system

Colour codes

WH	White	**OG**	Orange
BU	Blue	**RD**	Red
GY	Grey	**PK**	Pink
YE	Yellow	**GN**	Green
BN	Brown	**VT**	Violet
BK	Black	**SR**	Silver
NA	Natural	**LG**	Light green

Key to items

1 Battery no.1
2 Battery no.2
5 Engine fusebox
 R4 = main beam relay
 R6 = dip beam relay
 R13 = ignition relay
6 Ignition switch
7 Passenger fusebox
15 Stop light switch
16 Reversing light switch

17 High level brake light
18 LH rear light unit
 a = stop light
 b = reversing light
 c = tail light
19 RH rear light unit
 (as above)
20 Light switch
 a = side/headlight

21 LH headlight unit
 a = side light
 b = dip beam
 c = main beam
22 RH headlight unit
 (as above)
23 LH number plate light
24 RH number plate light

25 Multifunction switch
 a = dip/main/flasher switch

Diagram 3

H33926

Typical stop & reversing lights

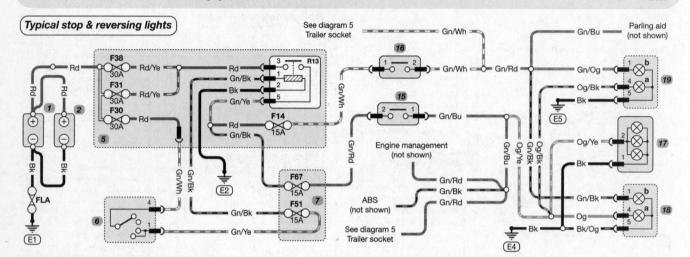

Typical side, tail & number plate lights

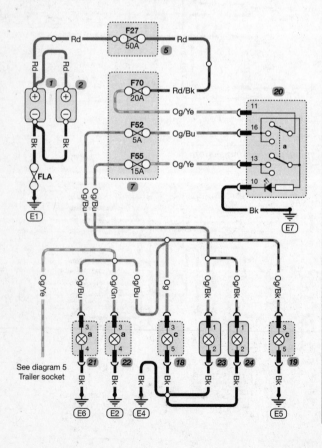

Typical headlights

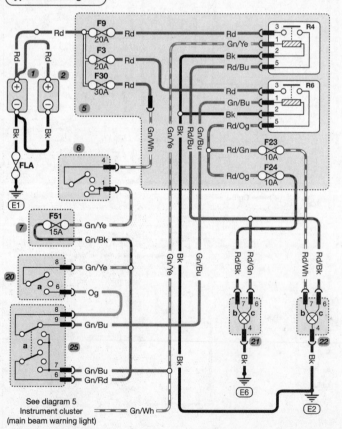

Colour codes

WH	White	**OG**	Orange
BU	Blue	**RD**	Red
GY	Grey	**PK**	Pink
YE	Yellow	**GN**	Green
BN	Brown	**VT**	Violet
BK	Black	**SR**	Silver
NA	Natural	**LG**	Light green

Key to items

1 Battery no.1
2 Battery no.2
5 Engine fusebox
   R13 = ignition relay
6 Ignition switch
7 Passenger fusebox
13 Auxiliary fusebox
   AR2 = RH direction indicator relay
   AR4 = LH direction indicator relay
18 LH rear light unit
   d = direction indicator
   e = foglight

19 RH rear light unit
   (as above)
20 Light switch
   a = side/headlight
   b = headlight levelling adjuster
   c = front/rear foglight
21 LH headlight unit
   d = headlight levelling
22 RH headlight unit
   d = headlight levelling
25 Multifunction switch
   b = direction indicator switch

Diagram 4

28 Hazard warning switch
29 Direction indicator flasher unit
30 LH front direction indicator
31 RH front direction indicator
32 LH indicator side repeater
33 RH indicator side repeater
34 LH front foglight
35 RH front foglight

H33927

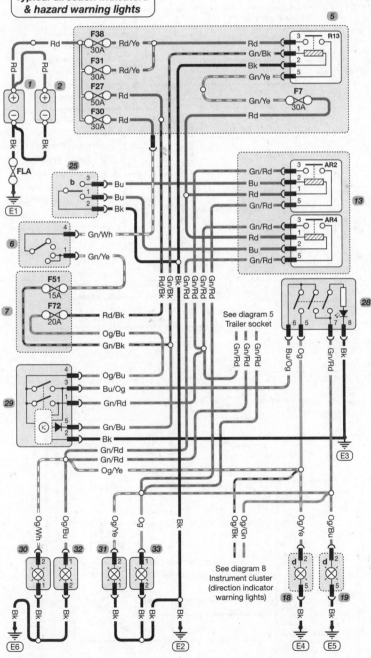

Typical direction indicators & hazard warning lights

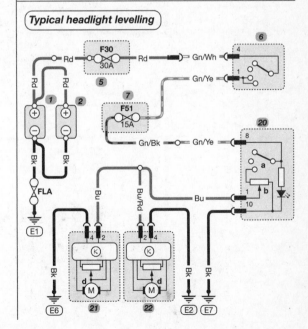

Typical front & rear foglights

Typical headlight levelling

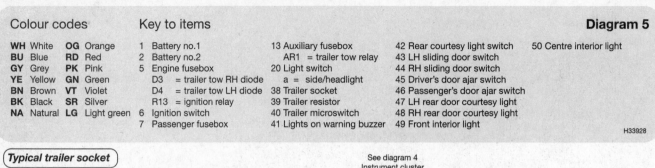

Colour codes

WH	White	OG	Orange
BU	Blue	RD	Red
GY	Grey	PK	Pink
YE	Yellow	GN	Green
BN	Brown	VT	Violet
BK	Black	SR	Silver
NA	Natural	LG	Light green

Key to items

1 Battery no.1
2 Battery no.2
5 Engine fusebox
   D3 = trailer tow RH diode
   D4 = trailer tow LH diode
   R13 = ignition relay
6 Ignition switch
7 Passenger fusebox

13 Auxiliary fusebox
   AR1 = trailer tow relay
20 Light switch
   a = side/headlight
38 Trailer socket
39 Trailer resistor
40 Trailer microswitch
41 Lights on warning buzzer

42 Rear courtesy light switch
43 LH sliding door switch
44 RH sliding door switch
45 Driver's door ajar switch
46 Passenger's door ajar switch
47 LH rear door courtesy light
48 RH rear door courtesy light
49 Front interior light

50 Centre interior light

Diagram 5

H33928

Typical trailer socket

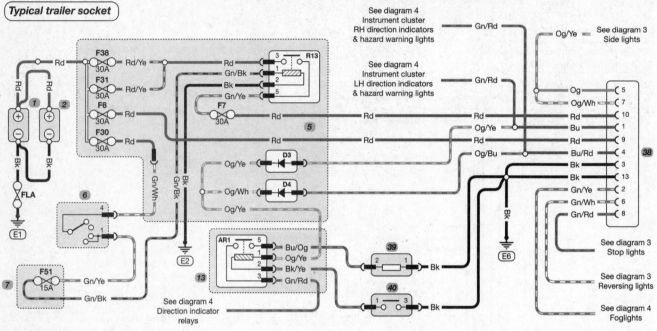

Typical interior lighting - models without central locking

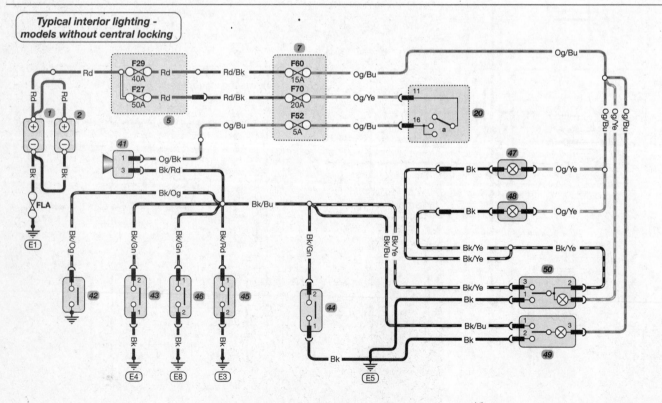

Colour codes

WH	White	**OG**	Orange
BU	Blue	**RD**	Red
GY	Grey	**PK**	Pink
YE	Yellow	**GN**	Green
BN	Brown	**VT**	Violet
BK	Black	**SR**	Silver
NA	Natural	**LG**	Light green

Key to items

1 Battery no.1
2 Battery no.2
5 Engine fusebox
  R13 = ignition relay
6 Ignition switch
7 Passenger fusebox
  a   = rear door ajar buzzer
  R18 = interior light relay
  R19 = rear door warning buzzer relay
20 Light switch
  a = side/headlight

41 Lights on warning buzzer
43 LH sliding door switch
44 RH sliding door switch
45 Driver's door ajar switch
47 LH rear door courtesy light
48 RH rear door courtesy light
49 Front interior light
50 Centre interior light
54 Rear door stepwell light
55 LH sliding door light 1

56 LH sliding door light 2
57 RH sliding door light 1
58 RH sliding door light 2
59 Driver's door lock assembly
60 Passenger's door lock assembly
61 Rear door lock assembly
62 Central locking control unit

Diagram 6

H33929

Typical interior lighting - models with central locking

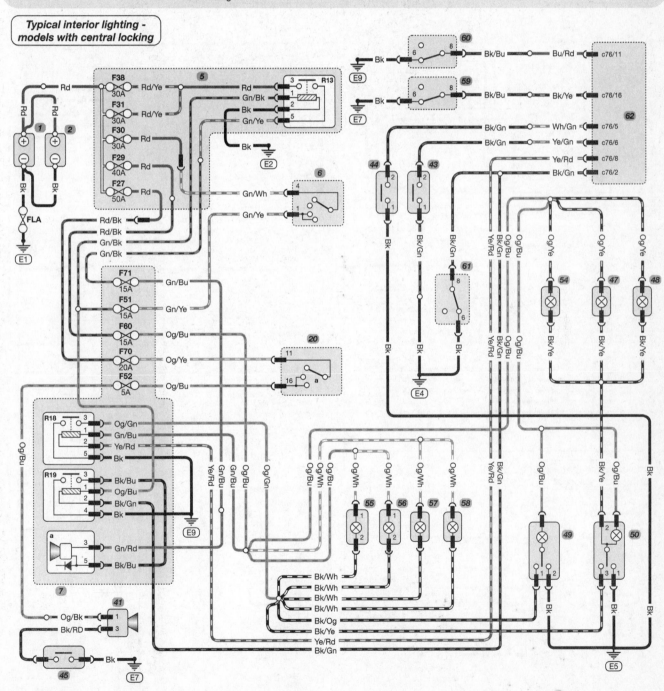

Colour codes

WH	White	OG	Orange
BU	Blue	RD	Red
GY	Grey	PK	Pink
YE	Yellow	GN	Green
BN	Brown	VT	Violet
BK	Black	SR	Silver
NA	Natural	LG	Light green

Key to items

1 Battery no.1
2 Battery no.2
5 Engine fusebox
　R13 = ignition relay
6 Ignition switch
7 Passenger fusebox
　R22 = heated rear window/mirror relay

20 Light switch
　a = side/headlight
　d = interior lighting dimmer
65 Heater panel
　a = heater blower switch
66 Heater blower resistors
67 Heater blower motor

68 Cigar lighter
69 Accessory socket
70 Heated rear window (with tailgate)
71 LH heated rear window (without tailgate)
72 RH heated rear window (without tailgate)
73 Heated rear window switch

Diagram 7

H33930

Typical heater blower

Typical heated rear window

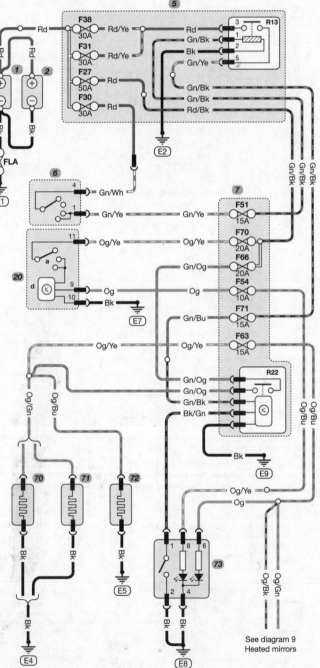

Typical cigar lighter & accessory socket

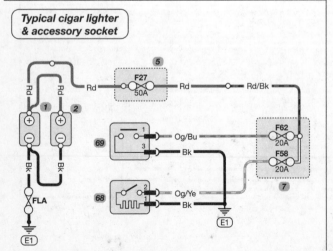

Colour codes

WH	White	**OG**	Orange
BU	Blue	**RD**	Red
GY	Grey	**PK**	Pink
YE	Yellow	**GN**	Green
BN	Brown	**VT**	Violet
BK	Black	**SR**	Silver
NA	Natural	**LG**	Light green

Key to items

1 Battery no.1
2 Battery no.2
5 Engine fusebox
  R13 = ignition relay
6 Ignition switch
7 Passenger fusebox
20 Light switch
  a = side/headlight
  d = interior lighting dimmer
75 Low brake fluid switch
76 Oil pressure switch
77 Fuel gauge sender unit

78 Instrument cluster
  a = instrument illumination
  b = LH indicator warning light
  c = RH indicator warning light
  d = main beam warning light
  e = fuel gauge
  f = anti-slosh module
  g = speedometer
  h = coolant temperature gauge
  i = tachometer
  j = low fuel warning light
  k = coolant temp. warning light

  l = low brake fluid/handbrake warning light
  m = ABS warning light
  n = airbag failure warning light
  o = airbag system warning light
  p = durashift warning light
  q = alternator warning light
  r = oil pressure warning light
  s = engine immobiliser warning light
  t = maintenance indicator warning light
  u = glow plug warning light
  v = clock
  w = trip computer

Diagram 8

H33931

Typical Instrument cluster

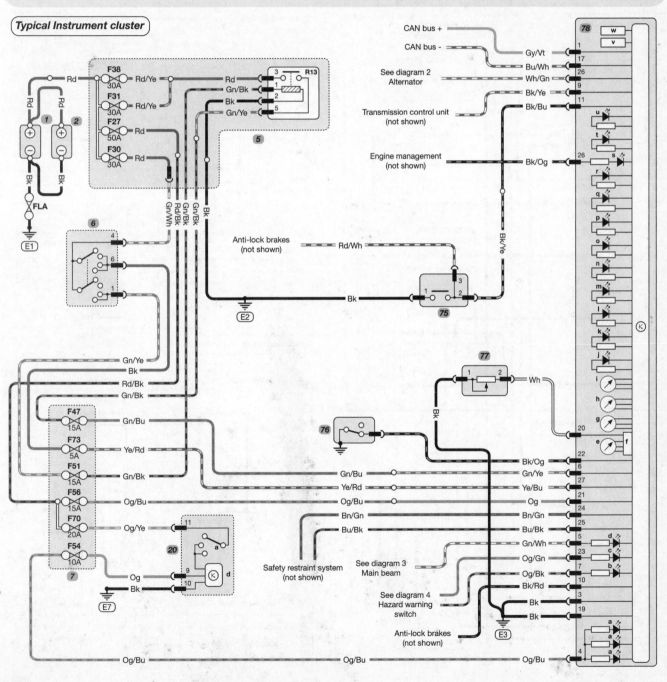

Colour codes

WH	White	**OG**	Orange
BU	Blue	**RD**	Red
GY	Grey	**PK**	Pink
YE	Yellow	**GN**	Green
BN	Brown	**VT**	Violet
BK	Black	**SR**	Silver
NA	Natural	**LG**	Light green

Key to items

1   Battery no.1
2   Battery no.2
5   Engine fusebox
   R13 = ignition relay
6   Ignition switch
7   Passenger fusebox
   R14 = windscreen wiper relay
   R21 = rear wiper relay

20 Light switch
   a = side/headlight
   d = interior lighting dimmer
25 Multifunction switch
   c = front wiper
   d = rear wash/wipe
   e = front washer
80 Front/rear washer pump

81 Front wiper motor
82 Rear wiper motor
83 Audio unit
84 LH front speaker
85 RH front speaker
86 Mirror control switch
87 Driver's door mirror
88 Passenger's door mirror

Diagram 9

H33932

Typical wash/wipe

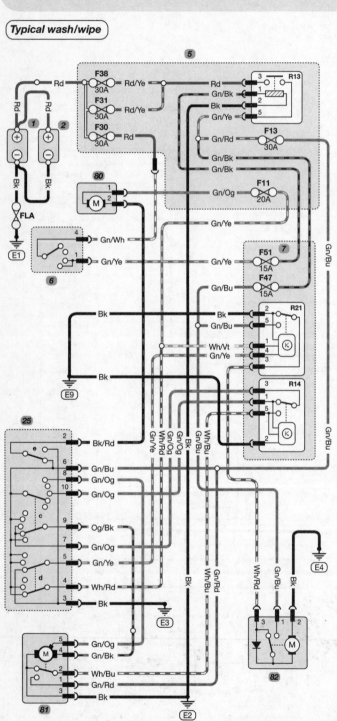

Typical audio system

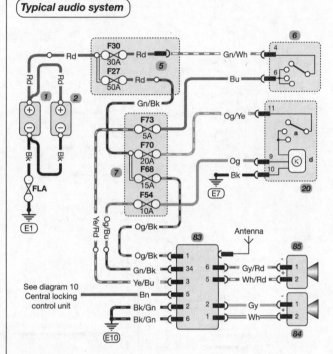

See diagram 10
Central locking
control unit

Typical electric mirrors

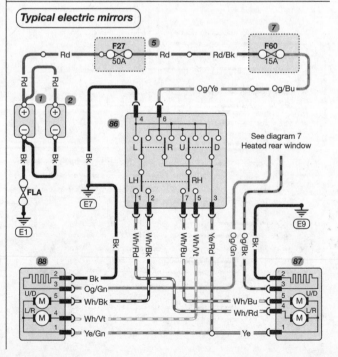

See diagram 7
Heated rear window

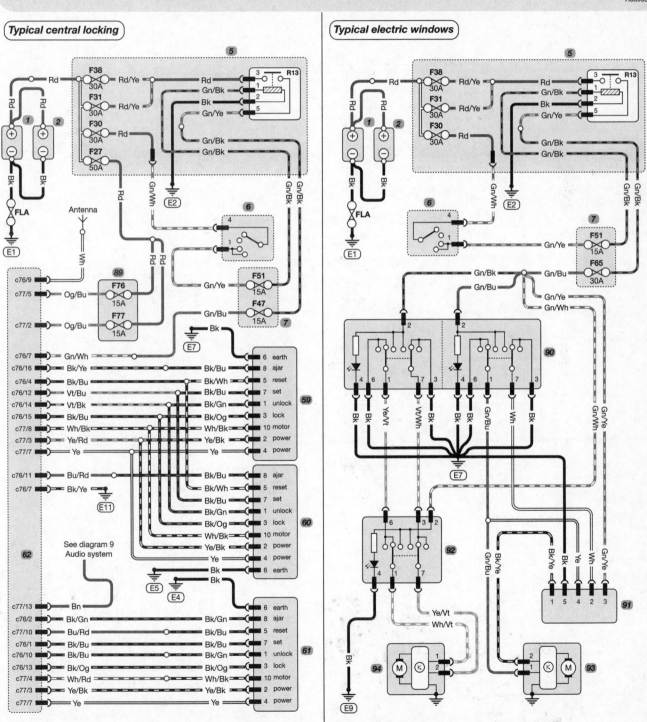

Colour codes

WH	White	OG	Orange
BU	Blue	RD	Red
GY	Grey	PK	Pink
YE	Yellow	GN	Green
BN	Brown	VT	Violet
BK	Black	SR	Silver
NA	Natural	LG	Light green

Key to items

1 Battery no.1
2 Battery no.2
5 Engine fusebox
   R13 = ignition relay
6 Ignition switch
7 Passenger fusebox
59 Driver's door lock assembly
60 Passenger's door lock assembly
61 Rear door lock assembly
62 Central locking control unit
89 Auxiliary fuses
90 Electric window master switch
91 Driver's one touch control unit
92 Passenger's window switch
93 Driver's window motor
94 Passenger's window motor

Diagram 10

H33933

Typical central locking

Typical electric windows

Dimensions and weights

Note: *All figures are approximate and may vary according to model. Refer to manufacturer's data for exact figures.*

Dimensions

Overall length:
  Van and Torneo:
    Short wheelbase . . . . 4834 mm
    Medium wheelbase . . . . 5201 mm
    Long wheelbase . . . . 5651 mm
  Chassis cab/Flatbed truck:
    Short wheelbase . . . . 5225 mm
    Medium wheelbase . . . . 5675 to 5692 mm
    Long wheelbase . . . . 6042 to 6575 mm
Overall width (excluding door mirrors):
  Van and Torneo . . . . 1974 mm
  Chassis cab/Flatbed truck . . . . 2198 mm
Overall height (unladen):
  Van and Torneo:
    Low roof . . . . 1984 to 2055 mm
    Semi-high roof . . . . 2299 to 2365 mm
    Extra high roof . . . . 2542 to 2587 mm
  Chassis cab/Flatbed truck . . . . 1974 to 2051 mm
Wheelbase:
  Van and Torneo:
    Short wheelbase . . . . 2933 mm
    Medium wheelbase . . . . 3300 mm
    Long wheelbase . . . . 3750 mm
  Chassis cab/Flatbed truck:
    Short wheelbase . . . . 3137 mm
    Medium wheelbase . . . . 3504 mm
    Long wheelbase . . . . 3954 mm
Front track . . . . 1737 mm
Rear track:
  Van and Torneo . . . . 1700 to 1710 mm
  Chassis cab/Flatbed truck:
    With single rear wheels . . . . 1700 to 1710 mm
    With twin rear wheels . . . . 1642 mm

Weights

Kerb weight . . . . Refer to information contained on the vehicle identification plate

Conversion factors

Length (distance)

Inches (in)	x 25.4	= Millimetres (mm)	x 0.0394	= Inches (in)
Feet (ft)	x 0.305	= Metres (m)	x 3.281	= Feet (ft)
Miles	x 1.609	= Kilometres (km)	x 0.621	= Miles

Volume (capacity)

Cubic inches (cu in; in³)	x 16.387	= Cubic centimetres (cc; cm³)	x 0.061	= Cubic inches (cu in; in³)
Imperial pints (Imp pt)	x 0.568	= Litres (l)	x 1.76	= Imperial pints (Imp pt)
Imperial quarts (Imp qt)	x 1.137	= Litres (l)	x 0.88	= Imperial quarts (Imp qt)
Imperial quarts (Imp qt)	x 1.201	= US quarts (US qt)	x 0.833	= Imperial quarts (Imp qt)
US quarts (US qt)	x 0.946	= Litres (l)	x 1.057	= US quarts (US qt)
Imperial gallons (Imp gal)	x 4.546	= Litres (l)	x 0.22	= Imperial gallons (Imp gal)
Imperial gallons (Imp gal)	x 1.201	= US gallons (US gal)	x 0.833	= Imperial gallons (Imp gal)
US gallons (US gal)	x 3.785	= Litres (l)	x 0.264	= US gallons (US gal)

Mass (weight)

Ounces (oz)	x 28.35	= Grams (g)	x 0.035	= Ounces (oz)
Pounds (lb)	x 0.454	= Kilograms (kg)	x 2.205	= Pounds (lb)

Force

Ounces-force (ozf; oz)	x 0.278	= Newtons (N)	x 3.6	= Ounces-force (ozf; oz)
Pounds-force (lbf; lb)	x 4.448	= Newtons (N)	x 0.225	= Pounds-force (lbf; lb)
Newtons (N)	x 0.1	= Kilograms-force (kgf; kg)	x 9.81	= Newtons (N)

Pressure

Pounds-force per square inch (psi; lbf/in²; lb/in²)	x 0.070	= Kilograms-force per square centimetre (kgf/cm²; kg/cm²)	x 14.223	= Pounds-force per square inch (psi; lbf/in²; lb/in²)
Pounds-force per square inch (psi; lbf/in²; lb/in²)	x 0.068	= Atmospheres (atm)	x 14.696	= Pounds-force per square inch (psi; lbf/in²; lb/in²)
Pounds-force per square inch (psi; lbf/in²; lb/in²)	x 0.069	= Bars	x 14.5	= Pounds-force per square inch (psi; lbf/in²; lb/in²)
Pounds-force per square inch (psi; lbf/in²; lb/in²)	x 6.895	= Kilopascals (kPa)	x 0.145	= Pounds-force per square inch (psi; lbf/in²; lb/in²)
Kilopascals (kPa)	x 0.01	= Kilograms-force per square centimetre (kgf/cm²; kg/cm²)	x 98.1	= Kilopascals (kPa)
Millibar (mbar)	x 100	= Pascals (Pa)	x 0.01	= Millibar (mbar)
Millibar (mbar)	x 0.0145	= Pounds-force per square inch (psi; lbf/in²; lb/in²)	x 68.947	= Millibar (mbar)
Millibar (mbar)	x 0.75	= Millimetres of mercury (mmHg)	x 1.333	= Millibar (mbar)
Millibar (mbar)	x 0.401	= Inches of water (inH₂O)	x 2.491	= Millibar (mbar)
Millimetres of mercury (mmHg)	x 0.535	= Inches of water (inH₂O)	x 1.868	= Millimetres of mercury (mmHg)
Inches of water (inH₂O)	x 0.036	= Pounds-force per square inch (psi; lbf/in²; lb/in²)	x 27.68	= Inches of water (inH₂O)

Torque (moment of force)

Pounds-force inches (lbf in; lb in)	x 1.152	= Kilograms-force centimetre (kgf cm; kg cm)	x 0.868	= Pounds-force inches (lbf in; lb in)
Pounds-force inches (lbf in; lb in)	x 0.113	= Newton metres (Nm)	x 8.85	= Pounds-force inches (lbf in; lb in)
Pounds-force inches (lbf in; lb in)	x 0.083	= Pounds-force feet (lbf ft; lb ft)	x 12	= Pounds-force inches (lbf in; lb in)
Pounds-force feet (lbf ft; lb ft)	x 0.138	= Kilograms-force metres (kgf m; kg m)	x 7.233	= Pounds-force feet (lbf ft; lb ft)
Pounds-force feet (lbf ft; lb ft)	x 1.356	= Newton metres (Nm)	x 0.738	= Pounds-force feet (lbf ft; lb ft)
Newton metres (Nm)	x 0.102	= Kilograms-force metres (kgf m; kg m)	x 9.804	= Newton metres (Nm)

Power

Horsepower (hp)	x 745.7	= Watts (W)	x 0.0013	= Horsepower (hp)

Velocity (speed)

Miles per hour (miles/hr; mph)	x 1.609	= Kilometres per hour (km/hr; kph)	x 0.621	= Miles per hour (miles/hr; mph)

Fuel consumption*

Miles per gallon, Imperial (mpg)	x 0.354	= Kilometres per litre (km/l)	x 2.825	= Miles per gallon, Imperial (mpg)
Miles per gallon, US (mpg)	x 0.425	= Kilometres per litre (km/l)	x 2.352	= Miles per gallon, US (mpg)

Temperature

Degrees Fahrenheit = (°C x 1.8) + 32   Degrees Celsius (Degrees Centigrade; °C) = (°F - 32) x 0.56

It is common practice to convert from miles per gallon (mpg) to litres/100 kilometres (l/100km), where mpg x l/100 km = 282

Spare parts are available from many sources, including maker's appointed garages, accessory shops, and motor factors. To be sure of obtaining the correct parts, it will sometimes be necessary to quote the vehicle identification number. If possible, it can also be useful to take the old parts along for positive identification. Items such as starter motors and alternators may be available under a service exchange scheme – any parts returned should be clean.

Our advice regarding spare parts is as follows.

Officially appointed garages

This is the best source of parts which are peculiar to your car, and which are not otherwise generally available (eg, badges, interior trim, certain body panels, etc). It is also the only place at which you should buy parts if the vehicle is still under warranty.

Accessory shops

These are very good places to buy materials and components needed for the maintenance of your vehicle (oil, air and fuel filters, light bulbs, drivebelts, greases, brake pads/shoes, touch-up paint, etc). Components of this nature sold by a reputable shop are of the same standard as those used by the vehicle manufacturer.

Besides components, these shops also sell tools and general accessories, usually have convenient opening hours, charge lower prices, and can often be found close to home. Some accessory shops have parts counters where components needed for almost any repair job can be purchased or ordered.

Motor factors

Good factors will stock all the more important components which wear out comparatively quickly, and can sometimes supply individual components needed for the overhaul of a larger assembly (eg, brake seals and hydraulic parts, bearing shells, pistons, valves). They may also handle work such as cylinder block reboring, crankshaft regrinding, etc.

Tyre and exhaust specialists

These outlets may be independent, or members of a local or national chain. They frequently offer competitive prices when compared with a main dealer or local garage, but it will pay to obtain several quotes before making a decision. When researching prices, also ask what 'extras' may be added – for instance fitting a new valve and balancing the wheel are both commonly charged on top of the price of a new tyre.

Other sources

Beware of parts or materials obtained from market stalls, car boot sales or similar outlets. Such items are not invariably sub-standard, but there is little chance of compensation if they do prove unsatisfactory. In the case of safety-critical components such as brake pads, there is the risk not only of financial loss, but also of an accident causing injury or death.

Second-hand components or assemblies obtained from a car breaker can be a good buy in some circumstances, but this sort of purchase is best made by the experienced DIY mechanic.

Vehicle identification

Modifications are a continuing and unpublished process in vehicle manufacture, quite apart from major model changes. Spare parts manuals and lists are compiled upon a numerical basis, the individual vehicle numbers being essential to correct identification of the component required.

When ordering spare parts, always give as much information as possible. Quote the vehicle type, year of manufacture and vehicle identification and/or engine numbers as appropriate.

The *vehicle identification plate* is attached to the front door pillar (**see illustration**) and includes the Vehicle Identification Number (VIN), vehicle weight information and paint and trim colour codes.

The *Vehicle Identification Number* (VIN) is given on the vehicle identification plate. It is also stamped on the right-hand side of the engine compartment, and on a tag on the facia, so that it can be seen through the bottom corner of the windscreen. A symbol on the tag indicates how many air bags are fitted to the vehicle (**see illustration**).

The *engine number* on 2.0 litre engines, is stamped on a horizontal flat located on the front of the cylinder block, near the fuel injection pump (**see illustration**). On 2.4 litre engines, the engine number is stamped on a horizontal flat located on the rear, right-hand side of the cylinder block, just above the sump flange, and on the right-hand side of the cylinder head, above the exhaust manifold. The engine code is contained within the engine number.

Engine codes are as follows:

2.0 litre engines

DuraTorq-Di (75 PS – direct injection) D3FA
DuraTorq-Di (85 PS – direct injection) F3FA
DuraTorq-Di (100 PS – direct injection) . . . . ABFA
DuraTorq-TDCi (125 PS – common rail injection) . . . . FIFA

2.4 litre engines

DuraTorq-Di (75 PS – direct injection) F4FA
DuraTorq-Di (90 PS – direct injection) . . . . D2FA, D2FB and HEFA
DuraTorq-Di (115 PS – direct injection) . . . . FXFA
DuraTorq-Di (120 PS – direct injection) . . . . D4FA and DFFA
DuraTorq-Di (125 PS – direct injection) . . . . DOFA
DuraTorq-TDCi (135 PS – common rail injection) H9FA

Vehicle identification plate attached to the front door pillar

The VIN number is also stamped on a tag on the facia, so that it can be seen through the bottom corner of the windscreen

The engine number on 2.0 litre engines is stamped on a horizontal flat located on the front of the cylinder block

Whenever servicing, repair or overhaul work is carried out on the car or its components, observe the following procedures and instructions. This will assist in carrying out the operation efficiently and to a professional standard of workmanship.

Joint mating faces and gaskets

When separating components at their mating faces, never insert screwdrivers or similar implements into the joint between the faces in order to prise them apart. This can cause severe damage which results in oil leaks, coolant leaks, etc upon reassembly. Separation is usually achieved by tapping along the joint with a soft-faced hammer in order to break the seal. However, note that this method may not be suitable where dowels are used for component location.

Where a gasket is used between the mating faces of two components, a new one must be fitted on reassembly; fit it dry unless otherwise stated in the repair procedure. Make sure that the mating faces are clean and dry, with all traces of old gasket removed. When cleaning a joint face, use a tool which is unlikely to score or damage the face, and remove any burrs or nicks with an oilstone or fine file.

Make sure that tapped holes are cleaned with a pipe cleaner, and keep them free of jointing compound, if this is being used, unless specifically instructed otherwise.

Ensure that all orifices, channels or pipes are clear, and blow through them, preferably using compressed air.

Oil seals

Oil seals can be removed by levering them out with a wide flat-bladed screwdriver or similar implement. Alternatively, a number of self-tapping screws may be screwed into the seal, and these used as a purchase for pliers or some similar device in order to pull the seal free.

Whenever an oil seal is removed from its working location, either individually or as part of an assembly, it should be renewed.

The very fine sealing lip of the seal is easily damaged, and will not seal if the surface it contacts is not completely clean and free from scratches, nicks or grooves. If the original sealing surface of the component cannot be restored, and the manufacturer has not made provision for slight relocation of the seal relative to the sealing surface, the component should be renewed.

Protect the lips of the seal from any surface which may damage them in the course of fitting. Use tape or a conical sleeve where possible. Lubricate the seal lips with oil before fitting and, on dual-lipped seals, fill the space between the lips with grease.

Unless otherwise stated, oil seals must be fitted with their sealing lips toward the lubricant to be sealed.

Use a tubular drift or block of wood of the appropriate size to install the seal and, if the seal housing is shouldered, drive the seal down to the shoulder. If the seal housing is unshouldered, the seal should be fitted with its face flush with the housing top face (unless otherwise instructed).

Screw threads and fastenings

Seized nuts, bolts and screws are quite a common occurrence where corrosion has set in, and the use of penetrating oil or releasing fluid will often overcome this problem if the offending item is soaked for a while before attempting to release it. The use of an impact driver may also provide a means of releasing such stubborn fastening devices, when used in conjunction with the appropriate screwdriver bit or socket. If none of these methods works, it may be necessary to resort to the careful application of heat, or the use of a hacksaw or nut splitter device.

Studs are usually removed by locking two nuts together on the threaded part, and then using a spanner on the lower nut to unscrew the stud. Studs or bolts which have broken off below the surface of the component in which they are mounted can sometimes be removed using a stud extractor. Always ensure that a blind tapped hole is completely free from oil, grease, water or other fluid before installing the bolt or stud. Failure to do this could cause the housing to crack due to the hydraulic action of the bolt or stud as it is screwed in.

When tightening a castellated nut to accept a split pin, tighten the nut to the specified torque, where applicable, and then tighten further to the next split pin hole. Never slacken the nut to align the split pin hole, unless stated in the repair procedure.

When checking or retightening a nut or bolt to a specified torque setting, slacken the nut or bolt by a quarter of a turn, and then retighten to the specified setting. However, this should not be attempted where angular tightening has been used.

For some screw fastenings, notably cylinder head bolts or nuts, torque wrench settings are no longer specified for the latter stages of tightening, "angle-tightening" being called up instead. Typically, a fairly low torque wrench setting will be applied to the bolts/nuts in the correct sequence, followed by one or more stages of tightening through specified angles.

Locknuts, locktabs and washers

Any fastening which will rotate against a component or housing during tightening should always have a washer between it and the relevant component or housing.

Spring or split washers should always be renewed when they are used to lock a critical component such as a big-end bearing retaining bolt or nut. Locktabs which are folded over to retain a nut or bolt should always be renewed.

Self-locking nuts can be re-used in non-critical areas, providing resistance can be felt when the locking portion passes over the bolt or stud thread. However, it should be noted that self-locking stiffnuts tend to lose their effectiveness after long periods of use, and should then be renewed as a matter of course.

Split pins must always be replaced with new ones of the correct size for the hole.

When thread-locking compound is found on the threads of a fastener which is to be re-used, it should be cleaned off with a wire brush and solvent, and fresh compound applied on reassembly.

Special tools

Some repair procedures in this manual entail the use of special tools such as a press, two or three-legged pullers, spring compressors, etc. Wherever possible, suitable readily-available alternatives to the manufacturer's special tools are described, and are shown in use. In some instances, where no alternative is possible, it has been necessary to resort to the use of a manufacturer's tool, and this has been done for reasons of safety as well as the efficient completion of the repair operation. Unless you are highly-skilled and have a thorough understanding of the procedures described, never attempt to bypass the use of any special tool when the procedure described specifies its use. Not only is there a very great risk of personal injury, but expensive damage could be caused to the components involved.

Environmental considerations

When disposing of used engine oil, brake fluid, antifreeze, etc, give due consideration to any detrimental environmental effects. Do not, for instance, pour any of the above liquids down drains into the general sewage system, or onto the ground to soak away. Many local council refuse tips provide a facility for waste oil disposal, as do some garages. If none of these facilities are available, consult your local Environmental Health Department, or the National Rivers Authority, for further advice.

With the universal tightening-up of legislation regarding the emission of environmentally-harmful substances from motor vehicles, most vehicles have tamperproof devices fitted to the main adjustment points of the fuel system. These devices are primarily designed to prevent unqualified persons from adjusting the fuel/air mixture, with the chance of a consequent increase in toxic emissions. If such devices are found during servicing or overhaul, they should, wherever possible, be renewed or refitted in accordance with the manufacturer's requirements or current legislation.

Note: It is antisocial and illegal to dump oil down the drain. To find the location of your local oil recycling bank, call this number free.

OIL CARE · FOLLOW THE CODE

OIL BANK LINE
0800 66 33 66
www.oilbankline.org.uk

The jack supplied with the vehicle tool kit should only be used for changing roadwheels – see *Wheel changing* at the front of this manual. Ensure the jack head is correctly engaged before attempting to raise the vehicle. When carrying out any other kind of work, raise the vehicle using a hydraulic jack, and always supplement the jack with axle stands positioned under the vehicle jacking points.

When jacking up the vehicle with a trolley jack, position the jack head under one of the relevant jacking points. **Do not** jack the vehicle under the sump or any of the steering or suspension components. Supplement the jack using axle stands **(see illustrations)**.

⚠️ *Warning: Never work under, around, or near a raised vehicle, unless it is adequately supported in at least two places.*

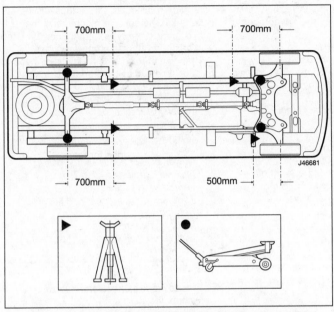

Jacking and supporting points for Van and Torneo models

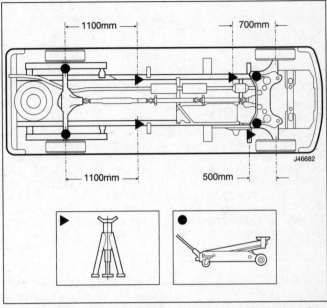

Jacking and supporting points for Chassis cab/Flatbed truck models

Disconnecting the battery

Numerous systems fitted to the vehicle require battery power to be available at all times, either to ensure their continued operation (such as the clock) or to maintain control unit memories which would be erased if the battery were to be disconnected. Whenever the battery is to be disconnected therefore, first note the following, to ensure that there are no unforeseen consequences of this action:

a) First, on any vehicle with central locking, it is a wise precaution to remove the key from the ignition, and to keep it with you, so that it does not get locked in, if the central locking should engage accidentally when the battery is reconnected.

b) Depending on vehicle and specification, the Ford anti-theft alarm system may be of the type which is automatically activated when the vehicle battery is disconnected and/or reconnected. To prevent the alarm sounding on models so equipped, switch the ignition on, then off, and disconnect the battery within 15 seconds. If the alarm is activated when the battery is reconnected, deactivate the alarm by locking and unlocking one of the front doors.

c) If a security-coded audio unit is fitted, and the unit and/or the battery is disconnected, the unit will not function again on reconnection until the correct security code is entered. Details of this procedure, which varies according to the unit fitted, are given in the vehicle audio system operating instructions. Ensure you have the correct code before you disconnect the battery. If you do not have the code or details of the correct procedure, but can supply proof of ownership and a legitimate reason for wanting this information, a Ford dealer may be able to help.

d) The engine management powertrain control module (PCM) is of the 'self-learning' type, meaning that as it operates, it also monitors and stores the settings which give optimum engine performance under all operating conditions. When the battery is disconnected, these settings are lost and the PCM reverts to the base settings programmed into its memory at the factory. On restarting, this may lead to the engine running/idling roughly for a short while, until the PCM has re-learned the optimum settings. This process is best accomplished by taking the vehicle on a road test (for approximately 15 minutes), covering all engine speeds and loads, concentrating mainly in the 2500 to 3500 rpm region.

e) On all models, when reconnecting the battery after disconnection, switch on the ignition and wait 10 seconds to allow the electronic vehicle systems to stabilise and re-initialise.

Introduction

A selection of good tools is a fundamental requirement for anyone contemplating the maintenance and repair of a motor vehicle. For the owner who does not possess any, their purchase will prove a considerable expense, offsetting some of the savings made by doing-it-yourself. However, provided that the tools purchased meet the relevant national safety standards and are of good quality, they will last for many years and prove an extremely worthwhile investment.

To help the average owner to decide which tools are needed to carry out the various tasks detailed in this manual, we have compiled three lists of tools under the following headings: *Maintenance and minor repair*, *Repair and overhaul*, and *Special*. Newcomers to practical mechanics should start off with the *Maintenance and minor repair* tool kit, and confine themselves to the simpler jobs around the vehicle. Then, as confidence and experience grow, more difficult tasks can be undertaken, with extra tools being purchased as, and when, they are needed. In this way, a *Maintenance and minor repair* tool kit can be built up into a *Repair and overhaul* tool kit over a considerable period of time, without any major cash outlays. The experienced do-it-yourselfer will have a tool kit good enough for most repair and overhaul procedures, and will add tools from the *Special* category when it is felt that the expense is justified by the amount of use to which these tools will be put.

Maintenance and minor repair tool kit

The tools given in this list should be considered as a minimum requirement if routine maintenance, servicing and minor repair operations are to be undertaken. We recommend the purchase of combination spanners (ring one end, open-ended the other); although more expensive than open-ended ones, they do give the advantages of both types of spanner.

☐ *Combination spanners:*
   Metric - 8 to 19 mm inclusive
☐ *Adjustable spanner - 35 mm jaw (approx.)*
☐ *Spark plug spanner (with rubber insert) - petrol models*
☐ *Spark plug gap adjustment tool - petrol models*
☐ *Set of feeler gauges*
☐ *Brake bleed nipple spanner*
☐ *Screwdrivers:*
   Flat blade - 100 mm long x 6 mm dia
   Cross blade - 100 mm long x 6 mm dia
   Torx - various sizes (not all vehicles)
☐ *Combination pliers*
☐ *Hacksaw (junior)*
☐ *Tyre pump*
☐ *Tyre pressure gauge*
☐ *Oil can*
☐ *Oil filter removal tool*
☐ *Fine emery cloth*
☐ *Wire brush (small)*
☐ *Funnel (medium size)*
☐ *Sump drain plug key (not all vehicles)*

Repair and overhaul tool kit

These tools are virtually essential for anyone undertaking any major repairs to a motor vehicle, and are additional to those given in the *Maintenance and minor repair* list. Included in this list is a comprehensive set of sockets. Although these are expensive, they will be found invaluable as they are so versatile - particularly if various drives are included in the set. We recommend the half-inch square-drive type, as this can be used with most proprietary torque wrenches.

The tools in this list will sometimes need to be supplemented by tools from the *Special* list:

☐ *Sockets (or box spanners) to cover range in previous list (including Torx sockets)*
☐ *Reversible ratchet drive (for use with sockets)*
☐ *Extension piece, 250 mm (for use with sockets)*
☐ *Universal joint (for use with sockets)*
☐ *Flexible handle or sliding T "breaker bar" (for use with sockets)*
☐ *Torque wrench (for use with sockets)*
☐ *Self-locking grips*
☐ *Ball pein hammer*
☐ *Soft-faced mallet (plastic or rubber)*
☐ *Screwdrivers:*
   Flat blade - long & sturdy, short (chubby), and narrow (electrician's) types
   Cross blade - long & sturdy, and short (chubby) types
☐ *Pliers:*
   Long-nosed
   Side cutters (electrician's)
   Circlip (internal and external)
☐ *Cold chisel - 25 mm*
☐ *Scriber*
☐ *Scraper*
☐ *Centre-punch*
☐ *Pin punch*
☐ *Hacksaw*
☐ *Brake hose clamp*
☐ *Brake/clutch bleeding kit*
☐ *Selection of twist drills*
☐ *Steel rule/straight-edge*
☐ *Allen keys (inc. splined/Torx type)*
☐ *Selection of files*
☐ *Wire brush*
☐ *Axle stands*
☐ *Jack (strong trolley or hydraulic type)*
☐ *Light with extension lead*
☐ *Universal electrical multi-meter*

Sockets and reversible ratchet drive

Brake bleeding kit

Torx key, socket and bit

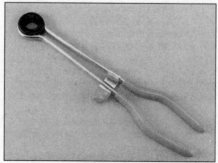
Hose clamp

Angular-tightening gauge

Special tools

The tools in this list are those which are not used regularly, are expensive to buy, or which need to be used in accordance with their manufacturers' instructions. Unless relatively difficult mechanical jobs are undertaken frequently, it will not be economic to buy many of these tools. Where this is the case, you could consider clubbing together with friends (or joining a motorists' club) to make a joint purchase, or borrowing the tools against a deposit from a local garage or tool hire specialist. It is worth noting that many of the larger DIY superstores now carry a large range of special tools for hire at modest rates.

The following list contains only those tools and instruments freely available to the public, and not those special tools produced by the vehicle manufacturer specifically for its dealer network. You will find occasional references to these manufacturers' special tools in the text of this manual. Generally, an alternative method of doing the job without the vehicle manufacturers' special tool is given. However, sometimes there is no alternative to using them. Where this is the case and the relevant tool cannot be bought or borrowed, you will have to entrust the work to a dealer.

☐ Angular-tightening gauge
☐ Valve spring compressor
☐ Valve grinding tool
☐ Piston ring compressor
☐ Piston ring removal/installation tool
☐ Cylinder bore hone
☐ Balljoint separator
☐ Coil spring compressors (where applicable)
☐ Two/three-legged hub and bearing puller
☐ Impact screwdriver
☐ Micrometer and/or vernier calipers
☐ Dial gauge
☐ Stroboscopic timing light
☐ Dwell angle meter/tachometer
☐ Fault code reader
☐ Cylinder compression gauge
☐ Hand-operated vacuum pump and gauge
☐ Clutch plate alignment set
☐ Brake shoe steady spring cup removal tool
☐ Bush and bearing removal/installation set
☐ Stud extractors
☐ Tap and die set
☐ Lifting tackle
☐ Trolley jack

Buying tools

Reputable motor accessory shops and superstores often offer excellent quality tools at discount prices, so it pays to shop around.

Remember, you don't have to buy the most expensive items on the shelf, but it is always advisable to steer clear of the very cheap tools. Beware of 'bargains' offered on market stalls or at car boot sales. There are plenty of good tools around at reasonable prices, but always aim to purchase items which meet the relevant national safety standards. If in doubt, ask the proprietor or manager of the shop for advice before making a purchase.

Care and maintenance of tools

Having purchased a reasonable tool kit, it is necessary to keep the tools in a clean and serviceable condition. After use, always wipe off any dirt, grease and metal particles using a clean, dry cloth, before putting the tools away. Never leave them lying around after they have been used. A simple tool rack on the garage or workshop wall for items such as screwdrivers and pliers is a good idea. Store all normal spanners and sockets in a metal box. Any measuring instruments, gauges, meters, etc, must be carefully stored where they cannot be damaged or become rusty.

Take a little care when tools are used. Hammer heads inevitably become marked, and screwdrivers lose the keen edge on their blades from time to time. A little timely attention with emery cloth or a file will soon restore items like this to a good finish.

Working facilities

Not to be forgotten when discussing tools is the workshop itself. If anything more than routine maintenance is to be carried out, a suitable working area becomes essential.

It is appreciated that many an owner-mechanic is forced by circumstances to remove an engine or similar item without the benefit of a garage or workshop. Having done this, any repairs should always be done under the cover of a roof.

Wherever possible, any dismantling should be done on a clean, flat workbench or table at a suitable working height.

Any workbench needs a vice; one with a jaw opening of 100 mm is suitable for most jobs. As mentioned previously, some clean dry storage space is also required for tools, as well as for any lubricants, cleaning fluids, touch-up paints etc, which become necessary.

Another item which may be required, and which has a much more general usage, is an electric drill with a chuck capacity of at least 8 mm. This, together with a good range of twist drills, is virtually essential for fitting accessories.

Last, but not least, always keep a supply of old newspapers and clean, lint-free rags available, and try to keep any working area as clean as possible.

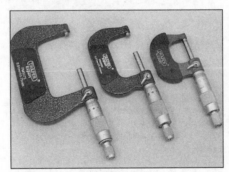

Micrometers

Dial test indicator ("dial gauge")

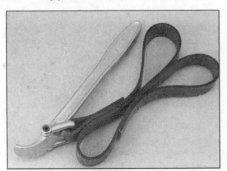

Strap wrench

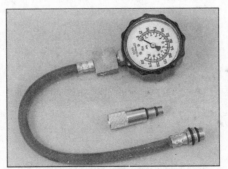

Compression tester

Fault code reader

This is a guide to getting your vehicle through the MOT test. Obviously it will not be possible to examine the vehicle to the same standard as the professional MOT tester. However, working through the following checks will enable you to identify any problem areas before submitting the vehicle for the test.

It has only been possible to summarise the test requirements here, based on the regulations in force at the time of printing. Test standards are becoming increasingly stringent, although there are some exemptions for older vehicles.

An assistant will be needed to help carry out some of these checks.

The checks have been sub-divided into four categories, as follows:

1 Checks carried out **FROM THE DRIVER'S SEAT**

2 Checks carried out **WITH THE VEHICLE ON THE GROUND**

3 Checks carried out **WITH THE VEHICLE RAISED AND THE WHEELS FREE TO TURN**

4 Checks carried out on **YOUR VEHICLE'S EXHAUST EMISSION SYSTEM**

---

1 Checks carried out **FROM THE DRIVER'S SEAT**

Handbrake

☐ Test the operation of the handbrake. Excessive travel (too many clicks) indicates incorrect brake or cable adjustment.
☐ Check that the handbrake cannot be released by tapping the lever sideways. Check the security of the lever mountings.

Footbrake

☐ Depress the brake pedal and check that it does not creep down to the floor, indicating a master cylinder fault. Release the pedal, wait a few seconds, then depress it again. If the pedal travels nearly to the floor before firm resistance is felt, brake adjustment or repair is necessary. If the pedal feels spongy, there is air in the hydraulic system which must be removed by bleeding.

☐ Check that the brake pedal is secure and in good condition. Check also for signs of fluid leaks on the pedal, floor or carpets, which would indicate failed seals in the brake master cylinder.
☐ Check the servo unit (when applicable) by operating the brake pedal several times, then keeping the pedal depressed and starting the engine. As the engine starts, the pedal will move down slightly. If not, the vacuum hose or the servo itself may be faulty.

Steering wheel and column

☐ Examine the steering wheel for fractures or looseness of the hub, spokes or rim.
☐ Move the steering wheel from side to side and then up and down. Check that the steering wheel is not loose on the column, indicating wear or a loose retaining nut. Continue moving the steering wheel as before, but also turn it slightly from left to right.
☐ Check that the steering wheel is not loose on the column, and that there is no abnormal

movement of the steering wheel, indicating wear in the column support bearings or couplings.

Windscreen, mirrors and sunvisor

☐ The windscreen must be free of cracks or other significant damage within the driver's field of view. (Small stone chips are acceptable.) Rear view mirrors must be secure, intact, and capable of being adjusted.

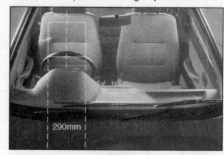

☐ The driver's sunvisor must be capable of being stored in the "up" position.

Seat belts and seats

Note: *The following checks are applicable to all seat belts, front and rear.*

☐ Examine the webbing of all the belts (including rear belts if fitted) for cuts, serious fraying or deterioration. Fasten and unfasten each belt to check the buckles. If applicable, check the retracting mechanism. Check the security of all seat belt mountings accessible from inside the vehicle.

☐ Seat belts with pre-tensioners, once activated, have a "flag" or similar showing on the seat belt stalk. This, in itself, is not a reason for test failure.

☐ The front seats themselves must be securely attached and the backrests must lock in the upright position.

Doors

☐ Both front doors must be able to be opened and closed from outside and inside, and must latch securely when closed.

2 Checks carried out WITH THE VEHICLE ON THE GROUND

Vehicle identification

☐ Number plates must be in good condition, secure and legible, with letters and numbers correctly spaced – spacing at (A) should be at least twice that at (B).

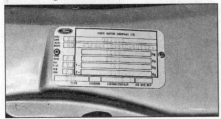

☐ The VIN plate and/or homologation plate must be legible.

Electrical equipment

☐ Switch on the ignition and check the operation of the horn.

☐ Check the windscreen washers and wipers, examining the wiper blades; renew damaged or perished blades. Also check the operation of the stop-lights.

☐ Check the operation of the sidelights and number plate lights. The lenses and reflectors must be secure, clean and undamaged.

☐ Check the operation and alignment of the headlights. The headlight reflectors must not be tarnished and the lenses must be undamaged.

☐ Switch on the ignition and check the operation of the direction indicators (including the instrument panel tell-tale) and the hazard warning lights. Operation of the sidelights and stop-lights must not affect the indicators - if it does, the cause is usually a bad earth at the rear light cluster.

☐ Check the operation of the rear foglight(s), including the warning light on the instrument panel or in the switch.

☐ The ABS warning light must illuminate in accordance with the manufacturers' design. For most vehicles, the ABS warning light should illuminate when the ignition is switched on, and (if the system is operating properly) extinguish after a few seconds. Refer to the owner's handbook.

Footbrake

☐ Examine the master cylinder, brake pipes and servo unit for leaks, loose mountings, corrosion or other damage.

☐ The fluid reservoir must be secure and the fluid level must be between the upper (**A**) and lower (**B**) markings.

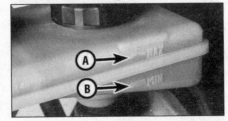

☐ Inspect both front brake flexible hoses for cracks or deterioration of the rubber. Turn the steering from lock to lock, and ensure that the hoses do not contact the wheel, tyre, or any part of the steering or suspension mechanism. With the brake pedal firmly depressed, check the hoses for bulges or leaks under pressure.

Steering and suspension

☐ Have your assistant turn the steering wheel from side to side slightly, up to the point where the steering gear just begins to transmit this movement to the roadwheels. Check for excessive free play between the steering wheel and the steering gear, indicating wear or insecurity of the steering column joints, the column-to-steering gear coupling, or the steering gear itself.

☐ Have your assistant turn the steering wheel more vigorously in each direction, so that the roadwheels just begin to turn. As this is done, examine all the steering joints, linkages, fittings and attachments. Renew any component that shows signs of wear or damage. On vehicles with power steering, check the security and condition of the steering pump, drivebelt and hoses.

☐ Check that the vehicle is standing level, and at approximately the correct ride height.

Shock absorbers

☐ Depress each corner of the vehicle in turn, then release it. The vehicle should rise and then settle in its normal position. If the vehicle continues to rise and fall, the shock absorber is defective. A shock absorber which has seized will also cause the vehicle to fail.

Exhaust system

☐ Start the engine. With your assistant holding a rag over the tailpipe, check the entire system for leaks. Repair or renew leaking sections.

3 Checks carried out
WITH THE VEHICLE RAISED AND THE WHEELS FREE TO TURN

Jack up the front and rear of the vehicle, and securely support it on axle stands. Position the stands clear of the suspension assemblies. Ensure that the wheels are clear of the ground and that the steering can be turned from lock to lock.

Steering mechanism

☐ Have your assistant turn the steering from lock to lock. Check that the steering turns smoothly, and that no part of the steering mechanism, including a wheel or tyre, fouls any brake hose or pipe or any part of the body structure.
☐ Examine the steering rack rubber gaiters for damage or insecurity of the retaining clips. If power steering is fitted, check for signs of damage or leakage of the fluid hoses, pipes or connections. Also check for excessive stiffness or binding of the steering, a missing split pin or locking device, or severe corrosion of the body structure within 30 cm of any steering component attachment point.

Front and rear suspension and wheel bearings

☐ Starting at the front right-hand side, grasp the roadwheel at the 3 o'clock and 9 o'clock positions and rock gently but firmly. Check for free play or insecurity at the wheel bearings, suspension balljoints, or suspension mountings, pivots and attachments.
☐ Now grasp the wheel at the 12 o'clock and 6 o'clock positions and repeat the previous inspection. Spin the wheel, and check for roughness or tightness of the front wheel bearing.

☐ If excess free play is suspected at a component pivot point, this can be confirmed by using a large screwdriver or similar tool and levering between the mounting and the component attachment. This will confirm whether the wear is in the pivot bush, its retaining bolt, or in the mounting itself (the bolt holes can often become elongated).

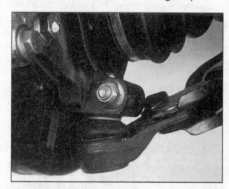

☐ Carry out all the above checks at the other front wheel, and then at both rear wheels.

Springs and shock absorbers

☐ Examine the suspension struts (when applicable) for serious fluid leakage, corrosion, or damage to the casing. Also check the security of the mounting points.
☐ If coil springs are fitted, check that the spring ends locate in their seats, and that the spring is not corroded, cracked or broken.
☐ If leaf springs are fitted, check that all leaves are intact, that the axle is securely attached to each spring, and that there is no deterioration of the spring eye mountings, bushes, and shackles.

☐ The same general checks apply to vehicles fitted with other suspension types, such as torsion bars, hydraulic displacer units, etc. Ensure that all mountings and attachments are secure, that there are no signs of excessive wear, corrosion or damage, and (on hydraulic types) that there are no fluid leaks or damaged pipes.
☐ Inspect the shock absorbers for signs of serious fluid leakage. Check for wear of the mounting bushes or attachments, or damage to the body of the unit.

Driveshafts (fwd vehicles only)

☐ Rotate each front wheel in turn and inspect the constant velocity joint gaiters for splits or damage. Also check that each driveshaft is straight and undamaged.

Braking system

☐ If possible without dismantling, check brake pad wear and disc condition. Ensure that the friction lining material has not worn excessively, (A) and that the discs are not fractured, pitted, scored or badly worn (B).

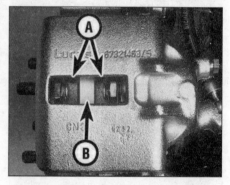

☐ Examine all the rigid brake pipes underneath the vehicle, and the flexible hose(s) at the rear. Look for corrosion, chafing or insecurity of the pipes, and for signs of bulging under pressure, chafing, splits or deterioration of the flexible hoses.
☐ Look for signs of fluid leaks at the brake calipers or on the brake backplates. Repair or renew leaking components.
☐ Slowly spin each wheel, while your assistant depresses and releases the footbrake. Ensure that each brake is operating and does not bind when the pedal is released.

☐ Examine the handbrake mechanism, checking for frayed or broken cables, excessive corrosion, or wear or insecurity of the linkage. Check that the mechanism works on each relevant wheel, and releases fully, without binding.

☐ It is not possible to test brake efficiency without special equipment, but a road test can be carried out later to check that the vehicle pulls up in a straight line.

Fuel and exhaust systems

☐ Inspect the fuel tank (including the filler cap), fuel pipes, hoses and unions. All components must be secure and free from leaks.

☐ Examine the exhaust system over its entire length, checking for any damaged, broken or missing mountings, security of the retaining clamps and rust or corrosion.

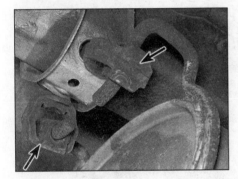

Wheels and tyres

☐ Examine the sidewalls and tread area of each tyre in turn. Check for cuts, tears, lumps, bulges, separation of the tread, and exposure of the ply or cord due to wear or damage. Check that the tyre bead is correctly seated on the wheel rim, that the valve is sound and properly seated, and that the wheel is not distorted or damaged.

☐ Check that the tyres are of the correct size for the vehicle, that they are of the same size and type on each axle, and that the pressures are correct.

☐ Check the tyre tread depth. The legal minimum at the time of writing is 1.6 mm over at least three-quarters of the tread width. Abnormal tread wear may indicate incorrect front wheel alignment.

Body corrosion

☐ Check the condition of the entire vehicle structure for signs of corrosion in load-bearing areas. (These include chassis box sections, side sills, cross-members, pillars, and all suspension, steering, braking system and seat belt mountings and anchorages.) Any corrosion which has seriously reduced the thickness of a load-bearing area is likely to cause the vehicle to fail. In this case professional repairs are likely to be needed.

☐ Damage or corrosion which causes sharp or otherwise dangerous edges to be exposed will also cause the vehicle to fail.

4 Checks carried out on YOUR VEHICLE'S EXHAUST EMISSION SYSTEM

Petrol models

☐ The engine should be warmed up, and running well (ignition system in good order, air filter element clean, etc).

☐ Before testing, run the engine at around 2500 rpm for 20 seconds. Let the engine drop to idle, and watch for smoke from the exhaust. If the idle speed is too high, or if dense blue or black smoke emerges for more than 5 seconds, the vehicle will fail. Typically, blue smoke signifies oil burning (engine wear); black smoke means unburnt fuel (dirty air cleaner element, or other fuel system fault).

☐ An exhaust gas analyser for measuring carbon monoxide (CO) and hydrocarbons (HC) is now needed. If one cannot be hired or borrowed, have a local garage perform the check.

CO emissions (mixture)

☐ The MOT tester has access to the CO limits for all vehicles. The CO level is measured at idle speed, and at 'fast idle' (2500 to 3000 rpm). The following limits are given as a general guide:

At idle speed – Less than 0.5% CO
At 'fast idle' – Less than 0.3% CO
Lambda reading – 0.97 to 1.03

☐ If the CO level is too high, this may point to poor maintenance, a fuel injection system problem, faulty lambda (oxygen) sensor or catalytic converter. Try an injector cleaning treatment, and check the vehicle's ECU for fault codes.

HC emissions

☐ The MOT tester has access to HC limits for all vehicles. The HC level is measured at 'fast idle' (2500 to 3000 rpm). The following limits are given as a general guide:

At 'fast idle' – Less then 200 ppm

☐ Excessive HC emissions are typically caused by oil being burnt (worn engine), or by a blocked crankcase ventilation system ('breather'). If the engine oil is old and thin, an oil change may help. If the engine is running badly, check the vehicle's ECU for fault codes.

Diesel models

☐ The only emission test for diesel engines is measuring exhaust smoke density, using a calibrated smoke meter. The test involves accelerating the engine at least 3 times to its maximum unloaded speed.

Note: *On engines with a timing belt, it is VITAL that the belt is in good condition before the test is carried out.*

☐ With the engine warmed up, it is first purged by running at around 2500 rpm for 20 seconds. A governor check is then carried out, by slowly accelerating the engine to its maximum speed. After this, the smoke meter is connected, and the engine is accelerated quickly to maximum speed three times. If the smoke density is less than the limits given below, the vehicle will pass:

Non-turbo vehicles: 2.5m-1
Turbocharged vehicles: 3.0m-1

☐ If excess smoke is produced, try fitting a new air cleaner element, or using an injector cleaning treatment. If the engine is running badly, where applicable, check the vehicle's ECU for fault codes. Also check the vehicle's EGR system, where applicable. At high mileages, the injectors may require professional attention.

Engine

- [ ] Engine fails to rotate when attempting to start
- [ ] Engine rotates, but will not start
- [ ] Engine difficult to start when cold
- [ ] Engine difficult to start when hot
- [ ] Starter motor noisy or excessively-rough in engagement
- [ ] Engine starts, but stops immediately
- [ ] Engine idles erratically
- [ ] Engine misfires at idle speed
- [ ] Engine misfires throughout the driving speed range
- [ ] Engine hesitates on acceleration
- [ ] Engine stalls
- [ ] Engine lacks power
- [ ] Engine backfires
- [ ] Oil pressure warning light illuminated with engine running
- [ ] Engine runs-on after switching off
- [ ] Engine noises

Cooling system

- [ ] Overheating
- [ ] Overcooling
- [ ] External coolant leakage
- [ ] Internal coolant leakage
- [ ] Corrosion

Fuel and exhaust systems

- [ ] Excessive fuel consumption
- [ ] Fuel leakage and/or fuel odour
- [ ] Excessive noise or fumes from exhaust system

Clutch

- [ ] Pedal travels to floor – no pressure or very little resistance
- [ ] Clutch fails to disengage (unable to select gears)
- [ ] Clutch slips (engine speed increases, with no increase in vehicle speed)
- [ ] Judder as clutch is engaged
- [ ] Noise when depressing or releasing clutch pedal

Transmission

- [ ] Noisy in neutral with engine running
- [ ] Noisy in one particular gear
- [ ] Difficulty engaging gears
- [ ] Jumps out of gear
- [ ] Vibration
- [ ] Lubricant leaks

Driveshafts

- [ ] Vibration when accelerating or decelerating
- [ ] Clicking or knocking noise on turns (at slow speed on full-lock)

Propeller shaft

- [ ] Vibration when accelerating or decelerating
- [ ] Noise (grinding or high-pitched squeak) when moving slowly
- [ ] Noise (knocking or clicking) when accelerating or decelerating

Rear axle

- [ ] Roughness or rumble from the rear of the vehicle (perhaps less with the handbrake slightly applied)
- [ ] Noise (high-pitched whine) increasing with road speed
- [ ] Noise (knocking or clicking) when accelerating or decelerating
- [ ] Lubricant leaks

Braking system

- [ ] Vehicle pulls to one side under braking
- [ ] Noise (grinding or high-pitched squeal) when brakes applied
- [ ] Excessive brake pedal travel
- [ ] Brake pedal feels spongy when depressed
- [ ] Excessive brake pedal effort required to stop vehicle
- [ ] Judder felt through brake pedal or steering wheel when braking
- [ ] Brakes binding
- [ ] Rear wheels locking under normal braking

Suspension and steering

- [ ] Vehicle pulls to one side
- [ ] Wheel wobble and vibration
- [ ] Excessive pitching and/or rolling around corners, or during braking
- [ ] Wandering or general instability
- [ ] Excessively-stiff steering
- [ ] Excessive play in steering
- [ ] Lack of power assistance
- [ ] Tyre wear excessive

Electrical system

- [ ] Battery will not hold a charge for more than a few days
- [ ] Ignition/no-charge warning light remains illuminated with engine running
- [ ] Ignition/no-charge warning light fails to come on
- [ ] Lights inoperative
- [ ] Instrument readings inaccurate or erratic
- [ ] Horn inoperative, or unsatisfactory in operation
- [ ] Windscreen wipers inoperative, or unsatisfactory in operation
- [ ] Windscreen washers inoperative, or unsatisfactory in operation
- [ ] Electric windows inoperative, or unsatisfactory in operation
- [ ] Central locking system inoperative, or unsatisfactory in operation

Introduction

The vehicle owner who does his or her own maintenance according to the recommended service schedules should not have to use this section of the manual very often. Modern component reliability is such that, provided those items subject to wear or deterioration are inspected or renewed at the specified intervals, sudden failure is comparatively rare. Faults do not usually just happen as a result of sudden failure, but develop over a period of time. Major mechanical failures in particular are usually preceded by characteristic symptoms over hundreds or even thousands of miles. Those components which do occasionally fail without warning are often small and easily carried in the vehicle.

With any fault-finding, the first step is to decide where to begin investigations. Sometimes this is obvious, but on other occasions, a little detective work will be necessary. The owner who makes half a dozen haphazard adjustments or replacements may be successful in curing a fault (or its symptoms), but will be none the wiser if the fault recurs, and ultimately may have spent more time and money than was necessary. A calm and logical approach will be found to be more satisfactory in the long run. Always take into account any warning signs or abnormalities that may have been noticed in the period preceding the fault – power loss, high or low gauge readings, unusual smells, etc – and remember that failure of components such as fuses may only be pointers to some underlying fault.

The pages which follow provide an easy-reference guide to the more common problems which may occur during the operation of the vehicle. These problems and their possible causes are grouped under headings denoting various components or systems, such as Engine, Cooling system, etc. The general Chapter which deals with the problem is also shown in brackets; refer to the relevant part of that Chapter for system-specific information. Whatever the fault, certain basic principles apply. These are as follows:

Verify the fault. This is simply a matter of being sure that you know what the symptoms are before starting work. This is particularly important if you are investigating a fault for someone else, who may not have described it very accurately.

Don't overlook the obvious. For example, if the vehicle won't start, is there fuel in the tank? (Don't take anyone else's word on this particular point, and don't trust the fuel gauge either!) If an electrical fault is indicated, look for loose or broken wires before digging out the test gear.

Cure the disease, not the symptom. Substituting a flat battery with a fully-charged one will get you off the hard shoulder, but if the underlying cause is not attended to, the new battery will go the same way.

Don't take anything for granted. Particularly, don't forget that a 'new' component may itself be defective (especially if it's been rattling around in the boot for months), and don't leave components out of a fault diagnosis sequence just because they are new or recently-fitted. When you do finally diagnose a difficult fault, you'll probably realise that all the evidence was there from the start.

Consider what work, if any, has recently been carried out. Many faults arise through careless or hurried work. For instance, if any work has been performed under the bonnet, could some of the wiring have been dislodged or incorrectly routed, or a hose trapped? Have all the fasteners been properly tightened? Were new, genuine parts and new gaskets used? There is often a certain amount of detective work to be done in this case, as an apparently-unrelated task can have far-reaching consequences.

Diesel fault diagnosis

The majority of starting problems on small diesel engines are electrical in origin. The mechanic who is familiar with petrol engines but less so with diesel may be inclined to view the diesel's injectors and pump in the same light as the spark plugs and distributor, but this is generally a mistake.

When investigating complaints of difficult starting for someone else, make sure that the correct starting procedure is understood and is being followed. Some drivers are unaware of the significance of the preheating warning light – many modern engines are sufficiently forgiving for this not to matter in mild weather, but with the onset of winter, problems begin.

As a rule of thumb, if the engine is difficult to start but runs well when it has finally got going, the problem is electrical (battery, starter motor or preheating system). If poor performance is combined with difficult starting, the problem is likely to be in the fuel system. The low-pressure (supply) side of the fuel system should be checked before suspecting the injectors and high-pressure pump. The most common fuel supply problem is air getting into the system, and any pipe from the fuel tank forwards must be scrutinised if air leakage is suspected. Normally the pump is the last item to suspect, since unless it has been tampered with, there is no reason for it to be at fault.

Engine

Engine fails to rotate when attempting to start

☐ Battery terminal connections loose or corroded *(see Weekly checks)*
☐ Battery discharged or faulty (Chapter 5)
☐ Broken, loose or disconnected wiring in the starting circuit (Chapter 5)
☐ Defective starter solenoid or ignition switch (Chapter 5 or 12)
☐ Defective starter motor (Chapter 5)
☐ Starter pinion or flywheel ring gear teeth loose or broken (Chapter 2A, 2B or 5)
☐ Engine earth strap broken or disconnected (Chapter 5)
☐ Engine suffering 'hydraulic lock' (eg from water drawn into the engine after traversing flooded roads, or from a serious internal coolant leak) – consult a main dealer for advice

Engine rotates, but will not start

☐ Fuel tank empty
☐ Battery discharged (engine rotates slowly) (Chapter 5)
☐ Battery terminal connections loose or corroded *(see Weekly checks)*
☐ Immobiliser fault, or 'uncoded' ignition key being used (Chapter 12 or Roadside repairs)
☐ Preheating system faulty (Chapter 5)
☐ Fuel injection/engine management system fault (Chapter 4A or 4B)
☐ Air in fuel system (Chapter 4A)
☐ Major mechanical failure (Chapter 2A, 2B, or 2C)

Engine difficult to start when cold

☐ Battery discharged (Chapter 5)
☐ Battery terminal connections loose or corroded *(see Weekly checks)*
☐ Preheating system faulty (Chapter 5)
☐ Fuel injection/engine management system fault (Chapter 4A or 4B)
☐ Wrong grade of engine oil used *(Weekly checks, Chapter 1)*
☐ Low cylinder compression (Chapter 2A or 2B)
☐ Air in fuel system (Chapter 4A)

Engine difficult to start when hot

☐ Air filter element dirty or clogged (Chapter 1)
☐ Fuel injection/engine management system fault (Chapter 4A or 4B)
☐ Low cylinder compression (Chapter 2A or 2B)
☐ Air in fuel system (Chapter 4A)

Starter motor noisy or excessively-rough in engagement

☐ Starter pinion or flywheel ring gear teeth loose or broken (2A, 2B or 5)
☐ Starter motor mounting bolts loose or missing (Chapter 5)
☐ Starter motor internal components worn or damaged (Chapter 5)

Engine starts, but stops immediately

☐ Fuel injection/engine management system fault (Chapter 4A or 4B)

Engine idles erratically

☐ Air filter element clogged (Chapter 1)
☐ Uneven or low cylinder compression (Chapter 2A or 2B)
☐ Camshaft lobes worn (Chapter 2A or 2B)
☐ Fuel injection/engine management system fault (Chapter 4A or 4B)
☐ Air in fuel system (Chapter 4A)

Engine misfires at idle speed

☐ Faulty injector(s) (Chapter 4A)
☐ Uneven or low cylinder compression (Chapter 2A or 2B)
☐ Disconnected, leaking, or perished crankcase ventilation hoses (Chapter 4B)
☐ Fuel injection/engine management system fault (Chapter 4A or 4B)

Engine misfires throughout the driving speed range

☐ Fuel filter choked (Chapter 1)
☐ Fuel tank vent blocked, or fuel pipes restricted (Chapter 4A or 4B)
☐ Faulty injector(s) (Chapter 4A)
☐ Uneven or low cylinder compression (Chapter 2A or 2B)
☐ Blocked catalytic converter (Chapter 4B)
☐ Fuel injection/engine management system fault (Chapter 4A or 4B)
☐ Engine overheating (Chapter 3)

Engine (continued)

Engine hesitates on acceleration

- [ ] Faulty injector(s) (Chapter 4A)
- [ ] Fuel injection/engine management system fault (Chapter 4A or 4B)

Engine stalls

- [ ] Fuel filter choked (Chapter 1)
- [ ] Fuel tank vent blocked, or fuel pipes restricted (Chapter 4A or 4B)
- [ ] Faulty injector(s) (Chapter 4A)
- [ ] Fuel injection/engine management system fault (Chapter 4A or 4B)

Engine lacks power

- [ ] Air filter element blocked (Chapter 1)
- [ ] Fuel filter choked (Chapter 1)
- [ ] Fuel pipes blocked or restricted (Chapter 4A or 4B)
- [ ] Engine overheating (Chapter 3)
- [ ] Accelerator pedal position sensor faulty (Chapter 4A)
- [ ] Faulty injector(s) (Chapter 4A)
- [ ] Uneven or low cylinder compression (Chapter 2A or 2B)
- [ ] Fuel injection/engine management system fault (Chapter 4A or 4B)
- [ ] Blocked catalytic converter (Chapter 4B)
- [ ] Brakes binding (Chapter 1 or 9)
- [ ] Clutch slipping (Chapter 6)

Engine backfires

- [ ] Fuel injection/engine management system fault (Chapter 4A or 4B)
- [ ] Blocked catalytic converter (Chapter 4B)

Oil pressure warning light illuminated with engine running

- [ ] Low oil level, or incorrect oil grade (see Weekly checks)
- [ ] Faulty oil pressure warning light switch, or wiring damaged (Chapter 2A or 2B)
- [ ] Worn engine bearings and/or oil pump (Chapter 2A, 2B or 2C)
- [ ] High engine operating temperature (Chapter 3)
- [ ] Oil pump pressure relief valve defective (Chapter 2A, 2B or 2C)
- [ ] Oil pump pick-up strainer clogged (Chapter 2A or 2B)

Engine runs-on after switching off

- [ ] Excessive carbon build-up in engine (Chapter 2A, 2B or 2C)
- [ ] High engine operating temperature (Chapter 3)
- [ ] Fuel injection/engine management system fault (Chapter 4A or 4B)

Engine noises

Pre-ignition (pinking) or knocking during acceleration or under load

- [ ] Excessive carbon build-up in engine (Chapter 2A, 2B or 2C)
- [ ] Fuel injection/engine management system fault (Chapter 4A or 4B)
- [ ] Faulty injector(s) (Chapter 4A)

Whistling or wheezing noises

- [ ] Leaking exhaust manifold gasket or pipe-to-manifold joint (Chapter 4A)
- [ ] Leaking vacuum hose (Chapter 4A, 4B or 9)
- [ ] Blowing cylinder head gasket (Chapter 2A or 2B)
- [ ] Partially blocked or leaking crankcase ventilation system (Chapter 4B)

Tapping or rattling noises

- [ ] Worn valve gear or camshaft(s) (Chapter 2A, 2B or 2C)
- [ ] Ancillary component fault (coolant pump, alternator, etc) (Chapter 3, 5, etc)

Knocking or thumping noises

- [ ] Worn big-end bearings (regular heavy knocking, perhaps less under load) (Chapter 2C)
- [ ] Worn main bearings (rumbling and knocking, perhaps worsening under load) (Chapter 2C)
- [ ] Piston slap – most noticeable when cold, caused by piston/bore wear (Chapter 2C)
- [ ] Ancillary component fault (coolant pump, alternator, etc) (Chapter 3, 5, etc)
- [ ] Engine mountings worn or defective (Chapter 2A or 2B)
- [ ] Front suspension or steering components worn (Chapter 10)

Cooling system

Overheating

- [ ] Insufficient coolant in system (see Weekly checks)
- [ ] Thermostat faulty (Chapter 3)
- [ ] Radiator core blocked, or grille restricted (Chapter 3)
- [ ] Cooling fan faulty (Chapter 3)
- [ ] Inaccurate cylinder head temperature sensor (Chapter 3 or 4A)
- [ ] Airlock in cooling system (Chapter 1 or 3)
- [ ] Expansion tank pressure cap faulty (Chapter 1 or 3)
- [ ] Engine management system fault (Chapter 4A or 4B)

Overcooling

- [ ] Thermostat faulty (Chapter 3)
- [ ] Inaccurate cylinder head temperature sensor (Chapter 3 or 4A)
- [ ] Cooling fan faulty (Chapter 3)
- [ ] Engine management system fault (Chapter 4A or 4B)

External coolant leakage

- [ ] Deteriorated or damaged hoses or hose clips (Chapter 1)
- [ ] Radiator core or heater matrix leaking (Chapter 3)
- [ ] Expansion tank pressure cap faulty (Chapter 1 or 3)
- [ ] Coolant pump internal seal leaking (Chapter 3)
- [ ] Coolant pump gasket leaking (Chapter 3)
- [ ] Boiling due to overheating (Chapter 3)
- [ ] Cylinder block core plug leaking (Chapter 2C)

Internal coolant leakage

- [ ] Leaking cylinder head gasket (Chapter 2A or 2B)
- [ ] Cracked cylinder head or cylinder block (Chapter 2A, 2B or 2C)

Corrosion

- [ ] Infrequent draining and flushing (Chapter 1)
- [ ] Incorrect coolant mixture or inappropriate coolant type (Chapter 1)

Fuel and exhaust systems

Excessive fuel consumption

- [ ] Air filter element dirty or clogged (Chapter 1)
- [ ] Fuel injection system fault (Chapter 4A or 4B)
- [ ] Engine management system fault (Chapter 4A or 4B)
- [ ] Crankcase ventilation system blocked (Chapter 4B)
- [ ] Tyres under-inflated (see Weekly checks)
- [ ] Brakes binding (Chapter 1 or 9)
- [ ] Fuel leak, causing apparent high consumption (Chapter 1, 4A or 4B)

Fuel leakage and/or fuel odour

- [ ] Damaged or corroded fuel tank, pipes or connections (Chapter 4A or 4B)

Excessive noise or fumes from exhaust system

- [ ] Leaking exhaust system or manifold joints (Chapter 1 or 4A)
- [ ] Leaking, corroded or damaged silencers or pipe (Chapter 1 or 4A)
- [ ] Broken mountings causing body or suspension contact (Chapter 1 or 4A)

Clutch

Pedal travels to floor – no pressure or very little resistance

- [ ] Air in hydraulic system/faulty master or slave cylinder (Chapter 6)
- [ ] Faulty hydraulic release system (Chapter 6)
- [ ] Faulty clutch release/slave cylinder (Chapter 6)
- [ ] Broken diaphragm spring in clutch pressure plate (Chapter 6)

Clutch fails to disengage (unable to select gears)

- [ ] Air in hydraulic system/faulty master or release/slave cylinder (Chapter 6)
- [ ] Faulty hydraulic release system (Chapter 6)
- [ ] Clutch disc sticking on transmission input shaft splines (Chapter 6)
- [ ] Clutch disc sticking to flywheel or pressure plate (Chapter 6)
- [ ] Faulty pressure plate assembly (Chapter 6)
- [ ] Clutch release mechanism worn or incorrectly assembled (Chapter 6)

Clutch slips (engine speed increases, with no increase in vehicle speed)

- [ ] Faulty hydraulic release system (Chapter 6)
- [ ] Clutch disc linings excessively worn (Chapter 6)
- [ ] Clutch disc linings contaminated with oil or grease (Chapter 6)
- [ ] Faulty pressure plate or weak diaphragm spring (Chapter 6)

Judder as clutch is engaged

- [ ] Clutch disc linings contaminated with oil or grease (Chapter 6)
- [ ] Clutch disc linings excessively worn (Chapter 6)
- [ ] Faulty or distorted pressure plate or diaphragm spring (Chapter 6).
- [ ] Worn or loose engine or transmission mountings (Chapter 2A or 2B)
- [ ] Clutch disc hub or transmission input shaft splines worn (Chapter 6)

Noise when depressing or releasing clutch pedal

- [ ] Faulty clutch release/slave cylinder (Chapter 6)
- [ ] Worn or dry clutch pedal bushes (Chapter 6)
- [ ] Faulty pressure plate assembly (Chapter 6)
- [ ] Pressure plate diaphragm spring broken (Chapter 6)
- [ ] Broken clutch disc cushioning springs (Chapter 6)

Manual transmission

Noisy in neutral with engine running

- [ ] Lack of oil (Chapter 7A or 7B)
- [ ] Input shaft bearings worn (noise apparent with clutch pedal released, but not when depressed) (Chapter 7A or 7B)*
- [ ] Clutch release/slave cylinder faulty (noise apparent with clutch pedal depressed, possibly less when released) (Chapter 6)

Noisy in one particular gear

- [ ] Worn, damaged or chipped gear teeth (Chapter 7A or 7B)*

Difficulty engaging gears

- [ ] Clutch fault (Chapter 6)
- [ ] Worn, damaged, or poorly-adjusted gearchange (Chapter 7A or 7B)
- [ ] Lack of oil (Chapter 7A or 7B)
- [ ] Worn synchroniser units (Chapter 7A or 7B)*

Jumps out of gear

- [ ] Worn, damaged, or poorly-adjusted gearchange (Chapter 7A or 7B)
- [ ] Worn synchroniser units (Chapter 7A or 7B)*
- [ ] Worn selector forks (Chapter 7A or 7B)*

Vibration

- [ ] Lack of oil (Chapter 7A or 7B)
- [ ] Worn bearings (Chapter 7A or 7B)*

Lubricant leaks

- [ ] Leaking driveshaft or selector shaft oil seal (Chapter 7A)
- [ ] Leaking housing joint (Chapter 7A or 7B)*
- [ ] Leaking input shaft oil seal (Chapter 7A or 7B)*

*Although the corrective action necessary to remedy the symptoms described is beyond the scope of the home mechanic, the above information should be helpful in isolating the cause of the condition, so that the owner can communicate clearly with a professional mechanic.

Driveshafts

Vibration when accelerating or decelerating

☐ Worn inner constant velocity joint (Chapter 8)
☐ Bent or distorted driveshaft (Chapter 8)
☐ Worn intermediate shaft bearing (Chapter 8)

Clicking or knocking noise on turns (at slow speed on full-lock)

☐ Worn outer constant velocity joint (Chapter 8)
☐ Lack of constant velocity joint lubricant, possibly due to damaged gaiter (Chapter 8)

Propeller shaft

Vibration when accelerating or decelerating

☐ Propeller shaft out of balance or incorrectly fitted (Chapter 8)
☐ Propeller shaft flange bolts loose (Chapter 8)
☐ Excessive wear in universal joints (Chapter 8)
☐ Excessive wear in centre bearings (Chapter 8)

Noise (grinding or high-pitched squeak) when moving slowly

☐ Excessive wear in universal joints (Chapter 8)
☐ Excessive wear in centre bearings (Chapter 8)

Noise (knocking or clicking) when accelerating or decelerating

☐ Propeller shaft flange bolts loose (Chapter 8)
☐ Excessive wear in universal joints (Chapter 8)
☐ Excessive wear in centre bearings (Chapter 8)

Rear axle

Roughness or rumble from the rear of the vehicle (perhaps less with the handbrake slightly applied)

☐ Rear hub bearings worn (Chapter 8)
☐ Differential pinion flange bolts loose (Chapter 8)
☐ Loose rear spring U-bolts (Chapter 8)
☐ Roadwheel nuts loose (Chapter 1 and 10)

Lubricant leaks

☐ Leaking oil seal (Chapter 8)
☐ Leaking differential housing cover joint (Chapter 8)

Braking system

Note: *Before assuming that a brake problem exists, make sure that the tyres are in good condition and correctly inflated, that the front wheel alignment is correct, and that the vehicle is not loaded with weight in an unequal manner. Apart from checking the condition of all pipe and hose connections, any faults occurring on the anti-lock braking system should be referred to a Ford dealer for diagnosis.*

Vehicle pulls to one side under braking

☐ Worn, defective, damaged or contaminated brake pads/shoes on one side (Chapter 1 or 9)
☐ Seized or partially-seized brake caliper/wheel cylinder piston (Chapter 1 or 9)
☐ A mixture of brake pad/shoe lining materials fitted between sides (Chapter 1 or 9)
☐ Brake caliper mounting bolts loose (Chapter 9)
☐ Worn or damaged steering or suspension components (Chapter 1 or 10)

Noise (grinding or high-pitched squeal) when brakes applied

☐ Brake pad/shoe friction lining material worn down to wear sensor or metal backing (Chapter 1 or 9)
☐ Excessive corrosion of brake disc/drum (may be apparent after the vehicle has been standing for some time (Chapter 1 or 9)
☐ Foreign object (stone chipping, etc) trapped between brake disc and shield (Chapter 1 or 9)

Excessive brake pedal travel

☐ Faulty master cylinder (Chapter 9)
☐ Air in hydraulic system (Chapter 1 or 9)
☐ Faulty vacuum servo unit (Chapter 9)
☐ Faulty vacuum pump (Chapter 9)
☐ Disconnected, damaged or insecure brake servo vacuum hose (Chapter 9)

Brake pedal feels spongy when depressed

☐ Air in hydraulic system (Chapter 1 or 9)
☐ Deteriorated flexible rubber brake hoses (Chapter 1 or 9)
☐ Master cylinder mounting nuts loose (Chapter 9)
☐ Faulty master cylinder (Chapter 9)

Excessive brake pedal effort required to stop vehicle

☐ Faulty vacuum servo unit (Chapter 9)
☐ Faulty vacuum pump (Chapter 9)
☐ Disconnected, damaged or insecure brake servo vacuum hose (Chapter 9)
☐ Primary or secondary hydraulic circuit failure (Chapter 9)
☐ Seized brake caliper/wheel cylinder piston (Chapter 9)
☐ Brake pads/shoes incorrectly fitted (Chapter 9)
☐ Incorrect grade of brake pads/shoes fitted (Chapter 9)
☐ Brake pad/shoe linings contaminated (Chapter 1 or 9)

Judder felt through brake pedal or steering wheel when braking

Note: *Under heavy braking on models equipped with ABS, vibration may be felt through the brake pedal. This is a normal feature of ABS operation, and does not constitute a fault.*

☐ Excessive run-out or distortion of discs/drums (Chapter 1 or 9)
☐ Brake pad/shoe linings worn (Chapter 1 or 9)
☐ Brake caliper mounting bolts loose (Chapter 9)
☐ Wear in suspension or steering components or mountings (Chapter 1 or 10)
☐ Front wheels out of balance (see *Weekly checks*)

Brakes binding

☐ Seized brake caliper/wheel cylinder piston (Chapter 9)
☐ Faulty master cylinder (Chapter 9)

Rear wheels locking under normal braking

☐ Rear brake shoe linings contaminated or damaged (Chapter 1 or 9)
☐ Rear brake drum warped (Chapter 1 or 9)

Suspension and steering

Note: *Before diagnosing suspension or steering faults, be sure that the trouble is not due to incorrect tyre pressures, mixtures of tyre types, or binding brakes.*

Vehicle pulls to one side

- ☐ Defective tyre *(see Weekly checks)*
- ☐ Excessive wear in suspension or steering components (Chapter 1 or 10)
- ☐ Incorrect front wheel alignment (Chapter 10)
- ☐ Accident damage to steering or suspension components (Chapter 1 or 10)

Wheel wobble and vibration

- ☐ Front wheels out of balance (vibration felt mainly through the steering wheel) *(see Weekly checks)*
- ☐ Rear wheels out of balance (vibration felt throughout the vehicle) *(see Weekly checks)*
- ☐ Roadwheels damaged or distorted *(see Weekly checks)*
- ☐ Faulty or damaged tyre *(see Weekly checks)*
- ☐ Worn steering or suspension joints, bushes or components (Chapter 1 or 10)
- ☐ Wheel nuts loose (Chapter 1)

Excessive pitching and/or rolling around corners, or during braking

- ☐ Defective shock absorbers (Chapter 1 or 10)
- ☐ Broken or weak spring and/or suspension component (Chapter 1 or 10)
- ☐ Worn or damaged anti-roll bar or mountings (Chapter 1 or 10)

Wandering or general instability

- ☐ Incorrect front wheel alignment (Chapter 10)
- ☐ Worn steering or suspension joints, bushes or components (Chapter 1 or 10)
- ☐ Roadwheels out of balance *(see Weekly checks)*
- ☐ Faulty or damaged tyre *(see Weekly checks)*
- ☐ Wheel nuts loose (Chapter 1)
- ☐ Defective shock absorbers (Chapter 1 or 10)
- ☐ Power steering system fault (Chapter 10)

Excessively-stiff steering

- ☐ Seized steering linkage balljoint or suspension balljoint (Chapter 1 or 10)
- ☐ Incorrect front wheel alignment (Chapter 10)
- ☐ Steering rack damaged (Chapter 10)
- ☐ Power steering system fault (Chapter 10)

Excessive play in steering

- ☐ Worn steering column/intermediate shaft joints (Chapter 10)
- ☐ Worn track rod balljoints (Chapter 1 or 10)
- ☐ Worn steering rack (Chapter 10)
- ☐ Worn steering or suspension joints, bushes or components (Chapter 1 or 10)

Lack of power assistance

- ☐ Power steering system fault (Chapter 10)
- ☐ Faulty steering rack (Chapter 10)

Tyre wear excessive

Tyres worn on inside or outside edges

- ☐ Tyres under-inflated (wear on both edges) *(see Weekly checks)*
- ☐ Incorrect camber or castor angles (wear on one edge only) (Chapter 10)
- ☐ Worn steering or suspension joints, bushes or components (Chapter 1 or 10)
- ☐ Excessively-hard cornering or braking
- ☐ Accident damage

Tyre treads exhibit feathered edges

- ☐ Incorrect toe-setting (Chapter 10)

Tyres worn in centre of tread

- ☐ Tyres over-inflated *(see Weekly checks)*

Tyres worn on inside and outside edges

- ☐ Tyres under-inflated *(see Weekly checks)*

Tyres worn unevenly

- ☐ Tyres/wheels out of balance *(see Weekly checks)*
- ☐ Excessive wheel or tyre run-out
- ☐ Worn shock absorbers (Chapter 1 10)
- ☐ Faulty tyre *(see Weekly checks)*

Electrical system

Note: *For problems associated with the starting system, refer to the faults listed under 'Engine' earlier in this Section.*

Battery will not hold a charge for more than a few days

- ☐ Battery defective internally (Chapter 5)
- ☐ Battery terminal connections loose or corroded *(see Weekly checks)*
- ☐ Auxiliary drivebelt worn or faulty automatic adjuster (Chapter 1)
- ☐ Alternator not charging at correct output (Chapter 5)
- ☐ Alternator or voltage regulator faulty (Chapter 5)
- ☐ Short-circuit causing continual battery drain (Chapter 5 or 12)

Ignition/no-charge warning light remains illuminated with engine running

- ☐ Auxiliary drivebelt broken, worn, or or faulty automatic adjuster (Chapter 1)
- ☐ Internal fault in alternator or voltage regulator (Chapter 5)
- ☐ Broken, disconnected, or loose wiring in charging circuit (Chapter 5 or 12)

Ignition/no-charge warning light fails to come on

- ☐ Warning light bulb blown (Chapter 12)
- ☐ Broken, disconnected, or loose wiring in warning light circuit (Chapter 5 or 12)
- ☐ Alternator faulty (Chapter 5)

Lights inoperative

- ☐ Bulb blown (Chapter 12)
- ☐ Corrosion of bulb or bulbholder contacts (Chapter 12)
- ☐ Blown fuse (Chapter 12)
- ☐ Faulty relay (Chapter 12)
- ☐ Broken, loose, or disconnected wiring (Chapter 12)
- ☐ Faulty switch (Chapter 12)

Instrument readings inaccurate or erratic

Fuel or temperature gauges give no reading

- ☐ Faulty gauge sender unit (Chapter 3 or 4A)
- ☐ Wiring open-circuit (Chapter 12)
- ☐ Faulty gauge (Chapter 12)

Electrical system (continued)

Fuel or temperature gauges give continuous maximum reading

☐ Faulty gauge sender unit (Chapter 3 or 4A)
☐ Wiring short-circuit (Chapter 12)
☐ Faulty gauge (Chapter 12)

Horn inoperative, or unsatisfactory in operation

Horn operates all the time

☐ Horn push either earthed or stuck down (Chapter 12)
☐ Horn cable-to-horn push earthed (Chapter 12)

Horn fails to operate

☐ Blown fuse (Chapter 12)
☐ Cable or connections loose, broken or disconnected (Chapter 12)
☐ Faulty horn (Chapter 12)

Horn emits intermittent or unsatisfactory sound

☐ Cable connections loose (Chapter 12)
☐ Horn mountings loose (Chapter 12)
☐ Faulty horn (Chapter 12)

Windscreen wipers inoperative, or unsatisfactory in operation

Wipers fail to operate, or operate very slowly

☐ Wiper blades stuck to screen, or linkage seized or binding (Chapter 12)
☐ Blown fuse (Chapter 12)
☐ Battery discharged (Chapter 5)
☐ Cable or connections loose, broken or disconnected (Chapter 12)
☐ Faulty relay (Chapter 12)
☐ Faulty wiper motor (Chapter 12)

Wiper blades sweep over too large or too small an area of the glass

☐ Wiper blades incorrectly fitted, or wrong size used (see *Weekly checks*)
☐ Wiper arms incorrectly positioned on spindles (Chapter 12)
☐ Excessive wear of wiper linkage (Chapter 12)
☐ Wiper motor or linkage mountings loose or insecure (Chapter 12)

Wiper blades fail to clean the glass effectively

☐ Wiper blade rubbers dirty, worn or perished (see *Weekly checks*)
☐ Wiper blades incorrectly fitted, or wrong size used (see *Weekly checks*)
☐ Wiper arm tension springs broken, or arm pivots seized (Chapter 12)
☐ Insufficient windscreen washer additive to adequately remove road film (see *Weekly checks*)

Windscreen washers inoperative, or unsatisfactory in operation

One or more washer jets inoperative

☐ Blocked washer jet
☐ Disconnected, kinked or restricted fluid hose (Chapter 12)
☐ Insufficient fluid in washer reservoir (see *Weekly checks*)

Washer pump fails to operate

☐ Broken or disconnected wiring or connections (Chapter 12)
☐ Blown fuse (Chapter 12)
☐ Faulty washer switch (Chapter 12)
☐ Faulty washer pump (Chapter 12)

Washer pump runs for some time before fluid is emitted from jets

☐ Faulty one-way valve in fluid supply hose (Chapter 12)

Electric windows inoperative, or unsatisfactory in operation

Window glass will only move in one direction

☐ Faulty switch (Chapter 12)

Window glass slow to move

☐ Battery discharged (Chapter 5)
☐ Regulator seized or damaged, or in need of lubrication (Chapter 11)
☐ Door internal components or trim fouling regulator (Chapter 11)
☐ Faulty motor (Chapter 11)

Window glass fails to move

☐ Blown fuse (Chapter 12)
☐ Faulty relay (Chapter 12)
☐ Broken or disconnected wiring or connections (Chapter 12)
☐ Faulty motor (Chapter 11)

Central locking system inoperative, or unsatisfactory in operation

Complete system failure

☐ Remote handset battery discharged, where applicable
☐ Blown fuse (Chapter 12)
☐ Faulty relay (Chapter 12)
☐ Broken or disconnected wiring or connections (Chapter 12)
☐ Faulty motor (Chapter 11)

Latch locks but will not unlock, or unlocks but will not lock

☐ Remote handset battery discharged, where applicable
☐ Faulty master switch (Chapter 12)
☐ Broken or disconnected latch operating rods or levers (Chapter 11)
☐ Faulty relay (Chapter 12)
☐ Faulty motor (Chapter 11)

One solenoid/motor fails to operate

☐ Broken or disconnected wiring or connections (Chapter 12)
☐ Faulty operating assembly (Chapter 11)
☐ Broken, binding or disconnected latch operating rods or levers (Chapter 11)
☐ Fault in door latch (Chapter 11)

Note: *References throughout this index are in the form "**Chapter number**" • "**Page number**". So, for example, 2C•15 refers to page 15 of Chapter 2C.*

Note: *References throughout this index are in the form "**Chapter number**" • "**Page number**". So, for example, 2C•15 refers to page 15 of Chapter 2C.*

Note: *References throughout this index are in the form* "**Chapter number**" • "**Page number**". *So, for example, 2C•15 refers to page 15 of Chapter 2C.*

Note: *References throughout this index are in the form* **"Chapter number"** • **"Page number"**. *So, for example, 2C•15 refers to page 15 of Chapter 2C.*

Haynes Manuals – The Complete UK Car List

Title	Book No.
ALFA ROMEO Alfasud/Sprint (74 - 88) up to F *	0292
Alfa Romeo Alfetta (73 - 87) up to E *	0531
AUDI 80, 90 & Coupe Petrol (79 - Nov 88) up to F	0605
Audi 80, 90 & Coupe Petrol (Oct 86 - 90) D to H	1491
Audi 100 & 200 Petrol (Oct 82 - 90) up to H	0907
Audi 100 & A6 Petrol & Diesel (May 91 - May 97) H to P	3504
Audi A3 Petrol & Diesel (96 - May 03) P to 03	4253
Audi A4 Petrol & Diesel (95 - 00) M to X	3575
Audi A4 Petrol & Diesel (01 - 04) X to 54	4609
AUSTIN A35 & A40 (56 - 67) up to F *	0118
Austin/MG/Rover Maestro 1.3 & 1.6 Petrol (83 - 95) up to M	0922
Austin/MG Metro (80 - May 90) up to G	0718
Austin/Rover Montego 1.3 & 1.6 Petrol (84 - 94) A to L	1066
Austin/MG/Rover Montego 2.0 Petrol (84 - 95) A to M	1067
Mini (59 - 69) up to H *	0527
Mini (69 - 01) up to X	0646
Austin/Rover 2.0 litre Diesel Engine (86 - 93) C to L	1857
Austin Healey 100/6 & 3000 (56 - 68) up to G *	0049
BEDFORD CF Petrol (69 - 87) up to E	0163
Bedford/Vauxhall Rascal & Suzuki Supercarry (86 - Oct 94) C to M	3015
BMW 316, 320 & 320i (4-cyl) (75 - Feb 83) up to Y *	0276
BMW 320, 320i, 323i & 325i (6-cyl) (Oct 77 - Sept 87) up to E	0815
BMW 3- & 5-Series Petrol (81 - 91) up to J	1948
BMW 3-Series Petrol (Apr 91 - 99) H to V	3210
BMW 3-Series Petrol (Sept 98 - 03) S to 53	4067
BMW 520i & 525e (Oct 81 - June 88) up to E	1560
BMW 525, 528 & 528i (73 - Sept 81) up to X *	0632
BMW 5-Series 6-cyl Petrol (April 96 - Aug 03) N to 03	4151
BMW 1500, 1502, 1600, 1602, 2000 & 2002 (59 - 77) up to S *	0240
CHRYSLER PT Cruiser Petrol (00 - 03) W to 53	4058
CITROËN 2CV, Ami & Dyane (67 - 90) up to H	0196
Citroën AX Petrol & Diesel (87 - 97) D to P	3014
Citroën Berlingo & Peugeot Partner Petrol & Diesel (96 - 05) P to 55	4281
Citroën BX Petrol (83 - 94) A to L	0908
Citroën C15 Van Petrol & Diesel (89 - Oct 98) F to S	3509
Citroën C3 Petrol & Diesel (02 - 05) 51 to 05	4197
Citroen C5 Petrol & Diesel (01-08) Y to 08	4745
Citroën CX Petrol (75 - 88) up to F	0528
Citroën Saxo Petrol & Diesel (96 - 04) N to 54	3506
Citroën Visa Petrol (79 - 88) up to F	0620
Citroën Xantia Petrol & Diesel (93 - 01) K to Y	3082
Citroën XM Petrol & Diesel (89 - 00) G to X	3451
Citroën Xsara Petrol & Diesel (97 - Sept 00) R to W	3751
Citroën Xsara Picasso Petrol & Diesel (00 - 02) W to 52	3944
Citroen Xsara Picasso (03-08)	4784
Citroën ZX Diesel (91 - 98) J to S	1922
Citroën ZX Petrol (91 - 98) H to S	1881
Citroën 1.7 & 1.9 litre Diesel Engine (84 - 96) A to N	1379
FIAT 126 (73 - 87) up to E *	0305
Fiat 500 (57 - 73) up to M *	0090
Fiat Bravo & Brava Petrol (95 - 00) N to W	3572
Fiat Cinquecento (93 - 98) K to R	3501
Fiat Panda (81 - 95) up to M	0793
Fiat Punto Petrol & Diesel (94 - Oct 99) L to V	3251
Fiat Punto Petrol (Oct 99 - July 03) V to 03	4066
Fiat Punto Petrol (03-07) 03 to 07	4746
Fiat Regata Petrol (84 - 88) A to F	1167
Fiat Tipo Petrol (88 - 91) E to J	1625
Fiat Uno Petrol (83 - 95) up to M	0923
Fiat X1/9 (74 - 89) up to G *	0273
FORD Anglia (59 - 68) up to G *	0001

Title	Book No.
Ford Capri II (& III) 1.6 & 2.0 (74 - 87) up to E *	0283
Ford Capri II (& III) 2.8 & 3.0 V6 (74 - 87) up to E	1309
Ford Cortina Mk I & Corsair 1500 ('62 - '66) up to D*	0214
Ford Cortina Mk III 1300 & 1600 (70 - 76) up to P *	0070
Ford Escort Mk I 1100 & 1300 (68 - 74) up to N *	0171
Ford Escort Mk I Mexico, RS 1600 & RS 2000 (70 - 74) up to N *	0139
Ford Escort Mk II Mexico, RS 1800 & RS 2000 (75 - 80) up to W *	0735
Ford Escort (75 - Aug 80) up to V *	0280
Ford Escort Petrol (Sept 80 - Sept 90) up to H	0686
Ford Escort & Orion Petrol (Sept 90 - 00) H to X	1737
Ford Escort & Orion Diesel (Sept 90 - 00) H to X	4081
Ford Fiesta (76 - Aug 83) up to Y	0334
Ford Fiesta Petrol (Aug 83 - Feb 89) A to F	1030
Ford Fiesta Petrol (Feb 89 - Oct 95) F to N	1595
Ford Fiesta Petrol & Diesel (Oct 95 - Mar 02) N to 02	3397
Ford Fiesta Petrol & Diesel (Apr 02 - 07) 02 to 57	4170
Ford Focus Petrol & Diesel (98 - 01) S to Y	3759
Ford Focus Petrol & Diesel (Oct 01 - 05) 51 to 05	4167
Ford Galaxy Petrol & Diesel (95 - Aug 00) M to W	3984
Ford Granada Petrol (Sept 77 - Feb 85) up to B *	0481
Ford Granada & Scorpio Petrol (Mar 85 - 94) B to M	1245
Ford Ka (96 - 02) P to 52	3570
Ford Mondeo Petrol (93 - Sept 00) K to X	1923
Ford Mondeo Petrol & Diesel (Oct 00 - Jul 03) X to 03	3990
Ford Mondeo Petrol & Diesel (July 03 - 07) 03 to 56	4619
Ford Mondeo Diesel (93 - 96) L to N	3465
Ford Orion Petrol (83 - Sept 90) up to H	1009
Ford Sierra 4-cyl Petrol (82 - 93) up to K	0903
Ford Sierra V6 Petrol (82 - 91) up to J	0904
Ford Transit Petrol (Mk 2) (78 - Jan 86) up to C	0719
Ford Transit Petrol (Mk 3) (Feb 86 - 89) C to G	1468
Ford Transit Diesel (Feb 86 - 99) C to T	3019
Ford Transit Diesel (00-06)	4775
Ford 1.6 & 1.8 litre Diesel Engine (84 - 96) A to N	1172
Ford 2.1, 2.3 & 2.5 litre Diesel Engine (77 - 90) up to H	1606
FREIGHT ROVER Sherpa Petrol (74 - 87) up to E	0463
HILLMAN Avenger (70 - 82) up to Y	0037
Hillman Imp (63 - 76) up to R *	0022
HONDA Civic (Feb 84 - Oct 87) A to E	1226
Honda Civic (Nov 91 - 96) J to N	3199
Honda Civic Petrol (Mar 95 - 00) M to X	4050
Honda Civic Petrol & Diesel (01 - 05) X to 55	4611
Honda CR-V Petrol & Diesel (01-06)	4747
Honda Jazz (01 - Feb 08) 51 - 57	4735
HYUNDAI Pony (85 - 94) C to M	3398
JAGUAR E Type (61 - 72) up to L *	0140
Jaguar MkI & II, 240 & 340 (55 - 69) up to H *	0098
Jaguar XJ6, XJ & Sovereign; Daimler Sovereign (68 - Oct 86) up to D	0242
Jaguar XJ6 & Sovereign (Oct 86 - Sept 94) D to M	3261
Jaguar XJ12, XJS & Sovereign; Daimler Double Six (72 - 88) up to F	0478
JEEP Cherokee Petrol (93 - 96) K to N	1943
LADA 1200, 1300, 1500 & 1600 (74 - 91) up to J	0413
Lada Samara (87 - 91) D to J	1610
LAND ROVER 90, 110 & Defender Diesel (83 - 07) up to 56	3017
Land Rover Discovery Petrol & Diesel (89 - 98) G to S	3016
Land Rover Discovery Diesel (Nov 98 - Jul 04) S to 04	4606
Land Rover Freelander Petrol & Diesel (97 - Sept 03) R to 53	3929
Land Rover Freelander Petrol & Diesel (Oct 03 - Oct 06) 53 to 56	4623

Title	Book No.
Land Rover Series IIA & III Diesel (58 - 85) up to C	0529
Land Rover Series II, IIA & III 4-cyl Petrol (58 - 85) up to C	0314
MAZDA 323 (Mar 81 - Oct 89) up to G	1608
Mazda 323 (Oct 89 - 98) G to R	3455
Mazda 626 (May 83 - Sept 87) up to E	0929
Mazda B1600, B1800 & B2000 Pick-up Petrol (72 - 88) up to F	0267
Mazda RX-7 (79 - 85) up to C *	0460
MERCEDES-BENZ 190, 190E & 190D Petrol & Diesel (83 - 93) A to L	3450
Mercedes-Benz 200D, 240D, 240TD, 300D & 300TD 123 Series Diesel (Oct 76 - 85)	1114
Mercedes-Benz 250 & 280 (68 - 72) up to L *	0346
Mercedes-Benz 250 & 280 123 Series Petrol (Oct 76 - 84) up to B *	0677
Mercedes-Benz 124 Series Petrol & Diesel (85 - Aug 93) C to K	3253
Mercedes-Benz A-Class Petrol & Diesel (98-04) S to 54	4748
Mercedes-Benz C-Class Petrol & Diesel (93 - Aug 00) L to W	3511
Mercedes-Benz C-Class (00-06)	4780
MGA (55 - 62) *	0475
MGB (62 - 80) up to W	0111
MG Midget & Austin-Healey Sprite (58 - 80) up to W *	0265
MINI Petrol (July 01 - 05) Y to 05	4273
MITSUBISHI Shogun & L200 Pick-Ups Petrol (83 - 94) up to M	1944
MORRIS Ital 1.3 (80 - 84) up to B	0705
Morris Minor 1000 (56 - 71) up to K	0024
NISSAN Almera Petrol (95 - Feb 00) N to V	4053
Nissan Almera & Tino Petrol (Feb 00 - 07) V to 56	4612
Nissan Bluebird (May 84 - Mar 86) A to C	1223
Nissan Bluebird Petrol (Mar 86 - 90) C to H	1473
Nissan Cherry (Sept 82 - 86) up to D	1031
Nissan Micra (83 - Jan 93) up to K	0931
Nissan Micra (93 - 02) K to 52	3254
Nissan Micra Petrol (03-07) 52 to 57	4734
Nissan Primera Petrol (90 - Aug 99) H to T	1851
Nissan Stanza (82 - 86) up to D	0824
Nissan Sunny Petrol (May 82 - Oct 86) up to D	0895
Nissan Sunny Petrol (Oct 86 - Mar 91) D to H	1378
Nissan Sunny Petrol (Apr 91 - 95) H to N	3219
OPEL Ascona & Manta (B Series) (Sept 75 - 88) up to F *	0316
Opel Ascona Petrol (81 - 88)	3215
Opel Astra Petrol (Oct 91 - Feb 98)	3156
Opel Corsa Petrol (83 - Mar 93)	3160
Opel Corsa Petrol (Mar 93 - 97)	3159
Opel Kadett Petrol (Nov 79 - Oct 84) up to B	0634
Opel Kadett Petrol (Oct 84 - Oct 91)	3196
Opel Omega & Senator Petrol (Nov 86 - 94)	3157
Opel Rekord Petrol (Feb 78 - Oct 86) up to D	0543
Opel Vectra Petrol (Oct 88 - Oct 95)	3158
PEUGEOT 106 Petrol & Diesel (91 - 04) J to 53	1882
Peugeot 205 Petrol (83 - 97) A to P	0932
Peugeot 206 Petrol & Diesel (98 - 01) S to X	3757
Peugeot 206 Petrol & Diesel (02 - 06) 51 to 06	4613
Peugeot 306 Petrol & Diesel (93 - 02) K to 02	3073
Peugeot 307 Petrol & Diesel (01 - 04) Y to 54	4147
Peugeot 309 Petrol (86 - 93) C to K	1266
Peugeot 405 Petrol (88 - 97) E to P	1559
Peugeot 405 Diesel (88 - 97) E to P	3198
Peugeot 406 Petrol & Diesel (96 - Mar 99) N to T	3394
Peugeot 406 Petrol & Diesel (Mar 99 - 02) T to 52	3982

* Classic reprint